BMW F800 & F650
Service and Repair Manual

by Phil Mather

Models covered

(4872-296)

F800 S. 798cc. 2006 to 2010
F800 ST. 798 cc. 2006 to 2010
F650 GS. 798 cc. 2007 to 2010
F800 GS. 798 cc. 2007 to 2010
F800 R. 798 cc. 2009 to 2010

© Haynes Publishing 2010

A book in the **Haynes Service and Repair Manual Series**

ISBN 978 1 84425 872 7

British Library Cataloguing in Publication Data
A catalogue record for this book is available from the British Library

Library of Congress Control Number 2010920500

ABCDE
FGHIJ
KLMNO
PQ

Printed in the USA

Haynes Publishing
Sparkford, Yeovil, Somerset BA22 7JJ, England

Haynes North America, Inc
861 Lawrence Drive, Newbury Park, California 91320, USA

Haynes Publishing Nordiska AB
Box 1504, 751 45 UPPSALA, Sweden

Contents

LIVING WITH YOUR BMW

Introduction

BMW – They did it their way	Page	0•4
Acknowledgements	Page	0•7
About this manual	Page	0•7
Safety first!	Page	0•8
Identification numbers	Page	0•9
Buying spare parts	Page	0•9
Model development	Page	0•15
Bike spec	Page	0•16

Pre-ride checks

Coolant level	Page	0•10
Engine oil level	Page	0•11
Suspension, steering and drive chain or belt	Page	0•11
Brake fluid levels	Page	0•12
Legal and safety	Page	0•13
Tyres	Page	0•14

MAINTENANCE

Routine maintenance and servicing

Specifications	Page	1•2
Lubricants and fluids	Page	1•2
Maintenance schedule	Page	1•3
Component locations	Page	1•4
Maintenance procedures	Page	1•7

Contents

REPAIRS AND OVERHAUL

Engine, transmission and associated systems
Engine, clutch and transmission .... Page **2•1**

Cooling system .... Page **3•1**

Engine management system .... Page **4•1**

Chassis components
Frame and suspension .... Page **5•1**

Brakes, wheels and final drive .... Page **6•1**

Fairing and bodywork .... Page **7•1**

Electrical system
.... Page **8•1**

Wiring diagrams
.... Page **8•28**

REFERENCE

Tools and Workshop Tips .... Page **REF•2**

Security .... Page **REF•20**

Lubricants and fluids .... Page **REF•23**

Conversion factors .... Page **REF•26**

MOT Test Checks .... Page **REF•27**

Storage .... Page **REF•32**

Fault Finding .... Page **REF•35**

Technical Terms Explained .... Page **REF•44**

Index
.... Page **REF•48**

BMW – They did it their way

by Julian Ryder

BMW - Bayerische Motoren Werke

If you were looking for a theme tune for BMW's engineering philosophy you'd have to look no further than Francis Albert Sinatra's best known ditty: 'I did it my way.' The Bayerische Motoren Werke, like their countrymen at Porsche, takes precious little notice of the way anyone else does it, point this out to a factory representative and you will get a reply starting: 'We at BMW... '. The implication is clear.

It was always like that. The first BMW motorcycle, the R32, was, according to motoring sage L J K Setright: 'the first really outstanding post-War design, argued from first principles and uncorrupted by established practice. It founded a new German school of design, it established a BMW tradition destined to survive unbroken from 1923 to the present day.' That tradition was, of course, the boxer twin. The nickname 'boxer' for an opposed twin is thought to derive from the fact that the pistons travel horizontally towards and away from each other like the fists of boxers.

Before this first complete motorcycle, BMW had built a horizontally-opposed fore-and-aft boxer engine for the Victoria company of Nuremburg. It was a close copy of the British Douglas motor which the company's chief engineer Max Friz admired, a fact the company's official history confirms despite what some current devotees of the marque will claim. In fact BMW didn't really want to make motorcycles at all, originally it was an aero-engine company - a fact celebrated in the blue-and-white tank badge that is symbolic of a propeller. But in Germany after the Treaty of Versailles such potentially warlike work was forbidden to domestic companies and BMW had to diversify, albeit reluctantly.

Friz was known to have a very low opinion of motorcycles and chose the Douglas to copy simply because he saw it as fundamentally a good solution to the engineering problem of powering a two-wheeler. In the R32 the engine was arranged with the crankshaft in-line with the axis of the bike and the cylinders sticking out into the cooling airflow, giving a very low centre-of-gravity and perfect vibration-free primary balance. It wasn't just the motor's layout that departed from normal practice, the clutch was a single-plate type as used in cars, final drive was by shaft and the rear

wheel could be removed quickly. The frame and suspension were equally sophisticated, but the bike was quite heavy. Most of that description could be equally well applied to any of the boxer-engined bikes BMW made in the next 70-plus years.

Development within the surprisingly flexible confines of the boxer concept was quick. The second BMW, the R37 of 1925, retained the 68 x 68 mm Douglas bore and stroke but had overhead valves in place of the side valves. In 1928 two major milestones were passed. First, BMW acquired the car manufacturer Dixi and started manufacturing a left-hand-drive version of the Austin 7 under license. Secondly, the larger engined R62 and R63 appeared, the latter being an OHV sportster that would be the basis of BMW's sporting and record-breaking exploits before the Second World War.

The 1930s was the era of speed records on land, on sea and in the air, and the name of Ernst Henne is in the record books no fewer than ten times: eight for two-wheeled exploits, twice for wheel-on-a-stick 'sidecar' world records. At first he was on the R63 with supercharging, but in 1936 he

F800 S

switched to the 500 cc R5, high-pushrod design reminiscent of the latest generation of BMW twins. Chain-driven camshafts operated short pushrods which opened valves with hairpin - not coil - springs. A pure racing version of this motor also appeared, this time with shaft and bevel-gear driven overhead camshafts, but with short rockers operating the valves so the engine can't be called a true DOHC design. Again with the aid of a blower, this was the motor that powered the GP 500s of the late '30s to many wins including the 1939 Senior TT. After the War, this layout would re-emerge in the immortal Rennsport.

From 1939 to 1945 BMW were fully occupied making military machinery, notably the R75 sidecar for the army. The factory didn't restart production until 1948, and then only with a lightweight single. There was a false start in 1950 and a slump in sales in 1953 that endangered the whole company, before the situation was rescued by one of the truly classic boxers. Their first post-War twin had been the R51/2, and naturally it was very close to the pre-War model although simplified to a single-camshaft layout. Nevertheless, it was still a relatively advanced OHV design not a sidevalve sidecar tug which enabled a face-lift for the 1955 models to do the marketing trick.

The 1955 models got a swinging arm - at both ends. The old plunger rear suspension was replaced by a swinging arm while leading-link Earles forks adorned the front. Thus were born the R50, the R60 and the R69. The European market found these new bikes far too expensive compared to British twins but America saved the day, buying most of the company's output. The car side of the company also found a product the market wanted, a small sports-car powered by a modified bike engine, thus BMW's last crisis was averted

In 1960 the Earles fork models were updated and the R69S was launched with more power, closer transmission ratios and those funny little indicators on the ends of the handlebars. Very little changed during the '60s, apart from US export models getting telescopic forks, but in 1970 everything changed...

The move to Spandau and a new line of Boxers

BMW's bike side had outgrown its site in Munich at the company's head-quarters, so, taking advantage of government subsidies for enterprises that located to what was then West Berlin, surrounded by the still Communist DDR, BMW built a new motorcycle assembly plant at Spandau in Berlin. It opened in 1969, producing a completely new range of boxers, the 5-series, which begat the 6-series, which begat the 7-series.

In 1976, at the same time as the launch of the 7-series the first RS boxer appeared. It's hard to believe now, but it was the only fully

F800 ST

faired motorcycle, and it set the pattern for all BMWs, not just boxers, to come. The RS suffix came to mean a wonderfully efficient fairing that didn't spoil a sporty riding position. More sedate types could buy the RT version with a massive but no less efficient fairing that protected a more upright rider. Both bikes could carry luggage in a civilised fashion, too, thanks to purpose-built Krauser panniers. Both the RT and RS were uncommonly civilised motorcycles for their time.

When the boxer got its next major makeover in late 1980 BMW did something no-one thought possible, they made a boxer trail bike, the R80G/S. This wasn't without precedent as

various supermen had wrestled 750 cc boxers to honours in the ISDT and in '81 Hubert Auriol won the Paris-Dakar on a factory boxer. Some heretics even dared to suggest the roadgoing G/S was the best boxer ever.

The K-series

By the end of the '70s the boxer was looking more and more dated alongside the opposition, and when the motorcycle division's management was shaken up at the beginning of 1979 the team working on the boxer replacement was doubled in size. The first new bike wasn't

F650 GS

launched until late '83, but when it was it was clear that BMW had got as far away from the boxer concept as possible.

The powerplant was an in-line water-cooled DOHC four just like all the Japanese opposition, but typically BMW did it their way by aligning the motor so its crank was parallel to the axis of the bike and lying the motor on it side. In line with their normal practice, there was a car-type clutch, shaft drive and a single-sided swinging arm. It was totally novel yet oddly familiar. And when RT and RS version were introduced to supplement the basic naked bike, the new K-series 'flying bricks' felt even more familiar.

It was clear that BMW wanted the new four, and the three-cylinder 750 that followed it, to be the mainstay of the company's production - but in a further analogy with Porsche the customers simply wouldn't let go of the old boxer. Just as Porsche were forced to keep the 911 in production so BMW had to keep the old air-cooled boxer going by pressure from their customers. It kept going until 1995, during which time the K-bikes had debuted four-valve heads and ABS. And when the latest generation of BMWs appeared in 1993 what were they? Boxers. Granted they were four-valve, air/oil-cooled and equipped with non-telescopic fork front ends, but they were still boxers. And that high camshaft, short pushrod layout looked remarkably similar to something that had gone before...

The New 4-valve Boxers

Even by BMW's standards, the new-generation Boxers were a shock. Maybe we shouldn't have been surprised after the lateral thinking that gave us the K-series, but the way in which the men from Munich took the old opposed-twin Boxer concept that launched the company and projected it into the 21st-Century was nothing short of breath-taking in its audacity. About the only design features the old and new Boxers had in common was that they both had two wheels and two cylinders. The 4-valve engine was produced in 850 and 1100 cc version, with the later eventually being upgraded to 1150 cc for GS, R, RS and RT versions, and stretched further to 1200 cc for the C model made famous in the 007 film Golden Eye.

The new bikes mixed old and new technology in a very clever way. Fuel injection and four-valve heads were very cutting edge, high camshafts operating pushrods (for ground clearance) and air cooling (albeit with some substantial help from oil) was not. The really revolutionary stuff was in the chassis department: Telelever at the front and Paralever at the rear bolted to the motor via tubular steel sub-frames and nothing in the way of a conventional frame in the middle. The Telelever front fork is carried on a couple of wishbones with anti-dive built into the linkage. Rear Paralever suspension uses a single-sided swingingarm with a shaft drive running inside it which forms not quite a parallelogram shaped

F800 GS

system with a tie-arm running from just below to the swinging arm pivot to the rear hub. It ensures the rear axle moves in an (almost) straight line and suppresses the old BMW habit of the rear end rising when the throttle is opened. The styling was also anything but safe; the old cliché of the boring BMW was blown out of the water.

Singles and Parallel Twins

BMW have never been a factory that follows fashion, nor have they ever taken much notice of what anyone else does. Much like their fellow individualists at Porsche they have stuck with a hallmark design (albeit with a bit of pressure from their loyal customers) that none of their competitors would want, or dare, to emulate. What other car maker has produced a rear-engined flat four in recent years? And has any other bike maker even considered for a moment making a horizontally-opposed twin?

BMW's problem wasn't keeping their old customers, once they'd got them on Boxer

twins they tended to stay, it was getting them in the first place. Hence the first deviation from the norm was a single, the F650, a bike that was consciously meant to be different and appeal to a new type of customer. The theory was that new, younger customers would stick with BMW once they'd sampled the high quality of the firm's products and dealer network.

The other revolutionary aspect of the F650 was that it was produced in close cooperation with another manufacturer, Aprilia. It used the same Rotax-based engine as one of the Italian company's bikes and was assembled in Italy. But perhaps the biggest deviation from company philosophy was the F650's final drive: for the first time a BMW motorcycle did not have shaft drive. Heresy of heresies! It had a nasty, messy, inefficient chain. It didn't matter, BMW sold over 30,000 F650s in the first three model years.

Revolutionary as the F650 was, its development followed the usual BMW pattern: after the first unfortunately named Funduro

F800 R

came the ST tourer and the GS on/off roader. Radicalism returned with the CS model, a full-on roadster with cast wheels aimed at the scooter rider trading up and the urban professional.

The success of the single meant that BMW had an obvious gap in the range between the F650 and the big Boxer twins.

Enter the F800, in its way just as radical a departure as the little bike. A parallel-twin BMW? Who'd have thought it? When the whole world, led by the British industry, was making parallel twins, BMW engineers would have shut the factory rather than make one. The all-new motor was developed with, and is assembled by, Rotax then shipped to Germany to be assembled into the bikes.

The F800 S and ST were intended to do another thing that the company had

previously eschewed, appeal directly to buyers of mainstream Japanese bikes. Hence the conventional telescopic forks rather than the Telelever fitted to the Boxers, and belt final drive that meant the owner didn't have the maintenance he/she would have to do with a chain and of course it is considerably lighter than a shaft. And lightness was one of the key design objectives of the F800.

Bikes designed to be all things to all men often end up bland, not the F800. It started like as the half-faired S and the touring-oriented ST before getting the GS treatment in its second model year (with a lower powered option rather confusingly called the F650 alongside). The next F800 model was another revolutionary step; the R model, which like the GS models had chain drive and a conventional double-sided swinging arm. The motor got a

few tweaks and shorter gearing to compete in the naked middleweight sector beloved of newly qualified riders and those who do a lot of riding in town. The world's best stunt rider, Christian Pfeiffer, started using an F800S and the modifications he made for his shows helped in development of the R. BMW even marketed a limited-edition Pfeiffer replica. There's something else you never thought would happen: staid old BMW involved with a stunt rider?

Would anyone be stupid enough to describe BMW as staid transport for boring old blokes anymore? Does any other factory make a range as radical as BMW's GS and HP flat twins, or the 650 singles and 800 twins. Thought not. And that's before you even think about the astonishing S1000RR that is rewriting the Superbike rule book.

Acknowledgements

Our thanks are due to CW Motorcycles of Dorchester who supplied the machines featured in the illustrations throughout this manual. We would also like to thank NGK

Spark Plugs (UK) Ltd for supplying the colour spark plug condition photographs, the Avon Rubber Company for supplying information on tyre fitting and Draper

Tools Ltd for some of the workshop tools shown.

Thanks are also due to Julian Ryder who wrote the introduction BMW – They did it their way.

About this Manual

The aim of this manual is to help you get the best value from your motorcycle. It can do so in several ways. It can help you decide what work must be done, even if you choose to have it done by a dealer; it provides information and procedures for routine maintenance and servicing; and it offers diagnostic and repair procedures to follow when trouble occurs.

We hope you use the manual to tackle the work yourself. For many simpler jobs, doing it yourself may be quicker than arranging an appointment to get the motorcycle into a dealer and making the trips to leave it and pick it up. More importantly, a lot of money can be saved by avoiding the expense the shop must pass on to you to cover its labour and overhead costs. An added benefit is the sense of satisfaction and accomplishment that you feel after doing the job yourself.

References to the left or right side of the motorcycle assume you are sitting on the seat, facing forward.

We take great pride in the accuracy of information given in this manual, but motorcycle manufacturers make alterations and design changes during the production run of a particular motorcycle of which they do not inform us. No liability can be accepted by the authors or publishers for loss, damage or injury caused by any errors in, or omissions from, the information given.

Illegal Copying

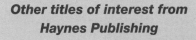

Other titles of interest from Haynes Publishing

Building the Ultimate Adventure Motorcycle
ISBN
978 1 84425 836 9
Book No. H4836

The BMW Story
Racing and production motorcycles from 1923 to the present day
ISBN
978 1 85960 854 8
Book No. H854

Professional mechanics are trained in safe working procedures. However enthusiastic you may be about getting on with the job at hand, take the time to ensure that your safety is not put at risk. A moment's lack of attention can result in an accident, as can failure to observe simple precautions.

There will always be new ways of having accidents, and the following is not a comprehensive list of all dangers; it is intended rather to make you aware of the risks and to encourage a safe approach to all work you carry out on your bike.

Asbestos

● Certain friction, insulating, sealing and other products - such as brake pads, clutch linings, gaskets, etc. - contain asbestos. Extreme care must be taken to avoid inhalation of dust from such products since it is hazardous to health. If in doubt, assume that they do contain asbestos.

Fire

● Remember at all times that petrol is highly flammable. Never smoke or have any kind of naked flame around, when working on the vehicle. But the risk does not end there - a spark caused by an electrical short-circuit, by two metal surfaces contacting each other, by careless use of tools, or even by static electricity built up in your body under certain conditions, can ignite petrol vapour, which in a confined space is highly explosive. Never use petrol as a cleaning solvent. Use an approved safety solvent.

● Always disconnect the battery earth terminal before working on any part of the fuel or electrical system, and never risk spilling fuel on to a hot engine or exhaust.

● It is recommended that a fire extinguisher of a type suitable for fuel and electrical fires is kept handy in the garage or workplace at all times. Never try to extinguish a fuel or electrical fire with water.

Fumes

● Certain fumes are highly toxic and can quickly cause unconsciousness and even death if inhaled to any extent. Petrol vapour comes into this category, as do the vapours from certain solvents such as trichloro-ethylene. Any draining or pouring of such volatile fluids should be done in a well ventilated area.

● When using cleaning fluids and solvents, read the instructions carefully. Never use materials from unmarked containers - they may give off poisonous vapours.

● Never run the engine of a motor vehicle in an enclosed space such as a garage. Exhaust fumes contain carbon monoxide which is extremely poisonous; if you need to run the engine, always do so in the open air or at least have the rear of the vehicle outside the workplace.

The battery

● Never cause a spark, or allow a naked light near the vehicle's battery. It will normally be giving off a certain amount of hydrogen gas, which is highly explosive.

● Always disconnect the battery ground (earth) terminal before working on the fuel or electrical systems (except where noted).

● If possible, loosen the filler plugs or cover when charging the battery from an external source. Do not charge at an excessive rate or the battery may burst.

● Take care when topping up, cleaning or carrying the battery. The acid electrolyte, evenwhen diluted, is very corrosive and should not be allowed to contact the eyes or skin. Always wear rubber gloves and goggles or a face shield. If you ever need to prepare electrolyte yourself, always add the acid slowly to the water; never add the water to the acid.

Electricity

● When using an electric power tool, inspection light etc., always ensure that the appliance is correctly connected to its plug and that, where necessary, it is properly grounded (earthed). Do not use such appliances in damp conditions and, again, beware of creating a spark or applying excessive heat in the vicinity of fuel or fuel vapour. Also ensure that the appliances meet national safety standards.

● A severe electric shock can result from touching certain parts of the electrical system, such as the spark plug wires (HT leads), when the engine is running or being cranked, particularly if components are damp or the insulation is defective. Where an electronic ignition system is used, the secondary (HT) voltage is much higher and could prove fatal.

Remember...

✗ **Don't** start the engine without first ascertaining that the transmission is in neutral.

✗ **Don't** suddenly remove the pressure cap from a hot cooling system - cover it with a cloth and release the pressure gradually first, or you may get scalded by escaping coolant.

✗ **Don't** attempt to drain oil until you are sure it has cooled sufficiently to avoid scalding you.

✗ **Don't** grasp any part of the engine or exhaust system without first ascertaining that it is cool enough not to burn you.

✗ **Don't** allow brake fluid or antifreeze to contact the machine's paintwork or plastic components.

✗ **Don't** siphon toxic liquids such as fuel, hydraulic fluid or antifreeze by mouth, or allow them to remain on your skin.

✗ **Don't** inhale dust - it may be injurious to health (see Asbestos heading).

✗ **Don't** allow any spilled oil or grease to remain on the floor - wipe it up right away, before someone slips on it.

✗ **Don't** use ill-fitting spanners or other tools which may slip and cause injury.

✗ **Don't** lift a heavy component which may be beyond your capability - get assistance.

✗ **Don't** rush to finish a job or take unverified short cuts.

✗ **Don't** allow children or animals in or around an unattended vehicle.

✗ **Don't** inflate a tyre above the recommended pressure. Apart from overstressing the carcass, in extreme cases the tyre may blow off forcibly.

✔ **Do** ensure that the machine is supported securely at all times. This is especially important when the machine is blocked up to aid wheel or fork removal.

✔ **Do** take care when attempting to loosen a stubborn nut or bolt. It is generally better to pull on a spanner, rather than push, so that if you slip, you fall away from the machine rather than onto it.

✔ **Do** wear eye protection when using power tools such as drill, sander, bench grinder etc.

✔ **Do** use a barrier cream on your hands prior to undertaking dirty jobs - it will protect your skin from infection as well as making the dirt easier to remove afterwards; but make sure your hands aren't left slippery. Note that long-term contact with used engine oil can be a health hazard.

✔ **Do** keep loose clothing (cuffs, ties etc. and long hair) well out of the way of moving mechanical parts.

✔ **Do** remove rings, wristwatch etc., before working on the vehicle - especially the electrical system.

✔ **Do** keep your work area tidy - it is only too easy to fall over articles left lying around.

✔ **Do** exercise caution when compressing springs for removal or installation. Ensure that the tension is applied and released in a controlled manner, using suitable tools which preclude the possibility of the spring escaping violently.

✔ **Do** ensure that any lifting tackle used has a safe working load rating adequate for the job.

✔ **Do** get someone to check periodically that all is well, when working alone on the vehicle.

✔ **Do** carry out work in a logical sequence and check that everything is correctly assembled and tightened afterwards.

✔ **Do** remember that your vehicle's safety affects that of yourself and others. If in doubt on any point, get professional advice.

● If in spite of following these precautions, you are unfortunate enough to injure yourself, seek medical attention as soon as possible.

Frame and engine numbers

The frame number is stamped into the right-hand side of the steering head. The engine number is stamped into the right-hand crankcase half just below the alternator cover. Both of these numbers should be recorded and kept in a safe place so they can be given to law enforcement officials in the event of a theft. The VIN plate is fixed to the right-hand side of the steering head.

The frame and engine numbers should also be kept in a handy place (such as with your driver's licence) so they are always available when purchasing or ordering parts for your machine.

The procedures in this manual identify models by name (e.g. GS, S, ST or R) and by year of manufacture/engine number when there are model year differences.

Buying spare parts

Once you have found all the identification numbers, record them for reference when buying parts. Since the manufacturers change specifications, parts and vendors (companies that manufacture various components on the machine), providing the ID numbers is the only way to be reasonably sure that you are buying the correct parts.

Whenever possible, take the worn part to the dealer so direct comparison with the new component can be made. Along the trail from the manufacturer to the parts shelf, there are numerous places that the part can end up with the wrong number or be listed incorrectly.

The two places to purchase new parts for your motorcycle – the franchised or main dealer and the parts/accessories store – differ in the type of parts they carry. While dealers can obtain every single genuine part for your motorcycle, the accessory store is usually limited to normal high wear items such as tyres, brake pads, spark plugs and lubes etc. Rarely will an accessory outlet have major suspension components, camshafts, transmission gears, or engine cases.

Used parts can be obtained from breakers yards for roughly half the price of new ones, but you can't always be sure of what you're getting. Once again, take your worn part to the breaker for direct comparison, or when ordering by mail order make sure that you can return it if you are not happy.

Whether buying new, used or rebuilt parts, the best course is to deal directly with someone who specialises in your particular make.

The engine number is stamped into the right crankcase half just below the alternator cover

Frame number and VIN plate on S, ST and R models.

Frame number and VIN plate on GS models.

Note: *The Pre-ride checks outlined in your rider's manual cover those items which should be inspected before each journey. These checks should be made with the ignition off.*

Coolant level

> ⚠️ *Warning: DO NOT remove the radiator pressure cap to add coolant. Topping up is done via the coolant reservoir tank filler. DO NOT leave open containers of coolant about, as it is poisonous.*

Before you start:

✔ Make sure you have a supply of coolant available (a mixture of 50% distilled or soft water and 50% corrosion inhibited ethylene glycol nitrite-free anti-freeze is needed).
✔ Always check the coolant level when the engine is **cold**.
✔ Support the motorcycle upright on level ground.
✔ The coolant reservoir is behind the right-hand bodywork side panel.
✔ On S and ST models, the coolant level is visible via a cut-out in the panel. If topping-up is necessary, remove the panel for access (see Chapter 7).
✔ On GS and R models the coolant level is visible when the reservoir is viewed from the front.

Bike care:

● Use only the specified coolant mixture. It is important that anti-freeze is used in the system all year round, and not just in the winter. Do not top the system up using only water, as the system will become too diluted.
● Do not overfill the reservoir. If the coolant is significantly above the MAX level line at any time, the surplus should be siphoned or drained off to prevent the possibility of it being expelled out of the overflow hose.
● If the coolant level falls steadily, check the system for leaks (see Chapter 1). If no leaks are found and the level continues to fall, it is recommended that the machine is taken to a BMW dealer for a pressure test.

GS and R models

1 With the motorcycle vertical and level, the coolant level should lie between the MAX and MIN level lines (arrowed) marked on the reservoir. If necessary, remove the right-hand bodywork side panel for access (see Chapter 7).

2 If the coolant level is on or below the MIN line, remove the reservoir filler cap.

3 Top the reservoir up with the recommended coolant mixture almost to the MAX level line, using a suitable funnel if required. Fit and tighten the cap. If removed, install the side panel.

S and ST models

1 With the motorcycle vertical and level, the coolant level should be above the MIN level line (arrowed) marked on reservoir (the MAX level line is only visible with the right-hand bodywork side panel removed).

2 If the coolant level is on or below the MIN line, remove the side panel (see Chapter 7), then unscrew the reservoir filler cap.

3 Top the reservoir up with the recommended coolant mixture almost to the MAX level line, using a suitable funnel if required. Fit and tighten the cap, then install the side panel.

Engine oil level

Before you start:

✔ Support the motorcycle upright on level ground.

✔ Make sure the engine is at **normal operating temperature**. Allow the engine to idle until the cooling fan starts, then run the engine for a further one minute before checking the oil level. If you check the oil level when the engine is cold or only warm you will get a false reading.

✔ The oil level is measured using a dipstick attached to the filler cap that screws into the clutch cover on the left-hand side of the engine. On GS models, the filler cap is at the front of the cover. On S, ST and R models the filler cap is at the rear of the cover.

✔ Wipe the area around the filler cap clean before unscrewing it from the cover.

Bike care:

● If you have to add oil frequently, check whether there are any oil leaks from the engine joints, oil seals and gaskets, or from the oil cooler. If not, the engine could be burning oil, in which case there will be white smoke coming out of the exhaust (see *Fault Finding*).

The correct oil

● Modern, high-revving engines place great demands on their oil. It is very important that the correct oil for your bike is used.

● Always top up with a good quality motorcycle oil – do not use motor oils designed for car engines. Do not overfill the engine.

Oil type	SAE 10W/40 mineral motorcycle oil of API classification SF, SG or SH.

1 Unscrew the filler cap, withdraw the dipstick and wipe it clean – GS model shown.

2 Unscrew the filler cap, withdraw the dipstick and wipe it clean – S, ST and R models shown.

3 Insert the dipstick into its hole and rest the filler cap on the cover, but do not screw it in.

4 Withdraw the dipstick – the oil level should lie between the MAX and MIN level lines on the dipstick.

5 If the level is near, on or below the MIN line, top up with the recommended grade and type of oil so the level lies approximately mid-way between the MAX and MIN lines. **Do not overfill.** If necessary, drain off any excess oil (see Chapter 1). On completion, tighten the filler cap securely. Repeat the warm-up procedure and re-check the level.

Suspension, steering and drive chain or belt

Suspension and Steering:

● Check that the front and rear suspension operates smoothly without binding (see Chapter 1).

● Check that the rear shock absorber is adjusted as required (see Chapter 5).

● Check that the steering moves smoothly from lock to lock.

Drive chain – GS and R models:

● Check that the chain isn't too loose or too tight, and adjust it if necessary (see Chapter 1).

● If the chain looks dry, lubricate it (see Chapter 1).

Drive belt – S and ST models:

● Examine the belt for broken teeth, splits, cracks and fraying.

● Check the belt tension at the appropriate service interval (see Chapter 1).

Brake fluid levels

> **Warning: Brake fluid can harm your eyes and damage painted surfaces, so use extreme caution when handling and pouring it and cover surrounding surfaces with rag. Do not use fluid that has been standing open for some time, as it is hygroscopic (absorbs moisture from the air) which can cause a dangerous loss of braking effectiveness.**

Before you start:

✔ The front brake fluid reservoir is on the right-hand handlebar. When checking the fluid level turn the handlebars so the reservoir is level.

✔ On GS models the rear brake fluid reservoir is located on the right-hand side below the fuel tank. On S, ST and R models, the rear brake fluid reservoir is located on the right-hand side alongside the rear shock absorber.

✔ Make sure you have the correct hydraulic fluid. DOT 4 is recommended.

✔ Wrap a rag around the reservoir being worked on to ensure that any spillage does not come into contact with painted surfaces.

Bike care:

● The fluid in the front and rear brake fluid reservoirs will drop at a very slow rate as the brake pads wear down. If the fluid level is low check the brake pads for wear (see Chapter 1), and replace them with new ones if necessary (see Chapter 6). Do not top the reservoir up until the new pads have been fitted, and then check to see if topping-up is still necessary – when the caliper pistons are pushed back to accommodate the extra thickness of the pads some fluid will be displaced back into the reservoir.

● MIN and MAX level lines are marked on the reservoirs. Note that the MAX level on the front reservoir is only visible once the cap has been removed.

● If either fluid reservoir requires repeated topping-up there could be a leak somewhere in the system, which must be investigated immediately.

● Check for signs of fluid leakage from the hydraulic hoses and/or brake system components – if found, rectify immediately (see Chapter 1).

● Check the operation of both brakes before taking the machine on the road; if there is evidence of air in the system (spongy feel to lever or pedal), it must be bled (see Chapter 6).

Front brake fluid level

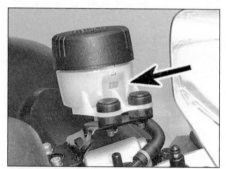

1 The front brake fluid level is visible through the window in the reservoir body – it must be above the MIN level line.

2 To top-up, press the locking tabs in and unscrew the cap.

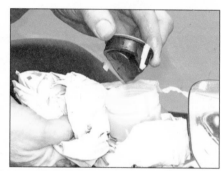

3 Remove the diaphragm plate and diaphragm.

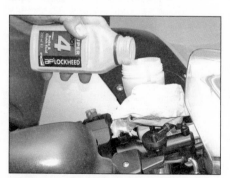

4 Top-up with new DOT 4 brake fluid, until the level is just below the MAX level line. Do not overfill and take care to avoid spills (see **Warning** above).

5 Wipe any moisture off the diaphragm (arrowed) with a clean paper towel.

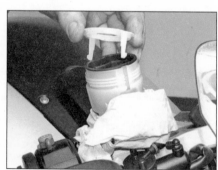

6 Ensure that the diaphragm is correctly seated before installing the diaphragm plate and cover. Tighten the cap securely.

Rear brake fluid level

1 The rear brake fluid level is visible through the reservoir body – it must be between the MAX and MIN level lines.

2 If the level is near, on or below the MIN line, unscrew the cap . . .

3 . . . and remove the diaphragm plate and diaphragm.

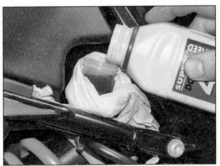

4 Top-up with new DOT 4 brake fluid, until the level is just below the MAX level line. Do not overfill and take care to avoid spills (see **Warning** on page 0•12).

5 Wipe any moisture off the diaphragm with a clean paper towel. Ensure that the diaphragm is correctly seated, then install the cap and tighten it securely.

Legal and safety

Lighting and signalling:

● Take a minute to check that the headlight, sidelight, tail light, brake light, licence plate light, instrument lights and turn signals all work correctly.
● Check that the horn sounds when the button is pressed.
● A working speedometer, graduated in mph, is a statutory requirement in the UK.

Safety:

● Check that the throttle twistgrip rotates smoothly when opened and snaps shut when released, in all steering positions. Also check for the correct amount of freeplay (see Chapter 1).
● Check that the brake lever and pedal, clutch lever and gearchange lever operate smoothly. Lubricate them at the specified intervals or when necessary (see Chapter 1). Check for the correct amount of freeplay in the clutch cable (see Chapter 1).
● Check that there is good pressure in both front and rear brake systems when lever or pedal is applied.
● Check that the engine shuts off when the kill switch is operated.
● Check that the stand return springs hold the stand up securely when retracted.

Fuel:

● This may seem obvious, but check that you have enough fuel to complete your journey. If you notice signs of fuel leakage – rectify the cause immediately.
● Ensure you use the correct grade fuel – see *Specifications* in Chapter 4.

Tyres

The correct pressures:

● The tyres must be checked when **cold**, not immediately after riding. Note that incorrect tyre pressures will cause abnormal tread wear and unsafe handling. Low tyre pressures may cause the tyre to slip on the rim or come off.

● Use an accurate pressure gauge. Many forecourt gauges are wildly inaccurate. If you buy your own, spend as much as you can justify on a quality gauge.

● Proper air pressure will increase tyre life and provide maximum stability and ride comfort.

Tyre care:

● Check the tyres carefully for cuts, tears, embedded nails or other sharp objects and excessive wear. Operation of the motorcycle with excessively worn tyres is extremely hazardous, as traction and handling are directly affected.

● Check the condition of the tyre valve and ensure the dust cap is in place and tight.

● Pick out any stones or nails which may have become embedded in the tyre tread. If left, they will eventually penetrate through the casing and cause a puncture.

● If tyre damage is apparent, or unexplained loss of pressure is experienced, seek the advice of a tyre fitting specialist without delay.

● Check the wheel rims and spokes for damage. The spoke tension on wire-spoked wheels can change; refer to Chapter 1 if you suspect spoke tension is incorrect.

Tyre tread depth:

● At the time of writing UK law requires that tread depth must be at least 1 mm over 3/4 of the tread breadth all the way around the tyre, with no bald patches. Many riders, however, consider 2 mm tread depth minimum to be a safer limit. BMW recommend a minimum of 2 mm on the front and 3 mm on the rear for normal speeds, but note that German law requires a minimum of 1.6 mm for each tyre.

● Many tyres now incorporate wear indicators in the tread. Identify the location marking on the tyre sidewall (either an arrow, triangle, the letters TWI, or the manufacturer's logo) to locate the indicator bar and replace the tyre if the tread has worn down to the bar.

Model	Front	Rear
F800 S and ST models	36 psi (2.5 Bar)	40 psi (2.8 Bar)
F800 R models	36 psi (2.5 Bar)	42 psi (2.9 Bar)
F800/650 GS models – rider only	32 psi (2.2 Bar)	36 psi (2.5 Bar)
F800/650 GS models – with passenger and luggage	32 psi (2.2 Bar)	42 psi (2.9 Bar)

1 Remove the dust cap from the valve, and do not forget to fit the cap after checking the pressure.

2 Use an accurate gauge and make sure the tyres are **cold**.

3 Measure tread depth at the centre of the tyre using a depth gauge.

4 Tyre tread wear indicator location marking (arrowed).

F800 S

The F800 S was launched in May, 2006, effectively filling the gap between the F650 singles and the R1200 Boxer twins in the BMW model line-up.

Styled as a sports bike, although fitted with only a half fairing, it was powered by a newly designed 798 cc parallel twin engine that was developed in conjunction with the Austrian Rotax factory. The engine featured chain driven double overhead camshafts, actuating four valves per cylinder, a deep, semi-dry sump lubrication system and liquid cooling that incorporated an oil cooler acting as a heat exchanger between the lubrication and cooling systems. Two dual rotor, trochoidal oil pumps were driven off the back of the clutch and the water pump was located on the cylinder head and driven by the intake camshaft.

To counteract the vibration associated with parallel twin engine designs, a third connecting rod was fitted to the crankshaft. This was part of a balancing arm assembly, working within the crankcases in the opposite direction to the two conventional rods.

The clutch was a conventional cable-operated, wet multi-plate unit and the gearbox was 6-speed. Drive to the rear wheel was by a toothed belt and pulleys.

The engine was fuel-injected, the large-volume air filter housing and various engine management system sensors occupying the space normally taken-up by the fuel tank. The tank itself was located inside the rear sub-frame, underneath the seat, with the filler cap in the body panel on the right-hand side. This feature was disguised by bodywork panels that covered both sides and the centre of the machine forward of the seat.

The engine was housed in a twin spar aluminium frame. Front suspension was by conventional telescopic forks and rear suspension by a single-sided swingarm with two-way adjustable shock absorber. The swingarm pivoted directly off the rear of the crankcases. The wheels were cast aluminium.

An optional low seat height version was available on request.

The front brake system featured two 320 mm discs and four-piston Brembo calipers. The rear brake system had a single piston sliding caliper acting on a 265 mm disc. The brake hoses were braided stainless steel and ABS was available as an optional extra.

All the machine's electronics were designed using CAN-bus technology with linked engine management and general vehicle electronics systems for co-ordinated running and fault-finding.

F800 ST

The F800 ST was launched at the same time as the F800S, equipped as a touring version with full fairing, taller screen, higher handlebars and a rear luggage rack.

F800 GS

Launched late in 2007, the F800 GS was an off-road styled machine based around the 798 cc parallel twin engine of the S and ST models. Although there were some detail changes to the engine, such as the relocating of the oil filler cap to the front of the clutch cover, the main difference from previous models was an all-new tubular steel trellis frame with upside-down front forks and double-sided swingarm.

The swingarm pivots were located in the frame and both wheels were wire spoked with tubed, dual purpose tyres. The front brake system featured two 300 mm discs and two piston sliding calipers. The rear brake system had a single piston sliding caliper acting on a 265 mm disc. ABS was available as an optional extra and ABS operation could be cancelled when riding off-road.

The bodywork reflected the styling of other off-road BMWs with an extension at the front end acting as a secondary upper mudguard, a short screen and asymmetrical high and low beam headlights incorporated in a single unit. An LED tail light was fitted as standard.

A major concession to off-road use was the adoption of chain and sprocket drive to the rear wheel.

In celebration of 30 years of the original R80G/S introduced in 1980, BMW released an anniversary special edition F800 GS in 2010. This model sports white paintwork and a red seat, like the Paris-Dakar version of the original G/S model. In practical terms, it had a bash plate and hand guards as standard.

F650 GS

Launched at the same time as the F800 GS, the F650 utilised the same 798 cc engine, despite its title, and same trellis frame. It was, however, detuned, producing less horse-power, and shorter, conventional telescopic front forks and smaller, cast aluminium wheels lowered ground clearance. Overall weight was reduced by fitting only one front disc brake and the omission of the secondary air system.

A 30th Anniversary model was available in 2010. It had white paintwork and a red seat, with a sump guard and hand guards as standard.

F800 R

Launched in January 2009, the F800 R combined the engine and twin spar chassis of the S/ST models with the double-sided swingarm and chain final drive of the GS models. The GS asymmetrical headlight was used and the area of bodywork was much reduced, giving the machine a 'naked' roadster appearance.

Front suspension was by conventional telescopic forks. The front brake system featured two 320 mm discs and four piston Brembo calipers. The rear brake system had a single piston sliding caliper acting on a 265 mm disc. ABS was available as an optional extra.

A limited, special edition version was produced in late 2009, based on the machine used by stunt champion Christian Pfeiffer.

Weights and dimensions

	F800 S	F800 ST	F650 GS	F800 GS	F800 R
Overall length	2082 mm	2195 mm	2280 mm	2320 mm	2082 mm
Overall width	860 mm	860 mm	890 mm	945 mm	812 mm
Overall height	1155 mm	1225 mm	1240 mm	1350 mm	1240 mm
Wheelbase	1466 mm	1466 mm	1575 mm	1578 mm	1520 mm
Seat height					
Standard seat	820 mm	820 mm	820 mm	880 mm	825 mm
Low seat	790 mm	790 mm	790 mm	850 mm	755 mm
Weight (wet)	204 kg	204 kg	199 kg	207 kg	199 kg
Max. load	201 kg	201 kg	237 kg	236 kg	201 kg
Max gross weight	405 kg	405 kg	436 kg	443 kg	405 kg

Engine

Type . . . Four-stroke parallel twin cylinder
Capacity . . . 798 cc
Bore . . . 82 mm
Stroke . . . 75.6 mm
Compression ratio . . . 12.0 to 1
Valves per cylinder . . . 4
Cooling system . . . Liquid cooled
Clutch . . . Wet multi-plate
Transmission . . . Six-speed constant mesh
Final drive
  F800 S and ST . . . Belt and pulleys
  F650 GS, F800 GS and F800 R . . . Chain and sprockets
Camshafts . . . DOHC, chain-driven
Fuel system . . . Fuel injection
Ignition system . . . BMS-KP computer-controlled with integrated EWS immobiliser

Chassis

Frame type
  F800 S, ST and R . . . Aluminium twin spar
  F650 GS and F800 GS . . . Tubular steel trellis

Chassis (continued)

Rake and Trail

F800 S and ST . . . . 26.2°, 94.6 mm

F650 GS . . . . 26.0°, 97.0 mm

F800 GS . . . . 26.0°, 117.0 mm

F800 R . . . . 25.0°, 91.0 mm

Fuel tank capacity (including reserve)

F800 S, ST, F650 GS and F800 GS . . . . 16.0 litres (res. 4 litres)

F800 R . . . . 16.0 litres (res. 2 litres)

Front suspension

F800 S and ST

Type . . . . 43 mm oil-damped, conventional telescopic forks

Travel . . . . 140 mm

F650 GS

Type . . . . 43 mm oil-damped, conventional telescopic forks

Travel . . . . 180 mm

F800 GS

Type . . . . 45 mm oil-damped, upside-down telescopic forks

Travel . . . . 230 mm

F800 R

Type . . . . 43 mm oil-damped, conventional telescopic forks

Travel . . . . 125 mm

Rear suspension

F800 S and ST

Type . . . . Aluminium single-sided swingarm

Travel . . . . 140 mm

F650 GS

Type . . . . Aluminium double-sided swingarm

Travel . . . . 170 mm

F800 GS

Type . . . . Aluminium double-sided swingarm

Travel . . . . 215 mm

F800 R

Type . . . . Aluminium double-sided swingarm

Travel . . . . 125 mm

Single shock absorber (all models)

Adjustment . . . . Spring pre-load and rebound damping

Wheels

F800 S and ST

Front . . . . 3.50 x 17 MT H2

Rear . . . . 5.50 x 17 MT H2

F650 GS

Front . . . . 2.50 x 19 MT H2

Rear . . . . 3.50 x 17 MT H2

F800 GS

Front . . . . 2.15 x 21 MT H2

Rear . . . . 4.25 x 17 MT H2

F800 R

Front . . . . 3.50 x 17 MT H2

Rear . . . . 5.50 x 17 MT H2

Tyres

F800 S and ST

Front 120/70-ZR 17

Rear 180/55-ZR 17

F650 GS

Front . . . . 110/80-R 19 (59V) TL

Rear . . . . 140/80-R 17 (69V) TL

F800 GS

Front . . . . 90/90- 21 (54V), tubed

Rear . . . . 150/70-R 17 (69V), tubed

F800 R

Front 120/70-ZR 17

Rear 180/55-ZR 17

Front brake

F800 S, ST and R . . . . Twin 320 mm floating discs with four piston calipers

F650 GS . . . . Single 300 mm fixed disc with two piston sliding caliper

F800 GS . . . . Twin 300 mm floating discs with two piston sliding calipers

Rear brake . . . . Single 265 mm fixed disc with single piston sliding caliper

Chapter 1
Routine maintenance and servicing

Contents

	Section			Section
Air filter	11	Engine wear assessment		see Chapter 2
Brake fluid level check	see *Pre-ride checks*	Fuel system		14
Brake system	5	Nuts and bolts		8
Clutch and throttle cables	4	General lubrication		7
Coolant level check	see *Pre-ride checks*	Spark plugs		12
Cooling system	15	Steering head bearings		6
Drive belt and pulleys (S and ST models)	2	Suspension		13
Drive chain and sprockets (GS and R models)	1	Valve clearances		10
Engine oil and filter	3	Wheels and wheel bearings		9
Engine oil level check	see *Pre-ride checks*			

Degrees of difficulty

| **Easy,** suitable for novice with little experience | **Fairly easy,** suitable for beginner with some experience | **Fairly difficult,** suitable for competent DIY mechanic | **Difficult,** suitable for experienced DIY mechanic | **Very difficult,** suitable for expert DIY or professional |

Engine

Idle speed	1200 to 1300 rpm
Spark plug type	NGK DCPR 8E
Spark plug electrode gap	0.8 to 0.9 mm
Valve clearances (COLD engine)	
Intake valves	0.18 to 0.26 mm
Exhaust valves	0.27 to 0.35 mm

Chassis

Drive chain slack	
F650 GS and F800 R models	30 to 40 mm
F800 GS models	35 to 45 mm
Drive belt tension	
F800 S and ST models	see text
Clutch cable freeplay	1 mm
Throttle cable freeplay	1 to 2 mm
Tyre pressures (cold)	see Pre-ride checks
Brake pad friction material minimum thickness	1 mm

Lubricants and fluids

Engine oil	see Pre-ride checks
Engine oil capacity	approx 3.0 litres
Brake fluid	DOT 4
Drive chain	Aerosol chain lubricant suitable for O-ring chains
Steering head bearings	Multi-purpose grease with EP2 rating
Swingarm pivot bearings	Multi-purpose grease with EP2 rating
Bearing seal lips	Multi-purpose grease
Gearchange lever/rear brake pedal/footrest pivots	Teflon spray
Clutch and front brake lever pivots	Teflon spray
Sidestand and centrestand pivots	Teflon spray
Cables	Aerosol cable lubricant

Torque settings

Drive belt adjuster screw (S and ST models)	10 Nm
Drive belt eccentric adjuster clamp screws (S and ST models)	
Initial torque	10 Nm
Final torque	30 Nm
Engine oil drain plug	40 Nm
Engine oil filter	14 Nm
Fork clamp bolts (top yoke)	
GS models	19 Nm
All other models	20 Nm
Rear axle nut (GS and R models)	100 Nm
Spark plugs	18 Nm
Steering head bearing adjuster	
Initial setting	25 Nm
Final setting	10 Nm
Steering stem clamp bolt	
GS models	19 Nm
All other models	25 Nm

Note: *The Pre-ride checks outlined in the owner's manual cover those items which should be inspected before every ride. Also perform the pre-ride inspection at every maintenance interval (in addition to the procedures listed). The intervals listed below are the intervals recommended by the manufacturer for the models covered in this manual.*

Pre-ride
☐ See *'Pre-ride checks'* at the beginning of this manual.

After the initial 600 miles (1000 km)
Note: *This check is usually performed by a BMW dealer after the first 600 miles (1000 km) from new. Thereafter, maintenance is carried out according to the following intervals of the schedule.*

Every 600 miles (1000 km)
☐ Check, adjust, clean and lubricate the drive chain – GS and R models (Section 1)

After the initial 6,000 miles (10,000 km), then every 12,000 miles (20,000 km)
☐ Have fault code memory read by BMW dealer
☐ Check the drive belt and pulleys – S and ST models (Section 2)
☐ Change the engine oil and oil filter (Section 3)
☐ Check and adjust the clutch and throttle cable freeplay (Section 4)
☐ Check the brake pads and discs for wear (Section 5)
☐ Check the brake system (Section 5)
☐ Check and adjust the steering head bearings (Section 6)
☐ Check and lubricate the clutch, gearchange and brake levers, the brake pedal, centrestand and sidestand pivots, and the cables (Section 7)
☐ Check the tightness of all nuts, bolts and fasteners (Section 8)
☐ Check the lights and signalling equipment (see Chapter 8)
☐ Check the wheels and wheel bearings (Section 9)

Every 12,000 miles (20,000 km)
Carry out all the items under the 6,000 mile (10,000 km) check, plus the following:
☐ Check and adjust the valve clearances (Section 10)
☐ Fit a new air filter element (Section 11)

Every 24,000 miles (40,000 km)
Carry out all the items under the 6,000 mile (10,000 km) check, plus the following:
☐ Fit new spark plugs (Section 12)
☐ Fit a new drive belt and rear pulley coupling dampers – S and ST models (see Chapter 6)

Every year
Note: *The following service items should be carried out once a year irrespective of the mileage covered.*
☐ Check the battery (see Chapter 8)
☐ Check the front and rear suspension (Section 13)
☐ Check the fuel system (Section 14)
☐ Check the cooling system (Section 15)
☐ Change the brake fluid – initially after the first year, then every 2 years (see Chapter 6)

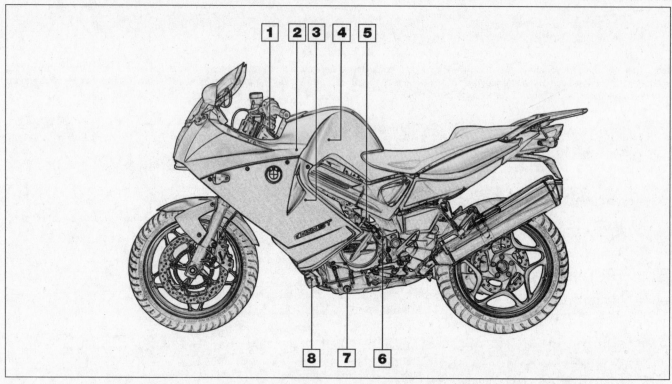

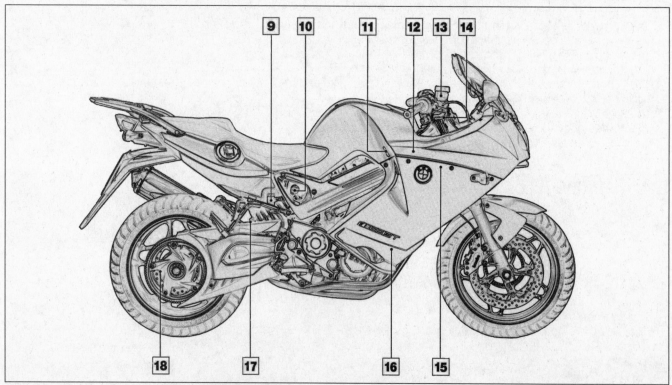

Component locations – F800 ST (and F800 S) models

1 Steering head bearing
adjuster
2 Battery
3 Valve cover, spark plugs and
secondary air system hoses
4 Air filter

5 Clutch cable adjuster
6 Engine oil dipstick/filler
7 Engine oil drain plug
8 Engine oil filter
9 Rear brake fluid
reservoir

10 Rear shock pre-load
adjuster
11 Coolant level inspection slot
12 Coolant reservoir
13 Front brake fluid reservoir
14 Throttle cable adjuster

15 Radiator pressure cap
16 Coolant drain point on oil
cooler
17 Rear shock damping adjuster
18 Drive belt eccentric adjuster
screw

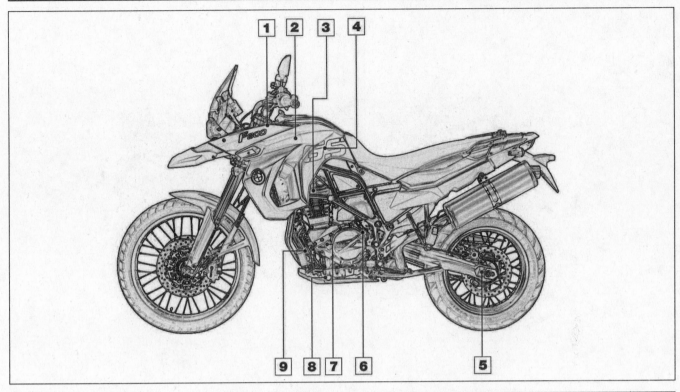

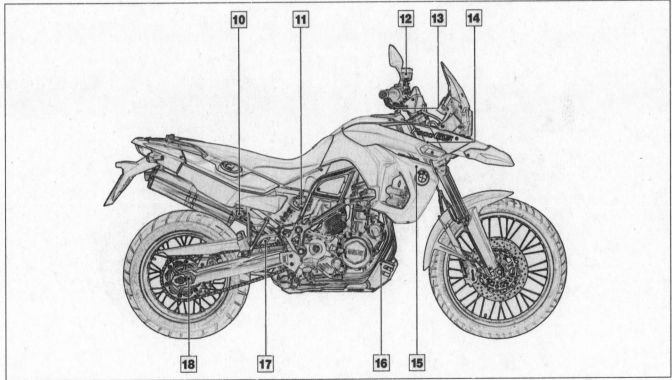

Component locations – F800 GS (and F650 GS) models

1 Steering head bearing
  adjuster
2 Battery
3 Valve cover, spark plugs and
  secondary air system hoses
4 Air filter

5 Drive chain adjuster
6 Clutch cable adjuster
7 Engine oil dipstick/filler
8 Engine oil drain plug
9 Coolant drain point on oil
  cooler

10 Rear brake fluid reservoir
11 Rear shock pre-load
   adjuster
12 Front brake fluid reservoir
13 Throttle cable adjuster
14 Coolant reservoir

15 Radiator pressure cap
16 Engine oil filter
17 Rear shock damping
   adjuster
18 Drive chain adjuster

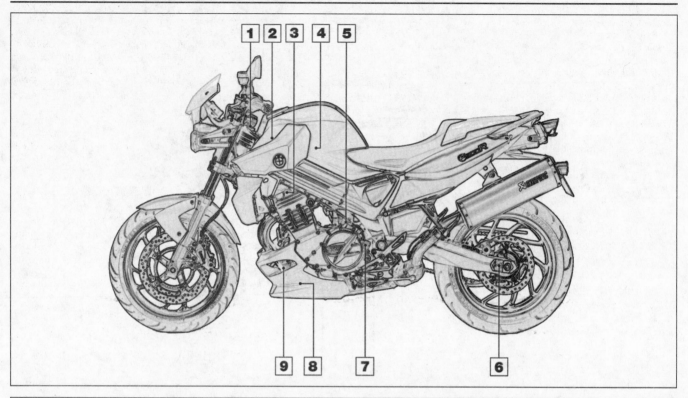

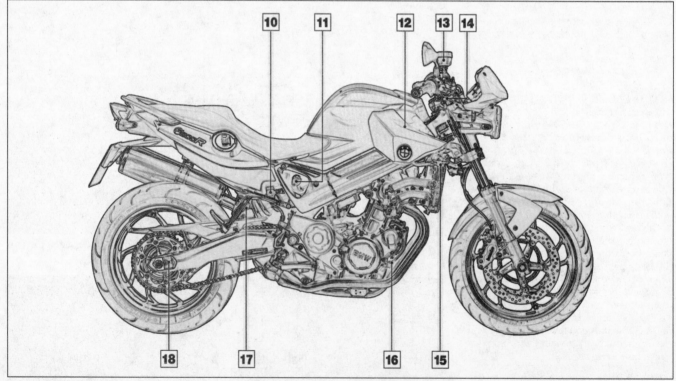

Component locations – F800 R model

1 Steering head bearing
  adjuster
2 Battery
3 Valve cover, spark plugs
  and secondary air system
  hoses

4 Air filter
5 Clutch cable adjuster
6 Drive chain adjuster
7 Engine oil dipstick/filler
8 Engine oil drain plug
9 Engine oil filter

10 Rear brake fluid reservoir
11 Rear shock pre-load adjuster
12 Coolant reservoir
13 Front brake fluid reservoir
14 Throttle cable adjuster
15 Radiator pressure cap

16 Coolant drain point on oil
   cooler
17 Rear shock damping
   adjuster
18 Drive chain adjuster

1 This Chapter is designed to help the home mechanic maintain his/her motorcycle for safety, economy, long life and peak performance.

2 Deciding where to start or plug into the routine maintenance schedule depends on several factors. If your motorcycle has been maintained according to the warranty standards and has just come out of warranty, start routine maintenance as it coincides with the next mileage or calendar interval. If you have owned the machine for some time but have never performed any maintenance on it, start at the nearest interval and include some additional procedures to ensure that nothing important is overlooked. If you have just had a major engine overhaul, then start the maintenance routine from the beginning. If you have a used machine and have no knowledge of its history or maintenance record, combine all the checks into one large service initially and then settle into the specified maintenance schedule. Note that each procedure is covered as a separate item but may include removal of parts for access (such as body panels) that may need to be removed for another procedure in the same service interval – to avoid more work than necessary read through all items you intend to carry out so you know what you need to do.

3 Before beginning any maintenance or repair, the machine should be cleaned thoroughly. Cleaning will help ensure that dirt does not get where it shouldn't when parts are removed or disassembled and will allow you to detect wear and damage that could otherwise easily go unnoticed.

4 Certain maintenance information is sometimes printed on labels attached to the motorcycle. If the information on the labels differs from that included here, use the information on the label.

---

1 Drive chain and sprockets (GS and R models)

Caution: If the machine is continually ridden in wet or dusty conditions, the drive chain should be checked, cleaned and lubricated more frequently.

1 A neglected drive chain won't last long and will quickly damage the sprockets. Routine chain lubrication and adjustment isn't difficult and will ensure maximum chain and sprocket life.

Clean and lubricate the chain

2 Clean the chain using a dedicated aerosol cleaner that will not damage the O-rings, or paraffin (kerosene), using a soft brush to work out any dirt. Wipe the cleaner off the chain and allow it to dry, using compressed air if available. If the chain is excessively dirty, follow the procedure in Chapter 6 to remove it and allow it to soak in the paraffin or solvent. *Caution: Don't use petrol (gasoline), an unsuitable solvent or other cleaning fluids which might damage the internal sealing properties of the chain. Don't use high-pressure water to clean the chain. The entire process shouldn't take longer than ten minutes, otherwise the O-rings could be damaged.*

3 The best time to lubricate the chain is after the motorcycle has been ridden. When the chain is warm, the lubricant will penetrate the joints between the side plates better than when cold. **Note:** *BMW specifies an aerosol chain lube that it is suitable for O-ring (sealed) chains; do not use any other chain lubricants – the solvents could damage the chain's sealing rings.* Apply the lubricant to the area where the sideplates overlap – not the middle of the rollers **(see illustration)**.

HAYNES HiNT *Apply the lubricant to the top of the lower chain run, so centrifugal force will work the oil into the chain when the bike is moving. After applying the lubricant, let it soak in a few minutes before wiping off any excess.*

⚠ *Warning: Take care not to get any lubricant on the tyres or brake system components. If any of the lubricant inadvertently contacts them, clean it off thoroughly using a suitable solvent or dedicated brake cleaner before riding the machine.*

Check chain slack

4 To check the chain, support the bike on its sidestand with no weight applied. Shift the transmission to neutral.

5 Push up on the bottom run of the chain midway between the two sprockets and measure the slack, then compare your measurement to that listed in this Chapter's Specifications **(see illustrations)**. As the chain stretches with wear, periodic adjustment will be necessary (see below).

1.3 Apply the lubricant where the sideplates overlap

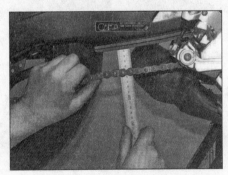

1.5b ... then push the chain up to measure the slack

6 Since the chain will rarely wear evenly, rotate the rear wheel so that another section of chain can be checked – do this several times to check the entire length of chain, and mark the tightest spot.

Caution: Riding the bike with excess slack in the chain could lead to damage, or in extreme cases it could jump off the rear sprocket.

7 In some cases where lubrication has been neglected, corrosion and dirt may cause the links to bind and kink, which effectively shortens the chain's length and makes it tight **(see illustration)**. Thoroughly clean and work free any such links, then highlight them with a marker pen or paint. Take the bike for a ride.

8 After the bike has been ridden, repeat the measurement for slack in the highlighted area. If the chain has kinked again and is still

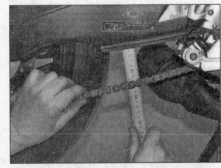

1.5a Hold a ruler midway between the two sprockets ...

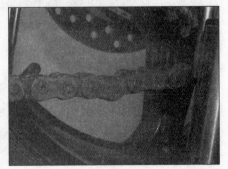

1.7 Neglect has caused the links in this chain to kink

1.9 Try to lift the chain off the rear sprocket

1.10 Check the drive chain slider (arrowed) for wear

tight, replace it with a new one (see Chapter 6). A rusty, kinked or worn chain will damage the sprockets and can damage transmission bearings. If in any doubt as to the condition of a chain, it is far better to install a new one than risk damage to other components and possibly yourself.

9 Check the entire length of the chain for damaged rollers, loose links and pins, and missing O-rings and replace it with a new one if necessary. Try to lift the chain off the rear sprocket at a position midway around the sprocket **(see illustration)**. If the chain lifts clear of the sprocket teeth it is worn out and should be renewed. Check the sprockets for wear (see Step 16). **Note:** *Never install a new chain on old sprockets, and never use the old chain if you install new sprockets – replace the chain and sprockets as a set.*

10 Inspect the drive chain slider on the front of the swingarm for excessive wear and damage **(see illustration)**. Replace the slider with a new one if necessary (see Chapter 5).

Adjust chain slack

11 Rotate the rear wheel so that the chain is positioned with the tightest point at the centre of its bottom run (see Step 6). Support the bike on its sidestand.

12 Slacken the rear axle nut **(see illustration)**.

13 Loosen the locknut on the left and right-hand chain adjusters, then turn both adjusters evenly and a little at a time until the amount of freeplay specified at the beginning of the Chapter is obtained at the centre of the bottom run of the chain **(see illustration)**. If the chain was slack turn the adjusters anti-clockwise; if the chain was tight turn them clockwise.

14 Following adjustment, check the alignment of the adjuster plates with the index marks on both sides of the swingarm **(see illustration 1.12)**. It is important the plates are in the same position otherwise the rear wheel will be out of alignment with the front (see *Wheel alignment* in Chapter 6). If there is a difference in the positions of the adjuster plates, adjust one so that its position is exactly the same as the other, then check the chain freeplay again and readjust if necessary.

15 When adjustment is complete, counter-hold the adjusters to prevent them turning and tighten the locknuts **(see illustration 1.13)**. Tighten the axle nut to the torque setting specified at the beginning of this Chapter. Recheck the chain adjustment as above.

Check sprocket wear

16 Remove the front sprocket cover (see Chapter 6). Check the teeth on the front and

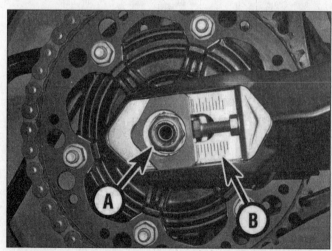

1.12 Slacken the axle nut (A). Note the index marks (B)

1.13 Adjuster locknut (A) and chain adjuster (B)

1.16a Check the teeth on the front . . .

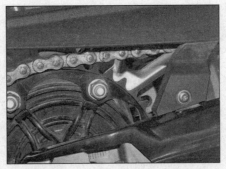

1.16b . . . and rear sprockets

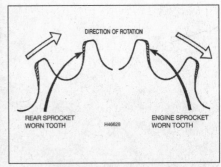

1.16c Check the sprockets in the area indicated to see if they are worn excessively

rear sprockets for wear **(see illustrations)**. If the sprocket teeth are worn excessively, follow the procedure in Chapter 6 to renew the chain and both sprockets as a set.

2 Drive belt and pulleys (S and ST models)

Check belt and pulley wear

1 Support the bike on its centrestand or an auxiliary stand. Shift the transmission into neutral.

2 Remove the lower belt guard and the front pulley cover (see Chapter 6).

3 Check the teeth on the belt and pulleys for wear and damage, and inspect the belt for any splits, cracks or fraying **(see illustration)**. Rotate the rear wheel to check the entire length of the belt. If necessary, replace the belt and/or pulleys with new ones (see Chapter 6). **Note:** *A new drive belt should be fitted at the appropriate service interval.*

Check belt tension

Special tool: *A belt tension tester (BMW Part No. 27 1 541) is required for this procedure (see Step 7). In an emergency, apply a load to the belt using a spring balance and measure the deflection (see Step 10).*

Note: *This procedure must be undertaken with the machine at room temperature.*

4 Support the bike on its centrestand or an auxiliary stand – make sure no load is on the rear suspension. Shift the transmission into neutral.

2.3 Check the teeth on the belt and pulleys for wear

5 If not already done, remove the lower belt guard (see Chapter 5, Section 13).

6 Turn the rear wheel until the paint mark on the rear pulley is pointing to the rear **(see illustration)**.

7 Turn the pre-load adjuster on the tension tester to align with mark 10 on the scale **(see illustration)**. Depress the tester stop and slide the top edge of the tester over the belt, midway between the pulleys **(see illustration)**. Ensure the tester engages correctly with the belt teeth.

8 If belt tension is correct, the upper reference

2.6 Paint mark (arrowed) should be pointing to the rear

2.7a Set the pre-load adjuster as described

2.7b Fit the tension tester midway between the pulleys

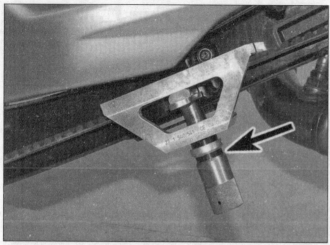

2.8 Read the scale against the upper reference edge (arrowed)

2.9a Loosen the eccentric adjuster clamp screws (arrowed)

2.9b Turn the adjuster screw clockwise

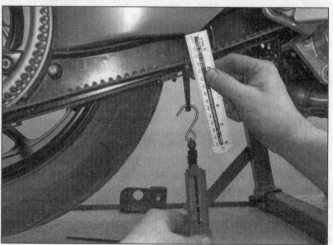

2.10 Measuring belt slack with a spring balance

edge of the tester will be aligned with mark 5.5 on the scale **(see illustration)**.

Adjust belt slack

9 If the belt tension requires adjustment, first loosen the eccentric adjuster clamp screws by no more than one full turn **(see illustration)**. If not already done, install the tension tester (see Steps 5 to 7). Now turn the adjuster screw clockwise until the upper reference edge of the tester is aligned with mark 5.5 on the scale **(see illustration)**. **Note 1:** *Only a small amount of adjustment is normally required. If the correct belt tension cannot be achieved a new belt will have to be fitted.* **Note 2:** *A new drive belt should be fitted at the appropriate service interval.*

10 If the belt tension tester is not available, follow the procedure in Steps 4 to 6, then measure belt slack as follows. Using a cable-tie, attach a spring balance to the belt, midway between the pulleys, then apply a pull of 5 kg and measure the belt deflection **(see illustration)**. On the machine photographed,

with the belt tension correctly adjusted, a deflection of 32 mm was recorded. If the deflection is greater than this figure, follow the procedure in Step 9 to loosen the eccentric adjuster clamp screws. Now turn the adjuster screw clockwise 1/4 turn at a time until the tension is correct (see **Notes** above).

Caution: Belt tension increases as load is applied to the rear suspension. Over-tightening the belt during adjustment will lead to rapid belt wear and damage to the transmission bearings.

11 When adjustment is complete, tighten the adjuster clamp screws to the initial torque setting specified at the beginning of this Chapter. Now tighten the screws to the final torque setting. Back-off the adjuster screw and check the torque setting of the clamp screws, then tighten the adjuster screw to the specified torque.

12 Install the lower belt guard.

13 If the belt was adjusted without the use of the service tool, have the tension checked by a BMW dealer at your earliest convenience.

3 Engine oil and filter

Warning: Be careful when draining the oil, as the exhaust pipes, the engine, and the oil itself can cause severe burns.

1 Regular oil and filter changes are the single most important maintenance procedure you can perform. The oil not only lubricates the internal parts of the engine, transmission and clutch, but it also acts as a coolant, a cleaner, a sealant, and a protector. Because of these demands, the oil takes a terrific amount of abuse and should be drained and the engine refilled with new oil of the correct type and

HAYNES HINT *Saving a little money on the difference in cost between a good oil and a cheap oil won't pay off if the engine is damaged.*

3.4a Unscrew the plug and drain the oil

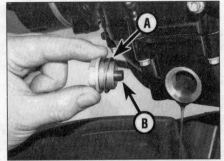

3.4b Note the sealing washer (A) and magnet (B)

3.6a Use a filter adapter . . .

grade at the specified service interval. A new oil filter should be fitted at the same time.

2 Before changing the oil, warm up the engine so the oil will drain easily. On GS models, if fitted, remove the large sump guard (see Chapter 7). On R models, if fitted, remove the belly panel.

3 Support the bike in an upright position on level ground. Unscrew the oil filler cap from the clutch cover to vent the crankcase and to act as a reminder that there is no oil in the engine (see *Pre-ride checks*). Check the condition of the O-ring on the filler cap and replace it with a new one if it is damaged or worn.

4 Place a drain tray below the left-hand side of the engine, then unscrew the oil drain plug and allow the oil to flow into the tray **(see illustration)**. Note the sealing washer and magnet on the drain plug **(see illustration)**. Clean any particles of metal swarf off the magnet and discard the washer as a new one must be fitted.

> **HAYNES HINT**
> *To help determine whether any abnormal or excessive engine wear is occurring, place a strainer between the engine and the drain tray so that any debris in the oil is filtered out and can be examined. If there are flakes or chips of metal in the oil or on the drain plug magnet, then something is drastically wrong internally and the engine will have to be disassembled for inspection and repair. If there are pieces of fibre-like material in the oil, the clutch is wearing excessively and should be checked.*

3.6b . . . to unscrew the oil filter

5 When the oil has completely drained, fit a new sealing washer to the drain plug, screw the plug into the sump and tighten it to the torque setting specified at the beginning of this Chapter. Do not overtighten it as the threads in the sump are easily damaged.

6 Place the drain tray below the oil filter on the front of the engine. Clean the crankcase around the filter, then unscrew the filter using a filter adapter (BMW service tool Part No. 11 4 661 or an aftermarket alternative) **(see illustrations)**. Tip any residual oil into the drain tray **(see illustration)**.

7 Lubricate the seal of the new filter with clean engine oil, then screw it onto the engine by hand until the seal seats **(see illustrations)**. Using the filter adapter (DO NOT use a strap or chain type removing tool), tighten the filter to the specified torque setting.

8 Refill the engine with the correct amount and type of oil (see *Pre-ride checks*). With the

3.6c Tip any residual oil into the drain tray

motorcycle supported upright on level ground, the oil level should lie between the MIN and MAX level lines on the dipstick with the filler cap fully unscrewed and resting on the cover. Install the filler cap.

> **HAYNES HINT**
> *Saving a little money on the difference between good and cheap oils won't pay off if the engine is damaged as a result.*

9 Start the engine and ensure that the oil pressure warning light goes out after a few seconds. Run until it reaches normal operating temperature and the radiator fan comes on, then allow it to run for a further minute. Turn the engine OFF.

10 Recheck the oil level and top-up if necessary. Tighten the filler cap securely.

11 If removed, install the sump guard (GS models) or the belly panel (R models).

12 The old oil drained from the engine cannot be re-used and should be disposed of properly. Check with your local refuse disposal company, disposal facility or environmental agency to see whether they will accept the used oil for recycling. Don't pour used oil into drains or onto the ground.

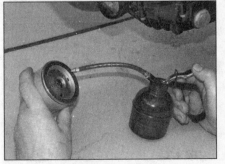

3.7a Lubricate the filter seal . . .

3.7b . . . then screw the new filter on by hand

4.3 Measure the gap (arrowed)

4.4 Loosen the locknuts (arrowed) on the adjuster

4 Clutch and throttle cables

Clutch cable

1 Check that the clutch lever operates smoothly and easily.

2 If the clutch lever operation is heavy or stiff, remove the cable (see Chapter 2, Section 15) and lubricate it (see below). Check that the inner cable slides freely and easily in the outer cable. If not, fit a new cable. Install the lubricated or new cable (see Chapter 2) and adjust the freeplay as follows.

3 Periodic adjustment is necessary to compensate for wear in the clutch plates and stretch of the cable. Turn the handlebars all the way to the left, then pull the outer cable gently and measure the gap between the end of the outer cable and the handlebar lever **(see illustration)**. Check that the gap (freeplay) is as specified at the beginning of this Chapter.

4 If adjustment is required, loosen the locknuts on the adjuster on the lower end of the cable **(see illustration)**. To reduce freeplay, thread the upper locknut towards the adjuster bracket. To increase freeplay, thread the lower locknut towards the adjuster bracket. Ensure the handlebars are turned all the way to the left while making the adjustment.

5 When the correct adjustment has been achieved, tighten the locknuts against the bracket. Turn the handlebars from left-to-right and back again a few times and check the adjustment.

6 If all the cable adjustment has been taken-up, fit a new cable (see Chapter 2).

7 The clutch lever has a span adjuster which alters the distance of the lever from the handlebar **(see illustration)**. Each setting is indexed – push the lever gently forwards and turn the adjuster clockwise to increase the distance or anti-clockwise to reduce the distance.

Throttle cable

8 Make sure the throttle cable operates smoothly and freely with the front wheel turned at various angles. The throttle twistgrip should return automatically from fully open to fully closed when released.

9 If action is sticky, this is probably due to a cable fault. Remove the cable (see Chapter 4) and lubricate it (see below). Check that the inner cable slides freely and easily in the outer cable. If not, fit a new cable.

10 With the cable removed, make sure the twistgrip turns freely on the handlebar – dirt combined with a lack of lubrication can cause the action to be stiff. If necessary, remove, clean and lubricate the twistgrip (see Chapter 5).

11 With the cable operating smoothly, check for freeplay by noting the amount of twistgrip rotation before the pulley on the throttle bodies moves **(see illustration)**.

4.7 Clutch lever span adjuster (arrowed)

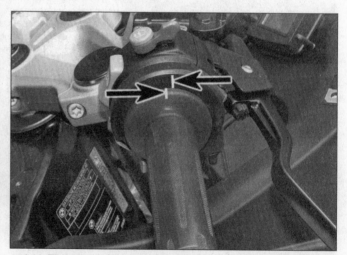

4.11 Throttle cable freeplay is measured in terms of twistgrip rotation

12 If adjustment is required, loosen the lockring on the adjuster on the upper end of the cable **(see illustration)**. To reduce freeplay, thread the adjuster out from the cable elbow. To increase freeplay, thread the adjuster towards the cable elbow.

13 When the correct adjustment has been achieved, tighten the lockring. Turn the handlebars from lock to lock a few times and check the adjustment.

14 If all the cable adjustment has been taken up, fit a new cable (see Chapter 4).

⚠ *Warning: Turn the handlebars all the way through their travel with the engine idling – idle speed should not change. If it does, the throttle cable may be routed incorrectly. Correct this condition before riding the bike.*

Cable lubrication

Special tool: *A cable lubricating adapter is necessary for this procedure.*

15 To lubricate the cables, disconnect the relevant cable at its upper end, then lubricate it with a pressure adapter and aerosol lubricant cable lube **(see illustrations)**.

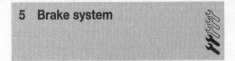

5 Brake system

Brake pads and discs

1 Each brake pad has wear indicators, in the form of cut-outs in the friction material on the front pads and a chamfered edge on the rear pads **(see illustrations)**. The wear indicators should be visible by looking at the edges of the friction material, but an accumulation of road dirt and brake dust could make them difficult to see.

2 If the indicators aren't visible it is advisable either to displace the calipers or remove the pads for inspection (see Chapter 6). **Note:** *Some after-market pads may use different*

4.12 Throttle cable adjuster lockring (arrowed)

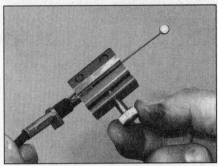

4.15b Ensure the adapter grips the inner and outer cables firmly

indicators to those on the original equipment. BMW specifies a minimum thickness of 1 mm for the friction material **(see illustration)**.

3 If the pads are worn to the minimum thickness they must be replaced with new ones (see Chapter 6). **Note:** *It is advisable to fit new pads before they become this worn.* If the pads are wearing unevenly, displace the caliper(s) and check the operation of the pistons.

4 Inspect the surface of the brake discs for scoring and check for a lip around the outer edge of the disc – evidence that the disc has worn (see Chapter 6).

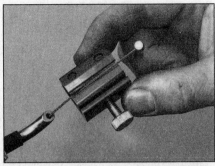

4.15a Fitting the cable lubricating adapter onto the inner cable

4.15c Connect the can of cable lubricant to the adapter

5.1a Front brake pad wear indicators

5.1b Rear brake pad wear indicator

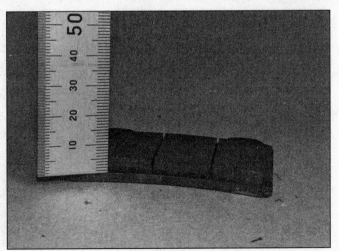

5.2 Measuring pad friction material – front pad shown

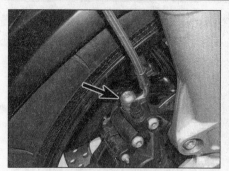

5.8a Check the front . . .

5.8b . . . and rear brake hose unions

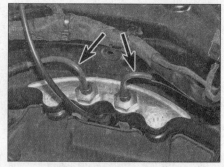

5.9a ABS front brake pipes behind steering head

Brake system check

5 A routine general check of the brake system will ensure that any problems are discovered and remedied before the rider's safety is jeopardised.

6 Check the brake lever and pedal for loose fixings, improper or rough action, excessive play, bends, and other damage. Replace any damaged parts with new ones (see Chapter 6). Clean and lubricate the lever and pedal pivots if their action is stiff or rough (see Section 7). If the lever or pedal is spongy, bleed the brakes (see Chapter 6).

7 Make sure the fluid level in the reservoirs is correct (see *Pre-ride checks*).

8 Make sure all brake component fasteners are tight. Look for leaks at the hose and pipe connections and ensure they are tightened securely **(see illustrations)**.

9 On models with ABS, remove the bodywork as required (see Chapter 7) and check the brake pipes, the pipe joints and the control unit for signs of fluid leakage and for any dents or cracks in the pipes **(see illustrations)**.

10 The braided hoses used on the machines covered in this manual are generally maintenance-free. However, they can be damaged if they are pinched or crushed, as in a crash. Ensure the hoses are routed clear of the steering and suspension components. Inspect the hoses between the front and rear fluid reservoirs and the master cylinders. These will deteriorate with age. Squeeze the hoses and check for cracks or splits in the surface, and renew them as necessary. New hose clips will have to be fitted at the same time (see Chapter 6).

11 Always replace the banjo union sealing washers with new ones when fitting new hoses. Refill the system with new brake fluid and bleed the system as described in Chapter 6.

12 Make sure the brake light operates when the brake lever or pedal is applied. If it fails to operate properly, check the bulb and if necessary the switches (see Chapter 8).

13 The front brake lever has a span adjuster which alters the distance of the lever from the handlebar **(see illustration)**. Each setting is indexed – push the lever gently forwards and turn the adjuster clockwise to increase the distance or anti-clockwise to reduce the distance.

Brake fluid change

14 The brake fluid should be changed at the specified service interval or whenever a master cylinder or caliper is disconnected – see Chapter 6 for details. Ensure that all the old fluid is pumped from the system and that the level in the fluid reservoir is checked and the brakes tested before riding the motorcycle.

Brake caliper and master cylinder seals

15 Brake system seals will deteriorate with age and lose their effectiveness, leading to sticky operation of the brake master cylinders or the pistons in the brake calipers, or to fluid loss. Internal components are not listed for the master cylinders – if one becomes faulty a new master cylinder will have to be fitted.

16 Caliper seals are listed for the front and rear brakes on GS models and for the rear brake

only on S, ST and R models. Otherwise, a new caliper will have to be fitted. Check with your dealer as to the availability of replacement seal kits or individual parts and refer to Chapter 6 for details of brake component overhaul.

6 Steering head bearings

1 Steering head bearings can become dented, rough or loose during normal use of the machine. In extreme cases, worn or loose steering head bearings can cause steering wobble – a condition that is potentially dangerous. Bearings that are too tight will cause handling problems.

Check freeplay

2 Support the motorcycle upright using an auxiliary stand if necessary, then position an additional support under the engine so that the front wheel is off the ground. Ensure the bike is held securely.

3 Point the front wheel straight-ahead and slowly move the handlebars from lock to lock. Any dents or roughness in the bearing races will be felt and if the bearings are too tight the bars will not move smoothly and freely. If the bearings are damaged they should be replaced with new ones (see Chapter 5). If the bearings are too tight, adjust them as described below.

4 Next, grasp the bottom of the forks and gently pull and push them forward and backward **(see illustration)**. Any looseness or

5.9b Check the pipe joints on the ABS control unit

5.13 Front brake lever span adjuster (arrowed)

6.4 Checking for play in the steering head bearings

6.6 Bearing adjuster bolt – GS models

6.7 Top yoke fork clamp bolts – R models

freeplay in the steering head bearings will be felt as front-to-rear movement of the forks. If play is felt, adjust the bearings as follows.

HAYNES HiNT *Make sure you are not mistaking any movement between the bike and stand, or between the stand and the ground, for freeplay in the bearings. Do not pull and push the forks too hard – a gentle movement is all that is needed. Freeplay between the fork tubes due to worn bushes can also be misinterpreted as steering head bearing play – do not confuse the two.*

Adjustment

5 Support the motorcycle upright with the front wheel on the ground.
6 On GS models, follow the procedure In Chapter 5 to displace the handlebars to access the bearing adjuster bolt **(see illustration)**.
7 On R models, follow the procedure In Chapter 5 to loosen the handlebar clamp bolts, then rotate the handlebars to access the fork clamp bolts in the top yoke **(see illustration)**.
8 On all models, loosen the fork clamp bolts on both sides in the top yoke **(see illustration)**. Loosen the steering stem clamp bolt **(see illustration)**.
9 Prise out the blanking cap from the bearing adjuster bolt **(see illustration)**.
10 Loosen the adjuster bolt approximately one turn, then tighten it to the initial torque setting specified at the beginning of this Chapter. Turn the steering from lock-to-lock three times to settle the bearings. Next, loosen the bolt through an angle of 60° (1/6th of a turn), then tighten it to the final torque setting **(see illustration)**.
Caution: Take great care not to apply excessive pressure because this will cause premature failure of the bearings.
11 Tighten the steering stem clamp bolt and

the fork clamp bolts to the specified torque settings
12 Turn the steering from lock-to-lock a few times, then check the adjustment and re-adjust if necessary.
13 Install the blanking cap.
14 On GS and R models, follow the procedure In Chapter 5 to install the handlebars.
15 If the bearings cannot be correctly adjusted, remove the steering stem and check the bearings and races (see Chapter 5).

Lubrication

16 Over time the grease in the bearings

6.8a Loosen the top yoke fork clamp bolts . . .

6.9 Prise out the blanking cap

will be dispersed, washed out or will harden allowing the ingress of dirt and water.
17 Although not a scheduled service item, the steering head should be disassembled periodically and the bearings cleaned and re-greased (see Chapter 5).

7 General lubrication

1 Since the controls, stands, footrests and various other components of a motorcycle are exposed to the elements, they should be

6.8b . . . and the steering stem clamp bolt

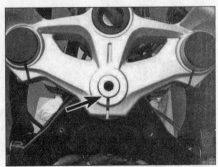

6.10 Use the bolt (arrowed) to adjust the bearings

checked and lubricated periodically to ensure safe and trouble-free operation.

2 The footrest pivots, clutch and brake lever pivots, brake pedal and gearchange lever pivots and linkage and sidestand and centrestand pivot (as applicable) should be lubricated frequently.

3 In order for the lubricant to be applied where it will do the most good, the component should be disassembled (see Chapter 5).

4 The lubricant recommended by BMW for each application is listed at the beginning of this Chapter. If an aerosol lubricant is used, it can be applied to the pivot joint gaps and will usually work its way into the areas where friction occurs, so less disassembly of the component is needed (however it is always better to do so and clean off all corrosion, dirt and old lubricant first).

5 If motor oil or light grease is being used, apply it sparingly as it may attract dirt (which could cause the controls to bind or wear at an accelerated rate).

8 Nuts and bolts

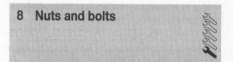

1 Since vibration of the machine tends to loosen fasteners, all nuts, bolts, screws, etc. should be periodically checked for proper tightness.

2 Pay particular attention to the following, referring to the relevant Chapter:
● Spark plug(s)
● Oil and coolant drain bolts
● Lever and pedal bolts
● Handlebar clamp bolts
● Footrest and footrest bracket bolts
● Sidestand/centrestand pivot bolts and mounting bolts
● Engine mounting bolts
● Shock absorber bolts; swingarm pivot bolt and nut

● Front fork clamp bolts (top and bottom yoke) and fork top bolts
● Steering stem clamp bolt
● Front axle and axle clamp bolts
● Rear axle nut (GS and R models)
● Rear wheel bolts (S and ST models)
● Front and rear sprocket/pulley nuts
● Drive belt eccentric adjuster clamp screws
● Brake caliper and master cylinder mounting bolts
● Brake hose banjo bolts and caliper bleed valves
● Brake disc bolts
● Exhaust system bolts/nuts

3 If a torque wrench is available, use it along with the torque settings given at the beginning of this and other Chapters.

9 Wheels and wheel bearings

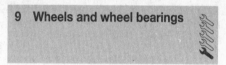

Wire spoked wheels

1 Check the spokes for damage and corrosion. A broken or bent spoke must be replaced with a new one immediately because the load taken by it will be transferred to adjacent spokes which may in turn fail.

2 Check spoke tension by tapping each one lightly with a screwdriver and noting the sound produced – each one should make the same sound. Tight, properly tensioned spokes will make a sharp ringing sound, loose ones will produce a lower, dull sound. If a spoke needs adjustment turn the adjuster at the rim using a spoke key or an open-ended spanner **(see illustration)**.

3 Unevenly tensioned spokes will promote rim misalignment – refer to information on wheel runout in Chapter 6 and have the wheel checked by a BMW dealer or wheel building specialist.

4 Check that the wheel balance weights are fixed firmly to the wheel rim. If you suspect

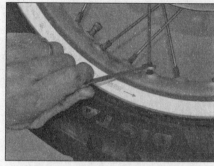
9.2 Tighten loose spokes carefully to avoid damage

that a weight has fallen off, have the wheel rebalanced by a motorcycle tyre specialist.

5 Check front and rear wheel alignment as described in Chapter 6.

Cast wheels

6 Cast wheels are virtually maintenance free, but they should be kept clean and checked periodically for cracks and other damage. Also check the wheel runout and alignment (see Chapter 6).

7 Never attempt to repair damaged cast wheels; they must be renewed if damaged.

8 Check that the wheel balance weights are fixed firmly to the wheel rim **(see illustration)**. If you suspect that a weight has fallen off, have the wheel rebalanced by a motorcycle tyre specialist.

Tyres

9 Check the tyre condition and tread depth thoroughly (see *Pre-ride checks*).

10 Make sure that both valves have a dust cap fitted. Check the valve for signs of damage. If tyre deflation occurs and it is not due to a slow puncture, the valve core may be loose or air could be leaking past the valve seal. Check that the core is tight **(see illustration)**. To check for air leaks from the valve, smear soapy water over the open end – escaping air will form bubbles in the water.

9.8 Balance weights must be fixed firmly to the wheel rim

9.10 Check the valve core for air leaks

9.13a Checking for play in the front . . .

9.13b . . . and rear wheel bearings

10.4 Timing mark alignment – No. 1 piston at TDC

11 If the valve core is thought to be faulty, support the machine with the wheel to be worked on off the ground. Unscrew the core from the valve housing and thread a new one in its place. Inflate the tyre to the correct pressure (see *Pre-ride checks*). Check that the tyre is properly seated all around the wheel rim.

> **HAYNES HiNT** *A valve core tool can be made quite easily by cutting a slot into the threaded end of a bolt using a hacksaw – the bolt must fit inside the valve housing and the slot must be deep enough to locate around the flat sides of the core and grip it.*

Wheel bearings

12 Wheel bearings will wear over a considerable mileage and should be checked periodically to avoid handling problems.
13 Support the motorcycle upright using an auxiliary stand so that the wheel being examined is off the ground. When checking the front wheel bearings, turn the handlebars to full lock on one side so you have something to push against. Check for any play in the bearings by pushing and pulling the wheel against the hub **(see illustrations)**. Also rotate the wheel and check that it turns smoothly and without any grating noises.
14 If any play is detected in the hub, or if

the wheel does not rotate smoothly (and this is not due to brake or drive chain/belt drag), the wheel should be removed and the bearings inspected for wear or damage (see Chapter 6). Note that on belt-drive S and ST models, the rear wheel bearings are contained in the belt tension eccentric adjuster assembly in the rear end of the swingarm (see Chapter 6).

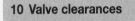

10 Valve clearances

Special tool: *A set of blade-type feeler gauges is necessary for this job (see Step 6).*

Check

1 The engine must be completely cool for this maintenance procedure.
2 Follow the procedure in Chapter 2 to remove the valve cover. Note that it is not necessary to remove the secondary air system reed valves.
3 Make a chart or sketch of the valve positions so that a note of each clearance can be made against the relevant valve. The intake valves are on the back of the cylinder head and the exhaust valves are on the front.
4 To check the valve clearances the engine must be turned in the direction of normal rotation until the No. 1 piston is at top dead centre (TDC) on the compression stroke – all four valves for that cylinder closed. To do this, support the machine with the rear wheel off the ground, engage first gear and

turn the engine by rotating the rear wheel. Alternatively, remove the alternator cover (see Chapter 8) and turn the alternator rotor bolt in a clockwise direction. The engine is in the correct position when the 'I/N' and 'E/X' timing marks (only I and E will be visible) on the camshaft sprockets are facing each other and parallel with the sealing surface of the cylinder head **(see illustration)**.
5 With the camshaft sprockets in this position, check the clearances on the No. 1 cylinder intake and exhaust valves.
6 Insert a feeler gauge of the same thickness as the correct valve clearance (see *Specifications* at the beginning of this Chapter) between the camshaft lobe and the follower of each valve and check that it is a firm sliding fit – you should feel a slight drag when the you pull the gauge out **(see illustration)**. If not, use the feeler gauges to obtain the exact clearance. Record the measured clearance on the chart. **Note:** *The intake and exhaust valve clearances are different.*
7 Now rotate the engine (crankshaft) 360° clockwise so that the timing marks on the camshaft sprockets (only N and X will be visible) are facing *away* from each other and parallel with the sealing surface of the cylinder head **(see illustration)** – the No. 2 piston should now be at TDC with all valves closed. Check the clearances on the No. 2 cylinder intake and exhaust valves and record them on the chart **(see illustration)**.
8 When all clearances have been measured

10.6 Checking the clearance on No. 1 cylinder valves

10.7a Timing mark alignment – No. 2 piston at TDC

10.7b Checking the clearance on No. 2 cylinder valves

10.10a Retrieve the shim either from the top of the valve . . .

10.10b . . . or from inside the follower

10.11a Size mark etched on the shim

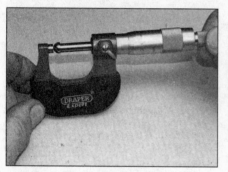

10.11b Measuring the shim with a micrometer

10.14 Lower the follower onto the valve

and recorded, identify whether the clearance on any valve falls outside the specified range. If it does, the shim between the cam follower and the valve must be replaced with one of a thickness which will restore the correct clearance.

Adjustment

9 Changing the shims requires removal of the camshafts (see Chapter 2). Place rags over the spark plug holes, cam chain tunnel and oil galleries to prevent a shim from dropping into the engine on removal. Work on one valve at a time.

10 Raise the follower and retrieve the shim either from the top of the valve or from inside the follower using either a magnet or a screwdriver with a dab of grease on it **(see**

illustrations). Do not allow the shim to fall into the engine.

11 A size mark should be etched on the side of the shim, but you should measure the shim to check whether it has worn **(see illustrations)**.

12 Calculate the size of the shim required – if the clearance measured was too big you need a shim that is thicker than the existing shim by the amount that the clearance was too great; if the clearance was too small you need a shim that is thinner than the existing shim by the amount that the clearance was too small.

13 Shims are available from 4.60 mm to 5.70 mm thick in increments of 0.05 mm. **Note:** *If the required shim is greater than 5.70 mm (the largest available), the valve is probably not*

seating correctly due to a build-up of carbon deposits and should be checked and cleaned or resurfaced as required (see Chapter 2).

14 Prior to installation, smear the curved top of the shim with a dab of grease, then press it into the appropriate follower – the grease will hold it in position. Check that the shim is correctly seated, then lower the follower onto the valve **(see illustration)**.

15 Repeat the process for any other valves as required, then install the camshafts (see Chapter 2).

16 Rotate the crankshaft clockwise several turns to seat the new shim(s), then check the valve clearances again.

17 Install the valve cover (see Chapter 2).

18 Install the remaining components in the reverse order of removal.

11 Air filter

Caution: If the machine is continually ridden in wet or dusty conditions, the filter should be changed more frequently.

1 Remove the seat and bodywork centre panel; on GS models remove both side panels, on all other models remove the left-hand side panel (see Chapter 7).

2 On GS models, undo the screws securing the filter cover and remove the cover, then lift out the filter element **(see illustrations)**.

11.2a Undo the screws . . .

11.2b . . . securing the cover . . .

11.2c . . . and lift out the filter element

11.3a Pull up the clips . . .

11.3b . . . to release the intake pipe . . .

11.3c . . . and lift out the filter element

11.6 Ensure the filter element is properly seated – GS models

11.7a Fit the filter element into the intake pipe – S, ST and R models

11.7b Install the clips securely

3 On S, ST and R models, pull up the clips securing the intake pipe, then lift off the pipe assembly and filter element **(see illustrations)**.

4 The filter element is not designed to be cleaned – fit a new element at the specified service interval (see *Caution* above).

5 Clean the inside of the filter cover or intake pipe assembly as applicable.

6 On GS models, fit the filter element into the housing, making sure it is properly seated **(see illustration)**. Install the cover and tighten the cover screws securely **(see illustrations 11.2b and a)**.

7 On S, ST and R models, fit the filter element into the intake pipe, locate the assembly on the air intake housing and secure it with the clips **(see illustrations)**.

8 Install the remaining components in the reverse order of removal.

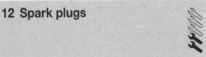

12 Spark plugs

Note: *The spark plug caps are integral with the ignition HT coils. To avoid damaging the wiring, always disconnect the wiring connectors before removing the coils. Do not attempt to lever the coils off the plugs or pull them off with pliers – use the special tool. Do not drop the coils.*

Special tools: *An ignition HT coil puller and a wire or blade-type feeler gauge are necessary for this job (see Steps 6 and 12).*

Removal

1 Make sure your spark plug socket is the correct size before attempting to remove the plugs (see Step 7).

2 Remove the seat, bodywork centre panel and both side panels (see Chapter 7).

3 Remove the battery (see Chapter 8).

4 Remove the air filter housing assembly (see Chapter 4).

5 Check that the cylinder location is marked on both coil wiring connectors and mark them accordingly if not **(see illustration)**. Disconnect the connectors.

6 Clean the area around the coil seals to prevent any dirt falling into the spark plug channels, then pull the coils off the spark plugs using the service tool (Part No. 12 3 561) **(see illustrations)**. **Note:** *If the coils are*

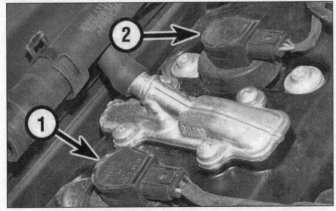

12.5 Mark the coil connectors with the cylinder number

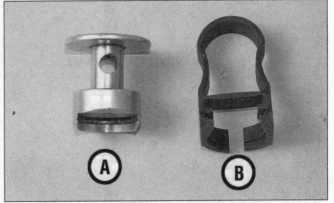

12.6a BMW service tool (A) and ignition coil puller (B)

12.6b Using the service tool

12.6c Using the ignition coil puller

12.7 Unscrew the plugs from the cylinder head

stuck in the plug channels squirt penetrating fluid into the gap between the coils and the valve cover, then twist them carefully and ease them out.

7 Using a 16 mm deep socket type wrench, unscrew the plugs from the cylinder head **(see illustration)**.

Check

8 New spark plugs should be fitted at the specified service interval. However, if a running problem develops between services, check the plugs as follows.

9 Lay the plugs out in relation to their cylinders; if either plug shows up a problem it will then be easy to identify the troublesome cylinder.

10 Look for excessive deposits and evidence of a cracked or chipped insulator around the centre electrode. Compare your spark plugs to the colour spark plug reading chart on the inside rear cover. Inspect the ceramic insulator body for cracks and other damage. Check the threads and the sealing washer.

11 Make sure the plugs are the correct type and heat range as specified at the beginning of this Chapter. Examine the electrodes for wear – both the centre and side electrodes

should have square edges and the side electrode should be of uniform thickness. If the electrodes are not excessively worn, and any deposits can be easily removed with a wire brush, the plugs can be re-used. If in doubt concerning the condition of the plugs, replace them with new ones, as the expense is minimal.

12 Before installing the plugs, check the gap between the electrodes **(see illustration)**. Compare the gap to that specified and adjust as necessary. If the gap must be adjusted, bend the side electrode and be very careful not to chip or crack the insulator nose **(see illustration)**.

Installation

13 Always install the correct type and heat range of spark plug for your machine (see *Specifications* at the beginning of this Chapter).

14 Check the gap between the electrodes (see Step 12) and make sure the sealing washer is in place on the plug.

15 Fit the plug into the end of the tool, then use the tool to insert the plug **(see illustration 12.7)**. Since the cylinder head is made of aluminium, which is soft and easily damaged, thread the

plugs as far as possible into the head turning the tool by hand. Once the plugs are finger-tight, the job can be finished with a spanner on the tool supplied or a socket drive.

> **HAYNES HiNT** *As the plugs are quite recessed, slip a short length of hose over the end of the plug to use as a tool to thread it into place. The hose will grip the plug well enough to turn it, but will start to slip if the plug begins to cross-thread in the hole – this will prevent damaged threads.*

16 If a torque wrench is available, tighten the spark plugs to the torque setting specified at the beginning of this Chapter. Otherwise, tighten them according the instructions on the box – generally if new plugs are being used, tighten them by 1/2 a turn after the washer has seated, and if the old plugs are being reused, tighten them by 1/8 to 1/4 turn after they have seated. Do not over-tighten the spark plugs.

17 Install the ignition coils, pressing them down firmly onto the spark plugs so that the seals are tight against the valve cover, and connect the connectors **(see illustration 12.5)**.

12.12a Using a wire type gauge to measure the spark plug electrode gap

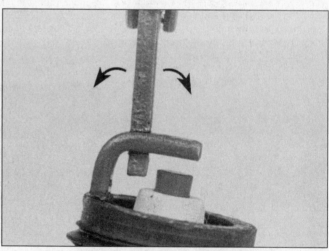

12.12b Bend the side electrode to adjust the gap

13.2 Checking the action of the front suspension

13.4 Check around the seals (arrowed) for oil leakage

18 Install the remaining components in the reverse order of removal.

Stripped plug threads in the cylinder head can be repaired with a Heli-Coil insert – see 'Tools and Workshop Tips' in the Reference section.

13 Suspension

1 The suspension components must be maintained in top operating condition to ensure rider safety. Loose, worn or damaged suspension parts decrease the motorcycle's stability and control.

Front suspension check

2 While standing alongside the motorcycle, apply the front brake and push on the handlebars to compress the forks several times **(see illustration)**. See if they move up-and-down smoothly without binding. If binding is felt, the forks should be disassembled and inspected (see Chapter 5).
3 Inspect the fork inner tubes for scratches, corrosion and pitting which will cause premature seal failure – if the damage is excessive, new tubes should be installed (see Chapter 5). Minor rust spots can be treated and cleaned up using metal polish.
4 Inspect the fork inner tube around the dust seal for signs of oil leakage, then carefully lever the seal off using a flat-bladed screwdriver and inspect the area around the fork oil seal **(see illustration)**. If leakage is evident, the fork oil should be drained and refilled to the specified level and the oil seals should be renewed (see Chapter 5).
5 If there is evidence of corrosion between the oil seal retaining ring and its groove in the fork

outer tube, remove the fork leg and fit new dust seals (see Chapter 5). Prior to fitting the dust seals, spray the oil seal retaining ring and groove with a penetrative lubricant, otherwise the ring will be difficult to remove when needed. Wipe away any surplus lubricant.
6 Check the tightness of all suspension bolts to be sure none have worked loose, referring to the torque settings specified at the beginning of Chapter 5.

Front fork oil change

7 The fork oil will degrade over a period of time and lose its damping qualities. Although not a scheduled service item, the oil should be changed after the machine has covered a high mileage, or the forks should be drained and refilled with fresh oil whenever the seals are renewed (see Chapter 5).

Rear suspension check

8 Inspect the rear shock absorber for fluid leakage and tightness of its mountings. If leakage is found, the shock must be replaced with a new one (see Chapter 5).
9 With the aid of an assistant to support the bike, compress the rear suspension several times. It should move up and down freely

13.11 Checking the rear shock for freeplay

without binding. If any binding is felt, the worn or faulty component must be identified and checked (see Chapter 5). The problem could be due to either the shock absorber or the swingarm.
10 Support the motorcycle on an auxiliary stand so that the rear wheel is off the ground. Grab the swingarm and rock it from side-to-side – there should be no discernible movement at the rear. If there's a little movement or a slight clicking can be heard, check the tightness of the swingarm pivot bolt, referring to the torque setting specified at the beginning of Chapter 5, then re-check for movement.
11 Next, grasp the top of the rear wheel and pull it upwards – there should be no discernible freeplay before the shock absorber begins to compress **(see illustration)**. Any freeplay felt in either check indicates worn bearings in the swingarm, or worn shock absorber mountings. The worn components must be identified and replaced with new ones (see Chapter 5).
12 To make an accurate assessment of the swingarm bearings, remove the rear wheel (see Chapter 6). Now follow the procedure in Chapter 5, Section 13, and check for wear (freeplay) in the bearings.
13 Next, move the swingarm up and down through its full travel. It should move freely, without any binding or rough spots. If there is any play in the swingarm bearings, or if the swingarm does not move freely, remove the swingarm and inspect the pivot bolt, bearing sleeves and bearings (see Chapter 5).

Rear suspension bearing lubrication

14 Over time the grease in the bearings will be dispersed, washed out or will harden allowing the ingress of dirt and water.
15 Although not a scheduled service item, the swingarm should be removed periodically and the bearings cleaned and re-greased (see Chapter 5).

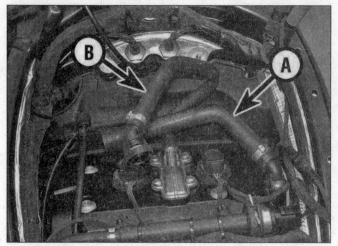

14.4a Check the engine breather hose (A) and secondary air system hose (B)

14.4b Note the clip used to secure the hose to the fuel rail

14 Fuel system

⚠ **Warning: Petrol (gasoline) is extremely flammable, so take extra precautions when you work on any part of the fuel system. Don't smoke or allow open flames or bare light bulbs near the work area, and don't work in a garage where a natural gas-type appliance is present. If you spill any fuel on your skin, rinse it off immediately with soap and water. When you perform any kind of work on the fuel system, wear safety glasses and have a fire extinguisher suitable for a Class B type fire (flammable liquids) on hand.**

General check

1 Remove the seat, bodywork centre panel and both side panels (see Chapter 7).
2 Remove the battery (see Chapter 8).
3 Remove the air filter housing (see Chapter 4).
4 Check the entire fuel system, especially the hose from the tank to the fuel rail and the fuel injector unions on the fuel rail, for signs of leaks, deterioration or damage. Also check the engine breather hose and, on all models except the F650 GS, the secondary air system hose **(see illustrations)**. Renew any hose that is cracked or deteriorated with a new one. **Note:** *Non-reuseable type hose clips should be replaced with new ones if they have been loosened. Special pliers are required to close these clips (see Chapter 4).*
5 If there are any leaks between the injectors and the throttle body, remove the injectors and fit a new seals and O-rings (see Chapter 4).
6 Check around the fuel filler neck, the fuel pump and the fuel safety valve on the fuel tank for signs of leaks. Where necessary,

remove the component and renew the seal (see Chapter 4)
7 Machines fitted with a catalytic converter should have the exhaust gas checked by a dealer – special equipment is needed.

Fuel strainer

8 Cleaning and inspection of the fuel strainer is advised after a particularly high mileage has been covered, although no service interval is specified by BMW. It is also necessary if fuel starvation is suspected.
9 The strainer is located on the bottom of the fuel pump – remove the pump from the fuel tank and clean the strainer as described in Chapter 4. In addition, note that a fuel filter is integral with the pump assembly and is not listed as a separate item.

15 Cooling system

⚠ **Warning: The engine must be cool before beginning this procedure.**

1 Remove the seat, bodywork centre panel and right-hand side panel (see Chapter 7).
2 Check the entire cooling system for

15.2 Check the coolant hoses and hose connections

evidence of leaks. Examine each coolant hose along its length, looking for cracks, abrasions and other damage **(see illustration)**. Squeeze each hose at various points to see whether it has become hardened – the hoses should be firm yet pliable, and should return to their original shape when released. If necessary, replace them with new ones (see Chapter 3).
3 Check each cooling system connection, the inlet and outlet unions on the water pump and radiator, and the pipe unions on the oil cooler on the front of the engine **(see illustration)**. Check the thermostat housing union on the lower, right-hand side of the radiator. Make sure all hose clips and joint screws are tight – if leaks persist, disassemble the components and renew the sealing gasket or O-ring (see Chapter 3, Section 8).
4 To prevent leakage of coolant from the cooling system into the lubrication system and vice versa, two seals are fitted on the water pump shaft inside the pump body. If either seal fails, coolant or oil can escape via a drain hole in the cylinder head below the location of the pump (see Chapter 3).
5 Check the radiator for leaks and other damage. Leaks in the radiator leave tell-tale scale deposits or coolant stains on the outside of the core below the leak. If leaks are noted, have the radiator repaired or replace it with a

15.3 Check the oil cooler pipe unions (arrowed)

15.8a Turn the radiator cap anti-clockwise . . .

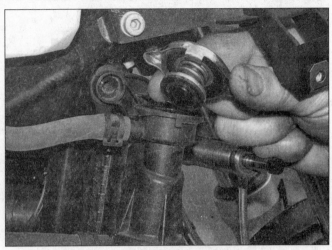

15.8b . . . then press down and twist to remove it

new one – do not use a liquid leak stopping compound to try to repair leaks.

6 Check the radiator fins for mud, dirt and insects, which may impede the flow of air through the radiator. If the fins are dirty, remove the radiator (see Chapter 3) and clean it using water or low pressure compressed air directed through the fins from the back of the radiator. If the fins are bent or distorted, straighten them carefully with a screwdriver. If airflow is restricted by bent or damaged fins over more than 20% of the radiator's surface area, replace the radiator with a new one.

7 Check the condition of the coolant in the system. If it is rust-coloured or if accumulations of scale are visible, drain, flush and refill the system with new coolant (see Chapter 3).

8 Remove the pressure cap from the radiator filler neck by turning it anti-clockwise until it reaches the stop. Now press down on the cap and continue turning it until it can be removed (see illustrations).

 Warning: Do not remove the pressure cap when the engine is hot. It is good practice to cover

the cap with a heavy cloth and turn the cap slowly anti-clockwise. If you hear a hissing sound (indicating that there is still pressure in the system), wait until it stops, then continue turning the cap until it can be removed.

9 Check the cap seal for cracks and other damage (see illustration). If in doubt about the pressure cap's condition, have it tested by a BMW dealer or fit a new one.

10 Check the antifreeze content of the coolant with an antifreeze hydrometer (see illustration). If the system has not been topped-up with the correct coolant mixture (see *Pre-ride checks*) the coolant will be too weak to offer adequate protection. If the hydrometer indicates a weak mixture, drain and refill the system (see Chapter 3).

11 Fit the cap by turning it clockwise until it reaches the first stop then push down on it and continue turning until it can turn no further (see illustration).

12 Start the engine and let it reach normal operating temperature, then check the system for leaks. As the coolant temperature

15.9 Check the cap seal

increases, the electric fan (mounted on the back of the radiator) should come on automatically and the temperature should begin to drop. If it does not, refer to Chapter 3 and check the fan and fan circuit carefully.

13 If the coolant level is consistently low, and no evidence of leaks can be found, have the entire system pressure checked by a BMW dealer.

15.10 Checking the coolant with an antifreeze hydrometer

15.11 Tighten the radiator cap against the stop (arrowed)

Chapter 2
Engine, clutch and transmission

Contents

	Section
Alternator	see Chapter 8
Balancer assembly	20
Cam chain tensioner	7
Camshafts and followers	8
Cam chain, tensioner and guide blades	9
Clutch	14
Clutch cable	15
Component access	2
Connecting rod and crankshaft bearing information	21
Connecting rods and big-end bearings	22
Crankcases	19
Crankshaft and main bearings	23
Cylinder head and valve overhaul	11
Cylinder head removal and installation	10
Engine overhaul information	5
Engine removal and installation	4
Engine wear assessment	3
External gearchange mechanism	17
Gear position sensor	see Chapter 4
General information	1

	Section
Ignition timing sensor	see Chapter 4
Oil and filter change	see Chapter 1
Oil cooler	12
Oil level check	see Pre-ride checks
Oil pressure switch	see Chapter 8
Oil pumps	16
Oil sump, strainer and pressure regulator	18
Pistons and cylinders	24
Piston rings	25
Running-in procedure	29
Selector drum and forks	28
Spark plugs	see Chapter 1
Starter clutch and gears	13
Starter motor	see Chapter 8
Transmission shaft overhaul	27
Transmission shafts and output shaft oil seal	26
Valve clearance check and adjustment	see Chapter 1
Valve cover	6
Water pump	see Chapter 3

Degrees of difficulty

Easy, suitable for novice with little experience	Fairly easy, suitable for beginner with some experience	Fairly difficult, suitable for competent DIY mechanic	Difficult, suitable for experienced DIY mechanic	Very difficult, suitable for expert DIY or professional

Specifications

General

Type	Four-stroke twin
Capacity	798 cc
Bore	82 mm
Stroke	75.6 mm
Compression ratio	12 to 1
Camshafts	DOHC, chain-driven
Cylinder identification	No. 1 left-hand, No. 2 right-hand
Clutch	Wet multi-plate
Transmission	Six-speed constant mesh
Final drive	
F650 GS, F800 GS and F800R	Chain
F800 S and ST	Belt
Cooling system	Liquid cooled
Lubrication	Dry sump, 2 trochoid pumps

Cylinder compression
Standard (when new) . . . .   217.5 psi (15 Bar)
Minimum . . . .   145 psi (10 Bar)

Lubrication system
Minimum oil pressure (oil @ 80°C)
   At idle speed. . . . .   17.4 psi (1.2 Bar)
   At 5000 rpm . . . .   50.7 psi (3.5 Bar)

Camshafts
Camshaft lobe height – intake and exhaust
   Standard. . . . .   36.64 to 36.66 mm
   Service limit (min) . . . .   36.52 mm
Camshaft journal diameter
   Standard. . . . .   24.99 to 25.0 mm
   Service limit (min) . . . .   24.97 mm
Camshaft holder bore diameter (max) . . . .   25.06 mm
Oil clearance
   Standard. . . . .   0.020 to 0.050 mm
   Service limit (max) . . . .   0.080 mm

Camchain tensioner and guide blades
Chain track depth (max). . . . .   0.8 mm

Valves, guides and springs
Valve clearances. . . . .   see Chapter 1
Valve stem runout
   Service limit at stem. . . . .   0.02 mm
   Service limit at head. . . . .   0.04 mm
Valve head diameter
   Intake . . . .   32.0 mm
   Exhaust. . . . .   27.5 mm
Valve stem diameter
   Intake valve
      Standard. . . . .   4.973 mm
      Service limit (min) . . . .   4.950 mm
   Exhaust valve
      Standard. . . . .   4.963 mm
      Service limit (min) . . . .   4.940 mm
Guide bore diameter
   Intake and exhaust valves
      Standard. . . . .   5.00 to 5.012 mm
Stem-to-guide radial clearance
   Intake valve
      Standard. . . . .   0.020 to 0.044 mm
      Service limit . . . .   0:07 mm
   Exhaust valve
      Standard. . . . .   0.030 to 0.054 mm
      Service limit . . . .   0.08 mm
Seat width
   Intake
      Standard. . . . .   1.05 to 1.35 mm
      Service limit . . . .   1.80 mm
   Exhaust
      Standard. . . . .   1.25 to 1.55 mm
      Service limit . . . .   2.50 mm
Valve spring free length
   Standard. . . . .   50.85 mm
   Service limit (min) . . . .   49.50 mm

Cylinder head
Warpage (max). . . . .   0.03 to 0.06 mm

Cylinder bore
Bore (measured 31 to 36 mm below top edge, across three points)
    Standard.. 81.993 to 82.007 mm
    Service limit (max) .... 82.03 mm

Piston
Piston diameter (measured across bottom edge of piston, at 90° to piston pin axis)
    Standard.. 81.94 to 81.96 mm
    Service limit (min) .... 81.92 mm
Piston-to-bore clearance
    Standard.. 0.03 to 0.06 mm
    Service limit (max) .... 0.10 mm
Piston pin clearance in connecting rod small-end
    Standard.. 0.01 to 0.025 mm
    Service limit (max) .... 0.04 mm

Crankshaft and bearings
End-float
    Standard.. 0.15 to 0.30 mm
    Service limit .... 0.45 mm
Main bearing oil clearance
    Standard.. 0.03 to 0.06 mm
    Service limit .... 0.10 mm

Connecting rod
Side clearance
    Standard.. 0.10 to 0.25 mm
    Service limit .... 0.30 mm
Big-end bearing oil clearance
    Standard.. 0.026 to 0.062 mm
    Service limit .... 0.080 mm

Balancer assembly
Connecting rod big-end bearing oil clearance
    Standard.. 0.044 to 0.080 mm
    Service limit .... 0.090 mm
Balancer rod shaft oil clearance
    Standard.. 0.005 to 0.020 mm
    Service limit .... 0.040 mm

Clutch
Friction plate thickness
    Standard.. 3.42 to 3.58 mm
    Service limit .... 3.40 mm
Friction plate tab width
    Inner and outer plates.................................. 13.0 mm
    All other plates .... 14.0 mm
Housing short slot width
    Standard.. 14.1 mm
    Service limit .... 14.4 mm
Plain plate thickness .... 1.45 to 1.55 mm
Plain plate warpage (max) .... 0.15 mm
Pull rod length
    With thrust washer .... 45.2 mm
    Without thrust washer .... 44.0 mm
Spring free length
    Standard.. 63.0 mm
    Service limit .... 60.0 mm

Oil pressure regulator
Spring free length.. 18.0 mm

Selector drum and forks
Selector fork end thickness (min)............................... 5.60 mm
Selector fork guide pin OD (min) .... 6.25 mm

Transmission
Gear ratios (no. of teeth)
  F800 S and ST
    Primary reduction...................................... 1.943 to 1 (35/68)
    Final reduction .... 2.353 to 1 (34/80)
    1st gear.. 2.462 to 1 (13/32)
    2nd gear... 1.750 to 1 (16/28)
    3rd gear... 1.381 to 1 (21/29)
    4th gear... 1.174 to 1 (23/27)
    5th gear... 1.042 to 1 (24/25)
    6th gear... 0.960 to 1 (25/24)
  F650GS and F800 GS
    Primary reduction...................................... 1.943 to 1 (35/68)
    Final reduction
      F650 GS .... 2.412 to 1 (17/41)
      F800 GS .... 2.625 to 1 (16/42)
    1st gear.. 2.462 to 1 (13/32)
    2nd gear... 1.750 to 1 (16/28)
    3rd gear... 1.381 to 1 (21/29)
    4th gear... 1.174 to 1 (23/27)
    5th gear... 1.042 to 1 (24/25)
    6th gear... 0.960 to 1 (25/24)
  F800 R
    Primary reduction...................................... 1.943 to 1 (35/68)
    Final reduction .... 2.350 to 1 (20/47)
    1st gear.. 2.462 to 1 (13/32)
    2nd gear... 1.750 to 1 (16/28)
    3rd gear... 1.381 to 1 (21/29)
    4th gear... 1.227 to 1 (22/27)
    5th gear... 1.130 to 1 (23/26)
    6th gear... 1.042 to 1 (24/25)

Torque settings
Balancer assembly connecting rod cap bolts
  Initial setting .... 10 Nm
  Second setting .... 50 Nm
  Final setting .... + 70°
Balancer assembly cover bolts .... 12 Nm
Cam chain tensioner blade pivot bolt .... 10 Nm
Cam chain tensioner cap bolt .... 40 Nm
Camshaft holder nuts.................................. 10 Nm
Camshaft sprocket bolts .... 50 Nm
Clutch cover bolts .... 12 Nm
Clutch nut... 180 Nm
Clutch spring bolts .... 10 Nm
Connecting rod big-end bearing cap bolts
  Initial setting .... 10 Nm
  Second setting .... 20 Nm
  Final setting .... + 70°
Crankcase bolts
  Lower half 8 mm main bearing bolts
    Initial setting .... 15 Nm
    Final setting .... + 80°
  Upper half 8 mm bolts................................ 30 Nm
  Upper and lower half 6 mm bolts........................ 12 Nm
Crankshaft main bearing cap bolts
  Initial setting .... 15 Nm
  Final setting .... + 45°
Cylinder head 10 mm bolts
  Initial setting .... 10 Nm
  Second setting .... 20 Nm
  Final setting .... + 110°
Cylinder head 6 mm bolts .... 10 Nm

Torque settings (continued)

Engine mountings
    F800 S, ST and R models

Adjuster	5 Nm max.
Adjuster locknut	100 Nm
Upper mounting bolts, right-hand side	
Initial setting	30 Nm
Final setting	40 Nm
Upper mounting bolts, left-hand side	40 Nm
Swinging arm clamp bolts	40 Nm
F650 GS and F800 GS models	
Upper front mounting bolts	66 Nm
Upper rear mounting bolts	40 Nm
Lower rear mounting bolts	38 Nm
Gearchange mechanism stopper arm bolt	10 Nm
Oil cooler centre bolt	30 Nm
Oil cooler mounting/flange bolts	10 Nm
Oil pump cover bolts	12 Nm
Oil sump bolts	12 Nm
Selector drum cam centre bolt	10 Nm
Starter clutch bolts	35 Nm
TDC locating pin tool blanking bolt	25 Nm
Valve cover bolts	10 Nm
Water pump drive gear bolt	30 Nm

---

1 General information

The engine is a liquid-cooled, vertical twin cylinder. Each cylinder has four valves that are operated by double overhead camshafts, chain driven off the left-hand end of the crankshaft. A third connecting rod is fitted to the crankshaft midway between the two conventional rods. This third rod is connected to a balance arm, the purpose of which is to reduce engine vibration.

The engine/transmission is a unit assembly constructed from aluminium alloy. The crankcase divides horizontally, the cylinders being integral with the upper crankcase half.

Engine oil is retained in a specially designed reservoir within the crankcase and is pressure-fed via two, dual rotor trochoidal oil pumps to oil jets in the gearbox and to the engine bearings. The oil pumps are driven off the back of the clutch. An oil cooler is located on the front of the crankcase.

The alternator is on the right-hand end of the crankshaft and the rotor carries the starter clutch and the ignition timing triggers. The water pump is on the right-hand side of the cylinder head, and is driven by the intake camshaft.

Power from the crankshaft is routed to the transmission via the clutch. The clutch is of the wet, multi-plate type and is gear-driven off the crankshaft. The clutch is operated by cable. The transmission is a six-speed, constant-mesh unit. Final drive to the rear wheel is by chain and sprockets on GS and R models, and by belt and pulleys on S and ST models.

2 Component access

Operations possible with the engine in the frame

The components and assemblies listed below can be removed without having to remove the engine from the frame. If however, a number of areas require attention at the same time, removal of the engine is recommended.

    Valve cover
    Cam chain tensioner and blades
    Camshafts
    Clutch
    Alternator/starter clutch
    Oil cooler
    Oil pumps
    Oil sump, strainer and pressure regulator
    Gearchange mechanism
    Starter motor
    Water pump
    Transmission output shaft oil seal

Operations requiring engine removal

It is necessary to remove the engine from the frame to gain access to the following components.

    Cam chain
    Connecting rods
    Crankshaft and bearings
    Cylinder head
    Balancer assembly
    Pistons
    Selector drum and forks
    Transmission shafts

3 Engine wear assessment

Cylinder compression check

Special tool: *A compression gauge is needed – they are available from good automotive tool suppliers. Get the type that threads into the spark plug hole (make sure it comes with an adapter with the same thread size (12 mm) and reach (19 mm) as the spark plug – it is very important the reach is not longer as the piston could contact it). Depending on the outcome of the initial test, a squirt-type oil can may also be needed.*

Note: *Due to removal of the air filter housing for this test a number of sensors must be disconnected. When the ignition is switched on, these will register as fault codes in the engine control unit memory. The memory should be cleared by a BMW dealer using the appropriate diagnostic equipment at the next service interval.*

1 Poor engine performance may be caused by leaking valves, incorrect valve clearances, a leaking head gasket, or worn piston, piston rings or cylinder wall. A cylinder compression check will highlight these conditions and can also indicate the presence of excessive carbon deposits in the cylinder head. A leakdown test (for which special equipment is needed – consult a BMW dealer) will pinpoint the actual cause(s) of the problem.

2 Start by making sure the valve clearances are correctly set (see Chapter 1) and that the cylinder head bolts are tightened to the correct torque setting (see Section 10).

3.4 Install the compression tester as described

3.12 Set-up for checking the engine oil pressure

3 Run the engine until it is at normal operating temperature. Stop the engine, then follow the procedure in Chapter 1 to remove the spark plugs, taking care not to burn your hands on the hot components.

4 Fit the adaptor and gauge into the No. 1 cylinder spark plug hole **(see illustration)**. Place a rag over the open No. 2 cylinder spark plug hole to prevent atomised fuel escaping.

5 Temporarily install the air filter housing, reconnect the sensors, and install the battery. Turn the ignition ON and open the throttle fully. Crank the engine over on the starter motor for a few seconds until the gauge reading stabilises and take a note of the reading. Turn the ignition OFF. Transfer the compression gauge and adaptor to the other cylinder and repeat the procedure.

6 Compare the readings obtained with those in the *Specifications* at the beginning of this Chapter. If they fall within the specified range and are relatively equal, the engine is in good condition. Install the components in the reverse order of removal.

7 If the readings are close to or below the minimum limit, or one cylinder differs markedly from the other, further investigation is required. To determine the cause of low compression, inject a small quantity of engine oil into the spark plug hole of the suspect cylinder with a pump-type oil can – this will temporarily seal the piston rings. Repeat the compression test. If the result shows a noticeable increase in pressure this confirms that the cylinder bore, piston or rings are worn (see Sections 12 to 14). If there is no change in the reading, the cylinder head gasket or valves are leaking (see Sections 10 and 11).

8 Although unlikely with the use of modern fuels, a high compression reading indicates excessive carbon deposits in the combustion chamber area. Remove the cylinder head and clean all carbon off the pistons, head and valves (see Sections 10 and 11).

Engine oil pressure check

Special tool: *An oil pressure gauge and adapter (which screws into the oil gallery) are needed – they are available from good automotive tool suppliers.*
Note: *When the ignition is switched on*

during this test, the disconnected oil pressure switch will register as a fault code in the engine control unit memory. The memory should be cleared by a BMW dealer using the appropriate diagnostic equipment at the next service interval.

9 If there is any doubt about the performance of the engine lubrication system an oil pressure check must be carried out. The check provides useful information about the state of wear of the engine.

10 The oil pressure warning light should come on when the ignition switch is turned ON and extinguish a few seconds after the engine is started. If the oil pressure light comes on whilst the engine is running, low oil pressure is indicated – stop the engine immediately and check the oil level (see *Pre-ride checks*). If the oil level is good an oil pressure check must be carried out.

11 Warm the engine up to normal operating temperature then stop it.

12 Remove the oil pressure switch (see Chapter 8) and screw the gauge adapter in its place. Connect the oil pressure gauge to the adapter **(see illustration)**.

13 Start the engine and allow it idle, and note the reading on the gauge. Briefly increase the engine speed to 5000 rpm and again note the gauge reading. In each case the oil pressure should be similar to that given in the *Specifications* at the beginning of this Chapter.

14 Stop the engine. Unscrew the gauge and adapter from the crankcase and install the oil pressure switch (see Chapter 8).

 Warning: Be careful when removing the pressure gauge adapter as the engine will be hot.

15 If the pressure is significantly lower than the standard, first make sure that the correct grade of oil is being used. Next, check for a blocked filter or oil strainer, pressure regulator stuck open, or damaged oil pump or pump drive mechanism (see Sections 16 and 18). If all those items are good, it is likely the bearing oil clearances are excessive and the engine needs to be overhauled.

16 If the pressure is too high, either the wrong grade of oil is being used, the pressure regulator is stuck closed or an oil passage is clogged.

| 4 | Engine removal and installation |

Caution: The engine is heavy. Engine removal and installation should be carried out with the aid of at least one assistant; personal injury or damage could occur if the engine falls or is dropped.

Removal

All models

Special tools: *A jack will be required to support the engine. A means of lifting the frame off the engine unit, such as an automotive engine hoist, will also be required.*

1 Support the bike upright on level ground. Work can be made easier by raising the machine to a suitable working height on an hydraulic ramp or platform. However, note that in the final stage of disassembly, the frame will have to be lifted off the engine unit. Make sure the motorcycle is secure and will not topple over (also see *Tools and Workshop Tips* in the Reference section).

2 During the removal procedure, make a careful note of the routing of all cables, wiring and hoses and of any ties, clips or clamps that secure or guide them, so everything can be returned to its original location. Keep nuts, bolts and washers with the parts they secure.

3 Remove the seat and rear panels, bodywork centre panel and both side panels (see Chapter 7). On ST models, remove the lower side panel brackets, on GS models remove the sump guard (see Chapter 7).

4 Remove the battery (see Chapter 8).

5 On S and ST models, have an assistant apply the rear brake, then loosen the rear wheel bolts and the rear pulley nut – they are very tight and loosening them once the rear brake lever has been displaced may prove difficult (see Chapter 6). Disconnect the drive belt from the front pulley and, if required, loosen the front pulley bolt (see Chapter 6).

6 On GS and R models, if required, loosen the front sprocket bolt (see Chapter 6) – it is very tight and loosening it once the rear brake lever has been displaced may prove difficult. Disconnect the drive chain from the front sprocket (see Chapter 6).

7 Trace the wiring from the sidestand switch and disconnect it at the connector. Release the wiring from any clips or ties and feed it back to the switch (see Chapter 5). On GS models, remove the gearchange lever; on all other models, release the gearchange lever from the gearchange arm and remove the left-hand rider's footrest bracket assembly (see Chapter 5).

8 If the engine is dirty, particularly around its mountings, wash it thoroughly. This will make work much easier and rule out the possibility of dirt falling into some vital component.

9 Drain the engine oil – if required remove the oil filter (see Chapter 1).

4.17 Disconnect the earth lead terminal

4.18a Trace the wiring from the camshaft position sensor . . .

4.18b . . . and disconnect it at the connector

10 Drain the coolant and remove the reservoir (see Chapter 3).

11 Remove the radiator and the radiator hoses, then undo the screws securing the heat shield and remove it (see Chapter 3). On GS models, remove the water pump housing and pump impeller (see Chapter 3).

12 Remove the air filter housing and the throttle bodies (see Chapter 4). Plug the engine intake manifolds with clean rag.

13 Remove the exhaust system (see Chapter 4).

14 Check that the cylinder location is marked on both ignition coil wiring connectors and mark them accordingly if not. Disconnect the connectors and pull the coils off the spark plugs (see Chapter 1).

15 Refer to Section 15 and detach the clutch cable from the engine.

16 Remove the regulator/rectifier and its mounting bracket (see Chapter 8).

17 Detach the lead from the starter motor terminal and, if required, remove the starter motor (see Chapter 8). Disconnect the earth lead terminal from the front of the crankcase **(see illustration)**.

18 Trace the wiring from the camshaft position sensor and disconnect it at the connector **(see illustrations)**. Remove the camshaft position sensor (see Chapter 4).

19 Disconnect the oil pressure switch and

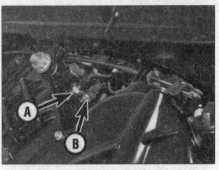

4.19 Oil pressure switch (A) and coolant temperature sensor (B)

coolant temperature sensor wiring connectors from the back of the cylinder head **(see illustration)**.

20 Release the wiring from the cable-ties on the top of the crankcase **(see illustration)**. Disconnect the ignition timing sensor wiring connector, then disconnect the gear position sensor wiring connector (see Chapter 4). Trace the alternator wiring from the back of the alternator cover and disconnect it at the connector (see Chapter 8).

21 Free the loom side of all wiring from any clips or ties to the engine and secure it clear, noting its routing.

22 On machines equipped with ABS, undo the nuts securing the ABS modulator to its

4.20 Release the wiring from the cable-ties

mounting bracket, then ease the stud on the underside of the modulator out from the grommet in the top of the bracket **(see illustration)**.

23 Position a jack centrally underneath the engine unit. Raise the jack to take the weight of the engine, but make sure it is not lifting the bike and taking the weight of that as well. The idea is to support the engine so that there is no pressure on the mounting bolts, allowing them to be easily withdrawn. Strap the engine to the jack so that it will not topple in any direction when the frame is lifted clear. Secure the frame to a suitable hoist, once again ensuring there is no pressure on the engine mounting bolts **(see illustration)**.

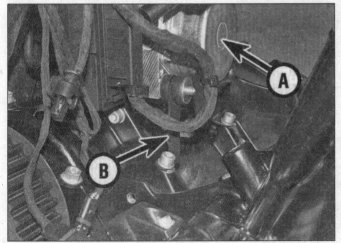

4.22 Ease the ABS modulator off its bracket

4.23 Set-up for lifting the frame off the engine

4.27 Remove the swingarm clamp bolts

4.28 Remove the upper front and rear mounting bolts, left-hand side

4.29 Loosen the locknuts (arrowed) and back-off the adjusters

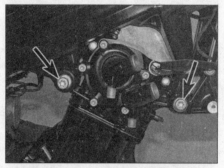

4.30a Remove the upper front and rear mounting bolts, right-hand side . . .

4.30b . . . noting the position of the washers

4.31 Support the engine and lift off the frame

24 Remove the rear wheel (see Chapter 6).
25 Remove the swingarm and rear shock absorber (see Chapter 5).
26 Check around the engine unit to make sure everything that needs to be detached or disconnected is free and clear. Have an assistant ready to support the engine while the mounting bolts are removed (see *Caution* above).

F800 S, ST and R models

27 Remove the swingarm clamp bolts, noting the position of the washers (see illustration).
28 Remove the upper front and rear mounting bolts on the left-hand side, noting the position of the washers (see illustration).
29 Loosen the adjuster locknuts and back off the adjusters anti-clockwise to create clearance between the adjusters and the cylinder head (see illustration).
30 Remove the upper front and rear mounting bolts on the right-hand side, noting the position of the washers (see illustrations).
31 Lift the frame and front suspension off the engine unit (see illustration).

GS models

32 Remove the blanking plugs from the upper engine mounting bolt locations (see illustration).
33 Remove the upper front and rear and lower rear mounting bolts on the left-hand side (see illustrations).

4.32 Remove the blanking plugs

4.33a Remove the upper front and rear . . .

4.33b . . . and lower rear mounting bolts, left-hand side

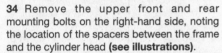

4.34a Remove the upper front and rear mounting bolts, right-hand side . . .

4.34b . . . noting the position of the spacers on the front . . .

4.34c . . . . and rear bolts between the frame and the engine

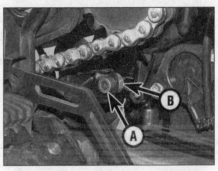

4.35 Remove the lower rear mounting bolt (A) right-hand side, noting the spacer (B)

34 Remove the upper front and rear mounting bolts on the right-hand side, noting the location of the spacers between the frame and the cylinder head (see illustrations).

35 Remove the lower rear mounting bolt on the right-hand side, noting the location of the spacer (see illustration).

36 Lift the frame and front suspension off the engine unit (see illustration 4.31).

Installation

37 Secure the engine on the jack, then raise it so the mounting points can be easily aligned with the mounting points for the frame and swingarm.

38 Lower the frame onto the engine unit so that the mounting points align. Make sure no wires get trapped.

F800 S, ST and R models

39 Slide the swingarm shaft into position in the clamps on the rear of the crankcase, then install the swingarm clamp bolts and washers and tighten them lightly (see illustration 4.27).

40 Install the upper front and rear mounting bolts and washers on the right-hand side and tighten them to the initial torque setting specified at the beginning of this Chapter (see illustration 4.30a).

41 Loosen the swingarm clamp bolts so that they are finger-tight, then tighten the front clamp bolts to the specified torque setting.

42 Tighten the upper front and rear right-hand mounting bolts to the final specified torque setting.

43 On the left-hand side, turn the adjusters clockwise and tighten them against the cylinder head to the specified torque setting, then tighten the adjuster locknuts to the specified torque setting (see illustration 4.29).

44 Install the upper front and rear mounting bolts and washers on the left-hand side and tighten them to the specified torque setting (see illustration 4.28).

45 Loosen the front swingarm clamp bolts and withdraw the swingarm shaft. Install the shock absorber and swingarm (see Chapter 5). Now go to Step 51.

GS models

46 Install the upper front and rear and

lower rear mounting bolts on the left-hand side and tighten them to the torque settings specified at the beginning of this Chapter (see illustrations 4.33a and b).

47 Install the upper front and rear mounting bolts on the right-hand side – don't forget to fit the spacers between the frame and the cylinder head (see illustration 4.34a, b and c). Tighten the bolts to the specified torque setting.

48 Install the lower rear right-hand mounting bolt and spacer and tighten it to the specified torque setting (see illustration 4.35).

49 Install the upper engine mounting bolt blanking plugs.

50 Install the shock absorber and swingarm (see Chapter 5).

All models

51 The remainder of the installation procedure is the reverse of removal, noting the following:
● Make sure all wires, cables and hoses are correctly routed and connected, and secured by any clips or ties.
● Adjust the throttle and clutch cable freeplay (see Chapter 1).
● On S and ST models adjust the drive belt tension; on GS and R models adjust the drive chain (see Chapter 1).
● Refill the engine with oil and coolant (see Chapter 1 and Pre-ride checks).
● Start the engine and check that there are no coolant leaks. **Note:** Perform this check before installing the bodywork side panels.

---

5 Engine overhaul information

1 Before you start, read through the relevant Section(s) of this manual to familiarise yourself with the scope and requirements of the job. Overhauling an engine is not all that difficult, but it is time consuming. Check on the availability of parts and make sure that any necessary special tools are obtained in advance. Most procedures can be done with workshop hand tools, although a number of precision measuring tools are required for inspecting parts to determine if they are worn.

Disassembly

2 Before disassembling the engine, the external surfaces of the unit should be thoroughly cleaned and degreased. This will prevent contamination of the engine internals, and will also make working a lot easier and cleaner. A high flash-point solvent, such as paraffin (kerosene) can be used, or better still, a proprietary engine cleaner such as Gunk. Use a paraffin brush or old paintbrush to work the solvent into the recesses of the engine casings. Take care to exclude solvent or water from the electrical components and intake and exhaust ports.

⚠️ *Warning: The use of petrol (gasoline) as a cleaning agent should be avoided because of the risk of fire.*

3 When the engine is clean and dry, clear a suitable area for working – a workbench is desirable for all operations once a component has been removed from the machine. Gather a selection of small containers and plastic bags so that parts can be grouped together in an easily identifiable manner. Some paper and a pen should be at hand so that notes can be made and labels attached where necessary. A supply of clean rag is also required. If the engine has been removed from the bike (see Section 4), have an assistant help you lift it onto the workbench.

4 When removing components note that great force is seldom required unless specified. Checking the torque setting of the nut or bolt being removed will indicate how tight it is, and

6.5 Remove the radiator heat shield – GS models

6.6 Remove the radiator heat shield – S model shown

6.8a Undo the screw (arrowed) . . .

therefore how much force should be needed. In many cases, a component's reluctance to be removed is indicative of an incorrect approach or removal method – if in any doubt, re-read the text. In cases where fasteners have corroded, apply penetrating oil or WD-40 before disassembly.

5 Keep 'mated' parts together (e.g. camshafts and followers, valve assemblies, pistons and connecting rods, clutch plates etc. that have been in contact with each other during engine operation). These 'mated' parts must be reused or renewed as assemblies.

6 A complete engine/transmission strip should be done in the following general order with reference to the appropriate Sections of this manual.

 Remove the valve cover
 Remove the camshafts
 Remove the cam chain blades
 Remove the water pump
 Remove the starter motor (see Chapter 8)
 Remove the alternator (see Chapter 8)
 Remove the starter clutch
 Remove the clutch
 Remove the gearchange mechanism
 Remove the oil pumps
 Remove the cylinder head

 Remove the oil sump
 Separate the crankcase halves
 Remove the balancer assembly
 Remove the connecting rods and pistons
 Remove the crankshaft and cam chain
 Remove the transmission shafts
 Remove the selector drum and forks

Reassembly

7 Reassembly is accomplished by reversing the general disassembly sequence.

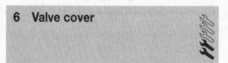

6 Valve cover

Note: The valve cover can be removed with the engine in the frame. If the engine has been removed, ignore the steps which do not apply.

Removal

1 Remove the seat, bodywork centre panel and both side panels (see Chapter 7).
2 Remove the battery (see Chapter 8).
3 Remove the air filter housing and disconnect

the throttle cable from the throttle body pulley (see Chapter 4).
4 Displace the radiator (see Chapter 3). Secure the radiator with cable-ties to avoid straining the coolant hoses.
5 On GS models, follow the procedure in Chapter 3 to remove the radiator heat shield **(see illustration)**.
6 On S, ST and R models, follow the procedure in Chapter 3 to remove the radiator heat shield **(see illustration)**.
7 If required, the secondary air system reed valves can be removed at this stage (see Steps 14 and 15). Alternatively, remove the reed valves once the valve cover is off the machine.
8 Undo the screw securing the engine breather union and remove the union and breather hose **(see illustrations)**. Note the location of the O-ring on the union and discard it as new one must be fitted on reassembly.
9 Remove both ignition coils and spark plugs (see Chapter 1).
10 Disconnect the lower end of the throttle cable from the throttle body pulley and release the cable from the bracket on the throttle body assembly **(see illustration)**.
11 Undo the bolts securing the valve

6.8b . . . and remove the breather assembly

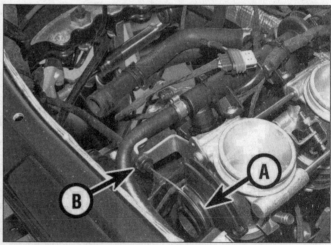

6.10 Throttle body pulley (A) and cable bracket (B)

6.11a Unscrew the valve cover bolts . . .

6.11b . . . and remove them . . .

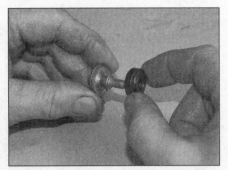

6.11c . . . noting how the sealing washers fit

cover, noting the location of the sealing washers **(see illustrations)**. Discard the washers as new ones must be fitted on reassembly.

12 Lift the valve cover off the cylinder head **(see illustration)**. If it is stuck, tap around the joint with a soft-faced mallet to dislodge it – don't try to lever it off with a screwdriver as the sealing surfaces will be damaged. Discard the cover gasket and secondary air system gasket as new ones must be fitted **(see illustrations)**.

13 Remove the engine breather seal and discard it as a new one must be fitted **(see illustration)**.

14 On all models except F650 GS, undo the screws securing the reed valve cover and lift the cover off **(see illustrations)**. Lift out the reed valves, noting which way round they

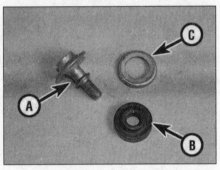

6.11d Valve cover bolt (A), sealing washer (B) and cupped washer (C)

are fitted **(see illustration)**. Take care not to damage the sealing surface of the valves as no gasket is fitted.

6.12a Lift off the valve cover

15 Inspect the reed valves for damage and gum and carbon deposits. If necessary, clean the reeds and stopper plates carefully with a

6.12b Note the location of the cover gasket . . .

6.12c . . . and the secondary air system gasket

6.13 Remove the engine breather seal

6.14a Undo the bolts securing the reed valve cover . . .

6.14b . . . and lift the cover off

6.14c Note which way round the reed valves are fitted

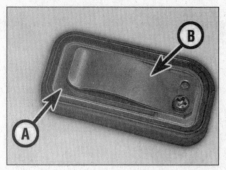

6.15a Reed valve (A) and stopper plate (B)

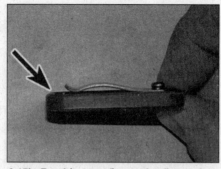

6.15b Reed (arrowed) must lay flat against the valve body

6.17 Apply thread-locking compound to the reed valve cover screws

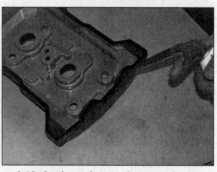

6.19 Apply sealant to the area shown

head and valve cover with a suitable solvent to remove all traces of old sealant and gasket. If a scraper is used, take care not to scratch or gouge the soft aluminium.

17 Install the reed valves reed side down and install the cover (**see illustrations 6.14c and b**). Clean the threads of the cover screws, apply a suitable non-permanent thread-locking compound and tighten the screws securely (**see illustration**).

18 Install a new engine breather seal and secondary air system gasket (**see illustrations 6.13 and 12c**).

19 Lay the new gasket onto the valve cover, making sure it locates correctly in its groove, then apply a suitable, non-permanent sealant to the area shown (**see illustration**).

20 Position the cover on the cylinder head carefully, making sure the gasket stays in position. Install the cover bolts with new sealing washers, then tighten the bolts evenly and in a criss-cross sequence to the torque setting specified at the beginning of this Chapter.

21 Install the remaining components in the reverse order of removal.

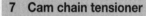

7 Cam chain tensioner

Note: *The cam chain tensioner can be removed with the engine in the frame.*

Removal

1 The tensioner is on the back of the cylinder head on the left-hand side (**see illustration**). If required, remove the left-hand bodywork side panel for access (see Chapter 7).

2 Unscrew the tensioner cap bolt and remove the sealing washer (**see illustration**). Check the condition of the sealing washer and replace it with a new one if necessary.

3 Withdraw the tensioner spring and pushrod from the cylinder head (**see illustrations**).

 Warning: Do not turn the engine with the tensioner removed.

4 Inspect the spring for damage and the pushrod for wear and score marks (**see illustration**). If either component is in poor condition, renew it.

suitable solvent (**see illustration**). The reeds should lay flat against the valve body – if the reeds have become distorted, fit a new valve assembly (**see illustration**). For further information on the secondary air system and

the system control valve, refer to Chapter 4, Section 3.

Installation

16 Clean the mating surfaces of the cylinder

7.1 Location of the cam chain tensioner

7.2 Note the sealing washer on the cap bolt

7.3a Withdraw the spring . . .

7.3b . . . and tensioner pushrod

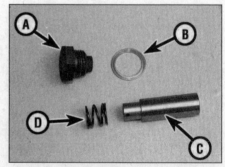

7.4 Cam chain tensioner cap bolt (A), sealing washer (B), pushrod (C) and spring (D)

8.2 Timing mark alignment – No. 1 piston at TDC

8.3a Unscrew the blanking bolt

Installation

5 Install the tensioner pushrod and spring **(see illustrations 7.3b and a)**.

6 Fit a new sealing washer onto the cap bolt if required, then install the bolt and tighten it to the torque setting specified at the beginning of this Chapter.

8 Camshafts and followers

Note: *The camshafts can be removed with the engine in the frame.*
Special tools: *A top dead centre (TDC) locating tool will be required for this procedure*

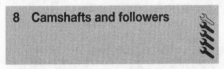

(see Step 3). Plastigauge will be required to measure the camshaft journal oil clearances (see Step 12).

Removal

1 Remove the valve cover, secondary air system gasket and the engine breather seal (see Section 6). Stuff clean rag into the spark plug holes to prevent anything dropping into the engine.

2 Turn the engine in the direction of normal rotation until the No. 1 piston is at top dead centre (TDC) on the compression stroke – all the valves for that cylinder closed. To do this, support the machine with the rear wheel off the ground, engage first gear and turn the engine by rotating the rear wheel. Alternatively,

remove the alternator cover (see Chapter 8) and turn the alternator rotor bolt in a clockwise direction. The engine is in the correct position when the 'I/N' and 'E/X' timing marks on the camshaft sprockets are facing each other and parallel with the sealing surface of the cylinder head **(see illustration)**; note that only the I and E with be visble.

3 To ensure that the engine is held precisely at TDC during this procedure, a slot is cut into the left-hand web of the crankshaft. Undo the blanking bolt on the left-hand side of the crankcase and discard the sealing washer **(see illustration)**. The slot should be visible by shining a light through the bolt hole – rock the crankshaft slowly backwards-and-forwards to locate the centre of the slot, then screw a suitable locating tool into the hole so that the tapered end aligns with the slot and tighten it finger-tight. BMW produces a service tool for this purpose (Part No. 11 6 570) **(see illustration)**. Alternatively a tool can be made from a high tensile M8 x 1.25 bolt, approx 50 mm long with its end ground to a blunt taper as shown **(see illustration)**. With the tool correctly installed it should not be possible to turn the crankshaft **(see illustration)**.

4 Unscrew the camshaft holder nuts, slackening them diagonally and a little at

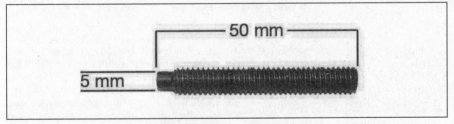

8.3b The BMW service tool

8.3c Installing the BMW service tool

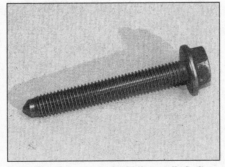

8.3d Grind the end of a high tensile bolt as shown

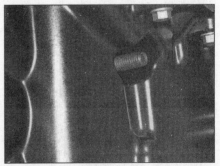

8.3e Installed position of the TDC locating tool

8.4a **Unscrew the camshaft holder nuts**

8.4b **Remove the upper cam chain guide . . .**

8.4c **. . . and the camshaft holder**

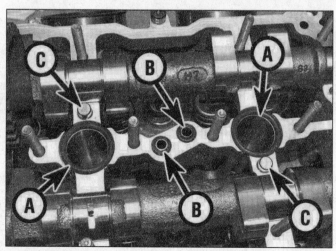

8.4d **Spark plug hole seals (A), camshaft holder seals (B) and dowels (C)**

a time **(see illustration)**. Remove the nuts and lift off the upper cam chain guide and camshaft holder **(see illustrations)**. Remove the spark plug hole and camshaft holder seals and discard them as new ones must be fitted **(see illustration)**. Note the location of the dowels and remove them if they are loose.

5 Remove the cam chain tensioner (see Section 7).
6 Carefully ease both camshafts out from their bearing seats in the cylinder head. Remove the intake camshaft first – disengage the sprocket from the chain and lift the camshaft out **(see illustration)**, then lift out the exhaust

camshaft **(see illustration)**. Secure the cam chain to prevent it dropping down into the engine **(see illustration)**.
7 The camshafts are not marked for identification, but the sprockets are marked **(see illustration 8.2)** and the coolant pump drive gear is located on the right-hand

8.6a **Remove the intake camshaft . . .**

8.6b **. . . and then the exhaust camshaft**

8.6c **Secure the cam chain with a length of bent wire**

8.7 Coolant pump drive gear (A) and engine breather seal (B)

8.8 Removing the shim with a magnet – note the position of the cam follower (arrowed)

end of the intake camshaft – remove the engine breather seal if not already done **(see illustration)**. The lobe on the right-hand end of the exhaust camshaft is the trigger for the camshaft position sensor (see Chapter 4, Section 17).

8 If the cam followers and shims are being removed from the cylinder head, obtain a container which is divided into eight compartments, and label each compartment with the location of a valve, i.e. No.1 cylinder intake or exhaust camshaft, left or right valve. If a container is not available, use labelled plastic bags (egg cartons or ice cube trays do very well too!). Lift up each cam follower and retrieve the shim from either the top of the valve or from inside the follower using either a magnet or a screwdriver with a dab of grease on it **(see illustration)**. Do not allow the shims to fall into the engine.

9 Mark the followers so that they can be returned to their original positions if required. Draw the E-clip off one end of the follower shaft and slide the nearest follower off, then slide the shaft and the other follower out from the cylinder head **(see illustrations)**. Slide the follower back onto the shaft for safekeeping. Discard the E-clips as new ones must be used on reassembly.

Inspection

10 Inspect the bearing surfaces of the camshaft holder and the cylinder head **(see illustration)**. Look for score marks, deep scratches and evidence of spalling (a pitted appearance). If wear or damage is found, inspect the corresponding journals on the camshafts and check the oil passages for clogging.

11 Check the camshaft lobes for heat discoloration (blue appearance), score marks, chipped areas, flat spots and spalling. Measure the height of each lobe with a micrometer **(see illustration)** and compare

the results with the specifications listed at the beginning of this Chapter. If damage is noted or wear is excessive, the camshaft must be replaced with a new one.

12 Next, check the camshaft journal oil clearances – these are measured with a product known as Plastigauge. First clean the camshafts and the bearing surfaces in the cylinder head and camshaft holder with a clean lint-free cloth.

13 Lay each camshaft in its correct location in the cylinder head with the lobes clear of the valves – there is no need to fit the chain round the sprockets.

8.9a Remove the E-clip (arrowed) . . .

8.9b . . . and the nearest follower . . .

8.9c . . . then withdraw the shaft and other follower

8.10 Inspect the bearing surfaces for wear and damage

8.11 Measuring camshaft lobe height

8.14 Lay Plastigauge (arrowed) along the camshaft journal

8.17 Compare the width of the crushed Plastigauge with the scale

8.18a Measuring camshaft journal diameter

14 Cut lengths of Plastigauge slightly shorter than the camshaft journals and lay one length on each journal, parallel with the camshaft centreline **(see illustration)**.

15 If removed, install the camshaft holder dowels. Install the camshaft holder and tighten the nuts evenly and a little at a time in a criss-cross sequence to the torque setting specified at the beginning of this Chapter **(see illustration 8.4a)**. **Note:** *It is important that the camshafts do not rotate during this procedure to avoid distorting the Plastigauge.*

16 Now undo the holder nuts evenly and a little at a time, and lift the holder off carefully.

17 To determine the oil clearance, compare the crushed Plastigauge (at its widest point) with the printed Plastigauge scale **(see illustration)**.

18 Compare the results with this Chapter's *Specifications*. If any oil clearance is greater than the service limit, measure the diameter

8.18b Measuring the camshaft holder bore diameter

of the appropriate camshaft journal(s) **(see illustration)**. If the journal is worn below the service limit a new camshaft will have to be fitted. If the camshaft journals are good, then the internal diameter of the holders is worn and a new holder and cylinder head will be required. To confirm your findings, install the camshaft holder without the camshafts and measure the internal diameter of the holder bores **(see illustration)**. Compare the results to the *Specifications*. Subtract the diameter of the appropriate camshaft journal from the matching bore diameter to find the oil clearance.

19 Inspect the bearing surface of the cam followers for wear. If the surface of a follower is in poor condition a new one must be fitted. The followers should be a sliding fit on their shafts – apply clean engine oil to the shaft, slide on the follower and check for any freeplay between the two. If the clearance is excessive renew the components.

20 Check the camshaft sprockets for wear, chipped teeth and other damage **(see illustration)**. If necessary, undo the bolts securing the sprockets and lift them off, noting the location of the sprocket pin. The sprockets are marked I/N (intake) and E/X (exhaust) – mark the camshafts to aid reassembly.

21 Check the water pump drive gear for wear, chipped teeth and other damage **(see illustration)**. If necessary, undo the bolt and washer securing the drive gear and lift it off. **Note:** *The bolt has a left-hand thread – to undo it turn it clockwise.* If the drive gear is in need of renewal, then the driven gear on the water pump should also be renewed (see Chapter 3, Section 8).

22 Prior to installation, clean the threads of the sprocket bolts and apply a suitable, non-permanent thread locking compound. Ensure the new sprockets are fitted the correct way round with the timing marks facing out and align the sprocket pins with the holes in the camshaft flanges. Tighten the bolts to the torque setting specified at the beginning of this Chapter.

23 Clean the threads of the water pump drive gear bolt and apply a suitable, non-permanent thread locking compound. Install the gear on the right-hand end of the intake camshaft, then fit the bolt and washer. Tighten the bolt, turning it anti-clockwise, to the specified torque setting.

24 If the camshaft sprockets are worn, the chain and the drive sprocket on the crankshaft are probably worn as well and should be checked (see Sections 9 and 23).

25 Inspect the cam chain guides and tensioner blade (see Section 9).

Installation

26 If removed, lubricate the cam follower shafts with engine oil and install the shafts and followers in the cylinder head (see Step 9). Secure the assemblies with new E-clips **(see illustrations 8.9c, b and a)**. Install the E-clips with the convex side towards the cam follower. **Note:** *If new cam followers have been fitted the valve clearances must be checked and adjusted accordingly.*

27 Smear the curved top of each shim with a dab of grease, then press it into the appropriate follower – the grease will hold it in position. Check that the shim is correctly seated, then lower the follower onto the valve **(see illustration)**. **Note:** *It is most important*

8.20 Inspect the sprocket teeth. Note location of sprocket pin (arrowed)

8.21 Inspect the pump drive gear teeth. Retaining bolt has left-hand thread

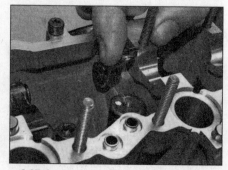

8.27 Lower the follower onto the valve

8.30 Lubricate the bearing surfaces with engine oil

8.31 Install the exhaust camshaft with the E/X mark as shown

8.32 Install the intake camshaft with the I/N mark as shown

8.34a Install the new spark plug hole seals . . .

that the shims are returned to their original valves otherwise the valve clearances will be inaccurate.

28 Make sure the contact surfaces of the cylinder head and camshaft holder are clean and dry. If removed, install the camshaft holder dowels **(see illustration 8.4d)**.

29 Check that the crankshaft is locked in position at TDC (see Step 3). If both camshafts have been removed, install the exhaust camshaft first.

30 Lubricate the bearing surfaces on the camshafts and in the cylinder head and holder with engine oil **(see illustration)**.

31 Keeping the front run of the cam chain taut, manoeuvre the exhaust camshaft into position with the 'E/X' mark on the camshaft sprocket facing the rear, parallel with the sealing surface on the cylinder head **(see illustration)**. Engage the chain on the sprocket, ensuring there is no slack in the front run between the crankshaft and the sprocket, but do not press the camshaft down fully into position at this stage.

32 Manoeuvre the intake camshaft into

position with the 'I/N' mark on the camshaft sprocket facing the front, parallel with the sealing surface on the cylinder head **(see illustration)**. Engage the chain on the sprocket, ensuring there is no slack between the two sprockets.

33 Ensure the 'I/N' and 'E/X' marks are facing each other and parallel with the sealing surface of the cylinder head (note that only the I and E will be visible above the head surface), then

press both camshafts down into the cylinder head, ensuring the water pump drive gear is correctly engaged with the pump driven gear. Check the alignment of the sprockets **(see illustration 8.32)**.

34 Lubricate the new spark plug hole seals and camshaft holder seals with a smear of oil and install them in the head **(see illustrations)**. Install the camshaft holder, pressing it down firmly **(see illustration)**. Install the upper

8.34b . . . and camshaft holder seals

8.34c Install the camshaft holder

8.37 Camshaft holder nut TIGHTENING sequence

9.7 Removing the front guide blade

cam chain guide, then tighten the holder nuts finger-tight (see illustrations 8.4b and a).
35 Install the cam chain tensioner (see Section 7).
36 Check that the timing marks are still in exact alignment as described in Step 33. If the marks are out of alignment, verify which camshaft is misaligned, then remove the cam chain tensioner and camshaft holder. Disengage the chain from the camshaft sprocket, then move the camshaft round as required. Refit the cam chain, camshaft holder and frame and check the marks again (see illustrations 8.2).
Caution: If the marks are not aligned exactly as described, the valve timing will be incorrect and the valves may strike the pistons, causing extensive damage to the engine.
37 Tighten the camshaft holder nuts to the specified torque setting in the numerical sequence shown (see illustration).
38 Unscrew the TDC locating tool and refit the blanking bolt using a new sealing washer; tighten the blanking bolt to the specified torque setting (see illustrations 8.3c and a).
39 Turn the engine through two full turns and check again that all the timing marks still align (see Step 2). Check the valve clearances and adjust them if necessary (see Chapter 1).
40 Install the remaining components in the reverse order of removal. If required, check the oil level and top-up as necessary (see Pre-ride checks).

9 Cam chain, tensioner and guide blades

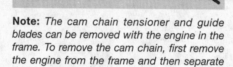

Note: The cam chain tensioner and guide blades can be removed with the engine in the frame. To remove the cam chain, first remove the engine from the frame and then separate the crankcase halves.

Upper guide blade

1 Follow the procedure in Section 6 to remove the valve cover.
2 Follow the procedure in Section 8 to position the No. 1 piston at top dead centre (TDC) on the compression stroke. This reduces the pressure on the camshaft holder.
3 Unscrew the nuts securing the upper cam chain guide and lift it off (see illustration 8.4b).
4 Inspect the working surface of the guide for wear. If there are grooves in the surface and they exceed the service limit, a new guide blade should be fitted (see Specifications at the beginning of this Chapter). Note: Wear in

the guide blade indicates a loose chain, either due to a faulty cam chain tensioner, worn tensioner blade or wear in the chain itself. Check the tensioner (see Section 7), tensioner blade (see Steps 10 to 13) and cam chain (see Steps 15 to 17).
5 Installation is the reverse of removal.

Front guide blade

6 Follow the procedure in Section 8 to remove the camshafts.
7 Note the location of the front guide blade, then draw it out of the engine (see illustration).
8 Inspect the guide blade for wear and renew it if necessary (see Step 4).
9 Installation is the reverse of removal, noting the following:
● Ensure that the top of the guide blade is level with the sealing surface of the cylinder head before installing the camshafts (see illustration).

Tensioner blade

10 Follow the procedure in Section 8 to remove the camshafts.
11 Remove the clutch cover (see Section 14).
12 Unscrew the pivot bolt and draw the tensioner blade out of the engine (see illustrations).

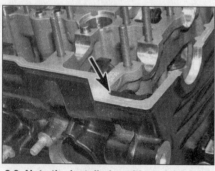

9.9 Note the installed position of the front guide blade

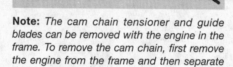 

9.12a Unscrew the pivot bolt . . .

9.12b . . . and lift out the tensioner blade

13 Inspect the tensioner blade for wear and renew it if necessary (see Step 4).

14 Installation is the reverse of removal, noting the following:

● Prior to installation, clean the threads of the pivot bolt and apply a suitable non-permanent, thread locking compound **(see illustration)**

● Tighten the pivot bolt to the torque setting specified at the beginning of this Chapter.

Cam chain

15 Except in cases of oil starvation, the cam chain wears very little. If the chain has stretched excessively and can no longer be correctly tensioned by the cam chain tensioner, it is likely that the chain guide and tensioner blades will be worn and in need of renewal as well. Also check the condition of the camshaft sprockets (see Section 8) and crankshaft sprocket.

16 To inspect the chain, first follow the procedure in Section 8 to remove the camshafts.

17 Check all round the chain – if there is any discernible slack between the links, or if there is any doubt about its condition, fit a new chain **(see illustration)**.

18 To renew the chain, follow the procedure in Section 23 to remove the crankshaft, then lift the chain off the crankshaft sprocket. Inspect the teeth of the crankshaft sprocket. If there are any signs of wear or damage, a new crankshaft will have to be fitted. **Note:** *If the crankshaft is going to be removed and the cam chain is going to be reused when the*

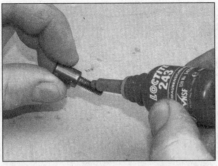

9.14 Thread lock the tensioner blade pivot bolt

engine is reassembled, mark the chain so that it can be installed the original way round.

19 Installation is the reverse of removal.

10 Cylinder head removal and installation

Note: *To remove the cylinder head the engine must be removed from the frame.*
Special tool: *A torque angle gauge will be required to tighten the cylinder head bolts (see Tools and Workshop Tips).*

Removal

1 Follow the procedure in Section 4 and remove the engine from the frame.

2 Remove the camshafts, followers and shims (see Section 8).

3 Remove the front cam chain guide blade (see Section 9).

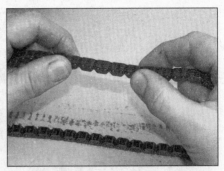

9.17 Checking for play between the links of the cam chain

4 The cylinder head is secured by two 6 mm bolts and six 10 mm bolts. First unscrew and remove the 6 mm bolts **(see illustration)**. Now unscrew and remove the 10 mm bolts, slackening them evenly and a little at a time in a criss-cross pattern starting from the outside **(see illustration)**.

5 Lift the head up off the cylinder block, passing the cam chain down the tunnel **(see illustration)**. If the head is stuck, tap around the joint faces with a soft-faced mallet. Do not attempt to free the head by inserting a screwdriver between the head and block mating surfaces – you'll damage them.

6 Secure the cam chain over the tensioner blade to prevent it falling into the engine and remove the cylinder head gasket **(see illustrations)**. Stuff a clean rag into the cam chain tunnel to prevent any dirt falling in.

7 If they are loose, remove the dowels from the front and rear corners of the cylinder block for safekeeping **(see illustration)**. If either

10.4a 6 mm bolts are located on the left-hand side of the head

10.4b Location of the 10 mm cylinder head bolts

10.5 Lifting off the cylinder head

10.6a Remove the cylinder head gasket

10.6b Cam chain is secured with a cable-tie

10.7 Location of cylinder head dowels (arrowed)

10.15a Cylinder head 10 mm bolt TIGHTENING sequence

10.15b Using a torque angle gauge

appears to be missing it is probably stuck in the underside of the cylinder head.

8 Inspect the cylinder head gasket and the mating surfaces on the cylinder head and block for signs of leakage, which could indicate that the head is distorted. If necessary, check the cylinder head with a straight-edge (see Section 11). Discard the old head gasket as a new one must be fitted on reassembly.

9 Clean all traces of old gasket material from the cylinder head and block. If a scraper is used, take care not to scratch or gouge the soft aluminium. Be careful not to let any of the gasket material fall into the cylinder bores or the oil and coolant passages.

> **HAYNES HiNT** *Refer to Tools and Workshop Tips for details of gasket removal methods.*

Installation

10 If removed, install the two dowels into the cylinder block **(see illustration 10.7)**.

11 Remove any rag from the cam chain tunnel and check that the lower end of the cam chain is properly located around the crankshaft sprocket.

12 Lay the new head gasket onto the block, locating it over the dowels and making sure all the holes are correctly aligned **(see illustration 10.6a)**.

13 With the help of an assistant, keep the cam chain taut and pass it up through the tunnel in the head while the head is lowered onto the block. Ensure the head locates onto the dowels, then secure the cam chain **(see illustration 8.6c)**.

14 Install the cylinder head bolts and tighten them finger-tight **(see illustrations 10.4a and b)**.

15 Tighten the six 10 mm bolts first, following the numerical sequence shown **(see illustration)**. Tighten the bolts in three stages to the torque settings specified at the beginning of this Chapter. Use a torque angle gauge to tighten the bolts to the final setting **(see illustration)**.

16 Now tighten the two 6 mm bolts to the specified torque setting.

17 Install the remaining components in the reverse order of removal.

11 Cylinder head and valve overhaul

Special tools: *A valve spring compressor (small enough for motorcycle engines) will be required for this procedure (see Step 9). Hose clip pliers will be needed to install the intake adapters, if removed (see Step 38)*

1 Because of the complex nature of this job and the special tools and equipment required, most owners leave servicing of the valves, valve seats and valve guides to a professional. However, you can make an initial assessment of whether the valves are seating correctly, and therefore sealing, by pouring a small amount of solvent into each of the valve ports. If the solvent leaks past any valve into the combustion chamber area the valve is not seating correctly and sealing.

2 With a valve spring compressor you can also remove the valves and associated components from the cylinder head, clean them and check them for wear to assess the extent of the work needed, and, unless seat cutting or guide replacement is required, grind in the valves and reassemble them in the head.

3 A dealer service department or specialist engineer can renew the guides and re-cut the valve seats.

4 After the valve service has been performed, be sure to clean it very thoroughly before installation on the engine to remove any metal particles or abrasive grit that may still be present from the valve service operations. Use compressed air, if available, to blow out all the holes and passages.

Disassembly

5 Before proceeding, arrange to label and store the valves along with their related components in such a way that they can be returned to their original locations without getting mixed up **(see illustration)**. Either

1 Spring seat
2 Spring
3 Spring retainer
4 Collets
5 Valve stem seal
6 Valve

11.5 Valve components

11.7 Intake adapters are secured by non-reuseable clamps

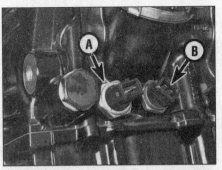

11.8 Location of the oil pressure switch (A) and coolant temperature sensor (B)

11.9a Ensure the valve spring compressor fits the spring retainer . . .

use the same container as the cam followers and shims are stored in (see Section 8), or obtain a separate container and label each compartment accordingly.

6 Follow the procedure in Chapter 3 to remove the water pump.

7 The intake adapters are secured with non-reuseable clamps – if the adapters need to be removed, ease the clamps open with a flat-bladed screwdriver and draw the adapters off, noting how they fit **(see illustration)**. New clamps will have to be used on installation.

8 If required, unscrew the oil pressure switch and the coolant temperature sensor **(see illustration)**.

9 Compress the valve spring on the first valve with a spring compressor, making sure it is correctly located onto each end of the valve assembly. On the top of the valve the adaptor needs to be about the same size as the spring retainer **(see illustration)**. On the underside of the head make sure the plate on the compressor only contacts the valve and not the soft aluminium of the head **(see illustration)** – if the plate is too big for the valve, use a spacer between them. Do not compress the spring any more than is absolutely necessary.

10 Remove the collets, using a magnet or a screwdriver with a dab of grease on it **(see illustration)**.

11 Carefully release the valve spring compressor and remove the spring retainer, the spring and the spring seat, noting which way up each component fits **(see illustrations)**.

11.9b . . . and the valve head correctly

11.10 Removing the valve collets

12 Pull the valve out from the underside of the head **(see illustration)**. If the valve binds in the guide and won't pull through, push it back into the head and deburr the area around

the collet groove with a very fine file **(see illustration)**.

13 Pull the valve stem seal off the top of the valve guide with pliers and discard it

11.11a Remove the spring retainer . . .

11.11b . . . the valve spring, noting the paint marks (arrowed) . . .

11.11c . . . and the spring seat

11.12a Pull the valve out carefully

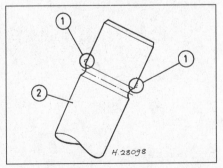

11.12b If the valve stem (2) won't pull through the guide, deburr the area above the collet groove (1)

11.13 Remove the valve stem seal

11.19 Checking the head gasket mating surface for warpage

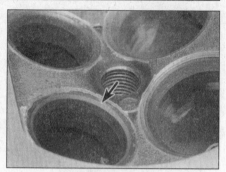

11.20a Examine the valve seats in the combustion chamber

(the old seals should never be reused) **(see illustration)**.

14 Repeat the procedure for the remaining valves. Remember to keep the parts for each valve together so they can be reinstalled in the same location.

15 Clean the cylinder head with solvent and dry it thoroughly. Compressed air will speed the drying process and ensure that all holes and recessed areas are clean. **Note:** *Do not use a wire brush mounted in a drill motor to clean the combustion chamber as the head material is soft and may be scratched or eroded away by the wire brush.*

16 Clean all of the valve springs, collets, retainers and spring seats with solvent and dry them thoroughly. Do the parts from one valve at a time so that no mixing of parts between valves occurs.

17 Remove any carbon deposits that may have formed on the valve head using a scraper or a motorised wire brush. Again, make sure the valves do not get mixed up.

Inspection

18 Inspect the head very carefully for cracks and other damage. If cracks are found, a new head is required.

19 Using a precision straight-edge and a feeler gauge check the head gasket mating surface for warpage **(see illustration)**. Refer to *Tools and Workshop Tips* in the Reference section for details of how to use the straight-edge. If the head is warped beyond the maximum specified at the beginning of this Chapter, consult your BMW dealer or take it to a specialist repair shop for rectification.

20 Examine the valve seats in the combustion chamber **(see illustration)**. If they are pitted, cracked or burned, the head will require work beyond the scope of the home mechanic. Measure the valve seat width and compare it to the specifications **(see illustration)**. If it exceeds the service limit, or if it varies around its circumference, consult your BMW dealer or take the head to a specialist repair shop for rectification.

21 Examine the head of each valve for cracks, pits and burned spots. Measure the diameter of each valve head and compare the results with the specifications **(see illustration)** – if any valve is worn undersize it should be replaced with a new one.

22 Check the valve stem and the collet groove area for wear and damage **(see illustration)**. Check the end of the stem for pitting and excessive wear.

23 Rotate the valve and check for any obvious indication that it is bent. Using V-blocks and a dial gauge, measure the valve stem runout and compare the results to the specification **(see illustration)**. If the measurement exceeds the service limit a new valve must be fitted.

24 Working on one valve and guide at a time, fit a valve into its guide until the stem end reaches the top of the guide, so that its head is above the seat **(see illustration)**. Mount a dial gauge against the side of the valve head and measure the amount of radial clearance (wobble) between the valve stem and its guide in two perpendicular directions.

25 If the clearance exceeds the service limit,

11.20b Measuring the valve seat width

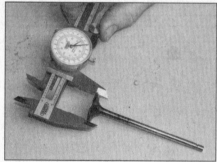

11.21 Measuring the diameter of the valve head

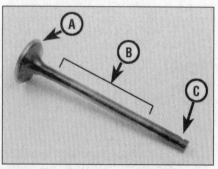

11.22 Valve head (A), stem (B) and collet groove (C)

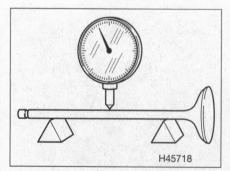

H45718

11.23 Measuring valve stem runout

11.24 Install the valve and mount the tip of the dial gauge against the side of the valve head

11.25a Measuring valve stem diameter

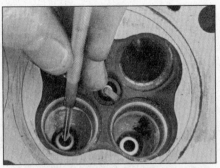

11.25b Measuring the valve guide inside diameter with a small hole gauge

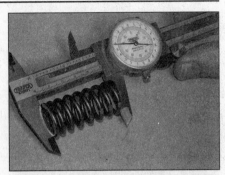

11.26 Measuring valve spring free length

remove the valve and measure the valve stem diameter **(see illustration)**. Also measure the inside diameter of the guide with a small hole gauge and micrometer **(see illustration)**. Measure the guides at each end and at the centre to determine if they are worn unevenly. Replace any component that is worn beyond its specifications with a new one. If the valve guide is within specifications, but is worn unevenly, it should be renewed.

26 Check the end of each valve spring for wear and pitting. Measure the spring free length and compare it to the specifications **(see illustration)**. If any spring is shorter than the service limit renew the springs as a set.

27 Stand each spring upright on a flat surface and check it for bend with a set square **(see illustration)**. If the bend in any spring is excessive, fit a new set of springs.

28 Check the spring seats, retainers and collets for obvious wear and cracks. Any questionable parts should not be reused, as extensive damage will occur in the event of failure during engine operation.

29 If the inspection indicates that no overhaul work is required, the valve components can be reinstalled in the head.

Reassembly

30 Working on one valve at a time, lubricate the valve with engine oil and install it in the head. Check that the valve moves up and down freely in the guide.

31 Slide a suitable plastic sleeve over the upper end of the valve stem, then slide the new valve stem seal down over the sleeve. The purpose of the plastic sleeve is to prevent the

11.27 Check that the springs are not bent

edges of the collet groove damaging the inside of the stem seal – electrical heat shrink sleeving is ideal. If a suitable sleeve is not available, take great care when installing the seal.

32 If used, remove the sleeve, then using an appropriate sized deep socket, press the seal over the end of the valve guide until it is felt to clip into place **(see illustration)**.

33 Install the valve spring seat with its shouldered side facing up **(see illustration)**. Install the valve spring with its paint marks at the top, followed by the spring retainer, with its shouldered side facing down into the top of the spring **(see illustrations 11.11b and a)**.

34 Apply a small amount of grease to the collets to help hold them in place. Compress the spring with the valve spring compressor and install the collets **(see illustration 11.10)**. When compressing the spring, depress it only as far as is absolutely necessary to slip the collets into place. Make certain that

11.32 Press the seal into place with a suitable deep socket

the collets are securely located in the collet groove and release the spring compressor **(see illustration)**.

35 Repeat the procedure for the remaining valves. Remember to keep the parts for each valve together and separate from the other valves so they can be reinstalled in the same location.

36 Support the cylinder head on blocks so the valves can't contact the work surface, then tap the end of each valve stem lightly to seat the collets in their grooves **(see illustration)**.

> **HAYNES HiNT** *Check for proper sealing of the valves by pouring a small amount of solvent into each of the valve ports.*
> *If the solvent leaks past any valve into the combustion chamber the valve grinding operation on that valve should be repeated.*

11.33 Shouldered side of the spring seat faces up

11.34 Installed position of the valve collets

11.36 Tap each valve stem lightly to seat the collets

37 If removed, install the coolant temperature sensor and oil pressure switch **(see illustration 11.8)**. Tighten them to the specified torque settings (Chapters 3 and 8).

38 If removed, install the intake adapters with new clamps, then tighten the clamps with special hose clip pliers **(see illustration 11.7)**. **Note:** *It is essential that the clamps are tightened securely to prevent air leaks.*

39 Install the water pump (see Chapter 3).

40 After the cylinder head and camshafts have been installed, check the valve clearances and adjust as required (see Chapter 1).

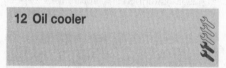

12 Oil cooler

Note: *The oil cooler can be removed with the engine in the frame. If the engine has been removed, ignore the steps which do not apply.*

Removal

1 The oil cooler is located on the front of the engine. If the casing around the oil cooler is

12.4a Bolts securing coolant pipes – GS models

12.4b Bolts securing coolant pipes – S, ST and R models

dirty, wash it thoroughly – this will make work much easier and rule out the possibility of dirt getting inside.

2 Drain the engine oil and remove the oil filter (see Chapter 1).

3 Drain the cooling system (see Chapter 3). On ST models, remove the lower left-hand bodywork side panel (see Chapter 7).

4 Undo the bolts securing both coolant pipes to the oil cooler flange and disconnect the pipes,

noting the O-rings **(see illustrations)**. Discard the O-rings as new ones must be fitted.

5 If required, release the clips securing the coolant pipe connectors to the water pump and remove the pipes **(see illustrations)**.

6 On GS models, the oil cooler flange is integral with the crankcase. Undo the bolts securing the oil cooler to the flange and remove the oil cooler **(see illustration)**. Discard the cooler gasket **(see illustration 12.7f)**.

12.4c Note the location of the O-ring (arrowed)

12.5a Disconnect the coolant pipes (arrowed) from the pump . . .

12.5b . . . and lift them off

12.6 Bolts (arrowed) secure oil cooler – GS models

12.7a Undo the centre bolt (arrowed) . . .

12.7b . . . and the flange bolt to the cooler assembly

12.7c Note the location of the O-ring

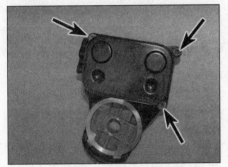

12.7d Undo the bolts (arrowed) . . .

12.7e . . . and remove the cooler

12.7f Discard the cooler gasket

7 On all other models, unscrew the oil filter centre bolt and the cooler flange bolt and lift the cooler assembly off **(see illustrations)**. Note the location of the O-ring and discard it as a new one must be fitted **(see illustration)**. Undo the bolts securing the cooler to the flange and lift the cooler off **(see illustrations)**. Discard the cooler gasket **(see illustration)**.

8 Drain out any residual oil, then wash the components with solvent and dry them thoroughly. Compressed air will speed the drying process and ensure that all holes and recessed areas are clean.

Installation

9 On GS models, ensure the mating surface of the crankcase is clean.

10 On all models, fit a new cooler gasket into the groove in the cooler flange, then install the cooler and tighten the mounting bolts to the

torque setting specified at the beginning of this Chapter.

11 On S, ST and R models, fit a new flange O-ring into the groove in the flange **(see illustration 12.7c)**. Ensure the mating surface of the crankcase is clean, then install the cooler assembly and tighten the flange bolt to the specified torque **(see illustration 12.7b)**. Clean the threads of the oil filter centre bolt and apply a suitable non-permanent thread locking compound **(see illustration)**. Tighten the centre bolt to the specified torque setting.

12 Fit new O-rings onto the unions on the lower ends of the coolant pipes **(see illustration)**. If removed, fit the coolant pipes onto the water pump – ensure the hose clips are on the pipes and push the flexible connectors all the way onto the pump unions.

13 Align the pipes with the oil cooler flange and press them in carefully, taking care not

to damage the O-rings. Tighten the mounting bolts to the specified torque setting **(see illustrations 12.4c, b and a)**.

14 If removed, secure the coolant pipe connectors to the water pump (see Chapter 3).

15 Install the oil filter, then fill the engine with oil and coolant to the correct levels (see Chapter 1 and *Pre-ride checks*).

16 Start the engine and check that there are no oil or coolant leaks. **Note:** *On ST models, perform this check before installing the lower bodywork side panels.*

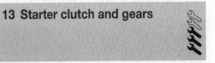

13 Starter clutch and gears

Note: *The starter clutch can be removed with the engine in the frame. If the engine has been removed, ignore the steps which do not apply.* **Special tools:** *A top dead centre (TDC) locating tool (see Section 8) and a puller to draw the alternator rotor off the crankshaft (see Chapter 8) will be required for this procedure.*

Check

1 The operation of the starter clutch can be checked while it is in situ. Remove the starter motor (see Chapter 8). Check that the reduction gear is able to rotate freely clockwise as you look at it from the left-hand side via the starter motor aperture, but locks when rotated anti-clockwise. If not, the starter clutch is faulty and should be removed for inspection.

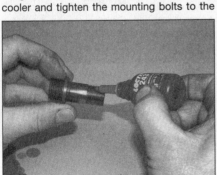

12.11 Thread lock the oil cooler centre bolt

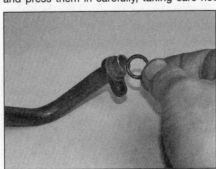

12.12 Fit new O-rings onto the coolant pipe unions

13.5a Remove the large plain washer . . .

13.5b . . . then draw the starter driven gear off the crankshaft

13.5c Turn the gear clockwise to release the starter clutch

Removal

2 Remove the spark plugs (see Chapter 1). Stuff clean rag into the spark plug holes to prevent anything dropping into the engine.

3 Remove the alternator cover (see Chapter 8).

4 Follow the procedure in Chapter 8 to remove the alternator rotor.

5 Remove the large plain washer from the starter idler gear shaft, then draw the starter driven gear off the crankshaft, noting how it fits **(see illustrations)**. If the driven gear came off with the alternator rotor, lay the rotor assembly face down on the workbench and draw the driven gear out from the back of the rotor, turning the gear clockwise to release the starter clutch **(see illustration)**.

6 Note the alignment between the idler gear and the reduction gear, then draw them off their shafts **(see illustration)**.

Inspection

7 Wash the components with solvent and dry them thoroughly.

8 Inspect the teeth of the driven gear, reduction and idler gears **(see illustration)**. Renew the gears as a set if worn or chipped teeth are discovered on related gears. Also check the idler and reduction gear shafts for damage, and check that the gears are not a loose fit on them **(see illustration)**. Check the teeth on the starter motor shaft (see Chapter 8).

9 Refer to *Tools and Workshop Tips* in the *Reference* section and inspect the rollers of the needle bearing in the driven gear hub and the corresponding surface on the crankshaft **(see illustration)**. Inspect the outer surface of the hub where it fits into the starter clutch for wear. If the bearing is worn it must be renewed; if the gear hub is damaged a new gear must be fitted.

10 Check the condition of the sprags in the starter clutch – they should be free to rotate in the housing **(see illustration)**. If they are sticking, or the surfaces are pitted, renew the clutch assembly. Counter-hold the rotor, unscrew the clutch housing bolts and lift the assembly off, noting how it fits **(see illustration)**. Prior to installation, clean the threads of the housing bolts and apply a suitable non-permanent thread-locking compound (BMW recommends Loctite 648). Install the clutch assembly, ensuring the flange on the sprag cage faces towards the rotor. Tighten the housing bolts to the torque setting specified at the beginning of this Chapter.

11 To check the operation of the starter clutch, lay the rotor face down on the workbench and install the driven gear, turning it clockwise to free the clutch sprags **(see illustration 13.5c)**. The driven gear should

13.6 Starter idler gear (A) and reduction gear (B)

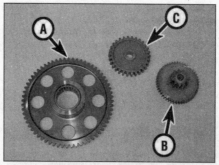

13.8a Starter driven gear (A), reduction gear (B) and idler gear (C)

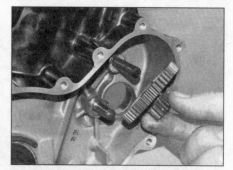

13.8b Gears should be a sliding fit on their shafts

13.9 Inspect the needle bearing (A) and the outer surface of the hub (B)

13.10a Check the starter clutch sprags

13.10b Starter clutch housing bolts (arrowed)

13.13 Ensure that all the gears are correctly engaged

14.3 Remove the oil filler cap and dipstick

rotate freely in a clockwise direction and lock against the rotor when turned anti-clockwise. If it doesn't, the starter clutch is faulty and must be renewed.

Installation

12 Lubricate the idler and reduction gear shafts with engine oil. Install the reduction gear with the smaller pinion outermost, then install the idler gear **(see illustration 13.6)**. **Note:** *The larger pinion on the reduction gear should engage with the starter motor teeth.*
13 Lubricate the driven gear needle bearing with engine oil and slide it onto the crankshaft – ensure the teeth of the driven gear, idler and reduction gear are correctly engaged **(see illustration)**. Install the large plain washer on the idler gear shaft **(see illustration 13.5a)**.
14 Lubricate the starter clutch with engine oil, ensuring the tapered inner section of the alternator rotor remains oil-free, then follow the procedure in Chapter 8 to install the rotor.

15 Once the rotor bolt has been tightened, don't forget to unscrew the TDC locating tool and refit the blanking bolt using a new sealing washer.
16 Install the remaining components in the reverse order of removal. If required, check the oil level and top-up as necessary (see *Pre-ride checks*).

14 Clutch

Note 1: *The clutch can be removed with the engine in the frame. If the engine has been removed, ignore the steps which don't apply.*
Note 2: *The clutch nut lock washer must be discarded and a new one used on installation – it is best to obtain the new washer in advance.*
Special tools: *A clutch centre locking tool*

is required for this procedure (see Steps 8 and 9). A top dead centre (TDC) locating tool is also required (see Step 8).

Removal

1 On F800 ST models, remove the left-hand bodywork side panel (see Chapter 7).
2 As applicable, remove the gearchange lever or disconnect the gearchange arm from the gearchange shaft (see Chapter 5).
3 Remove the oil filler cap and dipstick **(see illustration)**.
4 Disconnect the clutch cable from the actuating arm and bracket on the clutch cover (see Section 15).
5 Place a drain tray below the clutch cover to catch any residual oil. Unscrew the cover bolts and remove the cover **(see illustrations)**. **Note:** *There are 16 cover bolts on GS models and 17 on S, ST and R models. Note the location of the thrust washer on the gearchange shaft – if it is stuck*

14.5a Unscrew the cover bolts . . .

14.5b . . . and remove the cover

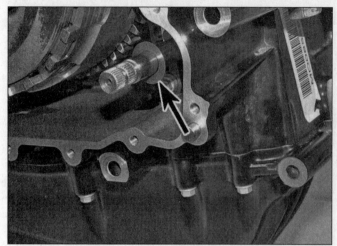

14.5c Note the location of the thrust washer (arrowed)

14.5d Remove the gasket, noting the location of the cover dowels (arrowed)

14.6a Undo the spring bolts in a criss-cross pattern . . .

14.6b . . . then remove the bolts, washers and springs

inside the cover, slide it back onto the shaft **(see illustration)**. Remove the cover gasket and discard it; note the position of the cover dowels and remove them for safe-keeping if they are loose **(see illustration)**.

6 Undo the clutch spring bolts a little at a time in a criss-cross pattern, then remove the bolts, washers and springs **(see illustrations)**.

7 Remove the clutch pressure plate, thrust washer where fitted, and pullrod **(see illustration)**. Note that the thrust washer is only fitted to the longer pull rod used on early type clutches (see *Specifications* at the beginning of this Chapter). Note the location of the tabs on the outer clutch friction plate – these locate in the offset short slots in the clutch housing **(see illustration)**. **Note:** *Specifications differ slightly between early and late type clutches*

and it is important to identify which type your machine has, both for reassembling the clutch correctly and for ordering new components. On early type clutches, one of the offset short slots in the housing is marked with red paint and the tab on the outer friction plate that fits in this slot is stamped 'C'. The innermost friction plate is also stamped 'C' and the innermost plain plate has a notch on the outside edge. On late type clutches, the tabs on the outer and inner friction plates are narrower than on the other friction plates and the innermost plain plate has a notch on the outside edge. It is important to keep all the clutch plates in order during inspection.

8 If a clutch locking tool is available (BMW service tool Part No. 21 4 601), pull out the first four friction and plain plates, noting how they fit, then install the locking tool – ensure the outer tabs on the tool engage in the long slots in the clutch housing. Install the TDC locating tool (see Section 8, Step 3). It is not necessary to remove the valve cover – remove the alternator cover (see Chapter 8) then, with

14.7a Remove the pressure plate and pullrod

14.7b Outer friction plate tabs locate in the offset short slots (arrowed)

14.9a Using a commercially available tool to hold the clutch centre

14.9b Unscrew the nut . . .

the aid of an assistant, turn the alternator rotor bolt in a clockwise direction until the slot cut into the left-hand web of the crankshaft is visible through the bolt hole. Note: *Considerable pressure will be required to undo the clutch centre nut – ensure the locating tool is correctly installed before proceeding.* The transmission output shaft is now locked and cannot turn. Undo the clutch centre nut and remove the locking washer, then draw the clutch assembly off the transmission input shaft. Note the location of the two needle bearings and the bearing spacer inside the

centre of the clutch housing. Now go to Step 11.
9 If the BMW service tool is not available, draw out the clutch plates noting how they fit (see **Note** in Step 7 above). To undo the clutch centre nut, the transmission input shaft must be locked. On GS and R models (chain final drive), if the engine is in the frame, temporarily install the gearchange lever and engage a high gear, then have an assistant hold the rear brake on hard. Alternatively, and on S and ST models (belt final drive), a commercially available tool can be used

to hold the clutch centre whilst the nut is loosened **(see illustration)**. Unscrew the nut and remove the lock washer – a new washer must be fitted on reassembly **(see illustrations)**.
10 Slide the clutch centre and the splined spacer off the input shaft **(see illustrations)**.
11 Draw off the clutch housing – note the location of the oil pump drive gear on the back of the housing and the location of the two needle roller bearings and the bearing spacer inside the centre of the clutch housing **(see illustrations)**.

14.9c . . . and remove the lock washer

14.10a Slide off the clutch centre . . .

14.10b . . . and the splined spacer

14.11a Remove the clutch housing . . .

14.11b . . . noting the location of the oil pump drive gear . . .

14.11c . . . and the needle roller bearings and spacer

14.12 Note the location of the thrust washer

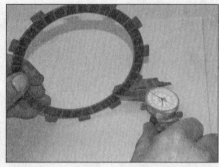

14.13 Measure the thickness of the friction plates

14.14 Check the plain plates for warpage

12 If required, slide the thrust washer off the shaft **(see illustration)**.

Inspection

13 After an extended period of service the clutch friction plates will wear and promote clutch slip. Measure the thickness of each friction plate using a Vernier caliper **(see illustration)**. If any plate has worn to or beyond the service limits given in *Specifications* at the beginning of this Chapter, or if any of the plates smell burnt or are glazed, the clutch plates must be renewed with a new set.

14 The plain plates should not show any signs of excess heating (bluing). Check for warpage using a flat surface and feeler gauges **(see illustration)**. If any plate exceeds the

maximum permissible amount of warpage, or shows signs of bluing, the clutch plates must be replaced with a new set.

15 Measure the width of the offset short slots and compare the result with the specifications **(see illustration)**. Inspect the clutch assembly for burrs and indentations in the slots in the housing and on the corresponding tabs on the friction plates **(see illustration)**. Similarly check for wear between the inner teeth of the plain plates and the slots in the clutch centre **(see illustration)**. Wear of this nature will cause clutch drag and slow disengagement during gear changes as the plates will snag when the pressure plate is lifted. With care a small amount of wear can be corrected by dressing with a fine file, but if this is

excessive the worn components should be renewed.

16 Ensure the threads for the spring bolts in the clutch centre are in good condition and check for wear on the centre splines **(see illustration)**.

17 Refer to *Tools and Workshop Tips* in the *Reference* section and inspect the needle roller bearings and the bearing surfaces in the clutch housing and on the transmission shaft **(see illustrations)**. If there are any signs of wear, pitting or other damage the affected parts must be renewed.

18 The clutch housing incorporates a cush-drive mechanism – check that the springs are not loose or broken and that there is no backlash between the housing

14.15a Check the width of the offset short slots (arrowed)

14.15b Check for wear between the friction plates and the clutch housing

14.15c Check for wear between the plain plates and the clutch centre

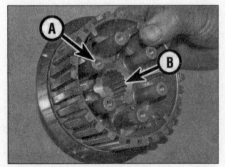

14.16 Inspect the threads (A) and centre splines (B)

14.17a Inspect the bearings . . .

14.17b . . . and the bearing surfaces

14.18 Check for backlash between primary driven gear (A) and clutch housing (B)

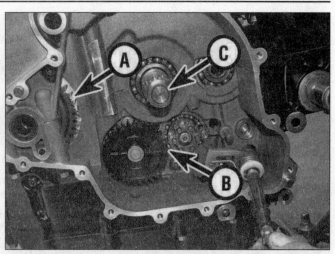

14.19 Location of primary drive gear (A). Note oil pump driven gear (B) and oil jet (C)

14.20 Note how the tabs on the oil pump drive gear locate

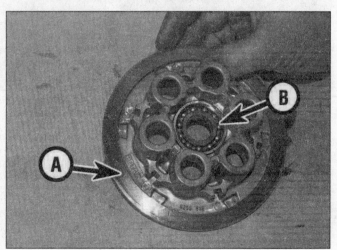

14.21 Check pressure plate surface (A) and pullrod bearing (B)

and the primary driven gear, otherwise replace the housing with a new one **(see illustration)**.

19 Check the teeth of the primary driven gear on the back of the clutch housing and the corresponding teeth of the primary drive gear on the crankshaft **(see illustration)**. Replace the clutch housing with a new one if any teeth are worn or chipped. The primary drive gear is an integral part of the crankshaft – if the gear is damaged, take the crankshaft to a BMW dealer or specialist engineer for assessment (see Section 23 for removal of the crankshaft).

20 Check the oil pump drive and driven gear teeth, and the tabs on the drive gear that locate on the back of the clutch housing **(see illustration)**.

21 Check the surface of the pressure plate and the pullrod bearing for signs of wear, damage or roughness and renew any parts as necessary **(see illustration)**. Refer to *Tools and Workshop Tips* in the *Reference* section for details of bearing removal and installation.

The bearing is lubricated by oil fed through a small jet in the end of the transmission input shaft **(see illustration 14.19)**. To ensure the jet is clear, blow through it with compressed air.

22 Inspect the pullrod and the corresponding

bearing surface on the clutch actuating shaft for wear **(see illustration)**.

23 If there is freeplay between the shaft and its bearings in the clutch cover, or evidence of oil leakage at the top of the shaft, note the location of the return spring **(see illustration)**,

14.22 Inspect the pullrod for wear

14.23a Note the location of the return spring (arrowed)

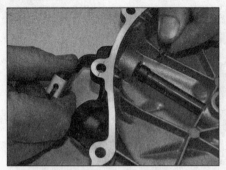

14.23b Remove the E-clip . . .

14.23c . . . and pull the shaft out of the cover

14.23d Inspect the shaft . . .

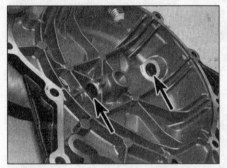

14.23e . . . and the needle bearings (arrowed)

14.23f Lever out the old seal with a flat-bladed screwdriver

14.24 Measure clutch spring free length

then remove the E-clip and pull the shaft out of the cover (see illustration). Inspect the shaft and the needle bearings in the cover for wear and damage and renew any parts as necessary (see illustrations). The seal can be renewed by levering the old one out with a flat-bladed screwdriver and pressing the new one in (see illustration). Refer to *Tools and Workshop Tips* in the Reference Section for details of removing and installing needle bearings. Lubricate the bearings with oil and the seal lips with grease before installing the shaft and securing it with a new E-clip.

24 Measure the free length of each clutch spring using a Vernier caliper (see illustration). Stand each spring upright on a flat surface and check it for bend by placing a set square against it. If any spring is shorter than the specified service limit, or if the bend in any spring is excessive, replace all the springs as a set.

Installation

25 Remove all traces of old gasket from the crankcase and clutch cover surfaces.
26 Ensure the thrust washer is located on the transmission input shaft (see illustration 14.12).
27 Lubricate the needle bearings with engine

oil and fit the bearings and spacer into the clutch housing (see illustration 14.11c). Fit the oil pump drive gear onto the back of the clutch housing ensuring the tabs locate correctly – there should be no backlash between the gear and the housing (see illustration 14.11b).
28 Slide the clutch housing onto the input shaft (see illustration 14.11a). Make sure that the primary drive and driven gear teeth and the oil pump drive and driven gear teeth engage – if necessary, rock the clutch housing and the oil pump driven gear backwards and forwards until the teeth are felt to engage (see illustrations).

14.28a Ensure the primary drive gear (arrowed) . . .

14.28b . . . and oil pump driven gear (arrowed) are correctly engaged

14.32 Fit a new lock washer and thread-lock the clutch centre nut

14.33a Install the innermost plain plate – note the notch (arrowed) . . .

14.33b . . . followed by the innermost friction plate

29 Slide the splined spacer onto the shaft (see illustration 14.10b). Lubricate the shaft splines with a smear of molybdenum grease then wipe the threads with a solvent soaked rag and install the clutch centre (see illustration 14.10a).

30 If the BMW service tool is available for locking the clutch, install the first five plain and friction plates, referring to **Note** in Step 7. The innermost plain plate is installed first. **Note:** *Install all plain plates with the sharp edge facing in.* Next install the innermost friction plate, then continue to alternate plain and friction plates to build up the clutch, finishing with the fifth friction plate from the inside. **Note:** *Coat each friction plate with engine oil prior to installation.*

31 Install the clutch locking tool, pressing it firmly into place. If removed, reinstall the TDC locating tool. Fit a new lock washer on the input shaft and apply a suitable non-permanent thread-locking compound (BMW recommends Loctite 648) to the shaft threads – ensure no locking compound blocks the oil jet in the shaft. Install the clutch centre nut and tighten it to the torque setting specified at the beginning of this Chapter. Remove the locking tool and install the remaining four

plain and friction plates. Don't forget that the tabs on the outer friction plate locate in the offset short slots in the housing (see illustration 14.7b). Now go to Step 34.

32 If the BMW service tool is not available, fit a new lock washer and apply a suitable non-permanent thread-locking compound (BMW recommends Loctite 648) to the input shaft threads (see illustration) – ensure no locking compound blocks the oil jet in the shaft. Install the clutch centre nut finger tight. Using the method employed on removal to lock the input shaft (see Step 9), tighten the nut to the torque setting specified at the beginning of this Chapter.

33 Install the clutch plates, referring to **Note** in Step 7. The innermost plain plate is installed first (see illustration). **Note:** *Install all plain plates with the sharp edge facing in.* Next install the innermost friction plate (see illustration), then continue to alternate plain and friction plates to build up the clutch. **Note:** *Coat each friction plate with engine oil prior to installation.* Don't forget that the tabs on the outer friction plate locate in the offset short slots in the housing (see illustration 14.7b).

34 Lubricate the pullrod bearing in the pressure plate with oil. On early type clutches, fit the thrust washer onto the pullrod. Insert the pullrod through the bearing from the back of the pressure plate (see illustration 14.7a).

35 Fit the pressure plate onto the clutch, then install the springs, bolts and washers (see illustration 14.6b). Tighten the bolts evenly in a criss-cross pattern to the specified torque setting.

36 Ensure the thrust washer is located on the gearchange shaft (see illustration 14.5c). Ensure that the oilways are clean (see illustration). If removed, install the cover dowels, then fit a new cover gasket, making sure it locates correctly onto the dowels (see illustration 14.5d).

37 Align the flat face on the clutch pullrod as shown (see illustration). Install the clutch cover carefully, ensuring the pullrod and the actuating shaft are mated correctly – if the cover will not lay flat against the crankcase, check the position of the pullrod and actuating shaft before installing the cover bolts. **Note:** *With the cover correctly installed, the clutch actuating arm should align with the clutch cable.*

14.36 Ensure that the oilways (arrowed) are clean

14.37a Align the flat face on the clutch pullrod as shown

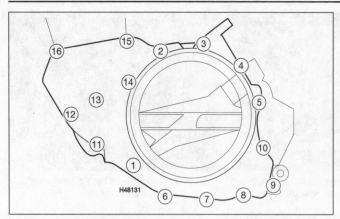

14.37b Tightening sequence for clutch cover bolts – GS models

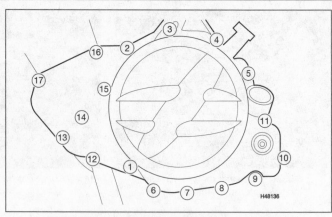

14.37c Tightening sequence for clutch cover bolts – S, ST and R models

Tighten the cover bolts evenly in the sequence shown to the specified torque **(see illustrations)**.

38 Install the remaining components in the reverse order of removal.

39 Check the oil level and top-up as necessary (see *Pre-ride checks*). Adjust the clutch cable freeplay (see Chapter 1).

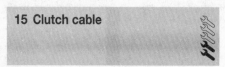

15 Clutch cable

1 Remove the air filter housing (see Chapter 4).
2 Loosen the adjuster locknuts on the lower end of the clutch cable to slacken the cable, then disconnect the inner cable end from the clutch actuating arm **(see illustration)**. Unscrew the lower locknut from the adjuster and slip the cable out through the slot in the back of the bracket **(see illustration)**.

3 Pull the cable out from the handlebar bracket and detach the end of the inner cable from the handlebar lever **(see illustrations)**.

15.2a Loosen the adjuster locknuts

15.2b Slip the cable out through the slot in the bracket

15.3a Pull the cable out from the handlebar bracket . . .

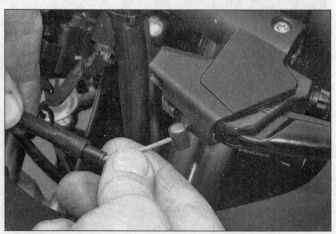

15.3b . . . and detach the inner cable from the handlebar lever

16.4a Remove the circlip . . .

16.4b . . . and washer

16.5a Position the slot horizontal . . .

4 Remove the cable from the machine, noting its routing through the radiator heat shield.

 Before removing the cable from the bike, tape the lower end of the new cable to the upper end of the old cable. Slowly pull the lower end of the old cable out, guiding the new cable down into position. Using this method will ensure the cable is routed correctly.

16.5b . . . lever the driven gear off . . .

16.5c . . . and withdraw the drive pin (arrowed)

5 Installation is the reverse of removal. Apply grease to the cable ends. Make sure the cable is correctly routed. Adjust the amount of clutch lever freeplay (see Chapter 1). Tighten the locknuts against the bracket on completion.

16 Oil pumps

Note: *The oil pumps can be removed with the engine in the frame. If the engine has been removed, ignore the steps which don't apply.*
1 There are two oil pumps inside the crankcases – a feed pump on the left-hand side behind the clutch and a scavenge pump

on the right-hand side behind the front pulley or sprocket cover. Work on one pump at a time and keep the parts from each pump separate.

Removal

2 Drain the engine oil (see Chapter 1).

Feed pump

3 Remove the clutch (see Section 14). Note the location of the oil pump drive gear on the back of the clutch housing **(see illustration 14.11b)**.
4 Remove the circlip and washer securing the pump driven gear **(see illustrations)**. Discard the circlip as a new one must be used.

5 Position the driven gear so that the retaining slot for the drive pin is horizontal, then carefully lever the gear off the pin – on assembly, the gear is a snap fit on the pin **(see illustrations)**. Withdraw the drive pin from the pump shaft **(see illustration)**.
6 Undo the bolts securing the pump cover and remove it **(see illustration)**. Note the location of the cover dowel and remove it for safekeeping if it is loose **(see illustration)**.
7 Note the location of the inner and outer pump rotors and the punch marks on the outer facing sides of both rotors, then draw the rotors out of the pump housing **(see**

16.6a Undo the pump cover bolts

16.6b Note the location of the cover dowel

16.7a Outer facing sides of rotors have punch marks

16.7b Note how inner rotor locates over its drive pin . . .

16.7c . . . then remove the pin

illustration). Note how the inner rotor locates over its drive pin, then remove the pin (see illustrations).The pump shaft cannot be removed unless the scavenge pump rotors are removed (see below).

Scavenge pump

8 On GS and R models remove the front sprocket cover (see Chapter 6). On S and ST models remove the front pulley cover (see Chapter 6).

9 Clean the area around the pump cover thoroughly to avoid dirt getting inside the pump, then undo the bolts securing the cover and ease it off (see illustrations). Discard the cover O-ring as a new one must be fitted (see illustration).

10 Note the location of the inner and outer pump rotors and the punch marks on the outer facing sides of both rotors, then draw the rotors out of the pump housing (see illustrations). Note how the inner rotor locates over its drive pin, then remove the pin (see illustrations).

11 Withdraw the pump shaft from the crankcases (see illustration).

Inspection

12 Clean all the components in solvent.

13 Inspect the pump shaft, rotors and housings for scoring and wear. No specifications are available for measuring the

16.9a Undo the pump cover bolts . . .

16.9b . . . and lift the cover off

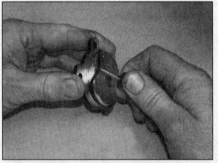

16.9c Discard the cover O-ring

16.10a Note the location of the inner and outer pump rotors

16.10b Draw out the outer rotor . . .

16.10c . . . and the inner rotor, noting how it locates . . .

16.10d . . . over the drive pin (arrowed) in the shaft

16.11 Withdraw the pump shaft

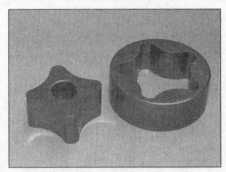

16.13 Always renew the pump rotors in matched sets

17.2 Location of the gearchange shaft and selector arm assembly

17.3 Return spring locating pin (A) and selector arm pawls (B)

clearance between the rotors, but if there is any evidence of damage the rotors should be renewed in sets **(see illustration)**.
14 Inspect the oil pump drive (on back of clutch housing) and driven gears for wear and damage to the teeth **(see illustration 14.20)**. Ensure the driven gear is a good fit on the shaft and drive pin (see Step 5).

Installation

Note: *Lubricate all pump components with engine oil prior to installation.*

Scavenge pump

15 Install the pump shaft from the right-hand side, then fit the inner rotor drive pin and rotor, and the outer rotor – ensure the punch marks on the rotors are facing out **(see illustrations 16.11, 10d, c, b and a)**.
16 Ensure the mating surfaces of the pump housing and cover are clean. Fit a new O-ring into the groove in the cover and lubricate it with a smear of oil, then install the cover **(see illustration 16.9b)**. Tighten the cover bolts evenly to the torque setting specified at the beginning of this Chapter.
17 Install the remaining components in the reverse order of removal.

Feed pump

18 Fit the inner rotor drive pin and rotor, and the outer rotor – ensure the punch

marks on the rotors are facing out **(see illustrations 16.7c, b and a)**.
19 Ensure the mating surfaces of the pump housing and cover are clean. If removed, install the cover dowel, then install the cover **(see illustrations 16.6b and a)**. Tighten the cover bolts evenly to the torque setting specified at the beginning of this Chapter.
20 Install the drive pin for the driven gear **(see illustration 16.5c)**. Slide the gear onto the shaft so that the slot in the back of the gear aligns with the pin, then press the gear onto the shaft – it should snap onto the pin.
21 Install the washer and secure the gear with a new circlip **(see illustrations 16.4b and a)**. Ensure the circlip is correctly located in its groove – if the groove is not clearly visible, the gear has not been pressed onto the shaft far enough.
22 Install the clutch (Section 14).
23 Fill the engine with oil to the correct level (see Chapter 1 and *Pre-ride checks*). Start the engine and ensure that the oil pressure warning light goes out after a few seconds.

17 External gearchange mechanism

Note: *The external gearchange mechanism can be removed with the engine in the frame.*

If the engine has been removed, ignore the steps which don't apply.

Removal

1 Make sure the transmission is in neutral, then remove the clutch cover (see Section 14).
2 The gearchange shaft and selector arm assembly are located on the right-hand side of the crankcase behind the clutch **(see illustration)**. The shaft can be withdrawn from this position – however, if the gearchange cam or stopper cam require attention it is first necessary to remove the clutch (see Section 14).
3 Note how the gearchange shaft return spring fits on each side of the locating pin in the casing, and how the pawls on the selector arm locate onto the pins on the end of the selector drum cam **(see illustration)**. Draw the shaft assembly out of the casing
4 Note the location of the stopper arm spring ends and how the roller on the arm locates in the neutral detent on the selector drum cam **(see illustration)**. Loosen the bolt securing the stopper arm, then release the spring tension on the arm and remove it **(see illustration)**. If fitted, note the location of the chamfered washer between the spring and the crankcase.

17.4a Stopper arm spring ends (A) and roller (B)

17.4b Removing the stopper arm as described

17.5a Inspect the selector arm assembly. Note the shaft return spring (A) and the selector arm spring (B)

17.5b Check the six selector drum pins (arrowed) for wear

17.5c Check the gearchange shaft for wear and damage

Inspection

5 Check the selector arm for cracks, distortion and wear of its pawls, and check for any corresponding wear on the pins on the selector drum cam (see illustrations). Check that the gearchange shaft is straight and that the splines on the end of the shaft are undamaged (see illustration). If necessary, fit a new gearchange shaft and selector arm assembly.

6 Inspect the shaft return spring and the selector arm spring for fatigue, wear or damage (see illustration 17.5a). If any is found, they must be replaced with new ones.

To renew the return spring, first slide off the thrust washer, then remove both circlips and discard them as new ones must be used (see illustration). Slide off the plastic sleeve (see illustration). Note how the ends of the return spring locate either side of the tab on the selector plate, then remove the spring (see illustration 17.5a). Fit the new spring, then fit the sleeve into the spring and secure it with a new circlip – open the circlip only enough to slide it along the shaft (see illustration). Fit the second new circlip and the thrust washer (see illustration 17.6a). Note: Ensure the circlips are correctly located in their grooves.

7 Check the stopper arm return spring for fatigue and wear and ensure that the stopper arm roller turns freely (see illustration). Renew any components that are worn or damaged. Also check the detents in the selector drum cam for wear (see illustration 17.5b). To renew the cam, unscrew the centre bolt and pull the cam off, noting the position of the locating pin. Install the new cam and tighten the centre bolt to the torque setting specified at the beginning of this Chapter.

8 Check the condition of the shaft oil seal in the clutch cover. If it is damaged, deteriorated or shows signs of leakage it must be replaced with a new one – lever out the old seal with a seal hook or screwdriver (see illustration 14.23f). Press or drive the new seal squarely into place using your fingers, a seal driver or suitable socket.

Installation

9 Make sure the transmission is in neutral. If fitted, install the chamfered washer with its chamferd side towards the casing. Assemble the washer, stopper arm, sleeve and spring on the stopper arm bolt (see illustration 17.7) and install the assembly. Make sure the arm is located on the sleeve and that the straight end of the spring is against the casing and the hooked end is around the arm, then tighten the pivot bolt to the torque setting specified at

17.6a Remove the thrust washer and circlips (arrowed)

17.6b Slide off the plastic sleeve

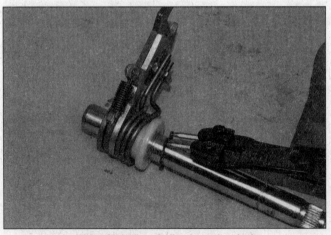

17.6c Slide the circlip along the shaft

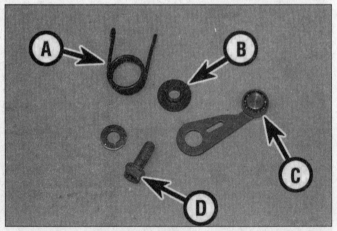

17.7 Stopper arm return spring (A), sleeve (B), roller (C) and bolt (D)

the beginning of this Chapter **(see illustration 17.4a)**. Check that the roller is located in the neutral detent on the cam and that the stopper arm moves freely.

10 Install the gearchange shaft. Ensure that the return spring fits on each side of the locating pin in the casing and the pawls on the selector arm locate onto the pins on the end of the selector drum cam **(see illustration 17.3)**.

11 Install the remaining components in the reverse order of removal.

18.6a Remove the sump

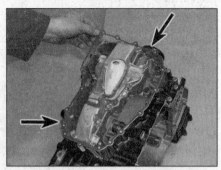

18.6b Remove the gasket, noting the dowels (arrowed)

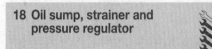

18 Oil sump, strainer and pressure regulator

Note: The oil sump, strainer and pressure regulator can be removed with the engine in the frame. If the engine has been removed, ignore the steps which don't apply.

Removal

1 On GS models, remove the sump guard (see Chapter 7).

2 On S, ST and R models remove the left and right-hand rider's footrest brackets (see Chapter 5).

3 Remove the exhaust system (see Chapter 4).

4 Drain the engine oil (see Chapter 1).

5 Unscrew the sump bolts, loosening them evenly in a criss-cross pattern to prevent distortion **(see illustrations 18.14a or b)**.

6 Remove the sump **(see illustration)**. Remove

the gasket and discard it as a new one must be fitted on reassembly – note the location of the dowels and remove them for safe-keeping if they are loose **(see illustration)**.

7 Release the tabs securing the strainer cover carefully, then lift out the cover noting the location of the seal **(see illustrations)**. Discard the seal as a new one must be fitted. Lift out the strainer gauze **(see illustration)**.

8 To access the pressure regulator it is first necessary to remove the cover for the balancer rod assembly. If the engine is in the frame, position a drain tray below the cover to catch any residual oil, then unscrew the cover bolts, loosening them evenly in a criss-cross pattern to prevent distortion **(see illustration 18.12)**. Remove the cover **(see illustration)**. Remove the gasket and discard it as a new one must be fitted on reassembly **(see illustration)**. Note the location of the pressure regulator in

the recess in the cover and lift the valve and spring out **(see illustration)**.

Inspection

9 Clean the sump and balancer assembly cover thoroughly with a suitable solvent. Remove all traces of old gasket from the crankcase, sump and cover sealing surfaces.

10 Wash the strainer gauze and its cover with solvent and remove any debris caught in the mesh, using compressed air if available. Inspect the gauze for any signs of damage and renew it if necessary.

11 Measure the free length of the pressure regulator spring and compare it to the specification at the beginning of this Chapter. If the spring is shorter than specified, renew it. Clean the pressure regulator components. Assemble the valve and spring, then press the valve into its recess in the rod cover and ensure

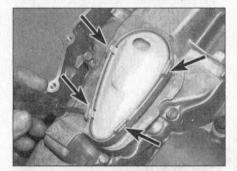

18.7a Release the tabs securing the strainer cover . . .

18.7b . . . then lift out the cover, noting the seal (arrowed)

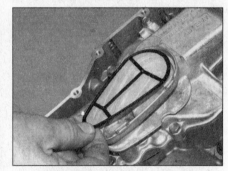

18.7c Lift out the strainer gauze

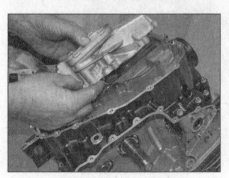

18.8a Remove the cover

18.8b Remove the cover gasket

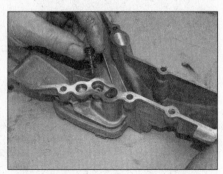

18.8c Note the location of the pressure regulator valve and spring

18.11 Inspect the pressure regulator valve seat (arrowed)

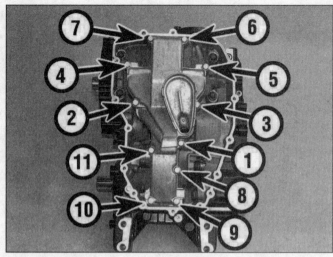

18.12 Tightening sequence for the balancer assembly cover bolts

that it returns under spring pressure. If there is any doubt about the condition of the spring, fit a new one. Check that the valve seat in the underside of the crankcase is clean (see illustration).

Installation

12 Press the pressure regulator into its recess in the balancer assembly cover. Fit a new gasket onto the cover or crankcase as is convenient – if required, use a few dabs of grease to hold it in place (see illustration 18.8b). Clean the threads of the cover bolts and apply a suitable non-permanent thread-locking compound (BMW recommends Loctite 243), then install the cover and secure it with the bolts. Tighten the bolts in the order shown to the torque setting specified at the beginning of this Chapter (see illustration).

13 Fit a new seal onto the strainer cover (see illustration 18.7b). Press the strainer gauze fully into its housing, then fit the cover ensuring all the tabs clip into place (see illustrations 18.7c and a).

14 Fit a new gasket onto the sump or crankcase as is convenient – if required, use a few dabs of grease to hold it in place. Install the sump and secure it with the bolts. Tighten the bolts in the order shown to the torque setting specified at the beginning of this Chapter (see illustrations).

15 Fit the exhaust system (see Chapter 4).

16 Fill the engine with oil to the correct level (see Chapter 1 and *Pre-ride checks*). Start the engine and ensure that the oil pressure warning light goes out after a few seconds.

17 Install the remaining components in the reverse order of removal.

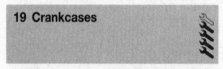

19 Crankcases

Note 1: *To separate the crankcase halves the engine must be removed from the frame.*
Note 2: *The four 8 mm main bearing bolts must be discarded and new ones used on*

installation – it is best to obtain the new bolts in advance (see Step 9).
Special tool: *A torque angle gauge is required for this procedure (see Step 31).*

1 To access the connecting rods, crankshaft, balancer assembly, gearchange selector drum and forks and transmission shafts, the crankcase must be split into two halves.

Separation

2 Remove the engine from the frame (see Section 4).

3 Before the crankcases can be separated the following components must be removed:

    Starter motor (see Chapter 8)
    Oil cooler (Section 12)
    Cylinder head (Section 10)
    Alternator (see Chapter 8)
    Clutch (Section 14)
    Gearchange shaft and selector arm (Section 17)
    Oil pumps, if required (Section 16)
    Oil sump and balancer assembly cover (Section 18)

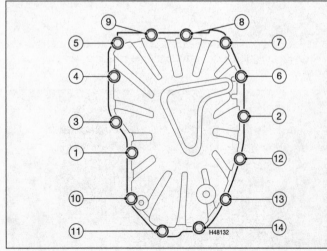

18.14a Tightening sequence for the sump bolts – GS models

18.14b Tightening sequence for the sump bolts – S, ST and R models

19.4 Upper crankcase half bolts – numbers indicate TIGHTENING sequence

19.5 Unscrew the bolts in the upper crankcase half evenly in a criss-cross sequence

4 Make a cardboard template punched with holes to match all the bolts in the upper crankcase half – as each bolt is removed, store it in its relative position on the template **(see illustration)**. This will ensure all bolts are installed in the correct location on reassembly.

5 Unscrew the fourteen bolts in the upper crankcase half evenly, a little at a time and in a criss-cross sequence until they are finger-tight, then remove them and fit them in the template **(see illustration)**.

6 Turn the engine upside down.

7 Lift out the pin securing the balancer rod shaft, then screw a suitable bolt into the end of the shaft and pull the shaft out **(see illustrations)**. Lift the free end of the rod out from the crankcase.

8 Make a cardboard template punched with holes to match all the bolts in the lower crankcase half **(see illustration)**.

9 Unscrew the nine bolts in the lower crankcase half evenly, a little at a time and in a criss-cross sequence until they are finger-tight, then remove them and fit them in the template **(see illustration)**. **Note:** *The four 8 mm bolts support the crankshaft main bearings. These* *are stretch bolts – use the old bolts for the crankshaft oil clearance check (see Section 23) but use new bolts on final reassembly.*

10 Carefully lift the lower crankcase half off the upper half, using a soft-faced hammer to tap around the joint to initially separate

19.7a Lift out the pin . . .

19.7b . . . then pull the shaft (arrowed) out

19.8 Lower crankcase half bolts – numbers indicate TIGHTENING sequence

19.9 Unscrew the bolts in the lower crankcase half evenly in a criss-cross sequence

19.10 Lift the lower crankcase half off carefully

19.11 Only remove the bearing shells if they are loose

the halves if necessary **(see illustration)**. Support the balancer rod so that it does not fall and damage the sealing surface of the upper crankcase half. **Note:** *If the halves do not separate easily, make sure all fasteners have been removed. Do not try and separate the halves by levering between the crankcase mating surfaces as they are easily damaged and will leak on reassembly.*

11 The lower crankcase will come away leaving the balancer assembly, crankshaft and transmission input and output shafts in the upper crankcase. The gearchange selector drum and forks are located in the lower crankcase. Take care not to dislodge the outer main bearing shells which should remain in their seats in the lower crankcase – remove the shells if they are loose, but keep them in order **(see illustration)**.

12 Remove the seal from the right-hand end of the transmission output shaft and discard it. **Note:** *The new seal should be fitted after the crankcase halves have been reassembled – see Section 26.*

13 Refer to the relevant Sections of this Chapter for removal and installation of the

balancer assembly (Section 20), connecting rods and pistons (Section 22), crankshaft (Section 23), transmission shafts (Section 26) and selector drum and forks (Section 28). Check all components and their bearings for wear as described in those Sections.

Inspection

14 Remove all traces of old sealant from the mating surfaces of the crankcases **(see illustration)**. Carefully clean up minor damage to the surfaces with a fine file.

15 Note the location of the crankcase dowels and remove them for safekeeping if they are loose **(see illustration)**. Clean the crankcases thoroughly with solvent and dry them with compressed air. Blow out all oil passages with compressed air.

Caution: Be very careful not to nick or gouge the crankcase mating surfaces or oil leaks will result. Check both crankcase halves very carefully for cracks and other damage.

16 Small cracks or holes in aluminium castings can be repaired with an epoxy resin adhesive as a temporary measure. Permanent

repairs can only be done by argon-arc welding, and only a specialist in this process is in a position to advise on the economy or practical aspect of such a repair, although low-temperature DIY weld kits are available for small repairs. If any damage is found that can't be repaired, renew the crankcase halves as a set.

17 Damaged threads can be reclaimed by using a diamond section wire insert, of the Heli-Coil type, which is easily fitted after drilling and re-tapping the affected thread.

18 Sheared bolts or screws can usually be removed with extractors, which consist of a tapered, left-hand thread screw of very hard steel. These are inserted into a pre-drilled hole and usually succeed in dislodging the most stubborn bolt or screw – see *Tools and Workshop Tips* in the *Reference* section.

 Always clean the crankcases thoroughly after any repair work to ensure no dirt or metal swarf is trapped inside when the engine is rebuilt.

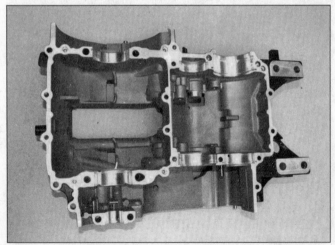

19.14 Clean off old sealant from the crankcase mating surfaces

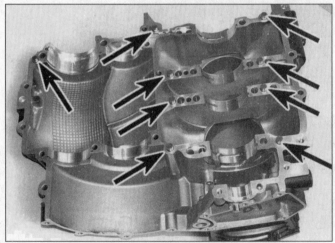

19.15 Note the location of the crankcase dowels

Reassembly

19 Support the upper crankcase securely on the work surface. Ensure that all components and their bearings are in place in the upper crankcase, including the cam chain **(see illustration 23.5)**.

20 If removed, fit the locating dowels into the upper crankcase **(see illustration 19.15)**.

21 Ensure that all components are in place in the lower crankcase, including the outer main bearing shells **(see illustration 19.11)**.

22 Lubricate the crankshaft big-end and main bearings, and the balancer assembly bearings, with engine oil.

23 Make sure the transmission input and output shafts and their bearings are correctly installed (see Section 26).

24 Make sure the transmission is in neutral – the input and output shafts should rotate freely and the selector drum stopper arm should rest in the neutral detent on the selector drum cam **(see illustration 17.4a)**.

25 Wipe the mating surfaces of both crankcase halves with a rag soaked in high flash-point solvent to remove all traces of oil. Apply a thin coating of suitable sealant to the mating surface of the lower crankcase **(see illustration)**.

Caution: Apply the sealant only to the shaded areas. Do not apply an excessive amount of sealant as it will ooze out when the case halves are assembled and may obstruct oil passages. Do not apply the sealant on or too close to any of the bearing shells or surfaces.

26 Support the balancer rod and carefully fit the lower crankcase onto the upper crankcase, making sure the dowels all align correctly **(see illustration)**.

27 Check that the lower crankcase is correctly seated **(see illustration)**.

Caution: The crankcase halves should fit together without being forced. If the casings are not correctly seated, remove the lower crankcase half and investigate

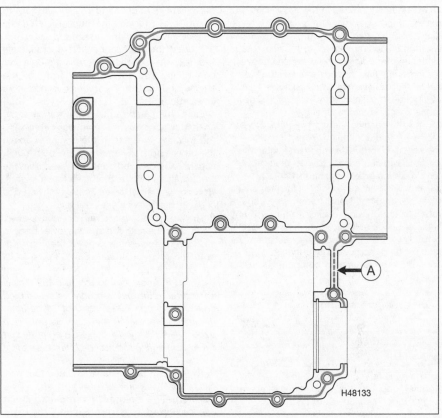

19.25 Apply sealant to the lower crankcase mating surface. Apply sealant to outside edge at (A) to avoid oilway in upper crankcase half

the problem. Do not attempt to pull the casings together using the crankcase bolts as the casing will crack and be ruined.

28 Lubricate the underside of the heads of the new 8 mm main bearing bolts with engine oil and install the bolts finger-tight **(see illustration 19.8)**. Install the five 6 mm lower crankcase bolts finger-tight.

29 Press the free end of the balancer rod down into the crankcase, install the balancer

rod shaft and secure it with the pin **(see illustrations 19.7b and a)**.

30 Turn the engine the right way up. Install the fourteen upper crankcase bolts finger-tight **(see illustration 19.4)**.

31 Turn the engine upside down and support it securely, or have an assistant hold it, while the 8 mm main bearing bolts (numbered 1 to 4) are tightened to the torque setting specified at the beginning of this Chapter **(see illustration**

19.26 Install lower crankcase – note position of balancer rod (arrowed)

19.27 Ensure lower crankcase is correctly seated

19.8). Tighten the bolts in the order shown to the initial torque setting, then, using an angle gauge, tighten the bolts in the same order in one continuous movement to the final torque setting. **Note:** *If tightening is paused between the initial and final settings, slacken the bolt to below the initial setting and start again.*

32 Tighten the 6 mm bolts in the order shown to the specified torque setting.

33 Turn the engine the right way up. Tighten the two 8 mm bolts (numbered 10 and 11) to the specified torque setting, then tighten the 6 mm bolts in numerical order to the specified torque setting **(see illustration 19.4)**.

34 With all crankcase bolts tightened, check that the crankshaft and transmission shafts rotate smoothly and easily. If there are any signs of undue stiffness, tight or rough spots, or of any other problem, the fault must be rectified before proceeding further.

35 Install the remaining components in the reverse order of removal.

20 Balancer assembly

Note: *To remove the balancer assembly the engine must be removed from the frame.*
Special tool: *A torque angle gauge is required for this procedure (see Step 17).*

Removal

1 Follow the procedure in Section 19 to separate the crankcase halves.

2 Using paint or a marker pen, mark across the balancer connecting rod-to-cap join to ensure that the rod and cap are fitted the correct way around on reassembly.

3 Protect the front edge of the crankcase with a clean rag, then position the balancer connecting rod towards the front of the engine and loosen the upper cap bolt **(see illustration)**.

4 Lay some clean rag over the transmission shafts and position the balancer connecting rod towards the rear of the engine. Loosen the other cap bolt, then remove both bolts, separate the cap and connecting rod from the crankshaft and lift them off **(see illustrations)**. **Note:** *If the cap appears stuck, tap it on one end with a hammer while pulling it.*

5 The upper bearing shell will come away with the connecting rod and the lower bearing shell will remain in the cap. Fit the cap back onto the rod and install the bolts to keep the components together. **Note:** *The joint between the connecting rod and the cap is a fractured joint that can only be assembled one way round. Take care not to damage the joint surfaces – if the surfaces are not a perfect match they will not rejoin properly and a new connecting rod assembly will have to be fitted.*

6 The old cap bolts should be used for an oil clearance check only (see Step 11).

Caution: The connecting rod cap bolts are designed to stretch when they are tightened. NEVER use the old bolts for final installation.

7 Do not try to separate the balancer rod from the connecting rod.

Inspection

8 Inspect the assembly for cracks and other obvious damage. Check for any freeplay between the balancer rod and the connecting rod – if necessary, have the assembly checked by a BMW dealer.

9 The balancer rod shaft should be a sliding fit in the eye in the end of the rod – check for any freeplay between the two **(see illustration)**. Measure the outside diameter of the shaft and the inside diameter of the rod eye (see *Tools and Workshop Tips* in the *Reference* section). Subtract the rod diameter from the eye diameter to calculate the oil clearance and compare the result with the specification at the beginning of this Chapter. If the clearance is greater than the service limit, renew the complete assembly.

10 Refer to Section 21 and examine the connecting rod big-end bearing shells. If they are scored, badly scuffed or appear to have seized, new shells must be installed. Always renew the shells as a set. If any are badly damaged, check the crankshaft journal. Evidence of extreme heat, such as discoloration, indicates that lubrication failure has occurred. Be sure to check the oil pump, pressure regulator and all oil holes and passages thoroughly before reassembling the engine. Remove the bearing shells by pushing their centres to the side then lifting them out **(see illustration)**.

11 Whether new bearing shells are being fitted or the original ones are being re-used, the connecting rod big-end bearing oil clearance should be checked prior to

20.3 Position the balancer connecting rod as described and loosen the upper cap bolt

20.4a Loosen the other cap bolt . . .

20.4b . . . separate the cap and connecting rod . . .

20.4c . . . and lift them off the crankshaft

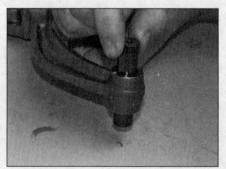

20.9 Checking the balancer rod shaft for freeplay

20.10 Remove the shells by carefully pushing them to one side

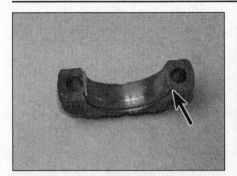

20.14 Tab (arrowed) must locate in notch

20.17 Using an angle gauge to tighten the cap bolt

reassembly – follow the procedure in Section 22. Compare the result with the specification at the beginning of this Chapter. If the clearance is greater than the service limit, renew the complete assembly.

Installation

12 If a new balancer assembly is being fitted use all the new components. Clean everything with solvent to remove any anti-rust coating, then dry it all using compressed air.

13 Ensure that the backs of the bearing shells, the bearing seats in the cap and rod and the crankshaft journal are clean. If new shells are being fitted, ensure that all traces of protective grease are removed using paraffin (kerosene). Dry the shells, with a clean, lint-free cloth.

14 Install the shells, making sure the tab on each shell engages the notch in the cap or rod **(see illustration)**. Take care not to touch any bearing surfaces with your fingers.

15 Lubricate the underside of the heads and the threads of the new cap bolts with engine oil.

16 Lubricate the shells and crankshaft journal with engine oil. Fit the connecting rod and cap onto the journal, ensuring that the rod is fitted the correct way round and that the previously made markings align (see Step 2). Ensure that the two halves of the fractured joint are a perfect fit, then install the cap bolts and tighten them finger-tight **(see illustrations 20.4b, a and 20.3)**.

17 Protect the front edge of the crankcase with a clean rag, then position the balancer connecting rod towards the front of the engine. Ensure that the engine is supported securely, or have an assistant hold it, and tighten the upper cap bolt in three stages to the torque settings specified at the beginning of this Chapter. Tighten the bolt to the initial setting, then to the second setting, and then, using an angle gauge, tighten it in one continuous movement to the final torque setting **(see illustration)**. **Note:** *If tightening is paused between the second and final settings, slacken the bolt to below the second setting and start again.*

18 Lay some clean rag over the transmission shafts and position the balancer connecting rod towards the rear of the engine. Follow the same procedure to tighten the other cap bolt

19 Check that the rod rotates smoothly and freely on the crankshaft. If there are any signs of roughness or tightness, remove the balancer assembly and re-check the bearing clearance. Sometimes tapping the cap bolts will relieve tightness.

20 Install the remaining components in the reverse order of removal.

21 Connecting rod and crankshaft bearing information

1 Even though new connecting rod big-end bearings and crankshaft main bearings are generally fitted during engine overhaul, the old bearings should be retained for close examination as they may reveal valuable information about the condition of the engine.

2 Bearing failure occurs mainly due to the presence of dirt or other foreign particles, lack of lubrication, overloading the engine or corrosion. Regardless of the cause of bearing failure, it must be corrected before the engine is reassembled to prevent it from happening again.

3 When examining the bearings, lay them out on a clean surface in the same general position as their location on the crankshaft journals. This will enable you to match any noted bearing problems with the corresponding crankshaft journal.

4 Dirt and other foreign particles get into the engine in a variety of ways. They may be left in the engine during assembly or they may pass through filters or breathers, then get into the oil and from there into the bearings. Metal chips from machining operations and normal engine wear are often present. Abrasives are sometimes left in engine components after reconditioning operations, especially when parts are not thoroughly cleaned using the proper cleaning methods.

5 Whatever the source, foreign objects often end up imbedded in the soft bearing material and are easily recognised. Large particles will not embed in the bearing and will score or gouge the bearing and journal. The best prevention for this cause of bearing failure is to clean all parts thoroughly and keep everything spotlessly clean during engine

reassembly. Regular oil and filter changes are also recommended.

6 Lack of lubrication or lubrication breakdown has a number of interrelated causes. Excessive heat (which thins the oil), overloading (which squeezes the oil from the bearing face) and oil leakage or throw off (from excessive bearing clearances, worn oil pump or high engine speeds) all contribute to lubrication breakdown. Blocked oil passages, a damaged pump or pressure regulator will starve a bearing of lubrication and destroy it. When lack of lubrication is the cause of bearing failure, the bearing material is wiped or extruded from the steel backing of the bearing. Temperatures may increase to the point where the steel backing and the journal turn blue from overheating. Refer to *Tools and Workshop Tips* in the *Reference* section at the end of this manual for bearing fault finding.

7 Riding habits can have a definite effect on bearing life. Full throttle/low speed operation, or labouring the engine, puts very high loads on bearings, which tend to squeeze out the oil film. These loads cause the bearings to flex, which produces fine cracks in the bearing face (fatigue failure). Eventually the bearing material will loosen in pieces and tear away from the steel backing. Short trip riding leads to corrosion of bearings, as insufficient engine heat is produced to drive off the condensed water and corrosive gases produced. These products collect in the engine oil, forming acid and sludge. As the oil is carried to the engine bearings, the acid attacks and corrodes the bearing material.

8 Incorrect bearing installation during engine assembly will lead to bearing failure as well. Tight fitting bearings which leave insufficient bearing oil clearances result in oil starvation. Dirt or foreign particles trapped behind a bearing shell result in high spots on the bearing which lead to failure.

9 To avoid bearing problems, clean all parts thoroughly before reassembly, double check all bearing clearance measurements and lubricate the new bearings with clean engine oil during installation.

22 Connecting rods and big-end bearings

Note 1: *To remove the connecting rods the engine must be removed from the frame and the crankcase halves separated.*
Special tool: *A torque angle gauge is required for this procedure (see Step 30).*

Removal

1 Follow the procedure in Section 19 to separate the crankcase halves.

2 If the connecting rods are being removed as part of a general overhaul, first remove the balancer assembly (see Section 20) and lift out the transmission output and input shafts (see Section 26).

22.3 Measuring the big-end side clearance

22.5 Mark the cylinder identity on the cap-to-connecting rod joint

3 Before detaching the connecting rods from the crankshaft, measure the big-end side clearance on each rod with a feeler gauge **(see illustration)**. If the clearance on either rod is greater than the service limit listed in the Specifications at the beginning of this Chapter, renew the rod and check the clearance again. If the clearance is still excessive, replace the crankshaft with a new one.
4 Support the upper crankcase half with sufficient clearance below the top of the cylinders to allow for removal of the pistons and connecting rods.
5 Using paint or a marker pen, mark the cylinder identity on each connecting rod and cap next to the cap-to-connecting rod join to ensure that the cap and rod are fitted the correct way around on reassembly **(see illustration)**.
6 Working on one connecting rod at a time,

unscrew the cap bolts and remove the cap, complete with the lower bearing shell, from the crankshaft **(see illustrations). Note:** *If the cap appears stuck, tap it on one end with a hammer while pulling it.*
7 Detach the rod, complete with the upper bearing shell, from the crankshaft, then push the rod and piston assembly out through the top of the cylinder. Fit the cap back onto the rod and install the bolts to keep the components together **(see illustration)**. **Note:** *The joint between the connecting rod and the cap is a fractured joint that can only be assembled one way round. Take care not to damage the joint surfaces – if the surfaces are not a perfect match they will not come-together properly and a new connecting rod assembly will have to be fitted.*
8 The old cap bolts should be used for an oil clearance check only (see Step 13).

Caution: *The connecting rod cap bolts are designed to stretch when they are tightened. NEVER use the old bolts for final installation.*
9 Follow the procedure in Section 24 to remove the pistons.

Inspection

10 Check the connecting rods for cracks and other obvious damage. Have the rods checked for twist and bend by a BMW dealer if you are in doubt about their straightness.
11 Follow the procedure in Section 24 and check for freeplay between each piston pin and its connecting rod small-end. If either small-end is worn beyond its service limit, a new pair of connecting rods will have to be fitted.
12 Refer to Section 21 and examine the connecting rod big-end bearing shells. If they are scored, badly scuffed or appear to have seized, new shells must be installed. Always renew the shells as a set. If any are badly damaged, check the corresponding crankshaft journal. Evidence of extreme heat, such as discoloration, indicates that lubrication failure has occurred. Be sure to check the oil pump, pressure regulator and all oil holes and passages thoroughly before reassembling the engine. Remove the bearing shells by pushing their centres to the side, then lifting them out **(see illustration)**.

Oil clearance check

13 Whether new bearing shells are being fitted or the original ones are being re-used, the connecting rod big-end bearing oil clearance should be checked prior to reassembly. Bearing oil clearance is measured with a product known as Plastigauge.
14 Working on one connecting rod at a time, remove the bearing shells from the rod and cap, keeping them in order. Clean the backs of the bearing shells, the bearing locations in both the connecting rod and cap, and the crankshaft big-end journal with a suitable solvent. If new shells are being fitted, ensure that all traces of protective grease are removed using paraffin (kerosene). Dry the shells, with a clean, lint-free cloth.
15 Press the bearing shells into their locations, ensuring that the tab on each shell engages the notch in the connecting rod or cap **(see illustration)**. Make sure the bearings

22.6a Undo the cap bolts . . .

22.6b . . . and remove the cap

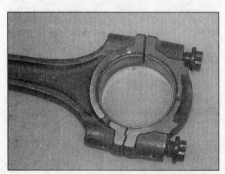

22.7 Keep the connecting rod components together

22.12 Remove the shells by carefully pushing them to one side

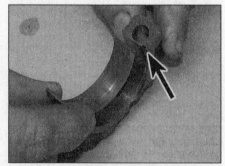

22.15 Align the tab with the notch (arrowed)

22.16 Lay Plastigauge (arrowed) along the big-end journal

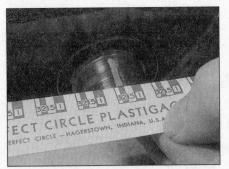

22.20 Compare the width of the crushed Plastigauge with the scale

22.24 Measuring the crankshaft big-end journal diameter

are fitted in the correct locations and take care not to touch any shell's bearing surface with your fingers.

16 Lock the crankshaft so that it cannot rotate. Cut a length of appropriate size Plastigauge – it should be slightly shorter than the width of the big-end journal – and place it on the centreline of the journal to be checked **(see illustration)**. Do not place Plastigauge over the oil holes in the journal.

17 Fit the connecting rod and cap onto the journal, ensuring that the rod is fitted the correct way round and that the previously made markings align (see Step 5). **Note:** *It is essential that, throughout this procedure, the connecting rod does not rotate on the crankshaft.*

18 Ensure that the two halves of the fractured joint are a perfect fit. Lubricate the underside of the heads and the threads of the old cap bolts with engine oil, then install them and tighten them in two stages to the second torque setting specified at the beginning of this Chapter – if necessary, have an assistant hold the crankshaft.

19 Undo the bolts and remove the cap and connecting rod from the crankshaft, again taking great care that the rod does not rotate on the crankshaft.

20 To determine the oil clearance, compare the crushed Plastigauge (at its widest point) with the printed Plastigauge scale **(see illustration)**. Compare the result with this Chapter's *Specifications*.

21 If the bearing shells and journal are in

good condition the oil clearance will be within the standard specified range.

22 Carefully scrape away all traces of the Plastigauge from the big-end journal and bearing shells using a fingernail or other object which will not score the bearing surfaces.

23 If, using the old bearing shells, the oil clearance is between the standard specified maximum and the service limit, replace the old shells with new ones, then check the oil clearance again. The new clearance may exceed the standard specified maximum slightly, but it must not be less than the standard specified minimum, otherwise bearing seizure may occur.

24 If, using the old bearing shells, the oil clearance exceeds the service limit, but the crankshaft journal shows no signs of wear or damage, measure the journal diameter in several places to ensure it has not worn out-of-round **(see illustration)**. If the journal is good, replace the old shells with new ones, then check the oil clearance again. If the clearance still exceeds the service limit, the crankshaft is worn and a new one must be fitted.

Installation

25 Follow the procedure in Section 24 to install the pistons on the connecting rods.

26 Follow the procedure in Steps 14 and 15 to ensure the components are clean and install the bearing shells correctly.

27 Working on one piston/connecting rod assembly at a time, follow the procedure

in Section 24 to fit the assemblies into the cylinders.

28 Lubricate the shells and crankshaft journal with engine oil. Draw the connecting rod up onto the crankshaft, ensuring that the rod is fitted the correct way round **(see illustration)**. Fit the cap ensuring that the previously made markings align **(see illustrations 22.6b and 5)**.

29 Lubricate the underside of the heads and the threads of the new cap bolts with engine oil. Ensure that the two halves of the fractured joint are a perfect fit, then install the cap bolts and tighten them finger-tight **(see illustration 22.6a)**.

30 Ensure that the engine is supported securely, or have an assistant hold it, and tighten the cap bolts in three stages to the torque settings specified at the beginning of this Chapter **(see illustration)**. Tighten both bolts to the initial setting, then to the second setting, and then, using an angle gauge, tighten them in one continuous movement to the final torque setting **(see illustration)**. **Note:** *If tightening is paused between the second and final settings, slacken the bolt to below the second setting and start again.*

31 Check that the rod rotates smoothly and freely on the crankshaft. If there are any signs of roughness or tightness, tap on the cap with a hammer – this should relieve stress and free it up. If it doesn't, recheck the bearing clearance.

32 Fit the other piston/connecting rod assembly.

33 Install the remaining components in the reverse order of removal.

22.28 Draw the connecting rod up onto the crankshaft

22.30a Tighten the cap bolts (arrowed) in three stages

22.30b Using an angle gauge to tighten the connecting rod cap bolts

23.3 Check for crankshaft end-float

23.4a Note the numbers (arrowed) and mark the main bearing caps . . .

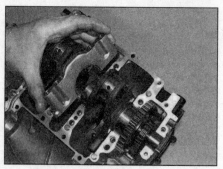

23.4b . . . then remove the caps

23 Crankshaft and main bearings

Note 1: *To remove the crankshaft the engine must be removed from the frame and the crankcase halves separated.*

Note 2: *The 8 mm crankshaft cap bolts must be discarded and new ones used on installation – it is best to obtain the new bolts in advance.*

Special tool: *A torque angle gauge is required for this procedure (see Step 28).*

Removal

1 Follow the procedure in Section 19 to separate the crankcase halves.

2 Remove the balancer assembly (see Section 20) and lift out the transmission output and input shafts (see Section 26). Remove the connecting rod and piston assemblies (see Section 22).

3 Before removing the crankshaft from the upper crankcase half, check for any end-float on the crankshaft **(see illustration)**. Measure the end-float between one of the inner crankshaft webs and the adjacent side of the crankcase and compare the result with the specification at the beginning of this Chapter. If the end-float is greater than the service limit, have the crankshaft and crankcase checked by a BMW dealer.

4 Note the numbers cast in the crankcase forward of the crankshaft main bearing caps and mark the caps using paint or a marker pen to ensure correct reassembly, then undo the cap bolts evenly and lift the caps off **(see illustrations)**. The old cap bolts should be used for an oil clearance check only (see Step 11).

5 Mark the cam chain so that it can to installed the same way round, then lift out the crankshaft taking care not to dislodge the main bearing shells **(see illustration)**. Lift off the cam chain (see Section 9 for inspection details).

Inspection

6 Clean the crankshaft with a suitable solvent, paying particular attention to flush out the oil passages. If available, blow the crank dry with compressed air, and also blow through the oil passages.

7 Inspect the primary drive gear and cam chain sprocket for wear or damage **(see illustration)**. If any of the gear or sprocket teeth are excessively worn, chipped or broken, the crankshaft must be renewed. **Note:** *If wear or damage is found, also inspect the primary driven gear on the clutch housing (see Section 14) or the cam chain and camshaft sprockets (see Section 9).*

8 Refer to Section 21 and examine the main bearing shells **(see illustrations)**. Don't forget the outer main bearing shells in the lower crankcase half **(see illustration 19.11)**. If they are scored, badly scuffed or appear to have been seized, new shells must be installed. Always renew the main bearing shells as a set.

9 The crankshaft journals should be given a close visual examination, paying particular attention where damaged bearings have been discovered. If the journals are scored or pitted in any way, a new crankshaft will be required. Place the crankshaft on V-blocks and check the runout at the centre main bearing journals using a dial gauge (see *Tools and Workshop Tips* in the *Reference* Section) **(see illustration)**. If the runout is excessive, a

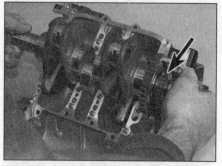

23.5 Lift out the crankshaft – note the cam chain (arrowed)

23.7 Primary drive gear (A) and cam chain sprocket (B)

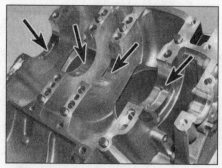

23.8a Examine the bearing shells in the crankcases . . .

23.8b . . . and in the bearing caps

23.9 Check crankshaft runout at the centre main bearing journals

23.10 Remove the shells by carefully pushing them to one side

23.14 Tab on the shell engages in the notch (arrowed)

23.16 Lay a strip of Plastigauge along the centreline of each journal

new crankshaft must be fitted; consult a BMW dealer if runout appears to be significant.

10 Remove the bearing shells from both crankcase halves and from the bearing caps by pushing their centres to the side, then lifting them out **(see illustration)**. Keep the shells in order so that they can be fitted in their original locations for the oil clearance check.

Oil clearance check

11 Whether new bearing shells are being fitted or the original ones are being reused, the main bearing oil clearance should be checked prior to reassembly. Bearing oil clearance is measured with a product known as Plastigauge.

12 Clean the backs of the bearing shells, the bearing seats in both crankcase halves and the bearing caps, and the main bearing journals on the crankshaft. If new shells are being fitted, ensure that all traces of protective grease are removed using paraffin (kerosene). Dry the shells, with a clean, lint-free cloth.

13 Remove all traces of old sealant from the crankcase mating surfaces with a suitable solvent and clean the threads of the crankcase bolts.

14 Press the bearing shells into their seats, ensuring that the tab on each shell engages in the notch in the crankcase or bearing cap **(see illustration)**. Make sure the bearings are fitted in the correct locations and take care not to touch bearing surfaces with your fingers.

15 Lay the crankshaft in position in the upper crankcase half. If removed, fit the dowels into the crankcase **(see illustration 19.15)**.

16 Lock the crankshaft so that it cannot rotate. Cut four lengths of the appropriate size Plastigauge – they should be slightly shorter than the width of the crankshaft journals – then place a length of Plastigauge along the centreline of each journal **(see illustration)**. Do not place Plastigauge over the oil holes in the crankshaft.

17 Carefully fit the main bearing caps, ensuring they are the correct way round **(see illustrations 23.4b and a)**. Tighten the old cap bolts to the initial torque setting specified at the beginning of this Chapter in the order shown **(see illustration)**. **Note:** *It is essential that, throughout this procedure, the crankshaft does not rotate in the crankcase.* Next, fit

the lower crankcase half onto the upper crankcase, ensuring that the Plastigauge is not disturbed. Make sure the dowels locate correctly and that the lower crankcase half is correctly seated. Follow the procedure in Section 19 to install and tighten the old 8 mm main bearing bolts to the initial torque setting in the order shown **(see illustration 19.8)**.

18 Unscrew the crankcase bolts in the **reverse** order of the tightening sequence and remove them. Carefully lift off the lower crankcase half, making sure the Plastigauge is not disturbed. Next, undo the main bearing cap bolts evenly and lift the caps off.

19 Compare the width of the crushed Plastigauge on each crankshaft journal to the printed Plastigauge scale to obtain the main bearing oil clearance **(see illustration 22.20)**. Compare the oil clearance to the specifications at the beginning of this Chapter.

20 If the bearing shells and journal are in good condition the oil clearance will be within the standard specified range.

21 Carefully scrape away all traces of the Plastigauge from the journal and bearing shells using a fingernail or other object which will not score the bearing surfaces.

22 If, using the old bearing shells, the oil clearance is between the standard specified maximum and the service limit, replace the old shells with new ones, then check the oil clearance again. The new clearance may exceed the standard specified maximum slightly, but it must not be less than the standard specified minimum, otherwise bearing seizure may occur.

23 If, using the old bearing shells, the oil clearance exceeds the service limit, but the crankshaft journals show no signs of wear or damage, measure the journal diameters in several places to ensure they have not worn out-of-round **(see illustration)**. If the journals are good, replace the old shells with new ones, then check the oil clearance again. If the clearance still exceeds the service limit the crankshaft is worn and a new one must be fitted.

Installation

24 Follow the procedure in Steps 12 to 14 to ensure the components are clean and install the bearing shells correctly.

25 Lubricate the shells and crankshaft journals with engine oil.

26 Fit the cam chain over the crankshaft sprocket, ensuring it is the correct way round, then lay the crankshaft in position in the upper crankcase half **(see illustration 23.5)**. If removed, fit the dowels into the crankcase **(see illustration 19.15)**.

27 Fit the main bearing caps, ensuring they are the correct way round **(see illustration 23.4a)**. Lubricate the underside of the heads and the threads of the new cap bolts with engine oil.

28 Ensure that the engine is supported securely, or have an assistant hold it, and tighten the cap bolts in the order shown in two stages to the torque settings specified at the beginning of this Chapter **(see illustration 23.17)**. Tighten both bolts to the initial setting, then, using an angle gauge, tighten

23.17 TIGHTENING sequence for the main bearing cap bolts

23.23 Measuring the crankshaft main bearing journal diameter

23.28 Using a torque angle gauge to tighten the main bearing cap bolts

24.2 Arrows point towards the front of the engine

24.3 Note location of circlip tab (arrowed)

them in one continuous movement to the final torque setting (see illustration). Note: *If tightening is paused between the second and final settings, slacken the bolt to below the second setting and start again.*

29 Follow the procedure in Section 22 to install the connecting rod and piston assemblies.

30 Install the transmission shafts (see Section 26).

31 Install the balancer assembly (see Section 20)

32 Reassemble the crankcase halves (see Section 19).

24 Pistons and cylinders

Note: *To remove the pistons the engine must be removed from the frame and the crankcase halves separated. The cylinders are integral with the upper crankcase half.*

Removal

1 Follow the procedure in Section 19 to separate the crankcase halves.

2 Follow the procedure in Section 22 to remove the piston/connecting rod assemblies. Mark both pistons so that they can be assembled onto the correct connecting rods. Note that the tops of the pistons are stamped with an arrow which points to the front (exhaust) side of the engine (see illustration).

3 Working on one piston at a time, note how the tab on each circlip securing the piston pin

locates in the notch in the piston, then carefully prise out one of the circlips using a small flat-bladed screwdriver (see illustration).

4 Push the piston pin out from the other side to free the piston from the connecting rod (see illustration). Note: *BMW advises that it may be necessary to heat the piston to aid removal of the pin.* Remove the other circlip and discard them both as new ones must be used. Fit the pin back into the piston so that related parts don't get mixed up.

HAYNES HiNT *If the piston pin is a tight fit in the piston bosses, use a hot air gun to expand the alloy piston sufficiently to release its grip on the pin. If the piston pin is particularly stubborn, extract it using a drawbolt tool, but be careful to protect the piston's working surfaces.*

5 Using your thumbs or a thin blade, carefully remove the rings from the piston (see illustration). Do not nick or gouge the piston in the process. Note which way up each ring fits and in which groove as they must be installed in their original positions if being reused (see Section 25). Note: *It is good practice to fit new piston rings when an engine is being overhauled.*

6 Clean all traces of carbon from the top of the piston. A hand-held wire brush or a piece of fine emery cloth can be used once most of the deposits have been scraped away. Do not, under any circumstances, use a wire brush mounted in a drill motor; the piston material is soft and will be eroded away by the wire brush.

7 Use a piston ring groove cleaning tool to remove any carbon deposits from the ring grooves. If a tool is not available, a piece broken off an old ring will do the job. Be very careful to remove only the carbon deposits. Do not remove any metal and do not nick or gouge the sides of the ring grooves.

8 Once the carbon has been removed, clean the piston with a suitable solvent and dry it thoroughly. If the identification previously marked on the piston is cleaned off, be sure to re-mark it with the correct identity. Make sure the oil return holes at the back of the oil ring groove are clear.

Inspection

9 Carefully inspect each piston for cracks around the skirt, at the pin bosses and at the ring lands (between the ring grooves). Also check that the circlip grooves are not damaged. Normal piston wear appears as even, vertical wear on the thrust surfaces of the piston. If the skirt is scored or scuffed, the engine may have been suffering from overheating and/or abnormal combustion, which causes excessively high operating temperatures. The oil pumps should be checked thoroughly.

10 In extreme cases, a hole in the top of the piston or burned areas around the edge of the piston crown indicate that pre-ignition or knocking under load have occurred, although the ECU should detect problems with the fuel or ignition systems long before serious damage takes place. Check the symptoms of poor running in *Fault Finding* in the *Reference* section.

11 Inspect the cylinder walls carefully for scratches and score marks (see illustration).

24.4 Remove the piston pin to free the piston

24.5 Using a thin blade to remove the piston rings

24.11 Inspect the cylinder walls (arrowed) for damage

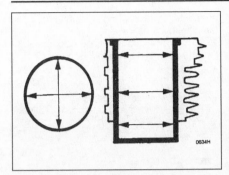

24.12a Measure the cylinder bore in the directions shown . . .

24.12b . . . using a telescoping gauge

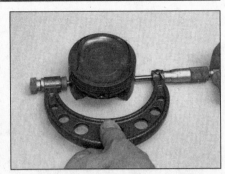

24.13 Measuring the piston diameter

12 Using a telescoping bore gauge and a micrometer, check the dimensions of the cylinders to assess the amount of wear, taper and ovality. Measure just below the top edge, in the centre and just above the bottom edge of the bore, both parallel to and across the crankshaft axis (see illustrations). Compare the results with *Specifications* at the beginning of this Chapter. If either cylinder is worn beyond the service limit, is oval or tapered, new crankcases will have to be fitted.

13 Check the piston-to-bore clearance – make sure the piston is matched to its correct cylinder. Measure the cylinder bore 31 to 36 mm below the top edge, across three points to obtain an average bore diameter (see illustration 24.12b). Measure the piston across the bottom of the skirt and at 90° to the piston pin axis (see illustration). Subtract the piston diameter from the bore diameter to obtain the clearance. If it is greater than the figure specified at the beginning of this Chapter, check whether it is the bore or piston that is worn. If the piston diameter is less that the service limit, new pistons and rings should be fitted.

14 Measure the external diameter of the pin at each end and in the centre to check for uneven wear (see illustrations). Apply clean engine oil to the piston pin, insert it into the piston and check for freeplay between the two (see illustration). The pin should be a sliding fit – if there is any freeplay or uneven wear a new pin should be fitted. Note: *Two types of piston pin are fitted to the machines covered in this manual. A plain, unpolished pin is fitted directly into the connecting rod small end; a*

highly polished pin is fitted into a small-end bush in the connecting rod. Check which type you have before ordering new parts.

15 Measure the internal diameter of the pin bore in connecting rod small-end (see illustration). Subtract the pin diameter from the bore diameter to determine the pin clearance, then compare the result with the specification at the beginning of this Chapter. If the clearance is greater than the service limit, and there is no evidence of wear on the pin, it is likely the small-end has worn and a new set of connecting rods will have to be fitted. Have the components checked by a BMW dealer.

Installation

16 Inspect and install the piston rings (see Section 25).

17 Working on one piston at a time, lubricate the piston pin, the piston pin bore and the connecting rod small-end bore with engine oil.

24.14a Measure the piston pin at each end . . .

18 When fitting the piston onto the connecting rod, make sure the arrow faces the front of the engine (see Step 2).

19 Fit a *new* circlip into one side of the piston (do not reuse old circlips) – ensure the tab on the circlip locates in the notch in the piston (see illustration 24.3). Line up the piston on the connecting rod, and insert the piston pin from the other side (see illustration 24.4). Secure the pin with the other *new* circlip (see illustration). Note: *When fitting the circlips, compress them only just enough to fit them in the piston, and make sure they are properly seated in their grooves.*

20 Ensure the piston ring end gaps are correctly staggered (see Section 25), then lubricate the pistons, rings and cylinder bores with clean engine oil. Fit a piston ring compressor tool over the rings, ensuring they are all pressed back into their grooves.

21 Lower the piston/connecting rod assembly

24.14b . . . and in the centre to check for uneven wear

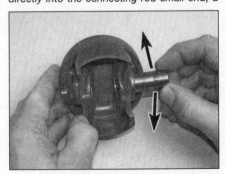

24.14c Checking the piston pin for freeplay

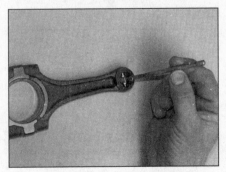

24.15 Measuring the internal diameter of the connecting rod small-end

24.19 Align the circlip to aid installation

24.21a Lower the assembly into the cylinder . . .

24.21b . . . rest the compressor on the top edge of the cylinder

24.22a Tap the piston down into the cylinder . . .

24.22b . . . until the ring compressor is free

into the cylinder, ensuring it is fitted the correct way round, and rest the lower edge of the compressor on the top edge of the cylinder (see illustrations).

22 Carefully press the piston down into the

cylinder – the rings must be fully compressed otherwise they will snag on the top edge of the cylinder and may break. If necessary, tap the top of the piston gently with a hammer handle until the piston has entered the bore

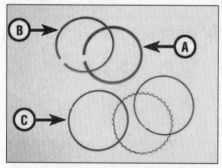

25.2a Top ring (A), second ring (B) and oil control ring (C)

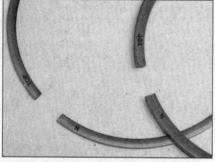

25.2b Markings on the top and second rings

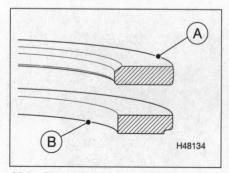

25.2c Piston ring cross sections – top ring (A) and second ring (B)

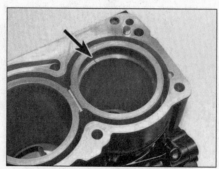

25.3 Fit the ring into the bore – note the end gap (arrowed)

completely and the ring compressor is free (see illustrations).

23 Follow the same procedure to install the other piston/connecting rod assembly.

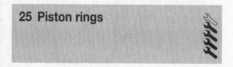

25 Piston rings

Inspection

1 It is good practice to replace the piston rings with new ones when an engine is being overhauled.

2 Lay out each piston with its ring set (see illustration). The upper surface of the top and second rings should be marked 'TOP' at one end (see illustration). On the machine used to illustrate this procedure, the upper surface of both rings was also marked 'N'. Note that the top and second rings have different cross-sections (see illustration).

3 No specifications are available for the piston rings, but before installing them onto the pistons it is worthwhile fitting them into the appropriate cylinder bore to ensure the ends do not touch or overlap when they are installed. Fit the top ring into its bore, setting it approximately 60 mm down from the top, and square it up with the bore wall by pushing it in with the top of the piston (see illustration). Note the gap between the ends of the ring. Repeat the procedure for the second ring, but not the three-piece oil control ring.

Installation

4 Install the oil control ring (lowest on the piston) first. It is composed of three separate components, namely the expander and the upper and lower side-rails. Check that the wire on the expander is positioned an equal distance either side of the end gap, then fit the expander into the groove (see illustrations). Next fit the lower side-rail – do not use a piston ring installation tool on the side-rails as they may be damaged. Instead, place one end of the side-rail into the groove between the expander and the ring land. Hold it firmly in place and slide a finger around the piston while pushing the rail into the groove (see

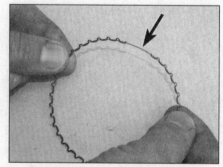

25.4a Note the location of the wire (arrowed) on the expander . . .

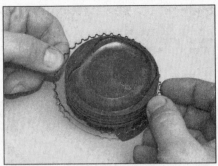

25.4b . . . then fit the expander into its groove

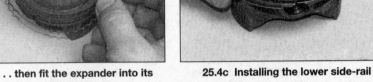

25.4c Installing the lower side-rail

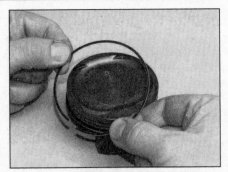

25.6a Fit the second ring onto the piston . . .

illustration). Install the upper side-rail in the same manner

5 After the components have been installed, check to make sure that both the upper and lower side-rails can be turned smoothly in the ring groove.

6 Fit the second ring into the middle groove in the piston with its mark facing up (see illustration 25.2b). Do not expand the ring any more than is necessary to slide it into place – if required, use a piston ring installation tool or thin blade to avoid breaking the ring (see illustrations).

7 Follow the same procedure to install the top ring into the top groove in the piston

8 Once the rings are correctly installed, check they move freely without snagging and stagger their end gaps as shown (see illustration). Note that none of the end gaps should align with the piston pin bore. The end gaps of the upper and lower oil control ring side rails should be 30° from each other. The end gaps of the second ring and top rings should be 120° from each other and 120° from the end gap of the oil control ring upper side rail.

26 Transmission shafts and output shaft oil seal

Note 1: To remove the transmission shafts the engine must be removed from the frame and the crankcase halves separated.

Note 2: The output shaft oil seal can be removed and a new one fitted with the engine

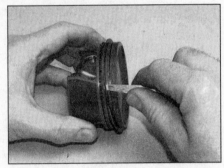

25.6b . . . then slide it into place with a thin blade

in the frame. If the engine has been removed, ignore the steps which do not apply.

Transmission shafts

Removal

1 Follow the procedure in Section 19 to separate the crankcase halves.

2 Note the location of the input and output shafts (see illustration). Note: Two variations of shaft bearing location are used on the machines covered in this manual. Check which type you have before ordering new parts.

3 Lift out the output shaft (see illustration). If fitted, note the location of the pin on the right-hand bearing and the position of the gaps in both bearing locating rings.

4 Lift out the input shaft (see illustration). If fitted, note the location of the pin on the right-hand bearing and the position of the gaps in both bearing locating rings.

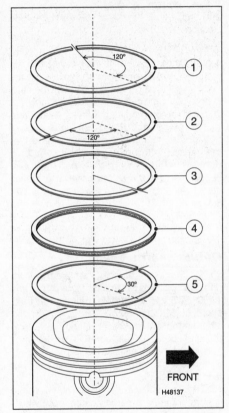

25.8 Stagger the ring end gaps as shown

1 Top ring
2 Second ring
3 Oil ring top side rail
4 Oil ring expander
5 Oil ring lower side rail

26.2 Location of the input (A) and output (B) shafts

26.3 Removing the output shaft – note the bearing locating pin (A) and locating ring (B)

26.4 Removing the input shaft

26.12 Removing the old output shaft seal

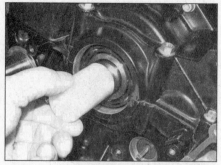

26.13 Cover the shaft splines to avoid damaging the seal

26.14 Lubricate the new seal prior to installation

5 If required, the shafts can be disassembled and inspected for wear or damage (see Section 27).

Installation

6 Install the input shaft. If fitted, ensure that the pin on the right-hand bearing is located in the notch in the upper crankcase and that the gaps in both bearing locating rings face upwards.

7 Install the output shaft. If fitted, ensure that the pin on the right-hand bearing is located in the notch in the upper crankcase and that the gaps in both bearing locating rings face upwards. **Note:** *The new output shaft seal should be fitted after the crankcase halves have been reassembled – see Steps 13 to 15.*

8 Check that the input and output shafts rotate freely.

9 Follow the procedure in Section 19 to reassemble the crankcase halves.

Output shaft oil seal

10 On S and ST models, remove the front drive belt pulley (see Chapter 6).

11 On GS and R models, remove the front sprocket (see Chapter 6).

12 To remove the old seal without separating the crankcase halves, carefully drill a small hole into the seal, install a self tapping screw, then use a pair of pliers to lever the seal out **(see illustration)**.

13 Before installing the new seal, cover the splines of the transmission output shaft with a plastic sheath or electrical tape to protect the inside lips of the new seal **(see illustration)**.

14 Lubricate the new seal with a smear of grease, then slide it over the shaft **(see illustration)**. Remove the sheath or tape.

26.15a Ensure the new seal is installed evenly

26.15b Installed position of the output shaft seal

15 Press the new seal into position evenly – if necessary, use a block of wood to drive it all the way into its housing **(see illustrations)**.

16 Install the remaining components in the reverse order of removal.

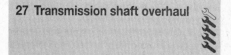

27 Transmission shaft overhaul

Note: *References to the right and left-hand ends of the transmission shafts are made as though they are installed in the engine and the engine is the correct way up.*

1 Remove the transmission shafts from the crankcase (see Section 26). Always disassemble the transmission shafts separately to avoid mixing up the components. When removing the needle bearings that sit between splined sections of shaft, spread their open

ends to clear the splines, but not so wide as to distort the cage. Note that new circlips must be used when rebuilding the shafts.

> **HAYNES HINT** *When disassembling the transmission shafts, place the parts on a long rod or thread a wire through them to keep them in order and facing the proper direction.*

Input shaft

Disassembly

2 To draw the bearing off the right-hand end of the shaft, position the legs of a puller behind the 6th gear pinion as shown **(see illustration)**. Protect the end of the shaft with a suitable bolt and draw the bearing off, noting which way round it is fitted **(see illustrations)**.

27.2a Set-up for removing the bearing – 6th gear pinion arrowed

27.2b Protect the end of the shaft with a suitable bolt . . .

27.2c . . . and draw the bearing off

27.3 Slide off the 2nd gear pinion – note the shoulder (arrowed)

27.4a Slide off the 6th gear pinion

27.4b Note the location of the needle bearing . . .

27.4c . . . then ease the ends apart . . .

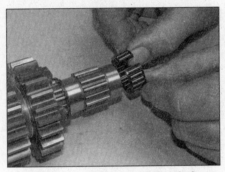

27.4d . . . and draw it off the shaft

27.5a Remove the circlip . . .

3 Slide off the 2nd gear pinion, noting which way round it is fitted **(see illustration)**.
4 Slide off the 6th gear pinion **(see illustration)**. Ease the ends of the needle bearing apart and draw it off **(see illustrations)**.
5 Remove the circlip securing the combined

3rd/4th gear pinion, then slide off the pinion, noting which way round it fits **(see illustrations)**.
6 Remove the circlip and thrust washer securing the 5th gear pinion, then slide the pinion off **(see illustrations)**.

7 The 1st gear pinion is integral with the shaft **(see illustration)**.
8 If required, draw the bearing off the left-hand end of the shaft – only remove the bearing if it is going to be renewed **(see illustration)**.

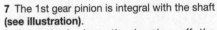

27.5b . . . and slide off the combined 3rd/4th gear pinion

27.6a Remove the circlip . . .

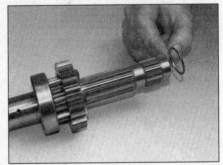

27.6b . . . thrust washer . . .

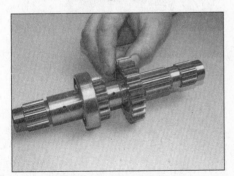

27.6c . . . and 5th gear pinion

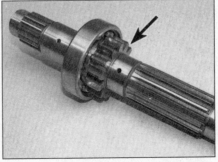

27.7 1st gear pinion is integral with the shaft

27.8 Only remove the bearing if it is to be renewed. Note the oil hole (arrowed)

27.10 Inspect the gear teeth for wear and damage

27.11 Inspect the dogs (arrowed) for wear and damage

27.18a Ensure the new circlip . . .

Inspection

9 Wash all the components in solvent and dry them thoroughly. Blow through the oil holes with compressed air, including the oil hole in the left-hand end of the shaft that supplies lubrication to the clutch release bearing **(see illustration 27.8)**.

10 Check the gear teeth for cracking, chipping, pitting and other obvious wear or damage **(see illustration)**. Any pinion that is damaged must be replaced with a new one. **Note:** *New gear pinions are supplied in sets – when renewing a pinion on the input shaft, the appropriate pinion on the output shaft must also be renewed.*

11 Inspect the dogs on the pinions for cracks, chips, and excessive wear, especially around the edges **(see illustration)**. Make sure mating gears engage properly. Always renew paired gears as a set.

12 Inspect the selector fork groove on the 3rd/4th gear pinion (see Section 28).
13 Check that each pinion moves freely on the shaft without excessive freeplay.
14 Check for signs of scoring and wear or bluing on the needle bearing, the bearing surfaces of the shaft and the gear pinions. This could be caused by overheating due to inadequate lubrication. Ensure that all the oil holes are clear. Renew any damaged components. The shaft is unlikely to sustain damage unless the engine or a transmission bearing has seized, or the machine has covered a very high mileage.
15 Inspect the shaft splines and circlip grooves for wear and renew the shaft if necessary.
16 Refer to *Tools and Workshop Tips* in the *Reference* Section to check the caged shaft bearings and renew either bearing if it is worn, loose or damaged. When the bearings are

being fitted, press them on carefully to avoid damage.

Reassembly

17 During reassembly, apply clean engine oil to the mating surfaces of the shaft and pinions. When installing the new circlips, do not expand their ends any further than is necessary. Install the stamped circlips so that the chamfered side faces the pinion it secures (see *Correct fitting of a stamped circlip* illustration in *Tools and Workshop Tips* of the *Reference* Section).
18 Slide the 5th gear pinion onto the shaft with its dogs facing away from the 1st gear pinion **(see illustration 27.6c)**. Slide on the thrust washer, then fit the new circlip, making sure that it locates correctly in the groove in the shaft **(see illustrations)**.
19 Slide the combined 3rd/4th gear pinion onto the shaft with the smaller 3rd gear pinion facing the 5th gear pinion **(see illustration 27.5b)**. Secure the pinion with a new circlip **(see illustration)**.
20 Install the needle bearing **(see illustrations 27.4d, c and b)**.
21 Slide the 6th gear pinion onto the bearing with its dogs facing towards the 4th gear pinion **(see illustration 27.4a)**.
22 Slide the 2nd gear pinion onto the shaft – the flat side should face away from the 6th gear pinion **(see illustration)**.
23 Press the bearing onto the end of the shaft using a driver or suitably-sized socket **(see illustration)**. Note that the sealed side should face out **(see illustration)**.

27.18b . . . is correctly located in its groove (arrowed)

27.19 Secure the combined 3rd/4th gear pinion with a new circlip

27.22 Install the 2nd gear pinion – flat side (arrowed) should face out

27.23a Drive on the bearing

27.23b Installed position of the shaft bearing

24 Check that all components have been correctly installed (**see illustration**).

Output shaft

Disassembly

25 Remove the circlip from the left-hand end of the shaft, then draw off the bearing and thrust washer (**see illustrations**).

26 Slide off the 1st gear pinion, its needle bearing and the thrust washer (**see illustrations**).

27 Slide off the 5th gear pinion (**see illustration**).

28 Remove the circlip securing the 3rd gear pinion, then slide the pinion off, noting which way round it fits (**see illustrations**).

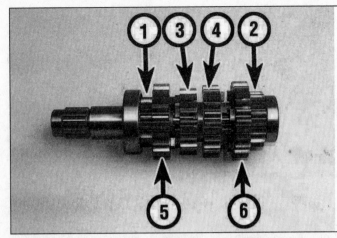

1	1st gear pinion
2	2nd gear pinion
3/4	Combined 3rd/4th gear pinion
5	5th gear pinion
6	6th gear pinion

27.24 Assembled input shaft

27.25a Remove the circlip . . .

27.25b . . . the bearing . . .

27.25c . . . and the thrust washer

27.26a Slide off the 1st gear pinion . . .

27.26b . . . the needle bearing . . .

27.26c . . . and the thrust washer

27.27 Slide off the 5th gear pinion – note the selector fork groove (arrowed)

27.28a Remove the circlip . . .

27.28b . . . and slide off the 3rd gear pinion

27.29 Slide off the 4th gear pinion

27.30a Remove the two needle bearings . . .

27.30b . . . and the circlip

29 Slide off the 4th gear pinion, noting which way round it fits **(see illustration)**.
30 Note the location of the two needle bearings and circlip, then remove them **(see illustrations)**.

31 Slide off the 6th gear pinion **(see illustration)**.
32 Remove the circlip securing the 2nd gear pinion, then slide the pinion off **(see illustrations)**.

33 Remove the needle bearing **(see illustration)**.
34 If required, draw the bearing off the right-hand end of the shaft – only remove the bearing if it is going to be renewed **(see illustration)**.

Inspection

35 Refer to Steps 9 to 16 above. Note that on the output shaft, the selector fork grooves are on the 5th and 6th gear pinions **(see illustration)**.

Reassembly

36 During reassembly, apply clean engine oil to the mating surfaces of the shaft and pinions. When installing the new circlips, do not expand their ends any further than is necessary. Install the stamped circlips so that the chamfered side faces the pinion it secures (see *Correct fitting of a stamped circlip* illustration in *Tools and Workshop Tips* of the *Reference* Section).
37 Install the needle bearing **(see illustration 27.33)**.
38 Slide the 2nd gear pinion onto the bearing and secure it with a new circlip **(see illustration)**.
39 Slide on the 6th gear pinion with the selector fork groove facing away from the 2nd gear pinion **(see illustration 27.31)**. Secure the pinion with a new circlip **(see illustration)**.

27.31 Slide off the 6th gear pinion

27.32a Remove the circlip . . .

27.32b . . . and slide off the 2nd gear pinion

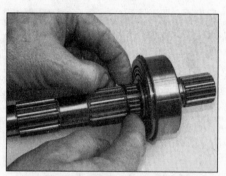

27.33 Ease off the needle bearing

27.34 Only remove the bearing if it is to be renewed

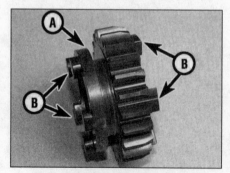

27.35 Selector fork groove (A) and dogs (B) – 6th gear shown

27.38 Ensure the 2nd gear circlip (arrowed) is correctly installed

27.39 Installed position of the 6th gear circlip

27.40 Installed position of the needle bearings

27.42a Note plain side of 3rd gear pinion

40 Install the two needle bearings **(see illustration)**.
41 Slide on the 4th gear pinion with the plain side facing away from the 6th gear pinion **(see illustration 27.29)**.
42 Slide on the 3rd gear pinion with the plain side facing the 4th gear pinion **(see illustration)**. Secure the pinion with a new circlip **(see illustration)**.
43 Slide on the 5th gear pinion with the selector fork groove facing the 3rd gear pinion **(see illustration 27.27)**.
44 Install the thrust washer, needle bearing and 1st gear pinion **(see illustrations 27.26c, b and a)**.
45 Install the thrust washer, then press the bearing onto the end of the shaft and secure it with a new circlip **(see illustration)**.
46 Check that all components have been correctly installed **(see illustration)**.

27.42b Secure 3rd gear pinion with new circlip

27.45 Installed position of the 1st gear circlip and bearing

28 Selector drum and forks

Note 1: *To remove the selector drum and forks the engine must be removed from the frame and the crankcase halves separated.*

Removal

1 Follow the procedure in Section 19 to separate the crankcase halves.
2 If not already done, remove the oil pumps (see Section 16), the selector drum stopper arm (see Section 17) and the neutral switch (see Chapter 8).
3 Note the arrangement between the input and output shaft selector forks and the selector drum **(see illustration)**. Before removing the selector forks, mark each one using paint or a marker pen to aid reassembly.
4 Support the input shaft selector fork and withdraw the fork rod from the casing, noting how the guide pin locates in the centre groove in the selector drum **(see illustration)**.
5 Withdraw the pin securing the rod for the

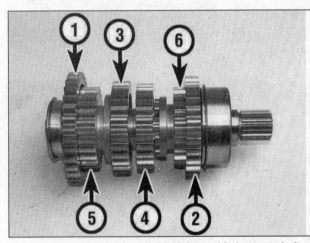

1 1st gear pinion
2 2nd gear pinion
3 3rd gear pinion
4 4th gear pinion
5 5th gear pinion
6 6th gear pinion

27.46 Assembled output shaft

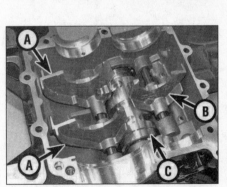

28.3 Output shaft selector forks (A), input shaft selector fork (B) and selector drum (C)

28.4 Remove the input shaft selector fork

28.5a Withdraw the pin

28.5b Note the location of the guide pins (arrowed)

28.5c Withdraw the rod and remove the right . . .

28.5d . . . and left-hand output shaft selector forks

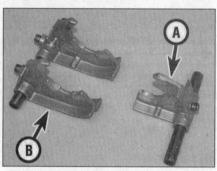

28.5e Input shaft (A) and output shaft (B) selector forks

28.6a Undo the screw (arrowed) . . .

28.6b . . . and remove the selector drum

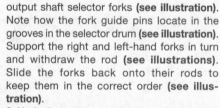

output shaft selector forks (see illustration). Note how the fork guide pins locate in the grooves in the selector drum (see illustration). Support the right and left-hand forks in turn and withdraw the rod (see illustrations). Slide the forks back onto their rods to keep them in the correct order (see illustration).

6 Undo the screw securing the selector drum and draw the drum out from the casing (see illustrations).

Inspection

7 Inspect the selector forks for any signs of wear or damage, especially around the fork ends where they engage with the grooves in the gear pinions (see illustration). Check that each fork fits correctly in its pinion groove (see illustration 27.35). If the forks are in any way damaged they must be replaced with new ones.

8 Measure the thickness of the fork ends and compare the results with the specifications at the beginning of this Chapter. If any are worn below the minimum thickness they must be renewed (see illustration). Check closely to ensure the forks are not bent.

9 Measure the thickness of the fork guide pins and compare the results with the

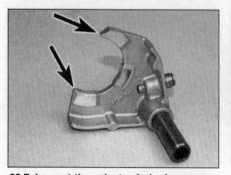

28.7 Inspect the selector forks for wear or damage

28.8 Measuring the thickness of the fork ends

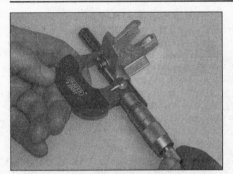

28.9 Measuring the thickness of the fork guide pins

28.10 Ensure the forks slide freely on their rods

28.11 Inspect the grooves for wear or damage

specifications at the beginning of this Chapter. If any are worn below the minimum thickness they must be renewed **(see illustration)**.

10 Check that the fork rods are straight by rolling them along a flat surface. A bent rod will cause difficulty in selecting gears and make the gearchange action heavy. Check that the forks are a sliding fit on their rods – there should be no freeplay or uneven wear **(see illustration)**. Renew any components that are worn or damaged.

11 Inspect the grooves in the selector drum for wear or damage – the guide pins must slide freely in the grooves without snagging **(see illustration)**.

12 Refer to *Tools and Workshop Tips* in the *Reference* Section to check the selector drum bearings and renew either bearing if it is worn, loose or damaged **(see illustration)**. To remove the right-hand bearing, use a hot air gun to heat the bearing housing to approximately 80°C, then tap the selector drum sharply against a wooden surface to dislodge the bearing. To install the new bearing, heat the housing again and press the new bearing in until it is level with the edge of the housing. To remove the left-hand bearing, first unscrew the centre bolt and pull the selector drum cam off **(see illustration)**. Note the position of the locating pin. Temporarily install the centre bolt and draw the bearing off with a puller. To install the new bearing, first heat it to approximately 80°C, then press it onto the end of the drum. Install the cam and tighten the centre bolt to the torque setting specified at the beginning of this Chapter.

28.12a Selector drum left (A) and right-hand (B) bearings

13 Check the condition of the neutral switch oil seal in the right-hand side of the casing. If it is damaged, deteriorated or shows signs of leakage it must be replaced with a new one – lever out the old seal with a seal hook or screwdriver **(see illustration)**. To avoid damaging the new seal, install it after the selector drum has been installed (see Step 20). Lubricate the new seal with a smear of engine oil, then press or drive it squarely into place using your fingers, a seal driver or suitable socket **(see illustrations)**.

Installation

14 Prior to installation, lubricate the components with engine oil.
15 Install the selector drum **(see illustration 28.6b)**. Clean the threads of the securing screw and apply a suitable non-permanent thread-locking compound (BMW recommends Loctite 243), then tighten the screw to the

28.12b Selector drum cam (A) and centre bolt (B)

torque setting specified at the beginning of this Chapter **(see illustration 28.6a)**.
16 Turn the drum to the neutral position and install the selector drum stopper arm (see Section 17).
17 Position the output shaft selector forks in the crankcase and slide the rod into position **(see illustrations 28.5d and c)**. Ensure the fork guide pins are correctly located in the outer grooves in the selector drum **(see illustration 28.5b)**. Secure the rod with the pin **(see illustration 28.5a)**.
18 Position the input shaft selector fork in the crankcase and slide the rod into position **(see illustration 28.4)**. Ensure the fork guide pin is correctly located in the centre groove in the selector drum. **Note:** *The rod is held in place by the left-hand (feed) oil pump cover.*
19 Check that the forks are correctly installed with the selector drum in the neutral position **(see illustration 28.3)**.

28.13a Removing the seal with a seal hook

28.13b Press the new seal in squarely . . .

28.13c . . . using a driver if necessary

20 Install the neutral switch oil seal (see Step 13), then install the neutral switch (see Chapter 8). Install the oil pumps (see Section 16).

21 Follow the procedure in Section 19 to reassemble the crankcase halves.

29 Running-in procedure

1 Make sure the engine oil and coolant levels are correct (see *Pre-ride checks*).

2 Make sure there is fuel in the tank. Turn the engine kill switch to the ON position and shift the gearbox into neutral. Turn the ignition ON.

3 Start the engine and allow it to idle until it reaches operating temperature.

⚠ *Warning: If the oil pressure warning light doesn't go off, or it comes on while the engine is running, stop the engine immediately.*

4 If a lubrication failure is suspected, stop the engine immediately and try to find the cause. If an engine is run without oil circulating, even for a short period of time, severe damage will occur.

5 Check carefully that there are no oil or coolant leaks and make sure the transmission and controls, especially the brakes, function properly before road testing the machine.

6 Treat the machine gently for the first few miles to make sure oil has circulated throughout the engine and any new parts installed have started to seat.

7 Upon completion of the road test, and after the engine has cooled down completely, recheck the valve clearances (see Chapter 1) and check the engine oil and coolant levels (see *Pre-ride checks*).

8 If a new piston and rings or a new crankshaft have been fitted, the bike will have to be run in as when new. This means greater use of the transmission and a restraining hand on the throttle, keeping engine speed below 5000 rpm and avoiding full throttle until at least 600 miles (1000 km) have been covered. There's no point in keeping to any set speed limit – the main idea is to keep from labouring (overloading) the engine. Between 600 and 1200 miles (1000 and 2000 km) gradually increase engine speeds, but again avoid labouring the engine, and do not use full throttle for prolonged periods. Experience is the best guide, since it's easy to tell when an engine is running freely.

Chapter 3
Cooling system

Contents

	Section		Section
Coolant change	2	General information	1
Coolant hoses	9	Radiator and pressure cap	6
Coolant level check	see Pre-ride checks	Temperature sensor	4
Coolant reservoir	7	Thermostat	5
Cooling fan	3	Water pump	8
Cooling system checks	see Chapter 1		

Degrees of difficulty

Easy, suitable for novice with little experience	**Fairly easy,** suitable for beginner with some experience	**Fairly difficult,** suitable for competent DIY mechanic	**Difficult,** suitable for experienced DIY mechanic	**Very difficult,** suitable for expert DIY or professional

Specifications

Coolant
Type	50% distilled or soft water, 50% corrosion inhibited ethylene glycol anti-freeze, nitrite-free
Capacity	approx.1.3 litres

Thermostat
Opening temperature	85°C

Radiator
Cap valve opening pressure	17 to 20 psi (1.2 to 1.4 Bar)

Torque settings
Coolant drain bolt in cylinder block	10 Nm
Coolant pipe-to-oil cooler	12 Nm
Temperature sensor	16 Nm
Water pump bolt	10 Nm
Water pump cover bolts	12 Nm

1 General information

The cooling system uses a water/anti-freeze coolant to carry excess heat away from the engine and maintain it at as constant an operating temperature as possible.

The cylinders and cylinder head are surrounded by a water jacket through which coolant is circulated by the water pump. The pump is located on the right-hand side of the cylinder head and is driven by the intake camshaft. Hot coolant passes from the engine to the radiator; it flows across the core of the radiator, and is then pumped back into the engine where the cycle is repeated.

A thermostat is fitted in the system to prevent the coolant flowing through the radiator when the engine is cold, therefore accelerating the speed at which the engine reaches normal operating temperature. Once the engine is hot enough, the thermostat opens and the coolant circulates as normal.

Coolant is also circulated through the oil cooler located on the front of the crankcases.

A cooling fan fitted to the back of the radiator aids temperature reduction in extreme conditions by drawing extra air through the radiator core. The fan motor and the temperature warning light in the instrument cluster are activated by the engine control unit (ECU), based on information received from the temperature sensor located in the rear of the cylinder head.

The complete cooling system is partially sealed and pressurised, the pressure being controlled by the spring-loaded radiator cap. By pressurising the coolant the boiling point is raised, preventing premature boiling in adverse conditions. The overflow pipe from the radiator is connected to a reservoir into which coolant is expelled under pressure.

The discharged coolant automatically returns to the radiator by the vacuum created as the engine cools.

⚠️ **Warning: Do not remove the pressure cap from the radiator when the engine is hot. Scalding hot coolant and steam may be blown out under pressure, which could cause serious injury. When the engine has cooled, place a thick rag, such as a hand towel, over the pressure cap; slowly rotate the cap anti-clockwise to the first stop. This procedure allows any residual pressure to escape. When the steam has stopped escaping, press down on the cap while turning it anti-clockwise and remove it. Note: Drain the coolant reservoir before removing the pressure cap.**

Caution: Do not allow anti-freeze to come in contact with your skin or painted surfaces of the motorcycle. Rinse off any spills immediately with plenty of water. Anti-freeze is highly toxic if ingested. Never leave anti-freeze lying around in an open container or in puddles on the floor; children and pets are attracted by its sweet smell and may drink it. Check with the local authorities about disposing of used anti-freeze. Many communities will have collection centres which will see that anti-freeze is disposed of safely.

Caution: At all times use the specified type of anti-freeze, and always mix it with distilled water in the correct proportion. The anti-freeze contains corrosion inhibitors which are essential to avoid damage to the cooling system. A lack of these inhibitors could lead to a build-up of corrosion which would block the coolant passages, resulting in overheating and severe engine damage. Distilled water must be used as opposed to tap water to avoid a build-up of scale which would also block the passages.

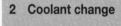

2 Coolant change

⚠️ *Warning: Allow the engine to cool completely before performing this operation. Also, don't allow*

2.3a Undo the screws – GS model shown

2.3b Undo the screw . . .

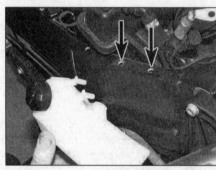
2.3c . . . and release the pegs from the holes (arrowed) – S model shown

2.3d Drain the coolant into a suitable container

anti-freeze to come into contact with your skin or the painted surfaces of the motorcycle. Rinse off spills immediately with plenty of water. Anti-freeze is highly toxic if ingested. Never leave anti-freeze lying around in an open container or in puddles on the floor; children and pets are attracted by its sweet smell and may drink it. Check with local authorities (councils) about disposing of anti-freeze. Many communities have collection centres which will see that anti-freeze is disposed of safely. Anti-freeze is also combustible, so don't store it near open flames.

Draining

1 Support the bike in an upright position on level ground.
2 Remove the seat, bodywork centre panel and right-hand side panel (see Chapter 7).

3 Undo the screw(s) securing the coolant reservoir, lift it off and drain the coolant into a suitable container (see illustrations). Fit the reservoir back onto the frame and secure it with the screw(s).
4 Remove the pressure cap from the radiator filler neck by turning it anti-clockwise until it reaches the stop. Now press down on the cap and continue turning it until it can be removed (see illustration).
5 Position a suitable container beneath the drain bolt on the front of the engine (see illustration). Unscrew the bolt and allow the coolant to completely drain from the system (see illustration). Retain the old sealing washer for use during flushing (if required). Note that a new sealing washer must be fitted on final installation.
6 Undo the bolt securing the lower coolant

2.4 Remove the radiator pressure cap

2.5a Undo the bolt (arrowed) . . .

2.5b . . . and drain the coolant

2.6a Disconnect the lower pipe – GS model shown

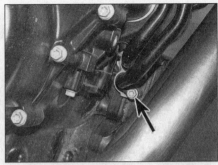

2.6b Disconnect the lower pipe . . .

2.6c . . . and drain the coolant – S model shown

2.6d Note the location of the O-ring

2.15 Fit a new sealing washer to the drain bolt

pipe to the oil cooler flange, disconnect the pipe and allow the coolant to drain **(see illustrations)**. Note the location of the O-ring – it may be on the pipe union or in the oil cooler flange **(see illustration)**. Temporarily install the pipe, using the old O-ring, and secure it with the bolt. Note that a new O-ring must be fitted on final installation.

Flushing

Note: *Under normal circumstances, i.e. where the coolant has been regularly changed and the correct mixture used, flushing should not be necessary. However if the coolant has become contaminated with rust, dirt or oil, all of which will be evident when the system is drained, the system should be flushed.*

7 Flush the system with clean tap water by inserting a hose in the radiator filler neck. Allow the water to run through the system until it is clear and flows out cleanly. If the radiator is extremely corroded, remove it (see Section 6) and have it cleaned by a specialist. Also flush the reservoir with clean water.

8 Ensure the drain hole in the front of the engine is clear, then install the drain bolt using the old sealing washer **(see illustration 2.5a)**.

9 Fill the cooling system via the radiator filler neck with clean water mixed with a flushing compound. Make sure the flushing compound is compatible with aluminium components, and follow the manufacturer's instructions carefully. Fit the radiator cap and coolant reservoir cap.

10 Start the engine and allow it to reach normal operating temperature. Let it run for about ten minutes.

11 Stop the engine. Let it cool for a while, then cover the pressure cap with a heavy rag and turn it anti-clockwise to the first stop, releasing any pressure that may be present in the system. Once the hissing stops, push down on the cap and remove it completely.

12 Drain the system (see Steps 3 to 6).

13 Repeat the procedure, this time flushing with clean water only.

Refilling

14 Fit a new O-ring onto the coolant pipe union, lubricate it with coolant, then press the union into the oil cooler flange and secure it with the bolt. Tighten the bolt to the torque

setting specified at the beginning of this Chapter **(see illustrations 2.6d, b and a)**.

15 Fit a new sealing washer onto the drain bolt and tighten it to the specified torque setting **(see illustration)**.

16 Undo the bleed bolt on the water pump cover, discard the old sealing washer and fit a new one **(see illustration)**. Install the bolt finger-tight.

17 Fill the system via the radiator filler neck with the correct coolant mixture (see *Specifications*). Pour the coolant in slowly to minimise the amount of air entering the system. When the coolant level reaches the radiator filler neck, tap and squeeze the hoses to dislodge any trapped air, then top-up the radiator **(see illustration)**.

18 Loosen the bleed bolt to free any trapped air. When coolant comes out, tighten the bolt

2.16 Fit a new sealing washer on the bleed bolt

2.17a Fill the system with the correct coolant mixture . . .

2.17b . . . until it reaches the radiator filler neck (arrowed)

2.18 Free any trapped air then tighten the bolt securely

3.3 Location of the fan wiring connector

securely **(see illustration)**. Top-up the radiator, then fit the pressure cap.

19 Fill the reservoir to just below the MAX level line (see *Pre-ride checks*). Install the reservoir cap.

20 Start the engine and allow it to reach normal operating temperature, let it run for a few minutes then shut it off. Let the engine cool, then check the level in the reservoir and top up if necessary.

21 Check the system for leaks.

22 Install the bodywork panels and the seat (see Chapter 7).

23 Do not dispose of the old coolant by pouring it down the drain. Instead pour it into a heavy plastic container, cap it tightly and take it into an authorised disposal site or service station – see *Warning* above.

3   Cooling fan

Check

1 If the engine is overheating and the cooling fan isn't coming on, first check the fan motor.
2 Where necessary, remove the right-hand bodywork side panel (see Chapter 7). The fan is located on the back of the radiator – check

that the fan rotor turns freely. If not, remove the radiator and inspect the fan assembly for damage (see Steps 5 and 6).

3 Release the cable-tie securing the fan wiring connector and disconnect the connector **(see illustration)**. Using a fully charged 12 volt battery and two jumper wires with suitable connectors, connect the battery to the fan side of the connector – the fan should operate.

4 If the fan works when connected to a battery, check the wiring and connector terminals for damage. If they are good, the temperature sensor could be faulty (see Section 4). **Note:** *Coolant temperature should be displayed on the instrument cluster and the engine warning symbol should illuminate if the ECU diagnoses a sensor fault. If the engine electronics circuit is not working correctly, have the system checked by a BMW dealer.*

Removal and installation

⚠ **Warning: The engine must be completely cool before carrying out this procedure.**

5 Remove the radiator (see Section 6).
6 Note the location of the fan assembly **(see illustration)**. The housing is secured to the top edge of the radiator by trim clips **(see illustration)**. Ease the centres of the trim clips out to release them **(see illustration)**, then remove the clips.

7 If not already done, undo the screw and nut securing the lower heat shield and the lower edge of the housing **(see illustration 6.7a and b)**. Lift the fan assembly off.
8 Installation is the reverse of removal.

4   Temperature sensor

1 The temperature sensor is part of the engine electronics circuit. The engine control unit (ECU) monitors signals from the sensor and electronically adjusts the fuel and ignition systems to suit running conditions. When the engine is cold, the ECU richens the fuel supply. When the engine is in danger of over-heating, the ECU activates the radiator fan.
2 Engine (coolant) temperature, measured by the sensor, is shown on the instrument cluster multi-function display. If the display fails due to a sensor fault, or if the ECU detects a sensor fault, the engine warning symbol will illuminate.

Check

3 BMW provides no test details for the temperature sensor. If it is thought to be faulty the best thing to do is to exchange it for one that is known to be good and see whether the fault clears. The condition of the sensor

3.6a Fan assembly is located on the back of the radiator

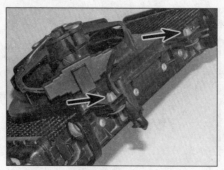

3.6b Housing is secured by trim clips (arrowed)

3.6c Ease out the centres to release the trim clips

4.4 Oil pressure sensor (A) and coolant temperature sensor (B)

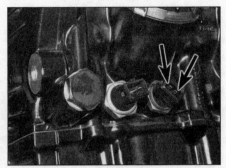

4.5 Measure resistance between the sensor terminals

can, however, be assessed by checking the resistance as follows.

4 The temperature sensor is located on the rear of the cylinder head, inboard of the cam chain tensioner and oil pressure switch **(see illustration)**. Disconnect the sensor wiring connector.

5 Using a multimeter set to the K-ohms scale, measure the resistance between the sensor terminals and note the result **(see illustration)**. On the machine used to illustrate this procedure, the resistance measured 3.17 K-ohms. If your reading differs widely, it is likely the sensor is faulty and a new one must be fitted (see Steps 8 to 12).

6 Once a new sensor has been installed, the fault code will remain in the ECU memory for a number of ignition ON/OFF cycles until it is automatically erased.

7 Alternatively, have the sensor checked by a BMW dealer. If a new sensor is fitted and the system is working correctly, they will delete the fault code.

Removal and installation

⚠ *Warning: The engine must be completely cool before carrying out this procedure.*

8 Drain the cooling system via the drain bolt on the front of the engine (see Section 2).

9 Disconnect the sensor wiring connector **(see illustration 4.4)**. Unscrew and remove the sensor.

10 Install the new sensor and tighten it to the torque setting specified at the beginning of this Chapter. Connect the wiring connector.

11 Refill the cooling system (see Section 2).

12 Start the engine, check the operation of the temperature sensor and check for coolant leaks.

5 Thermostat

1 The thermostat is located in the lower, right-hand side of the radiator – it is automatic in operation and shouldn't require attention. In the event of a failure, the valve will probably jam open, in which case the engine will take much longer than normal to warm up. Conversely, if the valve jams shut, the coolant will be unable to circulate through the radiator and the engine will overheat. Neither condition is acceptable, and the fault must be investigated promptly.

Removal

⚠ *Warning: The engine must be completely cool before carrying out this procedure.*

2 On all models except the F800 R, remove the seat, bodywork centre panel and right-hand side panel (see Chapter 7).

3 Drain the coolant via the drain bolt on the front of the engine (see Section 2).

4 Position a suitable container beneath the radiator to catch any residual coolant. Using a flat-bladed screwdriver, carefully prise out the clip securing the thermostat housing **(see illustrations)**. Ease the housing out from the radiator **(see illustrations)**. Discard the O-ring as a new one must be used **(see illustration)**.

5 Separate the thermostat and spring holder from the housing **(see illustration)**.

6 Note the location of the thermostat and

5.4a Use a flat-bladed screwdriver . . .

5.4b . . . to prise out the clip

5.4c Ease the thermostat housing . . .

5.4d . . . out from the radiator

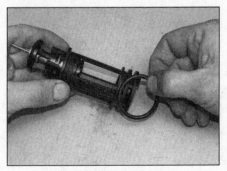

5.4e Renew the O-ring

5.5 Separate the thermostat and spring holder (arrowed) from the housing

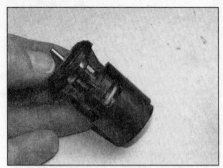

5.6a Note how the thermostat fits . . .

5.6b . . . then lift it out of the spring holder – thermostat (A) and spring holder (B)

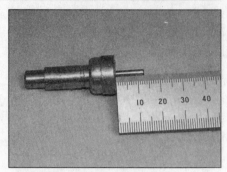

5.8 Chill the thermostat and measure the rod fully retracted

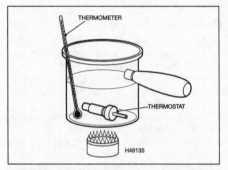

5.9 Set-up for heating the thermostat

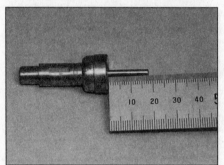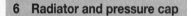

5.11 Measure the rod fully extended

spring, then lift the thermostat out **(see illustrations)**.

Check

7 Due to the thermostat's construction, it is not possible to check its operation visually. The thermostat can, however, be checked as follows, and the results compared to those obtained from the component used to illustrate this procedure.

8 Chill the thermostat to ensure the rod is fully retracted into the body – either leave it in a freezer or apply a freeze spray. Fully retracted, the rod measured 13 mm **(see illustration)**.

9 Now suspend the thermostat by a piece of wire in a container of water. Place a thermometer capable of reading temperatures up to 110°C in the water so that the bulb is close to the thermostat, and heat the water **(see illustration)**.

10 The specified opening temperature for the thermostat is 85°C. When the water reaches

this temperature, temporarily remove the thermostat and check the length of the rod – it should have started to extend from the thermostat body.

11 Return the thermostat to the water and continue heating for several minutes until the rod is fully extended. Remove the thermostat and check the length of the rod again. In our test the rod measured 18 mm fully extended **(see illustration)**.

12 If the thermostat is faulty a new one must be fitted. **Note:** *If the thermostat will not open (i.e. rod remains fully retracted) as an emergency measure only, it can be removed and the machine used without it. Take care when starting the engine from cold as it will take longer than usual to warm up. Ensure that a new thermostat is installed as soon as possible.*

Installation

13 Ensure that the spring and thermostat

are correctly installed in the holder – a new thermostat will be supplied with the holder as an assembly. Fit the holder into the housing **(see illustration 5.5)**.

14 Fit a new O-ring onto the housing **(see illustration 5.4e)**. Lubricate the O-ring with a smear of coolant, then insert the housing into the radiator and press it all the way in until the slots for the retaining clip are aligned.

15 Install the clip **(see illustration 5.4b)**.

16 Refill the cooling system (see Section 2).

17 Start the engine, check the operation of the thermostat and check for coolant leaks.

18 Install the remaining components in the reverse order of removal.

6 Radiator and pressure cap

Removal

⚠️ *Warning: The engine must be completely cool before carrying out this procedure.*

1 Drain the coolant via the drain bolt on the front of the engine (see Section 2).

2 On GS models, if fitted, remove the radiator screen (see Chapter 7).

3 On ST models, remove the left and right-hand lower side panels and inner panel (see Chapter 7). Undo the screw securing the left-hand heat shield and lift it off **(see illustrations)**.

4 Note how the cut-outs in the radiator inlet and outlet hoses align with the radiator unions **(see illustration)**. Release the clips securing

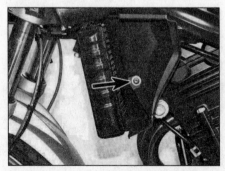

6.3a Undo the screw (arrowed) . . .

6.3b . . . and remove the heat shield

6.4a Note how the cut-outs (arrowed) align with the radiator unions

6.4b Release the clips . . .

6.4c . . . and slide them off the unions

6.5 Disconnect the hose to the filler neck

the hoses to the radiator and slide them off the radiator unions **(see illustration)**. Disconnect the hoses from the radiator. **Note:** *If required, the hoses can be disconnected from the water pump at the same time and removed completely (see Section 8).*

5 Release the clip securing the hose to the radiator filler neck and disconnect the hose **(see illustration)**.

6 If applicable, release the cable-tie securing the wiring to the upper left-hand radiator mounting **(see illustration)**.

7 Undo the screw and nut securing the lower heat shield and lift it off **(see illustrations)**.

8 Undo the bolt securing the lower right-hand side of the radiator, then draw the radiator to the right and off its mounting brackets **(see illustrations)**.

9 Disconnect the cooling fan wiring connector **(see illustration)**.

10 Note the location of the heat shield located behind the radiator and remove it if required. On GS models, unclip the camshaft position sensor wiring from the back of the shield,

then undo the screws securing the left-hand radiator bracket and bodywork side panel bracket **(see illustrations)**. Undo the screw securing the shield and lift it off, noting how

6.6 Release the wiring from the upper left-hand radiator mounting

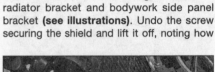

6.7a Undo the screw and nut . . .

6.7b . . . and remove the lower heat shield

6.8a Undo the bolt (arrowed) . . .

6.8b . . . and draw the radiator off its brackets

6.9 Disconnect the cooling fan wiring connector

6.10a Unclip the camshaft position sensor wiring

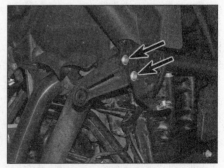

6.10b Undo the screws (arrowed) and remove the bracket

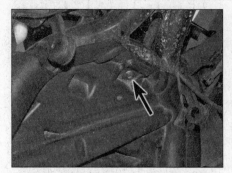

6.10c Undo the screw securing the shield . . .

6.10d . . . and lift it off

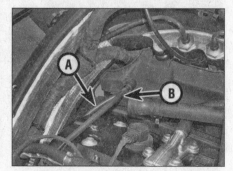

6.10e Note the position of the clutch (A) and throttle cable (B)

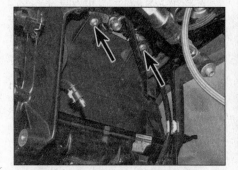

6.10f Undo the screws (arrowed) . . .

7.5 Disconnect the hose from the filler neck

8.1 Location of the water pump

it fits **(see illustrations)**. On all other models, note how the clutch cable and throttle cable locate in the left-hand side of the shield, then undo the mounting screws and lift it off, noting how it fits **(see illustrations)**.

Inspection

11 Note the arrangement of the rubber grommets in the radiator mounts. Replace the grommets with new ones if they are damaged, deformed or deteriorated.
12 If required, remove the cooling fan from the radiator (see Section 3). Follow the procedure in Chapter 1, Section 15, to check the radiator for damage
13 Check the condition of the coolant hoses and the hose clips (see Section 9).

Installation

14 Installation is the reverse of removal, noting the following.
● If removed, install the heat shield (see Step 10).
● Tighten the radiator mounting bolt securely **(see illustration 6.8a)**.
● Ensure the coolant hoses are correctly positioned and securely retained by their clips (see Steps 4 and 5).
● On completion, refill the cooling system and check for leaks (see Section 2).

Pressure checks

15 If problems such as overheating or loss of coolant occur, check the entire system as described in Chapter 1. The radiator cap opening pressure should be checked by a

BMW dealer with the special testers required to do the job. If the cap is defective, replace it with a new one.

7 Coolant reservoir

Removal

1 The coolant reservoir is located on the right-hand side of the machine behind the bodywork side panel – remove the panel for access (see Chapter 7).
2 Undo the screw(s) securing the reservoir and lift it off **(see illustrations 2.3a and b)**. On S, ST and R models, note how the pegs on the back of the reservoir locate in the frame **(see illustration 2.3c)**.
3 Unscrew the reservoir cap and drain the coolant into a suitable container.

4 Release the clip securing the radiator overflow hose to the union on the radiator filler neck **(see illustration 6.5)**.
5 Ease the hose off the union and remove the reservoir **(see illustration)**.

Installation

6 Installation is the reverse of removal, noting the following:
● Secure the overflow hose with its clip.
● Tighten the mounting bolt(s) securely.
● Fill the reservoir to just below the MAX level line (see *Pre-ride checks*).

8 Water pump

Check

1 The water pump is located on the right-hand side of the cylinder head **(see illustration)**. On all models except the F800 R, remove the seat, bodywork centre panel and right-hand side panel for access (see Chapter 7).
2 Check the area around the pump for signs of leakage.
3 To prevent leakage of coolant from the cooling system into the lubrication system and vice versa, two seals are fitted on the pump shaft. If either seal fails, a drain hole **(see illustration 8.18)** in the pump body between the seals allows coolant or oil to escape into the pump housing in the cylinder head. From

8.3a Drain hole in the pump housing . . .

8.3b . . . vents to the outside of the cylinder head

there it drains through a hole in the bottom of the housing **(see illustrations)**.

4 If on inspection the drain hole shows signs of leakage, a new pump must be fitted.

Removal

5 Drain the coolant via the drain bolt on the front of the engine (see Section 2).

6 Release the clips securing the radiator inlet and outlet hoses, and disconnect the hoses from the pump cover **(see illustration)**. **Note:**

If required, the hoses can be disconnected from the radiator at the same time and removed completely (see Section 6).

7 Release the clips securing the oil cooler hoses, and disconnect the hoses from the pump cover **(see illustration 8.6)**. **Note:** *If required, the coolant pipes can be disconnected from the cooler flange at the same time and removed completely (see Chapter 2, Section 12).*

8 Unscrew the pump cover bolts and remove the cover **(see illustrations)**. Remove the cover seal and discard it as a new one must be used **(see illustration)**.

9 Using a pair of long-nosed pliers inserted into the two holes in the pump impeller, turn the impeller anti-clockwise to unscrew it from the pump shaft **(see illustrations)**.

10 Undo the bolt securing the water pump

8.6 Disconnect the radiator hoses (A). Note the oil cooler hoses (B)

8.8a Unscrew the cover bolts . . .

8.8b . . . and remove the cover

8.8c Note the location of the cover seal

8.9a Unscrew the pump impeller . . .

8.9b . . . from the pump shaft

8.10a Undo the bolt (arrowed) . . .

8.10b . . . and withdraw the pump

and draw the pump out from its housing **(see illustrations)**.

11 Slide the driven gear off the drive pin on the inner end of the pump shaft **(see illustration)**. Note how the tabs on the washer underneath the drive pin retain the pin in the shaft.

12 Remove the pump body O-rings and

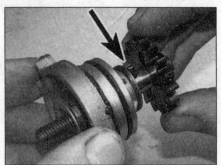

8.11 Remove the driven gear. Note how the washer tabs and drive pin (arrowed) align

discard them as new ones must be used **(see illustration)**.

Inspection

13 The pump shaft should turn freely without binding, but there should be no up-and-down play **(see illustration)**. Individual components

8.12 Remove the pump body O-rings

are not available – if the pump is worn or the internal seals are leaking, a new pump will have to be fitted.

14 Check the teeth of the driven gear for wear and damage and fit a new gear if necessary. Note that if the driven gear is in need of renewal, then the drive gear on the intake camshaft should also be renewed (see Chapter 2, Section 8).

15 Inspect the impeller for damage and renew it if necessary.

16 Check for corrosion or a build-up of scale in the pump cover and clean it if necessary.

Installation

17 Wipe the mating surfaces of the pump body and the cylinder head with a rag soaked in high flash-point solvent to remove all traces of old sealant.

18 Install new O-rings into the grooves in the pump body and lubricate them with a smear of grease **(see illustration)**.

8.13 Water pump (A), impeller (B) and driven gear (C)

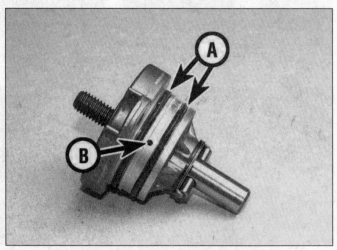

8.18 Fit new O-rings (A). Note the drain hole (B)

19 Apply a thin coating of suitable sealant to the mating surface of the pump body **(see illustration)**.
20 Ensure the tabs on the washer are aligned with the ends of the drive pin, then install the pump driven gear **(see illustration 8.11)**.
21 Align the pump body with its housing and press it in firmly **(see illustration 8.10b)**. If necessary, use a suitably-sized socket to drive the pump in fully **(see illustrations)**. Tighten the pump bolt to the torque setting specified at the beginning of this Chapter **(see illustration 8.10a)**.
22 Install the pump impeller finger-tight **(see illustration)**.
23 Install a new seal into the groove in the pump cover and lubricate it with a smear of grease **(see illustration 8.8c)**. Install the cover and tighten the bolts to the specified torque setting – don't forget to fit a new sealing washer on the bleed bolt **(see illustration 2.16)**.
24 Install the remaining components in the reverse order of removal.

9 Coolant hoses

Note: *When removing components of the cooling system, be prepared to catch any residual coolant.*

8.19 Apply a thin coating of sealant

8.21a Press the pump fully into its housing

8.21b Installed position of the water pump

8.22 Install the impeller finger-tight

Removal

1 Before removing a hose, drain the coolant (see Section 2).

2 All the hoses are secured by spring clips which can be expanded by squeezing their ears together with pliers or pipe grips **(see illustration)**. Slide the clips back along the hose and clear of the union **(see illustration)**.
Caution: The radiator unions are fragile. Do not use excessive force when attempting to remove the hoses.
3 If a hose proves stubborn, release it by rotating it on its union before working it off. If all else fails, cut the hose with a sharp knife – obviously this means replacing the hose with a new one. Hardened hoses should be renewed.
4 Discard the old hose clips if they are sprained or badly corroded – when in place the clips must grip the hoses tightly otherwise leakage will occur.

Installation

5 Slide the clips onto the hose and then work the hose on to its union as far as the spigot **(see illustrations)**.

 If the hose is difficult to push on its union, soften it by soaking it in very hot water, or alternatively a little soapy water on the union can be used as a lubricant.

6 Rotate the hose on its unions to settle it in position before sliding the clips into place to secure it.
7 Refill the cooling system with fresh coolant (see Section 2).

9.2a Using pipe grips . . .

9.2b . . . to slide the hose clips (arrowed) off the unions

9.5a Hose union spigots on the water pump . . .

9.5b . . . and on the radiator unions

Notes

Chapter 4
Engine management

Contents

	Section
Air filter	see Chapter 1
Air filter housing	2
Catalytic converter and oxygen sensor	12
Clutch switch	see Chapter 8
Engine management system and ECU.	15
Engine management system sensors	17
ECU removal and installation	16
Exhaust system	11
Fuel pressure sensor	7
Fuel pump, strainer and level sensor	5
Fuel rail and injectors	10

	Section
Fuel system check	see Chapter 1
Fuel tank	4
General information and precautions	1
Ignition HT coils	14
Ignition switch	see Chapter 8
Ignition system checks	13
Roll-over valve	6
Secondary air system control valve	3
Throttle bodies	9
Throttle cable	8
Sidestand switch	see Chapter 8

Degrees of difficulty

Easy, suitable for novice with little experience	**Fairly easy,** suitable for beginner with some experience	**Fairly difficult,** suitable for competent DIY mechanic	**Difficult,** suitable for experienced DIY mechanic	**Very difficult,** suitable for expert DIY or professional

Specifications

Fuel

Grade	Minimum 95 RON unleaded petrol/gasoline (F650 GS and F800 GS can use 91 RON if marked on filler cap)
Fuel tank capacity	
Total	16.0 litres
Reserve	
F800 S, ST, F800 GS and F650 GS	4.0 litres
F800 R	2.0 litres

Fuel injection system

Idle speed	see Chapter 1
Fuel pressure	36 to 72 psi (2.5 to 5.0 Bar)

Torque settings

Camshaft position sensor screw	10 Nm
Exhaust system	
Downpipe flange nuts	14 Nm
Exhaust mounting bolt	19 Nm
Silencer mounting bolt	19 Nm
Silencer-to-exhaust pipe ball clamp	35 Nm
Fuel pump retaining ring	35 Nm
Gear position sensor bolts	8 Nm
Ignition timing sensor screw	10 Nm
Oxygen sensor	45 Nm

1 General information and precautions

General information

All models covered in this manual are fitted with BMW's own digital engine management system (BMS-K) which monitors, controls and co-ordinates both the fuel and ignition system functions.

The system is operated by the engine electronics control unit (ECU). A second unit, the central vehicle electronics control unit (ZFE), is responsible for monitoring and control of all other electrical systems such as lighting, switches and accessories. The two units are linked for such functions as starting and engine immobilisation.

The ECU uses engine speed and throttle valve position as the basis for determining optimum engine operation. Additional data, supplied by temperature sensors, oil pressure and gear position sensors, and an exhaust gas analyser, when combined with control maps and correction values embedded within the ECU, fine tune injection volume and ignition timing to meet the engine's requirements in any given circumstance.

The engine management system has in-built diagnostic functions which record and store all data should a fault occur. If this happens, the engine warning light in the instrument cluster illuminates and, unless the fault is serious, the engine runs in emergency 'limp home' mode. Otherwise, the engine will stop. BMW advises that in 'limp home' mode, full engine power may not be available and the machine should be ridden accordingly. Have the machine checked by a BMW dealer – recorded faults can then be analysed using the BMW diagnostic tester and remedial action taken. Once the faulty component has been renewed, the fault code can be erased from the engine management system.

BMW provides no information on fault diagnosis or on testing any of the individual system components. However, before going to the effort and expense of visiting a dealer, first ensure that the relevant system wiring connectors are securely connected and free of corrosion – poor connections are the cause of the majority of problems. Also check the wiring itself for any obvious faults or breaks. Additionally, based on previous experience, we have been able to provide test specifications for some components obtained from machines used to illustrate diagnostic procedures in this manual. In the absence of diagnostic equipment, these should be of help in isolating a faulty component.

Because of their nature, individual system components cannot be repaired. Once the faulty component has been isolated, the only cure is to replace the part with a new one. Keep in mind that most electrical parts, once purchased, cannot be returned. To avoid unnecessary expense, make very sure the faulty component has been positively identified before buying a new part.

Fuel system

The fuel system consists of the fuel tank, fuel pump and filter, fuel hose, fuel rail and pressure sensor, fuel injectors, throttle bodies and throttle control cables, and the air intake system.

The fuel pump is housed inside the tank. A fuel strainer, filter and level sensor are fitted to the pump – the sensor operates the fuel gauge and low fuel warning on the instrument cluster.

There is an injector for both cylinders, housed in the throttle bodies. Cold starting, warm-up and engine idle speed are controlled by the ECU acting on information sent by the engine and intake air temperature sensors – there is no manual method (i.e. a choke) for assisting cold starting.

The exhaust system is a two-into-one design, incorporating an oxygen sensor and catalytic converter.

⚠️ **Warning: Petrol (gasoline) is extremely flammable, so take extra precautions when you work on any part of the fuel system. Don't smoke or allow open flames or bare light bulbs near the work area, and don't work in a garage where a natural gas-type appliance is present. If you spill any fuel on your skin, rinse it off immediately with soap and water. When you perform any kind of work on the fuel system, wear safety glasses and have a fire extinguisher suitable for a class B type fire (flammable liquids) on hand.**

Ignition system

All models are fitted with a digital inductive ignition system, which due to its lack of mechanical parts is totally maintenance free. The system comprises a trigger on the alternator rotor, a timing sensor, the ECU and two ignition coils. All models use the direct stick-type HT coils. The system incorporates ignition advance controlled by the ECU, which reacts to the information sent to it from the various sensors to provide the sparks at the optimum time

The system incorporates a safety interlock circuit which prevents the engine from being started when the sidestand is down, unless the gearbox is in neutral. The interlock circuit will also cut the ignition if a gear is selected whilst the engine is running and the sidestand is down, or if the sidestand is put down whilst the engine is running and in gear. A switch incorporated in the clutch lever allows the engine to be started in gear if the clutch is disengaged once the ignition has been switched on.

⚠️ **Warning: The very high output of the engine management system means that it can be very dangerous or even fatal to touch live components or terminals of any part of the system while in operation. Take care not to touch any part of the system when the engine is running, or even with it stopped and the ignition ON. Before working on an electrical component, make sure that the ignition switch is OFF, then disconnect the battery negative lead (-ve) and insulate it away from the battery terminal.**

Precautions

Always perform fuel-related procedures in a well-ventilated area to prevent a build-up of fumes.

Never work in a building containing a gas appliance with a pilot light, or any other form of naked flame. Ensure that there are no naked light bulbs or any sources of flame or sparks nearby.

Do not smoke (or allow anyone else to smoke) while in the vicinity of petrol (gasoline) or of components containing it. Remember the possible presence of vapour from these sources and move well clear before smoking.

Check all electrical equipment belonging to the house, garage or workshop where work is being undertaken (see the Safety first! section of this manual). Remember that certain electrical appliances such as drills, cutters etc. create sparks in the normal course of operation and must not be used near petrol (gasoline) or any component containing it. Again, remember the possible presence of fumes before using electrical equipment.

Always mop up any spilt fuel and safely dispose of the rag used.

Any stored fuel that is drained off during servicing work must be kept in sealed containers that are suitable for holding petrol (gasoline), and clearly marked as such; the containers themselves should be kept in a safe place. Note that this last point applies equally to the fuel tank if it is removed from the machine; also remember to keep its filler cap closed at all times.

Read the Safety first! section of this manual carefully before starting work.

Owners of machines used in the US, particularly California, should note that their machines must comply at all times with Federal or State legislation governing the permissible levels of noise and of pollutants such as unburnt hydrocarbons, carbon monoxide etc. that can be emitted by those machines. All vehicles offered for sale must comply with legislation in force at the date of manufacture and must not subsequently be altered in any way which will affect their emission of noise or of pollutants.

In practice, this means that adjustments may not be made to any part of the fuel, ignition or exhaust systems by anyone who is not authorised or mechanically qualified to do so, or who does not have the tools, equipment and data necessary to properly carry out the task. Also if any part of these systems is to be replaced it must be replaced with only genuine BMW components or by components which are approved under the relevant legislation. The machine must never be used with any part of these systems removed, modified or damaged.

2.1a Undo the screw . . .

2.1b . . . and remove the side cover – note the mounting pegs (arrowed)

2.3 Location of the IAT sensor wiring connector

2 Air filter housing

Note: *To change the air filter refer to Chapter 1, Section 11.*

Removal

GS models

1 Remove the seat, bodywork centre panel and both side panels (see Chapter 7). Undo the screws securing the left and right-hand side covers and lift them off **(see illustrations)**.

2 Remove the battery (see Chapter 8).
3 Disconnect the intake air temperature (IAT) sensor wiring connector **(see illustration)**.
4 Disconnect the idle actuator wiring connector **(see illustration)**.
5 Ease the idle air hoses off the unions on the throttle bodies **(see illustration)**.
6 On F800 GS models, disconnect the secondary air system valve wiring connector – the valve is located on the upper right-hand side of the housing. Disconnect the hose from the secondary air system valve. Release the wiring from the clip on the front edge of the housing.
7 Undo the screws and washers securing the front of the housing **(see illustration)**. Undo

the nuts securing the rear of the housing **(see illustration)**.
8 Ease the housing up off the throttle bodies and disconnect the engine breather hose from the housing **(see illustrations)**.
9 Cover the throttle body intakes with clean rag to prevent anything falling inside.

S, ST and R models

10 Remove the seat, bodywork centre panel and both side panels (see Chapter 7).
11 Follow the procedure in Chapter 1 to remove the air filter intake pipe assembly.
12 Remove the battery (see Chapter 8).
13 Displace the starter motor relay and support bracket (see Chapter 8).

2.4 Location of the idle actuator wiring connector

2.5 Ease the hoses off the unions on both sides

2.7a Undo the screws at the front . . .

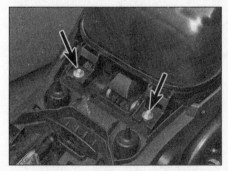

2.7b . . . and the nuts at the rear

2.8a Ease the housing off the throttle bodies . . .

2.8b . . . and disconnect the engine breather hose

2.14 Location of the IAT sensor wiring connector

2.15a Disconnect the secondary air system valve wiring connector

2.15b Release the wiring from the clip (arrowed)

2.15c Disconnect the secondary air system valve hose

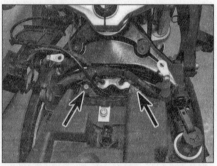

2.16a Undo the screws securing the front . . .

14 Disconnect the intake air temperature (IAT) sensor wiring connector **(see illustration)**.

15 Disconnect the secondary air system valve wiring connector, then release the wiring from the clip on the air filter housing **(see illustrations)**. Disconnect the hose from the secondary air system valve – note the quick-release catch **(see illustration)**.

16 Undo the screws securing the front and rear of the housing, noting the location of the washers **(see illustrations)**.

17 Ease the housing up off the throttle bodies and disconnect the idle actuator wiring connector **(see illustration)**.

18 Ease the idle air hoses off the unions on the throttle bodies **(see illustration)**.

19 Disconnect the engine breather hose from the housing **(see illustration)**.

20 Cover the throttle body intakes with clean rag to prevent anything falling inside.

Installation

21 Installation is the reverse of removal, noting the following:

● Don't forget to connect the engine breather and idle air hoses, and the idle speed actuator wiring connector, before fitting the housing onto the throttle bodies.
● Ensure the washers are located on the fixing screws.
● Ensure all the wiring connectors are secure.

2.16b . . . and rear of the housing . . .

2.16c . . . noting the location of the washers

2.17 Disconnect the idle actuator wiring connector

2.18 Disconnect the idle air hoses from the throttle bodies

2.19 Disconnect the engine breather hose

3.6 Check the security of the quick-release catch

3 Secondary air system control valve

Note: *This system is not fitted to the F650 GS model.*

1 A secondary air system is fitted to all machines covered in this manual except F650 GS models. The system is designed to reduce the amount of unburned hydrocarbons released in the exhaust gases.

2 The system consists of the control valve mounted on the air filter housing, the reed valves located in the valve cover, and the inter-connecting hose. The control valve is actuated electronically by the ECM.

3 Under certain operating conditions, the control valve allows filtered air to be drawn through it to the reed valves, and then via passages in the cylinder head into the exhaust ports. There the air mixes with the exhaust gases, allowing any remaining particles of fuel in the exhaust to be burnt. This process changes a considerable amount of hydrocarbons and carbon monoxide into relatively harmless carbon dioxide and water.

4 The reed valves prevent the flow of exhaust gases back into the control valve and air filter housing (see Chapter 2, Section 6).

5 To check the control valve, first remove the seat, bodywork centre panel and both side panels (see Chapter 7).

6 Ensure that the quick-release catch on the upper end of the hose connects the hose securely to the control valve **(see illustration)**.

7 No test details are provided for the valve, however its resistance can be measured with a multimeter set to the ohms scale as follows. Disconnect the valve wiring connector **(see illustration 2.15a)**. Measure the resistance between the control valve terminals – on the machine used to illustrate this procedure the resistance measured 19.8 ohms. If the result varies greatly it is likely that the valve is faulty – have it checked by a BMW dealer.

8 Remove the air filter housing (see Section 2) and check the condition of the hose and the hose connection on the reed valve cover **(see illustration)**. If the hose is damaged or a loose fit, renew it.

9 To remove the control valve, disconnect the wiring connector and the hose. Undo the screws securing the valve to the air filter housing and ease it out, noting the location of the O-ring.

10 Fit a new O-ring to the control valve, press the valve into the housing carefully and secure it with the screws.

11 Follow the procedure in Section 2 to install the air filter housing and connect the secondary air system hose and wiring connector.

4 Fuel tank

Warning: Refer to the precautions given in Section 1 before starting work.

1 Due to the design and location of the fuel tank, removal is beyond the scope of this manual. If the tank is damaged, have its condition assessed by a BMW dealer.

2 All repairs to the fuel tank should be carried out by a professional who has experience in this critical and potentially dangerous work. Even after cleaning and flushing of the fuel system, explosive fumes can remain and ignite during repair of the tank.

3 If the fuel tank is removed from the bike, it should not be placed in an area where sparks or open flames could ignite the fumes coming out of the tank. Be especially careful inside garages where a natural gas-type appliance is located, because the pilot light could cause an explosion.

5 Fuel pump, strainer and level sensor

1 The fuel pump, strainer and level sensor assembly is located inside the fuel tank. When the ignition is switched ON, it should be possible to hear the pump run for a few seconds until the system is up to pressure. If you can't hear anything, remove the seat (see Chapter 7) and check the pump connector and wiring **(see illustration)**.

2 If the wiring is good, remove the pump assembly and check that the internal wiring connectors are secure.

Removal

Special tool: *A pin wrench or similar suitable tool is required for this procedure (see Step 8).*

3 Disconnect the battery negative lead (see Chapter 8).

4 Due to the location of the pump, it may be necessary to drain some fuel out of the tank before removing the pump. Remove the filler cap and check the fuel content – if it is above

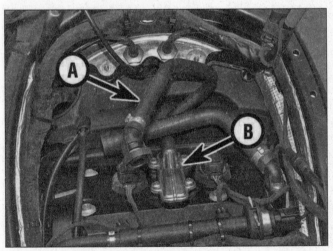

3.8 Secondary air system hose (A) and reed valve cover (B)

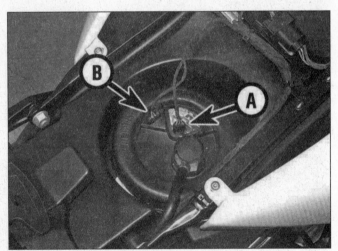

5.1 Fuel pump connector (A) and level sensor connector (B)

5.6 Disconnect the fuel hose

5.7 Lift off the cover

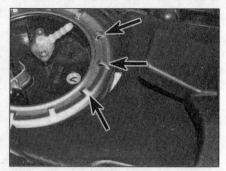

5.8a Use a tool that bears on the raised tabs . . .

5.8b . . . to unscrew the pump retaining ring . . .

5.8c . . . and lift the ring off

5.9a Ease the pump out carefully . . .

the level of the pump, empty any excess fuel using a commercially available pump.

5 On F800 GS models, if fitted, unscrew the fuel pump cover.

6 Disconnect the fuel pump and level sensor wiring connectors **(see illustration 5.1)**. Release the clip securing the fuel hose and disconnect the hose from the union on the top of the pump, being prepared to catch any residual fuel in some rag **(see illustration)**. Block the open end of the fuel hose with a suitable plug. Discard the hose clip as a new one must be fitted.

7 Lift off the protective cover **(see illustration)**.

8 Unscrew the pump retaining ring using a wrench that bears on the raised tabs on the ring **(see illustration)**. BMW produces a service tool for this purpose (Part No. 16 1 021). Alternatively a tool can be made by bolting two strips of steel together **(see illustration)**. Lift the ring off **(see illustration)**.

9 Ease the pump assembly out carefully by pulling on the tabs provided **(see illustration)**. Do not lever the pump out as the sealing

surface may be damaged. Note the locating tab on the rear edge of the pump rim **(see illustration)**. Take care not to damage the arm of the fuel level sensor float. Discard the pump seal as a new one must be fitted **(see illustration)**.

Check

Pump and strainer

10 Undo the screws securing the pump electronics unit, lift it off and disconnect

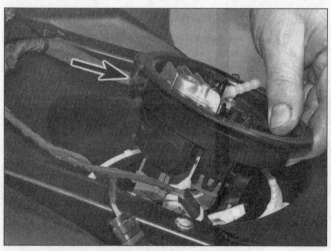

5.9b . . . noting the locating tab (arrowed)

5.9c Fit a new pump seal on installation

5.10a Undo the screws (arrowed) . . .

5.10b . . . lift off the electronics unit . . .

5.10c . . . and disconnect the wiring connector

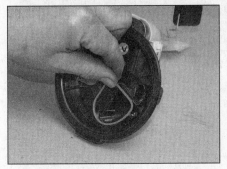

5.10d Note the location of the seal

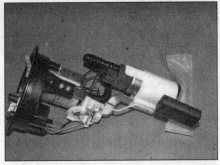

5.10e Inspect the wiring and terminals for damage

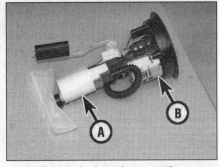

5.10f Ensure the hose between the pump (A) and filter (B) is secure

the wiring connector **(see illustrations)**. Discard the seal as a new one must be fitted **(see illustration)**. Inspect the external and internal wiring and terminals for damage **(see illustration)**. Ensure that the hose between the pump and the filter cartridge is secure **(see illustration)**.

11 No test details are provided for the pump, however its operation can be checked using a fully charged 12 volt battery and two insulated jumper wires. Connect the positive (+ve) battery terminal to the pump's positive terminal, and the negative (-ve) battery terminal to the pump's negative terminal. The pump should operate. If not, replace it with a new one. **Note 1:** *Do not allow the pump to run for more that a couple of seconds unloaded.* **Note 2:** *If a new fuel pump is fitted the machine must be taken to a BMW dealer so that the*

engine management system adaptation values can be reset to recognise the new pump. If the pump is good, have the electronics unit tested by a BMW dealer.

12 Allow the strainer element to dry, they use a soft brush to remove any dirt or sediment **(see illustration 5.13)**. If the strainer is heavily soiled, clean accumulated dirt out of the tank.

13 Inspect the strainer element for splits and holes – if any damage is found, ease the strainer off and fit a new one **(see illustration)**. If the strainer is damaged it is likely the filter cartridge has become clogged – the filter is an integral part of the pump assembly and is not listed as a separate item **(see illustration 5.10f)**.

Level sensor

14 If the sensor is thought to be faulty, first check that the float arm moves freely up and down.

15 Connect the probes of a multimeter set to the ohms x 100 scale to the sensor terminals and measure the resistance with the float in the tank full (up) position **(see illustration)**. Now move the float slowly to the tank empty (down) position **(see illustration)**.

16 If the sensor is working correctly, the meter should show a progressive change in the resistance. Although no test details are provided, on the machine used to illustrate this procedure the resistance in the tank full position measured 3.8 ohms and in the tank empty position measured 100.0 ohms.

17 If there is no difference in the results it is likely that the sensor is faulty and a new one must be fitted. Disconnect the sensor wiring connector, then undo the screws securing the sensor to the pump assembly. Installation is the reverse of removal.

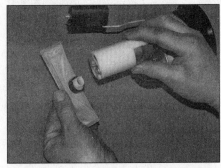

5.13 Ease the strainer off, noting how it fits

5.15a Float in tank full . . .

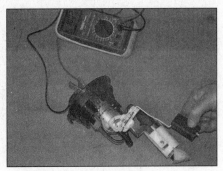

5.15b . . . and tank empty positions

5.18a Secure the fuel hose with a new clip

5.18b Ensure the hose is correctly routed

Installation

18 Installation is the reverse of removal, noting the following:

● Ensure the pump and tank mating surfaces are clean and dry.

● Ensure the pump assembly is installed the right way round **(see illustration 5.9b)**.

● If a suitable tool is available, tighten the retaining ring to the torque setting specified at the beginning of this Chapter.

● Don't forget to fit the protective cover.

● Secure the fuel hose with a new clip **(see illustration)**.

● Ensure the hose is correctly routed **(see illustration)**.

6.3 Location of the roll-over valve – S model shown

7.3a Measuring the fuel pressure sensor resistance

6 Roll-over valve

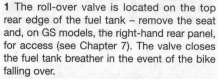

1 The roll-over valve is located on the top rear edge of the fuel tank – remove the seat and, on GS models, the right-hand rear panel, for access (see Chapter 7). The valve closes the fuel tank breather in the event of the bike falling over.

2 If the valve sticks in the closed position, or if the breather hose is trapped or blocked, fuel delivery will be restricted.

3 To remove the valve, first detach the

7.1 Location of the fuel pressure sensor (arrowed)

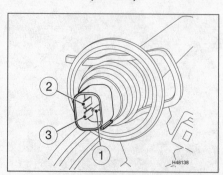

7.3b Pressure sensor connector terminal identification

breather hose **(see illustration)**. Undo the screws securing the valve to the tank, then lift off the valve and the O-ring. Discard the O-ring as a new one must be fitted.

4 Check the operation of the valve by holding it in the upright position and blowing through it – the valve should be open. Now tilt the valve on its side and blow through it – the valve should be closed.

5 Ensure that the breather hose is clear.

6 Installation is the reverse of removal. Tighten the screws evenly in a criss-cross pattern, taking care not to over-tighten them.

7 Fuel pressure sensor

 Warning: Refer to the precautions given in Section 1 before starting work.

1 The fuel pressure sensor is located on the right-hand end of the fuel rail **(see illustration)**. Remove the air filter housing for access (see Section 2).

2 Refer to *Fault Finding* at the end of this manual to identify the causes of poor fuel flow and low fuel pressure, including leakage from the fuel hose connections and between the fuel rail and injectors (see Section 10).

3 No test details are provided for the sensor, however its resistance can be measured with a multimeter set to the K-ohms scale as follows. Disconnect the sensor wiring connector and measure the resistance between the terminals on the sensor side of the connector **(see illustration)**. On the machine used to illustrate this procedure the resistance between terminals No. 2 and No. 3 measured 2.17 K-ohms and between terminals No. 1 and No. 3 measured 110.4 K-ohms **(see illustration)**. If the results vary greatly it is likely that the sensor is faulty – have it checked by a BMW dealer. **Note:** *Due to restricted access it may be necessary to displace the throttle bodies before testing or removing the fuel pressure sensor (see Section 9).*

7.4a Pull out the clip . . .

7.4b . . . then ease out the sensor

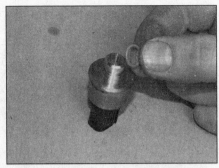

7.5 Note the location of the O-ring

4 The sensor is secured in the end of the fuel rail by a spring clip – have some rag handy to catch any residual fuel, then pull out the clip and ease the sensor out from the fuel rail **(see illustrations)**.

5 Note the location of the sensor O-ring and discard it as a new one must be fitted **(see illustration)**.

6 Installation is the reverse of removal, noting the following:

● Lubricate the new sensor O-ring with a smear of oil before installation.

● Press the sensor all the way in before fitting the spring clip.

● Fit a new clip if the old one is sprained or corroded.

Note: *If a new fuel pressure sensor is fitted the machine must be taken to a BMW dealer so that the engine management system adaptation values can be reset to recognise the new sensor.*

8 Throttle cable

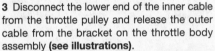

Removal

1 Remove the air filter housing (see Section 2).

2 Loosen the lockring on the adjuster on the upper end of the cable **(see illustration)**. Thread the adjuster towards the cable elbow to create maximum freeplay in the cable.

3 Disconnect the lower end of the inner cable from the throttle pulley and release the outer cable from the bracket on the throttle body assembly **(see illustrations)**.

4 Undo the screw securing the upper half of the twistgrip pulley housing and lift it off **(see illustrations)**.

5 Disconnect the end of the inner cable from the twistgrip pulley **(see illustration)**.

6 Unscrew the cable elbow retaining ring from

8.2 Throttle cable adjuster lockring (arrowed)

8.3a Disconnect the inner cable from the throttle pulley . . .

8.3b . . . and release the outer cable from the bracket (arrowed)

8.4a Undo the screw . . .

8.4b . . . and lift off the upper half of the pulley housing

8.5 End of the inner cable (arrowed)

8.6a Unscrew the retaining ring . . .

8.6b . . . and draw the cable out

the twistgrip housing and draw the cable out **(see illustrations)**.

7 Withdraw the cable from the machine, carefully noting its correct routing.

> **HAYNES HINT**
>
> *Tie string to the cable end so that it's drawn through with the old cable and used as a guide to draw the new cable into place.*

Installation

8 If required, lubricate the cable and the exposed inner cable ends (see Chapter 1).

9 Fit the upper end of the cable into the twistgrip housing and secure the elbow with the retaining ring – tighten the ring lightly at this stage **(see illustration 8.6b and a)**.

10 Fit the end of the inner cable into the twistgrip pulley, then install the upper half of

the housing and tighten the screw securely **(see illustrations 8.5, 4b and a)**.

11 Feed the cable through to the throttle body, making sure it is correctly routed – the cable must not interfere with any other component and should not be kinked or bent sharply. Now tighten the elbow retaining ring against the twistgrip housing.

12 Install the lower end of the outer cable in the bracket on the throttle body assembly, then hold the throttle pulley open and connect the end of the inner cable to the pulley **(see illustrations 8.3a and b)**.

13 Adjust the cable freeplay (see Chapter 1). Operate the throttle to check that it opens and closes freely. Turn the handlebars back and forth to make sure the cable doesn't cause the steering to bind.

14 Start the engine and check that the engine speed does not rise as the handlebars are turned. If it does, the throttle cable is routed

incorrectly. Correct the problem before riding the motorcycle.

15 Install the remaining components in the reverse order of removal.

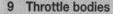

9 Throttle bodies

> ⚠ **Warning: Refer to the precautions given in Section 1 before starting work.**

Removal

1 Remove the air filter housing (Section 2).

2 Detach the cable from the throttle pulley (Section 8).

3 Disconnect the fuel injector wiring connectors and release the ties securing the wiring sub-loom to the throttle body assembly **(see illustration)**.

4 Undo the screw securing the earth lead terminal to the cylinder head **(see illustration)**.

5 Release the clip securing the fuel hose and disconnect the hose from the union on the end of the fuel rail, being prepared to catch any residual fuel in some rag **(see illustrations)**. Block the open end of the fuel hose with a suitable plug. Discard the hose clip as a new one must be fitted.

6 Disconnect the oil pressure switch and coolant temperature sensor wiring connectors **(see illustration)**.

7 Disconnect the fuel pressure sensor and throttle position sensor wiring connectors **(see illustration)**.

9.3 Disconnect the wiring connectors (arrowed) and release the cable-ties

9.4 Undo the screw securing the earth lead terminal

9.5a Release the clip securing the fuel hose . . .

9.5b . . . and disconnect the hose from the fuel rail

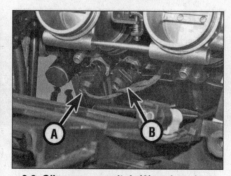

9.6 Oil pressure switch (A) and coolant temperature sensor (B) connectors

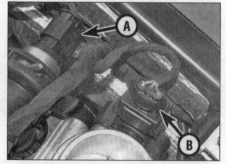

9.7 Fuel pressure sensor (A) and throttle position sensor (B) connectors

9.8a Throttle body clamps (arrowed) – S model shown

9.8b Throttle body clamp (arrowed) – F650 GS model shown

9.9 Ease the throttle body assembly out of the adapters

8 Loosen the clamps securing the throttle body assembly in the intake adapters (see illustrations). Note that two different types of clamp are used – on the F650 GS model used to illustrate this procedure, the clamps were of the non-reusable type. Ease the clamps open with a flat-bladed screwdriver; new clamps must be fitted on installation.
9 Ease the throttle body assembly out of the adapters and remove it (see illustration).
10 Cover the intake manifolds with clean rag to prevent anything falling inside.
11 If required, remove the fuel rail and injectors (see Section 10).

Cleaning

Caution: Use only a petroleum based solvent or dedicated injector cleaner for throttle body cleaning. Don't use caustic cleaners.

12 Ensure that only metal components are submerged in cleaning solvent and always follow manufacturers recommendations as to cleaning time (see illustration). If a spray cleaner is used, direct the spray into all passages.
13 After the cleaner has loosened and dissolved most of the varnish and other deposits, use a nylon-bristled brush to remove the stubborn deposits. Rinse the throttle bodies again, then dry them with compressed air.
14 Use compressed air to blow out all of the fuel and air passages.

Inspection

15 Check the throttle bodies for cracks or any

other damage which may result in air getting in.
16 Check that the throttle valves move smoothly and freely in the bodies. Inspect the valve shafts and throttle bodies for wear. Check the condition of the valve shaft spring. Do not tamper with the position of the stop screws on the valve shaft and throttle pulley (see illustration).
17 Only the fuel rail and injectors, and throttle position sensor are available as separate items. If any other components are worn or damaged, a new throttle body assembly will have to be fitted.
18 No test details are provided for the throttle position sensor, however its resistance can be measured with a multimeter set to the K-ohms scale as follows. Disconnect the sensor wiring connector and connect the meter probes to terminals No. 1 and No. 2 on the sensor side of the connector (see illustrations). Measure

the resistance with the throttle valves fully closed, then move the valves slowly to the fully open position.
19 If the sensor is working correctly, the meter should show a progressive change in the resistance. On the machine used to illustrate this procedure the resistance in the fully closed position measured 4.68 K-ohms and in the fully open position measured 1.51 K-ohms.
20 If there is no difference in the results it is likely that the sensor is faulty – have it checked by a BMW dealer. **Note:** *If a new throttle position sensor is fitted the machine must be taken to a BMW dealer so that the engine management system adaptation values can be reset to recognise the new sensor.*
21 Check the intake adapters for signs of cracking or deterioration and renew them if necessary (see illustration). Make sure the mating surfaces are clean before refitting.

9.12 Use cleaning solvents as directed

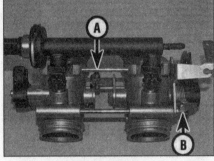

9.16 Valve shaft (A) and throttle pulley (B) stop screws

9.18a Measuring the throttle position sensor resistance

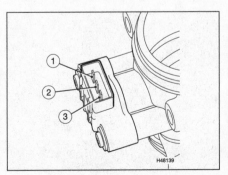

9.18b Throttle position sensor connector terminal identification

9.21 Check the condition of the intake adapters

9.22a Use the correct tool to tighten the hose clip

9.22b The installed hose clip should look like this

Installation

22 Installation is the reverse of removal, noting the following:

● Ensure the intake adapter clamps are correctly positioned for tightening.
● Make sure the throttle bodies are fully engaged with the intake adapters before tightening the clamps.
● Connect the wiring connectors as noted on removal.
● Don't forget to reconnect the earth terminal.
● Secure all the wiring sub-loom to the throttle body assembly **(see illustration 9.3)**.
● Secure the fuel hose with a new clip **(see illustrations)**.
● Check the operation of the throttle and adjust the cable freeplay (see Chapter 1).

● Run the engine and ensure that the fuel system is working correctly before riding the motorcycle.

10 Fuel rail and injectors

Warning: Refer to the precautions given in Section 1 before starting work.

Removal

1 Remove the air filter housing (Section 2).
2 The fuel rail and injectors can be removed once the throttle bodies have been removed (see Section) 9). Alternatively, follow the procedure in Section 9 to disconnect the fuel injector and fuel pressure sensor wiring

connectors, release the ties securing the wiring sub-loom to the fuel rail and disconnect the fuel hose from the union on the fuel rail.
3 Undo the screws securing the fuel rail to the throttle bodies **(see illustration)**.
4 Carefully lift the fuel rail assembly off the throttle bodies – the injectors will come away with the rail **(see illustration)**. Note the location of the injector seals **(see illustration)**.
5 Remove the spring clip from the injector, then pull the injector out of the rail, noting its alignment **(see illustrations)**. Note the location of the O-ring – discard the injector O-rings and seals as new ones must be fitted on reassembly

Inspection

6 Inspect the end of the fuel injector for accumulations of carbon and signs of damage **(see illustration)**. Check that the terminals in the wiring connector are clean.
7 Modern fuels contain detergents which should keep the injectors clean and free of gum or varnish from fuel residue. If an injector is suspected of being blocked, clean it through with injector cleaner. If the injector is clean but its performance is suspect, take it to a BMW dealer for assessment.
8 No test details are provided for the injectors, however their resistance can be measured with a multimeter set to the ohms scale as follows. If not already done, disconnect the injector wiring connector. Measure the resistance between the terminals on the injector side of the connector – on the machine used to illustrate this procedure the

10.3 Screws secure fuel rail to the throttle bodies

10.4a Lift the fuel rail assembly off the throttle bodies

10.4b Note location of the injector seals

10.5a Remove the spring clip . . .

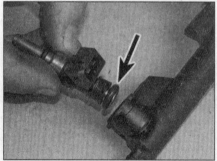

10.5b . . . and pull the injector out – note the O-ring

10.6 End of the injector should be free of carbon

10.9 Thread-lock the fuel rail screws

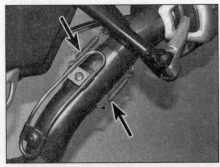

11.1 Release the holding springs (arrowed)

11.2a Counter-hold the mounting bolt . . .

resistance measured 12.4 ohms. If the result varies greatly it is likely that the injector is faulty – have it checked by a BMW dealer.

Installation

9 Installation is the reverse of removal, noting the following:
● Fit new O-rings and seals smeared lightly with engine oil.
● Make sure the injectors align correctly with the fuel rail (see illustration 10.5b).
● Secure the injectors with the clips (see illustration 10.5a).
● Make sure the injectors locate correctly in the throttle bodies (see illustration 10.4a).
● Clean the threads of the fuel rail screws and apply a suitable non-permanent thread-locking compound (see illustration).

11 Exhaust system

⚠️ **Warning: If the engine has been running the exhaust system will be very hot. Allow the system to cool before carrying out any work.**
Note: *Before starting work on the exhaust system spray all the nuts, mounting bolts and clamp bolts with penetrating fluid – many of them are exposed and are prone to corrosion.*

Silencer
GS and R models

1 Release the holding springs securing the silencer to the exhaust pipe (see illustration).

11.2b . . . and unscrew the nut on the inside of the bracket

2 Counter-hold the mounting bolt and unscrew the nut on the inside of the mounting bracket (see illustrations).
3 Support the silencer and remove the mounting bolt and washer, then draw the silencer off the exhaust pipe.
4 Inspect the bushing in the silencer support clamp and renew it if it is worn. If a new clamp is fitted, tighten the clamp bolts finger-tight until the silencer is installed and the clamp and mounting bracket are correctly aligned.
5 Prior to installation, clean the outside end of the exhaust pipe and the inside of the silencer front pipe and apply a smear of high temperature assembly grease.
6 Locate the silencer on the exhaust pipe and install the mounting bolt and washer, then tighten the nut finger-tight.
7 Ensure the tabs for the holding springs are aligned, then install the springs (see illustration).

11.7 Align tabs (arrowed) before installing spring

8 Check the alignment of the support clamp and bracket. If applicable, tighten the clamp bolts securely.
9 Tighten the mounting bolt to the torque setting specified at the beginning of this Chapter.

S and ST models

10 Loosen the ball clamp securing the silencer to the exhaust pipe, then counter-hold the mounting bolt and unscrew the nut on the inside of the mounting bracket (see illustration).
11 Support the silencer and remove the mounting bolt and washer, then draw the silencer off the exhaust pipe, noting how the two ends fit inside the ball clamp (see illustration).
12 Inspect the bushing in the silencer mounting bracket and renew it if it is worn (see illustration). If a new support clamp is

11.10 Location of the ball clamp (A) and mounting bolt (B)

11.11 Note how exhaust pipe and silencer front pipe locate inside ball clamp

11.12 Inspect the bushing in the silencer mounting bracket

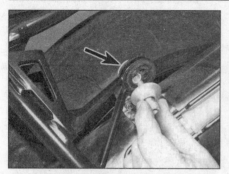

11.14 Note how the tab (arrowed) locates behind the mounting bracket

11.21 Location of the oxygen sensor

11.22a Counter-hold the mounting bolt . . .

11.22b . . . and unscrew the nut on the inside of the bracket

fitted, tighten the clamp bolts finger-tight until the silencer is installed and the clamp and mounting bracket are correctly aligned.

13 Prior to installation, clean the inside of the ball clamp and the outside ends of the exhaust pipe and silencer front pipe, and apply a smear of high temperature assembly grease.

14 Ensure the ball clamp is on the pipe. Align the silencer with the pipe and install the mounting bolt and washer – note that the tab on the support clamp locates behind the mounting bracket **(see illustration)**. Tighten the nut finger-tight.

15 Tighten the ball clamp to the torque setting specified at the beginning of this Chapter.

16 Check the alignment of the support clamp and bracket. If applicable, tighten the clamp bolts securely.

17 Tighten the mounting bolt to the specified torque setting.

Downpipes

Note: *On all models except the F650 GS, the rear section of the exhaust downpipe contains a three-way catalytic converter. Handle the downpipe with care when it is off the machine.*

GS and R models

18 Remove the silencer (see Steps 1 to 3).

19 Displace or remove the radiator to access the downpipe flange nuts (see Chapter 3).

20 Displace the regulator/rectifier to access the oxygen sensor wiring connector (see Chapter 8).

21 Trace the wiring from the oxygen sensor and disconnect it at the connector **(see illustration)**. Feed the wiring back to the sensor, noting its routing and freeing it from any ties.

22 Counter-hold the mounting bolt and unscrew the nut on the mounting bracket **(see illustrations)**. Remove the mounting bolt and washer.

23 Undo the downpipe flange nuts **(see illustration)**.

24 Detach the downpipes from the cylinder head and lift the exhaust off **(see illustration)**.

25 Remove the gaskets from the exhaust ports in the cylinder head and discard them as new ones must be used.

26 If required, remove the oxygen sensor (see Section 12).

27 Installation is the reverse of removal, noting the following:

● If removed, install the oxygen sensor.
● Fit new gaskets into the exhaust ports – the tabs on the gaskets will hold them in position.
● Fit the exhaust then install the downpipe flange nuts and mounting bolt finger-tight.
● Tighten the downpipe flange nuts evenly to the torque setting specified at the beginning of this Chapter.
● Tighten the exhaust mounting bolt and nut to the specified torque setting.
● Reconnect the oxygen sensor wiring connector. Secure the wiring as noted on removal.
● Run the engine and check that there are no exhaust gas leaks.

S and ST models

28 Remove the silencer (see Steps 10 and 11).

29 If the correct tool is available, unscrew

11.23 Exhaust downpipe flange nuts

11.24 Detach the downpipes and lift the exhaust off

11.29a Release the clip (arrowed) . . .

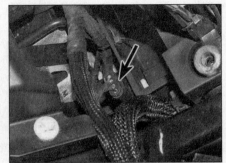

11.29b . . . and disconnect the connector

11.29c Feed the wiring back to the sensor

the oxygen sensor from the exhaust pipe (see Section 12). Alternatively, remove the seat and bodywork side panels to gain access to the oxygen sensor wiring connector (see Chapter 7). The connector is located on the back of the holder for the engine control unit (ECU) – access is extremely limited. On the machine used to illustrate this procedure it was first necessary to remove the central vehicle electronics (ZFE) unit and the ECU (see Section 16). Next, twist the clip securing the wiring connector to the ECU holder to release it, then draw the connector up and disconnect it **(see illustrations)**. Feed the wiring back to the sensor, noting its routing and freeing it from any ties **(see illustration)**.

30 On ST models, if not already done, remove the right-hand bodywork lower side panel (see Chapter 7).

31 Undo the downpipe flange nuts **(see illustration 11.23)**.

32 Detach the downpipes from the cylinder head and lift the exhaust off **(see illustration 11.24)**.

33 Remove the gaskets from the exhaust ports in the cylinder head and discard them as new ones must be used.

34 If required, remove the oxygen sensor (see Section 12).

35 Installation is the reverse of removal, noting the following:

● Fit new gaskets into the exhaust ports.
● Fit the exhaust then install the downpipe flange nuts finger-tight.
● Tighten the downpipe flange nuts evenly to the torque setting specified at the beginning of this Chapter.
● If removed, install the oxygen sensor.
● Reconnect the oxygen sensor wiring connector. Secure the wiring as noted on removal.
● Run the engine and check that there are no exhaust gas leaks.

12 Catalytic converter and oxygen sensor

Warning: If the engine has been running the exhaust system will be very hot. Allow the system to cool before carrying out any work.

Catalytic converter

1 A three-way catalytic converter located in the rear end of the exhaust downpipe. The purpose of the catalytic converter is to minimise the amount of pollutants which escape into the atmosphere. Hot exhaust gasses pass through the flow channels in the converter which are coated with a precious metal catalyst. The catalyst reduces nitrous oxides into nitrogen and oxygen, and oxidises unburned harmful hydrocarbons and carbon monoxide into water and carbon dioxide. The efficiency of the catalyst is reduced if the flow channels become clogged or if the precious metal coating becomes covered with carbon, lead or oil.

2 The catalytic converter is simple in operation and requires no maintenance.

● Always use unleaded fuel – the use of leaded fuel will destroy the converter.
● Do not use any fuel or oil additives.
● Keep the fuel and ignition systems in good order.
● Handle the exhaust downpipes with care when it is off the machine.

Oxygen sensor

3 The oxygen sensor measures exhaust gas oxygen content and relays this information to the ECU. The ECU compares exhaust gas oxygen content with the oxygen content in the ambient air and, depending on whether the engine is running rich or lean, adjusts the fuel/ air mixture accordingly.

4 The sensor is threaded into the exhaust pipe directly behind the engine unit **(see illustrations 11.21 and 29c)**.

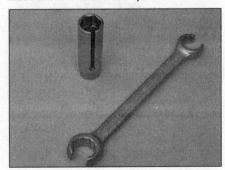

12.6 Slotted deep socket and special spanner for use on oxygen sensor

5 To remove the sensor, first disconnect the wiring connector (see Section 11).

6 Unscrew the sensor using the correct tool, taking care not to damage either the sensor or the exhaust pipe **(see illustration)**. If the sensor threads are corroded, soak them with penetrating oil before proceeding.

7 Deposits on the sensor tip are an indication of poor engine running – light rust coloured deposits indicate lead contamination through the use of the wrong fuel, black or dark brown deposits are a sign that oil is getting into the combustion chamber through worn valve stem seals or piston rings.

8 A contaminated sensor will send an inaccurate signal to the ECU, which should, in turn, illuminate the engine warning light in the instrument cluster. Do not attempt to clean the sensor – if it is contaminated, a new one will have to be fitted.

9 No test details are provided for the oxygen sensor, however the heater resistance can be measured with a multi-meter set to the ohms scale as follows. If not already done, disconnect the sensor wiring connector. Measure the resistance between the white wire terminals on the sensor side of the connector – on the machine used to illustrate this procedure the resistance measured 6.2 ohms. If the result varies greatly it is likely that the sensor is faulty – have it checked by a BMW dealer.

10 Before installing the oxygen sensor, clean the threads and lubricate them with a smear of high temperature assembly grease. If a suitable tool is available, tighten the sensor to the torque setting specified at the beginning of this Chapter.

11 Ensure that the terminals in the wiring connector are clean and make sure that the connection is secure.

13 Ignition system checks

Warning: Refer to the Warning given in Section 1 before starting work.

1 As no means of adjustment is available, any failure of the system can be traced to failure of a system component or a simple wiring fault.

Of the two possibilities, the latter is by far the most likely. In the event of failure, check the system in a logical fashion, as described below. **Note:** *Before making any tests, check that the battery is in good condition and fully charged.*

2 Ignition faults can be divided into two categories, namely those where the ignition system has failed completely, and those which are due to a partial failure. The likely faults are listed below, starting with the most probable source of failure. Work through the list systematically, referring to the subsequent sections for full details of the necessary checks and tests, where information is available.

● Loose, corroded or damaged wiring connections, broken or shorted wiring between any of the component parts of the ignition system (see Chapter 8).
● Faulty spark plug, dirty, worn or corroded plug electrodes, or incorrect gap between electrodes (see Chapter 1).
● Faulty ignition HT coil (see Section 14).
● Faulty ignition switch or engine kill switch (see Chapter 8).
● Faulty clutch switch or sidestand switch (see Chapter 7). Faulty gear position sensor (see Section 17).
● Incorrect ignition timing or faulty camshaft position sensor (see Section 17).
● Faulty engine control unit (ECU).

3 If the above checks don't reveal the cause of the problem, have the ignition system tested by a BMW dealer equipped with the diagnostic tester. The diagnostic tester permits full testing of the ignition system components and reads the ECU fault code memory.

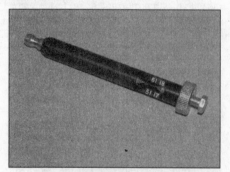

14.4 Spark gap tester tool

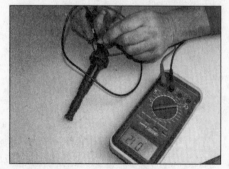

14.7a Measuring the HT coil primary resistance

14 Ignition HT coils

 ⚠ *Warning: Refer to the Warning given in Section 1 before starting work.*

1 Working on one HT coil at a time, follow the procedure in Chapter 1, Section 12, disconnect the wiring connector and pull the coil off the spark plug.

2 Ensure that the terminals inside the wiring connector are clean, then reconnect the wiring connector. Connect the coil to a new spark plug of the correct type and lay the plug on the engine with the threads contacting the engine. If necessary, hold the plug in position with an insulated tool.

⚠ *Warning: Do not remove the spark plugs from the engine to perform this check – atomised fuel being pumped out of the open spark plug hole could ignite, causing severe injury!*

3 Check that the kill switch is in the RUN position and the transmission is in neutral, then turn the ignition switch ON and turn the engine over on the starter motor. If the system is in good condition a regular, fat blue spark should be evident at the plug electrodes. If the spark appears thin or yellowish, or is non-existent, further investigation is necessary. Turn the ignition OFF. Repeat the check for the other coil.

4 The ignition system must be able to produce a spark which is capable of jumping a gap of at least 6 mm, although BMW provides no specification. A commercially available ignition spark gap tester tool will be required for this check **(see illustration)**.

5 Connect the coil to the protruding electrode on the test tool, and connect the tool to a good earth (ground) on the engine. Check that the kill switch is in the RUN position, turn the ignition switch ON and turn the engine over on the starter motor. If the system is in good condition a regular, fat blue spark should be seen to jump across the gap on the tool. Repeat the test for the other coil. If the test results are good the entire ignition system can be considered good. If the spark appears thin or yellowish, or is non-existent, further investigation is necessary.

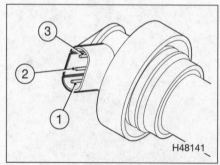

14.7b Ignition HT coil connector terminal identification

6 In order to determine conclusively that an ignition HT coil is defective, it should be tested by a BMW dealer equipped with the diagnostic tester. However, the coil can be checked visually for damage, and although no test details are provided, the primary and secondary coil resistances can be measured with a multimeter as follows.

7 Disconnect the wiring connector. To check the coil primary resistance, set the multimeter to the ohms x 1 scale and connect its probes to the outer terminals (Nos. 1 and 3) in the coil connector and note the result **(see illustrations)**. To check the coil secondary resistance, set the meter to the K-ohms scale and connect its probes to the middle terminal (No. 2) in the coil connector and to the spark plug terminal inside the coil **(see illustration)**.

8 On the machine used to illustrate this procedure the primary coil resistance measured between 1.2 and 1.4 ohms and the secondary coil resistance measured 5.3 K-ohms. If the results vary greatly it is likely that the coil is faulty – have it checked by a BMW dealer.

9 Follow the procedure in Chapter 1, Section 12, to install the ignition HT coils.

15 Engine management system and ECU

⚠ *Warning: Refer to the Warning given in Section 1 before starting work.*

1 For a general description of the system, see Section 1.

Diagnostic tester and fault identification

2 To diagnose the exact cause of a failure in the system, the BMW diagnostic tester, specifically designed for this system, is essential. Hence if a problem occurs, the motorcycle should be taken to a BMW dealer whenever possible.

3 The engine management system has in-built diagnostic functions which record and store all data should a fault occur. Recorded faults can then be checked using BMW's diagnostic tester, which analyses the data and identifies the exact fault.

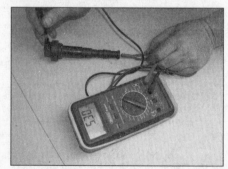

14.7c Measuring the coil secondary resistance

4 Should a fault occur, the engine warning light in the instrument cluster illuminates. If this happens, the management system switches itself into 'limp home' mode, so that in theory you should not be left stranded. Depending on the problem, it is possible that you will notice no difference in the running of the motorcycle. However, BMW advises that in 'limp home' mode, full engine power may not be available and the machine should be ridden accordingly.

5 In order to diagnose the problem and to turn the warning light off, the diagnostic tester is essential. Take your machine to a BMW dealer and have them check the system – it should not take long.

6 It is possible to perform certain tests and checks to identify a particular fault, but the difficulty is knowing in which part of the system the fault has occurred, and therefore where to start checking. Details on the location and function of the individual sensors can be found in Section 17.

Fault tracing

Note: *Disconnect the battery negative (-) lead (see Chapter 8) before carrying out any test on the wiring loom.*

7 If a fault is indicated, first check the wiring and connectors between the ECU and the various sensors and all their related components. It may be that a connector is dirty or corroded or has come loose – a dirty or corroded terminal or connector will affect the resistance in that circuit, which will distort the information going to the ECU, and therefore affect its output control signals. To deter corrosion, spray the wiring loom connector pins lightly with electrical contact cleaner.

8 A wire could be pinched and is shorting out – a continuity test of wires from connector to connector will locate this. Albeit a fiddly and laborious task, the only way to determine any wiring faults is to systematically work through the wiring diagrams at the end of Chapter 8 and test each individual wire and connector for continuity – all wires are colour-coded. The wiring diagrams show the terminal number for each wire on the ECU – match these to the terminals on the ECU connector when making the tests (see illustration 16.7b).

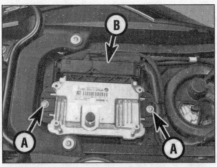
16.2 Location of the ECU on GS models. Note the mounting screws (A) and multi-pin connectors (B)

16.6b . . . then release the wiring connector

16 ECU removal and installation

⚠️ *Warning: Refer to the Warning given in Section 1 before starting work.*

Removal

1 Disconnect the battery negative (-ve) lead (see Chapter 8).

GS models

2 Remove the seat (see Chapter 7). The ECU is located on the frame to the rear of the fuel pump (see illustration).

3 Undo the screws securing the ECU brackets and lift it up.

16.6a Release the tie securing the ZFE wiring . . .

16.6c Lift the ZFE out of its holder

4 Release the ties securing the ECU wiring, then release the catches securing the two multi-pin wiring connectors and disconnect the connectors.

S, ST and R models

5 Remove the seat and both bodywork side panels (see Chapter 7).

6 Release the tie securing the wiring for the central vehicle electronics control unit (ZFE), then release the catch securing the ZFE wiring connector (see illustrations). Unhook the strap securing the ZFE and draw it out of its holder (see illustration).

7 Release the catches securing the two ECU multi-pin wiring connectors and disconnect the connectors (see illustrations).

8 Lift the ECU out of its holder (see illustration).

16.7a Disconnect the engine wiring harness connector . . .

16.7b . . . and the main wiring harness connector

16.8 Lift the ECU out of its holder

17.2 Location of the ignition timing sensor

17.3a Release the cable-tie . . .

17.3b . . . and disconnect the wiring connector

Installation

9 Installation is the reverse of removal, noting the following:

● Ensure that the terminals in the multi-pin connectors are clean and undamaged.
● Spray the connector pins lightly with electrical contact cleaner.
● Ensure the connectors are locked in position with the catches.

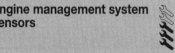

17 Engine management system sensors

Warning: Refer to the Warning given in Section 1 before starting work.

17.5a Undo the screw securing the ignition timing sensor . . .

Note 1: *Before disconnecting the wiring connector from any sensor, make sure the ignition is switched OFF, then disconnect the battery negative lead (see Chapter 8).*
Note 2: *Test specifications, where given, were obtained from machines used to illustrate the accompanying procedure.*
Note 3: *If a new sensor is fitted the machine must be taken to a BMW dealer so that the engine management system adaptation values can be reset to recognise the new component.*

Ignition timing sensor

Function

1 The sensor reads the position of the crankshaft and how fast it is turning. This

17.5b . . . and pull it out of the casing

information is used by the ECU to determine which cylinder is on its ignition stroke and when it should fire. The ECU combines engine speed with information from other sensors to determine fuelling and ignition requirements.

Removal and installation

2 The ignition timing sensor is located on the rear top edge of the alternator housing **(see illustration)**. On GS and R models, remove the front sprocket cover for access (see Chapter 6, Section 18). On S and ST models, remove the front pulley cover for access (see Chapter 6, Section 19).
3 Release the tie securing the wiring and disconnect the connector **(see illustrations)**.
4 No test details are provided for the sensor, however its resistance can be measured with a multimeter set to the ohms scale. Measure the resistance between the terminals on the sensor side of the connector – on the machine used to illustrate this procedure the resistance measured 667 ohms. If the result varies greatly it is likely that the sensor is faulty – have it checked by a BMW dealer.
5 Undo the screw securing the sensor and pull it out **(see illustrations)**. Note the location of the O-ring and discard it as a new one must be fitted **(see illustration)**.
6 The sensor is activated by the triggers on the outside of the alternator rotor **(see illustration)**. To inspect the triggers, follow the procedure in Chapter 8 and remove the cover.

17.5c Note the location of the O-ring

17.6 Sensor tip (A) and triggers (B)

17.9a Location of the camshaft position sensor – GS models

17.9b Location of the camshaft position sensor – S, ST and R models

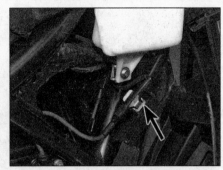

17.11a Sensor wiring connector – GS models

7 Installation is the reverse of removal, noting the following:
● Fit a new O-ring to the sensor and lubricate it with a smear of clean engine oil.
● Tighten the sensor screw to the torque setting specified at the beginning of this Chapter.
● Ensure the terminals in the wiring connector are clean.
● Ensure the wiring is securely connected.
● Renew any cable-ties.

Camshaft position sensor

Function

8 The sensor reads the position of the camshaft and how fast it is turning. This information is used by the ECU to determine which cylinder is on its ignition stroke and when it should fire.

Removal and installation

9 The camshaft position sensor is located on the right-hand side of the cylinder head, forward of the water pump (see illustrations).
10 Remove the right-hand bodywork side panel to access the sensor wiring connector (see Chapter 7).
11 On GS models, unclip the wiring connector from the back of the radiator heat shield (see illustration). On all other models, release the cable-tie securing the connector and free the wiring from the clip on the side of the air filter housing (see illustration). Disconnect the sensor wiring connector (see illustration).
12 No test details are provided for the sensor,

17.11b Sensor wiring connector – S, ST and R models

however its resistance can be measured with a multimeter set to the ohms scale. Measure the resistance between the terminals on the sensor side of the connector – on the machine used to illustrate this procedure the resistance measured 768 ohms. If the result varies greatly it is likely that the sensor is faulty – have it checked by a BMW dealer.
13 To access the sensor on GS models (see illustration 17.9a), first displace the upper coolant hose between the cylinder head and the radiator; on all other models (see illustration 17.9b), it may be necessary to displace both coolant hoses (see Chapter 3).
14 Undo the screw securing the sensor and pull it out (see illustrations). Note the location of the O-ring and discard it as a new one must be fitted (see illustration).
15 The sensor is activated by a trigger on the right-hand end of the exhaust camshaft. To inspect the trigger, follow the procedure

17.11c Disconnect the sensor wiring connector

in Chapter 2, Section 8, to remove the camshaft.
16 Installation is the reverse of removal, noting the following:
● Fit a new O-ring to the sensor and lubricate it with a smear of clean engine oil.
● Tighten the sensor screw to the torque setting specified at the beginning of this Chapter.
● Ensure the terminals in the wiring connector are clean.
● Ensure the wiring is securely connected.
● Renew any cable-ties.

Intake air temperature sensor
Function

17 The sensor reads the temperature of the air in the air filter housing. Because changes in temperature affect air density, the ECU uses the information to determine fuelling requirements.

17.14a Undo the screw securing the camshaft position sensor . . .

17.14b . . . and pull it out of the cylinder head

17.14c Note the location of the O-ring

17.18 Disconnect the IAT sensor wiring connector – GS models

17.19 Disconnect the IAT sensor wiring connector – S, ST and R models

Removal and installation

18 On GS models, the intake air temperature sensor is located at the rear of the air filter housing **(see illustration 2.3)**. Remove the bodywork centre panel to access the sensor (see Chapter 7). Disconnect the wiring connector **(see illustration)**.

19 On S, ST and R models, the intake air temperature sensor is located at the front of the air filter housing **(see illustration 2.14)**. Remove the bodywork centre panel to access the sensor (see Chapter 7). Disconnect the wiring connector **(see illustrations)**.

20 No test details are provided for the sensor, however its resistance can be measured with a multimeter set to the K-ohms scale. Measure the resistance between the terminals on the sensor side of the connector – on the machine used to illustrate this procedure the resistance measured 6.77 K-ohms **(see illustration)**. If the result varies greatly it is likely that the sensor is faulty – have it checked by a BMW dealer.

21 Draw the sensor out form the housing **(see illustration)**. Check the condition of the sensor O-ring and renew it if it is deformed or deteriorated.

22 Installation is the reverse of removal, noting the following:

● Lubricate the O-ring with a smear of clean engine oil.
● Ensure the terminals in the wiring connector are clean.
● Ensure the wiring is securely connected.

Idle actuator

Function

23 The idle actuator meters the engine's air supply when the throttle butterflies are closed, and ensures a smooth engine response when the throttle is first opened.

Removal and installation

24 On GS models, the idle actuator is located on the lower right-hand side of the air filter housing **(see illustration 2.4)**. Remove the right-hand bodywork side panel to access the actuator (see Chapter 7). Disconnect the wiring connector. Undo the screws securing the actuator and draw it out from the housing. Check the condition of the actuator O-ring and renew it if it is deformed or deteriorated.

25 On all other models, the idle actuator is located on the underside of the air filter housing **(see illustration 2.17)**. Follow the procedure in Section 2 to remove the housing, then undo the screws securing the actuator and lift it off together with the union for the air

hoses. Separate the union from the actuator and check the condition of the actuator O-ring – renew it if it is deformed or deteriorated.

26 No test details are available for the actuator – if it is thought to be faulty, first check the air hoses are in good condition and are securely connected. If the hoses are good, have the actuator checked by a BMW dealer.

27 Installation is the reverse of removal, noting the following:

● Lubricate the O-ring with a smear of clean engine oil.
● Ensure the air hoses securely connected.
● Ensure the terminals in the wiring connector are clean.
● Ensure the wiring is securely connected.

Gear position sensor

28 The sensor monitors the position of the selector drum in the gearbox and the ECU uses the information, combined with engine speed, to determine fuelling and ignition requirements.

Removal and installation

29 The gear position sensor is located on the lower right-hand side of the crankcase, below the front sprocket (GS and R models) or the front pulley (S and ST models) **(see illustration)**. Remove the sprocket or pulley cover, as

17.20 Measuring the IAT sensor resistance

17.21 Draw the sensor out from the housing

17.29 Location of the gear position sensor

17.31a Disconnect the connector . . .

17.31b . . . and unclip the wiring from the crankcase

applicable, for access (see Chapter 6). If the casing behind the cover is dirty, particularly on a chain-driven model, wash it thoroughly – this will make work much easier and rule out the possibility of dirt getting inside.

30 On GS models, displace the regulator/rectifier to access the sensor wiring connector (see Chapter 8).

31 On some S models, the sensor wiring connects directly into the sensor – release the wiring from the clip on the crankcase and disconnect the connector. On all other machines, trace the wiring to the connector and release the tie securing the wiring **(see illustration 17.3a)**. Disconnect the connector and unclip the wiring from the crankcase **(see illustrations)**.

32 No test details are available for the sensor – if it is thought to be faulty, first check the wiring and wiring connector. If they are good, have the sensor checked by a BMW dealer.

33 Undo the bolts securing the sensor and lift it off, noting how the selector drum shaft engages in the centre of the sensor **(see illustrations)**. Check the condition of the sensor O-ring and renew it if it is deformed or deteriorated **(see illustration)**.

34 Installation is the reverse of removal, noting the following:

● Lubricate the O-ring with a smear of clean engine oil.
● Tighten the sensor bolts to the torque setting specified at the beginning of this Chapter.

● Ensure the terminals in the wiring connector are clean.
● Ensure the wiring is securely connected.
● Renew any cable-ties and secure the wiring with the clip.

Fuel pressure sensor

35 See Section 7 for details.

Throttle position sensor

36 See Section 9 for details.

Oxygen sensor

37 See Section 12 for details.

Coolant temperature sensor

38 See Chapter 3 for details.

17.33a Undo the bolts securing the sensor . . .

17.33b . . . and lift it off

17.33c Note the location of the O-ring

Chapter 5
Frame and suspension

Contents

	Section		Section
Footrests, gearchange lever and brake pedal	3	Rear shock absorber adjustment	12
Fork oil change	7	Sidestand and centrestand	4
Fork overhaul	8	Sidestand switch	see Chapter 9
Fork removal and installation	6	Stand lubrication	see Chapter 1
Frame inspection and repair	2	Steering head bearing check and adjustment	see Chapter 1
General information	1	Steering head bearings and races	10
Handlebars and levers	5	Steering stem	9
Handlebar switches	see Chapter 9	Suspension check	see Chapter 1
Rear shock absorber	11	Swingarm	13

Degrees of difficulty

| Easy, suitable for novice with little experience | 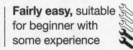 | Fairly easy, suitable for beginner with some experience | | Fairly difficult, suitable for competent DIY mechanic | | Difficult, suitable for experienced DIY mechanic | | Very difficult, suitable for expert DIY or professional | |

Specifications

Front forks

Fork leg installed height
F650 GS	fixed (see text)
F800 GS (above top yoke)	7.8 mm
F800 S and ST (above bottom yoke)	245 mm
F800 R (above top yoke)	14 mm

Fork oil type
F650 GS and F800 GS	SAE 7.5 fork oil
F800 S, ST and R	SAE 10 fork oil

Fork oil capacity (approx.)
F650 GS	530 ml
F800 GS	765 ml
F800 S and ST	520 ml
F800 R	584 ml

Fork oil level (see text)
F650 GS	100 mm
F800 GS	60 mm
F800 S and ST	120 mm
F800 R	94 mm

Fork spring free length
F650 GS	
Standard	378 to 382 mm
Service limit	376 mm
F800 GS	
Standard	473 to 477 mm
Service limit	471 mm
F800 S and ST	440 mm
F800 R	453 mm

Rear suspension

Spring pre-load adjustment
 F650 GS and F800 GS
  Min pre-load . . . . Turn adjuster fully anti-clockwise
  Max pre-load . . . . Turn adjuster fully clockwise
  Standard setting . . . . Min pre-load
 F800 S, ST and R
  Min pre-load . . . . Turn adjuster fully anti-clockwise
  Max pre-load . . . . Turn adjuster fully clockwise
  Standard setting . . . . 12 clicks back from min
Damping adjustment
 F650 GS
  Min . . . . Turn adjuster fully anti-clockwise
  Max . . . . Turn adjuster fully clockwise
  Standard setting . . . . 2 turns back from max
 F800 GS, S and ST
  Min . . . . Turn adjuster fully anti-clockwise
  Max . . . . Turn adjuster fully clockwise
  Standard setting . . . . 1 1/2 turns back from max
 F800 R
  Min . . . . Turn adjuster fully anti-clockwise
  Max . . . . Turn adjuster fully clockwise
  Standard setting . . . . 3/4 turn back from max

Torque settings

Brake pedal pivot bolt
 F650 GS and F800 GS . . . . 19 Nm
 F800 S, ST and R models . . . . 20 Nm
Brake lever pivot bolt . . . . 19 Nm
Clutch lever bracket bolts . . . . 5 Nm
Front brake master cylinder clamp bolts . . . . 5 Nm
Footrest bracket bolts
 F650 GS and F800 GS . . . . 38 Nm
 F800 S, ST and R models
  Left-hand . . . . 22 Nm
  Right-hand (M8 x 70 mm) . . . . 22 Nm
  Right-hand (M8 x 55 mm) . . . . 20 Nm
Fork damper bolt
 F650 GS and F800 GS . . . . 50 Nm
 F800 S, ST and R . . . . 20 Nm
Fork damper rod locknut (F800 GS) . . . . 20 Nm
Fork top bolt
 F800 GS . . . . 20 Nm
 F800 R . . . . 22 Nm
Fork clamp bolts
 F650 GS
  Top and bottom yoke . . . . 19 Nm
 F800 GS
  Top yoke . . . . 19 Nm
  Bottom yoke . . . . 20 Nm
 F800 S, ST and R
  Top yoke . . . . 20 Nm
  Bottom yoke . . . . 25 Nm
Gearchange arm pinch bolt – F800 S, ST and R models . . . . 9 Nm
Gearchange lever pinch bolt – F650 GS and F800 GS . . . . 8 Nm
Gearchange lever pivot bolt – F800 S, ST and R models . . . . 20 Nm
Handlebars
 F650 GS, F800 GS and F800 R
  Handlebar clamp bolts . . . . 28 Nm
 F800 S
  Handlebar locating screw . . . . 5 Nm
  Handlebar clamp bolts . . . . 9 Nm
 F800 ST
  Handlebar clamp bolts . . . . 20 Nm
Heel plate bolts – GS models . . . . 8 Nm
Rear sub-frame mounting bolts . . . . 50 Nm
Sidestand pivot bolt . . . . 40 Nm
Steering damper mounting bolts . . . . 20 Nm

Torque settings (contiued)

Steering head bearing adjuster bolt
  Initial setting . . . . 25 Nm
  Second setting . . . . 60° anti-clockwise
  Final setting . . . . 10 Nm
Steering stem clamp bolt (F650 GS and F800 GS) . . . . 19 Nm
Steering stem clamp bolt (F800 S, ST and R) . . . . 25 Nm
Shock absorber
  F650 GS and F800 GS
    Top and bottom mounting bolt . . . . 100 Nm
  F800 S, ST and R
    Top and bottom mounting bolt/nut . . . . 45 Nm
Swingarm pivot bolt nut – F650 GS, F800 GS . . . . 100 Nm
Swingarm shaft clamp bolts – F800 S, ST and R . . . . 40 Nm

1 General information

F650 GS and F800 GS models have tubular steel trellis frames which use the engine as a stressed member. On F800 S, ST and R models, the twin spar frame is made from aluminium.

Front suspension on F650 GS and F800 S, ST and R models is by conventional, oil-damped telescopic forks. Upside-down type forks are fitted to F800 GS models. The front forks on all models are non-adjustable.

At the rear, F650 GS, F800 GS and R models are equipped with an aluminium, twin-sided swingarm. F800 S and ST models have an aluminium, single-sided swingarm. Suspension movement is controlled by a single shock absorber mounted directly between the frame and the swingarm. The shock is adjustable for spring pre-load and rebound damping. On F800 S, ST and R models, the swingarm pivot shaft is held between clamps that are cast integrally with the crankcases.

2 Frame inspection and repair

1 The frame should not require attention unless accident damage has occurred. In most cases, fitting a new frame is the only satisfactory remedy for such damage. A few frame specialists have the jigs and other equipment necessary for straightening frames to the required standard of accuracy, but even then there is no simple way of assessing to what extent the frame may have been over stressed.
2 After a high mileage, examine the frame closely for signs of cracking or splitting at the welded joints. Loose engine mounting bolts can cause ovaling or fracturing of the mounting points. Minor damage can often be repaired by specialised welding, depending on the extent and nature of the damage.
3 Remember that a frame that is out of alignment will cause handling problems. If, as the result of an accident, misalignment is suspected, refer to Chapter 6 and check the wheel alignment first. If the frame is damaged, it will be necessary to strip the machine completely so the frame can be thoroughly checked by a specialist using a frame alignment jig.

3 Footrests, gearchange lever and brake pedal

Rider's footrests

1 The footrest is secured by the pivot pin (see illustration). Note the location of the footrest return spring, then remove the split pin on the underside of the footrest bracket, pull out the pivot pin and remove the footrest (see illustration). If required undo the screws and separate the rubber from the footrest – all components are available separately.
2 Installation is the reverse of removal. Apply a small amount of grease to the pivot pin and the sliding surfaces of mated parts. Secure the pivot pin with a new split pin.

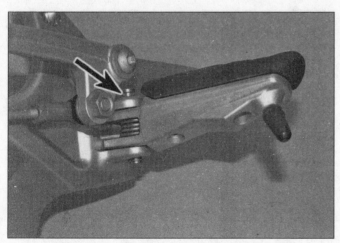
3.1a Rider's footrest is secured by the pivot pin

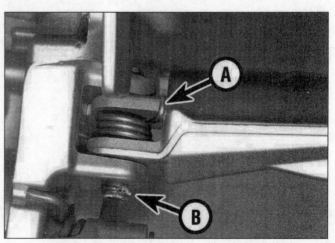
3.1b Note the return spring (A) and the split pin (B)

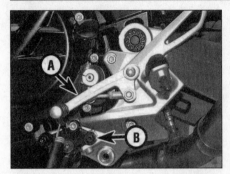

3.3a Gearchange lever (A) and sidestand bracket (B)

3.3b Release the wire clip . . .

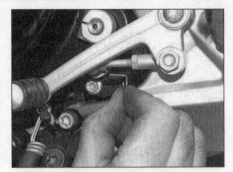

3.3c . . . and pull it out

3.4 Location of the sidestand switch wiring connector

3.5a Bracket mounting bolts – left-hand side

3.5b Note the location of the special washers

Footrest brackets

Left-hand

3 On S, ST and R models, the gearchange lever and the sidestand are mounted on the left-hand footrest bracket (see illustration). Before removing the bracket, release the wire clip securing the gearchange rod ball-and-socket to the gearchange arm and separate the rod from the arm (see illustrations).

4 Trace the wiring from the sidestand switch, located on the back of the stand bracket, and disconnect it at the connector (see illustration). Note the routing of the wiring. Release the wiring from any clips or ties and feed it back to the footrest bracket.

5 Undo the bracket mounting bolts (see illustration). Note the position of the bolts and the location of the special washers between the bracket and the frame (see illustration). Lift the bracket off, noting how the sidestand switch wiring is clipped to the back of the bracket (see illustration).

6 Follow the procedure in Step 23 to remove the gearchange lever. Follow the procedure in Section 4 to remove the sidestand.

7 Installation is the reverse of removal, noting the following:

● Secure the sidestand switch wiring with any clips or ties.

● Ensure the sidestand switch wiring connector is secure.

● Install the special washers on the bracket mounting bolts.

● Tighten the mounting bolts to the torque setting specified at the beginning of this Chapter.

● Ensure the gearchange rod ball-and-socket is secured with the wire clip.

Right-hand

8 On S, ST and R models, the rear brake pedal, master cylinder and brake switch are mounted on the right-hand footrest bracket (see illustration). Before removing the

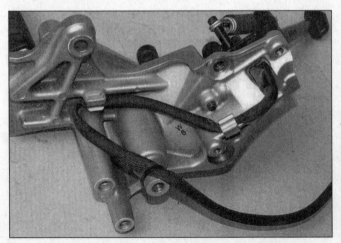

3.5c Note how the wiring is clipped to the bracket

3.8a Rear brake pedal (A) and master cylinder (B)

3.8b Release the clip and withdraw the clevis pin

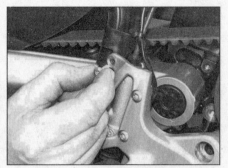

3.9a Undo the screw securing the brake hose guide

3.9b Undo the screws and nuts securing the master cylinder

3.10a Bracket mounting bolts – right-hand side

3.10b Note the location of the special washers

3.10c Note the brake light switch wiring

bracket, release the clip securing the clevis pin on the master cylinder pushrod, then withdraw the pin and separate the pushrod from the pedal **(see illustration)**.

9 On GS models, undo the screw securing the brake hose guide to the heel plate and undo the screws and nuts securing the master cylinder to the heel plate **(see illustrations)**.

10 Undo the bracket mounting bolts **(see illustration)**. Note the position of the bolts and the location of the special washers between the bracket and the frame **(see illustration)**. Lift the bracket off, noting how the brake light switch wiring is clipped to the back of the bracket **(see illustration)**. Undo the screw securing the switch and remove it **(see illustration)**.

11 Follow the procedure in Step 28 to remove the brake pedal.

12 Installation is the reverse of removal, noting the following:

● Secure the brake light switch wiring with any clips or ties.
● Install the special washers on the bracket mounting bolts.
● Tighten the mounting bolts to the torque setting specified at the beginning of this Chapter.

Heel plates – GS models

13 To remove the left-hand heel plate, undo the bolts securing the plate to the frame and lift it off **(see illustration)**.

14 The bolts securing the right-hand heel

plate also support the rear brake master cylinder **(see illustration)**. Undo the bolts and remove the plate, then temporarily install the bolts to support the master cylinder.

15 Installation is the reverse of removal. When installing the right-hand plate, clean the threads of the mounting bolts and apply a suitable non-permanent thread-locking compound. Tighten the bolts to the torque setting specified at the beginning of this Chapter.

Passenger's footrests

16 On S, ST and R models, the footrests are held in position (fully up or down) by a

3.10d Brake light switch mounting screw (arrowed)

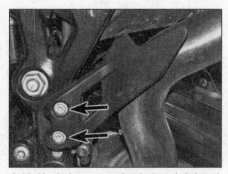

3.13 Heel plate mounting bolts – left-hand side

3.14 Heel plate mounting bolts – right-hand side

3.16 Location of the ball and detent plate

3.17 Pivot pin is secured by an E-clip

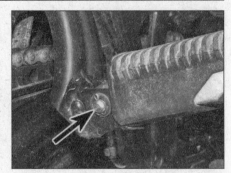

3.19 Pivot pin is secured by split pin and washer

spring-loaded ball and detent plate **(see illustration)**.

17 The footrest is secured by the pivot pin **(see illustration)**. Remove the E-clip on the underside of the footrest bracket, pull out the pivot pin and remove the footrest – take care not to loose the ball and spring. If required undo the screws and separate the rubber from the footrest – all components are available separately.

18 Installation is the reverse of removal. Apply a small amount of grease to the pivot pin and the sliding surfaces of mated parts. Check the operation of the detent ball, then secure the pivot pin using a new E-clip if required.

19 On GS models, the footrests are held in position (fully up or down) by the pressure of the footrest rubber against the bracket. Remove the split pin and washer on the rear of the footrest bracket, pull out the pivot pin and remove the footrest **(see illustration)**.

20 To remove the rubber, lift the end up and pull it off the footrest.

21 Installation is the reverse of removal. Apply a small amount of grease to the pivot pin and the sliding surfaces of mated parts. Secure the pivot pin with a new split pin.

Gearchange lever

Removal

22 On GS models, the lever is mounted on the end of the gearchange shaft – note the register mark on the casing that aligns with the slot in the lever **(see illustration)**. **Note:** *On some machines there are two register marks – see Step 24.* Unscrew and remove the pinch bolt and pull the lever off the shaft.

23 On all other models, the lever is mounted on the left-hand footrest bracket **(see illustration 3.3a)**. Follow the procedure in Step 3 to separate the rod from the gearchange arm. Undo the pivot bolt and washer and

pull the lever off **(see illustration)**. Note the location of the bush on the footrest bracket. Check for any wear in the bush and replace it with a new one if necessary.

24 To remove the gearchange arm, first note the register mark on the casing that aligns with the slot in the lever – if there are two marks, the slot should be aligned with the line on the casing **(see illustration)**. Unscrew and remove the pinch bolt and pull the arm off the shaft **(see illustration)**.

Installation

25 On GS models, installation is the reverse of removal. Tighten the pinch bolt to the torque setting specified at the beginning of this Chapter.

26 On all other models, installation of the gearchange arm is the reverse of removal. Tighten the pinch bolt to the torque setting specified at the beginning of this Chapter.

27 Before installing the lever, clean the threads of the pivot bolt and apply a suitable non-permanent thread-locking compound. Apply a smear of grease to the bush on the footrest bracket and the ball socket on the rod. Secure the lever with the pivot bolt and washer and tighten the bolt to the specified torque setting. Connect the rod ball-and-socket and secure it with the wire clip.

Brake pedal

Removal

28 Follow the procedure in Step 8 to separate the master cylinder pushrod from the pedal. Note the location of the pedal return spring – take care when removing the lever as it is held under tension **(see illustration)**. Undo the

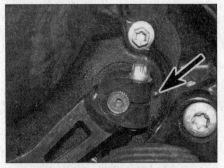

3.22 Register mark (arrowed) should align with slot in the lever

3.23 Gearchange lever pivot bolt

3.24a Register mark (arrowed) should align with slot in the lever

3.24b Remove the pinch bolt and pull the arm off

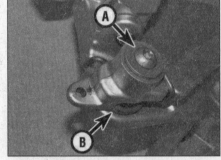

3.28 Brake pedal pivot bolt (A) and return spring (B)

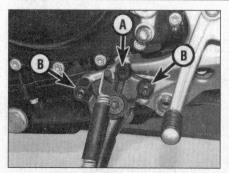

4.3 Footrest bracket bolt (A) and sidestand bracket bolts (B)

4.4a Nut (arrowed) secures sidestand switch

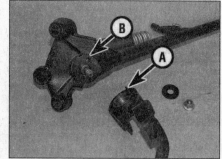

4.4b Note how tab (A) locates in hole (B)

pivot bolt and washer and lift the lever, pivot bush and spring off.

29 Check for any wear in the bush and replace it with a new one if necessary.

Installation

30 Before installing the pedal, clean the threads of the pivot bolt and apply a suitable non-permanent thread-locking compound. Apply a smear of grease to the bush. Assemble the lever, bush, pivot bolt and washer and spring, then secure the assembly to the machine ensuring the return spring locates correctly (see illustration 3.28).

31 Make sure the pedal locates correctly against the brake light switch, then tighten the pivot bolt to the torque setting specified at the beginning of this Chapter

32 Align the master cylinder pushrod with the pedal, install the clevis pin and secure the clip (see illustration 3.8b).

33 Check the operation of the rear brake light switch (see Chapter 8).

4 Sidestand and centrestand

Sidestand

Removal

1 Support the bike on the centrestand or an auxiliary stand.

2 If required, unhook the stand springs.

3 Undo the footrest bracket bolt that passes through the stand bracket, then loosen the bolts securing the stand (see illustration). Note the location of the special washer on the bracket bolt (see illustration 3.5b).

4 Support the stand and remove the bolts, then turn the stand over to access the nut securing the sidestand switch (see illustration). Remove the nut and washer, then lift the switch off, noting how it fits (see illustration).

5 If required, undo the pivot bolt and separate the stand from its bracket, noting the location of the pivot bush. Check for any wear in the bush and replace it with a new one if necessary.

Installation

6 Prior to installation, lubricate the stand bracket and pivot bush with a smear of grease.

7 Clean the threads of the pivot bolt and apply a suitable non-permanent thread-locking compound.

8 Fit the stand and bush onto the stand bracket, install the pivot bolt and tighten it to the torque setting specified at the beginning of this Chapter. Check that the stand pivots freely around the bolt.

9 Hook the upper ends of the springs over the lug on the bracket, then pull the springs down and hook them over the lug on the stand (see illustration). Note: It is essential that the springs are in good condition and are capable of holding the stand up when not in use.

10 Install the switch, ensuring the tab is correctly located (see illustration 4.4b).

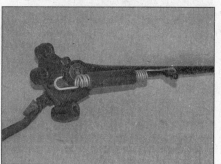

4.9 Installed position of the sidestand springs

4.11 Note how outside tab (arrowed) on switch locates

4.14a Location of centrestand springs

4.14b Remove the pivot bolts on both sides

Secure the switch with the washer and nut.

11 Install the stand, ensuring the switch is correctly located into the recess in the footrest bracket (see illustration).

12 Install the mounting bolts and tighten them securely. Install the footrest bracket bolt (see Section 3).

Centrestand

Removal

13 Support the bike securely on the sidestand or an auxiliary stand.

14 Unhook the stand springs (see illustration). Unscrew the nut and remove the washer from each pivot bolt (see illustration). Support the stand, remove the pivot bolts and remove the stand.

15 Remove the bush from each pivot. Check for any wear in the bushes and renew them if necessary.

Installation

16 Installation is the reverse of removal, noting the following:

● Clean the stand mounting brackets and pivot bushes.
● Lubricate the bushes with a smear of grease.
● Tighten the pivot bolts securely and check that the stand pivots freely around the bolts.
● Secure the spring ends correctly **(see illustration 4.14a)**.

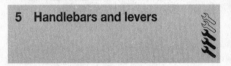

5 Handlebars and levers

Handlebars – S models

Removal

Note: *If required, the handlebars can be displaced individually once access has been gained to the screws securing the locating brackets (see Step 13). Secure the bars to ensure no strain is placed on the brake hose, clutch cable or wiring. Keep the brake fluid reservoir upright to prevent air entering the system.*

1 Remove the bodywork centre panel and both side panels to avoid damaging the paintwork (see Chapter 7).
2 Disconnect the front brake light switch wiring connector **(see illustration)**.
3 Undo both handlebar end-weight screws

5.5a Undo the screws (arrowed) . . .

5.2 Location of the front brake light switch connector

5.4a Screws secure front half of switch housing

5.5b . . . and remove the rear half of the switch housing

5.3 Handlebar end-weight screw

5.4b Disconnect the wiring connectors

and remove the weights, noting the location of the washers between the weights and the ends of the handlebar **(see illustration)**.
4 Undo the right-hand switch housing screws

and remove the front half **(see illustration)**. Displace the wiring connectors for the switch housing and, if fitted, the heated handlebar grip, and disconnect them **(see illustration)**.
5 Undo the screws securing the rear half of the switch housing and lift it off **(see illustrations)**.
6 Disconnect the throttle cable from the twistgrip pulley and pull the cable out of the housing (see Chapter 4).
7 Loosen the screw securing the twistgrip clamp **(see illustration)**. Draw the twistgrip off the handlebar.
8 Note the alignment punch mark for the front brake master cylinder clamp **(see illustration)**. Undo the bolts securing the bracket for the front brake master cylinder reservoir and the master cylinder clamp, then lift the assembly off **(see illustration)**.

5.7 Screw (arrowed) secures the twistgrip clamp

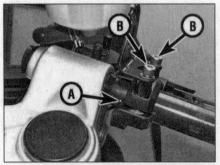

5.8a Alignment punch mark (A) and master cylinder clamp bolts (B)

5.8b Remove the brake master cylinder and reservoir assembly off

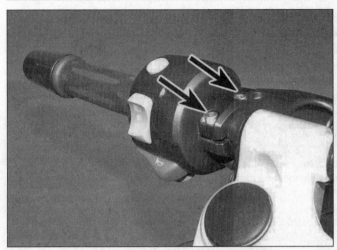

5.9a Clutch lever bracket bolts (arrowed)

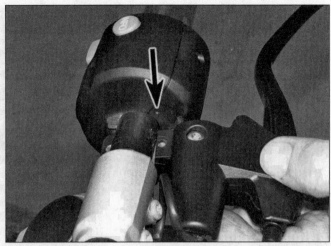

5.9b Alignment punch mark (arrowed)

Temporarily reassemble the clamp and reservoir bracket and secure the assembly clear of the handlebar to ensure no strain is placed on the brake hose. Keep the fluid reservoir upright to prevent air entering the system.

9 Undo the bolts securing the clutch lever bracket and remove it, noting the alignment mark on the switch housing **(see illustrations)**. If required, turn the lever over and disconnect the clutch switch wiring connector **(see illustration)**.

10 Undo the left-hand switch housing screws and remove the front half **(see illustrations)**. Displace the wiring connectors for the switch housing and, if fitted, the heated handlebar grip, and disconnect them **(see illustration)**.

11 Undo the screws securing the rear half of the switch housing and lift it off **(see illustrations)**.

12 Pull back the inner edge of the handlebar grip on the underside and undo the screw securing the grip **(see illustration)**. Draw the grip off the handlebar.

13 To remove the left and right-hand handlebars, undo the screw securing the locating bracket, then undo the clamp bolts

5.9c Clutch switch wiring connector

5.10a Undo the screws (arrowed) . . .

5.10b . . . and remove the front half of the switch housing

5.10c Disconnect the wiring connectors

5.11a Undo the screws (arrowed) . . .

5.11b . . . and remove the rear half of the switch housing

5.12 Undo the screw securing the grip

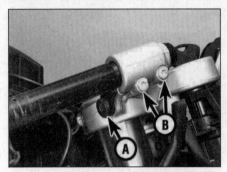

5.13 Undo screw (A) and clamp bolts (B)

5.14 Alignment mark on switch housing (arrowed)

5.19 Location of handlebar alignment mark – GS models

(see illustration). Draw the handlebar out of its mounting.

Installation

14 Installation is the reverse of removal, noting the following:
● Align the clutch lever bracket with the mark on the switch housing (see illustration 5.9b).
● Align the front brake master cylinder clamp with the punch mark on the handlebar (see illustration 5.8a).
● Align the mark on the right-hand switch housing with the mating surfaces of the front brake master cylinder clamp (see illustration).
● Tighten the handlebar, front brake master cylinder and clutch lever clamp/bracket bolts to the torque settings specified at the beginning of this Chapter.

Handlebars – GS, ST and R models

Removal

Note: If required, the handlebars can be displaced from the top yoke without displacing or removing the front brake master cylinder, clutch lever, cables or switch housings (see Steps 19 to 21). Secure the bars to ensure no strain is placed on the brake hose, clutch cable or wiring. Keep the brake fluid reservoir upright to prevent air entering the system.
15 Remove the bodywork centre panel and both side panels to avoid damaging the paintwork (see Chapter 7).
16 On GS and R models, remove the mirrors (see Chapter 7).
17 Cut any cable-ties on the handlebars.
18 Follow the procedure in Steps 2 to 12 to remove the end-weights, switch housings,

throttle twistgrip, front brake master cylinder, clutch lever and left-hand handlebar grip.
19 On GS models, loosen the handlebar clamp bolts, then support the handlebars and remove the bolts and clamps – note the alignment mark on the handlebars (see illustration).
20 On ST models, loosen the handlebar clamp bolts, then support the handlebars and remove the bolts and clamps – note the alignment mark on the handlebars (see illustration).
21 On R models, note the alignment marks on the front of the handlebar clamps (see illustration). Loosen the clamp bolts, then support the handlebars and remove the bolts and clamps – note the alignment marks on the handlebars (see illustration).

Installation

22 Installation is the reverse of removal, noting the following:
● Ensure the handlebar clamps are positioned correctly.
● Tighten the front clamp bolts first, then the rear clamp bolts
● Tighten the clamp bolts to the torque settings specified at the beginning of this Chapter.
● Note the points in Step 14 regarding the alignment between the front brake master cylinder and clutch lever clamps and the switch housings.
● Tighten the front brake master cylinder and clutch lever clamp/bracket bolts to the torque settings specified at the beginning of this Chapter.

Front brake lever

23 To remove the front brake lever, first undo the locknut on the underside of the lever pivot screw (see illustration). Pull out the pivot screw and withdraw the lever assembly from the bracket, noting the location of the spring between the lever and the pushrod pivot. Note the location of the bush for the pivot screw.
24 Prior to installation, apply silicone grease to the contact area between the pushrod tip and the brake lever, to the pivot screw and bush, and to the contact areas between the lever and its bracket.
25 To install the front brake lever, first insert

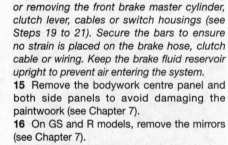

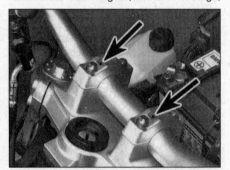

5.20 Location of handlebar alignment mark – ST models

5.21a Alignment marks (arrowed) on handlebar clamps – R models

5.21b Note handlebar alignment marks – R models

5.23 Undo locknut on the underside of brake lever pivot screw (arrowed)

5.27 Undo locknut on the underside of clutch lever pivot screw (arrowed)

the pushrod pivot into the bracket, ensuring the inner end of the pushrod locates against the master cylinder piston. Install the spring and bush in the pushrod pivot. Install the lever and secure it with the pivot screw and nut. Counter-hold the nut and tighten the screw securely. Ensure the lever moves smoothly.

26 Check the operation of the front brake before riding the motorcycle.

Clutch lever

27 To remove the clutch lever, first slacken the cable and disconnect it from the lever (see Chapter 2, Section 15). Undo the locknut on the underside of the pivot screw **(see illustration)**. Pull out the pivot screw and withdraw the lever assembly from the bracket.

28 Prior to installation, apply silicone grease to the pivot screw and to the contact areas between the lever and its bracket. Fit the lever into the bracket and secure it with the pivot screw and nut. Counter-hold the nut and tighten the screw securely. Ensure the lever moves smoothly.

29 Install the clutch cable and adjust the freeplay (see Chapter 1, Section 4).

---

6 Fork removal and installation

Removal

1 Remove the bodywork centre panel and both side panels to avoid damaging the paintwoork (see Chapter 7).

2 Remove the front wheel and, on machines equipped with ABS, displace the front wheel speed sensor (see Chapter 6).

3 Remove the front mudguard (see Chapter 7).

4 On R models, undo the bolts securing the fork brace and remove it **(see illustration)**.

5 Working on one fork leg at a time, note the routing of any cables, hoses and wiring around the forks. Note the position of the top of the fork tubes in relation to the top yoke.

6 On F650 GS models, a wire stop is held by the left-hand clamp bolt in the top yoke – the stop should rest on the cap in the top of the fork tube **(see illustration)**. The right-hand fork tube should be installed to match.

7 On S and ST models, the fork tubes are installed so that the distance between the top edge of the bottom yoke and the top edge of the tube measures 245 mm **(see illustration)**.

8 On R models, the distance between the top edge of the top bolt hex and the top edge of the top yoke measures 14 mm **(see illustration)**.

9 On F800 GS models, the distance between the top edge of the top yoke and the top

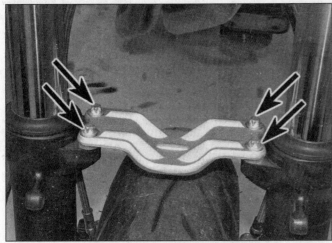

6.4 Bolts secure the front fork brace

6.6 Location of the wire stop – F650 GS models

6.7 Measuring fork tube installation – S and ST models

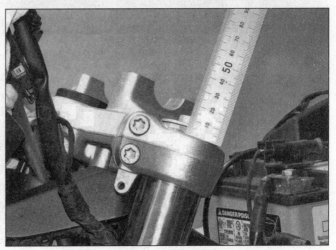

6.8 Measuring fork tube installation – R models

edge of the fork tube, excluding the top bolt, measures 7.8 mm.

10 Loosen the fork clamp bolt(s) in the top yoke (see illustrations).

11 On R and F800 GS models, if the fork is to be disassembled, or if the fork oil is being changed, loosen the fork top bolt (see illustration 6.10b).

12 Loosen the fork clamp bolts in the bottom yoke, then remove the fork leg by twisting it and pulling it downwards (see illustrations).

HAYNES HiNT *If the fork legs are seized in the yokes, spray the area with penetrating oil and allow time for it to soak in before trying again.*

Installation

13 Remove all traces of corrosion from the fork tube and the yokes. Slide the fork leg up through the bottom yoke and into the top yoke, making sure all cables, hoses and wiring are routed on the correct side of the leg.

14 Set the amount of protrusion of the fork tube above the top yoke as specified for your model (see Steps 6 to 9).

15 Tighten the fork clamp bolts in the bottom yoke evenly and a little at a time to the torque setting specified at the beginning of this Chapter (see illustration 6.12a).

16 On R and F800 GS models, if the fork has been dismantled or if the fork oil was changed, tighten the fork top bolt to the specified torque setting (see illustration 6.10b).

6.10a Top yoke fork clamp bolt – S model shown

17 Tighten the fork clamp bolt(s) in the top yoke to the specified torque (see illustrations 6.10a and b).

18 Install the remaining components in the reverse order of removal.

19 Check the operation of the front forks and brake before riding the motorcycle.

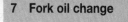
7 Fork oil change

Note: *After a high mileage the fork oil will deteriorate and its damping and lubrication qualities will be impaired. Always change the oil in both fork legs, working on one at a time.*

F800 S, ST, R and F650 GS models

1 Follow the procedure in Section 6 to remove

6.10b Top yoke fork clamp bolts – R model shown

the fork leg – on R models, make sure the top bolt is loosened while the leg is still clamped in the bottom yoke.

2 On S, ST and GS models, remove the cap from the top of the fork inner tube (see illustration). If any corrosion is evident, spray some penetrating fluid onto it, then tap the top plug with a hammer and drift to dislodge it. Press down on the top plug, which is under pressure from the fork spring, release the circlip from its groove, then slowly release pressure on the plug and lift it out (see illustrations).

3 On R models, support the fork leg in an upright position and unscrew the top bolt, noting that it is under pressure from the spring – it is best to use a ratchet tool and to keep constant downward pressure on the top bolt while unscrewing it (see illustration).

4 Check the condition of the O-ring on the

6.12a Loosen the clamp bolts in the bottom yoke . . .

6.12b . . . then remove the fork leg

7.2a Remove the cap from the inner tube

7.2b Press down on the plug to release the circlip . . .

7.2c . . . then lift the plug out

7.3 Unscrew the fork top bolt

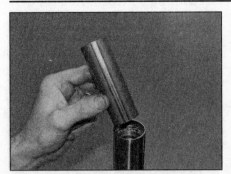

7.5a Remove the spacer . . .

7.5b . . . spring seat where fitted . . .

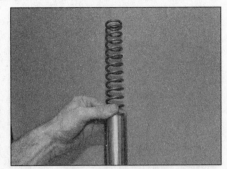

7.5c . . . and spring

top plug or top bolt – if it is deformed or deteriorated, fit a new one on reassembly.

5 Compress the inner tube into the outer tube and remove the spacer, spring seat on S, ST and R models, and spring **(see illustrations)**. Note which way up the spring fits – on S, ST and R models the closer wound coils should be at the bottom.

6 Invert the fork leg over a suitable container and pump the inner tube in-and-out of the outer tube to expel as much oil as possible.

7 Allow the fork leg to drain for several minutes. Wipe any excess oil off the spring and spacer. If the oil contains metal particles, disassemble the leg and inspect the fork components for signs of wear (see Section 8).

8 When the oil has drained, support the leg upright with the inner tube compressed into the outer tube. Slowly pour in the quantity and type of fork oil as specified at the beginning of this Chapter **(see illustration)**.

9 Pump the inner tube up-and-down several times to expel any trapped air **(see illustration)**. Secure the fork leg upright with the inner tube compressed into the outer tube, and let it to stand for several minutes to allow the oil level to stabilise.

10 Measure the oil level from the top of the inner tube **(see illustration)**. Add or subtract oil until it is at the level specified at the beginning of this Chapter.

11 When the oil level is correct, pull the inner tube out to its full extension and install the spring, ensuring it is fitted the correct way round (see Step 5). On S, ST and R models

7.8 Pour the measured amount of oil in slowly

fit the spring seat **(see illustration 7.5b)**. On all models, fit the spacer **(see illustration 7.5a)**.

12 If necessary, fit a new O-ring on the top plug or top bolt and lubricate it with a smear of fork oil.

13 On S, ST and GS models, fit the top plug into the inner tube, compressing the spring as you do, then push down to expose the groove and fit the circlip into it **(see illustrations 7.2c and b)**. Fit the cap **(see illustration 7.2a)**.

14 On R models, thread the top bolt into the inner tube, making sure it is not cross-threaded, and tighten it securely. **Note:** *The top bolt can be tightened to the specified torque setting once the fork leg has been installed on the bike and is securely held in the bottom yoke.*

15 Install the fork leg (see Section 6).

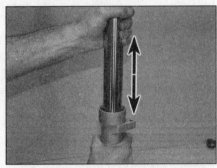

7.9 Pump the inner tube up-and-down to expel trapped air

F800 GS model

16 Follow the procedure in Section 6 to remove the fork leg – make sure the top bolt is loosened while the leg is still clamped in the bottom yoke.

17 Support the fork leg in an upright position and unscrew the top bolt. Check the condition of the O-ring on the top bolt – if it is deformed or deteriorated, fit a new one on reassembly.

18 Fit an open-ended spanner onto the top bolt locknut, then counter-hold the nut and loosen the top bolt **(see illustration)**.

19 Unscrew the top bolt from the damper assembly and remove the spring collar and the spring **(see illustrations)**. Withdraw the damper rod **(see illustration)**.

20 Invert the fork leg over a suitable container and pump the damper assembly in-and-out

7.10 Measure the fork oil level

7.18 Loosen the top bolt

7.19a Unscrew the top bolt . . .

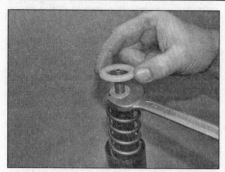

7.19b . . . and remove the spring collar . . .

7.19c . . . and the spring

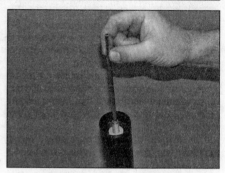

7.19d Withdraw the damper rod

to expel as much oil as possible. Note the location of the spacer that fits over the damper assembly.

 Warning: Do not pump the inner and outer tubes – if the tubes are pulled too far apart the internal seal will be damaged.

21 Allow the fork leg to drain for several minutes. Wipe any excess oil off the spring. If the oil contains metal particles, disassemble the leg and inspect the fork components for signs of wear (see Section 8).

22 When the oil has drained, support the leg upright with the outer tube compressed over the inner tube. Slide the spacer onto the damper assembly and install the damper rod. Slowly pour in the quantity and type of fork oil as specified at the beginning of this Chapter **(see illustration)**.

23 Pump the damper assembly in-and-out to ensure it is filled with oil. Carefully extend and compress the outer tube within the limits of normal travel to expel any trapped air, then secure the fork leg upright with the outer tube compressed over the inner tube, and let it to stand for several minutes to allow the oil level to stabilise.

24 Measure the oil level from the top of the inner tube. Add or subtract oil until it is at the level specified at the beginning of this Chapter.

25 When the oil level is correct, pull the damper out to its full extension and ensure the top bolt locknut is screwed on fully. Install the spring and spring collar, then press the spring

down and fit an open-ended spanner onto the top bolt locknut.

26 If necessary, fit a new O-ring on the top bolt and lubricate it with a smear of fork oil. Thread the top bolt onto the damper assembly, then counter-hold the top bolt and tighten the locknut. Remove the open-ended spanner.

27 Pull the outer tube up and screw the top bolt into the tube carefully, making sure it is not cross-threaded, and tighten it securely. **Note:** *The top bolt can be tightened to the specified torque setting once the fork leg has been installed on the bike and is securely held in the bottom yoke.*

28 Install the fork leg (see Section 6).

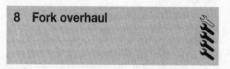

8 Fork overhaul

Note: *Always dismantle the fork legs separately to avoid interchanging parts. Store all components in separate, clearly marked containers.*

F800 S, ST, R and F650 GS models

Disassembly

1 Follow the procedure in Section 6 to remove the fork leg – on R models, make sure the top

bolt is loosened while the leg is still clamped in the bottom yoke.

2 Before dismantling the fork leg, loosen the damper bolt in the bottom of the outer tube. To do this, turn the leg upside down, compress the leg so that the fork spring exerts pressure on the internal damper assembly, then loosen the bolt **(see illustration)**. Alternatively, use an air wrench to loosen the bolt, or use a holding tool as described in Step 6.

3 On S, ST and GS models, follow the procedure in Section 7, Step 2, to remove the cap and plug from the fork inner tube. On R models, follow the procedure in Section 7, Step 3, to remove the top bolt.

4 Compress the inner tube into the outer tube and remove the spacer, spring seat on S, ST and R models, and spring. Note which way up the spring fits.

5 Invert the fork leg over a suitable container and drain the oil.

6 Remove the previously loosened damper bolt and its sealing washer from the bottom of the outer tube. Discard the washer as a new one must be fitted on reassembly. If the bolt could not be loosened earlier, a length of metal bar or wood dowel can be passed down through the fork inner tube and pressed hard against the top of the damper to hold it while the bolt is undone.

7 Tip the damper rod and rebound spring out of the fork **(see illustration)**. On S, ST and GS models, tip out the damper seat.

8 Using a small flat-bladed screwdriver, prise out the dust seal from the top of the outer

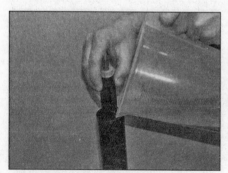

7.22 Pour the measured amount of oil in slowly

8.2 Loosen the damper bolt

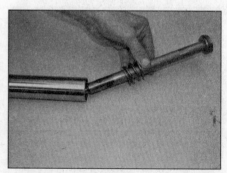

8.7 Tip out the damper rod and rebound spring

8.8 Prise out the dust seal

8.9 Ease out the oil seal retaining clip

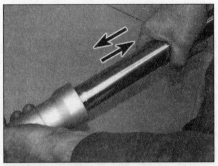

8.10a Repeatedly draw the tubes apart . . .

tube – discard the seal as a new one must be fitted on reassembly **(see illustration)**.

9 Ease out the oil seal retaining clip, taking care not to scratch the surface of the inner tube **(see illustration)**.

10 Grasp the inner tube in one hand and the outer tube in the other, then quickly and repeatedly draw the inner tube out until the oil seal, washer and top bush are displaced from the top of the outer tube by the bottom bush on the bottom of the inner tube **(see illustrations)**.

11 Draw the oil seal, washer and top bush off the inner tube. Discard the oil seal as a new one must be fitted on reassembly. Do not remove the bottom bush unless it is to be replaced with a new one.

12 On R models, tip the damper seat out of the outer tube **(see illustration)**.

Inspection

13 Clean all parts in a suitable solvent and blow them dry with compressed air, if available.

14 Check the surface of the fork inner tube for score marks, scratches, pitting and flaking of the finish, and excessive or abnormal wear. Look for dents in the tube and renew the tubes in both fork legs if any are found.

15 Check the inner tube for runout using V-blocks and a dial gauge. If the condition of the inner tube is suspect, have it checked by a BMW dealer or suspension specialist. BMW provides no specifications for runout.

 Warning: If the inner tube is bent or exceeds the runout limit, it should not be straightened; replace it with a new one.

8.10b . . . until the oil seal (1), washer (2) and top bush (3) are displaced by the bottom bush (4)

16 Inspect the inside surface of the outer tube and the working surface of each bush for score marks, scratches and signs of excessive wear. Renew the bushes as a set, particularly if excessive movement has been felt between the fork tubes (see Chapter 1). To remove the bottom bush, prise it apart at the slit using a flat-bladed screwdriver and slide it off **(see illustration)**. Make sure the new bushes seat properly.

17 Check the fork oil seal seat for nicks, gouges and scratches. If damage is evident, leaks will occur. Also check the oil seal washer for damage or distortion and replace it with a new one if necessary.

18 Check the fork spring for cracks and other damage. Measure the spring free length and compare the result with the specification at the beginning of this Chapter

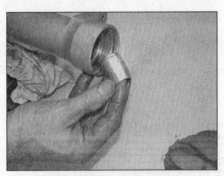

8.12 Tip out the damper seat – R models

(see illustration). If the spring is defective or has sagged below the figure given, fit new springs in both forks. Never fit only one new spring.

19 Check the damper, its piston ring and rebound spring for damage and wear, and renew them if necessary – all components are available separately **(see illustration)**.

Reassembly – S and ST models

20 Make sure the bottom bush is correctly located in its recess in the bottom of the inner tube **(see illustration 8.16)**.

21 Fit the rebound spring and damper seat onto the damper, then slide the damper assembly down to the bottom of the inner tube **(see illustration 8.7)**.

22 Lubricate the bottom bush and the inner surface of the outer tube with the specified

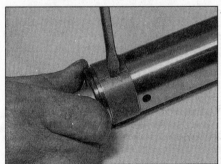

8.16 Remove the bottom bush by levering the ends apart

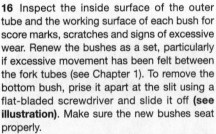

8.18 Measure the free length of the spring

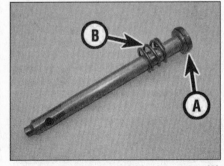

8.19 Damper assembly with piston ring (A) and rebound spring (B)

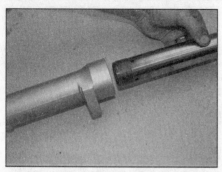

8.22 Slide the inner tube into the outer tube

8.23a Slide the top bush into the outer tube

8.23b Install the washer . . .

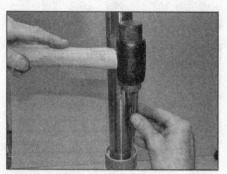

8.23c . . . and drive the bush in carefully

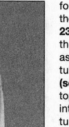

8.23d Check that the bush is correctly seated

fork oil. Slide the inner tube all the way into the outer tube (see illustration).

23 Lubricate the top bush with fork oil. Slide the bush down the inner tube and press it as far as possible into the top of the outer tube by hand, making sure it fits squarely (see illustration). Slide the washer onto the top of the bush, then carefully drive the bush into place using a suitable drift or length of tubing, or the BMW service tool (Part No. 313 691) (see illustrations). Take care not to mark the inner tube when driving the bush in. Remove the washer and make sure the bush is correctly seated, then refit the washer (see illustration).

24 Lubricate the new oil seal with fork oil. Slide the seal, with its marked side facing up, down the inner tube and press it as far as possible into the top of the outer tube by hand, making sure it fits squarely (see illustration). Carefully drive the seal into place using a suitable drift or length of tubing, or the BMW service tool. Take care not to mark the inner tube when driving the seal in. Make sure the seal is correctly seated – the groove for the retaining clip should be fully exposed (see illustration).

25 Fit the retaining clip, making sure it is correctly located in its groove (see illustration).

26 Fill the groove on the inside edge of the new dust seal with grease, then press the seal into place (see illustrations).

8.24a Fit the oil seal . . .

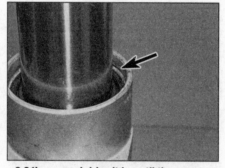

8.24b . . . and drive it in until the groove (arrowed) is visible

8.25 Fit the retaining clip into the groove

8.26a Fill the groove with grease . . .

8.26b . . . then press the dust seal into place

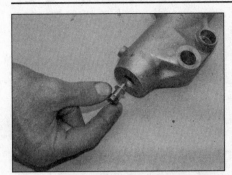

8.27 Fit a new sealing washer onto the damper bolt

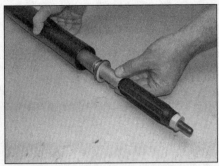

8.51 Withdraw the damper assembly from the fork tube

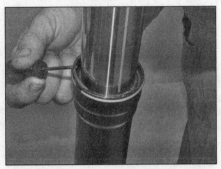

8.53 Ease out the oil seal retaining clip

27 Fit a new sealing washer onto the damper bolt (see illustration). Fit the bolt into the bottom of the outer tube, thread it into the bottom of the damper and tighten it to the torque setting specified at the beginning of this Chapter. If the damper rotates inside the tube as you tighten the bolt, use one of the methods described in Step 6 to hold it, or temporarily install the fork spring and spacer and use spring pressure.

28 Follow the procedure in Section 7 to fill the fork leg with the correct quantity and type of fork oil. Install the remaining components in the reverse order of removal.

Reassembly – F650 GS models

29 Make sure the bottom bush is correctly located in its recess in the bottom of the inner tube (see illustration 8.16).

30 Lubricate the bottom bush and the inner surface of the outer tube with the specified fork oil. Slide the inner tube all the way into the outer tube (see illustration 8.22).

31 Lubricate the top bush with fork oil. Slide the bush down the inner tube and press it as far as possible into the top of the outer tube by hand, making sure it fits squarely (see illustration 8.23a). Slide the washer onto the top of the bush, then carefully drive the bush into place using a suitable drift or length of tubing, or the BMW service tools (Part No. 31 3 650 and 31 1 511) (see illustrations 8.23b and c). Take care not to mark the inner tube when driving the bush in. Remove the washer and make sure the bush is correctly seated, then refit the washer (see illustration 8.23d).

32 Lubricate the new oil seal with fork oil. Slide the seal, with its marked side facing up, down the inner tube and press it as far as possible into the top of the outer tube by hand, making sure it fits squarely (see illustration 8.24a). Carefully drive the seal into place using a suitable drift or length of tubing, or the BMW service tools. Take care not to mark the inner tube when driving the seal in. Make sure the seal is correctly seated – the groove for the retaining clip should be fully exposed (see illustration 8.24b).

33 Fit the retaining clip, making sure it is correctly located in its groove (see illustration 8.25).

34 Fill the groove on the inside edge of the

new dust seal with grease, then press the seal into place (see illustrations 8.26a and b).

35 Fit the rebound spring and damper seat onto the damper, then slide the damper assembly down to the bottom of the inner tube (see illustration 8.7).

36 Fit a new sealing washer onto the damper bolt (see illustration 8.27). Fit the bolt into the bottom of the outer tube, thread it into the bottom of the damper and tighten it to the torque setting specified at the beginning of this Chapter. If the damper rotates inside the tube as you tighten the bolt, use one of the methods described in Step 6 to hold it, or temporarily install the fork spring and spacer and use spring pressure.

37 Follow the procedure in Section 7 to fill the fork leg with the correct quantity and type of fork oil. Install the remaining components in the reverse order of removal.

Reassembly – R models

38 Make sure the bottom bush is correctly located in its recess in the bottom of the inner tube (see illustration 8.16).

39 Slide the damper seat down to the bottom of the outer tube (see illustration 8.12).

40 Lubricate the bottom bush and the inner surface of the outer tube with the specified fork oil. Slide the inner tube all the way into the outer tube (see illustration 8.22).

41 Lubricate the top bush with fork oil. Slide the bush down the inner tube and press it as far as possible into the top of the outer tube by hand, making sure it fits squarely (see illustration 8.23a). Slide the washer onto the top of the bush, then carefully drive the bush into place using a suitable drift or length of tubing, or the BMW service tool (Part No. 313 691) (see illustrations 8.23b and c). Take care not to mark the inner tube when driving the bush in. Remove the washer and make sure the bush is correctly seated, then refit the washer (see illustration 8.23d).

42 Lubricate the new oil seal with fork oil. Slide the seal, with its marked side facing up, down the inner tube and press it as far as possible into the top of the outer tube by hand, making sure it fits squarely (see illustration 8.24a). Carefully drive the seal into place using a suitable drift or length of tubing, or the BMW service tool. Take care not to mark

the inner tube when driving the seal in. Make sure the seal is correctly seated – the groove for the retaining clip should be fully exposed (see illustration 8.24b).

43 Fit the retaining clip, making sure it is correctly located in its groove (see illustration 8.25).

44 Fill the groove on the inside edge of the new dust seal with grease, then press the seal into place (see illustrations 8.26a and b).

45 Fit the rebound spring onto the damper, then slide the damper assembly down to the bottom of the inner tube (see illustration 8.7).

46 Fit a new sealing washer onto the damper bolt (see illustration 8.27). Fit the bolt into the bottom of the outer tube, thread it into the bottom of the damper and tighten it to the torque setting specified at the beginning of this Chapter. If the damper rotates inside the tube as you tighten the bolt, use one of the methods described in Step 6 to hold it, or temporarily install the fork spring and spacer and use spring pressure.

47 Follow the procedure in Section 7 to fill the fork leg with the correct quantity and type of fork oil. Install the remaining components in the reverse order of removal.

F800 GS models

Disassembly

48 Follow the procedure in Section 6 to remove the fork leg – make sure the top bolt is loosened while the leg is still clamped in the bottom yoke.

49 Unscrew the damper bolt in the bottom of the inner tube. Note the sealing washer and discard it as a new one must be fitted. Drain the oil into a suitable container.

50 Follow the procedure in Section 7 to remove the top bolt, spring collar and spring. Drain out any residual oil, noting the location of the spacer that fits over the damper assembly.

51 Pull out the damper assembly and drain out any oil (see illustration).

52 Using a small flat-bladed screwdriver, prise out the dust seal from the bottom of the outer tube.

53 Ease out the oil seal retaining clip, taking care not to scratch the surface of the inner tube (see illustration).

8.54a Pull the inner and outer fork tubes apart

8.54b The oil seal, washer and both bushes will come out on the inner tube

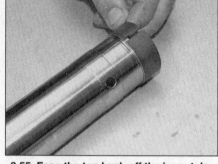

8.55 Ease the top bush off the inner tube

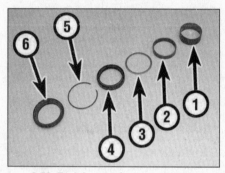

8.56 Fork inner tube components

1 Top bush
2 Bottom bush
3 Washer
4 Oil seal
5 Retaining clip
6 Dust seal

54 Grasp the inner tube in one hand and the outer tube in the other, then quickly and repeatedly draw the inner tube out until the oil seal, washer and bottom bush are displaced from the outer tube by the top bush on the inner tube (see illustrations).

55 Note the location of the top and bottom fork bushes. Ease the split in the top bush apart, then ease the bush off the inner tube (see illustration).

56 Slide off the bottom bush, washer, oil seal, seal retaining clip and dust seal (see illustration). Note which way round the seals are fitted, then discard them as new ones must be fitted.

Inspection

57 Clean all parts in a suitable solvent and blow them dry with compressed air, if available.

58 Check the surface of the fork inner tube for score marks, scratches, pitting and flaking of the finish, and excessive or abnormal wear. Look for dents in the tube and renew the tubes in both fork legs if any are found.

59 Check the inner tube for runout using V-blocks and a dial gauge. If the condition of the inner tube is suspect, have it checked by a BMW dealer or suspension specialist. BMW provides no specifications for runout.

⚠ Warning: If the inner tube is bent or exceeds the runout limit, it should not be straightened; replace it with a new one.

60 Inspect the inside surface of the outer tube and the working surface of each bush for score marks, scratches and signs of excessive wear. Renew the bushes as a set, particularly if excessive movement has been felt between the fork tubes (see Chapter 1).

61 Check the fork oil seal seat for nicks, gouges and scratches. If damage is evident, leaks will occur. Also check the oil seal washer for damage or distortion and replace it with a new one if necessary.

62 Check the fork spring for cracks and other damage. Measure the spring free length and compare the result with the specifications at the beginning of this Chapter (see illustration 8.18). If the spring is defective or has sagged, fit new springs in both forks. Never fit only one new spring.

63 Check that the damper rod slides freely in-and-out of the damper body. Note: If the fork inner tube has been bent, it is likely that the damper assembly will be damaged also.

Reassembly

64 Install the damper assembly in the inner tube. Fit a new sealing washer onto the damper bolt. Fit the bolt into the bottom of the inner tube, thread it into the bottom of the damper and tighten it to the torque setting specified at the beginning of this Chapter.

65 Wrap some tape around the top of the inner tube to protect the inside of the fork seal on assembly (see illustration).

66 Lubricate the inside of the new dust seal with a smear of fork oil, then slide it down over the inner tube, making sure that it is the correct way round (see illustration).

8.65 Tape around the top of the inner tube will protect the inside of the fork seal

8.66 Install the dust seal ensuring it is the correct way round

8.67 Slide on the oil seal retaining clip

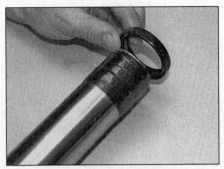

8.68a Install the oil seal . . .

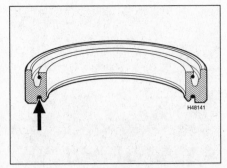

8.68b . . . ensuring the smaller recess (arrowed) faces the dust seal

8.69 Slide on the washer

8.70a Slide on the bottom bush . . .

8.70b . . . then install the top bush in its groove

67 Slide on the oil seal retaining clip **(see illustration)**.

68 Lubricate the inside of the new oil seal with a smear of fork oil, then slide it down over the inner tube, making sure that it is the correct way round – the smaller recess in the seal should face the dust seal **(see illustrations)**.

69 Slide on the washer, then remove the tape **(see illustration)**.

70 Lubricate the new fork bushes with fork oil. Slide on the bottom bush, then ease the top bush over the end of the inner tube and into its groove **(see illustrations)**.

71 Lubricate the inside of the outer tube with fork oil, then insert the inner tube. Slide the lower bush and washer into the bottom of the outer tube, then carefully tap around the washer with a small pin punch to ensure that the bush is located in its seat **(see illustrations)**. BMW provides a service

tool, Part No. 31 3 642, to drive the bush in.

72 Press the oil seal into its seat in the bottom of the outer tube – tap the seal lightly into place until the retaining clip groove is visible **(see illustration)**.

73 Install the oil seal retaining clip and ensure it is correctly seated in its groove **(see illustration)**.

74 Press the dust seal into its seat in the bottom of the tube **(see illustration)**. If

8.71a Slide the lower bush and washer into the bottom of the outer tube . . .

8.71b . . . then tap around the washer to ensure the bush is seated

8.72 Install the oil seal . . .

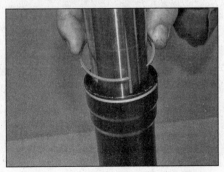

8.73 . . . and secure it with the clip

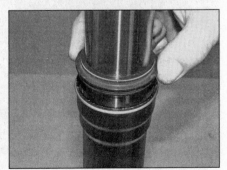

8.74 Press the dust seal into place

9.3a Undo the screws (arrowed) . . .

9.3b . . . and remove the cover

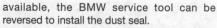

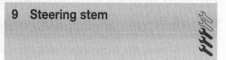

available, the BMW service tool can be reversed to install the dust seal.

75 Slide the spacer onto the damper assembly, then follow the procedure in Section 7 to fill the fork leg with the correct quantity and type of fork oil. Install the remaining components in the reverse order of removal.

9 Steering stem

Removal

1 Follow the procedure in Section 6 to remove the front forks (see Section 6).

2 On S, ST and R models, if required, the top fork yoke can be displaced with the handlebars in position. Alternatively, if the top yoke is to be removed, follow the procedure in Section 5 to displace the handlebars. On GS models, the handlebars must be displaced to gain access to the bearing adjuster bolt.

3 On GS models, undo the screws securing the cover to the underside of the bottom fork yoke **(see illustrations)**.

4 Remove the horn from the bottom yoke – all models except F650 GS (see Chapter 8).

5 Undo the screws securing the front brake hose union and/or the brake hose guide to the bottom yoke – all models except F800 GS **(see illustrations)**.

6 On S, ST and R models, undo the bolts securing the steering damper, noting the location of the cushion washers, and lift the damper off **(see illustrations)**.

7 Prise out the blanking cap from the bearing adjuster bolt **(see illustration)**.

8 Loosen the steering stem clamp bolt, then

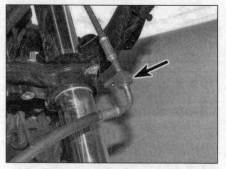

9.5a Undo screws (arrowed) – S model

9.5b Front brake hose union screw – R model

9.6a Location of the steering damper

9.5c Front brake hose union – F650 GS model

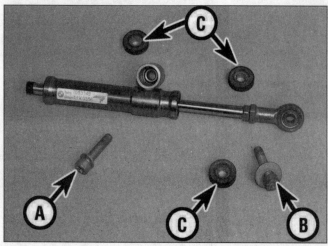

9.6b Damper mounting bolt (A), rod eye bolt (B) and cushion washers (C)

9.7 Prise out the blanking cap

9.8a Loosen the steering stem clamp bolt . . .

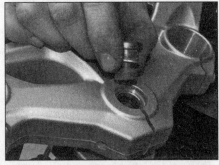

9.8b . . . then unscrew the adjuster bolt and washer

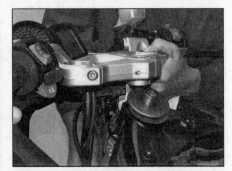

9.9a Lift off the top yoke

unscrew the adjuster bolt and washer **(see illustrations)**.

9 Support the bottom yoke and lift the top yoke up off the steering stem **(see illustration)**. On S, ST and R models, note the location of the steering lock on the underside of the top yoke **(see illustration)**.

10 Remove the bearing cover **(see illustration)**.

11 Lower the steering stem out of the steering head **(see illustration)**. Remove the upper bearing **(see illustration)**.

12 Remove all traces of old grease from the bearings and the races in the steering head and check them for wear or damage as described in Section 10.

13 On S, ST and R models, if required, the steering lock can be removed as follows. **Note:** *For security reasons the steering lock is retained by shear-head bolts which cannot be unscrewed using conventional tools. New bolts should be obtained before starting work.*

14 Where fitted, undo the screws securing the wiring connector cover, then disconnect the immobiliser antenna and ignition switch wiring connectors **(see illustrations)**. Remove the ignition switch (see Chapter 8, Section 16).

15 Secure the yoke in a soft-jawed vice with plenty of rag to protect it. Drill the heads off the

9.9b Note the location of the steering lock

9.10 Remove the bearing cover

9.11a Lower the steering stem out of the steering head

9.11b Remove the upper bearing

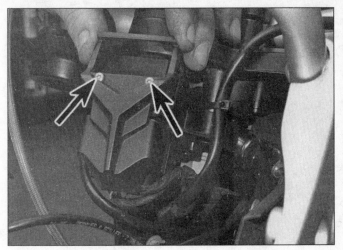

9.14a Undo the screws securing the cover

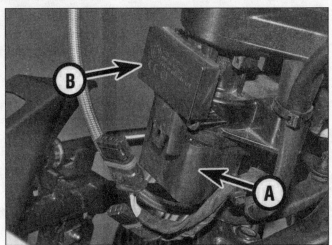

9.14b Ignition switch (A) and immobiliser antenna (B)

9.18 Install the upper bearing

9.19 Ensure all wiring and hoses are correctly routed

10.3 Check the bearing races for wear and damage

shear-head bolts and draw the assembly off. Note the location of the immobiliser antenna. Use a stud extractor to unscrew the remains of the bolts (see *Tools and Workshop Tips* in the *Reference* section).
16 Install the lock and immobiliser antenna in the reverse order of removal, tightening the new bolts until the heads break off. Install the ignition switch.

Installation

17 Smear a liberal quantity of multi-purpose grease onto the bearing races, and work some grease well into both the upper and lower bearings.
18 Lift the steering stem up through the steering head and install the upper bearing, pressing it down firmly **(see illustration)**. Support the bottom yoke and fit the bearing cover and the top yoke **(see illustrations 9.10 and 9a)**. Thread the adjuster bolt and washer into the steering stem and tighten it finger-tight **(see illustration 9.8b)**.
19 Ensure that all wiring and hoses are correctly routed around the bottom yoke **(see illustration)**.
20 Temporarily install the front forks and wheel, then follow the procedure in Chapter 1, Section 6, and adjust the steering head bearings.
21 With the bearings correctly adjusted, remove the wheel. Check that the amount of protrusion of both fork tubes above the top yoke is as specified for your model (see Section 6).

22 Install the remaining components in the reverse order of removal.

10 Steering head bearings and races

Inspection

1 Remove the steering stem (see Section 9).
2 Remove all traces of old grease from the roller bearings and check them for wear or damage – see *Tools and Workshop Tips* in the *Reference* Section.
3 Remove all traces of old grease from the bearing races in the steering head and check them for wear and damage **(see illustration)**. The races should be polished and free from indentations.
4 If there are any signs of wear or damage on any of the bearing components, both upper and lower bearing assemblies must be renewed as a set. **Note:** *Do not attempt to remove the outer races from the steering head or the lower bearing from the steering stem unless new bearings are being installed).*

Renewal

5 The outer races are an interference fit in the steering head and can be tapped out using a suitable drift located against the inner rim of the race **(see illustrations)**. Tap firmly and evenly around each race to ensure that it is driven out squarely.

6 Lubricate the new outer races with grease and install them both at the same time using a drawbolt arrangement **(see illustration)**. Ensure that the upper and lower drawbolt washers bear on the outer edges of the races only and do not contact the bearing surfaces.

> **HAYNES HINT** *Installation of new bearing outer races is made much easier if the races are left overnight in the freezer. This causes them to contract slightly making them a looser fit. Alternatively, use a freeze spray.*

7 Only remove the lower bearing from the steering stem if a new one is being fitted (see

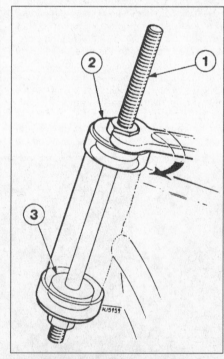
10.6 Drawbolt arrangement for installing steering head bearing races

1 Long bolt or threaded bar
2 Thick washer
3 Guide for lower race

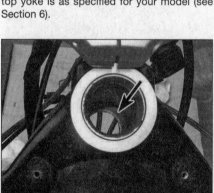
10.5a Inner rim of lower bearing outer race

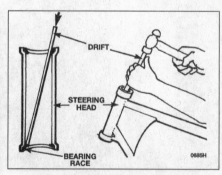
10.5b Drive the bearing races out locating the drift as shown

illustration). To remove the bearing, use two screwdrivers placed on opposite sides to work it free, or tap under it using a cold chisel. If the bearing is firmly in place it will be necessary to split it using an angle grinder – take care not to nick or gouge the steering stem.

8 Remove the dust seal from the bottom of the stem and replace it with a new one.

9 Grease the inside of the new bearing, then slide it down the steering stem. Tap the bearing into position using a length of tubing with an internal diameter slightly larger than the steering stem **(see illustration)**. Ensure that the tubing bears only on the inner edge of the bearing and does not contact the rollers.

10 Install the steering stem (see Section 9).

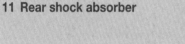

11 Rear shock absorber

Warning: Do not attempt to disassemble the shock absorber – improper disassembly could result in serious injury. No individual components are available for it.

Removal

Special tools: *On S, ST and R models, a means of lifting the rear sub-frame, such as an*

10.7 Location of the lower bearing

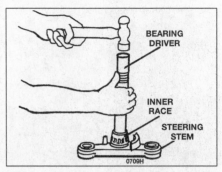

10.9 Install the new bearing with a suitable driver

automotive engine hoist (see Step 6), will be required.

1 Remove the seat and, on S, ST and R models, the seat cowling (see Chapter 7).

2 Remove the rear wheel (see Chapter 6).

GS models

3 Remove the bodywork centre panel and both side panels (see Chapter 7). Undo the screws securing the seat bridge on both sides **(see illustration)**. Ease the bridge up to access the upper shock absorber mounting bolt – if necessary, release the ties securing the wiring to the bridge.

4 Remove the exhaust silencer (see Chapter 4).

5 Undo the screws securing the chain guard, then unclip the guard from its front mounting and lift it off **(see illustrations)**. Undo the screws securing the top edge of the chain slider, then ease the slider up to access the lower shock absorber mounting bolt **(see illustration)**.

6 Unscrew the bolt securing the lower end of the shock to the swingarm **(see illustration)**. Support the swingarm, then withdraw the bolt and lower the swingarm carefully to avoid damage

7 Unscrew the bolt securing the top of the shock absorber. Support the shock and

11.3 Undo screws on both sides securing the seat bridge

11.5a Undo the screws securing the chain guard

11.5b Unclip the guard from its front mounting (arrowed)

11.5c Screws (arrowed) secure top edge of chain slider

11.6 Lower shock absorber mounting bolt

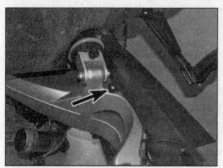

11.8a Upper belt guard fixing screws at rear . . .

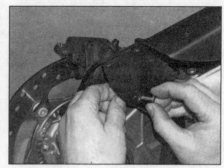

11.8b . . . and at back of guard

11.8c Unclip the guard from the brake hose cover . . .

11.8d . . . and lift it off – S and ST models

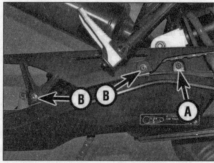

11.9a Loosen screw (A) and undo screws (B) . . .

withdraw the bolt, then manoeuvre the shock out.

S, ST and R models

8 On S and ST models, undo the screws securing the upper belt guard, then unclip the front and outer edge of the guard carefully and lift it off, noting how the front clips into the brake hose cover **(see illustrations)**.

9 On R models, loosen the inner screw securing the chain guard, then undo the outer screws and lift the guard off **(see illustrations)**.

10 Undo the screw and washer securing the rear shock pre-load adjuster and remove it **(see illustration)**. Undo the screw securing the rear brake fluid reservoir and support the reservoir clear of the rear sub-frame.

11 Where fitted, remove the plastic cap from the upper left-hand sub-frame mounting **(see illustration)**. Loosen both upper sub-frame mounting bolts **(see illustration 11.13)**.

12 Secure the rear sub-frame to a suitable hoist but ensure there is no pressure on the mounting bolts (see Chapter 2, Section 4).

13 Undo both lower sub-frame mounting bolts and remove the nuts, bolts and washers **(see illustration)**. Carefully raise the rear of the sub-frame, together with the fuel tank, to gain clearance for removal of the shock.

14 Undo the nut on the bolt securing the lower end of the shock to the swingarm **(see illustration)**. Support the swingarm, then withdraw the bolt and lower the swingarm carefully to avoid damage

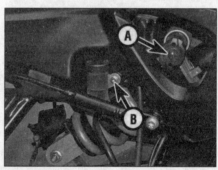

11.10 Remove the shock pre-load adjuster (A) and displace the brake fluid reservoir (B)

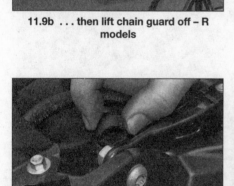

11.9b . . . then lift chain guard off – R models

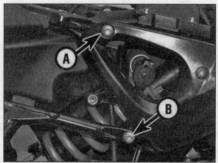

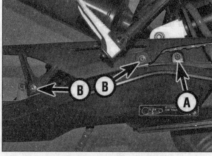

11.11 Remove the plastic cap

11.13 Loosen the upper sub-frame bolts (A) and remove the lower bolts (B) on both sides

11.14 Nut and bolt secure the lower end of the shock

15 Unscrew the bolt securing the top of the shock absorber **(see illustration)**. Support the shock and withdraw the bolt and sleeve, then manoeuvre the shock out **(see illustrations)**.

Inspection

16 Clean the shock absorber thoroughly, then inspect it for signs of damage and oil leakage. Check the spring for looseness, cracks or signs of fatigue. If the shock is thought to be faulty, or if it cannot be adjusted satisfactorily, have it checked by a BMW dealer.

17 Check the shock mountings and mounting bolts for wear or damage **(see illustration)**. Fit new mounting bolts if necessary.

18 On S, ST and R models, check the lower shock mounting bush on the swingarm (see Section 13).

Installation

19 Installation is the reverse of removal, noting the following:

● Apply multi-purpose grease to all pivot points.
● Clean the threads of the bottom mounting bolts and apply a suitable non-permanent thread-locking compound.
● Fit both top and bottom mounting bolts before tightening either of them.
● On S, ST and R models, clean the threads of the sub-frame mounting bolts and apply a suitable non-permanent thread-locking compound.
● Tighten all nuts/bolts to the torque settings specified at the beginning of the Chapter.

12 Rear shock absorber adjustment

1 The rear shock absorber is adjustable for spring pre-load and rebound damping. BMW recommends that adjustments to pre-load and damping are complimentary – an increase in pre-load requires firmer damping, a reduction in pre-load requires softer damping.

Spring pre-load

2 Spring pre-load is varied by turning the adjuster on the top, right-hand side of the

11.15a Top shock absorber mounting bolt (arrowed)

11.15b Withdraw the bolt and sleeve . . .

11.15c . . . and manoeuvre the shock out

11.17 Inspect the shock and mounting bolts for wear and damage

shock absorber. A key for this purpose is located under the seat **(see illustration)**.

3 Turn the key clockwise to increase pre-load and anti-clockwise to reduce it – see **Specifications** at the beginning of this Chapter.

Rebound damping

4 On GS models, rebound damping is varied by turning the adjuster on the lower, right-hand side of the shock absorber with a flat-bladed screwdriver **(see illustration)**.

5 On S, ST and R models, rebound damping is varied by turning the adjuster knob on the lower end of the shock absorber **(see illustration)**.

6 Turn the adjuster clockwise to increase damping and anti-clockwise to reduce it – see **Specifications** at the beginning of this Chapter.

13 Swingarm

Removal

1 Remove the rear wheel (see Chapter 6).

GS models

2 Undo the screw securing the brake hose

12.2 Use the key provided to adjust spring pre-load

12.4 Spring rebound damping adjuster – GS models

12.5 Spring rebound damping adjuster – S, ST and R models

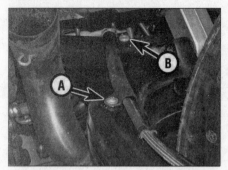

13.2a Undo cover screw (A), then draw cover out from front mounting (B) . . .

13.2b . . . and lift it off

13.5 Checking for wear in the swingarm bearings

13.6a Counter-hold the pivot bolt . . .

13.6b . . . and undo the nut and washer

13.7a Withdraw the pivot bolt . . .

cover, then unclip the cover from its front mounting and lift it off **(see illustrations)**.

3 Lift the rear brake caliper bracket off the swingarm and secure it to the rear sub-frame to avoid straining the brake hose.

4 Follow the procedure in Section 11, Steps 5 and 6, to remove the chain guard and the lower shock absorber mounting bolt.

5 To check the bearings, grasp the rear of the swingarm with one hand and place your other hand at the junction of the swingarm and the frame. Try to move the rear of the swingarm from side-to-side **(see illustration)**. Any wear (freeplay) in the bearings will be felt as forwards-and-backwards movement between the front of the swingarm and the frame.

6 Counter-hold the swingarm pivot bolt on the right-hand side, then undo the nut and remove the washer on the left-hand side **(see illustrations)**.

7 Withdraw the pivot bolt, then manoeuvre the swingarm out of the frame **(see illustrations)**.

S and ST models

8 Undo the screw securing the lower belt guard, then unclip the rear and front edges of the guard carefully and lift it off **(see illustrations)**.

9 Remove the rear pulley assembly (see Chapter 6).

13.7b . . . and manoeuvre the swingarm out

13.8a Screw (arrowed) secures lower belt guard

13.8b Unclip the rear . . .

13.8c . . . and lower edges . . .

13.8d . . . and lift the belt guard off

13.10a Remove the rear section of the belt guard . . .

13.10b . . . by removing the lower . . .

13.10c . . . and rear fixing screws

10 Follow the procedure in Section 11, Step 8, to remove the upper belt guard. Undo the screws securing the rear section of the belt guard and lift it off **(see illustrations)**. Undo the screws securing the brake hose cover and lift it off, noting how it fits **(see illustration)**.

11 Displace the rear brake caliper and bracket (see Chapter 6). Secure the caliper to the rear sub-frame to avoid straining the brake hose.

12 Remove the rear axle and eccentric adjuster assembly (see Chapter 6).

13 To check the bearings, grasp the rear of the swingarm with one hand and place your other hand at the junction of the swingarm and the frame. Try to move the rear of the swingarm from side-to-side. Any wear (freeplay) in the bearings will be felt as forwards-and-backwards movement between the front of the swingarm and the frame.

14 Ensure the centre section of the swingarm shaft is clean and free from corrosion **(see illustration)**.

15 Prise out the caps from both sides of the swingarm pivot **(see illustrations)**.

16 Remove the circlip from the left-hand end of the swingarm shaft **(see illustration)**. Discard the circlip as a new one must be fitted.

17 Loosen the swingarm shaft clamp bolts evenly **(see illustration 13.14)**.

18 Unscrew the lower shock absorber mounting nut and bolt (see Section 11, Step 14).

19 Withdraw the pivot shaft from the right-hand side and lift the swingarm out **(see illustrations)**.

13.10d Screws (arrowed) secure brake hose cover

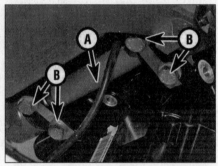

13.14 Ensure the centre section of the swingarm shaft (A) is clean. Note the clamp bolts (B)

13.15a Prise out . . .

13.15b . . . the swingarm pivot caps

13.16 Remove the circlip

13.19a Withdraw the pivot shaft . . .

13.19b . . . and lift the swingarm out

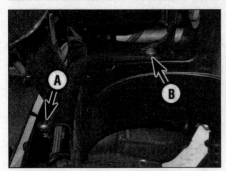

13.21a Undo cover screw (A), then draw cover out from the front mounting (B) . . .

13.21b . . . and lift it off

13.24a Withdraw the pivot shaft . . .

R models

20 Follow the procedure in Section 11, Step 9, to remove the chain guard.

21 Undo the screw securing the brake hose cover, then unclip the cover from its front mounting and lift it off **(see illustrations)**.

22 Lift the rear brake caliper bracket off the swingarm and secure it to the rear sub-frame to avoid straining the brake hose.

23 To check the bearings, grasp the rear of the swingarm with one hand and place your other hand at the junction of the swingarm and the frame. Try to move the rear of the swingarm from side-to-side **(see illustration 13.5)**. Any wear (freeplay) in the bearings will be felt as forwards-and-backwards movement between the front of the swingarm and the frame.

24 Follow the procedure in Steps 14 to 18, then withdraw the pivot shaft from the

right-hand side and lift the swingarm out **(see illustrations)**.

Inspection

25 Thoroughly clean the swingarm, removing all traces of dirt, corrosion and grease.

GS models

26 If required, undo the screws securing the chain slider and remove it **(see illustration)**. If it is badly worn or damaged, it should be replaced with a new one.

27 Check that the chain adjusters turn freely – if necessary, unscrew them and clean the threads or renew the adjuster bolts and locknuts **(see illustration)**. The plates scribed with the chain adjustment index marks are available as separate items if required.

28 Clean the swingarm pivot bolt and remove any corrosion using wire wool. Check that it is

straight by rolling it on a flat surface such as a piece of plate glass.

29 Inspect the swingarm closely, looking for obvious signs of wear such as heavy scoring, and cracks or distortion due to accident damage.

30 Lay the swingarm on the work surface and support it so that the pivot end is level (check this with a spirit level). Install the chain adjusters and the rear wheel axle and check that the axle is also level – if not, the swingarm is out of true and must be replaced with a new one.

31 The swingarm is fitted with two needle bearings in both sides **(see illustration)**. Working on one side at a time, withdraw the bearing sleeve and inspect it for wear and corrosion **(see illustration)**. If the sleeve is in poor condition, the sleeve and bearings should be renewed as a set.

32 Apply clean oil to the bearing sleeve, install it in the swingarm and check that it turns smoothly in the bearings. Slide the pivot bolt into place and check for any freeplay in the bearings. If the bearings do not turn smoothly and freely, or if there is excessive freeplay, they must be renewed – refer to *Tools and Workshop Tips (Section 5)* in the Reference section

33 If the bearings are in good condition, check the outer seals on both sides for wear and distortion – it is good practice to renew the seals whenever the swingarm is removed. Lever the seals out carefully to avoid damage, clean out any old grease, then lubricate the bearings with EP2 grease. Lubricate the new

13.24b . . . and lift the swingarm out

13.26 Undo the screws securing the chain slider

13.27 Chain adjusters should turn freely

13.31a Location of the swingarm needle bearings. Note the outer seal (arrowed)

13.31b Inspect the bearing sleeves

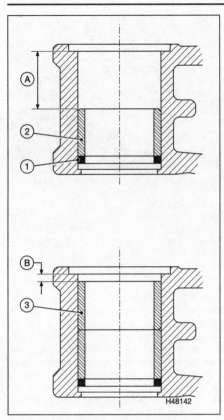

13.35 Swingarm bearing installation – GS models

1 Inner sealing ring
2 Inner bearing
3 Outer bearing
A Installed depth, inner bearing
B Installed depth, outer bearing

seals with a smear of grease and press them in carefully.

34 If new bearings are being fitted, support the swingarm on a firm surface and drive or press the old ones out from the inside of each pivot using a suitable tool. Note the location

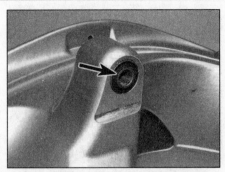

13.38 Shock absorber mounting bush

of the sealing rings on the outside and inside of the bearings and renew them.

35 The needle bearings are installed at specific depths, measured from the outside edge of the bearing housing **(see illustration)**. Study the diagram before installing the bearings and check the installed depths with a Vernier caliper. The new bearings should be pressed or drawn into their bores rather than driven into position. In the absence of a press, a suitable drawbolt tool can be made up as described in *Tools and WorkshopTips*. Ensure that the inner sealing ring is fitted before the inner bearing is installed and smear the bearings with grease to aid installation.

36 Once the outer bearing has been installed, fit the outer sealing ring and a new outer seal.

S and ST models

37 Inspect the swingarm closely, looking for obvious signs of wear such as heavy scoring, and cracks or distortion due to accident damage.

38 Inspect the mounting bush for the lower end of the shock absorber **(see illustration)**. If it is worn or damaged, support the swingarm and press the old bush out with a driver or suitably-sized socket. If necessary, heat the housing with a hot air gun to aid removal. Lubricate the new bush with a smear of grease to aid installation and press it into position.

13.40 Location of the swingarm needle bearing

39 Clean the swingarm shaft and remove any corrosion using wire wool. Check that it is straight by rolling it on a flat surface such as a piece of plate glass. Inspect the bearing surfaces for wear and corrosion. If the shaft is in poor condition, the shaft and bearings should be renewed as a set.

40 The swingarm is fitted with one needle bearing in both sides. Apply clean oil to the shaft, install it in the swingarm and check that it turns smoothly in the bearings without any freeplay **(see illustration)**. If the bearings do not turn smoothly and freely, or if there is excessive freeplay, they must be renewed – refer to *Tools and Workshop Tips (Section 5)* in the Reference section.

41 If the bearings are in good condition, inspect the inner thrust bushings on both sides for wear and renew them if necessary **(see illustration)**. Check the seals on both sides of each bearing for wear and distortion – it is good practice to renew the seals whenever the swingarm is removed. Lever the seals out carefully to avoid damage to the soft aluminium housing **(see illustration)**. Clean out any old grease, then lubricate the bearings with EP2 grease. Lubricate the new seals with a smear of grease and press them in carefully

42 If new bearings are being fitted, first remove the inner thrust bushings, then lever out the old seals **(see illustrations 13.41a and b)**. Support

13.41a Location of the inner thrust bushing

13.41b Lever the old seals out carefully

13.45a Location of the chain slider – R models

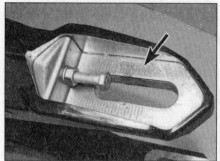

13.45b Check the chain adjusters. Note the scribed plate (arrowed)

13.45c Shock absorber mounting bush – R models

the swingarm on a firm surface and drive or press the old bearings out from the inside of each pivot using a suitable tool.

43 The bearings fit against a machined lip inside the swingarm pivot. They should be fitted from the outside and pressed or drawn into their bores until seated, rather than driven into position. In the absence of a press, a suitable drawbolt tool can be made up as described in *Tools and Workshop Tips*. Smear the bearings with grease to aid installation.

44 Install the new seals and inner thrust bushings.

R models

45 Follow the procedure in Steps 26 to 30, then inspect the mounting bush for the lower end of the shock absorber (see illustrations).

13.48 Installing the swingarm pivot bolt

13.59 Secure the swingarm shaft with a new circlip

46 The swingarm is fitted with one needle bearing in both sides. Follow the procedure in Steps 40 to 44 to inspect the bearings and thrust bushings and renew them if necessary.

Installation

GS models

47 If removed, fit the chain slider. Ensure the outer seals are in place and install the bearing sleeves (see illustrations 13.31a and b).

48 Clean the frame around the swingarm mountings. Loop the chain over the swigarm, then support the swingarm in position and install the pivot bolt from the right-hand side (see illustration).

49 Fit the washer and nut, then tighten the

13.57 Location of the inner thrust bushing – R models

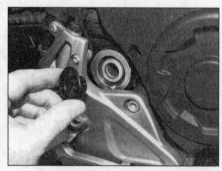

13.61 Install the swingarm pivot caps

nut to the torque setting specified at the beginning of this Chapter (see illustration 13.6b). Check that the swingarm moves freely up-and-down.

50 Install the remaining components in the reverse order of removal.

S and ST models

51 Ensure the inner thrust bushings are in place (see illustration 13.41a).

52 Clean the frame around the swingarm mountings. Loop the belt over the swingarm, then support the swingarm in position and install the shaft from the right-hand side (see illustration 13.19a).

53 Ensure the shaft is pressed all the way in and secure it with a new circlip (see illustration 13.16).

54 Tighten the swingarm shaft clamp bolts lightly, then tighten them to the torque setting specified at the beginning of this Chapter, tightening the two front bolts first (see illustration 13.14). Check that the swingarm moves freely up-and-down.

55 Install the swingarm pivot caps (see illustration 13.15b).

56 Install the remaining components in the reverse order of removal.

R models

57 Ensure the inner thrust bushings are in place (see illustration).

58 Clean the frame around the swingarm mountings. Loop the chain over the swingarm, then support the swingarm in position and install the shaft from the right-hand side (see illustration 13.24a).

59 Ensure the shaft is pressed all the way in and secure it with a new circlip (see illustration).

60 Tighten the swingarm shaft clamp bolts lightly, then tighten them to the torque setting specified at the beginning of this Chapter, tightening the two front bolts first (see illustration 13.14). Check that the swingarm moves freely up-and-down.

61 Install the swingarm pivot caps (see illustration).

62 Install the remaining components in the reverse order of removal.

Chapter 6
Brakes, wheels and final drive

Contents

	Section
Anti-lock brake system – ABS	10
Brake fluid level check	see Pre-ride checks
Brake hoses, pipes and fittings	11
Brake light switches	see Chapter 8
Brake pad wear check	see Chapter 1
Brake system bleeding and fluid change	12
Brake system check	see Chapter 1
Drive belt and pulleys – S and ST models	19
Drive chain and sprockets – GS and R models	18
Drive chain/belt check and adjustment	see Chapter 1
Front brake caliper	3
Front brake disc	4
Front brake master cylinder	5
Front brake pads	2
Front wheel	15
General information	1

	Section
Rear axle and eccentric adjuster assembly – S and ST models	21
Rear brake caliper	7
Rear brake disc	8
Rear brake master cylinder	9
Rear brake pads	6
Rear sprocket dampers (GS and R) and pulley coupling dampers (S and ST)	20
Rear wheel	16
Tyres	22
Tyre pressure, tread depth and condition	see Pre-ride checks
Wheel alignment check	14
Wheel bearing check	see Chapter 1
Wheel bearings	17
Wheel check	see Chapter 1
Wheel inspection and repair	13

Degrees of difficulty

Easy, suitable for novice with little experience	Fairly easy, suitable for beginner with some experience	Fairly difficult, suitable for competent DIY mechanic	Difficult, suitable for experienced DIY mechanic	Very difficult, suitable for expert DIY or professional

Specifications

Brakes

ABS sensor air gap	0.1 to 1.3 mm
Brake fluid type	DOT 4
Front caliper type	
F650 GS and F800 GS	Two piston sliding caliper
F800 S, ST and R	Four piston opposed caliper
Front disc diameter	
F650 GS and F800 GS	300 mm
F800 S, ST and R	320 mm
Front disc thickness	
F650 GS and F800 GS	
Standard	5.0 mm
Service limit	4.5 mm
F800 S, ST and R	
Standard	4.5 mm
Service limit	4.0 mm
Front disc maximum runout	0.15 mm
Rear brake pedal stop clearance	2.0 to 3.0 mm
Rear caliper type	Single piston sliding caliper
Rear disc diameter	265 mm
Rear disc thickness	
Standard	5.0 mm
Service limit	4.5 mm
Rear disc maximum runout	0.20 mm

Wheels

Wheel size

F800 S and ST	Front 3.50 x 17 MT H2, Rear 5.50 x 17 MT H2
F650 GS	Front 2.50 x 19 MT H2, Rear 3.50 x 17 MT H2
F800 GS	Front 2.15 x 21 MT H2, Rear 4.25 x 17 MT H2
F800 R	Front 3.50 x 17 MT H2, Rear 5.50 x 17 MT H2

Maximum wheel runout – front and rear

F800 GS (wire spoked wheels)

Axial (side-to-side)	1.7 mm
Radial (out-of-round).....................................	1.7 mm

All other models (cast wheels)

Axial (side-to-side)	1.5 mm
Radial (out-of-round).....................................	1.5 mm

Tyres

Tyre pressures	see *Pre-ride checks*

Tyre sizes*

F800 S and ST	Front 120/70-ZR 17, Rear 180/55-ZR 17
F650 GS	Front 110/80-R 19 (59V) TL, Rear 140/80-R 17 (69V) TL
F800 GS	Front 90/90- 21 (54V) tubed, Rear 150/70-R 17 (69V) tubed
F800 R	Front 120/70-ZR 17, Rear 180/55-ZR 17

*Refer to the Owners Handbook or the tyre information label on the swingarm for approved tyre brands.

Final drive – GS and R models

Drive chain slack and lubrication	see Chapter 1
Drive chain type	O-ring 525 5/8 x 5/16

Length

F650 GS and F800 GS	116 links
F800 R	120 links

Sprocket sizes

F650 GS	17 tooth front, 41 tooth rear
F800 GS	16 tooth front, 42 tooth rear
F800 R	20 tooth front, 47 tooth rear

Final drive – S and ST models

Drive belt slack...	see Chapter 1
Drive belt type	Contitech CTD 1903-C 11M-34
Pulley sizes..	34 tooth front, 80 tooth rear

Torque settings

Brake hose banjo bolts.......................................	24 Nm
Brake pipe gland nuts	14 Nm
Drive belt adjuster screw (S and ST models)	10 Nm

Drive belt eccentric adjuster clamp screws (S and ST models)

Initial torque	15 Nm
Final torque..	30 Nm

Front axle

GS models	30 Nm
S, ST and R models	50 Nm

Front axle clamp bolt(s)

GS models	19 Nm
S, ST and R models	20 Nm

Front brake caliper mounting bolts

GS models	38 Nm
S, ST and R models	30 Nm

Front brake disc bolts

F650 GS	11 Nm
F800 GS	8 Nm

S and ST models

Initial setting	12 Nm
Final setting	24 Nm
R models	19 Nm
Front brake master cylinder clamp bolts	5 Nm

Front pulley bolt – S and ST models

Initial setting	60 Nm
Final setting	+70°
Front sprocket bolt – GS and R models........................	50 Nm
Rear axle nut – GS and R models	100 Nm

Torque settings (continued)

Rear brake caliper bracket bolts – S and ST models...............	22 Nm
Rear brake disc bolts	
GS models	19 Nm
S, ST and R models	20 Nm
Rear brake master cylinder mounting bolts	
GS models	8 Nm
S, ST and R models	9 Nm
Rear pulley bolts/nuts – S and ST models....................	25 Nm
Rear pulley coupling nut – S and ST models..................	160 Nm
Rear sprocket nuts – GS and R models	
Initial setting	10 Nm
Final setting	+90° Nm
Rear wheel bolts – S and ST models.........................	60 Nm

1 General information

All models have hydraulically operated disc brakes. F800 S, ST and R models have twin front discs with four piston opposed calipers, F800 GS models have twin front discs with two piston sliding calipers, and F650 GS models have a single front disc with a two piston sliding caliper. All models are fitted with a single piston sliding caliper at the rear.

An anti-lock braking system (ABS), which prevents the wheels from locking up under hard braking, is available as an optional extra on all models covered in this manual. If required, the system can be switched off on GS models for off-road riding.

Drive to the rear wheel is by chain and sprockets on GS and R models, and by belt and pulleys on S and ST models. On GS and R models, the rear wheel hub incorporates a cush-drive. On S and ST models, cush-drive dampers are located in the rear pulleys on all models, and in the front pulleys on some market models.

F800 GS models are fitted with wire spoked wheels designed for tubed tyres only. All other models covered in this manual are fitted with cast alloy wheels designed for tubeless tyres only.

Note: *On ABS models, any work done on the brake system that involves bleeding the system afterwards requires the use of the BMW* diagnostic tester to restore braking action. Work on ABS components should either be carried out by a BMW dealer, or on completion of any work the machine should be transported (DO NOT ride) to a BMW dealer for the system to be reactivated and if necessary any fault codes cleared.

Caution: *Disc brake components rarely require disassembly. Do not disassemble components unless absolutely necessary. If a brake hose is loosened or disconnected, the union sealing washers must be replaced with new ones and the system must be bled upon reassembly. Do not use solvents on internal brake components. Solvents will cause the seals to swell and distort. Use only clean DOT 4 brake fluid. Use care when working with brake fluid as it can injure your eyes and it will damage painted surfaces and plastic parts.*

2 Front brake pads

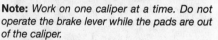

Note: *Work on one caliper at a time. Do not operate the brake lever while the pads are out of the caliper.*

Removal
GS models

1 Press the brake caliper against the disc to ease the pistons back into the caliper.
2 Note the location of the R-clip securing the pad pin, then pull out the clip **(see illustration)**.
3 Drive the pad pin out using a suitable punch, then ease the pads out, noting how they fit **(see illustrations)**.

S, ST and R models

4 Note the location of the R-clips securing the pad pins, then pull out the clips **(see illustrations)**.

2.2 Pull out the R-clip – GS models

2.3a Ease the outer . . .

2.3b . . . and inner pad out of the caliper

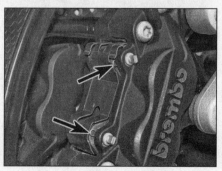

2.4a Note location of R-clips . . .

2.4b . . . then pull them out –
S, ST and R models

2.5a Withdraw the pad pins . . .

2.5b . . . and remove the caliper cover. Note the arrow on the cover

2.6 Draw the pads out of the caliper

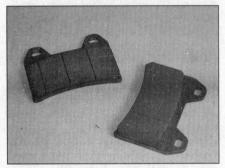

2.9 Clean the pads with a fine wire brush

5 Withdraw the pad pins and remove the caliper cover, noting how it fits **(see illustrations)**.

6 Ease the pads out, noting how they fit **(see illustration)**.

Inspection

7 Inspect the surface of each pad for contamination and check that the friction material has not worn beyond its service limit (see Chapter 1, Section 5). If any pad is worn down to, or beyond, the service limit wear indicator, is fouled with oil or grease, or is heavily scored or damaged, fit a set of new pads. **Note:** *It is not possible to degrease the friction material; if the pads are contaminated in any way they must be replaced with new ones.*

8 If the pads have worn unevenly, displace the caliper and check the operation of the pistons (see Section 3). If any piston appears seized, or on GS models, the caliper slider pins are seized, it will be necessary to overhaul the caliper (see Section 3).

9 If the pads are in good condition clean them carefully, using a fine wire brush which is completely free of oil and grease to remove all traces of road dirt and corrosion **(see illustration)**. Using a pointed instrument, dig out any embedded particles of foreign matter. If available, spray with a dedicated brake cleaner and/or compressed air to remove any dust.

10 Remove all traces of corrosion from the pad pin(s) and check for wear and damage **(see illustration)**.

11 If required, follow the procedure in Section 3 to displace the caliper, then spray the inside with dedicated brake cleaner to remove any dust. Note the location of the pad spring inside the caliper.

12 Check the condition of the brake disc (see Section 4).

13 If new pads are to be fitted, create room for them by pushing the pistons back into the caliper with a piece of wood, taking care not to lever against the brake disc. If the pistons are difficult to push back, temporarily displace the caliper (see Section 3). Install the old pads, then insert a large flat-bladed screwdriver between them and lever them apart to retract the pistons. Alternatively, use a commercially available piston spreader tool **(see illustration)**. If the brake master cylinder reservoir is full, it is advisable to remove the cover, plate and diaphragm and siphon out some fluid (see *Pre-ride checks*).

Installation

GS models

14 Locate the inner pad in the caliper, ensuring the friction material faces the disc **(see illustration 2.3b)**. Press the pad against the spring so that the holes in the pad and caliper align, then secure the pad with the pad pin.

15 Locate the outer pad in the caliper, ensuring the friction material faces the disc **(see illustration 2.3a)**. Press the pad against the spring so that the holes in the pad and caliper align, then secure the pad with the pad

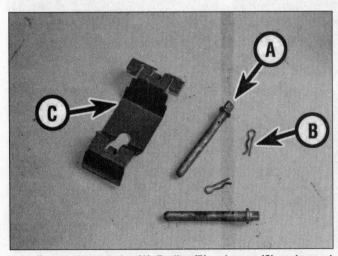

2.10 Ensure the pad pins (A), R-clips (B) and cover (C) are in good condition

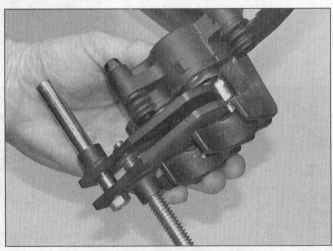

2.13 Using a piston spreader tool

pin, driving the pin all the way through **(see illustration)**.

16 Install the R-clip **(see illustration 2.2)**. Now go to Step 20.

S, ST and R models

17 Slide the pads into the caliper, ensuring the friction material faces the disc **(see illustration 2.6)**.

18 Install the caliper cover, ensuring it is the correct way round **(see illustration 2.5b)**. Align the holes in the pads with the holes in the caliper and insert the upper pad pin **(see illustration)**.

19 Press the pads down against the spring and insert the lower pad pin. Secure both pins with the R-clips **(see illustration 2.4a)**.

20 Operate the brake lever until the pads contact the disc. Check the brake fluid level in the reservoir and top-up if necessary (see *Pre-ride checks*).

21 Check the operation of the brake before riding the motorcycle.

---

3 Front brake caliper

Warning: If a caliper is in need of renewal or overhaul, all old brake fluid should be flushed from the system. Overhaul must be done in a spotlessly clean work area to avoid contamination and possible failure of the brake system. Do not, under any circumstances, use petroleum-based solvents to clean brake parts. Use clean DOT 4 brake fluid, dedicated brake cleaner or denatured alcohol only. To prevent damage from spilled brake fluid, always cover paintwork when working on the brake system.

Note 1: *Refer to Section 1 regarding the bleeding of the brake system on ABS models.*

Note 2: *If the caliper is being overhauled or renewed (usually due to sticking pistons or fluid leaks) read through the entire procedure first and make sure that you have obtained all the new parts required, and some new DOT 4 brake fluid. BMW only supply front brake caliper rebuild kits for GS models.*

2.15 Drive the pad pin through with a suitable punch

Note 3: *Work on one caliper at a time. Do not operate the brake lever while the caliper is off the disc.*

Removal

GS models

1 If the caliper is just being displaced, unscrew the caliper mounting bolts and slide the caliper off the disc **(see illustrations)**. On F800 GS models, if applicable, note how the mounting bolts for the left-hand caliper secure the bracket for the front wheel speed sensor cable. Secure the caliper to the motorcycle with a cable-tie to avoid straining the brake hose.

2 If the caliper is being completely removed, first remove the brake pads (see Section 2).

3 Note the alignment of the brake hose banjo union with the caliper **(see illustration)**. Unscrew the banjo bolt and detach the union – note the location of the sealing washers

3.1a Unscrew the caliper mounting bolts . . .

2.18 Insert the upper pad pin

and discard them as new ones must be fitted **(see illustration)**. On F800 GS models, note the twin hose arrangement on the left-hand side and the spacer located between the two banjo unions. **Note:** *If you are planning to overhaul the caliper and don't have a source of compressed air to blow out the pistons, just loosen the banjo bolt, then retighten it lightly at this stage. The brake system can be used to force the pistons out of the body once the caliper has been displaced.*

4 Wrap a small plastic bag around the banjo union and secure the hose in an upright position to minimise fluid loss.

5 Unscrew the caliper mounting bolts and slide the caliper off the disc (see Step 1).

S, ST and R models

6 If the caliper is just being displaced, unscrew the caliper mounting bolts and slide the caliper off the disc **(see illustration)**. If applicable, release the front wheel speed

3.1b . . . and slide the caliper off the disc

3.3a Note the alignment of the brake hose banjo union

3.3b Sealing washers are fitted both sides of the union

3.6a Unscrew the caliper mounting bolts . . .

3.6b ... and slide the caliper off the disc

3.6c Release the speed sensor cable from the clips (arrowed)

3.8 Note the alignment of the brake hose banjo union

sensor cable from the clips and ties securing it to the left-hand brake hose **(see illustration)**. Secure the caliper to the motorcycle with a cable-tie to avoid straining the brake hose.

7 If the caliper is being completely removed, first remove the brake pads (see Section 2).

8 Note the alignment of the brake hose banjo union with the caliper **(see illustration)**. Unscrew the banjo bolt and detach the union – note the location of the sealing washers and discard them as new ones must be fitted.

9 Wrap a small plastic bag around the banjo union and secure the hose in an upright position to minimise fluid loss.

10 Unscrew the caliper mounting bolts and slide the caliper off the disc (see Step 6).

Overhaul

GS models

11 Clean the exterior of the caliper with denatured alcohol or brake system cleaner. Have some clean rag ready to catch any spilled brake fluid.

12 Slide the caliper off its bracket **(see illustration)**. Note the location of the pad spring inside the caliper and the pad plate on the caliper bracket and remove them if required for cleaning or renewal **(see illustration)**.

13 Clean all traces of corrosion and hardened grease off the slider pins and examine the pin boots for cracks and splits. Replace the boots with new ones on reassembly if necessary.

14 Mark each piston and the caliper body to ensure that the pistons can be matched to their original bores on reassembly (see Step 20). Note the plastic plugs located in the outer ends of the pistons.

15 Displace the pistons as far as possible from the caliper body, either by pumping them out by operating the brake lever, or by easing them out using compressed air. If compressed air is used, place a wad of rag inside the caliper to act as a cushion and direct the air into the fluid inlet on the caliper **(see illustrations)**. Use only low pressure and make sure the pistons are displaced evenly, using a small piece of wood or thick card to block one while the other moves if necessary **(see illustration)**. Have some rag ready to catch any spilled brake fluid.

16 If a piston is stuck in its bore due to corrosion, the caliper should be replaced with a new one. Do not try to remove a piston by levering it out or by using pliers or grips.

17 Remove the outer dust seals and inner piston seals from the caliper bores using a soft wooden or plastic tool to avoid scratching the bores **(see illustration)**. Discard the seals as new ones must be fitted on reassembly.

18 Clean the pistons and bores with clean brake fluid. If compressed air is available, blow it through the fluid galleries in the caliper

3.12a Slide the caliper off its bracket

3.12b Location of pad spring (A) and pad plate (B)

3.15a Apply compressed air to the fluid inlet ...

3.15b ... until the pistons are displaced

3.15c Using thick card to block one piston

3.17 Remove the old seals carefully to avoid scratching the bores

3.20 Match the corresponding seals and pistons before installation

3.21 Fit the new seals into their grooves

3.22 Ease the pistons in carefully

to ensure they are clear (make sure the air is filtered and unlubricated).
Caution: Do not, under any circumstances, use a petroleum-based solvent to clean brake parts.

19 Inspect the caliper bores and pistons for signs of wear, corrosion, nicks and burrs. If surface defects are present, the caliper assembly must be replaced with a new one. On F800 GS models, if one caliper is in poor condition, the other front caliper should also be checked.

20 Note that there are two sizes of bore in the front caliper and care must therefore be taken to ensure that the correct size piston seals are fitted to the correct bores – the same applies when fitting the new dust seals and pistons **(see illustration)**.

21 Lubricate the new piston seals with the special grease supplied with the rebuild kit, or with clean brake fluid, and fit them into their grooves in the caliper bores **(see illustration)**. Follow the same procedure to install the new dust seals.

22 Lubricate the pistons and fit them, closed-end first (plastic plugs facing out), into the caliper bores, taking care not to displace the seals **(see illustration)**. Using your thumbs, push the pistons all the way in, making sure they enter the bore squarely.

23 Fit the pad spring into the caliper, ensuring it is the correct way round – the spring should be a tight fit, otherwise renew it **(see illustration 3.12b)**. Make sure the pad plate is located securely on the caliper bracket.

24 Make sure the slider pin boots are secure.

Lubricate the slider pins with a smear of silicone based grease.

25 Slide the caliper onto its bracket, making sure the boots locate correctly to provide a seal **(see illustration 3.12a)**.

S, ST and R models

26 No front brake caliper rebuild kits are available for these models. If the brake operation is faulty, first remove the brake pads and inspect them for contamination and evidence of uneven wear (see Section 2).

27 Working on one caliper at a time, displace the caliper and inspect the area around the pistons for signs of fluid leakage. Temporarily install the brake pads in the other caliper, then pull the brake lever carefully and check whether the pistons move out in the caliper being tested. If any of the pistons are seized, or there is leakage, the caliper is faulty and a new one must be fitted. If possible, have the condition of the caliper assessed by a BMW dealer.

Installation

GS models

28 Slide the caliper onto the disc and tighten the mounting bolts to the torque setting specified at the beginning of this Chapter **(see illustrations 3.1b and a)**. On F800 GS models, if applicable, don't forget to fit the bracket for the front wheel speed sensor cable on the left-hand side.

29 If removed, connect the brake hose(s) to the caliper using new sealing washers on each side of each banjo union **(see illustration 3.3b)**.

On F800 GS models you will need three washers for the two hoses on the right-hand side – don't forget to fit the spacer between the banjo unions. Align the hose(s) correctly **(see illustration 3.3a)**. Tighten the banjo bolt to the specified torque setting. Now go to Step 33.

S, ST and R models

30 Slide the caliper onto the disc and tighten the mounting bolts to the torque setting specified at the beginning of this Chapter **(see illustrations 3.6b and a)**.

31 If removed, connect the brake hose to the caliper using new sealing washers on each side of each banjo union. Align the hose(s) correctly **(see illustration 3.8)**. Tighten the banjo bolt to the specified torque setting.

32 If applicable, secure the front wheel speed sensor cable to the left-hand brake hose with the clips and ties noted on removal **(see illustration 3.6c)**.

33 If removed, install the brake pads (see Section 2).

34 Top up the master cylinder reservoir with new DOT 4 brake fluid (see *Pre-ride checks*) and bleed the system as described in Section 12. Check that there are no fluid leaks. On ABS models, refer to the **Note** in Section 1.

35 Check the operation of the brake before riding the motorcycle.

| 4 Front brake disc | |

Inspection

1 Inspect the surface of the disc for score marks and other damage **(see illustration)**. Light scratches are normal after use and won't affect brake operation, but deep grooves and heavy score marks will reduce braking efficiency and accelerate pad wear. If a disc is badly grooved it must be replaced with a new one.

2 The disc must not be machined or allowed to wear down to a thickness less than the service limit listed in this Chapter's Specifications. The minimum thickness is also stamped on the disc **(see illustration)**. Check the thickness of the disc with a micrometer.

4.1 Inspect the disc for score marks and damage

4.2 Minimum thickness is stamped on the disc

4.3 Set-up for checking disc runout

4.5a Support the wheel on wooden blocks

4.5b Loosen the disc retaining bolts evenly

3 To check if the disc is warped, position the bike on an auxiliary stand with the front wheel raised off the ground. Mount a dial gauge to the fork leg, with the gauge plunger touching the surface of the disc about 10 mm from the outer edge **(see illustration)**. Rotate the wheel and watch the gauge needle, comparing the reading with the limit listed in the Specifications at the beginning of this Chapter. If the runout is greater than the service limit, check the wheel bearings for play (see Chapter 1). If the bearings are worn, install new ones (see Section 17) and repeat this check. If the disc runout is still excessive, a new disc will have to be fitted.

Removal

4 Remove the wheel (see Section 15).
Caution: Don't lay the wheel down and allow it to rest on the disc – the disc could become warped. Set the wheel on wood blocks so the wheel rim supports the weight of the wheel.
5 If you are not replacing the disc with a new one, mark the relationship of the disc to the wheel, so it can be installed in the same position as originally fitted. Undo the disc retaining bolts, loosening them evenly and a little at a time in a criss-cross pattern to avoid distorting the disc **(see illustrations)**.
6 Note the location of any washers on the bolts. On F650 GS models, a washer is located between the disc and the hub. S and ST models have a combination of spacer (underneath the bolt head) followed by spring washer and thrust washer on top of the disc,

with a second thrust washer underneath the disc – BMW recommends that new thrust washers are fitted when the disc is installed.
7 On ABS models, note the location of the speed sensor rotor. On GS models the rotor is fitted on top of the disc; on S, ST and R models the rotor is fitted below the disc. On all models except the F650 GS, the rotor is mounted on the left-hand side of the hub.
8 Lift off the disc and the sensor rotor, as applicable.

Installation

9 Before installing the disc, make sure there is no dirt or corrosion where the disc seats on the hub. If the disc does not sit flat when it is bolted down, it will appear to be warped when checked or when the front brake is used. On ABS models, do the same where the disc seats on the sensor rotor.
10 Fit the disc onto the hub with its marked side facing out, aligning any previously made matchmarks. If applicable, fit the speed sensor rotor (see Step 7).
11 Clean the threads of the disc mounting bolts, then apply a suitable non-permanent thread-locking compound. Install the bolts, with their washers where fitted, and tighten them evenly and a little at a time in a criss-cross pattern to the torque setting specified at the beginning of this Chapter.
12 Clean the disc using acetone or brake system cleaner. If a new disc has been installed, remove any protective coating from its working surfaces and fit new brake pads (see Section 2).

13 Install the front wheel (see Section 15).
14 Operate the brake lever several times to bring the pads into contact with the disc. Check the operation of the brake before riding the motorcycle.

5 Front brake master cylinder

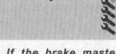

⚠️ *Warning: If the brake master cylinder is in need of renewal, all old brake fluid should be flushed from the system. Work on brake system components must be done in a spotlessly clean area to avoid contamination and possible failure of the brake system. Do not, under any circumstances, use petroleum-based solvents to clean brake parts. Use clean DOT 4 brake fluid, dedicated brake cleaner or denatured alcohol only. To prevent damage from spilled brake fluid, always cover paintwork when working on the brake system.*
Note 1: *Refer to Section 1 regarding the bleeding of the brake system on ABS models.*
Note 2: *If the master cylinder is being renewed (usually due to a sticking piston or fluid leaks) read through the entire procedure first and make sure that you have obtained all the new parts required, and some new DOT 4 brake fluid. BMW do not supply master cylinder rebuild kits.*

Removal

1 On GS and R models, remove the right-hand mirror (see Chapter 7).
2 If required, remove any bodywork panels to avoid damage from spilled brake fluid (see Chapter 7).
3 Disconnect the front brake light switch wiring connector **(see illustration)**.
4 If the master cylinder is just being displaced from the handlebar, make sure the fluid reservoir cover is secure. Undo the master cylinder clamp bolts, then wrap the master cylinder and reservoir assembly in some rag and position it clear of the handlebar **(see illustration)**. Make sure no strain is placed on the hydraulic hose. Keep the reservoir upright to prevent air entering the system.

5.3 Disconnect the front brake light switch connector

5.4 Undo the master cylinder clamp bolts

5.6 Clip secures fluid hose to master cylinder union

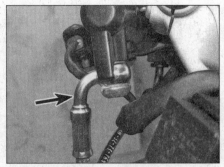

5.7 Note the alignment of the brake hose banjo union

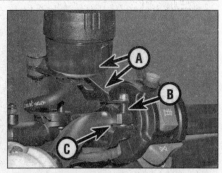

5.9 Reservoir and bracket assembly (A), clamp (B) and alignment mark (C)

5 If the master cylinder is being removed completely, unscrew the reservoir cap and remove the diaphragm plate and diaphragm (see *Pre-ride checks*). Siphon the brake fluid out into a suitable container and wipe any remaining fluid out of the reservoir with a clean rag. Inspect the reservoir diaphragm and fit a new one if it is damaged or deteriorated.
6 Release the clip securing the fluid hose to the union on the master cylinder **(see illustration)**. Have some rag to catch any residual fluid in the hose, then pull the hose off the union. Inspect the hose and fit a new one on installation if it is damaged or deteriorated.
7 Note the alignment of the brake hose banjo union with the master cylinder, then unscrew the banjo bolt and detach the hose **(see illustration)**. Note the location of the sealing washers and discard them as new ones must be fitted.
8 Wrap a small plastic bag around the banjo union and secure the hose in an upright position to minimise fluid loss.
9 Undo the master cylinder clamp bolts **(see illustration 5.4)**. Support the master cylinder/ brake lever, then lift off the reservoir and bracket assembly and remove the clamp **(see illustration)**. Note the alignment punch mark for the master cylinder clamp on the handlebar.
10 Remove the master cylinder/brake lever assembly. Follow the procedure in Chapter 5, Section 5, to remove the brake lever.
11 If required, undo the screws on the underside of the fluid hose union and remove the union – discard the O-ring as a new one must be fitted.

Installation
12 Installation is the reverse of removal, noting the following:
● Align the front brake master cylinder clamp with the punch mark on the handlebar **(see illustration 5.9)**.
● Tighten the clamp bolts to the torque setting specified at the beginning of this Chapter.
● Fit new sealing washers on each side of the banjo union.
● Align the hose as noted on removal.
● Tighten the banjo bolt to the torque setting specified at the beginning of this Chapter.
● Fill the fluid reservoir with new DOT 4 brake fluid (see *Pre-ride checks*).
● Refer to Section 12 and bleed the air from the system.
● Check the operation of the brake before riding the motorcycle.

6 Rear brake pads

Removal
GS and R models
1 Press the brake caliper against the disc to ease the piston back into the caliper **(see illustration)**.
2 Note the location of the R-clip securing the pad pin, then pull out the clip **(see illustration)**.
3 Drive the pad pin out using a suitable punch, then ease the pads out, noting how they fit **(see illustrations)**.
S and ST models
4 Remove the rear wheel (see Section 16).

6.1 Press the caliper against the disc to ease the piston back

6.2 Remove the R-clip (arrowed)

6.3a Drive out the pad pin . . .

6.3b . . . then ease the outer . . .

6.3c . . . and inner pad out of the caliper – GS and R

6.5 Pull out the R-clip (arrowed)

6.6a Drive out the pad pin (arrowed) and ease the inner . . .

5 Note the location of the R-clip securing the pad pin, then pull out the clip **(see illustration)**.
6 Drive the pad pin out from the right-hand side using a suitable punch, then ease the pads out, noting how they fit **(see illustrations)**.

Inspection

7 Inspect the surface of each pad for contamination and check that the friction material has not worn beyond its service limit (see Chapter 1, Section 5). If any pad is worn down to, or beyond, the service limit wear indicator, is fouled with oil or grease, or is heavily scored or damaged, fit a set of new pads. **Note:** *It is not possible to degrease the friction material; if the pads are contaminated in any way they must be replaced with new ones.*
8 If the pads have worn unevenly, displace the caliper and check that the slider pins are free and that the piston is not seized (see Section 7).
9 If the pads are in good condition clean them carefully, using a fine wire brush which is completely free of oil and grease to remove all traces of road dirt and corrosion. Using a pointed instrument, dig out any embedded particles of foreign matter. If available, spray with a dedicated brake cleaner and/or

compressed air to remove any dust.
10 Remove all traces of corrosion from the pad pin and check for wear and damage.
11 If required, follow the procedure in Section 7 to displace the caliper, then spray the inside with dedicated brake cleaner to remove any dust. Note the location of the pad spring inside the caliper.
12 Check the condition of the brake disc (see Section 8).
13 If new pads are to be fitted, create room for them by pushing the piston back into the caliper with a piece of wood, taking care not to lever against the brake disc. If the piston is difficult to push back, temporarily displace the caliper (see Section 7). Install the old pads, then insert a large flat-bladed screwdriver between them and lever them apart to retract the piston. Alternatively, use a commercially available piston spreader tool **(see illustration 2.13)**. If the brake master cylinder reservoir is full, it is advisable to remove the cover, plate and diaphragm and siphon out some fluid (see *Pre-ride checks*).

Installation

GS and R models

14 Locate the inner pad in the caliper, ensuring the friction material faces the disc **(see illustration 6.3c)**. Ensure the inner end of

6.6b . . . and outer pads out of the caliper – S and ST

the pad locates against the pad plate on the caliper bracket, then press the pad against the spring so that the holes in the pad and caliper align, and secure the pad with the pad pin **(see illustration)**.
15 Locate the outer pad in the caliper, ensuring the friction material faces the disc **(see illustration 6.3b)**. Press the pad against the spring so that the holes in the pad and caliper align, then secure the pad with the pad pin, driving the pin all the way through **(see illustration)**.
16 Install the R-clip **(see illustration)**. Now go to Step 21.

6.14 Locate pad against the pad plate (A) and install pad pin (B)

6.15 Drive the pin all the way through . . .

6.16 . . . and install the R-clip

S and ST models

17 Locate the inner pad in the caliper, ensuring the friction material faces the disc **(see illustration 6.6b)**. Ensure the inner end of the pad locates against the pad plate on the caliper bracket, then press the pad against the spring so that the holes in the pad and caliper align, and secure the pad with the pad pin.

18 Locate the outer pad in the caliper, ensuring the friction material faces the disc **(see illustration 6.6a)**. Press the pad against the spring so that the holes in the pad and caliper align, then secure the pad with the pad pin, driving the pin all the way through **(see illustrations)**.

19 Install the R-clip **(see illustration 6.5)**.

20 Install the rear wheel (see Section 16).

21 Operate the brake pedal until the pads contact the disc. Check the level of fluid in the reservoir and top-up if necessary (see *Pre-ride checks*).

22 Check the operation of the brake before riding the motorcycle.

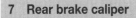
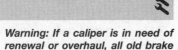

7 Rear brake caliper

Warning: If a caliper is in need of renewal or overhaul, all old brake fluid should be flushed from the system. Overhaul must be done in a spotlessly clean work area to avoid contamination and possible failure of the brake system. Do not, under any circumstances, use petroleum-based solvents to clean brake parts. Use clean DOT 4 brake fluid, dedicated brake cleaner or denatured alcohol only. To prevent damage from spilled brake fluid, always cover paintwork when working on the brake system.

Note 1: *Refer to Section 1 regarding the bleeding of the brake system on ABS models.*

Note 2: *If the caliper is being overhauled or renewed (usually due to a sticking piston or fluid leaks) read through the entire procedure first and make sure that you have obtained all the new parts required, and some new DOT 4 brake fluid.*

Note 3: *Do not operate the brake pedal while the caliper is off the disc.*

7.5a Note the alignment of the brake hose banjo union

6.18a Align the holes in the pad and caliper . . .

Removal

GS and R models

1 If the caliper is just being displaced, first remove the rear wheel (see Section 16). Note how the caliper bracket locates on the peg on the inside of the swingarm **(see illustration)**. Remove the brake hose cover (see Chapter 5, Section 13). Lift the caliper bracket assembly off and secure it to the motorcycle with a cable-tie to avoid straining the brake hose **(see illustration)**.

2 If the caliper is being completely removed, first remove the brake pads (see Section 6).

3 Remove the brake hose cover (see Chapter 5, Section 13).

4 Undo the bolt securing the speed sensor and displace the sensor **(see illustrations 10.10a and b)**.

5 Note the alignment of the brake hose banjo

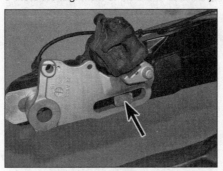

7.1a Caliper bracket locates on peg (arrowed)

7.5b Note the location of the sealing washers

6.18b . . . then drive the pin all the way through

union with the caliper **(see illustration)**. Unscrew the banjo bolt and detach the union – note the location of the sealing washers and discard them as new ones must be fitted **(see illustration)**. **Note:** *If you are planning to overhaul the caliper and don't have a source of compressed air to blow out the piston, just loosen the banjo bolt, then retighten it lightly at this stage. The brake system can be used to force the piston out of the body once the caliper has been displaced.*

6 Wrap a small plastic bag around the banjo union and secure the hose in an upright position to minimise fluid loss.

7 Remove the rear wheel and lift the caliper bracket assembly off **(see illustration)**.

S and ST models

8 Remove the rear wheel (see Section 16).

9 Follow the procedure in Chapter 5, Section 11, to remove the upper belt guard, then

7.1b Secure the caliper bracket to avoid straining the brake hose

7.7 Lift off the caliper bracket assembly

7.10a Undo the bolts . . .

7.10b . . . and slide the caliper off

7.17a Slide the caliper off its bracket –
GS model shown

7.17b Slide the caliper off its bracket –
S model shown

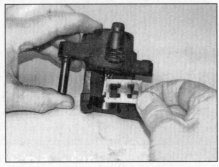

7.17c Location of the pad spring . . .

7.17d . . . and the pad plate (arrowed) –
GS model shown

remove the brake hose cover (see Chapter 5, Section 13).

10 If the caliper is just being displaced, undo the bolts securing the caliper bracket to the swingarm, then slide the caliper assembly off the disc **(see illustrations)**. Secure the assembly to the motorcycle with a cable-tie to avoid straining the brake hose.

11 If the caliper is being completely removed, first remove the brake pads (see Section 6).

12 Undo the bolt securing the speed sensor and displace the sensor **(see illustrations 10.10c and d)**.

13 Note the alignment of the brake hose banjo union with the caliper. Unscrew the banjo bolt and detach the union – note the location of the sealing washers and discard them as new ones must be fitted **(see illustration 7.5b)**. **Note:** *If you are planning to*

overhaul the caliper and don't have a source of compressed air to blow out the piston, just loosen the banjo bolt, then retighten it lightly at this stage. The brake system can be used to force the piston out of the body once the caliper has been displaced.

14 Wrap a small plastic bag around the banjo union and secure the hose in an upright position to minimise fluid loss.

15 Undo the bolts securing the caliper bracket to the swingarm, then slide the caliper assembly off the disc **(see illustrations 7.10a and b)**.

Overhaul

16 Clean the exterior of the caliper with denatured alcohol or brake system cleaner. Have some clean rag ready to catch any spilled brake fluid.

17 Slide the caliper off its bracket **(see illustrations)**. Note the location of the pad spring inside the caliper and the pad plate on the caliper bracket and remove them if required for cleaning or renewal **(see illustrations)**.

18 Clean all traces of corrosion and hardened grease off the slider pins and examine the pin boots for cracks and splits. Replace the boots with new ones on reassembly if necessary.

19 Displace the piston as far as possible from the caliper body, either by pumping it out by operating the brake pedal, or by easing it out using compressed air. If compressed air is used, place a wad of rag inside the caliper to act as a cushion and direct the air into the fluid inlet on the caliper **(see illustration)**. Use only low pressure and have some rag ready to catch any spilled brake fluid.

20 If a piston is stuck in its bore due to

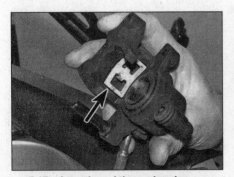

7.17e Location of the pad spring . . .

7.17f . . . and the pad plate (arrowed) –
S model shown

7.19 Apply compressed air to the fluid inlet

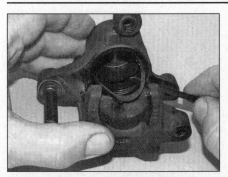

7.21 Remove the old seals carefully to avoid scratching the bores

7.24 Fit the new seals into their grooves

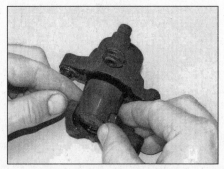

7.25 Ease the piston in carefully

corrosion, the caliper should be replaced with a new one. Do not try to remove a piston by levering it out or by using pliers or grips.

21 Remove the outer dust seal and inner piston seal from the caliper bore using a soft wooden or plastic tool to avoid scratching the bore **(see illustration)**. Discard the seals as new ones must be fitted on reassembly.

22 Clean the piston and bore with clean brake fluid. If compressed air is available, blow it through the fluid gallery in the caliper to ensure it is clear (make sure the air is filtered and unlubricated).

Caution: Do not, under any circumstances, use a petroleum-based solvent to clean brake parts.

23 Inspect the caliper bore and piston for signs of wear, corrosion, nicks and burrs. If surface defects are present, the caliper assembly must be replaced with a new one.

24 Lubricate the new piston seal with the special grease supplied with the rebuild kit, or with clean brake fluid, and fit it into its groove in the caliper bore **(see illustration)**. Follow the same procedure to install the new dust seal.

25 Lubricate the piston and fit it, closed-end first (plastic plug facing out), into the caliper bore, taking care not to displace the seals **(see illustration)**. Using your thumbs, push the piston all the way in, making sure it enters the bore squarely.

26 Fit the pad spring into the caliper, ensuring it is the correct way round – the spring should be a tight fit, otherwise renew it **(see illustrations 7.17c or e)**. Make sure the pad

plate is located securely on the caliper bracket **(see illustrations 7.17d or f)**.

27 Make sure the slider pin boots are secure. Lubricate the slider pins with a smear of silicone based grease.

28 Slide the caliper onto its bracket, making sure the boots locate correctly to provide a seal **(see illustration 7.17a and b)**.

Installation

GS and R models

29 Fit the caliper bracket assembly onto the peg on the inside of the swingarm **(see illustration 7.1a)**.

30 If removed, connect the brake hose to the caliper using new sealing washers on each side of each banjo union **(see illustration 7.5b)**. Align the hose correctly, then tighten the banjo bolt to the torque setting specified at the beginning of this Chapter.

31 Install the brake hose cover (see Chapter 5, Section 13).

32 Install the rear wheel (see Section 16).

33 Install the speed sensor and the brake pads. Now go to Step 40.

S and ST models

34 Slide the caliper onto the disc and tighten the mounting bolts to the torque setting specified at the beginning of this Chapter **(see illustrations 7.10b and a)**.

35 If removed, connect the brake hose to the caliper using new sealing washers on each side of each banjo union **(see illustration 7.5b)**. Align the hose correctly, then

tighten the banjo bolt to the torque setting specified at the beginning of this Chapter.

36 Install the speed sensor. Install the brake hose cover (see Chapter 5, Section 13).

37 Install the upper belt guard (see Chapter 5, Section 11).

38 If removed, install the brake pads (see Section 6).

39 Install the rear wheel (see Section 16).

40 Top up the master cylinder reservoir with new DOT 4 brake fluid (see *Pre-ride checks*) and bleed the system as described in Section 12. Check that there are no fluid leaks. On ABS models, refer to the **Note** in Section 1.

41 Check the operation of the brake before riding the motorcycle.

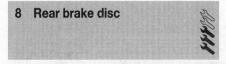

8 Rear brake disc

Inspection

1 Refer to Section 4 of this Chapter, noting that the dial gauge should be attached to the swingarm.

Removal

GS and R models

2 Remove the rear wheel (see Section 16).

Caution: Don't lay the wheel down and allow it to rest on the disc or sprocket – they could become warped. Set the wheel on wood blocks so the wheel rim supports the weight of the wheel.

3 If you are not replacing the disc with a new one, mark the relationship of the disc to the wheel, so it can be installed in the same position as originally fitted. Undo the disc retaining bolts, loosening them evenly and a little at a time in a criss-cross pattern to avoid distorting the disc **(see illustration)**. Note the location of any washers on the bolts.

4 The speed sensor rotor is installed underneath the disc mountings – note the fitment as an aid to installation **(see illustration)**. Lift off the disc and the sensor rotor.

S and ST models

5 Remove the rear wheel (see Section 16).

8.3 Loosen the disc retaining bolts evenly

8.4 Note the location of the speed sensor rotor

8.8 Location of the disc retaining bolts

8.9 Improved access to disc bolts with eccentric adjuster assembly removed

8.15 Minimum thickness marking (arrowed)

6 Displace the rear brake caliper (see Section 7).

7 If you are not replacing the disc with a new one, mark the relationship of the disc to the hub, so it can be installed in the same position as originally fitted.

8 If a suitable tool is available, undo the disc retaining bolts, loosening them evenly and a little at a time in a criss-cross pattern to avoid distorting the disc (see illustration). Lift off the disc and the speed sensor rotor.

9 Alternatively, remove the rear axle and eccentric adjuster assembly from the swingarm (see Section 21). Undo the disc retaining bolts, loosening them evenly and a little at a time in a criss-cross pattern to avoid distorting the disc (see illustration). Lift off the disc and the speed sensor rotor.

Installation

GS and R models

10 Before installing the disc, make sure there is no dirt or corrosion where the disc seats on the hub or the speed sensor rotor. If the disc does not sit flat when it is bolted down, it will appear to be warped when checked or when the rear brake is used.

11 Fit the sensor rotor and disc onto the hub. Fit the disc with its marked side facing out, aligning any previously made matchmarks.

12 Clean the threads of the disc mounting bolts, then apply a suitable non-permanent thread-locking compound. Install the bolts and tighten them evenly and a little at a time in a criss-cross pattern to the torque setting specified at the beginning of this Chapter.

13 Clean the disc using acetone or brake system cleaner. If a new disc has been installed, remove any protective coating from its working surfaces and fit new brake pads (see Section 6).

14 Install the rear wheel (see Section 16). Now go to Step 18.

S and ST models

15 Follow the procedure in Steps 10 and 11 to install the speed sensor rotor and disc, noting that the marked side of the disc should face the right-hand side of the machine (see illustration).

16 Follow the procedure in Steps 12 and 13 to secure the disc and tighten the mounting bolts, then clean the surface of the disc thoroughly.

17 Install the remaining components in the reverse order of removal.

18 Operate the brake pedal several times to bring the pads into contact with the disc. Check the operation of the brake before riding the motorcycle.

9 Rear brake master cylinder

⚠️ *Warning: If the brake master cylinder is in need of renewal, all old brake fluid should be flushed from the system. Work on brake system components must be done in a spotlessly clean area to avoid contamination and possible failure of the brake system. Do not,*

under any circumstances, use petroleum-based solvents to clean brake parts. Use clean DOT 4 brake fluid, dedicated brake cleaner or denatured alcohol only. To prevent damage from spilled brake fluid, always cover paintwork when working on the braking system.

Note 1: *Refer to Section 1 regarding the bleeding of the brake system on ABS models.*

Note 2: *If the master cylinder is being renewed (usually due to a sticking piston or fluid leaks) read through the entire procedure first and make sure that you have obtained all the new parts required, and some new DOT 4 brake fluid. BMW do not supply master cylinder rebuild kits.*

Removal

GS models

1 Release the clip securing the clevis pin on the master cylinder pushrod, then withdraw the pin and separate the pushrod from the pedal (see illustrations). If the clip is sprained, fit a new one on installation.

2 If the master cylinder is just being displaced, make sure the fluid reservoir cover is secure. Undo the reservoir mounting bolt and support the reservoir upright to prevent air entering the system (see illustration). Unclip the fluid hose from the frame and the brake pipe. Undo the master cylinder mounting bolts, lift off the heel plate and displace the master cylinder – note that movement is restricted by the rigid brake pipe.

3 If the master cylinder is being removed completely, undo the bolt securing the brake fluid reservoir (see illustration 9.2). Unscrew the reservoir cap and remove the diaphragm

9.1a Release the clip . . .

9.1b . . . and withdraw the pin

9.2 Fluid reservoir mounting bolt

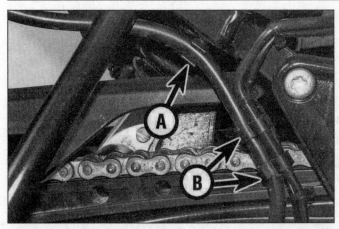

9.4 Unclip the fluid hose from the frame (A) and the brake pipe (B)

9.8 Separate the pushrod from the brake pedal

plate and diaphragm (see *Pre-ride checks*). Drain the brake fluid into a suitable container and wipe any remaining fluid out of the reservoir with a clean rag. Inspect the reservoir diaphragm and fit a new one if it is damaged or deteriorated.

4 Unclip the fluid hose from the frame and the brake pipe **(see illustration)**. Release the clip securing the fluid hose to the union on the master cylinder **(see illustration 9.11b)**. Discard the clip as a new one must be fitted. Have some rag to catch any residual fluid in the hose, then pull the hose off the union. Inspect the hose and fit a new one on installation if it is damaged or deteriorated.

5 Undo the brake pipe gland nut **(see illustration 9.12)**. Wrap a small plastic bag around the pipe end to minimise fluid loss.

6 Undo the master cylinder mounting bolts, lift off the heel plate and the master cylinder.

7 If required, ease the boot off the lower end of the master cylinder and withdraw the pushrod. Renew the boot on installation if it is damaged or deteriorated.

S, ST and R models

8 Release the clip securing the clevis pin on the master cylinder pushrod, then withdraw the pin and separate the pushrod from the pedal **(see illustration)**. If the clip is sprained, fit a new one on installation.

9 If the master cylinder is just being displaced, make sure the fluid reservoir cover is secure.

Undo the reservoir mounting bolt and support the reservoir upright to prevent air entering the system **(see illustration)**. Follow the procedure in Chapter 5, Section 3, to remove the right-hand footrest bracket – note that movement of the master cylinder is restricted by the rigid brake pipe.

10 If the master cylinder is being removed completely, undo the bolt securing the brake fluid reservoir **(see illustration 9.9)**. Unscrew the reservoir cap and remove the diaphragm plate and diaphragm (see *Pre-ride checks*). Drain the brake fluid into a suitable container and wipe any remaining fluid out of the reservoir with a clean rag. Inspect the reservoir diaphragm and fit a new one if it is damaged or deteriorated.

11 Undo the screw securing the brake hose guide to the footrest bracket **(see illustration)**. Release the clip securing the fluid hose to the union on the master cylinder **(see illustration)**. Discard the clip as a new one must be fitted. Have some rag to catch any residual fluid in the hose, then pull the hose off the union. Inspect the hose and fit a new one on installation if it is damaged or deteriorated.

12 Undo the brake pipe gland nut **(see illustration)**. Wrap a small plastic bag around the pipe end to minimise fluid loss.

13 Remove the right-hand footrest bracket (see Chapter 5, Section 3) – support the master cylinder as the bolts are withdrawn, then unclip the brake light switch wiring and lift the master cylinder off **(see illustration)**.

9.9 Fluid reservoir mounting bolt

9.11a Screw (arrowed) secures brake hose guide

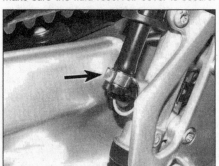

9.11b Clip secures fluid hose to master cylinder

9.12 Undo the brake pipe gland nut (arrowed)

9.13 Unclip the brake light switch wiring

10.2a Location of front wheel speed
sensor

10.2b Location of rear wheel speed sensor

10.2c Location of ABS modulator/control
unit (arrowed)

14 If required, ease the boot off the lower
end of the master cylinder and withdraw the
pushrod. Renew the boot on installation if it is
damaged or deteriorated.

Installation

15 Installation is the reverse of removal,
noting the following:
● Tighten the mounting bolts to the torque
  setting specified at the beginning of this
  Chapter.
● Tighten the brake pipe gland nut to the
  specified torque setting if the correct tools
  are available.
● Align the fluid hose as noted on removal.
● Fill the fluid reservoir with new DOT 4 brake
  fluid (see *Pre-ride checks*).
● Refer to Section 12 and bleed the air from
  the system.
● Check the operation of the rear brake light
  switch (see Chapter 8).
● Check the operation of the brake before
  riding the motorcycle.

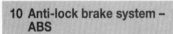

10 Anti-lock brake system –
ABS

 **Warning: The ABS works by
comparing the relative speed of
the wheels, and is programmed
using the wheel and tyre sizes
specified and fitted as standard. If
non-specified wheels or tyres are fitted the
control unit may become confused and the
system will not function correctly.**

General description

1 The anti-locking braking system (ABS) is
available as an optional extra (OE) on all the
machines covered in this manual.
2 ABS prevents the wheels from locking
up under hard braking or on uneven road
surfaces. A sensor on each wheel transmits
information about the speed of wheel rotation
to the ABS control unit **(see illustrations)**. If
the control unit senses that a wheel is about
to lock, it releases brake pressure to that
wheel momentarily via the ABS modulator,

thus preventing a skid **(see illustration)**.
When the modulator is activated, a pulsing
can be felt through the lever or pedal as the
brake pressure is released and reapplied as
required.
3 The ABS is self-checking, and is
automatically switched on with the ignition.
The warning light in the instrument cluster
illuminates and flashes intermittently until the
machine has moved off and the function of the
wheel speed sensors has been checked. The
warning light should then go off – if it remains
on, or comes on while riding, there is probably
a fault in the system
4 Stop the motorcycle and switch the ignition
OFF. Switch it ON again, start the engine and
ride the bike – if the light goes off then the
system is OK, but if the light remains on, or
comes on again, take the machine to a BMW
dealer for testing.
5 If the warning light does not come on when
the ignition is switched ON, take the machine
to a BMW dealer for testing.

Deactivating the ABS

6 On GS models it is possible, and preferable
when riding off-road, to switch the ABS off. To
do this, first ensure that the bike is stationary.
With the ignition ON, press and hold the ABS
button until the warning light illuminates, then
release the button immediately. The warning
light should remain ON (flashing) indicating
that the ABS has been deactivated.
7 The ABS will remain deactivated until the
ignition is switched OFF, and then ON again,

when the self-checking procedure will be
initiated (see Step 3). Alternatively, bring the
machine to a standstill, press and hold the
ABS button until the warning light goes off,
then release the button immediately.

Riding conditions

8 Note that under certain conditions the
warning light will come on, even though there
is no actual problem with the system. This can
occur if the machine is ridden continuously
on very bumpy roads, if the machine is ridden
with the front wheel off the ground, if the air
pressure in one tyre is extremely low, or if the
machine is placed on the centrestand or
an auxiliary stand with the engine running
and the rear wheel turning when the front is
stationary.
9 If this happens, stop the motorcycle and
turn the ignition OFF. Switch it ON again, start
the engine and ride the bike – the warning
light should go off.

Maintenance

10 Check regularly to ensure the tips of the
speed sensors are clean and that no dirt or
debris is trapped between the segments of
the sensor rotors **(see illustrations 10.2a
and b)**. If required, undo the bolt securing the
sensor and draw it out to check the condition
of the tip. The front wheel speed sensor is
mounted on the lower end of the front fork.
On GS and R models, the rear wheel speed
sensor is located on the left-hand side of the
brake caliper bracket **(see illustrations)**. On S

10.10a Undo the bolt (arrowed) . . .

10.10b . . . and remove the speed sensor –
GS and R models

10.10c Undo the bolt (arrowed) . . .

10.10d . . . and remove the speed sensor –
S and ST models

10.11 Measuring the sensor air gap

and ST models, the rear wheel speed sensor is located on the right-hand side of the brake caliper bracket **(see illustrations)** – if required, remove the rear wheel for access (see Section 16).

11 Measure the gap between the tip of each sensor and the rotor, then compare the results with the specification at the beginning of this chapter **(see illustration)**. No facility is provided for adjustment – if the gap is larger than specified, rotate the wheel to a different position and measure the gap again, and inspect the rotor for damage.

12 The speed sensor rotors are retained by the brake disc bolts – refer to Section 4 or 8 for removal and installation of the rotors.

13 ABS fault diagnosis and any other work on the system, including bleeding and changing the brake fluid, must be undertaken by a BMW dealer.

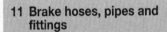

11 Brake hoses, pipes and fittings

Inspection

1 The braided hoses used on the machines covered in this manual are generally maintenance-free. However, they can be damaged and their condition should be checked periodically.

2 Inspect the banjo unions connected to the brake hoses – if they are rusted, scratched or cracked, fit new ones.

3 Inspect the hoses between the front and

rear fluid reservoirs and the master cylinders. These will deteriorate with age. Flex the hoses while looking for cracks, bulges and seeping hydraulic fluid. Check extra carefully around the area where the hoses connect and ensure the hose clips are secure and not corroded.

4 On models with ABS, also check the brake pipes for corrosion, dents or cracks **(see illustration)**. Inspect the pipe joints and gland nuts for corrosion and signs of fluid leakage **(see illustration)**.

Removal and installation

Note: *Refer to Section 1 regarding the bleeding of the brake system on ABS models.*

5 The brake hoses have banjo unions on each end. Cover the surrounding area with plenty of rags and unscrew the banjo bolt, noting the alignment of the union with the master cylinder or brake caliper **(see illustrations 3.3a, 5.7 and 7.5a)**. Free the hose from any clips or guides and remove it, noting its routing. Discard the sealing washers. **Note:** *Do not operate the brake lever or pedal while a brake hose is disconnected.*

6 Position the new hose, making sure it isn't twisted or otherwise strained, and ensure that it is correctly routed through any clips or guides and is clear of all moving components.

7 Check that the unions align correctly, then install the banjo bolts, using new sealing washers on both sides of the unions **(see illustration 3.3b and 7.5b)**. Tighten the banjo bolts to the torque setting specified at the beginning of this Chapter.

8 The brake pipe connected to the rear

brake master cylinder is secured by a gland nut – there is no sealing washer **(see illustration 9.12)**. Ensure the nut is tightened securely – tighten the nut to the specified torque setting if the correct tools are available.

9 On ABS models, the joints between the brake hoses and pipes, and where the pipes connect to the ABS modulator, are secured by gland nuts **(see illustrations 11.4a and b)**. There are no sealing washers. If required, unscrew the nuts to separate the hoses from the pipes and to detach the pipes from the modulator. When refitting them tighten the nuts to the specified torque setting if the correct tools are available.

10 Flush the old brake fluid from the system, refill with new DOT 4 brake fluid (see *Pre-ride checks*) and bleed the air from the system (see Section 12).

11 Check the operation of the brakes before riding the motorcycle.

12 Brake system bleeding and fluid change

Note 1: *Refer to Section 1 regarding the bleeding of the brake system on ABS models.*
Note 2: *If bleeding the system using the conventional method described does not work sufficiently well, it is advisable to obtain a vacuum-type brake bleeding tool (see illustration 12.18). Always follow the manufacturer's instructions when using a commercially available brake bleeding kit.*

Bleeding

1 Bleeding the brakes is simply the process of removing air from the brake fluid reservoir, the hose and the brake caliper. Bleeding is necessary whenever a brake system hydraulic connection is loosened, after a component or hose is replaced with a new one, or when the master cylinder or caliper is overhauled. Leaks in the system may also allow air to enter, but leaking brake fluid will reveal their presence and warn you of the need for repair.

2 To bleed the brakes, you will need some new DOT 4 brake fluid, a length of clear vinyl or plastic hose, a small container partially

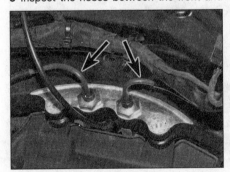

11.4a ABS pipes behind steering head – S model shown

11.4b Gland nut (arrowed) on ABS modulator

12.2a Set up for bleeding the front brake

12.2b Set up for bleeding the rear brake

12.4 Master cylinder bleed valve (arrowed) – R model shown

filled with clean brake fluid, some rags and a spanner to fit the brake caliper bleed valve (see illustrations). Brake bleeding kits for single person use are available, otherwise you will require help from an assistant.

3 Cover painted components to prevent damage in the event that brake fluid is spilled.

4 When bleeding the front brakes, note that some models have a bleed valve attached to the upper end of the master cylinder (see illustration). Apply the procedure in Step 6 to bleed air from the master cylinder end of the line first on these models.

5 In all other cases, refer to 'Pre-ride checks' and remove the reservoir cap, diaphragm plate and diaphragm, and slowly pump the brake lever (front brake) or pedal (rear brake) a few times, until no air bubbles can be seen floating up from the holes in the bottom of the reservoir. This bleeds the air from the master cylinder end of the line. Temporarily refit the reservoir cap.

6 Pull the dust cap off the bleed valve on the brake caliper (see illustration). Attach one end of the clear hose to the valve and submerge the other end in the clean brake fluid in the container (see illustration 12.2a or b). When bleeding the twin front brakes on F800 GS models, bleed the right-hand brake first. When bleeding the twin front brakes

on S, ST and R models, bleed the left-hand brake first. Note: To avoid damaging the bleed valve during the procedure, loosen it and then tighten it temporarily with a ring spanner before attaching the hose. With the hose attached, the valve can then be opened and closed either with an open-ended spanner, or by leaving the ring spanner located on the valve and fitting the hose above it.

7 Check the fluid level in the reservoir. Do not allow the fluid level to drop below the MIN mark during the procedure (see illustration).

8 Carefully pump the brake lever or pedal three or four times, then hold it in (front) or down (rear) and open the bleed valve. When the valve is opened, brake fluid will flow out of the caliper into the clear hose, and the lever will move toward the handlebar, or the pedal will move down. If there is air in the system there will be air bubbles in the brake fluid coming out of the caliper.

9 Tighten the bleed valve, then release the brake lever or pedal gradually. Top-up the reservoir and repeat the process until no air bubbles are visible in the brake fluid leaving the caliper, and the lever or pedal is firm when applied. On completion, disconnect the hose, check the bleed valve is tight (though do not overtighten it) and fit the dust cap.

HAYNES HiNT *If it is not possible to produce a firm feel to the lever or pedal, the fluid may be aerated. Let the brake fluid in the system stabilise for a few hours and then repeat the procedure when the tiny bubbles in the system have settled out.*

10 Top-up the reservoir, then install the diaphragm, diaphragm plate and cap (see Pre-ride checks). Wipe up any spilled brake fluid. Check the entire system for fluid leaks.

11 Check the operation of the brakes before riding the motorcycle.

Fluid change

12 Changing the brake fluid is a similar process to bleeding the brakes and requires the same materials plus a suitable tool for siphoning the fluid out of the reservoir. Also ensure that the container is large enough to take all the old fluid when it is flushed out of the system.

13 Follow Steps 3 and 6, then remove the reservoir cap, diaphragm plate and diaphragm and siphon the old fluid out of the reservoir. Fill the reservoir with new brake fluid, then carefully pump the brake lever or pedal three

12.6 Remove the dust cap

12.7 Don't allow the fluid to drop below the MIN level mark

or four times and hold it in (front) or down (rear) while opening the caliper bleed valve. When the valve is opened, brake fluid will flow out of the caliper into the clear tubing, and the lever will move toward the handlebar, or the pedal will move down.

14 Tighten the bleed valve, then release the brake lever or pedal gradually. Keep the reservoir topped-up with new fluid to above the MIN level at all times or air may enter the system and greatly increase the length of the task. Repeat the process until new fluid can be seen emerging from the caliper bleed valve.

 Old brake fluid is invariably much darker in colour than new fluid, making it easy to see when all old fluid has been expelled from the system.

15 Disconnect the hose, then make sure the bleed valve is tightened securely and install the dust cap.
16 Top-up the reservoir, then install the diaphragm, diaphragm plate, and cap (see *Pre-ride checks*). Wipe up any spilled brake fluid. Check the entire system for fluid leaks.
17 Check the operation of the brakes before riding the motorcycle.

Draining the system for overhaul

18 Draining the brake fluid is again a similar process to bleeding the brakes. The quickest and easiest way is to use a commercially available vacuum-type brake bleeding tool **(see illustration)**. Follow the procedure described above for changing the fluid, but quite simply do not put any new fluid into the reservoir.

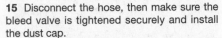
13 Wheel inspection and repair

1 In order to carry out a proper inspection of the wheels, it is necessary to support the bike upright so that the wheel being inspected is raised off the ground. Support the motorcycle on its centrestand or on an auxiliary stand. Clean the wheels thoroughly to remove mud and dirt that may interfere with the inspection procedure or mask defects. Make a general check of the wheels (see Chapter 1) and tyres (see *Pre-ride checks*).
2 Attach a dial gauge to the fork or the

12.18 Using a vacuum-type brake bleeding tool

swingarm and position its tip against the side of the wheel rim. Spin the wheel slowly and check the axial (side-to-side) runout of the rim **(see illustration)**.
3 In order to accurately check radial (out of round) runout with the dial gauge, remove the wheel from the machine, and the tyre from the wheel. With the axle clamped in a vice and the dial gauge positioned on the top of the rim, the wheel can be rotated to check the runout **(see illustration 13.2)**.
4 An easier, though slightly less accurate, method is to attach a stiff wire pointer to the fork or the swingarm and position the end a fraction of an inch from the wheel rim where the wheel and tyre join. If the wheel is true, the distance from the pointer to the rim will be constant as the wheel is rotated.
5 If wheel runout is excessive, on F800 GS models with wire spoked wheels, first make sure the spokes are properly tensioned (see Chapter 1). On all models check the wheel bearings. If all is good it may be that a new wheel is needed, but it is worth checking with a specialist first.
6 On models with cast wheels, inspect the wheels for cracks, flat spots on the rim and other damage. Look very closely for dents in the area where the tyre bead contacts the rim. Dents in this area may prevent complete sealing of the tyre against the rim, which leads to deflation of the tyre over a period of time. If damage is evident the wheel will have to be replaced with a new one. Never attempt to repair a damaged cast alloy wheel.
7 On F800 GS models with wire spoked wheels, regularly check the spokes as described in Chapter 1. Wheel rebuilding or spoke replacement must be left to a BMW dealer or wheel building specialist. A great deal of skill and some special equipment is

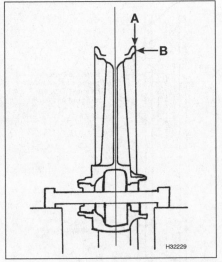
13.2 Check the wheel for radial (out-of-round) runout (A) and axial (side-to-side) runout (B)

required, and given the potential for poor handling and machine instability that could result from a poorly-built wheel, it is essential that owners do not attempt repairs themselves, unless suitably equipped and experienced.

14 Wheel alignment check

1 Misalignment of the wheels due to a bent frame or forks can cause strange and possibly serious handling problems. If the frame or forks are at fault, repair by a frame specialist or renewal are the only options.
2 To check wheel alignment you will need an assistant, a length of string or a perfectly straight piece of wood and a ruler. A plumb bob or spirit level for checking that the wheels are vertical will also be required.
3 In order to make a proper check of the wheels it is necessary to support the bike in an upright position, using an auxiliary stand. First ensure that the chain adjuster markings coincide on each side of the swingarm (see Chapter 1, Section 1) on chain drive models. Next, measure the width of both tyres at their widest points. Subtract the smaller measurement from the larger measurement, then divide the difference by two. The result is the amount of offset that should exist between the front and rear tyres on both sides of the machine.
4 If a string is used, have your assistant hold one end of it about halfway between the floor and the rear axle, with the string touching the back edge of the rear tyre sidewall.
5 Run the other end of the string forward and pull it tight so that it is roughly parallel to the floor. Slowly bring the string into contact with the front edge of the rear tyre sidewall, then turn the front wheel until it is parallel with the string. Measure the distance from the front tyre sidewall to the string **(see illustration)**.

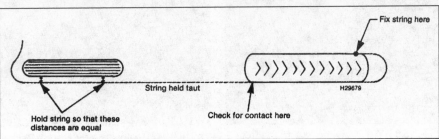
14.5 Wheel alignment check using string

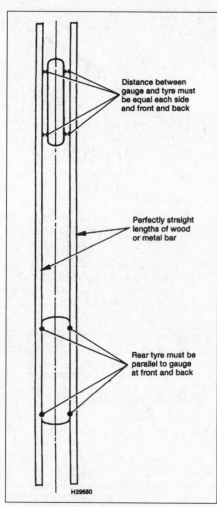

14.7 Wheel alignment check using a
straight-edge

6 Repeat the procedure on the other side of
the motorcycle. The distance from the front
tyre sidewall to the string should be equal on
both sides.

7 As previously mentioned, a perfectly
straight length of wood or metal bar may be
substituted for the string (see illustration).

8 If the distance between the string and tyre
is greater on one side, or if the rear wheel
appears to be out of alignment, have your

15.4 Loosen clamp bolt (A) and unscrew
axle (B)

machine checked by a BMW dealer or frame
specialist.

9 If the front-to-back alignment is correct, the
wheels still may be out of alignment vertically.

10 Using a plumb bob or spirit level, check
the rear wheel to make sure it is vertical. To do
this, hold the string of the plumb bob against
the tyre upper sidewall and allow the weight
to settle just off the floor. If the string touches
both the upper and lower tyre sidewalls and is
perfectly straight, the wheel is vertical. If it is
not, adjust the stand until it is.

11 Once the rear wheel is vertical, check the
front wheel in the same manner. If both wheels
are not perfectly vertical, the frame and/or
major suspension components are bent.

15 Front wheel

Removal

Special tool: *A 22 mm hex key is required to
unscrew and tighten the axle.*

1 Position the motorcycle on its centrestand
or an auxiliary stand so that the front wheel
is off the ground. Always make sure the
motorcycle is properly supported.

2 On ABS models, displace the front wheel
speed sensor (see Section 10).

3 Displace the front brake caliper(s) (see
Section 3). **Note:** *Do not operate the brake
lever while the caliper is off the disc.*

4 On F650 GS models, loosen the axle clamp

bolt on the bottom of the left-hand fork (**see
illustration**). Support the wheel, then unscrew
the axle using a hex key and withdraw it from
the left-hand side. Remove the wheel from
between the forks, and remove the spacers
from the both sides of the hub, noting how
they fit.

5 On F800 GS models, loosen the axle clamp
bolts on the bottom of the left and right-hand
forks. Support the wheel, then unscrew the
axle using a hex key and withdraw it from
the right-hand side. Remove the wheel from
between the forks, noting the 'direction of
rotation' arrow on the tyre, and remove the
spacer from the left-hand side of the hub.

6 On S, ST and R models, loosen the axle
clamp bolts on the bottom of the right-hand
fork, then support the wheel and unscrew
the axle using a hex key (**see illustration**).
Withdraw the axle from the right-hand side
(**see illustration**). Remove the wheel from
between the forks, noting the 'direction
of rotation' arrow on the tyre. Remove the
spacer from the left-hand side of the hub (**see
illustration**).

*Caution: Do not allow the wheel to rest on
the disc – it could become warped. If you
lay the wheel flat set it on wood blocks.*

Inspection

7 Clean the axle and remove any corrosion
using steel wool. Check the axle is straight
by rolling it on a flat surface such as a piece
of plate glass. If available, place the axle in
V-blocks and check for runout using a dial
gauge. No figure is given by BMW, but 0.2
mm is a typical service limit. Renew the axle if
it is bent.

8 Wipe any old grease off the bearing seals
and check the condition of the seals and the
wheel bearings (see Section 17).

9 Clean the spacer(s) and remove any
corrosion using steel wool.

Installation

10 Lubricate the axle and the lips of the
bearing seals with a smear of grease.
Install the spacer(s) as noted on removal (see
Step 4, 5 or 6.

11 Manoeuvre the wheel into position between
the forks. Ensure the 'direction of rotation'
arrow on the tyre is pointing correctly.

15.6a Loosen the clamp bolts (arrowed).
Note the hex key tool

15.6b Withdraw the axle from the
right-hand side

15.6c Remove the spacer from the
left-hand side

12 Lift the wheel and slide the axle into place – on F650 GS models, install the axle from the left-hand side, on all other models install the axle from the right-hand side. Ensure the axle is aligned with the hole in the opposite fork tube and thread it in carefully using a suitable hex key.

13 On GS models, tighten the axle to the torque setting specified at the beginning of this Chapter. Move the motorcycle off the stand and place a block of wood in front of the wheel. Bounce the front forks up-and-down a few times to settle the axle in position, then tighten the clamp bolt(s) to the specified torque setting.

14 On S, ST and R models, tighten the axle finger-tight, then follow the procedure in Step 13 to settle the axle in position. Tighten the axle to the torque setting specified at the beginning of this Chapter, then tighten the clamp bolts to the specified torque setting.

15 Install the front brake calipers (see Section 3).

16 On ABS-equipped machines install the front wheel speed sensor (see Section 10).

17 Check the operation of the brake before riding the motorcycle.

16 Rear wheel

GS and R models

Removal

1 Position the motorcycle on an auxiliary stand so that the rear wheel is off the ground. Always make sure the motorcycle is properly supported.

2 On ABS models, displace the rear wheel speed sensor (see Section 10).

3 Slacken the drive chain (see Chapter 1).

4 Remove the axle nut and washer **(see illustration)**.

5 Partially withdraw the axle and remove the right-hand chain adjuster plate, noting how it fits **(see illustration)**.

16.4 Remove the axle nut and washer

16.5 Remove the right-hand chain adjuster plate

16.6a Withdraw the axle and left-hand adjuster plate . . .

16.6b . . . and lower the wheel to the ground

6 Support the wheel, fully withdraw the axle and left-hand chain adjuster plate, then lower the wheel to the ground **(see illustrations)**.

7 Disengage the chain from the sprocket **(see illustration)**.

8 Draw the wheel back out of the swingarm. Detach the caliper bracket from the swingarm, noting how it locates **(see illustration 7.1a)**. Secure the caliper bracket assembly to the motorcycle with a cable-tie to avoid straining the brake hose **(see illustration 7.1b)**.

9 Remove the spacers from both sides of the hub, noting how they fit **(see illustrations)**.

Caution: Do not lay the wheel down and allow it to rest on the disc or the sprocket.

Set the wheel on wood blocks so the disc or the sprocket doesn't support the weight of the wheel. Do not operate the brake pedal with the wheel removed.

Inspection

10 Slide the left-hand chain adjuster plate off the axle. Clean the axle and remove any corrosion using steel wool. Check the axle is straight by rolling it on a flat surface such as a piece of plate glass. If available, place the axle in V-blocks and check for runout using a dial gauge. No figure is given by BMW, but 0.2 mm is a typical service limit. Renew the axle if it is bent.

11 Wipe any old grease off the bearing seals and check the condition of the seals and the wheel bearings (see Section 17). Lift out the sprocket coupling and check the bearing

16.7 Disengage the chain from the sprocket

16.9a Pull out the right-hand spacer

16.9b Pull out the left-hand spacer – note the lip (arrowed)

16.11 Check the bearing in the right-hand side of the hub

16.15 Ensure the head of the axle is correctly located in the adjuster plate

16.17a Manoeuvre the wheel into position

in the right-hand side of the wheel hub **(see illustration)**.

12 Check the condition of the sprocket coupling dampers (see Section 20).

13 Clean the spacers and remove any corrosion using steel wool.

Installation

14 Install the sprocket coupling (see Section 20).

15 Lubricate the axle and the lips of the bearing seals with a smear of grease. Press the spacers into the seals **(see illustrations 16.9a and b)**. Install the left-hand chain adjuster plate on the axle, ensuring the head of the axle is correctly located in the recess in the plate **(see illustration)**.

16 Make sure the caliper bracket is correctly located on the swingarm **(see illustration 7.1a)**.

17 Manoeuvre the wheel into position between the ends of the swingarm **(see illustration)**. Ensure there is enough space between the brake pads to allow installation of the disc **(see illustration)**. Lift the drive chain onto the sprocket **(see illustration 16.7)**.

18 Lift the wheel into position and slide the axle through from the left-hand side **(see illustration 16.6a)**. Push the axle all the way through **(see illustration)**. Install the right-hand chain adjuster plate, then fit the washer and axle nut finger-tight **(see illustrations 16.5 and 4)**.

19 Adjust the chain slack (see Chapter 1), then tighten the axle nut to the torque setting specified at the beginning of this Chapter.

20 On ABS models, install the rear wheel speed sensor (see Section 10).

21 Press the brake pedal several times to bring the pads back into contact with the

disc. Check the operation of the brakes before riding the bike.

S and ST models

Removal

22 Position the motorcycle on its centrestand or an auxiliary stand so that the rear wheel is off the ground. Always make sure the motorcycle is properly supported.

23 Remove the exhaust silencer (see Chapter 4).

24 Apply the rear brake and unscrew the wheel bolts **(see illustration)**.

25 Lift the wheel off the hub and lower it to the ground **(see illustration)**.

26 Check the condition of the seals and bearings in the rear axle and eccentric adjuster assembly (see Section 21).

Installation

27 Ensure there is no dirt or corrosion where the wheel seats on the hub.

28 Lift the wheel onto the hub and install the bolts finger-tight. Now tighten the bolts evenly, in a criss-cross sequence, to the torque setting specified at the beginning of this Chapter.

29 Install the silencer (see Chapter 4).

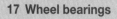
17 Wheel bearings

Caution: Don't lay the wheel down and allow it to rest on the brake disc (front) or the disc/sprocket (rear – GS and R only) – they could become warped. Set the wheel on wood blocks so the wheel rim supports the weight of the wheel.

Note: *Always renew the wheel bearings in sets, never individually. Avoid using a high pressure cleaner on the wheel bearing area.*

Special tools: *A hot air gun and an internal expanding puller with slide-hammer attachment is required to remove the bearings.*

Front wheel bearings

1 Remove the wheel (see Section 15).

2 Lever out the seals from the left and right-hand sides of the hub using a flat-bladed

16.17b Slide the brake disc between the pads

16.18 Push the axle all the way through

16.24 Unscrew the wheel bolts . . .

16.25 . . . and lift the wheel off the hub

17.2 Lever out the bearing seals

17.11 Using a socket to drive the bearing in

17.14 Driving the bearing out with a drift

screwdriver or a seal hook **(see illustration)**. Take care not to damage the hub. Discard the seals as new ones must be fitted on reassembly.

3 Inspect the bearings – check that the inner race turns smoothly and that the outer race is a tight fit in the hub (see *Tools and Workshop Tips* in the *Reference* section). **Note:** *Do not remove the bearings unless they are going to be replaced with new ones.*

GS models

4 If the bearings are worn, remove the left-hand bearing using an internal expanding puller with slide-hammer attachment (see *Tools and Workshop Tips*). Heat the bearing housing to approximately 100°C with a hot air gun to ease removal. Note that on F800 GS models, the left-hand bearing is retained by a circlip which must be removed first. If the circlip is corroded or sprained, fit a new one on installation.

5 Remove the spacer which fits between the bearings.

6 Either turn the wheel over and remove the right-hand bearing using the same procedure, or leave the wheel as it is and drive the bearing out from the top using a suitable drift.

7 Thoroughly clean the hub area of the wheel and inspect the bearing seats for scoring and wear. If the seats are damaged, consult a BMW dealer or wheel specialist before reassembling the wheel.

8 BMW advises that the new wheel bearings should be installed using the drawbolt method (see *Tools and Workshop Tips*). Install the new bearings marked sides facing out and heat the

bearing housing to approximately 100°C with a hot air gun to facilitate installation.

9 On F650 GS models, install the right-hand bearing first, the bearing spacer and then the left-hand bearing.

10 On F800 GS models, install the left-hand bearing first, the bearing spacer and then the right-hand bearing.

11 Ensure the bearings are fully seated in the hub. If a bearing driver or suitably-sized socket is used, ensure the driver bears only on the outer race of the bearing **(see illustration)**.

12 On F800 GS models, don't forget to secure the left-hand bearing with the circlip. Now go to Step 17.

S, ST and R models

13 If the bearings are worn, remove the right-hand bearing using an internal expanding puller with slide-hammer attachment (see *Tools and Workshop Tips*). Heat the bearing housing to approximately 100°C with a hot air gun to ease removal.

14 Remove the spacer which fits between the bearings, then drive the left-hand bearing out from the top using a suitable drift **(see illustration)**.

15 Clean the hub area and inspect the bearing seats (see Step 7).

16 The new wheel bearings should be installed using the drawbolt method (see *Tools and Workshop Tips*). Install the new bearings (marked sides facing out) and heat the bearing housing to approximately 100°C with a hot air gun to facilitate installation. Install the left-hand bearing, ensuring it is fully seated in the hub, then install the bearing spacer. Draw

the right-hand bearing into the hub until it contacts the bearing spacer – take care not to lift the left-hand bearing out of its housing.

All models

17 Allow the hub to cool. Apply a smear of grease to the new seals, then press them into place **(see illustration)**. Level the seals with the rim of the hub using a small block of wood if necessary **(see illustrations)**. On S, ST and R models, note that the left-hand seal has a larger inside diameter than the right-hand seal.

18 Clean the brake disc(s) using acetone or brake system cleaner, then install the wheel (see Section 15).

Rear wheel bearings

GS and R models

19 Remove the wheel (see Section 16). Lift the sprocket coupling out of the hub **(see illustration 16.11)**.

20 Lever out the seal from the left-hand side of the hub using a flat-bladed screwdriver or a seal hook **(see illustration 17.2)**. Take care not to damage the hub. Discard the seal as a new one should be fitted on reassembly.

21 Inspect the bearings in both sides of the hub – check that the inner race turns smoothly and that the outer race is a tight fit in the hub (see *Tools and Workshop Tips* in the *Reference* section). **Note:** *Do not remove the bearings unless they are going to be replaced with new ones.*

22 If the bearings are worn and need to be renewed, first remove the sprocket coupling dampers (see Section 20). Remove the circlip

17.17a Press the new seals in . . .

17.17b . . . then use a block of wood . . .

17.17c . . . to level them with the rim of the hub

17.22 Remove the circlip (arrowed)

17.35 Remove the bearing seal

17.37 Drive the bearing and spacer out from the inside

securing the left-hand bearing **(see illustration)**. Remove the left-hand bearing using an internal expanding puller with slide-hammer attachment (see *Tools and Workshop Tips*). Heat the bearing housing to approximately 100°C with a hot air gun to ease removal.

23 Remove the spacer which fits between the bearings.

24 Turn the wheel over and remove the remaining bearing using the same procedure.

25 Thoroughly clean the hub area of the wheel and inspect the bearing seats for scoring and wear. If the seats are damaged, consult a BMW dealer or wheel specialist before reassembling the wheel.

26 The new wheel bearings should be installed using the drawbolt method (see *Tools and Workshop Tips*). Install the new bearings (marked sides facing out) and heat the bearing housing to approximately 100°C with a hot air gun to facilitate installation.

27 Install the left-hand bearing first, ensuring it is fully seated in the hub, then install the bearing spacer. Draw the right-hand bearing into the hub until it contacts the bearing spacer – take care not to lift the left-hand bearing out of its housing.

28 Secure the left-hand bearing with the circlip – if the old circlip is corroded or sprained, fit a new one.

29 Allow the hub to cool. Apply a smear of grease to the new seal, then press it into the left-hand side of the hub. Level the seal with the rim of the hub using a small block of wood if necessary **(see illustrations 17.17a, b and c)**.

30 Check the condition of the sprocket coupling dampers (see Section 20).

31 Clean the brake disc using acetone or brake system cleaner, then install the wheel (see Section 16).

S and ST models

32 The rear wheel bearings are located inside the drive belt eccentric adjuster assembly. To check the bearings thoroughly, position the motorcycle on an auxiliary stand so that the rear wheel is off the ground. Displace the drive belt (see Section 19), then spin the wheel and ensure that the axle turns smoothly (see Chapter 1, Section 9).

33 If the bearings are worn or damaged, follow the procedure in Section 21 to remove the adjuster assembly. Take the assembly to a BMW dealer – disassembly requires special tools and is beyond the scope of this manual.

Sprocket or pulley coupling bearing(s)

F650 GS and R models

34 Remove the rear wheel (see Section 16). Lift the sprocket coupling out of the hub **(see illustration 16.11)**.

35 Lever out the bearing seal on the outside of the coupling using a flat-bladed screwdriver or a seal hook **(see illustration)**. Take care not to damage the rim of the coupling. Discard the seal as a new one should be fitted on reassembly.

36 Inspect the bearing – check that the inner races turn smoothly and that the outer race is a tight fit in the coupling (see *Tools and Workshop Tips* in the *Reference* section). **Note:** *Do not remove the bearing unless it is going to be replaced with a new one.*

37 If the bearing is worn, remove the circlip. Support the coupling on blocks of wood, sprocket side down. Heat the bearing housing to approximately 100°C with a hot air gun to facilitate removal and drive the spacer and bearing out from the inside using a bearing driver or socket **(see illustration)**.

38 Thoroughly clean the bearing seat and inspect it for scoring and wear. If the seat is damaged, consult a BMW dealer or wheel specialist before reassembling the wheel.

39 Heat the bearing housing to approximately 100°C with a hot air gun to facilitate installation. Install the spacer, then drive the new bearing, with its marked side facing out, into the coupling from the outside until it seats using a bearing driver or suitable socket (see *Tools and Workshop Tips*). Ensure that the driver or socket bears only on the outer race. Ensure the bearing is fitted squarely and all the way into the seat. Fit the circlip into its groove – if the old circlip is corroded or sprained, fit a new one.

40 Apply a smear of grease to the new seal, then press it into the coupling. Level the seal with the rim of the coupling using a small block of wood **(see illustrations 17.17a, b and c)**.

41 Check the condition of the sprocket coupling dampers (see Section 20).

42 Install the wheel (see Section 16).

F800 GS models

43 Remove the rear wheel (see Section 16). Lift the sprocket coupling out of the hub **(see illustration)**.

44 Drive the inner spacer out of the outer spacer using a suitable socket, then remove the outer spacer **(see illustrations)**.

17.43 Lift the sprocket coupling out of the hub

17.44a Drive the inner spacer out of the outer spacer . . .

17.44b . . . then remove the outer spacer

17.45 Levering out the coupling bearing seal

17.50a Fit the inner spacer from the inside . . .

17.50b . . . and drive it in until it seats

17.50c Press in the new bearing seal

17.50d Fit the outer spacer onto the inner spacer . . .

17.50e . . . then drive it in while supporting the inner spacer

45 Lever out the seal on the outside of the coupling using a flat-bladed screwdriver or a seal hook **(see illustration)**. Take care not to damage the rim of the coupling. Discard the seal as a new one should be fitted on reassembly.

46 Inspect the bearings – check that the inner races turn smoothly and that the outer races are a tight fit in the coupling (see *Tools and Workshop Tips* in the *Reference* section). **Note:** *Do not remove the bearings unless they are going to be replaced with new ones.*

47 If the bearings are worn, support the coupling on blocks of wood, sprocket side down. Heat the bearing housing to approximately 100°C with a hot air gun to facilitate removal. Move the centre spacer (between the two bearings) aside then drive the outer bearing out from the inside using a suitable drift located on the inner race, and moving it round so the bearing is driven out squarely. Remove the circlip and the spacer, then drive the inner bearing out using a socket on the inner race.

48 Thoroughly clean the bearing seat and inspect it for scoring and wear. If the seat is damaged, consult a BMW dealer or wheel specialist before reassembling the wheel.

49 Heat the bearing housing to approximately 100°C with a hot air gun to facilitate installation. Drive the new inner bearing, with its marked side facing out, into the coupling from the outside until it seats using a bearing driver or suitable socket (see *Tools and Workshop Tips*). Ensure that the driver or socket bears only on the outer race. Ensure the bearing is

fitted squarely and all the way into the seat. Fit the spacer and the circlip, then install the new outer bearing using the same procedure.

50 Press the inner spacer in from the inside until seated **(see illustrations)**. Apply a smear of grease to the new seal, then press it into the coupling **(see illustration)**. Level the seal with the rim of the coupling using a small block of wood. Support the inner spacer on a socket, then press the outer spacer onto the inner spacer until seated **(see illustrations)**.

51 Check the condition of the sprocket coupling dampers (see Section 20).

52 Install the wheel (see Section 16).

S and ST models

53 Remove the pulley coupling, then remove the backplate and dampers (see Section 20).

54 Inspect the bearing – check that the inner races turn smoothly and that the outer race is a tight fit in the coupling (see *Tools and Workshop Tips* in the *Reference* section).

17.55 Remove the circlip (arrowed)

Note: *Do not remove the bearing unless it is going to be replaced with a new one.*

55 If the bearing is worn, first remove the circlip **(see illustration)**. Turn the coupling over and drive the bearing out from the outside using a bearing driver or suitably-sized socket.

56 Thoroughly clean the bearing seat and inspect it for scoring and wear. If the seat is damaged, consult a BMW dealer or wheel specialist before reassembling the wheel.

57 Drive the new bearing, with its marked side facing out, into the coupling until it seats using a bearing driver or suitable socket (see *Tools and Workshop Tips*). Ensure that the driver or socket bears only on the outer race. Ensure the bearing is fitted squarely and all the way into the seat. Fit the circlip into its groove – if the old circlip is corroded or sprained, fit a new one.

58 Check the condition of the pulley coupling dampers (see Section 20).

59 Install the dampers and backplate, then install the pulley coupling (see Section 20).

18 Drive chain and sprockets – GS and R models

Drive chain

Note: *The drive chain fitted as original equipment is of the endless type (all links the same). If an aftermarket chain has been fitted which has a soft link, the chain can be split*

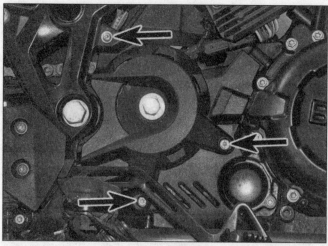

18.1a Front sprocket cover screws – GS models

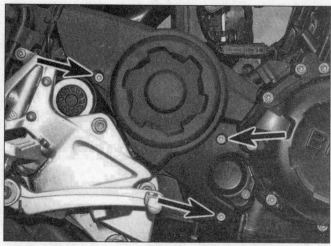

18.1b Front sprocket cover screws – R models

at the soft link and a new chain threaded into place; the procedure is given in Section 8 of 'Tools and Workshop Tips' in the Reference section of this manual.

Removal and installation

Note: *If the sprockets and chain are being renewed, loosen the front sprocket bolt before removing the drive chain (see Step 9).*

1 Undo the screws securing the front sprocket cover and lift it off **(see illustrations)**.
2 On R models, displace the right-hand footrest bracket (see Chapter 5, Section 3).

18.9a Unscrew the sprocket bolt . . .

18.11 Draw the sprocket off the shaft – note marking

3 Remove the swingarm (see Chapter 5).
4 Slip the chain off the front sprocket and remove it.
5 Refer to Chapter 1, Section 1, for details of routine chain cleaning. If the chain is extremely dirty, remove it from the motorcycle and soak it in paraffin (kerosene) or a dedicated chain cleaner for approximately five or six minutes, then clean it using a soft brush.
Caution: Don't use gasoline (petrol), solvent or other cleaning fluids which might damage its internal sealing properties. Don't use high-pressure water. Remove

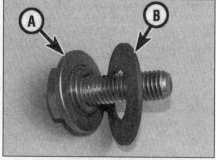

18.9b . . . and remove the shouldered (A) and spring (B) washers

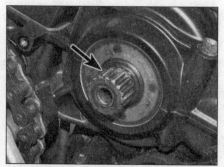

18.13 Clean and lubricate the transmission shaft

the chain, wipe it off, then blow dry it with compressed air immediately. The entire process shouldn't take longer than ten minutes – if it does, the O-rings in the chain rollers could be damaged.
6 Installation is the reverse of removal. Fit a new chain slider on the swingarm if the existing one is worn or damaged. On completion, follow the procedure in Chapter 1 to adjust and lubricate the chain.

Sprockets

7 Check both sprockets for wear (see Chapter 1, Section 1). If the sprockets need renewing, fit a new drive chain at the same time. Remove the front sprocket first.

Front sprocket

8 Remove the front sprocket cover (see Step 1).
9 Apply the rear brake, then unscrew the sprocket bolt and remove the shouldered and spring washers, noting how they fit **(see illustrations)**. If necessary heat the bolt to loosen the threadlock.
10 Fully slacken the drive chain as described in Chapter 1, or if the rear sprocket is being removed as well, remove the rear wheel (see Section 16). Otherwise disengage the chain from the rear sprocket.
11 Slip the chain off the front sprocket and draw the sprocket off the shaft, noting how it fits **(see illustration)**. If necessary, use a puller to draw the sprocket off (see *Tools and Workshop Tips* in the *Reference* section).
12 If the rear sprocket is being renewed, go to Step 19.
13 Prior to installation of the front sprocket, clean any corrosion or old grease off the shaft splines, then lubricate them with a smear of molybdenum grease (such as Optimoly TA) **(see illustration)**.
14 If the chain has been removed, install it now together with the swingarm. On R models, install the right-hand footrest bracket.
15 Engage the sprocket with the chain,

18.15 Install the sprocket and chain

18.17 Outside edge (arrowed) should touch the sprocket

18.20 Unscrew the sprocket nuts

ensuring the marked side is facing out, and slide it onto the shaft (see illustration).

16 If the chain was disengaged from the rear sprocket, fit it back on and adjust the tension as described in Chapter 1.

17 Clean the threads of the sprocket bolt. Install the shouldered washer and spring washer with the outside edge touching the sprocket (see illustration). Apply Loctite 243 to the bolt threads and tighten it to the torque setting specified at the beginning of this Chapter, using the rear brake to prevent the sprocket turning.

18 Fit the front sprocket cover (see Step 1). Check the chain slack as described in Chapter 1.

Rear sprocket

19 Remove the rear wheel and lift out the sprocket coupling (see Section 16).

20 Counter-hold the bolts then unscrew the nuts securing the sprocket to the coupling (see illustration). Remove the sprocket, noting which way round it fits.

21 Fit the sprocket onto the coupling with the marked side facing out.

22 Clean the threads of the bolts and apply a suitable non-permanent thread-locking compound. Fit the bolts and nuts and tighten them evenly and in a criss-cross sequence to the torque setting specified at the beginning of this Chapter.

23 Install the rear wheel (see Section 16).

19 Drive belt and pulleys – S and ST models

Drive belt

Removal and installation

1 Undo the screws securing the front pulley cover and lift it off (see illustration).

2 Remove the lower belt guard (see Chapter 5, Section 13).

3 Displace the right-hand footrest bracket (see Chapter 5, Section 3).

4 Loosen the drive belt adjuster clamp

screws by no more than one full turn, then back-off the adjuster screw several turns anti-clockwise (see illustration). Insert a suitable punch through the slot in the underside of the swingarm and into the hole in the eccentric adjuster assembly housing, then pull the punch towards the rear of the machine – this should rotate the assembly within the end of the swingarm and relieve any tension in the belt (see illustration).

5 If fitted, undo the screws securing the outer rim of the front pulley and lift it off (see illustrations).

6 If the belt is just being removed for maintenance and is not being renewed, note which way round it is fitted, or mark it with

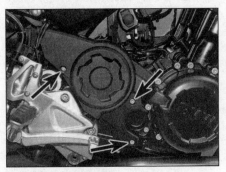

19.1 Front pulley cover screws

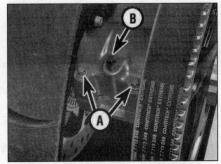

19.4a Adjuster clamp screws (A) and adjuster screw (B)

19.4b Use a punch to slacken the drive belt

19.5a Undo the screws . . .

19.5b . . . and remove the outer rim of the front pulley

19.6 Note which way round the belt is fitted

19.7a Slip the belt off the front pulley

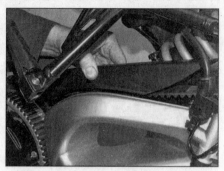

19.7b Ease the lower edge of the upper belt guard up . . .

19.7c . . . and manoeuvre the belt off

a pen or paint so that it can be installed the same way around **(see illustration)**.

7 Slip the belt off the front pulley and ease it behind the rear brake master cylinder **(see illustration)**. Ease the lower edge of the upper belt guard up and manoeuvre the belt off **(see illustrations)**. **Note:** *Take great care not to bend the belt sharply or twist it – this can damage the structure if the belt leading to premature failure.*

8 Refer to Chapter 1, Section 2, for details of routine drive belt checks. **Note:** *The drive belt should be renewed at the appropriate service interval – see Chapter 1.*

Installation

9 Installation is the reverse of removal. Once the belt is located on both pulleys, take up the initial slack using the punch in the hole in the underside of the eccentric adjuster – use light pressure to push the punch towards the front of the machine and turn the adjuster screw clockwise by hand to take up the clearance **(see illustrations 19.4b and 4a)**. Make final adjustments to the belt tension following the procedure in Chapter 1.

Pulleys

10 Check the teeth on the pulleys for wear and damage (see Chapter 1). The rear pulley coupling dampers should be renewed at the appropriate service interval.

Front pulley

Special tools: *A top dead centre (TDC) locating tool will be required for this procedure (see Chapter 2, Section 8). A suitable puller will be required to draw the pulley or pulley backplate off the transmission output shaft (see Steps 15 and 21).*

11 Follow the procedure in Steps 1 to 7 to displace the drive belt from the front pulley.

12 Two types of front pulley are fitted to the machines covered in this manual – either a one-piece pulley or a pulley assembly incorporating cush-drive dampers.

13 To remove the one-piece pulley, first follow the procedure in Chapter 2, Section 8, to lock the engine using the TDC locating tool. It is not necessary to remove the valve cover – with the aid of an assistant, and with the transmission in gear, use a spanner on the pulley centre bolt to turn the engine until the slot cut into the left-hand web of the crankshaft is visible. **Note:** *Considerable pressure will be required to undo the pulley centre bolt – ensure the locating tool is correctly installed before proceeding.*

14 Undo the pulley bolt and remove the washer **(see illustration 19.18)**.

15 To remove the pulley from the transmission shaft it is necessary to use a puller. BMW produces a service tool (Part No. 12 5 510) to do this – alternatively use a commercially available tool. Position a suitably-sized bolt or blanking piece over the end of the shaft, then install the puller fully onto the external threads on the centre of the pulley **(see illustration)**. With the transmission in gear and the engine locked, turn the puller centre bolt clockwise to draw the pulley off. Now go to Step 22.

16 On machines fitted with a front pulley assembly, first check the condition of the pulley coupling dampers as follows. Mark the pulley backplate and the adjacent pulley tooth with a line using a felt-tipped marker pen **(see illustration)**. Engage a gear, then grasp

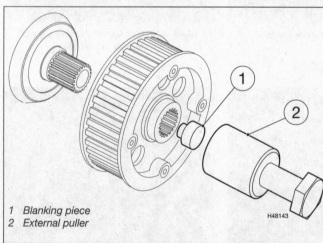

1 Blanking piece
2 External puller

H48143

19.15 Set-up for removing the front pulley

19.16 Make find reference marks across the pulley and backplate to assess damper wear

19.18 Undo the pulley bolt and remove the washer

19.19a Pull the pulley off the backplate . . .

19.19b . . . noting the location of the coupling dampers

the pulley and try to turn it forwards against the engine compression – if the paint marks separate by more than 1 mm the dampers are worn and must be renewed once the pulley has been removed.

17 The pulley centre bolt is very tight – to undo it, first follow the procedure in Chapter 2, Section 8, to lock the engine using the TDC locating tool. It is not necessary to remove the valve cover – with the aid of an assistant, and with the transmission in gear, use a spanner on the pulley centre bolt to turn the engine until the slot cut into the left-hand web of the crankshaft is visible. **Note:** *Considerable pressure will be required to undo the pulley centre bolt – ensure the locating tool is correctly installed before proceeding.*

18 Undo the pulley bolt and remove the washer **(see illustration)**.

19 Pull the pulley off the backplate, noting the location of the coupling dampers inside the pulley **(see illustrations)**. Lift out the dampers, noting how they fit **(see illustration)**.

20 Inspect the pulley and the centre bearing for wear – if necessary, fit a new pulley assembly, only the coupling dampers are available separately.

21 To remove the backplate from the transmission shaft it is necessary to use a puller. BMW produces a service tool (Part No. 27 1 551) to do this – alternatively use a commercially available tool **(see illustration)**. Position a suitably-sized nut or blanking piece over the end of the shaft, then install the puller fully onto the external threads on the centre of the backplate. With the transmission in gear and the engine locked, turn the puller centre bolt clockwise to draw the backplate off.

22 Prior to installation, clean any corrosion or old grease off the transmission shaft splines, then lubricate them with a smear of molybdenum grease (such as Optimoly TA) **(see illustration 18.13)**.

23 On machines fitted with a one-piece pulley, press the pulley onto the shaft, ensuring the lettering 'OUT' is facing out. If necessary, thread a suitable length of bar (thread size M12 x 1.5) into the end of the shaft, then use a thick washer and nut to ease the pulley onto the splines. When the pulley is fully installed, install the pulley bolt and washer. With the transmission in gear and the engine locked

19.19c Note how the pulley dampers fit

(see Step 13), tighten the pulley bolt to the torque setting specified at the beginning of this Chapter **(see illustration 19.24)**.

24 On machines fitted with a front pulley assembly, press the backplate onto the shaft – if necessary use the method described in Step 23 to install the backplate. Ensure the coupling dampers are correctly installed in the pulley, then press the pulley onto the backplate **(see illustrations 19.19b and a)**. Install the pulley bolt and washer. With the transmission in gear and the engine locked (see Step 17), tighten the pulley bolt to the torque setting specified at the beginning of this Chapter **(see illustration)**.

25 Unscrew the TDC locating tool and refit the blanking bolt using a new sealing washer (see Chapter 2, Section 8).

26 Follow the procedure in Step 9 to install the drive belt.

19.24 Using a torque angle gauge to tighten the pulley bolt

19.21 Installing the blanking piece and puller

Rear pulley

27 Follow the procedure in Steps 1 to 7 to displace the drive belt from the rear pulley.

28 Follow the procedure in Section 20 to remove the pulley coupling.

29 Counter-hold the bolts then unscrew the nuts securing the pulley to the coupling **(see illustration)**. Remove the pulley, noting which way round it fits.

30 Before installing the pulley, make sure there is no dirt or corrosion where the pulley seats on the coupling. If the pulley does not sit flat when it is bolted down, it will appear to be warped when the wheel is turned.

31 Fit the pulley onto the coupling making sure it is the correct way round – the lip on the rim should face the swingarm when the coupling is installed.

32 Clean the threads of the pulley bolts, then fit the bolts and tighten the nuts evenly and in

19.29 Undo the nuts and bolts securing the rear pulley

a criss-cross sequence to the torque setting specified at the beginning of this Chapter.

33 Install the pulley coupling but do not fit the belt at this stage (see Section 20).

34 If available, mount a dial gauge with a flat shoe on the pointer resting against the rear edge of the pulley. The shoe should be long enough to bridge two teeth on the pulley. Rotate the wheel and check the pulley radial (out of round) runout. Identify the lowest point on the pulley and mark it with a dab of paint – this mark should be used when checking belt tension (see Chapter 1). If a suitable dial gauge is not available, have the runout checked by a BMW dealer at your earliest convenience, then adjust the belt tension accordingly.

35 Install the drive belt (see Section 20).

20 Rear sprocket dampers (GS and R) and pulley coupling dampers (S and ST)

GS and R models

1 Remove the rear wheel (see Section 16). Check for freeplay between the sprocket coupling and the wheel hub by turning the sprocket. Any freeplay indicates worn damper segments.

Caution: Do not lay the wheel down on the disc as it could become warped. Lay the

20.2a Lift out the sprocket coupling . . .

20.2b . . . and check for signs of damage

wheel on wooden blocks so that the disc is off the ground.

2 Lift out the sprocket coupling leaving the dampers in position **(see illustration)**. Check the coupling for cracks or any obvious signs of damage **(see illustration)**.

3 Lift the damper segments from the hub and check them for cracks, hardening and general deterioration **(see illustration)**. Replace them with a new set if necessary.

4 Check the sprocket coupling bearing(s) (see Section 17).

5 Installation is the reverse of removal.

S and ST models

Special tool: *A 46 mm bi-hex socket is required for this procedure.*

6 Follow the procedure in Section 19, Steps 1 to 7, to displace the drive belt from the rear pulley.

7 Apply the rear brake and check for freeplay between the pulley coupling and the axle by turning the pulley **(see illustration)**. Any freeplay indicates worn damper segments. **Note:** *The coupling dampers should be renewed at the appropriate service interval – see Chapter 1.*

8 Remove the locking ring, noting how it locates **(see illustration)**.

9 Apply the rear brake and unscrew the coupling nut with the bi-hex socket **(see illustration)**. Remove the spacer, then draw the pulley coupling off the axle **(see illustrations)**.

10 Draw the backplate out from the bearing

20.3 Check the condition of the damper segments

20.7 Check for freeplay between the pulley coupling and the axle

20.8 Remove the locking ring

20.9a Unscrew the coupling nut . . .

20.9b . . . then remove the spacer . . .

20.9c . . . and draw the pulley coupling off the axle

in the centre of the coupling **(see illustration)**. Check the backplate for cracks or any obvious signs of damage.

11 Lift the damper segments from the coupling and check them for cracks, hardening and general deterioration **(see illustration)**. Replace them with a new set if necessary.

12 Examine the splines in the centre of the backplate for wear **(see illustration)**. Check the pulley coupling bearing (see Section 17).

13 Prior to installation, clean any corrosion or old grease off the axle and backplate splines, then lubricate them with a smear of molybdenum grease (such as Optimoly TA). Clean the axle threads.

14 Install the damper segments in the coupling and press in the backplate. Slide the pulley coupling onto the axle and install the spacer **(see illustrations 20.9c and b)**.

15 Apply Loctite 243 to the axle threads, then apply the rear brake and tighten the coupling nut to the torque setting specified at the beginning of this Chapter.

16 Install the locking ring, ensuring it is correctly seated in the groove around the outside of the bi-hex nut and that the cranked end is located through a convenient hole in the axle **(see illustration)**.

17 Install the drive belt (see Section 19).

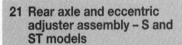

21 Rear axle and eccentric adjuster assembly – S and ST models

Removal

Note: *Disassembly requires special tools and is beyond the scope of this manual.*

1 Remove the rear wheel (see Section 16).

2 Remove the pulley coupling (see Section 20).

3 Displace the rear brake caliper (see Section 7).

4 Loosen the drive belt eccentric adjuster clamp screws, then unscrew and remove the adjuster screw **(see illustration)**.

5 Insert a suitable punch through the slot in the underside of the swingarm and into the hole in the eccentric adjuster assembly housing (see Section 19, Step 4). Adjust the position of the housing so that the cut-out in the lip on the left-hand side aligns with the pin on the swingarm **(see illustration)**.

6 Grasp the brake disc and draw the eccentric adjuster assembly out from the end of the swingarm **(see illustration)**.

7 If required, remove the brake disc (see Section 8).

Installation

8 Prior to installation, ensure the housing in the end of the swingarm is clean and free from corrosion **(see illustration)**.

9 If removed, install the brake disc (see Section 8).

10 Install the eccentric adjuster assembly from the left-hand side **(see illustration 21.6)**

20.10 Remove the backplate

20.11 Check the condition of the damper segments

20.12 Examine the splines (arrowed) for wear

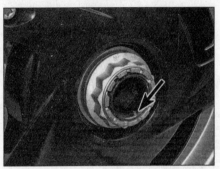

20.16 Installed position of the locking ring

21.4 Remove the adjuster screw

21.5 Cut-out (A) must align with the pin (B)

21.6 Draw the assembly out from the swingarm

21.8 Clean inside the housing – note adjustment slot (arrowed)

21.10 Installed position of the eccentric adjuster assembly

– ensure the cut-out in the lip of the housing aligns with the pin on the swingarm (see Step 5). Press the assembly all the way in **(see illustration)**.

11 Tighten the eccentric adjuster clamp screws evenly to the initial torque setting specified at the beginning of this Chapter. Install the adjuster screw hand tight, then tighten the clamp screws to the final torque setting specified. Note that final positioning of the eccentric adjuster assembly will be undertaken when the drive belt tension is adjusted.

12 Install the remaining components in the reverse order of removal. Clean the brake disc using acetone or brake system cleaner.

22 Tyres

General information

1 The wire-spoked wheels fitted on F800 GS models are designed to take tubed tyres. On all other models covered in this manual, the cast alloy wheels are designed to take tubeless tyres only. Tyre sizes are given in the *Introduction* at the beginning of this manual.

2 Refer to the *Pre-ride checks* listed at the beginning of this manual for tyre maintenance.

Fitting new tyres

3 When selecting new tyres, refer to the tyre information in the Owner's Handbook. Ensure that front and rear tyre types are compatible, of the correct size and correct speed rating – if necessary seek advice from a BMW dealer or tyre fitting specialist **(see illustration)**.

4 It is recommended that tyres are fitted by a motorcycle tyre specialist rather than attempted in the home workshop. This is particularly relevant in the case of tubeless tyres because the force required to break the seal between the wheel rim and tyre bead is substantial, and is usually beyond the capabilities of an individual working with normal tyre levers. Additionally, the specialist will be able to balance the wheels after tyre fitting.

5 Note that punctured tubeless tyres can in some cases be repaired. Seek the advice of a BMW dealer or a motorcycle tyre fitting specialist concerning tyre repairs.

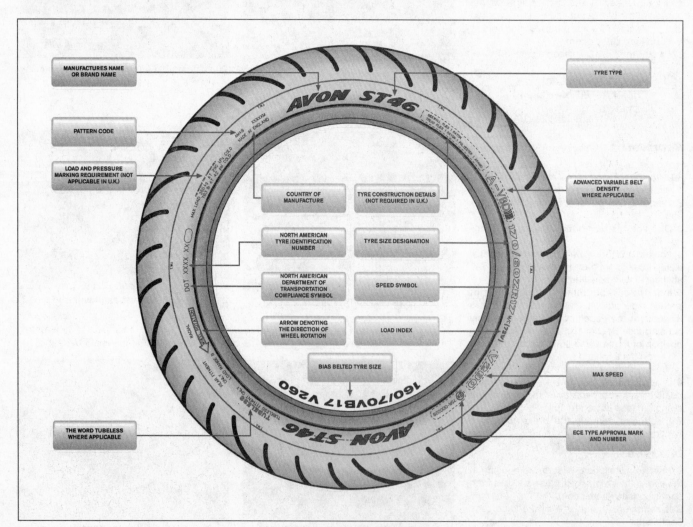

22.3 Common tyre sidewall markings

Chapter 7
Bodywork

Contents

	Section		Section
F650 GS and F800 GS models	2	F800 S and ST models	3
F800 R model	4	General information	1

Degrees of difficulty

Easy, suitable for novice with little experience		**Fairly easy,** suitable for beginner with some experience		**Fairly difficult,** suitable for competent DIY mechanic		**Difficult,** suitable for experienced DIY mechanic		**Very difficult,** suitable for expert DIY or professional	

1 General information

This Chapter covers the procedures necessary to remove and install the bodywork. Since many service and repair operations on these motorcycles require the removal of the body panels, the procedures are grouped here and referred to from other Chapters.

In the case of damage to the bodywork, it is usually necessary to remove the broken component and replace it with a new (or used) one. The material that the body panels are composed of doesn't lend itself to conventional repair techniques. Note that there are however some companies that specialise in 'plastic welding' and there are a number of bodywork repair kits now available for motorcycles.

When attempting to remove any body panel, first study it closely, noting any fasteners and associated fittings, to be sure of returning everything to its correct place on installation. In some cases the aid of an assistant will be required when removing panels, to help avoid the risk of damage to paintwork. Once the evident fasteners have been removed, try to withdraw the panel as described but DO NOT FORCE IT – if it will not release, check that all fasteners have been removed and try again.

When installing a body panel, first study it closely, noting any fasteners and associated fittings removed with it, to be sure of returning everything to its correct place. Check that all fasteners are in good condition, including the U-clips and Wellnuts **(see illustrations)**. Replace any faulty fasteners with new ones before the panel is reassembled. Check also that all mounting brackets are straight and repair them or replace them with new ones if necessary before attempting to install the panel.

Tighten the fasteners securely, but be careful not to overtighten any of them or the panel may break (not always immediately) due to the uneven stress.

2 F650 GS and F800 GS models

Seat

1 Insert the ignition key into the lock located below the front, left-hand side of the seat and turn it to unlock the seat **(see illustration)**.

1.1a Ensure all U-clips (arrowed) ...

1.1b ... and Wellnuts are in good condition

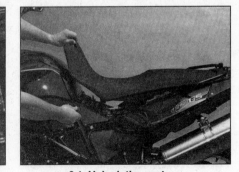

2.1 Unlock the seat ...

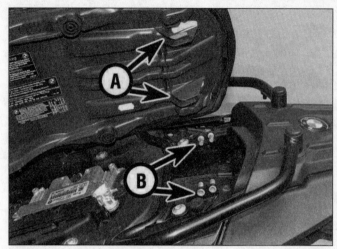

2.2 . . . and draw it forwards to release hooks (A) from tabs (B)

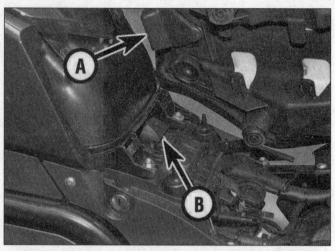

2.3 Tab (A) on seat base engages with latch mechanism (B)

2.5 Undo screw on both sides of ignition switch panel

2.6a Undo the screws (arrowed) . . .

2 Draw the seat forwards to release the hooks at the rear of the seat base from the tabs on the frame **(see illustration)**.

3 On installation, secure the hooks at the rear of the seat first, then press down on the front until the tab on the seat base engages with the latch mechanism **(see illustration)**.

Bodywork centre panel

4 Remove the seat (see Steps 1 and 2).
5 To remove the centre panel, first undo the screw on both sides of the ignition switch panel **(see illustration)**.
6 Undo the screws on the top of the centre panel, then lift the panel and disconnect the accessory socket wiring connector **(see illustrations)**.
7 Installation is the reverse of removal.

Screen

8 Undo the screws securing the screen, noting the location of the plastic washers, and lift the screen off **(see illustrations)**.
9 The screws are retained by Wellnuts located in the mounting brackets – if they are loose, new ones must be fitted **(see illustration 1.1b)**.
10 Installation is the reverse of removal. Renew any plastic washers that are hardened of cracked. Apply a smear of grease to the screw threads on installation.

2.6c . . . and disconnect the accessory socket connector

2.6b . . . then lift the centre panel . . .

2.8a Undo the screws (arrowed) . . .

2.8b . . . noting the location of the plastic washers . . .

2.8c . . . and lift the screen off

2.12a Undo the screws on both sides . . .

2.12b . . . and remove the upper front mudguard

2.13 Remove the joining piece

2.14a Undo the screws securing the underside . . .

2.14b . . . upper rear . . .

2.14c . . . and upper front edges of the panel

Bodywork side panels

11 Remove the seat, bodywork centre panel and screen (see Steps 1 to 8).
12 Undo the screws securing the upper front mudguard and lift it off **(see illustrations)**.
13 Undo the screws securing the joining piece across the front of the bodywork panels below the headlight unit **(see illustration)**.
14 Working on one panel at a time, undo the screws securing the underside, upper rear and upper front edges of the panel **(see illustrations)**. Support the panel and disconnect the turn signal wiring connector – in some cases it may be necessary to cut the wiring ties **(see illustrations)**.
15 Installation is the reverse of removal. Renew any wiring ties that were cut and check the operation of the turn signals before riding the motorcycle.

Passenger handles

16 Remove the seat (see Steps 1 and 2).

2.14d Disconnect the turn signal connector . . .

2.14e . . . cut any wiring ties . . .

2.14f . . . and lift the panel off

2.17a Prise out the blanking caps . . .

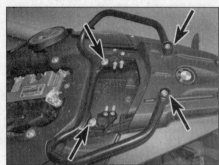

2.17b . . . then unscrew the bolts . . .

2.17c . . . and lift the handles off

2.21a Undo the screws . . .

2.21b . . . draw the top cover forwards and off

17 Prise out the blanking caps from the ends of the passenger handle mountings, then unscrew the bolts and lift the handles off **(see illustrations)**.

18 Installation is the reverse of removal.

Rear panels

19 Remove the seat (see Steps 1 and 2).

20 Remove the passenger handles (see Step 17).

21 Undo the screws securing the top cover, then draw it forwards and off **(see illustrations)**.

22 Undo the screws securing the right-hand side panel and lift it off, noting how the lower edge locates over the tab on the side of the fuel tank **(see illustrations)**.

23 Undo the screws securing the left-hand side panel and the screw securing the upper, left-hand side of the rear mudguard assembly **(see illustrations)**. Ease the rear edge of the side panel out from underneath the front edge of the mudguard and lift it off **(see illustration)**.

24 Installation is the reverse of removal.

Rear mudguard assembly

25 Remove the seat, passenger handles and rear panels (see above).

26 Note the location of the wiring for the tail light, licence plate light and turn signals **(see illustration)**. Release the wiring from the ties

2.22a Undo the screws (arrowed)

2.22b Lower edge of panel locates over tab (arrowed)

2.23a Undo the side panel screws . . .

2.23b . . . and the rear mudguard screw . . .

2.23c Ease rear edge of panel from underneath front edge of mudguard

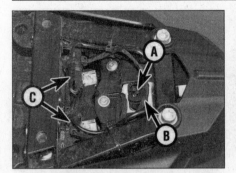

2.26a Tail light (A), licence plate light (B) and turn signal (C) wiring

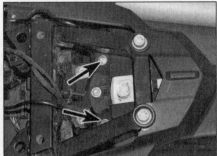

2.26b Screws secure mudguard assembly to frame and underseat panel

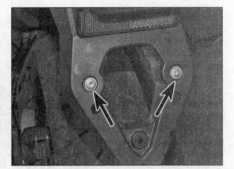

2.27a Undo screws securing rear mudguard . . .

and disconnect it at the connectors, including the connector on the top of the tail light unit. Undo the screws securing the mudguard assembly to the frame and the underseat panel **(see illustrations)**.

27 Remove the licence plate and undo the screws securing the mudguard to the underseat panel **(see illustration)**.

28 Undo the bolts securing the assembly to the frame, noting the location of the spacer and plain washer on each bolt, and lift the mudguard assembly off **(see illustrations)**.

29 Installation is the reverse of removal. Ensure the washers and spacers are correctly located on the mounting bolts. Secure the wiring as noted on removal and check the operation of the lights and turn signals before riding the motorcycle.

Front mudguard

30 On F650 GS models, undo the screws securing the mudguard on both sides, then draw it forwards and off **(see illustration)**.

31 On F800 GS models, first unclip the brake hose covers from the rear mudguard stays. Undo the screws securing the mudguard on both sides, then release the brake hoses from the rear stays and draw the mudguard forwards and off.

32 Installation is the reverse of removal.

Mirrors

33 Draw back the boot on the lower end of the mirror stem **(see illustration)**. The stem is held in an adapter that screws into the handlebar lever bracket. Use a spanner on the adapter hex to unscrew the mirror assembly.

Note that the adapter on the brake master cylinder side has a left-hand thread – turn the adapter *clockwise* to unscrew it.

34 Installation is the reverse of removal. Thread the adapter into the bracket and tighten it, turning the right-hand mirror adapter *anti-clockwise*.

35 To adjust the mirrors, counter-hold the adapter and loosen the adjuster hex above it. Position the mirror as required, then counter-hold the adapter and tighten the adjuster hex.

Sump guard

36 Unscrew the bolts and remove the sump guard.

37 Installation is the reverse of removal.

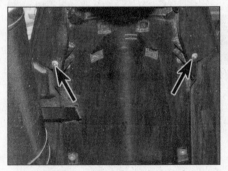

2.27b . . . to underseat panel

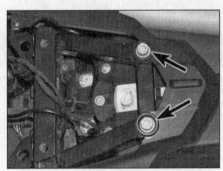

2.28a Undo the bolts (arrowed) . . .

2.28b . . . noting the location of the spacer and plain washer . . .

2.28c . . . then lift the mudguard assembly off

2.30 Screws secure front mudguard on both sides

2.33 Draw back the boot on the lower end of the mirror stem

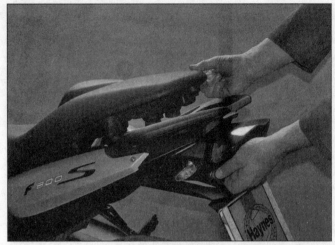

3.1 Unlock the seat . . .

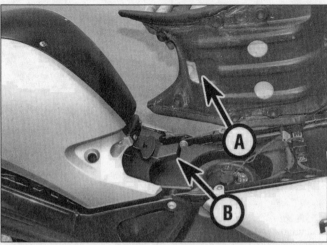

3.2 . . . and draw it rearwards to release slot (A) from tab (B)

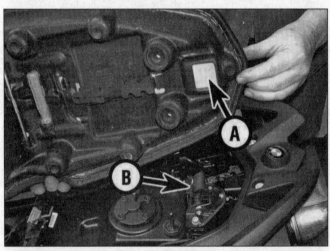

3.3 Slot (A) on seat base engages with latch mechanism (B)

3.5a Undo the screws along the sides . . .

3 F800 S and ST models

Seat

1 Insert the ignition key into the lock on the rear, left-hand side and turn it to unlock the seat **(see illustration)**.
2 Draw the seat rearwards to release the slot at the front of the seat base from the tab on the frame **(see illustration)**.
3 On installation, secure the slot at the front of the seat first, then press down on the rear until the slot in the rear of the seat base engages with the latch mechanism **(see illustration)**.

Bodywork centre panel

4 Remove the seat (see Steps 1 and 2).
5 Undo the screws securing the panel, then lift the panel off **(see illustrations)**.
6 Installation is the reverse of removal.

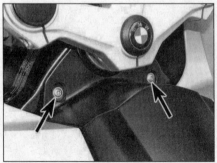

3.5b . . . at the front . . .

3.5c . . . and at the back . . .

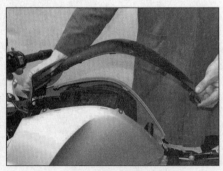

3.5d . . . then lift the centre panel off

3.9a Undo the screw (arrowed)

3.9b Undo the screws securing the underside . . .

3.9c . . . lower rear . . .

3.9d . . . and upper front edges of the side panel

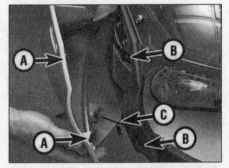

3.10a Release grommets (A) from pegs (B) – note wiring connector (C)

3.10b Lift the side panel off (S model)

Bodywork side panels

F800 S models

7 Remove the seat and the bodywork centre panel (see above).

8 Remove the left and/or right-hand mirror as appropriate (see Step 40).

9 Working on one panel at a time, undo the screw in the centre of the panel **(see illustration)**. Undo the screws securing the underside, lower rear and upper edge of the panel **(see illustrations)**.

10 Release the grommets on the front edge of the panel from the pegs on the headlight

assembly **(see illustration)**. Support the panel and disconnect the turn signal wiring connector **(see illustrations)**.

11 Installation is the reverse of removal. Check the operation of the turn signals before riding the motorcycle.

F800 ST models

12 Working on one side at a time, first remove each lower side panel as follows. Locate the turn signal wiring connector, release the cable-tie and disconnect the connector **(see illustrations)**.

13 Undo the screws securing the lower

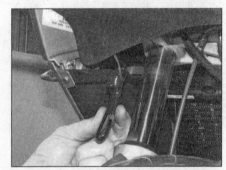

3.12a Locate the turn signal wiring connector . . .

3.12b . . . release the cable-tie . . .

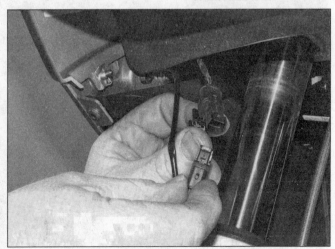

3.12c . . . and disconnect the connector

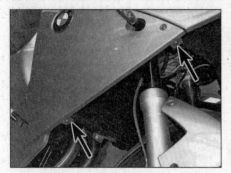

3.13a Screws (arrowed) secure lower front . . .

3.13b . . . and rear edges of the panel

3.14a Undo the screws (arrowed) . . .

3.14b . . . noting the location of the washers . . .

3.14c . . . and lift the lower side panel off (ST model)

front and rear edges of the panel **(see illustrations)**.

14 Undo the screws securing the top edge of the panel, noting the location of the washers, and lift the lower side panel off **(see illustrations)**.

15 Note the location of the radiator cowling **(see illustration)** – this should not be left unsupported once both lower side panels have been removed. Undo the nut a bolt securing the lower edge of the cowling, then undo the screw securing the rear top edge and lift the cowling off **(see illustrations)**.

16 Ensure that the mounting brackets on the front of the crankcase and behind the cylinder block are secure and that the U-clips are in good condition **(see illustrations)**.

3.15a Location of the radiator cowling (arrowed)

3.15b Undo the nut . . .

3.15c . . . and the screw . . .

3.15d . . . and lift the cowling off

3.16a Check the mounting brackets at the front . . .

3.16b . . . and rear of the engine

3.17 Ensure tab (arrowed) is pressed firmly into socket on the radiator

3.20a To remove the upper side panel . . .

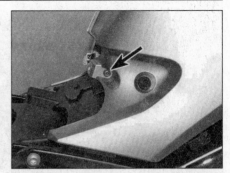

3.20b . . . undo screws securing the rear . . .

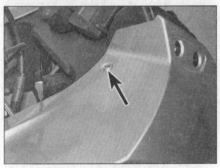

3.20c . . . and top edges

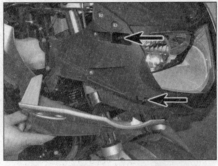

3.20d Release grommets from pegs (arrowed)

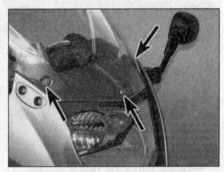

3.22a Undo the screws (arrowed) . . .

17 Installation is the reverse of removal. Prior to installing the right-hand lower side panel, ensure that the tab on the rear edge of the radiator cowling is pressed firmly into the socket on the right-hand side of the radiator **(see illustration)**. Check the operation of the turn signals before riding the motorcycle.
18 To remove the upper side panels, first remove the seat and the bodywork centre panel (see above).
19 Remove the left and/or right-hand mirror as appropriate (see Step 40).

20 Working on one panel at a time, undo the screws securing the rear and top edges **(see illustrations)**. Release the grommets on the front edge of the panel from the pegs on the headlight assembly and lift the panel off **(see illustration)**.
21 Installation is the reverse of removal.

Screen

22 Undo the screws securing the screen, noting the location of the plastic washers, and lift the screen off **(see illustrations)**.

23 Installation is the reverse of removal. Renew any plastic washers that are hardened of cracked. Apply a smear of grease to the screw threads on installation. The rubber mounted threaded inserts in the mounting panel are available as separate items if required.
24 Installation is the reverse of removal.

Passenger handles/rear carrier

25 Remove the seat (see above).
26 Unscrew the bolts and screws securing

3.22b . . . noting the location of the plastic washers . . .

3.22c . . . and lift the screen off

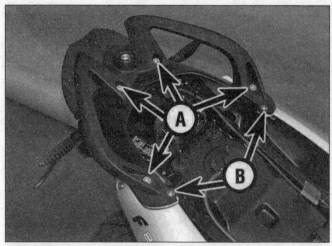

3.26a Bolts (A) and screws (B) secure passenger handles – S models

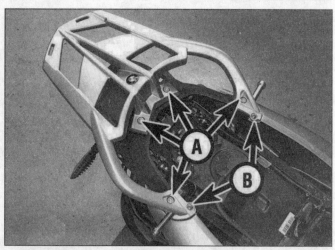

3.26b Bolts (A) and screws (B) secure rear carrier – ST models

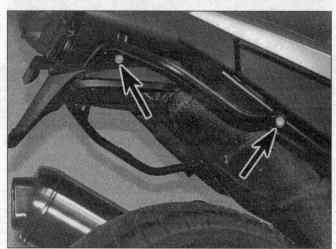

3.26c Bolts on both sides secure luggage bracket – ST models

3.29 Undo the screws (arrowed) . . .

the passenger handles/rear carrier and lift it off **(see illustrations)**. On ST models, if required, undo the bolts securing the luggage bracket and lift it off **(see illustration)**.

27 Installation is the reverse of removal.

Rear panels

⚠ **Warning: Petrol is extremely flammable. Read the precautions at the beginning of Chapter 4 before removing the fuel filler cap.**

28 Remove the seat (see above).

29 To remove the right-hand side panel, first open the fuel filler cap and identify the four counter-sunk screws securing the ring of the cap to the tank **(see illustration)**.

3.30 . . . and remove the filler cap

3.31a Undo the screws (arrowed) . . .

3.31b ... and lift the side panel off

3.33 Remove the left-hand side panel

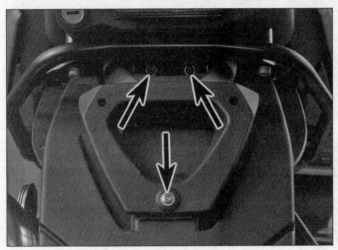

3.35a Undo the screws (arrowed) ...

3.35b ... and lift the rear mudguard off

30 Temporarily block the open fuel tank filler with clean rag. Undo the counter-sunk screws and lift the cap off **(see illustration)**.

31 Undo the screws securing the right-hand side panel and lift it off **(see illustrations)**.

32 Install the fuel filler cap.

33 Undo the screws securing the left-hand side panel and lift it off **(see illustrations)**.

34 Installation is the reverse of removal.

Rear mudguard

35 Remove the licence plate, undo the screws securing the mudguard to the licence plate bracket and lift the mudguard off **(see illustrations)**.

36 If required, undo the screws securing the licence plate bracket and lift the bracket off **(see illustrations)**.

37 Installation is the reverse of removal.

3.36a Undo screws (arrowed) at back ...

3.36b ... and under the seat ...

3.36c ... to release the licence plate bracket

3.38a Screws (arrowed) on both sides . . .

3.38b . . . secure the front mudguard

3.40a Undo the screws (arrowed) . . .

3.40b . . . and remove the mirror

4.8 Undo the screw (arrowed)

4.9a Ease the spring clip off the peg

4.9b Lift the side panel . . .

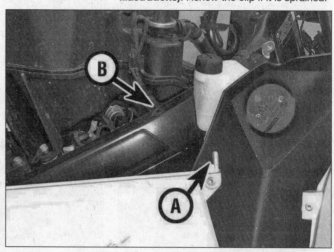

4.9c . . . to disengage the peg (A) from the hole in the frame rail (B)

Front mudguard

38 Undo the screws securing the mudguard on both sides, then draw it forwards and off **(see illustrations)**.
39 Installation is the reverse of removal.

Mirrors

40 Undo the screws securing the mirror and lift it off **(see illustrations)**.
41 Installation is the reverse of removal.

4   F800 R model

Seat

1 Insert the ignition key into the lock on the rear, left-hand side and turn it to unlock the seat **(see illustration 3.1)**.
2 Draw the seat rearwards to release the slot at the front of the seat base from the tab on the frame **(see illustration 3.2)**.
3 On installation, secure the slot at the front of the seat first, then press down on the rear until the latch mechanism engages with the slot in the rear of the seat base.

Bodywork centre panel

4 Remove the seat (see above).
5 Undo the screws securing the panel, then lift the panel off **(see illustrations 3.5a, b, c and d)**.
6 Installation is the reverse of removal.

Bodywork side panels

7 Remove the seat and the bodywork centre panel (see above).
8 Working on one panel at a time, undo the screw at the rear of the panel **(see illustration)**.
9 Ease the spring clip out from the groove in the front mounting peg and pull the tab off the peg **(see illustration)**. Lift the panel to disengage the peg on the lower edge from the hole in the top of the frame rail **(see illustrations)**. Renew the clip if it is sprained.

4.11a Undo the screws (arrowed) . . .

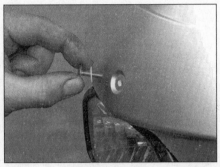

4.11b . . . noting the location of the plastic washers . . .

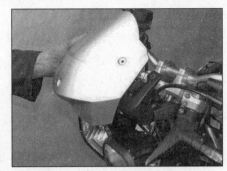

4.11c . . . and lift the windshield off

10 Installation is the reverse of removal. Ensure the peg on the lower edge of the panel is aligned with the hole in the top of the frame rail.

Windshield

11 Undo the screws securing the windshield, noting the location of the plastic washers, and lift the shield off **(see illustrations)**.

4.12 Screws (arrowed) secure the windshield bracket

12 Note the location of the windshield bracket. If required, undo the screws securing the bracket to the instrument cluster bracket and lift it off **(see illustration)**. The rubber mounted threaded inserts in the bracket are available as separate items if required.

13 Installation is the reverse of removal. Renew any plastic washers that are hardened

4.17a Note location of the front fork brace (arrowed)

of cracked. Apply a smear of grease to the screw threads on installation.

Passenger handles

14 Follow the procedure in Section 3, Steps 25 to 27.

Rear panels

15 Follow the procedure in Section 3, Steps 28 to 34.

Rear mudguard

16 Follow the procedure in Section 3, Steps 35 to 37.

Front mudguard

17 Note the location of the front fork brace **(see illustration)**. Undo the screws securing the mudguard on both sides, then draw it forwards and off **(see illustrations)**.

18 Installation is the reverse of removal.

Mirrors

19 Follow the procedure in Section 2, Steps 33 to 35.

4.17b Undo the screws on both sides . . .

4.17c . . . then draw the front mudguard forwards

Notes

Chapter 8
Electrical system

Contents

	Section
Air temperature sensor	14
Alternator	24
Battery	4
Brake light switches	11
Brake/tail light and licence plate light	8
Central vehicle electronics control unit – ZFE	2
Charging system check	23
Clutch switch	18
Electrical system fault finding	3
Gear position sensor	see Chapter 4
General information	1
Handlebar switches	19
Headlight and sidelight bulbs	6
Headlight unit	7
Horn	20
Ignition switch	16
Ignition system components	see Chapter 5
Instrument cluster	12
Lighting system check	5
Oil pressure switch	15
Regulator/rectifier	25
Sidestand switch	17
Speed sensor	13
Starter motor	22
Starter motor relay	21
Tail light and licence plate light	9
Turn signals	10
Wiring diagrams	26

Degrees of difficulty

Easy, suitable for novice with little experience | **Fairly easy,** suitable for beginner with some experience | **Fairly difficult,** suitable for competent DIY mechanic | **Difficult,** suitable for experienced DIY mechanic | **Very difficult,** suitable for expert DIY or professional

Specifications

Battery
Capacity .... 12 V, 14 Ah

Charging system
Max. power output 400W

Rear brake light switch
Switch-to-pedal clearance .... 2 to 3 mm

Bulbs

GS models
Headlight
High beam 12V, 55W H7
Low beam 12V, 55W H7
Sidelight 12V, 5W
Brake/tail light. . . . . LED
Licence plate light 12V, 5W
Turn signals
Standard. 12V, 10W
Optional equipment . . . . LED
Instrument and warning lights . . . . LED
S and ST models
Headlight
High beam 12V, 55W H7
Low beam 12V, 55W H7
Sidelight 12V, 5W
Brake/tail light. 12V, 21/5W
Turn signals
Standard. 12V, 10W
White signal lens. . . . . 12V, 10W RY amber
Optional equipment . . . . LED
Instrument and warning lights . . . . LED
R models
Headlight
High beam 12V, 55W H7
Low beam 12V, 55W H7
Sidelight 12V, 5W
Brake/tail light. 12V, 21/5W
Turn signals
Standard. 12V, 10W
White signal lens. . . . . 12V, 10W RY amber
OE equipment. . . . . LED
Instrument and warning lights . . . . LED

Torque settings

Alternator cover bolts. . . . . 12 Nm
Alternator rotor bolt . . . . 140 Nm
Alternator stator bolts. . . . . 10 Nm
Ignition switch security Torx screws – GS models. . . . . 19 Nm
Oil pressure switch. . . . . 20 Nm
Starter motor mounting bolts. . . . . 10 Nm

1 General information

General information

All models covered in this manual have a 12-volt electrical system charged by a three-phase alternator with a separate regulator/rectifier.

The regulator maintains the charging system output within the specified range to prevent overcharging, and the rectifier converts the ac (alternating current) output of the alternator to dc (direct current) to power the lights and other components and to charge the battery. The alternator rotor is mounted on the right-hand end of the crankshaft.

The starter motor is mounted on the front of the crankcase. The starting system includes the starter motor, battery, starter relay and switches. If the engine kill switch is in the RUN position and the ignition switch is ON, the starter relay allows the starter motor to operate only if the transmission is in neutral or, if the transmission is in gear, with the clutch lever pulled into the handlebar and the sidestand up.

CAN-bus technology

All models covered in this manual utilise Controlled Area Network (CAN)-bus technology to create an electronic information network between the control units, sensors and power-consuming components. This allows rapid and reliable data transfer around the network. It also allows comprehensive diagnosis of the entire system from one central point.

To reduce the amount of wiring in the network, all the components are designed to communicate via one or two wires. These wires are known as a 'data bus'. Each control unit (engine electronics control unit – ECU, central vehicle electronics control unit – ZFE, instrument cluster and, where fitted, ABS control unit and anti-theft warning system) has an integral transceiver which sends and receives data 'packets' along the bus. As the data packets travel between the units, each one examines the information and either acts upon it or ignores it, depending upon its relevance.

No fuses are fitted in the network – in the event of a short-circuit or component fault, the affected part of the network is isolated and switched off, leaving the rest of the network intact.

Note: *Keep in mind that electrical parts, once purchased, often cannot be returned. To avoid unnecessary expense, make very sure the faulty component has been positively identified before buying a replacement part.*

2 Central vehicle electronics control unit – ZFE

Description

1 The ZFE unit interacts between the battery power supply, the switches and the power

2.7 Unhook the strap (arrowed) securing the ZFE – GS models

2.8a Release the tie securing the ZFE wiring . . .

2.8b . . . then release the wiring connector

2.8c Lift the ZFE out of its holder – S, ST and R models

consuming components not related to the engine such as the lights and horn using the data bus principle. It also incorporates the functions of such items as turn signal and headlight relays, and protects the electrical systems from overload thus eliminating the need for fuses.

2 The ZFE does not have the fault identification function of the ECU – in the event of any failure in an electronics system, its memory should be analysed by a BMW dealer using the BMW diagnostic tester. Once the faulty component has been identified and renewed, the fault code can be erased from the engine management system.

3 Because of the nature of the components in the ZFE system, faults are often easy to diagnose. Details on the location and function of the individual components can be found in this Chapter.

Removal and installation

4 On GS models, the ZFE is located behind the steering head. On all other models it is located behind the air filter housing.

5 Remove the bodywork side panels (see Chapter 7).

6 On GS models, remove the battery; on all other models, disconnect the battery negative (-ve) lead (see Section 3).

7 On GS models, unhook the strap securing the ZFE **(see illustration)**. Release the tie securing the ZFE wiring, then release the catch securing the wiring connector and draw the ZFE out of its holder.

8 On S, ST and R models, release the tie securing the ZFE wiring, then release the catch securing the wiring connector **(see illustrations)**. Unhook the strap securing the ZFE and draw it out of its holder **(see illustration)**.

9 Installation is the reverse of removal, noting the following:
● Ensure that the terminals in the multi-pin connector are clean and undamaged.
● Spray the connector pins lightly with electrical contact cleaner.
● Ensure the connector is locked in position with the catch.

---

3 Electrical system fault finding

⚠️ *Warning: Make sure that the ignition switch is OFF and that the battery is disconnected before any electrical components are disconnected. Failure to do so will result in fault codes being recorded in the associated system and the need to have these erased using the BMW diagnostic tester. Depending upon the system concerned, the bike's performance may be affected.*

Fault finding

1 In the absence of test data, traditional probing with a multimeter should be avoided unless a specific result, as detailed in the text, is sought. The ZFE and the ECU are extremely sensitive to interference, and for the most part system checks should be confined to continuity tests of relevant sections of the wiring loom with the ignition switch OFF.

2 When testing for power supply to a component, always ensure that the multimeter is securely connected to the relevant wiring terminals before turning the ignition switch ON. It should be noted that in some cases, a test with the power ON may result in a fault being recorded by the ZFE.

3 If you don't have a multimeter it is highly advisable to obtain one – they are not expensive and will enable a full range of electrical tests to be made. Go for a modern digital one with LCD display as they are easier to use. A continuity tester and/or test light are useful for certain electrical checks as an alternative, though are limited in their usefulness compared to a multimeter **(see illustrations)**.

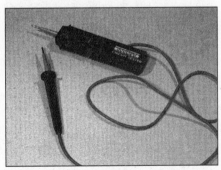

3.3b A battery powered continuity tester

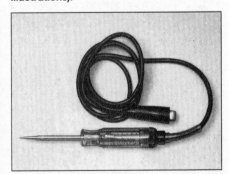

3.3c A simple test light can be used for voltage tests

3.3a A digital multimeter can be used for all electrical tests

4 If at all possible, have the machine checked by a BMW dealer – recorded faults can then be analysed using the BMW diagnostic tester and remedial action taken. Fault codes should be erased from the ZFE when the repair has been completed.

5 Note that if a new component is installed it will be necessary to reset the engine management system adaptation values to recognise the new component.

Simple wiring checks

6 Electrical problems often stem from simple causes, such as loose or corroded connections. Study the appropriate wiring diagram at the end of this Chapter to get a complete picture of what makes up that individual circuit.

7 Faults can often be tracked down by noting if other components related to that circuit are operating properly or not. If several components or circuits fail at one time, it may be that the fault lies in the earth (ground) connection, as several circuits are routed through the same earth connection.

8 Always check the condition of the wires and connections in the problem circuit. Intermittent failures can be especially frustrating, since you can't always duplicate the failure when it's convenient to test. In such situations, a good practice is to clean all connections in the affected circuit, whether or not they appear to be good. All of the connections and wires should also be wiggled to check for looseness which can cause intermittent failure.

Continuity checks

9 The term continuity describes the uninterrupted flow of electricity through an electrical circuit. Continuity can be checked with a multimeter set either to its continuity function (a beep is emitted when continuity is found), or to the resistance (ohms / Ω) function, or with a dedicated continuity tester. Both instruments are powered by an internal battery, therefore the checks are made with the ignition OFF. As a safety precaution, always disconnect the battery negative (-ve) lead

before making continuity checks, particularly if ignition switch checks are being made.

10 If using a multimeter, select the continuity function if it has one, or the resistance (ohms) function. Touch the meter probes together and check that a beep is emitted or the meter reads zero, which indicates continuity. If there is no continuity there will be no beep or the meter will show infinite resistance. After using the meter, always switch it OFF to conserve its battery.

11 A continuity tester can be used in the same way – its light should come on or it should beep to indicate continuity in the switch ON position, but should be off or silent in the OFF position.

12 Note that the polarity of the test probes doesn't matter for continuity checks, although care should be taken to follow specific test procedures if a diode or solid-state component is being checked.

Switch continuity checks

13 If a switch is at fault, trace its wiring to the wiring connectors. Separate the connectors and inspect them for security and condition. A build-up of dirt or corrosion here will most likely be the cause of the problem – clean up and apply a water dispersant such as WD40, or alternatively use a dedicated contact cleaner and protection spray.

14 If using a multimeter, select the continuity function if it has one, or the resistance (ohms / Ω) function, and connect its probes to the terminals in the connector **(see illustration)**. Simple ON/OFF type switches, such as brake light switches, only have two wires whereas combination switches, like the handlebar switches, have many wires. Study the wiring diagram to ensure that you are connecting to the correct pair of wires. Continuity should be indicated with the switch ON and no continuity with it OFF.

Wiring continuity checks

15 Many electrical faults are caused by damaged wiring, often due to incorrect routing or chaffing on frame components. Loose, wet or corroded wire connectors can also be the cause of electrical problems.

16 A continuity check can be made on a single length of wire by disconnecting it at each end and connecting the meter or

continuity tester probes to each end of the wire **(see illustration)**. Continuity (low or no resistance – zero ohms) should be indicated if the wire is good. If no continuity (high resistance) is shown, suspect a broken wire.

17 To check for continuity to earth in any earth wire connect one probe of your meter or tester to the earth wire terminal in the connector and the other to the frame, engine, or battery earth (-ve) terminal. Continuity (low or no resistance – zero ohms) should be indicated if the wire is good. If no continuity (high resistance) is shown, suspect a broken wire or corroded or loose earth point (see below).

Voltage checks

18 A voltage check can determine whether power is reaching a component. Use a multimeter set to the dc voltage scale, or a test light. The test light is the cheaper component, but the meter has the advantage of being able to give a voltage reading.

19 Connect the meter or test light in parallel, i.e. across the load **(see illustration)**.

20 First identify the relevant wiring circuit by referring to the wiring diagram at the end of this manual. If other electrical components share the same power supply, take note whether they are working correctly – this is useful information in deciding where to start checking the circuit.

21 If using a meter, check first that the meter leads are plugged into the correct terminals on the meter (red to positive (+ve), black to negative (-ve). Set the meter to the dc volts function, where necessary at a range suitable for the battery voltage – 0 to 20 volts dc. Connect the meter red probe (+ve) to the power supply wire and the black probe to a good metal earth (ground) on the motorcycle's frame or directly to the battery negative terminal. Battery voltage should be shown on the meter with the ignition switch, and if necessary any other relevant switch, ON.

22 If using a test light, connect its positive (+ve) probe to the power supply terminal and its negative (-ve) probe to a good earth (ground) on the motorcycle's frame. With the switch, and if necessary any other relevant switch, ON, the test light should illuminate.

23 If no voltage is indicated, work back towards the switch continuing to check for

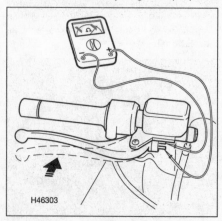

3.14 Testing a brake light switch for continuity

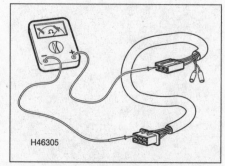

3.16 Testing for continuity in a wiring loom

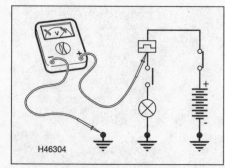

3.19 Connect the multimeter in parallel, or across the load, as shown

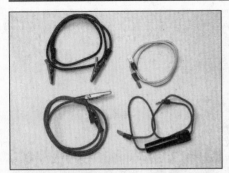

3.27 A selection of jumper wires for making earth (ground) checks

voltage. When you reach a point where there is voltage, you know the problem lies between that point and your last check point.

Earth (ground) checks

24 Earth connections are made either directly to the engine (such as the oil pressure switch which only has a positive feed) or to the engine or frame via the earth circuit of the appropriate wiring system (see *Wiring Diagrams* at the end of this Chapter).
25 Corrosion is a common cause of a poor earth connection, as is a loose earth terminal fastener.
26 If total or multiple component failure is experienced, check the security of the main earth lead from the negative (-ve) terminal of the battery, the earth leads bolted to the engine (at the front of the crankcase and the rear of the cylinder head), and the main earth

point(s) on the frame. If corroded, dismantle the connection and clean all surfaces back to bare metal. Remake the connection and prevent further corrosion from forming by smearing battery terminal grease over the connection.
27 To check the earth of a component, use an insulated jumper wire to temporarily bypass its earth connection (see illustration) – connect one end of the jumper wire to the earth terminal or metal body of the component and the other end to the motorcycle's frame. If the circuit works with the jumper wire installed, the earth circuit is faulty.
28 To check an earth wire first check for corroded or loose connections, then check the wiring for continuity (Steps 16 and 17) between each connector in the circuit in turn, and then to its earth point, to locate the break.

Caution: *Be extremely careful when handling or working around the battery. Always disconnect the battery negative (-ve) lead first, and reconnect it last.*

Removal and installation

Note: *Whenever the battery is disconnected, then reconnected, the engine management system service date must be reset by a BMW dealer equipped with the diagnostic tester.*
1 Make sure the ignition is switched OFF.

2 Remove the seat and the bodywork centre panel (see Chapter 7).
3 Unscrew the negative (-ve) terminal bolt and disconnect the lead from the battery, then unscrew the positive (+ve) terminal bolt and disconnect the lead (see illustrations).
4 Undo the battery holder screw(s) and displace the holder (see illustrations). If required, unclip the wiring and connectors from the holder.
5 Lift out the battery, noting which way round it is installed (see illustration).
6 On installation, ensure that the battery terminals and lead ends are clean. Install the battery so that the positive (+ve) and negative (-ve) terminals align with the appropriate leads.

HAYNES HiNT *Battery corrosion can be kept to a minimum by applying a layer of battery terminal grease or petroleum jelly (Vaseline) to the terminals after the leads have been connected. DO NOT use a mineral based grease.*

7 Install the battery holder and tighten the screws securely. Ensure the wiring is clipped to the holder (see illustrations 4.4a and b).
8 Reconnect the leads, connecting the positive (+ve) terminal first.
9 Install the remaining components in the reverse order of removal.
10 Have the service date reset by a BMW dealer.

4.3a Location of the battery – GS models

4.3b Location of the battery – S, ST and R models

4.3c Always disconnect the negative terminal first

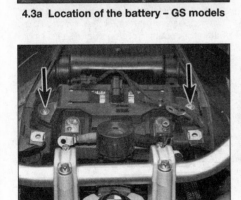

4.4a Battery holder screws – GS models

4.4b Battery holder screw – S, ST and R models

4.5 Note which way round the battery is fitted

4.12 Measuring battery voltage

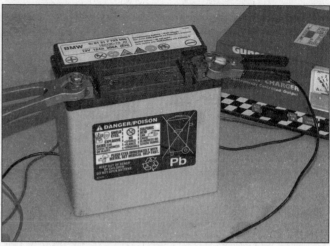

4.17 Check the battery connections before switching the charger on

Maintenance

11 All models covered in this manual are fitted with a sealed Absorbent Glass Mat (AGM) battery. All that should be done is to check that the terminals are clean and tight and that the casing is neither damaged nor leaking.

12 Check the condition of the battery by measuring the voltage present at the battery terminals. Connect the voltmeter positive (+ve) probe to the battery positive (+ve) terminal, and the negative (-ve) probe to the battery negative (-ve) terminal **(see illustration)**. When fully-charged there should be around 13.0 volts present. If the voltage falls below 12.3 volts, remove the battery and recharge it as described below.

13 If the machine is not in regular use, the on-board electronics and clock will gradually discharge the battery. Check the battery condition every four weeks and recharge it if necessary. BMW recommends the use their float-type trickle charger which is connected to the machine via the on-board socket. Alternatively, disconnect the battery and charge it from an external source as described below.

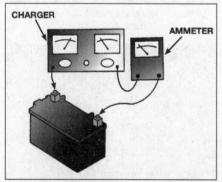

4.19 If the charger doesn't have an ammeter built-in, connect one in series as shown. Do not connect the ammeter between the battery terminals or it will be ruined

Charging

14 All models covered in this manual are fitted with an on-board socket that allows the battery to be charged without disconnecting the terminals and removing it from the machine. However, only the appropriate BMW Motorrad charger should be connected to the socket – some chargers may damage the bike's electronics. Under normal circumstances, the ZFE will monitor battery condition and switch the charger off when the battery is fully charged. If the battery is fully discharged it should be removed and connected to a charger in the conventional way – attempting to charge it via the on-board socket can damage the bike's electronics.

15 If the battery charger is to be connected to the battery terminals, remove the battery from the machine (see Steps 1 to 5).

16 Ensure that the charger is suitable for charging a 12V battery. **Note:** *Some battery chargers have an emergency high charging rate facility – this is not recommended for AGM type batteries.*

17 Ensure that the charger is switched off, then connect the positive (+ve) lead on the charger to the positive (+ve) terminal on the battery, and the negative (-ve) charger lead to the negative (-ve) battery terminal **(see illustration)**.

18 BMW provides no information regarding the charging rate. Refer to the instructions supplied with your battery charger. As a guide, a discharged battery should be charged at a low rate (approx. 1.5 amps) for 10 hours. Exceeding this figure can cause the battery to overheat, buckling the plates and rendering it useless.

19 Few owners will have access to an expensive current controlled charger, so if a normal domestic charger is used check that after a possible initial peak, the charge rate falls to a safe level **(see illustration)**. If the battery becomes hot during charging **STOP**. Further charging will cause damage.

20 If the recharged battery discharges rapidly when left disconnected it is likely that an internal short caused by physical damage has occurred. A new battery will be required. A good battery will tend to lose its charge at about 1% per day.

21 Install the battery (see Steps 6 to 10).

22 If the battery discharges while the machine is in regular use, either the battery is faulty or the charging system is defective. Refer to Section 23 to check the charging system.

5 Lighting system check

Note 1: *A warning on the instrument cluster will appear in the event of a bulb failure (see Step 4).*

Note 2: *If the ignition is switched ON for any checks, remember to switch it OFF again before proceeding further or removing any electrical component from the system.*

1 If a light fails first check the bulb (see relevant Section), and the bulb terminals in the holder. When checking for a blown filament in a bulb, it is advisable to back up a visual check with a continuity test of the filament as it is not always apparent that a bulb has blown. When testing for continuity, remember that on single terminal bulbs it is the metal body of the bulb that is the earth (ground).

2 If there is a problem with some or all the lights rather than just one, check the battery and the ignition switch, and where appropriate the light switch or turn signal switch (see Section 19). If the brake light fails to work also check the brake light switches (see Section 11).

3 If the problem persists, refer to the checks detailed in Section 3 and to the appropriate wiring diagram at the end of this Chapter. Check all the wiring, connectors and terminals in the circuit(s) for loose or broken connections and poor contacts. Check for voltage on

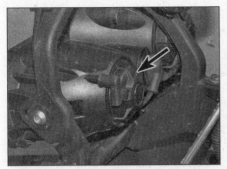

6.2a Headlight high beam bulb housing

6.2b Turn the cover anti-clockwise

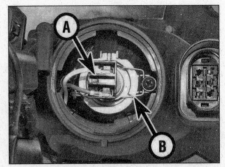

6.3 Pull off the wiring connector (A)
release the wire clip (B)

the supply side of the bulbholder and for
continuity between the bulbholder and earth
(ground).

Defective bulb warnings

4 In the event of a bulb failure, the warning
triangle symbol illuminates in the instrument
cluster and the word LAMP appears in the
multifunction display. Once the fault has been
corrected, the warning will be cancelled, but
a fault code will be stored in the ECU which
should be erased using the BMW diagnostic
tester.

6.6a Headlight low beam bulb housing

6.6b Turn the cover anti-clockwise

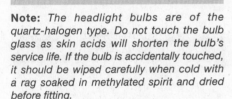

6 Headlight and sidelight bulbs

Note: *The headlight bulbs are of the
quartz-halogen type. Do not touch the bulb
glass as skin acids will shorten the bulb's
service life. If the bulb is accidentally touched,
it should be wiped carefully when cold with
a rag soaked in methylated spirit and dried
before fitting.*

GS and R models

Headlight

1 On R models, if required, remove the
windshield to improve access to the rear of
the headlight unit (see Chapter 7).
2 To remove the high beam (left-hand) bulb,
turn the bulb cover anti-clockwise **(see
illustrations)**.

3 Pull the wiring connector off the back of
the bulb, release the wire clip and remove the
bulb, noting how it fits **(see illustration)**.
4 Fit the bulb into the headlight, making sure
it locates correctly, and secure it in position
with the wire clip.
5 Connect the wiring connector, then install
the cover, turning it clockwise to lock it in
position.
6 To remove the low beam (right-hand)
bulb, turn the bulb cover anti-clockwise **(see
illustrations)**.
7 Pull the wiring connector off the back of
the bulb, release the wire clip and remove the
bulb, noting how it fits **(see illustration)**.
8 Fit the bulb into the headlight, making sure
it locates correctly, and secure it in position
with the wire clip.
9 Connect the wiring connector, then install
the cover, turning it clockwise to lock it in
position.

10 Check the operation of the headlight
before riding the motorcycle.

Sidelight

11 Remove the right-hand bulb cover **(see
illustration 6.6a and b)**.
12 Ease the bulbholder out from the back of
the reflector, then carefully pull the bulb out
(see illustrations). The bulb is of the capless
type.
13 Fit the bulb and check the operation of
the sidelight, then install the bulbholder and
the cover, turning it clockwise to lock it in
position.

> **HAYNES HINT** *Always use a paper towel or
> dry cloth when handling a
> new bulb to prevent injury if
> the bulb should break and to
> increase bulb life.*

6.7 Pull off the wiring connector (A)
release the wire clip (B)

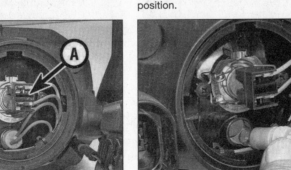

6.12a Ease the bulbholder out . . .

6.12b . . . then carefully pull out the
sidelight bulb

6.14 Turn handlebars for access to the rear of the headlight unit

6.15 Remove the high beam bulb cover

6.16a Pull off the wiring connector . . .

S and ST models

Headlight

14 Turn the handlebars to full left or right-hand lock for best access to the rear of the headlight unit **(see illustration)**.

15 To remove the high beam (left-hand) bulb, unclip the catch on the top of the bulb cover and lift it off, noting how it fits **(see illustration)**.

16 Pull the wiring connector off the back of the bulb, release the wire clip and remove the bulb, noting how it fits **(see illustrations)**.

17 Fit the bulb into the headlight, making sure it locates correctly, and secure it in position with the wire clip.

18 Connect the wiring connector, then install the cover, pressing it on firmly to secure the catch.

19 To remove the low beam (right-hand) bulb, unclip the catch on the top of the bulb cover and lift it off, noting how it fits.

20 Pull the wiring connector off the back of the bulb, release the wire clip and remove the bulb, noting how it fits **(see illustrations)**.

21 Fit the bulb into the headlight, making sure it locates correctly, and secure it in position with the wire clip.

22 Connect the wiring connector, then install the cover, pressing it on firmly to secure the catch.

23 Check the operation of the headlight before riding the motorcycle.

Sidelight

24 Disconnect the sidelight wiring connector. Turn the bulbholder anti-clockwise then pull it out from the back of the headlight unit, noting how it fits **(see illustration)**.

25 Carefully pull the bulb out **(see illustration)**. The bulb is of the capless type.

26 Fit the bulb, then align the bulbholder with the socket, push it in and turn it clockwise to lock it in position.

27 Connect the wiring connector and check the operation of the sidelight.

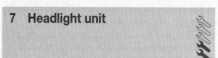

7 Headlight unit

Removal and installation

GS and R models

1 On GS models, remove the screen and the right-hand bodywork side panel (see Chapter 7).

6.16b . . . release the wire clip . . .

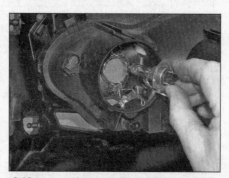

6.16c . . . and remove the high beam bulb

6.20a Pull off the wiring connector and release the wire clip . . .

6.20b . . . then withdraw the low beam bulb

6.24 Remove the sidelight bulbholder as described

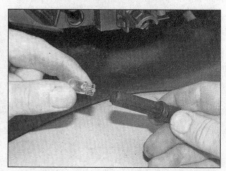

6.25 Carefully pull the capless bulb out

7.3 Note alignment of the headlight unit, then undo the mounting screws (arrowed)

7.4a Disconnect the headlight . . .

7.4b . . . and sidelight wiring connectors

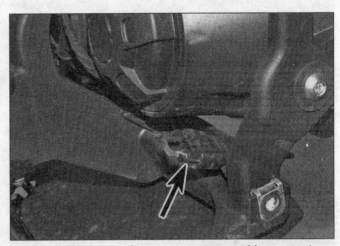

7.5a Location of the air temperature sensor wiring connector

2 On R models, remove the windshield (see Chapter 7).

3 Note the alignment of the headlight unit with its mounting bracket, then support the unit and undo the mounting screws **(see illustration)**.

4 Ease the unit forwards, disconnect the headlight and sidelight wiring connectors and lift the unit off **(see illustrations)**.

5 To remove the mounting bracket on GS models, if required, first remove the instrument cluster (see Section 12). Release the wiring loom from the ties on the bracket, noting how it fits. Disconnect the air temperature sensor wiring connector **(see illustration)**. Undo the screws and the central bolt securing the bracket and lift it off **(see illustrations)**.

6 To remove the mounting bracket on R models,

7.5b Undo the screws (arrowed) on both sides . . .

7.5c . . . and the bracket centre mounting bolt

7.6a Release the wiring from the tie

7.6b Note how the wiring is routed

7.6c Undo the screws securing the bracket . . .

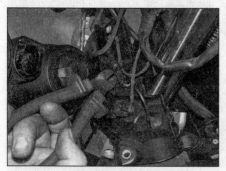

7.6d . . . then release the wiring ties

7.6e Disconnect the air temperature sensor wiring connector . . .

7.6f . . . and release the wiring from the clip on the bracket

7 Installation is the reverse of removal. Make sure the wiring is correctly routed, secured and connected. Check the operation of the headlight and sidelights, and front turn signals. Check the headlight aim (see Steps 15 and 16).

S and ST models

8 Remove the bodywork side panels and the screen (see Chapter 7).
9 Disconnect the air temperature sensor wiring connector (see illustration).
10 Support the headlight unit, then undo the screws securing the unit to the mounting bracket (see illustration).
11 Ease the unit forwards, disconnect the headlight and sidelight wiring connectors and lift the unit off (see illustrations).
12 If required, undo the screws securing the headlight in its housing, noting the location of the washers, and lift it out (see illustration).

7.9 Disconnect the air temperature sensor wiring connector

7.10 Undo the screws (arrowed) on both sides

if required, first release the wiring from the tie on the left-hand side of the bracket, noting how the wiring is routed (see illustrations). Undo the screws securing the bracket, then release the ties securing the turn signal wiring and

disconnect the connectors (see illustrations). Disconnect the air temperature sensor wiring connector, release the wiring from the clip on the bracket and lift the bracket off (see illustrations).

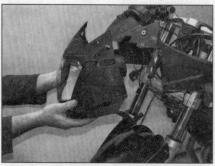

7.11a Disconnect the wiring connectors . . .

7.11b . . . and lift the headlight unit off

7.12 Screws secure the headlight in its housing

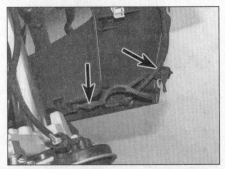

7.13a Release the wiring from the clips . . .

7.13b . . . then undo the bracket screws on both sides

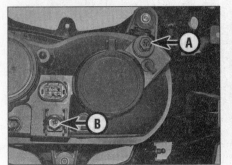

7.17a Headlight horizontal adjuster (A) and vertical adjuster (B)

7.17b Press lever down to lower headlight beam

13 To remove the mounting bracket, if required, first remove the instrument cluster (see Section 12). Release the wiring loom from the clips on the underside of the bracket, noting where it fits, then undo the screws securing the bracket and lift it off **(see illustrations)**.

14 Installation is the reverse of removal. Make sure the wiring is correctly routed and securely connected. Check the operation of the headlight and sidelights. Check the headlight aim (see Steps 15 and 17).

Headlight aim

Note: *An improperly adjusted headlight may cause problems for oncoming traffic or provide poor, unsafe illumination of the road ahead. Before adjusting the headlight aim, be sure to consult with local traffic laws and regulations – for UK models refer to MOT Test Checks in the Reference section.*

15 Before making any adjustment, check that the tyre pressures are correct and the rear suspension is adjusted as required. Make any adjustments to the headlight aim with the machine on level ground, with the fuel tank half full and with an assistant sitting on the seat. If the bike is usually ridden with a passenger on the back, have a second assistant to do this.

16 On GS and R models the headlight can only be adjusted vertically. Loosen the headlight mounting screws **(see illustration 7.3)** and move the headlight up or down as required, then tighten the screws securely.

17 On S and ST models, the headlight beam can be adjusted both horizontally and vertically.

Horizontal adjustment is made by turning the adjuster knob on the top right-hand side of the headlight unit, vertical adjustment is made by turning the adjuster knob on the lower edge of the unit **(see illustration)**. In addition, the

beam can be lowered when carrying a heavy load without altering the standard setting – press the adjuster lever down to lower the beam and move it back up to return to the pre-set setting **(see illustration)**.

8 Brake/tail light bulb and licence plate bulb

Brake/tail light bulb (S, ST and R models)

Note: *GS models are equipped with an LED brake/tail light as standard. It is optional on other models.*
1 Undo the lens screws and remove the lens **(see illustrations)**.
2 Push the bulb into the holder and twist it anti-clockwise to remove it **(see illustration)**.
3 Check the socket terminals for corrosion and clean them if necessary.
4 Line up the pins of the new bulb with the slots in the socket, then push the bulb in and turn it clockwise until it locks into place **(see illustration)**. **Note:** *It is a good idea to use a paper towel or dry cloth when handling the new bulb to prevent injury if the bulb should break and to increase bulb life.*
5 Fit the lens and tighten the screws securely.

Licence plate light bulb (GS models)

6 Undo the screw securing the cover on the underside of the rear mudguard and

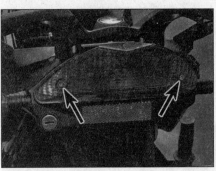

8.1a Undo the screws . . .

8.1b . . . and remove the lens

8.2 Push the bulb in and turn it anti-clockwise

8.4 Line up the pins on the bulb with the slots in the socket

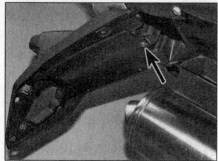

8.6a Undo the screw (arrowed) . . .

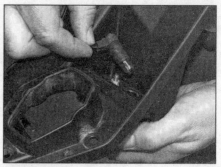

8.6b . . . and remove the cover

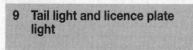

8.7 Ease the bulbholder out from the light unit

remove the cover, noting how it fits **(see illustrations)**.

7 Ease the bulbholder out from the back of the light unit, then carefully pull the bulb out **(see illustration)**. The bulb is of the capless type.

8 Fit the bulb and check the operation of the light, then install the bulbholder. Ensure the tabs on the lower edge of the cover are correctly located, then secure the cover with the screw.

9 Tail light and licence plate light

GS models

1 Remove the seat and the rear top cover (see Chapter 7).

2 Disconnect the tail light wiring connector **(see illustration)**.

3 Undo the screws securing the tail light unit and pull it out from the rear mudguard assembly **(see illustration)**.

4 To remove the licence plate light, first remove the cover on the underside of the rear mudguard, then ease out the bulbholder (see Section 8).

5 Undo the nuts securing the light unit and

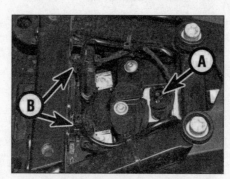

9.2 Tail light wiring connector (A). Note turn signal connectors (B)

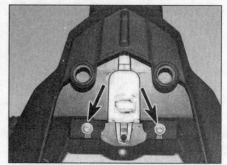

9.3 Screws secure the tail light unit

lift it off the rear mudguard assembly **(see illustration)**.

6 Installation is the reverse of removal. Check the operation of the tail and brake lights, and licence plate light.

S, ST and R models

7 Remove the seat, passenger handles and both rear panels (see Chapter 7).

8 Trace the wiring from the tail light, along the left-hand side of the frame, and disconnect it at the connector **(see illustration)**. Release the wiring from any ties. Disconnect the seat release cable from the lock.

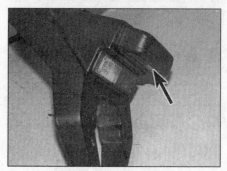

9.5a Licence plate light . . .

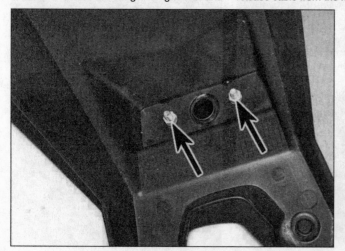

9.5b . . . is secured by nuts (arrowed)

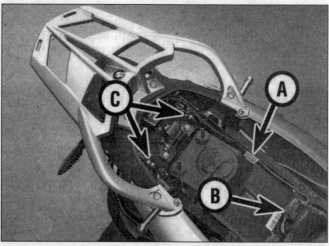

9.8 Trace tail light wiring (A) to the connector (B). Note turn signal connectors (C)

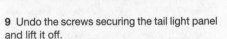

10.2a Undo the screw (arrowed) at the back of the unit . . .

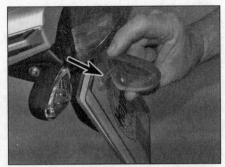

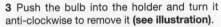

10.2b . . . and remove the lens – note how the tab locates

10.3 Push the bulb in and turn it anti-clockwise to remove it

9 Undo the screws securing the tail light panel and lift it off.
10 Undo the nuts securing the tail light unit, noting the washers and collars. Ease the light off the panel and disconnect the wiring connectors, noting how they fit.
11 Installation is the reverse of removal. Check the operation of the tail and brake lights, and rear turn signals.

10 Turn signals

Circuit check

1 Most turn signal problems are the result of a burned out bulb or corroded socket. This is especially true when the turn signals function properly in one direction, but fail to flash in the other direction. If this is the case, first check the bulbs, the sockets and the wiring connectors. If all the turn signals fail to work, check the switch and the wiring (see Sections 3 and 19). If no fault can be found have the machine checked by a BMW dealer – the turn signal relay is integral with the ZFE.

Bulb replacement

Note: *LED turn signals are optional equipment.*
2 Undo the screw securing the lens and detach it from the housing, noting how it fits **(see illustrations)**.

3 Push the bulb into the holder and turn it anti-clockwise to remove it **(see illustration)**.
4 Check the socket terminals for corrosion and clean them if necessary.
5 Line up the pins of the new bulb with the slots in the socket, then push the bulb in and turn it clockwise until it locks into place. **Note:** *The pins on amber turn signal bulbs (i.e. those used on models with white lenses) are offset, whereas those on a conventional clear glass bulb are 180° apart.*
6 Fit the lens onto the housing, making sure it locates correctly, and secure it with the screw. Do not overtighten the screw as it is easy to strip the threads or crack the lens.

Turn signal units

Front turn signals

7 On GS, S and ST models, remove the appropriate bodywork side panel (see Chapter 7). Undo the screw securing the turn signal and detach it from the panel.
8 On R models, first remove the headlight unit (see Section 7). Release the ties securing the turn signal wiring and disconnect the connectors **(see illustration 7.6d)**. Undo the screw securing the turn signal and detach it from the headlight bracket **(see illustration)**.
9 Installation is the reverse of removal. Check the operation of the turn signals.

Rear turn signals

10 On GS models, remove the seat and the rear top cover (see Chapter 7). Release the ties securing the turn signal wiring and disconnect

the connectors **(see illustration 9.2)**. Undo the screw securing the turn signal and detach it from the panel **(see illustration)**.
11 On S, ST and R models, remove the seat (see Chapter 7). Release the ties securing the turn signal wiring and disconnect the connectors **(see illustration 9.8)**. Undo the screw securing the turn signal and detach it from the tail light panel **(see illustration)**.
12 Installation is the reverse of removal. Check the operation of the turn signals.

11 Brake light switches

1 Before checking the switches, check the brake light circuit (see Section 3).

Front brake

2 The front brake light switch is located on the underside of the brake lever (see Chapter 5, Section 5).
3 To check the operation of the switch, first disconnect the wiring connector. Following the procedure in Section 3, test for continuity between the switch terminals – with the brake lever at rest, there should be no continuity. With the brake lever applied, there should be continuity. If the switch does not behave as described, replace it with a new one.
4 Undo the grub screw securing the switch and remove it, noting how it fits. Install the

10.8 Front turn signal is secured by screw (arrowed)

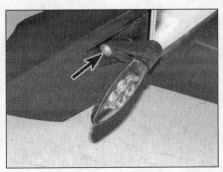

10.10 Screw (arrowed) secures rear turn signal – GS models

10.11 Screw (arrowed) secures rear turn signal – S, ST and R models

11.6a Undo the screw (arrowed) to remove the cover

11.6b Disconnect the wiring connector

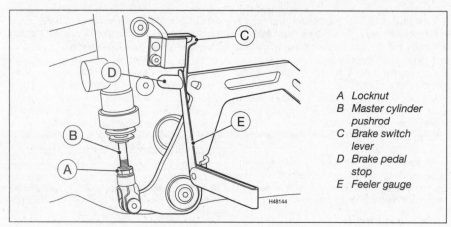

A Locknut
B Master cylinder pushrod
C Brake switch lever
D Brake pedal stop
E Feeler gauge

11.9 Measuring the switch-to-pedal clearance – GS models

With the brake pedal applied, there should be continuity. If the switch does not behave as described, replace it with a new one.

7 Follow the procedure in Chapter 5, Section 3, to remove the heel plate and access the switch. Undo the screw securing the switch and remove it, noting how it fits. Trace the wiring to the connector and release it from the ties.

8 Install the new switch, reconnect the wiring and secure it with new ties.

9 Temporarily install the screws securing the master cylinder without the heel plate. Measure the clearance between the switch lever and the brake pedal stop with a feeler gauge and compare the result with the specification at the beginning of this Chapter (see illustration). To adjust the clearance, loosen the locknut on the master cylinder pushrod clevis, then turn the pushrod until there is a small amount of play between the pedal, the switch lever and the pedal stop. Now turn the pushrod until the play is taken up and tighten the locknut.

10 Turn the ignition ON and check the operation of the switch.

11 Install the heel plate and the right-hand side cover.

S, ST and R models

12 The rear brake light switch is mounted on the back of the right-hand footrest bracket. To check the operation of the switch, first remove the right-hand bodywork side panel to access the wiring connector (see illustration). Disconnect the wiring connector, then following the procedure in Section 3, test for continuity between the terminals on the switch side of the connector – with the brake pedal at rest, there should be no continuity. With the brake pedal applied, there should be continuity. If the switch does not behave as described, replace it with a new one.

13 Follow the procedure in Chapter 5, Section 3, to remove the footrest bracket and access the switch. Undo the screw securing the switch and remove it, noting how it fits (see illustration). Trace the wiring to the connector

new switch, tighten the grub screw lightly and reconnect the wiring.

5 Turn the ignition ON and check the operation of the switch as follows. Pull the brake lever gently – the brake light should illuminate before pressure is felt in the lever, between 5 and 9 mm of lever travel at the ball end of the lever. Manually move the position of the switch until it is correct, then tighten the grub screw. Be careful not to over-tighten the grub screw otherwise the switch body could be damaged.

Rear brake

GS models

6 The rear brake light switch is mounted on the frame behind the right-hand heel plate. To check the operation of the switch, remove the right-hand side cover and disconnect the switch wiring connector (see illustrations). Following the procedure in Section 3, test for continuity between the terminals on the switch side of the connector – with the brake pedal at rest, there should be no continuity.

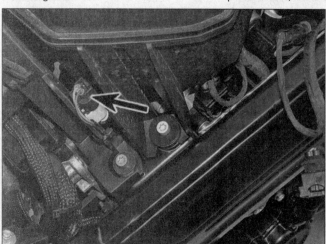

11.12 Rear brake light switch wiring connector – S, ST and R models

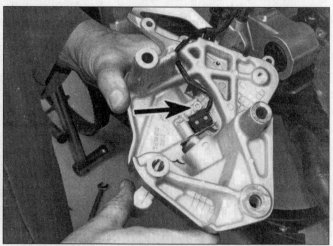

11.13 Brake light switch mounting screw (arrowed)

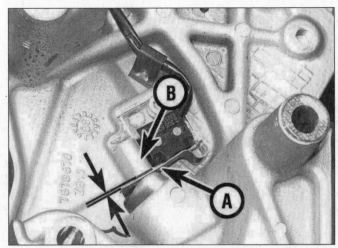

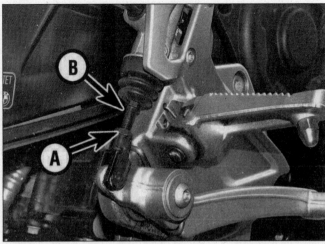

11.17a Measure the clearance between the switch lever (A) and the pedal stop (B)

11.17b Loosen locknut (A) and turn master cylinder pushrod (B)

and release it from the clips and ties – on the machine photographed it was necessary to remove the air filter housing to trace the wiring (see Chapter 4).

14 Install the new switch, reconnect the wiring and secure it with new ties.

15 Turn the ignition ON and check the operation of the switch – note that adjustment between the switch lever and the brake pedal can only be made once the footrest bracket has been installed and the brake pedal and master cylinder push rod are connected.

16 Install the footrest bracket and the right-hand bodywork side panel.

17 Measure the clearance between the switch lever and the brake pedal stop with a feeler gauge and compare the result with the specification at the beginning of this Chapter **(see illustration)**. To adjust the clearance, loosen the locknut on the master cylinder pushrod clevis **(see illustration)**. Turn the pushrod until there is a small amount of play between the pedal, the switch lever and the pedal stop. Now turn the pushrod until the play is taken up and tighten the locknut.

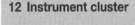

12 Instrument cluster

Note: *If the instruments are to be renewed, note that the machine's service and mileage history must first be downloaded onto the BMW diagnostic tester and the data uploaded to the new unit.*

1 On S and ST models, first follow the procedure in Section 7 and remove the headlight unit.

2 On GS models, first remove the screen (see Chapter 7).

3 On R models, remove the windshield and windshield bracket (see Chapter 7).

4 Ease off the spring clips securing the instrument cluster **(see illustration)**. If the clips are sprained or corroded, fit new ones on installation **(see illustration)**.

5 Lift the instrument cluster off its mounting, noting the location of the grommets, and disconnect the wiring connector **(see illustrations)**.

6 If required, undo the screws on the back of the housing and separate the two halves. The front and back of the housing and the instrument board are available as separate items.

7 Prior to installation, check that the mounting

12.4a Ease off the spring clips (arrowed)

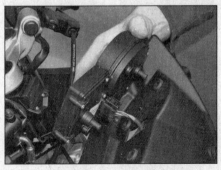

12.5a Lift off the instrument cluster . . .

grommets are in good condition and renew them if necessary.

8 Installation is the reverse of removal.

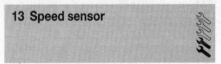

13 Speed sensor

1 On machines not fitted with ABS, the speed sensor rotor is retained by the rear brake disc bolts. On GS and R models, the speed sensor is located on the left-hand side of the brake

12.4b Examine the clips for damage and corrosion

12.5b . . . and disconnect the wiring connector

13.1a Location of the speed sensor – GS and R models

13.1b Location of the speed sensor – S and ST models

caliper bracket (see illustration). On S and ST models, the rear wheel speed sensor is located on the right-hand side of the brake caliper bracket (see illustration) – remove the rear wheel for access (see Chapter 6).

2 Maintenance is the same as for the rear ABS speed sensor (see Chapter 6, Section 10).

14 Air temperature sensor

1 The air temperature sensor reads the ambient air temperature and this is shown on the multi-function display in the instrument cluster. When the temperature first drops below 3°C the display automatically switches to temperature mode as a warning of the possibility of black ice. At any temperature below 3°C the display will flash continuously.

2 On GS models, the air temperature sensor is located on the right-hand side of the headlight

bracket (see illustration 7.5a). Remove the right-hand bodywork side panel for access (see Chapter 7).

3 On S and ST models, the air temperature sensor is located on the left-hand underside of the headlight unit (see illustration). Remove the left-hand bodywork side panel for access (see Chapter 7).

4 On R models, the air temperature sensor is located inside the headlight mounting bracket on the left-hand side (see illustration 7.6e). Remove the bracket for access (see Section 7).

5 No test details are provided for the sensor, however its resistance can be measured with a multimeter set to the K-ohms scale. Disconnect the wiring connector and measure the resistance between the terminals on the sensor side of the connector – on the machine photographed the resistance measured 6.48 K-ohms at 20°C (see illustration). If the result varies greatly it is likely that the sensor is faulty – have it checked by a BMW dealer.

6 Unclip the sensor from its mounting.

7 Installation is the reverse of removal, noting the following:
● Ensure the terminals in the wiring connector are clean.
● Ensure the wiring is securely connected.

15 Oil pressure switch

1 The oil pressure warning light in the instrument cluster should come on when the ignition switch is first turned ON as part of the instrument systems pre-ride check. The warning light should then go off when the check is complete. If the light does not come on there is a fault in the system – have the machine checked by a BMW dealer.

2 If the warning light does not go off, or comes on whilst the engine is running, stop the engine immediately and check the oil level (see Pre-ride checks). If the level is correct, have the oil pressure checked (see Chapter 2, Section 3).

3 If the oil level and oil pressure are good, start

14.3 Location of the air temperature sensor – S and ST models

14.5 Measuring the air temperature sensor resistance

15.3 Location of the oil pressure switch

15.5 Unscrew the oil pressure switch from the cylinder head

the engine and disconnect the oil pressure switch wiring connector (see illustration). With the wire detached, the warning light should be off. If it is illuminated, the wire between the switch and the ECU is earthed (grounded) at some point (see Section 3). If the wiring is good, the switch is defective and must be replaced with a new one.

Removal and installation

4 The oil pressure switch is located on the rear of the cylinder head, between the cam chain tensioner and the coolant temperature sensor.

5 If not already done, disconnect the wiring connector, then unscrew the switch from the head (see illustration).

6 Install the new switch and tighten it to the torque setting specified at the beginning of this Chapter. Ensure the wiring connector is secure.

7 Turn the ignition ON and check that the warning light works correctly (see Step 1). Start the engine and check that the oil pressure switch operates correctly without oil leakage.

16 Ignition switch

> **Warning: To prevent the risk of short circuits, disconnect the battery negative (–) lead before making any ignition switch checks.**

General

1 The ignition switch is part of an assembly that comprises the immobiliser antenna, the steering lock and the ignition switch.

2 Two ignition keys were supplied with each machine when new. The keys are security coded and contain an integral transponder. When a key is inserted into the ignition switch the security code is transmitted to the immobiliser (EWS) and the immobiliser is deactivated. Only the keys supplied with the machine will deactivate the immobiliser.

3 The keys should not be kept together – apart from the obvious risk of losing both

keys, the spare key may interfere with the enabling signal for starting and the EWS warning will appear on the instrument cluster multi-function display.

4 If a key is lost, or if a key loses its security code, a replacement can only be obtained from a BMW dealer. For security, the new key and the remaining original key can be re-coded by the dealer.

Check

5 On GS models, the ignition switch is located on the top of the frame behind the steering head. Remove the switch as described below to enable testing.

6 On S, ST and R models, the ignition switch is located on the front of the top yoke (see illustration). On S and ST models, remove the bodywork side panels and windscreen for access. On R models, remove the instrument cluster for access (see Section 12).

7 Where fitted, undo the screws securing the wiring connector cover, then disconnect the connector from the bottom of the switch assembly (see illustration).

16.6 Location of the ignition switch – S, ST and R models

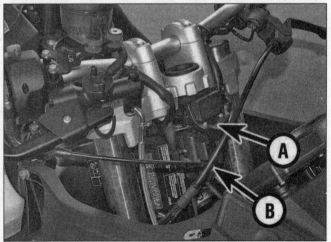

16.7 Remove the cover (A) then disconnect the connector (B)

16.10 Ignition switch on GS models is retained by a security Torx screw (arrowed) on each side

16.11 Undo the screws securing the ignition switch

17 Sidestand switch

Check

1 The sidestand switch is located on the back of the stand pivot. The switch is part of the starter interlock safety circuit which prevents or stops the engine running if the transmission is in gear whilst the sidestand is down, and prevents the engine from starting if the transmission is in gear unless the sidestand is up and the clutch lever is pulled in.

2 Trace the wiring back from the switch and disconnect it at the connector **(see illustration)** – on ST models, remove the lower left-hand bodywork side panel for access (see Chapter 7).

3 Using a multimeter or continuity tester, check the continuity between the terminal pairs on the switch side of the connector (see the *Wiring Diagrams* at the end of this Chapter).

4 If the switch does not perform as described it is faulty and must be replaced with a new one.

5 If the switch is good, check the wiring between the connector and the ECU.

Removal and installation

6 Loosen the sidestand mounting bolts **(see illustration)**.

7 Follow the procedure in Chapter 5, Section 3, to remove the left-hand footrest bracket. Unclip the wiring from the back of the bracket.

8 Note how the switch locates in the recess in the footrest bracket, then unscrew the sidestand mounting bolts and separate the sidestand from the footrest bracket **(see illustrations)**.

9 Remove the nut and washer securing the switch, then lift the switch off, noting how it fits **(see illustration)**.

10 Prior to installation, clean off any old grease and lubricate the stand bracket and pivot bush with a smear of grease (see Chapter 5, Section 4).

11 Install the switch, ensuring the tab is correctly located **(see illustration 17.9)**. Secure the switch with the washer and nut.

8 Using a multimeter or continuity tester, check the continuity between the terminal pairs on the switch side of the connector (see the *Wiring Diagrams* at the end of this Chapter). Continuity should exist between the terminals connected by a solid line on the diagram when the switch is in the indicated position.

9 If the switch fails any of the tests, replace it with a new one. **Note:** *If a new switch is being fitted, the BMW diagnostic tester must be used to register it with the ZFE.*

Removal and installation

10 On GS models, remove the bodywork side panels (see Chapter 7), the air filter housing (see Chapter 4) and the ZFE (see Section 2) for access. Remove the two security Torx screws and lift the switch off the frame to enable its

wiring to be disconnected **(see illustration)**; note that a special Torx bit will be required to engage this type of tamper-proof screw. On installation, tighen the Torx screws to the specified torque setting.

11 On S, ST and R models, remove the components described in Step 6, then, where fitted, undo the screws securing the ignition switch wiring connector cover, then disconnect the connector from the bottom of the switch assembly **(see illustration 16.7)**. Undo the screws securing the ignition switch and remove it, noting how it fits **(see illustration)**. The switch body/steering lock is retained to the underside of the top yoke by anti-tamper shear-head bolts; refer to Chapter 5, Section 9 for details of removal.

12 Check the operation of the switch after installation.

17.2 Location of the sidestand switch wiring connector

17.6 Loosen the sidestand mounting bolts

17.8a Note how the switch locates in the footrest bracket . . .

17.8b . . . then separate the sidestand from the bracket

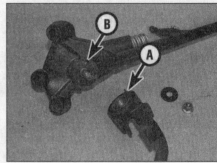

17.9 Note how tab (A) locates in hole (B)

12 Feed the wiring through the footrest bracket and install the sidestand **(see illustrations 17.8b and a)**; the mounting bolts can be tightened fully once the footrest bracket has been installed. Clip the wiring from the back of the bracket.
13 Install the footrest bracket (see Chapter 5, Section 3).
14 Tighten the sidestand mounting bolts securely.
15 Check the operation of the sidestand switch.

18 Clutch switch

Check

1 The clutch switch is located in the underside of the clutch lever bracket. The switch is part of the starter interlock safety circuit which prevents or stops the engine running if the transmission is in gear whilst the sidestand is down, and prevents the engine from starting if the transmission is in gear unless the sidestand is up and the clutch lever is pulled in.
2 Follow the procedure in Chapter 5, Section 5, to remove the clutch lever bracket. Turn the lever over and disconnect the clutch switch wiring connector **(see illustration)**.
3 Using a multimeter or continuity tester, check for continuity between the switch terminals. With the clutch lever pulled in, there should be continuity. With the clutch lever out, there should be no continuity.
4 If the switch does not perform as described it is faulty and must be replaced with a new one.
5 If the switch is good, check the wiring between the connector and the ECU.

Removal and installation

6 If not already done, remove the clutch lever bracket (see Step 2).
7 Undo the screw securing the switch and remove it, noting how it fits.
8 Installation is the reverse of removal.
9 Check the operation of the clutch switch.

19 Handlebar switches

Check

1 Generally speaking, the switches are reliable and trouble-free. Most troubles, when they do occur, are caused by dirty or corroded contacts, but wear and breakage of internal parts is a possibility that should not be overlooked.
2 Follow the procedure in Chapter 5, Section 5, to separate the two halves of the relevant switch housing and disconnect the switch wiring connectors.

18.2 Disconnect the clutch switch wiring connector

3 Using a multimeter or continuity tester, check for continuity between the terminals on the switch side of the connector with the switch in the ON or OFF position i.e. switch OFF – no continuity, switch ON – continuity (see the *Wiring Diagrams* at the end of this Chapter).
4 If the check indicates a problem exists, spray the switch contacts with electrical contact cleaner. If switch components are damaged or broken, it will be obvious when the switch is disassembled.
5 If the switch is good, remove the bodywork side panels (see Chapter 7) and check the wiring between the connector and the ZFE.

Removal and installation

6 Follow the procedure in Chapter 5, Section 5. On completion, check the operation of the switch.

20.1 Location of the horn (A) – GS models. Note the starter motor relay (B)

20.3 Location of the horn – R models

20 Horn

Check

1 On GS models, the horn is located on the left-hand side of the frame behind the steering head **(see illustration)**.
2 On S and ST models, the horn is located on the underside of the front fork bottom yoke **(see illustration)**.
3 On R models, the horn is located above the front fork bottom yoke **(see illustration)**.
4 On GS, S and ST models, remove the left-hand bodywork side panel for access (see Chapter 7). On R models, remove the headlight unit (see Section 7).
5 Disconnect the wiring connector and ensure the terminals are clean **(see illustration)**.
6 Using two jumper wires, apply voltage from a fully-charged 12V battery directly to the terminals on the horn. If the horn doesn't sound, replace it with a new one.
7 If the horn works when connected directly to a battery, check the horn circuit wiring (see Section 3 and the *Wiring Diagrams* at the end of this Chapter). If the wiring is good, check the handlebar switch (see Section 19).

Removal and installation

8 If not already done, remove the left-hand bodywork side panel or headlight unit, according to model (see Step 4).

20.2 Location of the horn – S and ST models

20.5 Check the horn connector and terminals

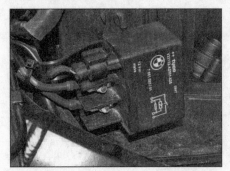

21.1 Starter motor relay – S model shown

21.2a Release the pin securing the relay . . .

21.2b . . . and displace the relay and bracket

9 Disconnect the wiring connector **(see illustration 20.5)**.
10 Unscrew the bracket bolt and remove the horn.
11 Installation is the reverse of removal. Check the operation of the horn.

21 Starter motor relay

Check

1 On GS models, the relay is located on the left-hand side of the frame behind the steering head **(see illustration 20.1)**. On all other models the relay is located on the left-hand side of the air filter housing **(see illustration)**. Remove the left-hand bodywork side panel for access (see Chapter 7).

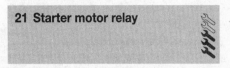

2 On S, ST and R models, release the pin securing the starter relay and displace the relay and support bracket **(see illustrations)**.
3 Unscrew the nut securing the starter motor (black) lead and position the lead away from the relay terminal. With the ignition switch ON, the engine kill switch in the RUN position, and the transmission in neutral, press the starter switch. The relay should be heard to click. Switch the ignition OFF.

4 If the relay doesn't click, remove it (see Steps 9 to 11) and test it as follows.
5 Set a multimeter to the ohms x 1 scale and connect it across the relay's starter motor (black) and battery (red) lead terminals. There should be no continuity. Using a fully-charged 12 volt battery and two insulated jumper wires, connect the battery to the small terminals on the relay. At this point the relay should be heard to click and the multimeter read 0 ohms (continuity). If this is the case the relay is good. If the relay does not click when battery voltage is applied and indicates no continuity (infinite resistance) across its terminals, it is faulty and must be replaced with a new one.
6 If the relay is good, check the leads from the battery to the relay, and from the relay to the starter motor, ensuring that the terminals are tight and corrosion-free.
7 Next check the wiring between the relay connector and the ECU (refer to Section 3 and the *Wiring Diagrams* at the end of this Chapter).

Removal and installation

8 If not already done, remove the left-hand bodywork side panel (see Chapter 7).
9 Ensure the ignition is OFF. Disconnect the battery negative lead (see Section 4).
10 On GS models, unscrew the nuts securing the starter motor and battery leads and

disconnect the leads from the terminals, noting how they fit **(see illustration 20.1)**. Disconnect the wiring connector. Undo the screws securing the relay to its bracket and lift it off.
11 On all other models, release the pin securing the starter relay and displace the relay and support bracket **(see illustration 21.2a and b)**. Unscrew the nuts securing the starter motor and battery leads and disconnect the leads from the terminals, noting how they fit. Disconnect the wiring connector.
12 Installation is the reverse of removal. Ensure the terminal nuts are tightened securely.

22 Starter motor

Removal and installation

1 The starter motor is located on the front of the engine. If the casing around the motor is dirty, wash it thoroughly – this will make work much easier and rule out the possibility of dirt getting inside.
2 Disconnect the battery negative lead (see Section 4).
3 Remove the cover from the starter motor terminal **(see illustration)**. Undo the nut

22.3a Remove the terminal cover

22.3b Disconnect the terminal lead (A) and the earth lead (B)

22.4 Undo the bolts securing the starter motor

22.5 Remove the O-ring

securing the lead to the motor terminal and detach the lead, then undo the screw securing the earth (ground) lead (see illustration).

4 Undo the bolts securing the starter motor to the crankcase and draw it out (see illustration).

5 Remove the O-ring on the end of the starter motor and discard it as a new one must be fitted (see illustration).

6 Installation is the reverse of removal, noting the following:

● Ensure the mounting position for the starter motor is clean.
● Ensure the O-ring is seated in its groove

and lubricate it with a smear of engine oil.
● Push the starter motor in firmly, ensuring the starter motor teeth engage correctly with those of the starter reduction gear.
● Tighten the mounting bolts to the torque setting specified at the beginning of this Chapter.
● Ensure the starter motor terminal and earth (ground) leads are securely connected.

Disassembly

7 Remove the starter motor (see Steps 1 to 5).

8 Note any alignment marks between the main housing and the front and rear covers, or make your own if they aren't clear (see illustration).

9 Unscrew the two long bolts, then remove the front cover (see illustrations). Note the location of the cover sealing ring.

10 Ease the armature out through the main housing, then grip the armature and rear cover and draw them out as an assembly (see illustrations). Note the location of the cover sealing ring.

11 Unscrew the terminal nut and remove the

22.8 Make alignment marks between the main housing and the covers

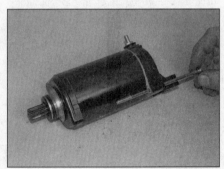

22.9a Unscrew the two long bolts . . .

22.9b . . . and remove the front cover – note the sealing ring (arrowed)

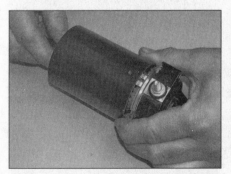

22.10a Ease the armature out through the main housing . . .

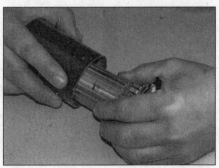

22.10b . . . then grip the armature and rear cover . . .

22.10c . . . and draw them out as an assembly

22.11a Unscrew the terminal nut . . .

22.11b . . . remove the insulating washer . . .

22.11c . . . and the O-ring

22.12a Note alignment between the long tabs (A) and the terminal (B) . . .

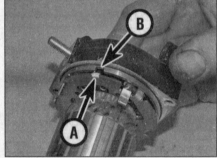

22.12b . . . and between the small tab (A) and the notch (B)

Inspection

14 The parts of the starter motor that are most likely to require attention are the brushes. No specifications are available, but if they are worn to the point where they no longer make good contact with the commutator, or are cracked, chipped, or otherwise damaged, fit a new brushplate assembly **(see illustration)**.

15 Inspect the commutator bars on the armature for scoring, scratches and discoloration **(see illustration)**. The commutator can be cleaned and polished with crocus cloth – do not use sandpaper or emery paper. After cleaning, wipe away any residue with a cloth soaked in electrical system cleaner or denatured alcohol. Also make sure the insulating mica between the bars is 0.5 mm below each bar – if not cut some of the insulating mica away using a fine file or saw blade **(see illustration)**.

insulating washer and the O-ring, noting how they fit **(see illustrations)**.

12 Note the alignment between the two long tabs on the brushplate and the terminal, and between the small tab and the notch in the rear cover **(see illustrations)**. Ease the rear cover off, pressing the terminal down through the hole in the cover **(see illustration)**. Lift off the insulator off the terminal and remove the thrust washers from the end of the armature **(see illustrations)**.

13 Ease the brushplate off the commutator.

22.12c Remove the rear cover

22.12d Lift the insulator off the terminal

22.12e Remove the thrust washers

22.14 Fit a new brushplate assembly if required

22.15a Inspect the commutator bars . . .

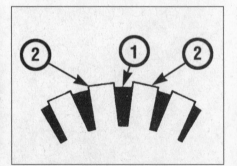

22.15b . . . and the depth of the mica (1) between the bars (2)

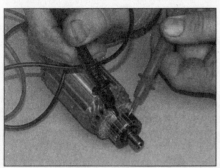

22.16a Check for continuity between the commutator bars

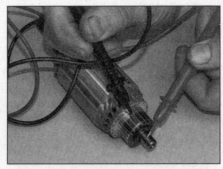

22.16b Check for continuity between the commutator bars and the armature

22.17 Inspect the gear teeth (A) and the bearing (B)

22.18 Inspect the front (A) and rear (B) covers

22.22a Hold the springs off the brushes as described

22.22b Install the brushplate onto the commutator

16 Using a multimeter or a continuity tester, check for continuity between the commutator bars **(see illustration)**. Continuity should exist between each bar and all of the others. Also, check for continuity between the commutator bars and the armature shaft **(see illustration)**. There should be no continuity. If the checks indicate otherwise, the armature is defective and a new starter motor will have to be fitted.

17 Check the front end of the armature shaft for worn, cracked, chipped and broken teeth **(see illustration)**. Check the bearing on the shaft (see *Tools and Workshop Tips* in the *Reference* section).

18 Inspect the front and rear covers for signs of cracks or wear, and check the oil seal in the front cover **(see illustration)**.

19 BMW do not list bearings or seals for the starter motor, but aftermarket parts are readily available from good suppliers, you just need

to remove the old ones and note the size markings.

20 Inspect the magnets in the main housing and the housing itself for cracks.

21 Inspect the terminal O-ring and cover sealing rings for signs of damage, deformation and deterioration and replace them with new ones if necessary.

Reassembly

22 Using four small screws or similar to hold the brush springs off the brushes, retract the brushes into their holders and install the brushplate onto the commutator, ensuring it is fitted the correct way round **(see illustrations)**. If necessary, ease the brushes onto the commutator using a small screwdriver, then remove the screws **(see illustrations)**.

23 Install the thrust washers and insulator **(see illustrations 22.12e and d)**.

24 Ensure the rear cover sealing ring is in place, then fit the terminal through the hole in the cover and install the cover ensuring the tabs align correctly **(see illustrations 22.12b and a)**. Install the O-ring and insulating washer and tighten the terminal nut securely **(see illustrations 22.11c, b and a)**.

25 Hold the armature and rear cover together firmly and slide on the main housing, ensuring the marks on the housing and cover align **(see illustrations 22.10b and a)**.

26 Ensure the front cover sealing ring is in place, then install the cover, ensuring the marks on the housing and cover align **(see illustration 22.9b)**.

27 Check the alignment marks made on removal are correctly aligned, then install the long bolts and tighten them securely.

28 Install the starter motor (see Step 6).

23 Charging system check

1 Accurate assessment of alternator output should be undertaken by a BMW dealer. However, a charging voltage output test can be undertaken as follows.

2 Make sure that the battery is fully charged (see Section 4).

3 Start the engine and run it at a fast idle. Using a multimeter set to the 0 to 20 volts DC scale, connect the positive (+ve) meter lead to the battery positive (+ve) terminal and

22.22c Ease the brushes onto the commutator . . .

22.22d . . . and remove the screws

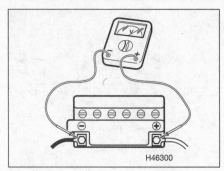

23.3 Regulated voltage check

24.3 Location of the alternator wiring connector – S, ST and R models

24.8 Alternator wiring exits at back of cover

the negative (-ve) lead to the negative (-ve) terminal (see illustration). The meter should indicate 13 to 15 volts.

4 Now switch on the headlight and select high beam – the voltage may drop momentarily, but should then return to the original indicated 13 to 15 volts.

5 If the output test indicates a voltage either lower or higher than the suggested range, it is likely that the alternator (see Section 24) or the regulator/rectifier (see Section 25) is faulty – have the charging system checked by a BMW dealer.

24 Alternator

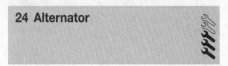

Check

1 The alternator is located on the right-hand side of the engine – the rotor is mounted on the crankshaft and the stator assembly is inside the right-hand cover.

2 On GS models, remove the right-hand side cover to access the wiring connector (see illustration 11.6a).

3 On S, ST and R models, displace the regulator/rectifier (see Section 25). The alternator wiring connector is clipped to the

underside of the ZFE holder (see illustration). Note: Access is extremely restricted – if necessary, remove the air filter housing (see Chapter 4).

4 Disconnect the wiring connector (three yellow wires).

5 Using a multimeter set to the ohms x 1 scale, check for a resistance between each of the wires on the alternator side of the connector, taking a total of three readings, then check for continuity between each terminal and earth (ground). If the stator coil windings are in good condition the three readings should be the same (BMW do not give a figure, but if the reading should not be very high), and there should be no continuity between any of the terminals and earth (ground). If not, the alternator stator coil assembly is faulty and should be replaced with a new one. Note: Before condemning the stator coils, check the fault is not due to damaged wiring between the connector and the coils.

Removal

Special tools: A top dead centre (TDC) locating tool will be required for this procedure (see Step 12). A suitable puller will be required to draw the alternator rotor off the crankshaft (see Step 14).

6 On ST models, remove the right-hand bodywork side panel (see Chapter 7).

7 On GS and R models, remove the front sprocket cover (see Chapter 6, Section 18). On S and ST models, remove the front pulley cover (see Chapter 6, Section 19).

8 If not already done, disconnect the alternator wiring connector (see Steps 2 to 4). Trace the wiring from the back of the alternator cover and release it from any clips or ties (see illustration). Feed the wiring back to the cover, noting its routing.

9 Loosen the alternator cover bolts evenly in the reverse of the tightening sequence (see illustration 24.31). Draw the cover off, noting that it will be restrained by the force of the rotor magnets (see illustration). Be prepared to catch any residual oil.

10 Discard the gasket as a new one must be used – note the location of the cover dowel and remove it if it is loose (see illustration).

11 Displace the ignition timing sensor to avoid the possibility of damage (see Chapter 4, Section 17).

12 To remove the rotor bolt, first follow the procedure in Chapter 2, Section 8, to lock the engine using the TDC locating tool. It is not necessary to remove the valve cover – with the aid of an assistant, turn the alternator rotor bolt in a clockwise direction until the slot cut into the left-hand web of the crankshaft is visible through the bolt hole. Note: Considerable pressure will be required

24.9 Draw the alternator cover off

24.10 Discard the old gasket – note location of cover dowel (arrowed)

24.13a Heat the rotor bolt to soften the locking compound

24.13b Loosen the bolt – apply steady pressure . . .

24.13c . . . then unscrew the bolt and washer

to undo the alternator bolt and draw the rotor off the crankshaft – using the TDC locating tool is by far the safest method of holding the crankshaft.

13 Unscrew the rotor bolt and remove the washer – if necessary, heat the bolt with a hot air gun to soften the locking compound on the bolt threads **(see illustrations)**.

14 To remove the rotor from the shaft it is necessary to use a rotor puller. BMW produces a service tool (Part No. 12 5 521) to do this – alternatively use a commercially available tool **(see illustration 24.15)**.

15 Using a hot air gun, heat the centre of the rotor to approximately 100°C, then thread the puller into the centre of the rotor and continue turning it clockwise to draw the rotor off **(see illustration)**. Remove the puller.

⚠ *Warning: The alternator rotor will be extremely hot at this stage – allow it to cool before handling it.*

16 If the starter driven gear came off with the rotor, lay the rotor face down on the workbench and draw the driven gear out (see Chapter 2, Section 13).

17 If required, remove the starter clutch from the rotor (see Chapter 2, Section 13).

18 Note the location of the Woodruff key in the tapered section of the crankshaft **(see illustration)**. The key should be a tight fit and should not be removed.

19 To remove the stator from the cover, first undo the screws securing the wiring clamp **(see illustration)**.

20 Undo the bolts securing the stator then lift it out, noting how the wiring grommet fits in the cover **(see illustrations)**.

Installation

Note: *Use the TDC locating tool to prevent the crankshaft from turning when the rotor bolt is tightened.*

21 Clean all traces of old gasket and sealant from the cover and crankcase mating surfaces.

22 Fit the stator into the cover, aligning the wiring grommet **(see illustration 24.20b)**.

23 Clean the threads of the stator bolts and wiring clamp screws, then apply a suitable non-permanent thread-locking compound. Tighten the bolts to the torque setting specified at the beginning of this Chapter and tighten the screws securely.

24 If removed, fit the starter clutch into the rotor (see Chapter 2, Section 13).

25 If removed, install the starter driven gear (see Chapter 2, Section 13).

26 Clean the tapered end of the crankshaft and the corresponding mating surface on the inside of the rotor thoroughly with a suitable solvent and clean cloth. Apply a thin coat of Loctite 648 to the crankshaft taper **(see illustration)**.

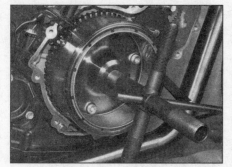

24.15 Using a universal puller to remove the alternator rotor

24.18 Note the location of the Woodruff key

24.19 Undo the screws securing the wiring clamp

24.20a Undo the bolts securing the stator . . .

24.20b . . . noting the location of the wiring grommet

24.26 Apply Loctite 648 to the crankshaft taper

24.27 Take care to align the slot in the rotor centre with the Woodruff key

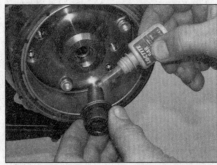

24.28 Thread lock the alternator rotor bolt

24.30 Apply sealant across the mating surface of the wiring grommet

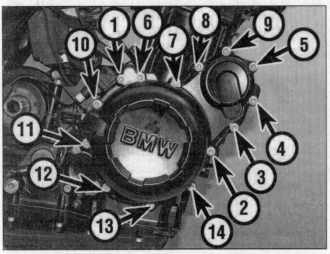

24.31 Alternator cover bolts TIGHTENING sequence

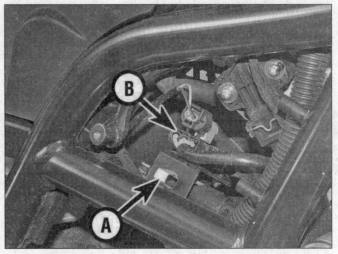

25.4 Battery (A) and alternator (B) wiring connectors

27 Make sure that no metal objects have attached themselves to the magnet on the inside of the rotor. Note the location of the Woodruff key in the crankshaft, then slide the rotor onto the shaft, locating the centre slot over the Woodruff key **(see illustration)**. If necessary, turn the starter driven gear anti-clockwise to allow the hub to fit into the starter clutch.

28 Clean the threads of the rotor bolt, then apply a suitable non-permanent thread-locking compound **(see illustration)**. Install the washer, then tighten the bolt to the torque setting specified at the beginning of this Chapter.

29 Unscrew the TDC locating tool and refit the blanking bolt using a new sealing washer (see Step 12).

30 Apply a smear of suitable sealant across the mating surface of the wiring grommet **(see illustration)**.

31 If removed, install the cover dowel, then install a new cover gasket **(see illustration 24.10)**. Install the alternator cover, noting that the rotor magnets will forcibly draw the cover on **(see illustration 24.9)**. Tighten the cover bolts evenly in the sequence shown to the specified torque setting **(see illustration)**.

32 Install the remaining components in the reverse order of removal. Check the oil level and top-up as necessary (see *Pre-ride checks*).

25 Regulator/rectifier

1 No test details are provided for the regulator/rectifier. If after testing the charging system as described in Section 23 it is thought to be faulty, have it checked by a BMW dealer.

2 The regulator/rectifier is located on the right-hand side above the transmission.

GS models

3 Remove the right-hand side cover to access the wiring connectors **(see illustrations 11.6a)**.

4 Release the battery wiring connector from its bracket and separate the connectors. Disconnect the battery and alternator wiring connectors **(see illustration)**.

5 Trace the wiring back to the regulator/rectifier and release it from any clips or ties **(see illustration)**. Feed the wiring back to the regulator/rectifier, noting its routing.

6 Either undo the bolts securing the regulator/rectifier to its mounting bracket, or the bolts securing the bracket to the frame, and lift it off.

7 Prior to installation, spray the connector terminals lightly with electrical contact cleaner **(see illustration)**.

8 Installation is the reverse of removal.

S, ST and R models

9 Remove the air filter housing (see Chapter 4).

25.5 Trace the wiring back to the regulator/rectifier (arrowed)

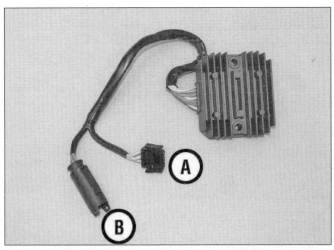

25.7 Spray alternator (A) and battery (B) connector terminals with electrical contact cleaner

25.10 Bolts secure regulator/rectifier to its mounting bracket

10 Undo the bolts securing the regulator/rectifier to its mounting bracket (see illustration).
11 Release the wiring from any ties and trace it back to the wiring connectors (see illustration). The alternator wiring connector is clipped to the underside of the ZFE holder (see illustration 24.3). The battery wiring connector is secured to the left-hand side of the ZFE holder (see illustration). Disconnect the wiring connectors and feed the wiring back to the regulator/rectifier, noting its routing.
12 If required, undo the screws securing the mounting bracket. Disconnect the accessory socket wiring connector and remove the bracket (see illustration).
13 Prior to installation, spray the connector terminals lightly with electrical contact cleaner (see illustration 25.7).
14 Installation is the reverse of removal.

26 Wiring diagrams

1 Starting, charging and engine management circuits are common to all models and presented in a single diagram. Other circuits such as lighting, instrumentation, ABS and controls are covered in separate diagrams for GS and S, ST, R models.
2 Connector plug terminal number details are given to aid testing and terminal identification. For the ECU the terminal numbers are represented in squares or circles to differentiate between the two connectors on the unit (see illustration). Study the wiring diagram and the two connectors on the ECU to determine the identity of the connector. The central vehicle electronics unit (ZFE) has one connector.
3 The components are drawn with a solid black outline where the unit connections are complete within that circuit. Where a hatched outline is used, their connections are shown on different circuits and thus the unit is not shown complete in any one circuit.
4 Wires can be identified by their colour and cross-sectional area, expressed in millimetres.
5 Internal connections within the wiring harness are respresented by full points with a DIN symbol alongisde, e.g. 31 denoting the earth (ground) circuit.

25.11a Release the wiring from any ties

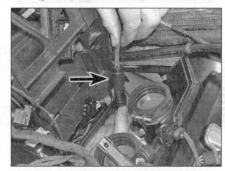

25.11b Release the battery wiring connector (arrowed)

25.12 Accessory socket wiring connector (arrowed)

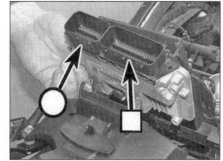

26.2 Terminal numbers are shown in circles or squares to identify the appropriate connector

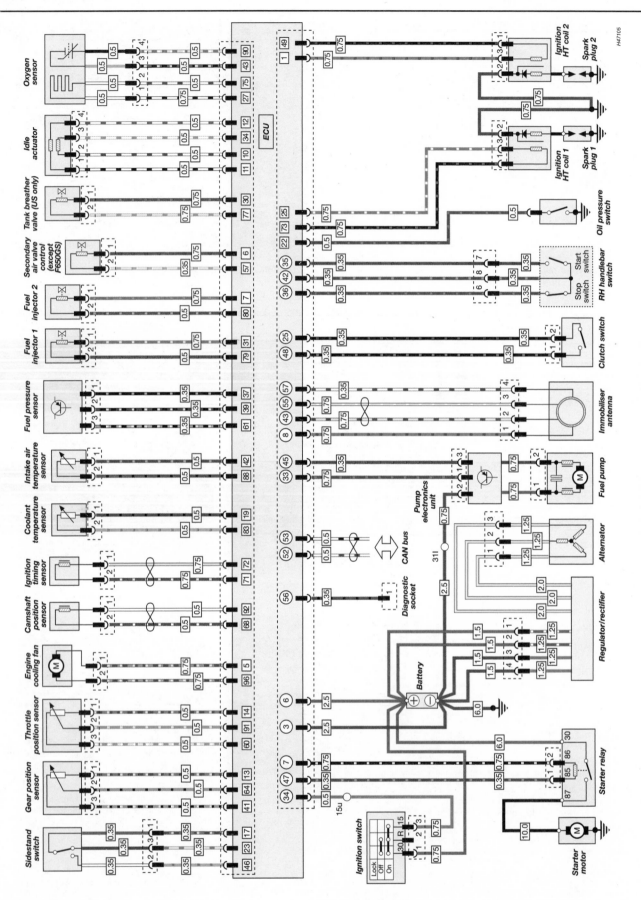

Starting, charging and engine management - all models

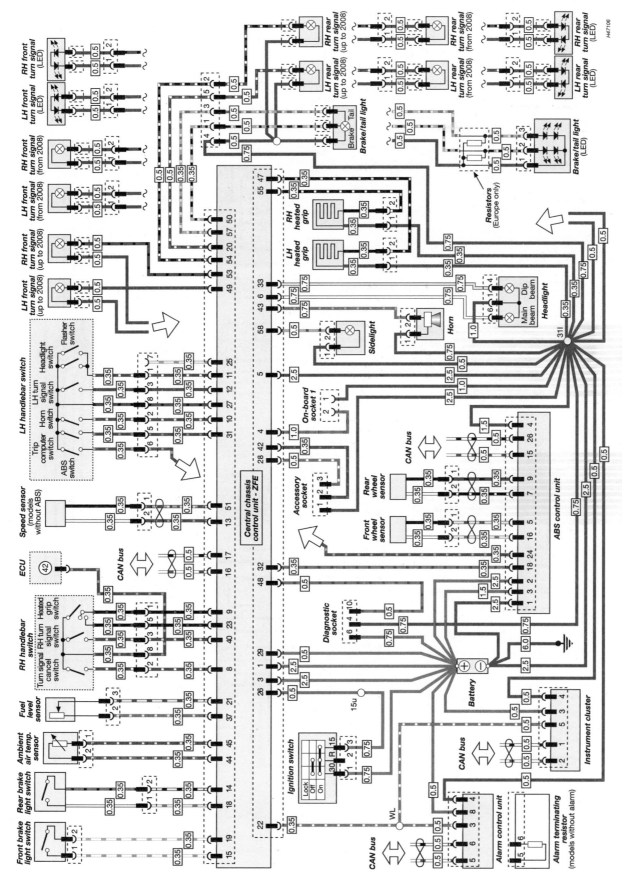

All other circuits - F800S, F800ST and F800R

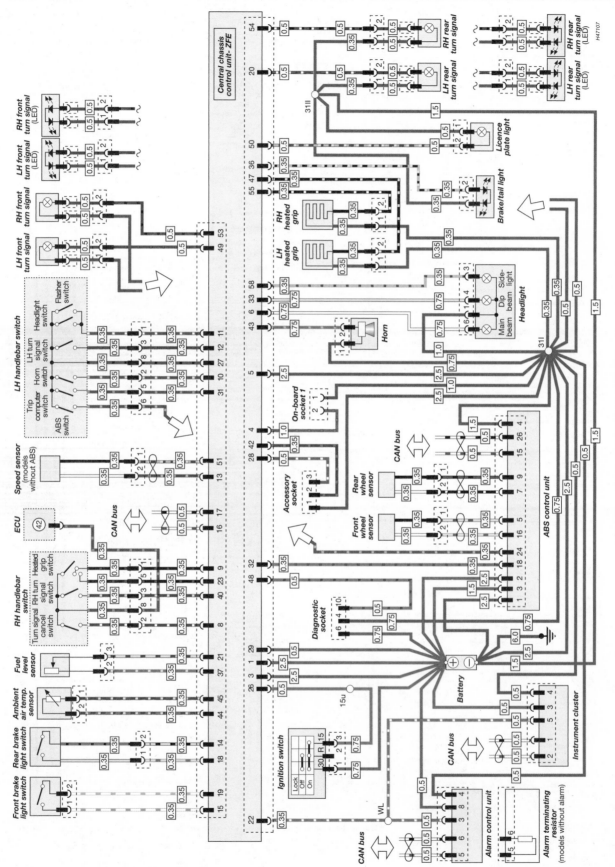

All other circuits - F650GS and F800GS

Reference

Tools and Workshop Tips

REF•2

● Building up a tool kit and equipping your workshop ● Using tools ● Understanding bearing, seal, fastener and chain sizes and markings ● Repair techniques

Security

REF•20

● Locks and chains ● U-locks ● Disc locks ● Alarms and immobilisers ● Security marking systems ● Tips on how to prevent bike theft

Lubricants and fluids

REF•23

● Engine oils ● Transmission (gear) oils ● Coolant/anti-freeze ● Fork oils and suspension fluids ● Brake/clutch fluids ● Spray lubes, degreasers and solvents

Conversion Factors

REF•26

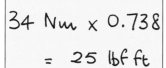

$$34 \ N_m \times 0.738$$
$$= 25 \ lbf \ ft$$

● Formulae for conversion of the metric (SI) units used throughout the manual into Imperial measures

MOT Test Checks

REF•27

● A guide to the UK MOT test ● Which items are tested ● How to prepare your motorcycle for the test and perform a pre-test check

Storage

REF•32

● How to prepare your motorcycle for going into storage and protect essential systems ● How to get the motorcycle back on the road

Fault Finding

REF•35

● Common faults and their likely causes ● How to check engine cylinder compression ● How to make electrical tests and use test meters

Technical Terms Explained

REF•44

● Component names, technical terms and common abbreviations explained

Index

REF•48

Buying tools

A toolkit is a fundamental requirement for servicing and repairing a motorcycle. Although there will be an initial expense in building up enough tools for servicing, this will soon be offset by the savings made by doing the job yourself. As experience and confidence grow, additional tools can be added to enable the repair and overhaul of the motorcycle. Many of the specialist tools are expensive and not often used so it may be preferable to hire them, or for a group of friends or motorcycle club to join in the purchase.

As a rule, it is better to buy more expensive, good quality tools. Cheaper tools are likely to wear out faster and need to be renewed more often, nullifying the original saving.

> **Warning: To avoid the risk of a poor quality tool breaking in use, causing injury or damage to the component being worked on, always aim to purchase tools which meet the relevant national safety standards.**

The following lists of tools do not represent the manufacturer's service tools, but serve as a guide to help the owner decide which tools are needed for this level of work. In addition, items such as an electric drill, hacksaw, files, soldering iron and a workbench equipped with a vice, may be needed. Although not classed as tools, a selection of bolts, screws, nuts, washers and pieces of tubing always come in useful.

For more information about tools, refer to the Haynes *Motorcycle Workshop Practice Techbook* (Bk. No. 3470).

Manufacturer's service tools

Inevitably certain tasks require the use of a service tool. Where possible an alternative tool or method of approach is recommended, but sometimes there is no option if personal injury or damage to the component is to be avoided. Where required, service tools are referred to in the relevant procedure.

Service tools can usually only be purchased from a motorcycle dealer and are identified by a part number. Some of the commonly-used tools, such as rotor pullers, are available in aftermarket form from mail-order motorcycle tool and accessory suppliers.

Maintenance and minor repair tools

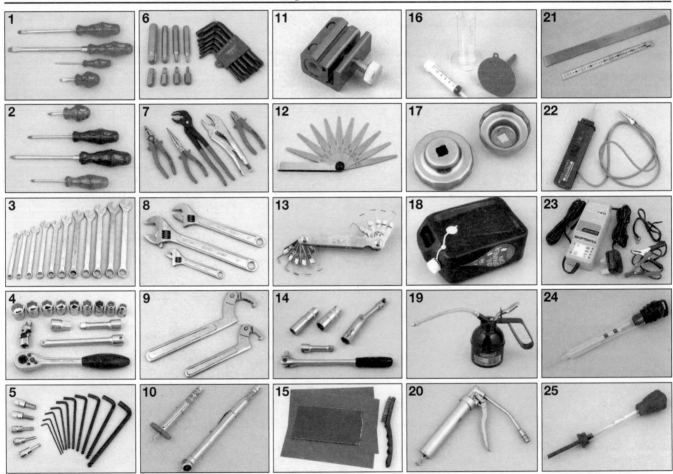

1 Set of flat-bladed screwdrivers
2 Set of Phillips head screwdrivers
3 Combination open-end and ring spanners
4 Socket set (3/8 inch or 1/2 inch drive)
5 Set of Allen keys or bits
6 Set of Torx keys or bits
7 Pliers, cutters and self-locking grips (Mole grips)
8 Adjustable spanners
9 C-spanners
10 Tread depth gauge and tyre pressure gauge
11 Cable oiler clamp
12 Feeler gauges
13 Spark plug gap measuring tool
14 Spark plug spanner or deep plug sockets
15 Wire brush and emery paper
16 Calibrated syringe, measuring vessel and funnel
17 Oil filter adapters
18 Oil drainer can or tray
19 Pump type oil can
20 Grease gun
21 Straight-edge and steel rule
22 Continuity tester
23 Battery charger
24 Hydrometer (for battery specific gravity check)
25 Anti-freeze tester (for liquid-cooled engines)

Repair and overhaul tools

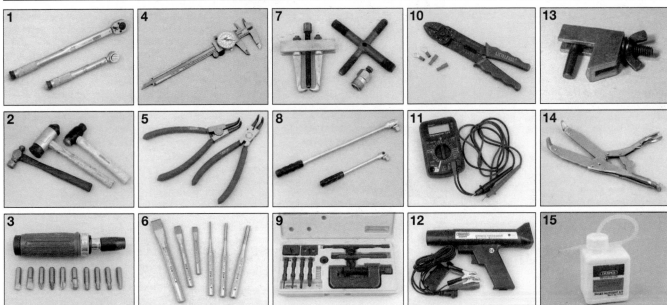

1 Torque wrench
(small and mid-ranges)
2 Conventional, plastic or
soft-faced hammers
3 Impact driver set

4 Vernier gauge
5 Circlip pliers (internal and
external, or combination)
6 Set of cold chisels
and punches

7 Selection of pullers
8 Breaker bars
9 Chain breaking/
riveting tool set

10 Wire stripper and
crimper tool
11 Multimeter (measures
amps, volts and ohms)
12 Stroboscope (for
dynamic timing checks)

13 Hose clamp
(wingnut type shown)
14 Clutch holding tool
15 One-man brake/clutch
bleeder kit

Specialist tools

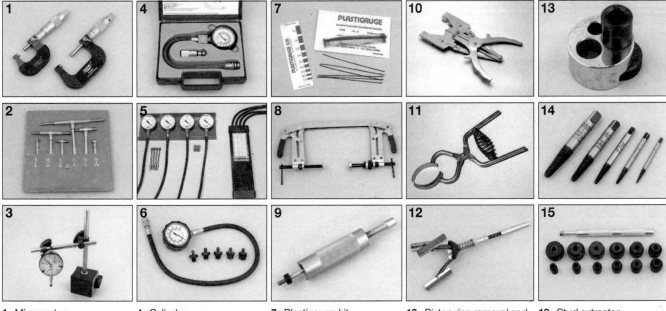

1 Micrometers
(external type)
2 Telescoping gauges
3 Dial gauge

4 Cylinder
compression gauge
5 Vacuum gauges (left) or
manometer (right)
6 Oil pressure gauge

7 Plastigauge kit
8 Valve spring compressor
(4-stroke engines)
9 Piston pin drawbolt tool

10 Piston ring removal and
installation tool
11 Piston ring clamp
12 Cylinder bore hone
(stone type shown)

13 Stud extractor
14 Screw extractor set
15 Bearing driver set

1 Workshop equipment and facilities

The workbench

● Work is made much easier by raising the bike up on a ramp - components are much more accessible if raised to waist level. The hydraulic or pneumatic types seen in the dealer's workshop are a sound investment if you undertake a lot of repairs or overhauls **(see illustration 1.1)**.

1.1 Hydraulic motorcycle ramp

● If raised off ground level, the bike must be supported on the ramp to avoid it falling. Most ramps incorporate a front wheel locating clamp which can be adjusted to suit different diameter wheels. When tightening the clamp, take care not to mark the wheel rim or damage the tyre - use wood blocks on each side to prevent this.
● Secure the bike to the ramp using tie-downs **(see illustration 1.2)**. If the bike has only a sidestand, and hence leans at a dangerous angle when raised, support the bike on an auxiliary stand.

1.2 Tie-downs are used around the passenger footrests to secure the bike

● Auxiliary (paddock) stands are widely available from mail order companies or motorcycle dealers and attach either to the wheel axle or swingarm pivot **(see illustration 1.3)**. If the motorcycle has a centrestand, you can support it under the crankcase to prevent it toppling whilst either wheel is removed **(see illustration 1.4)**.

1.3 This auxiliary stand attaches to the swingarm pivot

1.4 Always use a block of wood between the engine and jack head when supporting the engine in this way

Fumes and fire

● Refer to the Safety first! page at the beginning of the manual for full details. Make sure your workshop is equipped with a fire extinguisher suitable for fuel-related fires (Class B fire - flammable liquids) - it is not sufficient to have a water-filled extinguisher.
● Always ensure adequate ventilation is available. Unless an exhaust gas extraction system is available for use, ensure that the engine is run outside of the workshop.
● If working on the fuel system, make sure the workshop is ventilated to avoid a build-up of fumes. This applies equally to fume build-up when charging a battery. Do not smoke or allow anyone else to smoke in the workshop.

Fluids

● If you need to drain fuel from the tank, store it in an approved container marked as suitable for the storage of petrol (gasoline) **(see illustration 1.5)**. Do not store fuel in glass jars or bottles.

1.5 Use an approved can only for storing petrol (gasoline)

● Use proprietary engine degreasers or solvents which have a high flash-point, such as paraffin (kerosene), for cleaning off oil, grease and dirt - never use petrol (gasoline) for cleaning. Wear rubber gloves when handling solvent and engine degreaser. The fumes from certain solvents can be dangerous - always work in a well-ventilated area.

Dust, eye and hand protection

● Protect your lungs from inhalation of dust particles by wearing a filtering mask over the nose and mouth. Many frictional materials still contain asbestos which is dangerous to your health. Protect your eyes from spouts of liquid and sprung components by wearing a pair of protective goggles **(see illustration 1.6)**.

1.6 A fire extinguisher, goggles, mask and protective gloves should be at hand in the workshop

● Protect your hands from contact with solvents, fuel and oils by wearing rubber gloves. Alternatively apply a barrier cream to your hands before starting work. If handling hot components or fluids, wear suitable gloves to protect your hands from scalding and burns.

What to do with old fluids

● Old cleaning solvent, fuel, coolant and oils should not be poured down domestic drains or onto the ground. Package the fluid up in old oil containers, label it accordingly, and take it to a garage or disposal facility. Contact your local authority for location of such sites or ring the oil care hotline.

OIL CARE
FOLLOW THE CODE
OIL BANK LINE
0800 66 33 66
www.oilbankline.org.uk

Note: It is antisocial and illegal to dump oil down the drain. To find the location of your local oil recycling bank, call this number free.

In the USA, note that any oil supplier must accept used oil for recycling.

2 Fasteners -
screws, bolts and nuts

Fastener types and applications

Bolts and screws

● Fastener head types are either of hexagonal, Torx or splined design, with internal and external versions of each type **(see illustrations 2.1 and 2.2)**; splined head fasteners are not in common use on motorcycles. The conventional slotted or Phillips head design is used for certain screws. Bolt or screw length is always measured from the underside of the head to the end of the item **(see illustration 2.11)**.

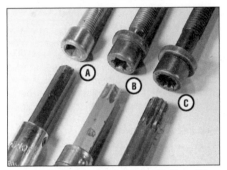

2.1 Internal hexagon/Allen (A), Torx (B) and splined (C) fasteners, with corresponding bits

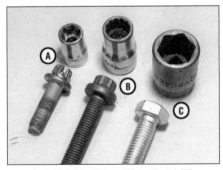

2.2 External Torx (A), splined (B) and hexagon (C) fasteners, with corresponding sockets

● Certain fasteners on the motorcycle have a tensile marking on their heads, the higher the marking the stronger the fastener. High tensile fasteners generally carry a 10 or higher marking. Never replace a high tensile fastener with one of a lower tensile strength.

Washers **(see illustration 2.3)**

● Plain washers are used between a fastener head and a component to prevent damage to the component or to spread the load when torque is applied. Plain washers can also be used as spacers or shims in certain assemblies. Copper or aluminium plain washers are often used as sealing washers on drain plugs.

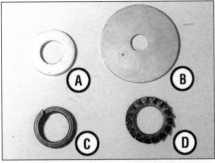

2.3 Plain washer (A), penny washer (B), spring washer (C) and serrated washer (D)

● The split-ring spring washer works by applying axial tension between the fastener head and component. If flattened, it is fatigued and must be renewed. If a plain (flat) washer is used on the fastener, position the spring washer between the fastener and the plain washer.

● Serrated star type washers dig into the fastener and component faces, preventing loosening. They are often used on electrical earth (ground) connections to the frame.

● Cone type washers (sometimes called Belleville) are conical and when tightened apply axial tension between the fastener head and component. They must be installed with the dished side against the component and often carry an OUTSIDE marking on their outer face. If flattened, they are fatigued and must be renewed.

● Tab washers are used to lock plain nuts or bolts on a shaft. A portion of the tab washer is bent up hard against one flat of the nut or bolt to prevent it loosening. Due to the tab washer being deformed in use, a new tab washer should be used every time it is disturbed.

● Wave washers are used to take up endfloat on a shaft. They provide light springing and prevent excessive side-to-side play of a component. Can be found on rocker arm shafts.

Nuts and split pins

● Conventional plain nuts are usually six-sided **(see illustration 2.4)**. They are sized by thread diameter and pitch. High tensile nuts carry a number on one end to denote their tensile strength.

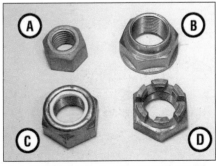

2.4 Plain nut (A), shouldered locknut (B), nylon insert nut (C) and castellated nut (D)

● Self-locking nuts either have a nylon insert, or two spring metal tabs, or a shoulder which is staked into a groove in the shaft - their advantage over conventional plain nuts is a resistance to loosening due to vibration. The nylon insert type can be used a number of times, but must be renewed when the friction of the nylon insert is reduced, ie when the nut spins freely on the shaft. The spring tab type can be reused unless the tabs are damaged. The shouldered type must be renewed every time it is disturbed.

● Split pins (cotter pins) are used to lock a castellated nut to a shaft or to prevent slackening of a plain nut. Common applications are wheel axles and brake torque arms. Because the split pin arms are deformed to lock around the nut a new split pin must always be used on installation - always fit the correct size split pin which will fit snugly in the shaft hole. Make sure the split pin arms are correctly located around the nut **(see illustrations 2.5 and 2.6)**.

2.5 Bend split pin (cotter pin) arms as shown (arrows) to secure a castellated nut

2.6 Bend split pin (cotter pin) arms as shown to secure a plain nut

Caution: If the castellated nut slots do not align with the shaft hole after tightening to the torque setting, tighten the nut until the next slot aligns with the hole - never slacken the nut to align its slot.

● R-pins (shaped like the letter R), or slip pins as they are sometimes called, are sprung and can be reused if they are otherwise in good condition. Always install R-pins with their closed end facing forwards **(see illustration 2.7)**.

**2.7 Correct fitting of R-pin.
Arrow indicates forward direction**

Circlips (see illustration 2.8)

● Circlips (sometimes called snap-rings) are used to retain components on a shaft or in a housing and have corresponding external or internal ears to permit removal. Parallel-sided (machined) circlips can be installed either way round in their groove, whereas stamped circlips (which have a chamfered edge on one face) must be installed with the chamfer facing away from the direction of thrust load **(see illustration 2.9)**.

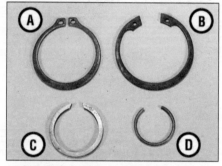

2.8 External stamped circlip (A), internal stamped circlip (B), machined circlip (C) and wire circlip (D)

● Always use circlip pliers to remove and install circlips; expand or compress them just enough to remove them. After installation, rotate the circlip in its groove to ensure it is securely seated. If installing a circlip on a splined shaft, always align its opening with a shaft channel to ensure the circlip ends are well supported and unlikely to catch **(see illustration 2.10)**.

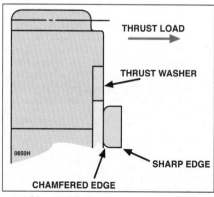

2.9 Correct fitting of a stamped circlip

THRUST LOAD

THRUST WASHER

SHARP EDGE

CHAMFERED EDGE

0650H

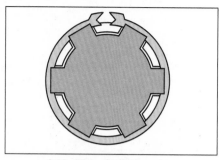

**2.10 Align circlip opening
with shaft channel**

● Circlips can wear due to the thrust of components and become loose in their grooves, with the subsequent danger of becoming dislodged in operation. For this reason, renewal is advised every time a circlip is disturbed.
● Wire circlips are commonly used as piston pin retaining clips. If a removal tang is provided, long-nosed pliers can be used to dislodge them, otherwise careful use of a small flat-bladed screwdriver is necessary. Wire circlips should be renewed every time they are disturbed.

Thread diameter and pitch

● Diameter of a male thread (screw, bolt or stud) is the outside diameter of the threaded portion **(see illustration 2.11)**. Most motorcycle manufacturers use the ISO (International Standards Organisation) metric system expressed in millimetres, eg M6 refers to a 6 mm diameter thread. Sizing is the same for nuts, except that the thread diameter is measured across the valleys of the nut.
● Pitch is the distance between the peaks of the thread **(see illustration 2.11)**. It is expressed in millimetres, thus a common bolt size may be expressed as 6.0 x 1.0 mm (6 mm thread diameter and 1 mm pitch). Generally pitch increases in proportion to thread diameter, although there are always exceptions.
● Thread diameter and pitch are related for conventional fastener applications and the accompanying table can be used as a guide. Additionally, the AF (Across Flats), spanner or socket size dimension of the bolt or nut **(see illustration 2.11)** is linked to thread and pitch specification. Thread pitch can be measured with a thread gauge **(see illustration 2.12)**.

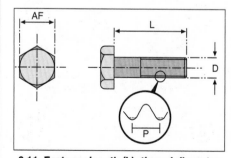

2.11 Fastener length (L), thread diameter (D), thread pitch (P) and head size (AF)

AF

L

D

P

**2.12 Using a thread gauge
to measure pitch**

AF size	Thread diameter x pitch (mm)
8 mm	M5 x 0.8
8 mm	M6 x 1.0
10 mm	M6 x 1.0
12 mm	M8 x 1.25
14 mm	M10 x 1.25
17 mm	M12 x 1.25

● The threads of most fasteners are of the right-hand type, ie they are turned clockwise to tighten and anti-clockwise to loosen. The reverse situation applies to left-hand thread fasteners, which are turned anti-clockwise to tighten and clockwise to loosen. Left-hand threads are used where rotation of a component might loosen a conventional right-hand thread fastener.

Seized fasteners

● Corrosion of external fasteners due to water or reaction between two dissimilar metals can occur over a period of time. It will build up sooner in wet conditions or in countries where salt is used on the roads during the winter. If a fastener is severely corroded it is likely that normal methods of removal will fail and result in its head being ruined. When you attempt removal, the fastener thread should be heard to crack free and unscrew easily - if it doesn't, stop there before damaging something.
● A smart tap on the head of the fastener will often succeed in breaking free corrosion which has occurred in the threads **(see illustration 2.13)**.
● An aerosol penetrating fluid (such as WD-40) applied the night beforehand may work its way down into the thread and ease removal. Depending on the location, you may be able to make up a Plasticine well around the fastener head and fill it with penetrating fluid.

**2.13 A sharp tap on the head of a fastener
will often break free a corroded thread**

● If you are working on an engine internal component, corrosion will most likely not be a problem due to the well lubricated environment. However, components can be very tight and an impact driver is a useful tool in freeing them (see illustration 2.14).

2.14 Using an impact driver to free a fastener

● Where corrosion has occurred between dissimilar metals (eg steel and aluminium alloy), the application of heat to the fastener head will create a disproportionate expansion rate between the two metals and break the seizure caused by the corrosion. Whether heat can be applied depends on the location of the fastener - any surrounding components likely to be damaged must first be removed (see illustration 2.15). Heat can be applied using a paint stripper heat gun or clothes iron, or by immersing the component in boiling water - wear protective gloves to prevent scalding or burns to the hands.

2.15 Using heat to free a seized fastener

● As a last resort, it is possible to use a hammer and cold chisel to work the fastener head unscrewed (see illustration 2.16). This will damage the fastener, but more importantly extreme care must be taken not to damage the surrounding component.

Caution: Remember that the component being secured is generally of more value than the bolt, nut or screw - when the fastener is freed, do not unscrew it with force, instead work the fastener back and forth when resistance is felt to prevent thread damage.

2.16 Using a hammer and chisel to free a seized fastener

Broken fasteners and damaged heads

● If the shank of a broken bolt or screw is accessible you can grip it with self-locking grips. The knurled wheel type stud extractor tool or self-gripping stud puller tool is particularly useful for removing the long studs which screw into the cylinder mouth surface of the crankcase or bolts and screws from which the head has broken off (see illustration 2.17). Studs can also be removed by locking two nuts together on the threaded end of the stud and using a spanner on the lower nut (see illustration 2.18).

2.17 Using a stud extractor tool to remove a broken crankcase stud

2.18 Two nuts can be locked together to unscrew a stud from a component

● A bolt or screw which has broken off below or level with the casing must be extracted using a screw extractor set. Centre punch the fastener to centralise the drill bit, then drill a hole in the fastener (see illustration 2.19). Select a drill bit which is approximately half to three-quarters the

2.19 When using a screw extractor, first drill a hole in the fastener . . .

diameter of the fastener and drill to a depth which will accommodate the extractor. Use the largest size extractor possible, but avoid leaving too small a wall thickness otherwise the extractor will merely force the fastener walls outwards wedging it in the casing thread.

● If a spiral type extractor is used, thread it anti-clockwise into the fastener. As it is screwed in, it will grip the fastener and unscrew it from the casing (see illustration 2.20).

2.20 . . . then thread the extractor anti-clockwise into the fastener

● If a taper type extractor is used, tap it into the fastener so that it is firmly wedged in place. Unscrew the extractor (anti-clockwise) to draw the fastener out.

> ⚠ *Warning: Stud extractors are very hard and may break off in the fastener if care is not taken - ask an engineer about spark erosion if this happens.*

● Alternatively, the broken bolt/screw can be drilled out and the hole retapped for an oversize bolt/screw or a diamond-section thread insert. It is essential that the drilling is carried out squarely and to the correct depth, otherwise the casing may be ruined - if in doubt, entrust the work to an engineer.

● Bolts and nuts with rounded corners cause the correct size spanner or socket to slip when force is applied. Of the types of spanner/socket available always use a six-point type rather than an eight or twelve-point type - better grip

2.21 Comparison of surface drive ring spanner (left) with 12-point type (right)

is obtained. Surface drive spanners grip the middle of the hex flats, rather than the corners, and are thus good in cases of damaged heads **(see illustration 2.21)**.

● Slotted-head or Phillips-head screws are often damaged by the use of the wrong size screwdriver. Allen-head and Torx-head screws are much less likely to sustain damage. If enough of the screw head is exposed you can use a hacksaw to cut a slot in its head and then use a conventional flat-bladed screwdriver to remove it. Alternatively use a hammer and cold chisel to tap the head of the fastener around to slacken it. Always replace damaged fasteners with new ones, preferably Torx or Allen-head type.

HAYNES HiNT

A dab of valve grinding compound between the screw head and screwdriver tip will often give a good grip.

Thread repair

● Threads (particularly those in aluminium alloy components) can be damaged by overtightening, being assembled with dirt in the threads, or from a component working loose and vibrating. Eventually the thread will fail completely, and it will be impossible to tighten the fastener.

● If a thread is damaged or clogged with old locking compound it can be renovated with a thread repair tool (thread chaser) **(see illustrations 2.22 and 2.23)**; special thread

2.22 A thread repair tool being used to correct an internal thread

2.23 A thread repair tool being used to correct an external thread

chasers are available for spark plug hole threads. The tool will not cut a new thread, but clean and true the original thread. Make sure that you use the correct diameter and pitch tool. Similarly, external threads can be cleaned up with a die or a thread restorer file **(see illustration 2.24)**.

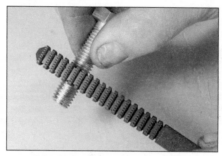

2.24 Using a thread restorer file

● It is possible to drill out the old thread and retap the component to the next thread size. This will work where there is enough surrounding material and a new bolt or screw can be obtained. Sometimes, however, this is not possible - such as where the bolt/screw passes through another component which must also be suitably modified, also in cases where a spark plug or oil drain plug cannot be obtained in a larger diameter thread size.

● The diamond-section thread insert (often known by its popular trade name of Heli-Coil) is a simple and effective method of renewing the thread and retaining the original size. A kit can be purchased which contains the tap, insert and installing tool **(see illustration 2.25)**. Drill out the damaged thread with the size drill specified **(see illustration 2.26)**. Carefully retap the thread **(see illustration 2.27)**. Install the

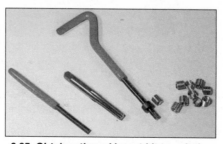

2.25 Obtain a thread insert kit to suit the thread diameter and pitch required

2.26 To install a thread insert, first drill out the original thread . . .

2.27 . . . tap a new thread . . .

2.28 . . . fit insert on the installing tool . . .

2.29 . . . and thread into the component . . .

2.30 . . . break off the tang when complete

insert on the installing tool and thread it slowly into place using a light downward pressure **(see illustrations 2.28 and 2.29)**. When positioned between a 1/4 and 1/2 turn below the surface withdraw the installing tool and use the break-off tool to press down on the tang, breaking it off **(see illustration 2.30)**.

● There are epoxy thread repair kits on the market which can rebuild stripped internal threads, although this repair should not be used on high load-bearing components.

Thread locking and sealing compounds

● Locking compounds are used in locations where the fastener is prone to loosening due to vibration or on important safety-related items which might cause loss of control of the motorcycle if they fail. It is also used where important fasteners cannot be secured by other means such as lockwashers or split pins.

● Before applying locking compound, make sure that the threads (internal and external) are clean and dry with all old compound removed. Select a compound to suit the component being secured - a non-permanent general locking and sealing type is suitable for most applications, but a high strength type is needed for permanent fixing of studs in castings. Apply a drop or two of the compound to the first few threads of the fastener, then thread it into place and tighten to the specified torque. Do not apply excessive thread locking compound otherwise the thread may be damaged on subsequent removal.

● Certain fasteners are impregnated with a dry film type coating of locking compound on their threads. Always renew this type of fastener if disturbed.

● Anti-seize compounds, such as copper-based greases, can be applied to protect threads from seizure due to extreme heat and corrosion. A common instance is spark plug threads and exhaust system fasteners.

3 Measuring tools and gauges

Feeler gauges

● Feeler gauges (or blades) are used for measuring small gaps and clearances (see illustration 3.1). They can also be used to measure endfloat (sideplay) of a component on a shaft where access is not possible with a dial gauge.

● Feeler gauge sets should be treated with care and not bent or damaged. They are etched with their size on one face. Keep them clean and very lightly oiled to prevent corrosion build-up.

3.1 Feeler gauges are used for measuring small gaps and clearances - thickness is marked on one face of gauge

● When measuring a clearance, select a gauge which is a light sliding fit between the two components. You may need to use two gauges together to measure the clearance accurately.

Micrometers

● A micrometer is a precision tool capable of measuring to 0.01 or 0.001 of a millimetre. It should always be stored in its case and not in the general toolbox. It must be kept clean and never dropped, otherwise its frame or measuring anvils could be distorted resulting in inaccurate readings.

● External micrometers are used for measuring outside diameters of components and have many more applications than internal micrometers. Micrometers are available in different size ranges, eg 0 to 25 mm, 25 to 50 mm, and upwards in 25 mm steps; some large micrometers have interchangeable anvils to allow a range of measurements to be taken. Generally the largest precision measurement you are likely to take on a motorcycle is the piston diameter.

● Internal micrometers (or bore micrometers) are used for measuring inside diameters, such as valve guides and cylinder bores. Telescoping gauges and small hole gauges are used in conjunction with an external micrometer, whereas the more expensive internal micrometers have their own measuring device.

External micrometer

Note: *The conventional analogue type instrument is described. Although much easier to read, digital micrometers are considerably more expensive.*

● Always check the calibration of the micrometer before use. With the anvils closed (0 to 25 mm type) or set over a test gauge (for

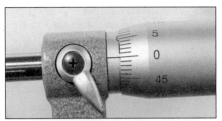

3.2 Check micrometer calibration before use

the larger types) the scale should read zero (see illustration 3.2); make sure that the anvils (and test piece) are clean first. Any discrepancy can be adjusted by referring to the instructions supplied with the tool. Remember that the micrometer is a precision measuring tool - don't force the anvils closed, use the ratchet (4) on the end of the micrometer to close it. In this way, a measured force is always applied.

● To use, first make sure that the item being measured is clean. Place the anvil of the micrometer (1) against the item and use the thimble (2) to bring the spindle (3) lightly into contact with the other side of the item (see illustration 3.3). Don't tighten the thimble down because this will damage the micrometer - instead use the ratchet (4) on the end of the micrometer. The ratchet mechanism applies a measured force preventing damage to the instrument.

● The micrometer is read by referring to the linear scale on the sleeve and the annular scale on the thimble. Read off the sleeve first to obtain the base measurement, then add the fine measurement from the thimble to obtain the overall reading. The linear scale on the sleeve represents the measuring range of the micrometer (eg 0 to 25 mm). The annular scale

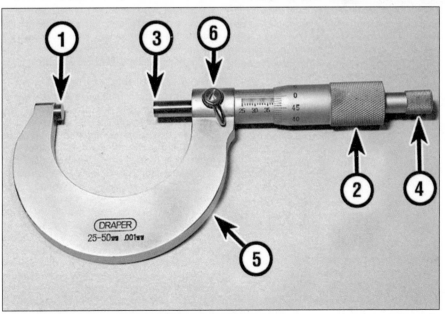

3.3 Micrometer component parts

1 Anvil	3 Spindle	5 Frame
2 Thimble	4 Ratchet	6 Locking lever

on the thimble will be in graduations of 0.01 mm (or as marked on the frame) - one full revolution of the thimble will move 0.5 mm on the linear scale. Take the reading where the datum line on the sleeve intersects the thimble's scale. Always position the eye directly above the scale otherwise an inaccurate reading will result.

In the example shown the item measures 2.95 mm **(see illustration 3.4)**:

Linear scale	2.00 mm
Linear scale	0.50 mm
Annular scale	0.45 mm
Total figure	**2.95 mm**

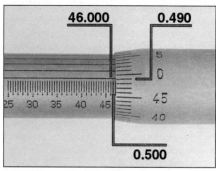

3.5 Micrometer reading of 46.99 mm on linear and annular scales . . .

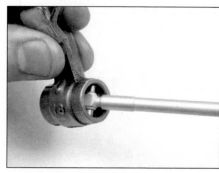

3.7 Expand the telescoping gauge in the bore, lock its position . . .

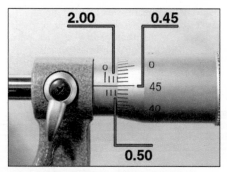

3.4 Micrometer reading of 2.95 mm

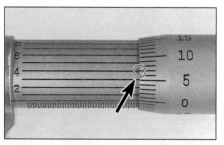

3.6 . . . and 0.004 mm on vernier scale

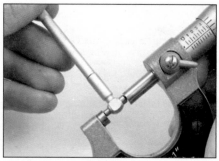

3.8 . . . then measure the gauge with a micrometer

Most micrometers have a locking lever (6) on the frame to hold the setting in place, allowing the item to be removed from the micrometer.
● Some micrometers have a vernier scale on their sleeve, providing an even finer measurement to be taken, in 0.001 increments of a millimetre. Take the sleeve and thimble measurement as described above, then check which graduation on the vernier scale aligns with that of the annular scale on the thimble **Note:** *The eye must be perpendicular to the scale when taking the vernier reading - if necessary rotate the body of the micrometer to ensure this.* Multiply the vernier scale figure by 0.001 and add it to the base and fine measurement figures.

In the example shown the item measures 46.994 mm **(see illustrations 3.5 and 3.6)**:

Linear scale (base)	46.000 mm
Linear scale (base)	00.500 mm
Annular scale (fine)	00.490 mm
Vernier scale	00.004 mm
Total figure	**46.994 mm**

Internal micrometer

● Internal micrometers are available for measuring bore diameters, but are expensive and unlikely to be available for home use. It is suggested that a set of telescoping gauges and small hole gauges, both of which must be used with an external micrometer, will suffice for taking internal measurements on a motorcycle.
● Telescoping gauges can be used to

measure internal diameters of components. Select a gauge with the correct size range, make sure its ends are clean and insert it into the bore. Expand the gauge, then lock its position and withdraw it from the bore **(see illustration 3.7)**. Measure across the gauge ends with a micrometer **(see illustration 3.8)**.
● Very small diameter bores (such as valve guides) are measured with a small hole gauge. Once adjusted to a slip-fit inside the component, its position is locked and the gauge withdrawn for measurement with a micrometer **(see illustrations 3.9 and 3.10)**.

Vernier caliper

Note: *The conventional linear and dial gauge type instruments are described. Digital types are easier to read, but are far more expensive.*
● The vernier caliper does not provide the precision of a micrometer, but is versatile in being able to measure internal and external diameters. Some types also incorporate a depth gauge. It is ideal for measuring clutch plate friction material and spring free lengths.
● To use the conventional linear scale vernier, slacken off the vernier clamp screws (1) and set its jaws over (2), or inside (3), the item to be measured **(see illustration 3.11)**. Slide the jaw into contact, using the thumb-wheel (4) for fine movement of the sliding scale (5) then tighten the clamp screws (1). Read off the main scale (6) where the zero on the sliding scale (5) intersects it, taking the whole number to the left of the zero; this provides the base measurement. View along the sliding scale and select the division which

3.9 Expand the small hole gauge in the bore, lock its position . . .

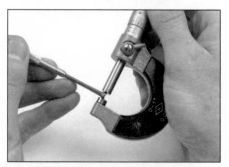

3.10 . . . then measure the gauge with a micrometer

lines up exactly with any of the divisions on the main scale, noting that the divisions usually represents 0.02 of a millimetre. Add this fine measurement to the base measurement to obtain the total reading.

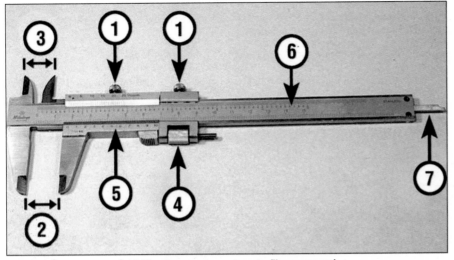

3.11 Vernier component parts (linear gauge)

1 *Clamp screws*	3 *Internal jaws*	5 *Sliding scale*	7 *Depth gauge*
2 *External jaws*	4 *Thumbwheel*	6 *Main scale*	

In the example shown the item measures 55.92 mm **(see illustration 3.12)**:

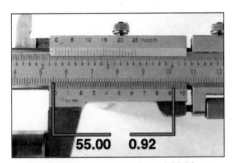

3.12 Vernier gauge reading of 55.92 mm

Base measurement	55.00 mm
Fine measurement	00.92 mm
Total figure	**55.92 mm**

● Some vernier calipers are equipped with a dial gauge for fine measurement. Before use, check that the jaws are clean, then close them fully and check that the dial gauge reads zero. If necessary adjust the gauge ring accordingly. Slacken the vernier clamp screw (1) and set its jaws over (2), or inside (3), the item to be measured **(see illustration 3.13)**. Slide the jaws into contact, using the thumbwheel (4) for fine movement. Read off the main scale (5) where the edge of the sliding scale (6) intersects it, taking the whole number to the left of the zero; this provides the base measurement. Read off the needle position on the dial gauge (7) scale to provide the fine measurement; each division represents 0.05 of a millimetre. Add this fine measurement to the base measurement to obtain the total reading.

In the example shown the item measures 55.95 mm **(see illustration 3.14)**:

Base measurement	55.00 mm
Fine measurement	00.95 mm
Total figure	**55.95 mm**

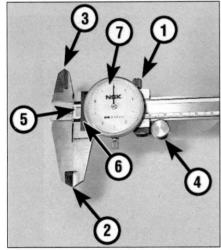

3.13 Vernier component parts (dial gauge)

1 *Clamp screw*	5 *Main scale*
2 *External jaws*	6 *Sliding scale*
3 *Internal jaws*	7 *Dial gauge*
4 *Thumbwheel*	

3.14 Vernier gauge reading of 55.95 mm

Plastigauge

● Plastigauge is a plastic material which can be compressed between two surfaces to measure the oil clearance between them. The width of the compressed Plastigauge is measured against a calibrated scale to determine the clearance.

● Common uses of Plastigauge are for measuring the clearance between crankshaft journal and main bearing inserts, between crankshaft journal and big-end bearing inserts, and between camshaft and bearing surfaces. The following example describes big-end oil clearance measurement.

● Handle the Plastigauge material carefully to prevent distortion. Using a sharp knife, cut a length which corresponds with the width of the bearing being measured and place it carefully across the journal so that it is parallel with the shaft **(see illustration 3.15)**. Carefully install both bearing shells and the connecting rod. Without rotating the rod on the journal tighten its bolts or nuts (as applicable) to the specified torque. The connecting rod and bearings are then disassembled and the crushed Plastigauge examined.

3.15 Plastigauge placed across shaft journal

● Using the scale provided in the Plastigauge kit, measure the width of the material to determine the oil clearance **(see illustration 3.16)**. Always remove all traces of Plastigauge after use using your fingernails.

Caution: Arriving at the correct clearance demands that the assembly is torqued correctly, according to the settings and sequence (where applicable) provided by the motorcycle manufacturer.

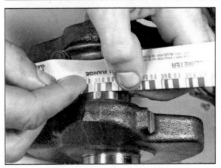

3.16 Measuring the width of the crushed Plastigauge

Dial gauge or DTI (Dial Test Indicator)

● A dial gauge can be used to accurately measure small amounts of movement. Typical uses are measuring shaft runout or shaft endfloat (sideplay) and setting piston position for ignition timing on two-strokes. A dial gauge set usually comes with a range of different probes and adapters and mounting equipment.

● The gauge needle must point to zero when at rest. Rotate the ring around its periphery to zero the gauge.

● Check that the gauge is capable of reading the extent of movement in the work. Most gauges have a small dial set in the face which records whole millimetres of movement as well as the fine scale around the face periphery which is calibrated in 0.01 mm divisions. Read off the small dial first to obtain the base measurement, then add the measurement from the fine scale to obtain the total reading.

In the example shown the gauge reads 1.48 mm **(see illustration 3.17)**:

Base measurement	1.00 mm
Fine measurement	0.48 mm
Total figure	**1.48 mm**

3.17 Dial gauge reading of 1.48 mm

● If measuring shaft runout, the shaft must be supported in vee-blocks and the gauge mounted on a stand perpendicular to the shaft. Rest the tip of the gauge against the centre of the shaft and rotate the shaft slowly whilst watching the gauge reading **(see illustration 3.18)**. Take several measurements along the length of the shaft and record the

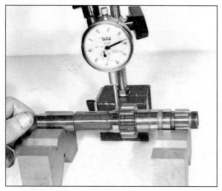

3.18 Using a dial gauge to measure shaft runout

maximum gauge reading as the amount of runout in the shaft. **Note:** *The reading obtained will be total runout at that point - some manufacturers specify that the runout figure is halved to compare with their specified runout limit.*

● Endfloat (sideplay) measurement requires that the gauge is mounted securely to the surrounding component with its probe touching the end of the shaft. Using hand pressure, push and pull on the shaft noting the maximum endfloat recorded on the gauge **(see illustration 3.19)**.

3.19 Using a dial gauge to measure shaft endfloat

● A dial gauge with suitable adapters can be used to determine piston position BTDC on two-stroke engines for the purposes of ignition timing. The gauge, adapter and suitable length probe are installed in the place of the spark plug and the gauge zeroed at TDC. If the piston position is specified as 1.14 mm BTDC, rotate the engine back to 2.00 mm BTDC, then slowly forwards to 1.14 mm BTDC.

Cylinder compression gauges

● A compression gauge is used for measuring cylinder compression. Either the rubber-cone type or the threaded adapter type can be used. The latter is preferred to ensure a perfect seal against the cylinder head. A 0 to 300 psi (0 to 20 Bar) type gauge (for petrol/gasoline engines) will be suitable for motorcycles.

● The spark plug is removed and the gauge either held hard against the cylinder head (cone type) or the gauge adapter screwed into the cylinder head (threaded type) **(see illustration 3.20)**. Cylinder compression is measured with the engine turning over, but not running - carry out the compression test as described in

3.20 Using a rubber-cone type cylinder compression gauge

Fault Finding Equipment. The gauge will hold the reading until manually released.

Oil pressure gauge

● An oil pressure gauge is used for measuring engine oil pressure. Most gauges come with a set of adapters to fit the thread of the take-off point **(see illustration 3.21)**. If the take-off point specified by the motorcycle manufacturer is an external oil pipe union, make sure that the specified replacement union is used to prevent oil starvation.

3.21 Oil pressure gauge and take-off point adapter (arrow)

● Oil pressure is measured with the engine running (at a specific rpm) and often the manufacturer will specify pressure limits for a cold and hot engine.

Straight-edge and surface plate

● If checking the gasket face of a component for warpage, place a steel rule or precision straight-edge across the gasket face and measure any gap between the straight-edge and component with feeler gauges **(see illustration 3.22)**. Check diagonally across the component and between mounting holes **(see illustration 3.23)**.

3.22 Use a straight-edge and feeler gauges to check for warpage

3.23 Check for warpage in these directions

● Checking individual components for warpage, such as clutch plain (metal) plates, requires a perfectly flat plate or piece or plate glass and feeler gauges.

4 Torque and leverage

What is torque?

● Torque describes the twisting force about a shaft. The amount of torque applied is determined by the distance from the centre of the shaft to the end of the lever and the amount of force being applied to the end of the lever; distance multiplied by force equals torque.

● The manufacturer applies a measured torque to a bolt or nut to ensure that it will not slacken in use and to hold two components securely together without movement in the joint. The actual torque setting depends on the thread size, bolt or nut material and the composition of the components being held.

● Too little torque may cause the fastener to loosen due to vibration, whereas too much torque will distort the joint faces of the component or cause the fastener to shear off. Always stick to the specified torque setting.

Using a torque wrench

● Check the calibration of the torque wrench and make sure it has a suitable range for the job. Torque wrenches are available in Nm (Newton-metres), kgf m (kilograms-force metre), lbf ft (pounds-feet), lbf in (inch-pounds). Do not confuse lbf ft with lbf in.

● Adjust the tool to the desired torque on the scale **(see illustration 4.1)**. If your torque wrench is not calibrated in the units specified, carefully convert the figure (see *Conversion Factors*). A manufacturer sometimes gives a torque setting as a range (8 to 10 Nm) rather than a single figure - in this case set the tool midway between the two settings. The same torque may be expressed as 9 Nm ± 1 Nm. Some torque wrenches have a method of locking the setting so that it isn't inadvertently altered during use.

● Install the bolts/nuts in their correct location and secure them lightly. Their threads must be clean and free of any old locking compound. Unless specified the threads and flange should be dry - oiled threads are necessary in certain circumstances and the manufacturer will take this into account in the specified torque figure. Similarly, the manufacturer may also specify the application of thread-locking compound.

● Tighten the fasteners in the specified sequence until the torque wrench clicks, indicating that the torque setting has been reached. Apply the torque again to double-check the setting. Where different thread diameter fasteners secure the component, as a rule tighten the larger diameter ones first.

● When the torque wrench has been finished with, release the lock (where applicable) and fully back off its setting to zero - do not leave the torque wrench tensioned. Also, do not use a torque wrench for slackening a fastener.

Angle-tightening

● Manufacturers often specify a figure in degrees for final tightening of a fastener. This usually follows tightening to a specific torque setting.

● A degree disc can be set and attached to the socket **(see illustration 4.2)** or a protractor can be used to mark the angle of movement on the bolt/nut head and the surrounding casting **(see illustration 4.3)**.

4.2 Angle tightening can be accomplished with a torque-angle gauge . . .

Loosening sequences

● Where more than one bolt/nut secures a component, loosen each fastener evenly a little at a time. In this way, not all the stress of the joint is held by one fastener and the components are not likely to distort.

● If a tightening sequence is provided, work in the REVERSE of this, but if not, work from the outside in, in a criss-cross sequence **(see illustration 4.4)**.

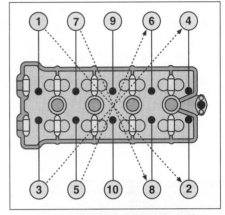

4.4 When slackening, work from the outside inwards

Tightening sequences

● If a component is held by more than one fastener it is important that the retaining bolts/nuts are tightened evenly to prevent uneven stress build-up and distortion of sealing faces. This is especially important on high-compression joints such as the cylinder head.

● A sequence is usually provided by the manufacturer, either in a diagram or actually marked in the casting. If not, always start in the centre and work outwards in a criss-cross pattern **(see illustration 4.5)**. Start off by securing all bolts/nuts finger-tight, then set the torque wrench and tighten each fastener by a small amount in sequence until the final torque is reached. By following this practice,

4.1 Set the torque wrench index mark to the setting required, in this case 12 Nm

4.3 . . . or by marking the angle on the surrounding component

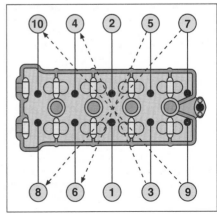

4.5 When tightening, work from the inside outwards

the joint will be held evenly and will not be distorted. Important joints, such as the cylinder head and big-end fasteners often have two- or three-stage torque settings.

Applying leverage

● Use tools at the correct angle. Position a socket wrench or spanner on the bolt/nut so that you pull it towards you when loosening. If this can't be done, push the spanner without curling your fingers around it **(see illustration 4.6)** - the spanner may slip or the fastener loosen suddenly, resulting in your fingers being crushed against a component.

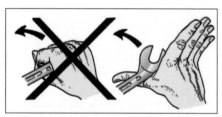

4.6 If you can't pull on the spanner to loosen a fastener, push with your hand open

● Additional leverage is gained by extending the length of the lever. The best way to do this is to use a breaker bar instead of the regular length tool, or to slip a length of tubing over the end of the spanner or socket wrench.
● If additional leverage will not work, the fastener head is either damaged or firmly corroded in place (see *Fasteners*).

5 Bearings

Bearing removal and installation

Drivers and sockets

● Before removing a bearing, always inspect the casing to see which way it must be driven out - some casings will have retaining plates or a cast step. Also check for any identifying markings on the bearing and if installed to a certain depth, measure this at this stage. Some roller bearings are sealed on one side - take note of the original fitted position.
● Bearings can be driven out of a casing using a bearing driver tool (with the correct size head) or a socket of the correct diameter. Select the driver head or socket so that it contacts the outer race of the bearing, not the balls/rollers or inner race. Always support the casing around the bearing housing with wood blocks, otherwise there is a risk of fracture. The bearing is driven out with a few blows on the driver or socket from a heavy mallet. Unless access is severely restricted (as with wheel bearings), a pin-punch is not recommended unless it is moved around the bearing to keep it square in its housing.

● The same equipment can be used to install bearings. Make sure the bearing housing is supported on wood blocks and line up the bearing in its housing. Fit the bearing as noted on removal - generally they are installed with their marked side facing outwards. Tap the bearing squarely into its housing using a driver or socket which bears only on the bearing's outer race - contact with the bearing balls/rollers or inner race will destroy it **(see illustrations 5.1 and 5.2)**.
● Check that the bearing inner race and balls/rollers rotate freely.

5.1 Using a bearing driver against the bearing's outer race

5.2 Using a large socket against the bearing's outer race

Pullers and slide-hammers

● Where a bearing is pressed on a shaft a puller will be required to extract it **(see illustration 5.3)**. Make sure that the puller clamp or legs fit securely behind the bearing and are unlikely to slip out. If pulling a bearing

5.3 This bearing puller clamps behind the bearing and pressure is applied to the shaft end to draw the bearing off

off a gear shaft for example, you may have to locate the puller behind a gear pinion if there is no access to the race and draw the gear pinion off the shaft as well **(see illustration 5.4)**.

> *Caution: Ensure that the puller's centre bolt locates securely against the end of the shaft and will not slip when pressure is applied. Also ensure that puller does not damage the shaft end.*

5.4 Where no access is available to the rear of the bearing, it is sometimes possible to draw off the adjacent component

● Operate the puller so that its centre bolt exerts pressure on the shaft end and draws the bearing off the shaft.
● When installing the bearing on the shaft, tap only on the bearing's inner race - contact with the balls/rollers or outer race with destroy the bearing. Use a socket or length of tubing as a drift which fits over the shaft end **(see illustration 5.5)**.

5.5 When installing a bearing on a shaft use a piece of tubing which bears only on the bearing's inner race

● Where a bearing locates in a blind hole in a casing, it cannot be driven or pulled out as described above. A slide-hammer with knife-edged bearing puller attachment will be required. The puller attachment passes through the bearing and when tightened expands to fit firmly behind the bearing **(see illustration 5.6)**. By operating the slide-hammer part of the tool the bearing is jarred out of its housing **(see illustration 5.7)**.
● It is possible, if the bearing is of reasonable weight, for it to drop out of its housing if the casing is heated as described opposite. If this

5.6 Expand the bearing puller so that it locks behind the bearing . . .

5.7 . . . attach the slide hammer to the bearing puller

method is attempted, first prepare a work surface which will enable the casing to be tapped face down to help dislodge the bearing - a wood surface is ideal since it will not damage the casing's gasket surface. Wearing protective gloves, tap the heated casing several times against the work surface to dislodge the bearing under its own weight **(see illustration 5.8)**.

5.8 Tapping a casing face down on wood blocks can often dislodge a bearing

● Bearings can be installed in blind holes using the driver or socket method described above.

Drawbolts

● Where a bearing or bush is set in the eye of a component, such as a suspension linkage arm or connecting rod small-end, removal by drift may damage the component. Furthermore, a rubber bushing in a shock absorber eye cannot successfully be driven out of position. If access is available to a engineering press, the task is straightforward. If not, a drawbolt can be fabricated to extract the bearing or bush.

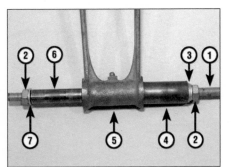

5.9 Drawbolt component parts assembled on a suspension arm

1 Bolt or length of threaded bar
2 Nuts
3 Washer (external diameter greater than tubing internal diameter)
4 Tubing (internal diameter sufficient to accommodate bearing)
5 Suspension arm with bearing
6 Tubing (external diameter slightly smaller than bearing)
7 Washer (external diameter slightly smaller than bearing)

5.10 Drawing the bearing out of the suspension arm

● To extract the bearing/bush you will need a long bolt with nut (or piece of threaded bar with two nuts), a piece of tubing which has an internal diameter larger than the bearing/bush, another piece of tubing which has an external diameter slightly smaller than the bearing/ bush, and a selection of washers **(see illustrations 5.9 and 5.10)**. Note that the pieces of tubing must be of the same length, or longer, than the bearing/bush.
● The same kit (without the pieces of tubing) can be used to draw the new bearing/bush back into place **(see illustration 5.11)**.

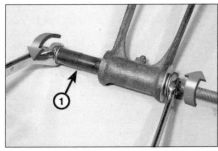

5.11 Installing a new bearing (1) in the suspension arm

Temperature change

● If the bearing's outer race is a tight fit in the casing, the aluminium casing can be heated to release its grip on the bearing. Aluminium will expand at a greater rate than the steel bearing outer race. There are several ways to do this, but avoid any localised extreme heat (such as a blow torch) - aluminium alloy has a low melting point.
● Approved methods of heating a casing are using a domestic oven (heated to 100°C) or immersing the casing in boiling water **(see illustration 5.12)**. Low temperature range localised heat sources such as a paint stripper heat gun or clothes iron can also be used **(see illustration 5.13)**. Alternatively, soak a rag in boiling water, wring it out and wrap it around the bearing housing.

> ⚠ **Warning: All of these methods require care in use to prevent scalding and burns to the hands. Wear protective gloves when handling hot components.**

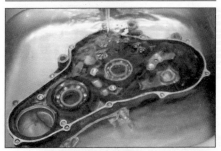

5.12 A casing can be immersed in a sink of boiling water to aid bearing removal

5.13 Using a localised heat source to aid bearing removal

● If heating the whole casing note that plastic components, such as the neutral switch, may suffer - remove them beforehand.
● After heating, remove the bearing as described above. You may find that the expansion is sufficient for the bearing to fall out of the casing under its own weight or with a light tap on the driver or socket.
● If necessary, the casing can be heated to aid bearing installation, and this is sometimes the recommended procedure if the motorcycle manufacturer has designed the housing and bearing fit with this intention.

● Installation of bearings can be eased by placing them in a freezer the night before installation. The steel bearing will contract slightly, allowing easy insertion in its housing. This is often useful when installing steering head outer races in the frame.

Bearing types and markings

● Plain shell bearings, ball bearings, needle roller bearings and tapered roller bearings will all be found on motorcycles (see illustrations 5.14 and 5.15). The ball and roller types are usually caged between an inner and outer race, but uncaged variations may be found.

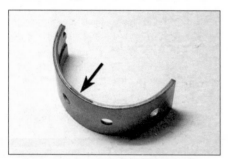

5.14 Shell bearings are either plain or grooved. They are usually identified by colour code (arrow)

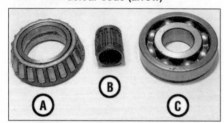

5.15 Tapered roller bearing (A), needle roller bearing (B) and ball journal bearing (C)

● Shell bearings (often called inserts) are usually found at the crankshaft main and connecting rod big-end where they are good at coping with high loads. They are made of a phosphor-bronze material and are impregnated with self-lubricating properties.
● Ball bearings and needle roller bearings consist of a steel inner and outer race with the balls or rollers between the races. They require constant lubrication by oil or grease and are good at coping with axial loads. Taper roller bearings consist of rollers set in a tapered cage set on the inner race; the outer race is separate. They are good at coping with axial loads and prevent movement along the shaft - a typical application is in the steering head.
● Bearing manufacturers produce bearings to ISO size standards and stamp one face of the bearing to indicate its internal and external diameter, load capacity and type (see illustration 5.16).
● Metal bushes are usually of phosphor-bronze material. Rubber bushes are used in suspension mounting eyes. Fibre bushes have also been used in suspension pivots.

5.16 Typical bearing marking

Bearing fault finding

● If a bearing outer race has spun in its housing, the housing material will be damaged. You can use a bearing locking compound to bond the outer race in place if damage is not too severe.
● Shell bearings will fail due to damage of their working surface, as a result of lack of lubrication, corrosion or abrasive particles in the oil (see illustration 5.17). Small particles of dirt in the oil may embed in the bearing material whereas larger particles will score the bearing and shaft journal. If a number of short journeys are made, insufficient heat will be generated to drive off condensation which has built up on the bearings.

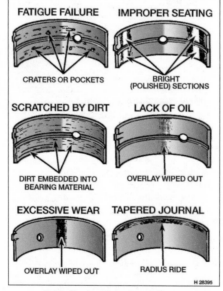

5.17 Typical bearing failures

● Ball and roller bearings will fail due to lack of lubrication or damage to the balls or rollers. Tapered-roller bearings can be damaged by overloading them. Unless the bearing is sealed on both sides, wash it in paraffin (kerosene) to remove all old grease then allow it to dry. Make a visual inspection looking to dented balls or rollers, damaged cages and worn or pitted races (see illustration 5.18).
● A ball bearing can be checked for wear by listening to it when spun. Apply a film of light oil to the bearing and hold it close to the ear - hold the outer race with one hand and spin the inner

5.18 Example of ball journal bearing with damaged balls and cages

5.19 Hold outer race and listen to inner race when spun

race with the other hand (see illustration 5.19). The bearing should be almost silent when spun; if it grates or rattles it is worn.

6 Oil seals

Oil seal removal and installation

● Oil seals should be renewed every time a component is dismantled. This is because the seal lips will become set to the sealing surface and will not necessarily reseal.
● Oil seals can be prised out of position using a large flat-bladed screwdriver (see illustration 6.1). In the case of crankcase seals, check first that the seal is not lipped on the inside, preventing its removal with the crankcases joined.

6.1 Prise out oil seals with a large flat-bladed screwdriver

● New seals are usually installed with their marked face (containing the seal reference code) outwards and the spring side towards the fluid being retained. In certain cases, such as a two-stroke engine crankshaft seal, a double lipped seal may be used due to there being fluid or gas on each side of the joint.

● Use a bearing driver or socket which bears only on the outer hard edge of the seal to install it in the casing - tapping on the inner edge will damage the sealing lip.

Oil seal types and markings

● Oil seals are usually of the single-lipped type. Double-lipped seals are found where a liquid or gas is on both sides of the joint.
● Oil seals can harden and lose their sealing ability if the motorcycle has been in storage for a long period - renewal is the only solution.
● Oil seal manufacturers also conform to the ISO markings for seal size - these are moulded into the outer face of the seal (see illustration 6.2).

6.2 These oil seal markings indicate inside diameter, outside diameter and seal thickness

7 Gaskets and sealants

Types of gasket and sealant

● Gaskets are used to seal the mating surfaces between components and keep lubricants, fluids, vacuum or pressure contained within the assembly. Aluminium gaskets are sometimes found at the cylinder joints, but most gaskets are paper-based. If the mating surfaces of the components being joined are undamaged the gasket can be installed dry, although a dab of sealant or grease will be useful to hold it in place during assembly.
● RTV (Room Temperature Vulcanising) silicone rubber sealants cure when exposed to moisture in the atmosphere. These sealants are good at filling pits or irregular gasket faces, but will tend to be forced out of the joint under very high torque. They can be used to replace a paper gasket, but first make sure that the width of the paper gasket is not essential to the shimming of internal components. RTV sealants should not be used on components containing petrol (gasoline).
● Non-hardening, semi-hardening and hard setting liquid gasket compounds can be used with a gasket or between a metal-to-metal joint. Select the sealant to suit the application: universal non-hardening sealant can be used on virtually all joints; semi-hardening on joint faces which are rough or damaged; hard setting sealant on joints which require a permanent bond and are subjected to high temperature and pressure. **Note:** *Check first if the paper gasket has a bead of sealant*

impregnated in its surface before applying additional sealant.
● When choosing a sealant, make sure it is suitable for the application, particularly if being applied in a high-temperature area or in the vicinity of fuel. Certain manufacturers produce sealants in either clear, silver or black colours to match the finish of the engine. This has a particular application on motorcycles where much of the engine is exposed.
● Do not over-apply sealant. That which is squeezed out on the outside of the joint can be wiped off, whereas an excess of sealant on the inside can break off and clog oilways.

Breaking a sealed joint

● Age, heat, pressure and the use of hard setting sealant can cause two components to stick together so tightly that they are difficult to separate using finger pressure alone. Do not resort to using levers unless there is a pry point provided for this purpose (see illustration 7.1) or else the gasket surfaces will be damaged.
● Use a soft-faced hammer (see illustration 7.2) or a wood block and conventional hammer to strike the component near the mating surface. Avoid hammering against cast extremities since they may break off. If this method fails, try using a wood wedge between the two components.

Caution: If the joint will not separate, double-check that you have removed all the fasteners.

7.1 If a pry point is provided, apply gently pressure with a flat-bladed screwdriver

7.2 Tap around the joint with a soft-faced mallet if necessary - don't strike cooling fins

Removal of old gasket and sealant

● Paper gaskets will most likely come away complete, leaving only a few traces stuck on

Most components have one or two hollow locating dowels between the two gasket faces. If a dowel cannot be removed, do not resort to gripping it with pliers - it will almost certainly be distorted. Install a close-fitting socket or Phillips screwdriver into the dowel and then grip the outer edge of the dowel to free it.

the sealing faces of the components. It is imperative that all traces are removed to ensure correct sealing of the new gasket.
● Very carefully scrape all traces of gasket away making sure that the sealing surfaces are not gouged or scored by the scraper (see illustrations 7.3, 7.4 and 7.5). Stubborn deposits can be removed by spraying with an aerosol gasket remover. Final preparation of

7.3 Paper gaskets can be scraped off with a gasket scraper tool . . .

7.4 . . . a knife blade . . .

7.5 . . . or a household scraper

7.6 Fine abrasive paper is wrapped around a flat file to clean up the gasket face

7.7 A kitchen scourer can be used on stubborn deposits

the gasket surface can be made with very fine abrasive paper or a plastic kitchen scourer **(see illustrations 7.6 and 7.7).**

● Old sealant can be scraped or peeled off components, depending on the type originally used. Note that gasket removal compounds are available to avoid scraping the components clean; make sure the gasket remover suits the type of sealant used.

8 Chains

Breaking and joining final drive chains

● Drive chains for all but small bikes are continuous and do not have a clip-type connecting link. The chain must be broken using a chain breaker tool and the new chain securely riveted together using a new soft rivet-type link. Never use a clip-type connecting link instead of a rivet-type link, except in an emergency. Various chain breaking and riveting tools are available, either as separate tools or combined as illustrated in the accompanying photographs - read the instructions supplied with the tool carefully.

> ⚠ **Warning: The need to rivet the new link pins correctly cannot be overstressed - loss of control of the motorcycle is very likely to result if the chain breaks in use.**

● Rotate the chain and look for the soft link. The soft link pins look like they have been

8.1 Tighten the chain breaker to push the pin out of the link . . .

8.2 . . . withdraw the pin, remove the tool . . .

8.3 . . . and separate the chain link

deeply centre-punched instead of peened over like all the other pins **(see illustration 8.9)** and its sideplate may be a different colour. Position the soft link midway between the sprockets and assemble the chain breaker tool over one of the soft link pins **(see illustration 8.1)**. Operate the tool to push the pin out through the chain **(see illustration 8.2)**. On an O-ring chain, remove the O-rings **(see illustration 8.3)**. Carry out the same procedure on the other soft link pin.

> *Caution: Certain soft link pins (particularly on the larger chains) may require their ends to be filed or ground off before they can be pressed out using the tool.*

● Check that you have the correct size and strength (standard or heavy duty) new soft link - do not reuse the old link. Look for the size marking on the chain sideplates **(see illustration 8.10)**.
● Position the chain ends so that they are engaged over the rear sprocket. On an O-ring

8.4 Insert the new soft link, with O-rings, through the chain ends . . .

8.5 . . . install the O-rings over the pin ends . . .

8.6 . . . followed by the sideplate

chain, install a new O-ring over each pin of the link and insert the link through the two chain ends **(see illustration 8.4)**. Install a new O-ring over the end of each pin, followed by the sideplate (with the chain manufacturer's marking facing outwards) **(see illustrations 8.5 and 8.6)**. On an unsealed chain, insert the link through the two chain ends, then install the sideplate with the chain manufacturer's marking facing outwards.
● Note that it may not be possible to install the sideplate using finger pressure alone. If using a joining tool, assemble it so that the plates of the tool clamp the link and press the sideplate over the pins **(see illustration 8.7)**. Otherwise, use two small sockets placed over

8.7 Push the sideplate into position using a clamp

8.8 Assemble the chain riveting tool over one pin at a time and tighten it fully

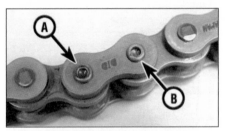

8.9 Pin end correctly riveted (A), pin end unriveted (B)

the rivet ends and two pieces of the wood between a G-clamp. Operate the clamp to press the sideplate over the pins.

● Assemble the joining tool over one pin (following the maker's instructions) and tighten the tool down to spread the pin end securely **(see illustrations 8.8 and 8.9)**. Do the same on the other pin.

 Warning: Check that the pin ends are secure and that there is no danger of the sideplate coming loose. If the pin ends are cracked the soft link must be renewed.

Final drive chain sizing

● Chains are sized using a three digit number, followed by a suffix to denote the chain type **(see illustration 8.10)**. Chain type is either standard or heavy duty (thicker sideplates), and also unsealed or O-ring/X-ring type.

● The first digit of the number relates to the pitch of the chain, ie the distance from the centre of one pin to the centre of the next pin **(see illustration 8.11)**. Pitch is expressed in eighths of an inch, as follows:

8.10 Typical chain size and type marking

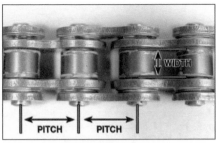

8.11 Chain dimensions

Sizes commencing with a 4 (eg 428) have a pitch of 1/2 inch (12.7 mm)
Sizes commencing with a 5 (eg 520) have a pitch of 5/8 inch (15.9 mm)
Sizes commencing with a 6 (eg 630) have a pitch of 3/4 inch (19.1 mm)

● The second and third digits of the chain size relate to the width of the rollers, again in imperial units, eg the 525 shown has 5/16 inch (7.94 mm) rollers **(see illustration 8.11)**.

9 Hoses

Clamping to prevent flow

● Small-bore flexible hoses can be clamped to prevent fluid flow whilst a component is worked on. Whichever method is used, ensure that the hose material is not permanently distorted or damaged by the clamp.

a) A brake hose clamp available from auto accessory shops **(see illustration 9.1)**.
b) A wingnut type hose clamp **(see illustration 9.2)**.

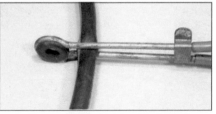

9.1 Hoses can be clamped with an automotive brake hose clamp . . .

9.2 . . . a wingnut type hose clamp . . .

c) Two sockets placed each side of the hose and held with straight-jawed self-locking grips **(see illustration 9.3)**.
d) Thick card each side of the hose held between straight-jawed self-locking grips **(see illustration 9.4)**.

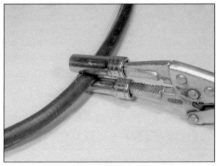

9.3 . . . two sockets and a pair of self-locking grips . . .

9.4 . . . or thick card and self-locking grips

Freeing and fitting hoses

● Always make sure the hose clamp is moved well clear of the hose end. Grip the hose with your hand and rotate it whilst pulling it off the union. If the hose has hardened due to age and will not move, slit it with a sharp knife and peel its ends off the union **(see illustration 9.5)**.

● Resist the temptation to use grease or soap on the unions to aid installation; although it helps the hose slip over the union it will equally aid the escape of fluid from the joint. It is preferable to soften the hose ends in hot water and wet the inside surface of the hose with water or a fluid which will evaporate.

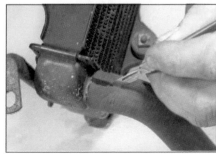

9.5 Cutting a coolant hose free with a sharp knife

Introduction

In less time than it takes to read this introduction, a thief could steal your motorcycle. Returning only to find your bike has gone is one of the worst feelings in the world. Even if the motorcycle is insured against theft, once you've got over the initial shock, you will have the inconvenience of dealing with the police and your insurance company.

The motorcycle is an easy target for the professional thief and the joyrider alike and the official figures on motorcycle theft make for depressing reading; on average a motorcycle is stolen every 16 minutes in the UK!

Motorcycle thefts fall into two categories, those stolen 'to order' and those taken by opportunists. The thief stealing to order will be on the look out for a specific make and model and will go to extraordinary lengths to obtain that motorcycle. The opportunist thief on the other hand will look for easy targets which can be stolen with the minimum of effort and risk.

Whilst it is never going to be possible to make your machine 100% secure, it is estimated that around half of all stolen motorcycles are taken by opportunist thieves. Remember that the opportunist thief is always on the look out for the easy option: if there are two similar motorcycles parked side-by-side, they will target the one with the lowest level of security. By taking a few precautions, you can reduce the chances of your motorcycle being stolen.

Security equipment

There are many specialised motorcycle security devices available and the following text summarises their applications and their good and bad points.

Once you have decided on the type of security equipment which best suits your needs, we recommended that you read one of the many equipment tests regularly carried out by the motorcycle press. These tests compare the products from all the major manufacturers and give impartial ratings on their effectiveness, value-for-money and ease of use.

No one item of security equipment can provide complete protection. It is highly recommended that two or more of the items described below are combined to increase the security of your motorcycle (a lock and chain plus an alarm system is just about ideal). The more security measures fitted to the bike, the less likely it is to be stolen.

Ensure the lock and chain you buy is of good quality and long enough to shackle your bike to a solid object

Lock and chain

Pros: *Very flexible to use; can be used to secure the motorcycle to almost any immovable object. On some locks and chains, the lock can be used on its own as a disc lock (see below).*

Cons: *Can be very heavy and awkward to carry on the motorcycle, although some types will be supplied with a carry bag which can be strapped to the pillion seat.*

● Heavy-duty chains and locks are an excellent security measure **(see illustration 1)**. Whenever the motorcycle is parked, use the lock and chain to secure the machine to a solid, immovable object such as a post or railings. This will prevent the machine from being ridden away or being lifted into the back of a van.

● When fitting the chain, always ensure the chain is routed around the motorcycle frame or swingarm **(see illustrations 2 and 3)**. Never merely pass the chain around one of the wheel rims; a thief may unbolt the wheel and lift the rest of the machine into a van, leaving you with just the wheel! Try to avoid having excess chain free, thus making it difficult to use cutting tools, and keep the chain and lock off the ground to prevent thieves attacking it with a cold chisel. Position the lock so that its lock barrel is facing downwards; this will make it harder for the thief to attack the lock mechanism.

Pass the chain through the bike's frame, rather than just through a wheel . . .

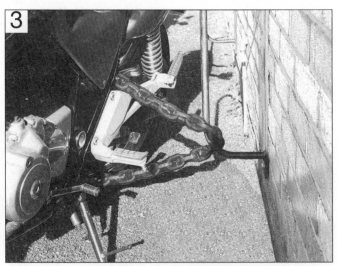

. . . and loop it around a solid object

U-locks

Pros: *Highly effective deterrent which can be used to secure the bike to a post or railings. Most U-locks come with a carrier which allows the lock to be easily carried on the bike.*

Cons: *Not as flexible to use as a lock and chain.*

● These are solid locks which are similar in use to a lock and chain. U-locks are lighter than a lock and chain but not so flexible to use. The length and shape of the lock shackle limit the objects to which the bike can be secured **(see illustration 4)**.

Disc locks

Pros: *Small, light and very easy to carry; most can be stored underneath the seat.*

Cons: *Does not prevent the motorcycle being lifted into a van. Can be very embarrassing if you*

U-locks can be used to secure the bike to a solid object – ensure you purchase one which is long enough

forget to remove the lock before attempting to ride off!

● Disc locks are designed to be attached to the front brake disc. The lock passes through one of the holes in the disc and prevents the wheel rotating by jamming against the fork/brake caliper **(see illustration 5)**. Some are equipped with an alarm siren which sounds if the disc lock is moved; this not only acts as a theft deterrent but also as a handy reminder if you try to move the bike with the lock still fitted.

● Combining the disc lock with a length of cable which can be looped around a post or railings provides an additional measure of security **(see illustration 6)**.

Alarms and immobilisers

Pros: *Once installed it is completely hassle-free to use. If the system is 'Thatcham' or 'Sold Secure-approved', insurance companies may give you a discount.*

Cons: *Can be expensive to buy and complex to install. No system will prevent the motorcycle from being lifted into a van and taken away.*

● Electronic alarms and immobilisers are available to suit a variety of budgets. There are three different types of system available: pure alarms, pure immobilisers, and the more expensive systems which are combined alarm/immobilisers **(see illustration 7)**.
● An alarm system is designed to emit an audible warning if the motorcycle is being tampered with.
● An immobiliser prevents the motorcycle being started and ridden away by disabling its electrical systems.
● When purchasing an alarm/immobiliser system, check the cost of installing the system unless you are able to do it yourself. If the motorcycle is not used regularly, another consideration is the current drain of the system. All alarm/immobiliser systems are powered by the motorcycle's battery; purchasing a system with a very low current drain could prevent the battery losing its charge whilst the motorcycle is not being used.

A typical disc lock attached through one of the holes in the disc

A disc lock combined with a security cable provides additional protection

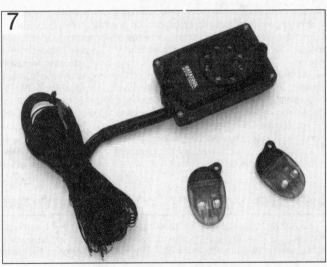

A typical alarm/immobiliser system

Indelible markings can be applied to most areas of the bike – always apply the manufacturer's sticker to warn off thieves

Chemically-etched code numbers can be applied to main body panels . . .

. . . again, always ensure that the kit manufacturer's sticker is applied in a prominent position

Security marking kits

Pros: *Very cheap and effective deterrent. Many insurance companies will give you a discount on your insurance premium if a recognised security marking kit is used on your motorcycle.*

Cons: *Does not prevent the motorcycle being stolen by joyriders.*

● There are many different types of security marking kits available. The idea is to mark as many parts of the motorcycle as possible with a unique security number **(see illustrations 8, 9 and 10)**. A form will be included with the kit to register your personal details and those of the motorcycle with the kit manufacturer. This register is made available to the police to help them trace the rightful owner of any motorcycle or components which they recover should all other forms of identification have been removed. Always apply the warning stickers provided with the kit to deter thieves.

Ground anchors, wheel clamps and security posts

Pros: *An excellent form of security which will deter all but the most determined of thieves.*

Cons: *Awkward to install and can be expensive.*

● Whilst the motorcycle is at home, it is a good idea to attach it securely to the floor or a solid wall, even if it is kept in a securely locked garage. Various types of ground anchors, security posts and wheel clamps are available for this purpose **(see illustration 11)**. These security devices are either bolted to a solid concrete or brick structure or can be cemented into the ground.

Permanent ground anchors provide an excellent level of security when the bike is at home

Security at home

A high percentage of motorcycle thefts are from the owner's home. Here are some things to consider whenever your motorcycle is at home:

✔ Where possible, always keep the motorcycle in a securely locked garage. Never rely solely on the standard lock on the garage door, these are usual hopelessly inadequate. Fit an additional locking mechanism to the door and consider having the garage alarmed. A security light, activated by a movement sensor, is also a good investment.

✔ Always secure the motorcycle to the ground or a wall, even if it is inside a securely locked garage.
✔ Do not regularly leave the motorcycle outside your home, try to keep it out of sight wherever possible. If a garage is not available, fit a motorcycle cover over the bike to disguise its true identity.
✔ It is not uncommon for thieves to follow a motorcyclist home to find out where the bike is kept. They will then return at a later date. Be aware of this whenever you are returning

home on your motorcycle. If you suspect you are being followed, do not return home, instead ride to a garage or shop and stop as a precaution.
✔ When selling a motorcycle, do not provide your home address or the location where the bike is normally kept. Arrange to meet the buyer at a location away from your home. Thieves have been known to pose as potential buyers to find out where motorcycles are kept and then return later to steal them.

Security away from the home

As well as fitting security equipment to your motorcycle here are a few general rules to follow whenever you park your motorcycle.
✔ Park in a busy, public place.
✔ Use car parks which incorporate security features, such as CCTV.

✔ At night, park in a well-lit area, preferably directly underneath a street light.
✔ Engage the steering lock.
✔ Secure the motorcycle to a solid, immovable object such as a post or railings with an additional lock. If this is not possible,

secure the bike to a friend's motorcycle. Some public parking places provide security loops for motorcycles.
✔ Never leave your helmet or luggage attached to the motorcycle. Take them with you at all times.

Lubricants and fluids

A wide range of lubricants, fluids and cleaning agents is available for motor-cycles. This is a guide as to what is available, its applications and properties.

Four-stroke engine oil

● Engine oil is without doubt the most important component of any four-stroke engine. Modern motorcycle engines place a lot of demands on their oil and choosing the right type is essential. Using an unsuitable oil will lead to an increased rate of engine wear and could result in serious engine damage. Before purchasing oil, always check the recommended oil specification given by the manufacturer. The manufacturer will state a recommended 'type or classification' and also a specific 'viscosity' range for engine oil.

● The oil 'type or classification' is identified by its API (American Petroleum Institute) rating. The API rating will be in the form of two letters, e.g. SG. The S identifies the oil as being suitable for use in a petrol (gasoline) engine (S stands for spark ignition) and the second letter, ranging from A to J, identifies the oil's performance rating. The later this letter, the higher the specification of the oil; for example API SG oil exceeds the requirements of API SF oil. **Note:** *On some oils there may also be a second rating consisting of another two letters, the first letter being C, e.g. API SF/CD. This rating indicates the oil is also suitable for use in a diesel engines (the C stands for compression ignition) and is thus of no relevance for motorcycle use.*

● The 'viscosity' of the oil is identified by its SAE (Society of Automotive Engineers) rating. All modern engines require multigrade oils and the SAE rating will consist of two numbers, the first followed by a W, e.g.

10W/40. The first number indicates the viscosity rating of the oil at low temperatures (W stands for winter – tested at –20°C) and the second number represents the viscosity of the oil at high temperatures (tested at 100°C). The lower the number, the thinner the oil. For example an oil with an SAE 10W/40 rating will give better cold starting and running than an SAE 15W/40 oil.

● As well as ensuring the 'type' and 'viscosity' of the oil match the recommendations, another consideration to make when buying engine oil is whether to purchase a standard mineral-based oil, a semi-synthetic oil (also known as a synthetic blend or synthetic-based oil) or a fully-synthetic oil. Although all oils will have a similar rating and viscosity, their cost will vary considerably; mineral-based oils are the cheapest, the fully-synthetic oils the most expensive with the semi-synthetic oils falling somewhere in-between. This decision is very much up to the owner, but it should be noted that modern synthetic oils have far better lubricating and cleaning qualities than traditional mineral-based oils and tend to retain these properties for far longer. Bearing in mind the operating conditions inside a modern, high-revving motorcycle engine it is highly recommended that a fully synthetic oil is used. The extra expense at each service could save you money in the long term by preventing premature engine wear.

● As a final note always ensure that the oil is specifically designed for use in motorcycle engines. Engine oils designed primarily for use in car engines sometimes contain additives or friction modifiers which could cause clutch slip on a motorcycle fitted with a wet-clutch.

Two-stroke engine oil

● Modern two-stroke engines, with their high power outputs, place high demands on their oil. If engine seizure is to be avoided it is essential that a high-quality oil is used. Two-stroke oils differ hugely from four-stroke oils. The oil lubricates only the crankshaft and piston(s) (the transmission has its own lubricating oil) and is used on a total-loss basis where it is burnt completely during the combustion process.

● The Japanese have recently introduced a classification system for two-stroke oils, the JASO rating. This rating is in the form of two letters, either FA, FB or FC – FA is the lowest classification and FC the highest. Ensure the oil being used meets or exceeds the recommended rating specified by the manufacturer.

● As well as ensuring the oil rating matches the recommendation, another consideration to make when buying engine oil is whether to purchase a standard mineral-based oil, a semi-synthetic oil (also known as a synthetic blend or synthetic-based oil) or a fully-synthetic oil. The cost of each type of oil varies considerably; mineral-based oils are the cheapest, the fully-synthetic oils the most expensive with the semi-synthetic oils falling somewhere in-between. This decision is very much up to the owner, but it should be noted that modern synthetic oils have far better lubricating properties and burn cleaner than traditional mineral-based oils. It is therefore recommended that a fully synthetic oil is used. The extra expense could save you money in the long term by preventing premature engine wear, engine performance will be improved, carbon deposits and exhaust smoke will be reduced.

● Always ensure that the oil is specifically designed for use in an injector system. Many high quality two-stroke oils are designed for competition use and need to be pre-mixed with fuel. These oils are of a much higher viscosity and are not designed to flow through the injector pumps used on road-going two-stroke motorcycles.

Transmission (gear) oil

● On a two-stroke engine, the transmission and clutch are lubricated by their own separate oil bath which must be changed in accordance with the Maintenance Schedule.
● Although the engine and transmission units of most four-strokes use a common lubrication supply, there are some exceptions where the engine and gearbox have separate oil reservoirs and a dry clutch is used.
● Motorcycle manufacturers will either recommend a monograde transmission oil or a four-stroke multigrade engine oil to lubricate the transmission.
● Transmission oils, or gear oils as they are often called, are designed specifically for use in transmission systems. The viscosity of these oils is represented by an SAE number, but the scale of measurement applied is different to that used to grade engine oils. As a rough guide a SAE90 gear oil will be of the same viscosity as an SAE50 engine oil.

Shaft drive oil
● On models equipped with shaft final drive, the shaft drive gears are will have their own oil supply. The manufacturer will state a recommended 'type or classification' and also a specific 'viscosity' range in the same manner as for four-stroke engine oil.
● Gear oil classification is given by the number which follows the API GL (GL standing for gear lubricant) rating, the higher the number, the higher the specification of the oil, e.g. API GL5 oil is a higher specification than API GL4 oil. Ensure the oil meets or

exceeds the classification specified and is of the correct viscosity. The viscosity of gear oils is also represented by an SAE number but the scale of measurement used is different to that used to grade engine oils. As a rough guide an SAE90 gear oil will be of the same viscosity as an SAE50 engine oil.
● If the use of an EP (Extreme Pressure) gear oil is specified, ensure the oil purchased is suitable.

Fork oil and suspension fluid

● Conventional telescopic front forks are hydraulic and require fork oil to work. To ensure the forks function correctly, the fork oil must be changed in accordance with the Maintenance Schedule.
● Fork oil is available in a variety of viscosities, identified by their SAE rating; fork oil ratings vary from light (SAE 5) to heavy (SAE 30). When purchasing fork oil, ensure the viscosity rating matches that specified by the manufacturer.
● Some lubricant manufacturers also produce a range of high-quality suspension fluids which are very similar to fork oil but are designed mainly for competition use. These fluids may have a different viscosity rating system which is not to be confused with the SAE rating of normal fork oil. Refer to the manufacturer's instructions if in any doubt.

Brake and clutch fluid
● All disc brake systems and some clutch systems are hydraulically operated. To ensure correct operation, the hydraulic fluid must be changed in accordance with the Maintenance Schedule.
● Brake and clutch fluid is classified by its DOT rating with most motorcycle manufacturers specifying DOT 3 or 4 fluid. Both fluid types are glycol-based and can be mixed together without adverse effect; DOT 4 fluid exceeds the requirements of DOT 3

fluid. Although it is safe to use DOT 4 fluid in a system designed for use with DOT 3 fluid, never use DOT 3 fluid in a system which specifies the use of DOT 4 as this will adversely affect the system's performance. The type required for the system will be marked on the fluid reservoir cap.
● Some manufacturers also produce a DOT 5 hydraulic fluid. DOT 5 hydraulic fluid is silicone-based and is not compatible with the glycol-based DOT 3 and 4 fluids. Never mix DOT 5 fluid with DOT 3 or 4 fluid as this will seriously affect the performance of the hydraulic system.

Coolant/antifreeze

● When purchasing coolant/antifreeze, always ensure it is suitable for use in an aluminium engine and contains corrosion inhibitors to prevent possible blockages of the internal coolant passages of the system. As a general rule, most coolants are designed to be used neat and should not be diluted whereas antifreeze can be mixed with distilled water to provide a coolant solution of the required strength. Refer to the manufacturer's instructions on the bottle.
● Ensure the coolant is changed in accordance with the Maintenance Schedule.

Chain lube
● Chain lube is an aerosol-type spray lubricant specifically designed for use on motorcycle final drive chains. Chain lube has two functions, to minimise friction between the final drive chain and sprockets and to prevent corrosion of the chain. Regular use of a good-quality chain lube will extend the life of the drive chain and sprockets and thus maximise the power being transmitted from the transmission to the rear wheel.

● When using chain lube, always allow some time for the solvents in the lube to evaporate before riding the motorcycle. This will minimise the amount of lube which will 'fling' off from the chain when the motorcycle is used. If the motorcycle is equipped with an 'O-ring' chain, ensure the chain lube is labelled as being suitable for use on 'O-ring' chains.

Degreasers and solvents

● There are many different types of solvents and degreasers available to remove the grime and grease which accumulate around the motorcycle during normal use. Degreasers and solvents are usually available as an aerosol-type spray or as a liquid which you apply with a brush. Always closely follow the manufacturer's instructions and wear eye protection during use. Be aware that many solvents are flammable and may give off noxious fumes; take adequate precautions when using them (*see Safety First!*).

● For general cleaning, use one of the many solvents or degreasers available from most motorcycle accessory shops. These solvents are usually applied then left for a certain time before being washed off with water.

Brake cleaner is a solvent specifically designed to remove all traces of oil, grease and dust from braking system components. Brake cleaner is designed to evaporate quickly and leaves behind no residue.

Carburettor cleaner is an aerosol-type solvent specifically designed to clear carburettor blockages and break down the hard deposits and gum often found inside carburettors during overhaul.

Contact cleaner is an aerosol-type solvent designed for cleaning electrical components. The cleaner will remove all traces of oil and dirt from components such as switch contacts or fouled spark plugs and then dry, leaving behind no residue.

Gasket remover is an aerosol-type solvent designed for removing stubborn gaskets from engine components during overhaul. Gasket remover will minimise the amount of scraping required to remove the gasket and therefore reduce the risk of damage to the mating surface.

Spray lubricants

● Aerosol-based spray lubricants are widely available and are excellent for lubricating lever pivots and exposed cables and switches. Try to use a lubricant which is of the dry-film type as the fluid evaporates, leaving behind a dry-film of lubricant. Lubricants which leave behind an oily residue will attract dust and dirt which will increase the rate of wear of the cable/lever.

● Most lubricants also act as a moisture dispersant and a penetrating fluid. This means they can also be used to 'dry out' electrical components such as wiring connectors or switches as well as helping to free seized fasteners.

Greases

● Grease is used to lubricate many of the pivot-points. A good-quality multi-purpose grease is suitable for most applications but some manufacturers will specify the use of specialist greases for use on components such as swingarm and suspension linkage bushes. These specialist greases can be purchased from most motorcycle (or car) accessory shops; commonly specified types include molybdenum disulphide grease, lithium-based grease, graphite-based grease, silicone-based grease and high-temperature copper-based grease.

Gasket sealing compounds

● Gasket sealing compounds can be used in conjunction with gaskets, to improve their sealing capabilities, or on their own to seal metal-to-metal joints. Depending on their type, sealing compounds either set hard or stay relatively soft and pliable.

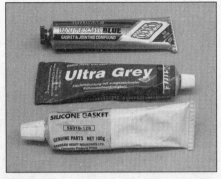

● When purchasing a gasket sealing compound, ensure that it is designed specifically for use on an internal combustion engine. General multi-purpose sealants available from DIY stores may appear visibly similar but they are not designed to withstand the extreme heat or contact with fuel and oil encountered when used on an engine (*see 'Tools and Workshop Tips' for further information*).

Thread locking compound

● Thread locking compounds are used to secure certain threaded fasteners in position to prevent them from loosening due to vibration. Thread locking compounds can be purchased from most motorcycle (and car) accessory shops. Ensure the threads of the both components are completely clean and dry before sparingly applying the locking compound (*see 'Tools and Workshop Tips' for further information*).

Fuel additives

● Fuel additives which protect and clean the fuel system components are widely available. These additives are designed to remove all traces of deposits that build up on the carburettors/injectors and prevent wear, helping the fuel system to operate more efficiently. If a fuel additive is being used, check that it is suitable for use with your motorcycle, especially if your motorcycle is equipped with a catalytic converter.

● Octane boosters are also available. These additives are designed to improve the performance of highly-tuned engines being run on normal pump-fuel and are of no real use on standard motorcycles.

Conversion factors

Length (distance)
Inches (in)	x 25.4	= Millimetres (mm)	x 0.0394	= Inches (in)
Feet (ft)	x 0.305	= Metres (m)	x 3.281	= Feet (ft)
Miles	x 1.609	= Kilometres (km)	x 0.621	= Miles

Volume (capacity)
Cubic inches (cu in; in³)	x 16.387	= Cubic centimetres (cc; cm³)	x 0.061	= Cubic inches (cu in; in³)
Imperial pints (Imp pt)	x 0.568	= Litres (l)	x 1.76	= Imperial pints (Imp pt)
Imperial quarts (Imp qt)	x 1.137	= Litres (l)	x 0.88	= Imperial quarts (Imp qt)
Imperial quarts (Imp qt)	x 1.201	= US quarts (US qt)	x 0.833	= Imperial quarts (Imp qt)
US quarts (US qt)	x 0.946	= Litres (l)	x 1.057	= US quarts (US qt)
Imperial gallons (Imp gal)	x 4.546	= Litres (l)	x 0.22	= Imperial gallons (Imp gal)
Imperial gallons (Imp gal)	x 1.201	= US gallons (US gal)	x 0.833	= Imperial gallons (Imp gal)
US gallons (US gal)	x 3.785	= Litres (l)	x 0.264	= US gallons (US gal)

Mass (weight)
Ounces (oz)	x 28.35	= Grams (g)	x 0.035	= Ounces (oz)
Pounds (lb)	x 0.454	= Kilograms (kg)	x 2.205	= Pounds (lb)

Force
Ounces-force (ozf; oz)	x 0.278	= Newtons (N)	x 3.6	= Ounces-force (ozf; oz)
Pounds-force (lbf; lb)	x 4.448	= Newtons (N)	x 0.225	= Pounds-force (lbf; lb)
Newtons (N)	x 0.1	= Kilograms-force (kgf; kg)	x 9.81	= Newtons (N)

Pressure
Pounds-force per square inch (psi; lbf/in²; lb/in²)	x 0.070	= Kilograms-force per square centimetre (kgf/cm²; kg/cm²)	x 14.223	= Pounds-force per square inch (psi; lbf/in²; lb/in²)
Pounds-force per square inch (psi; lbf/in²; lb/in²)	x 0.068	= Atmospheres (atm)	x 14.696	= Pounds-force per square inch (psi; lbf/in²; lb/in²)
Pounds-force per square inch (psi; lbf/in²; lb/in²)	x 0.069	= Bars	x 14.5	= Pounds-force per square inch (psi; lbf/in²; lb/in²)
Pounds-force per square inch (psi; lbf/in²; lb/in²)	x 6.895	= Kilopascals (kPa)	x 0.145	= Pounds-force per square inch (psi; lbf/in²; lb/in²)
Kilopascals (kPa)	x 0.01	= Kilograms-force per square centimetre (kgf/cm²; kg/cm²)	x 98.1	= Kilopascals (kPa)
Millibar (mbar)	x 100	= Pascals (Pa)	x 0.01	= Millibar (mbar)
Millibar (mbar)	x 0.0145	= Pounds-force per square inch (psi; lbf/in²; lb/in²)	x 68.947	= Millibar (mbar)
Millibar (mbar)	x 0.75	= Millimetres of mercury (mmHg)	x 1.333	= Millibar (mbar)
Millibar (mbar)	x 0.401	= Inches of water (inH₂O)	x 2.491	= Millibar (mbar)
Millimetres of mercury (mmHg)	x 0.535	= Inches of water (inH₂O)	x 1.868	= Millimetres of mercury (mmHg)
Inches of water (inH₂O)	x 0.036	= Pounds-force per square inch (psi; lbf/in²; lb/in²)	x 27.68	= Inches of water (inH₂O)

Torque (moment of force)
Pounds-force inches (lbf in; lb in)	x 1.152	= Kilograms-force centimetre (kgf cm; kg cm)	x 0.868	= Pounds-force inches (lbf in; lb in)
Pounds-force inches (lbf in; lb in)	x 0.113	= Newton metres (Nm)	x 8.85	= Pounds-force inches (lbf in; lb in)
Pounds-force inches (lbf in; lb in)	x 0.083	= Pounds-force feet (lbf ft; lb ft)	x 12	= Pounds-force inches (lbf in; lb in)
Pounds-force feet (lbf ft; lb ft)	x 0.138	= Kilograms-force metres (kgf m; kg m)	x 7.233	= Pounds-force feet (lbf ft; lb ft)
Pounds-force feet (lbf ft; lb ft)	x 1.356	= Newton metres (Nm)	x 0.738	= Pounds-force feet (lbf ft; lb ft)
Newton metres (Nm)	x 0.102	= Kilograms-force metres (kgf m; kg m)	x 9.804	= Newton metres (Nm)

Power
Horsepower (hp)	x 745.7	= Watts (W)	x 0.0013	= Horsepower (hp)

Velocity (speed)
Miles per hour (miles/hr; mph)	x 1.609	= Kilometres per hour (km/hr; kph)	x 0.621	= Miles per hour (miles/hr; mph)

Fuel consumption*
Miles per gallon, Imperial (mpg)	x 0.354	= Kilometres per litre (km/l)	x 2.825	= Miles per gallon, Imperial (mpg)
Miles per gallon, US (mpg)	x 0.425	= Kilometres per litre (km/l)	x 2.352	= Miles per gallon, US (mpg)

Temperature
Degrees Fahrenheit = (°C x 1.8) + 32   Degrees Celsius (Degrees Centigrade; °C) = (°F - 32) x 0.56

It is common practice to convert from miles per gallon (mpg) to litres/100 kilometres (l/100km), where mpg x l/100 km = 282

About the MOT Test

In the UK, all vehicles more than three years old are subject to an annual test to ensure that they meet minimum safety requirements. A current test certificate must be issued before a machine can be used on public roads, and is required before a road fund licence can be issued. Riding without a current test certificate will also invalidate your insurance.

For most owners, the MOT test is an annual cause for anxiety, and this is largely due to owners not being sure what needs to be checked prior to submitting the motorcycle for testing. The simple answer is that a fully roadworthy motorcycle will have no difficulty in passing the test.

This is a guide to getting your motorcycle through the MOT test. Obviously it will not be possible to examine the motorcycle to the same standard as the professional MOT tester, particularly in view of the equipment required for some of the checks. However, working through the following procedures will enable you to identify any problem areas before submitting the motorcycle for the test.

It has only been possible to summarise the test requirements here, based on the regulations in force at the time of printing. Test standards are becoming increasingly stringent, although there are some exemptions for older vehicles. More information about the MOT test can be obtained from the TSO publications, *How Safe is your Motorcycle* and *The MOT Inspection Manual for Motorcycle Testing*.

Many of the checks require that one of the wheels is raised off the ground. If the motorcycle doesn't have a centre stand, note that an auxiliary stand will be required. Additionally, the help of an assistant may prove useful.

Certain exceptions apply to machines under 50 cc, machines without a lighting system, and Classic bikes - if in doubt about any of the requirements listed below seek confirmation from an MOT tester prior to submitting the motorcycle for the test.

Check that the frame number is clearly visible.

Electrical System

Lights, turn signals, horn and reflector

✔ With the ignition on, check the operation of the following electrical components. **Note:** *The electrical components on certain small-capacity machines are powered by the generator, requiring that the engine is run for this check.*

a) *Headlight and tail light. Check that both illuminate in the low and high beam switch positions.*
b) *Position lights. Check that the front position (or sidelight) and tail light illuminate in this switch position.*
c) *Turn signals. Check that all flash at the correct rate, and that the warning light(s) function correctly. Check that the turn signal switch works correctly.*
d) *Hazard warning system (where fitted). Check that all four turn signals flash in this switch position.*
e) *Brake stop light. Check that the light comes on when the front and rear brakes are independently applied. Models first used on or after 1st April 1986 must have a brake light switch on each brake.*
f) *Horn. Check that the sound is continuous and of reasonable volume.*

✔ Check that there is a red reflector on the rear of the machine, either mounted separately or as part of the tail light lens.
✔ Check the condition of the headlight, tail light and turn signal lenses.

Headlight beam height

✔ The MOT tester will perform a headlight beam height check using specialised beam setting equipment **(see illustration 1)**. This equipment will not be available to the home mechanic, but if you suspect that the headlight is incorrectly set or may have been maladjusted in the past, you can perform a rough test as follows.
✔ Position the bike in a straight line facing a brick wall. The bike must be off its stand, upright and with a rider seated. Measure the height from the ground to the centre of the headlight and mark a horizontal line on the wall at this height. Position the motorcycle 3.8 metres from the wall and draw a vertical

Headlight beam height checking equipment

line up the wall central to the centreline of the motorcycle. Switch to dipped beam and check that the beam pattern falls slightly lower than the horizontal line and to the left of the vertical line **(see illustration 2)**.

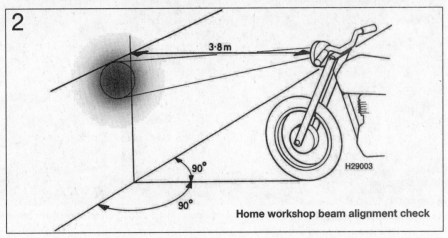

3·8 m

90°

90°

H29003

Home workshop beam alignment check

Exhaust System and Final Drive

Exhaust

✔ Check that the exhaust mountings are secure and that the system does not foul any of the rear suspension components.

✔ Start the motorcycle. When the revs are increased, check that the exhaust is neither holed nor leaking from any of its joints. On a linked system, check that the collector box is not leaking due to corrosion.

✔ Note that the exhaust decibel level ("loudness" of the exhaust) is assessed at the discretion of the tester. If the motorcycle was first used on or after 1st January 1985 the silencer must carry the BSAU 193 stamp, or a marking relating to its make and model, or be of OE (original equipment) manufacture. If the silencer is marked NOT FOR ROAD USE, RACING USE ONLY or similar, it will fail the MOT.

Final drive

✔ On chain or belt drive machines, check that the chain/belt is in good condition and does not have excessive slack. Also check that the sprocket is securely mounted on the rear wheel hub. Check that the chain/belt guard is in place.

✔ On shaft drive bikes, check for oil leaking from the drive unit and fouling the rear tyre.

Steering and Suspension

Steering

✔ With the front wheel raised off the ground, rotate the steering from lock to lock. The handlebar or switches must not contact the fuel tank or be close enough to trap the rider's hand. Problems can be caused by damaged lock stops on the lower yoke and frame, or by the fitting of non-standard handlebars.

✔ When performing the lock to lock check, also ensure that the steering moves freely without drag or notchiness. Steering movement can be impaired by poorly routed cables, or by overtight head bearings or worn bearings. The tester will perform a check of the steering head bearing lower race by mounting the front wheel on a surface plate, then performing a lock to lock check with the weight of the machine on the lower bearing (see illustration 3).

✔ Grasp the fork sliders (lower legs) and attempt to push and pull on the forks (see

Front wheel mounted on a surface plate for steering head bearing lower race check

illustration 4). Any play in the steering head bearings will be felt. Note that in extreme cases, wear of the front fork bushes can be misinterpreted for head bearing play.

✔ Check that the handlebars are securely mounted.

✔ Check that the handlebar grip rubbers are secure. They should by bonded to the bar left end and to the throttle cable pulley on the right end.

Front suspension

✔ With the motorcycle off the stand, hold the front brake on and pump the front forks up and down (see illustration 5). Check that they are adequately damped.

Checking the steering head bearings for freeplay

Hold the front brake on and pump the front forks up and down to check operation

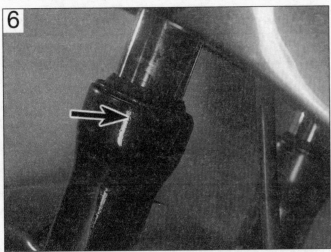

Inspect the area around the fork dust seal for oil leakage (arrow)

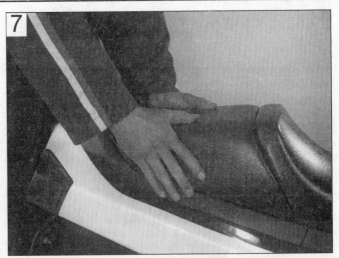

Bounce the rear of the motorcycle to check rear suspension operation

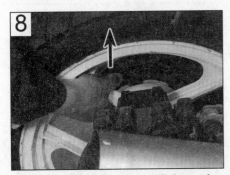

Checking for rear suspension linkage play

✔ Inspect the area above and around the front fork oil seals **(see illustration 6)**. There should be no sign of oil on the fork tube (stanchion) nor leaking down the slider (lower leg). On models so equipped, check that there is no oil leaking from the anti-dive units.

✔ On models with swingarm front suspension, check that there is no freeplay in the linkage when moved from side to side.

Rear suspension

✔ With the motorcycle off the stand and an assistant supporting the motorcycle by its handlebars, bounce the rear suspension **(see illustration 7)**. Check that the suspension components do not foul on any of the cycle parts and check that the shock absorber(s) provide adequate damping.

✔ Visually inspect the shock absorber(s) and check that there is no sign of oil leakage from its damper. This is somewhat restricted on certain single shock models due to the location of the shock absorber.

✔ With the rear wheel raised off the ground, grasp the wheel at the highest point and attempt to pull it up **(see illustration 8)**. Any play in the swingarm pivot or suspension linkage bearings will be felt as movement. **Note:** *Do not confuse play with actual suspension movement.* Failure to lubricate suspension linkage bearings can lead to bearing failure **(see illustration 9)**.

✔ With the rear wheel raised off the ground, grasp the swingarm ends and attempt to move the swingarm from side to side and forwards and backwards - any play indicates wear of the swingarm pivot bearings **(see illustration 10)**.

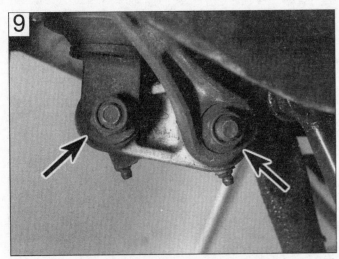

Worn suspension linkage pivots (arrows) are usually the cause of play in the rear suspension

Grasp the swingarm at the ends to check for play in its pivot bearings

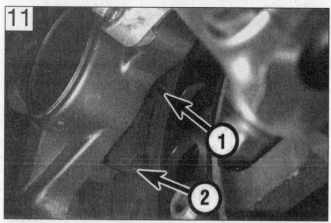

Brake pad wear can usually be viewed without removing the caliper. Most pads have wear indicator grooves (1) and some also have indicator tangs (2)

On drum brakes, check the angle of the operating lever with the brake fully applied. Most drum brakes have a wear indicator pointer and scale.

Brakes, Wheels and Tyres

Brakes

✔ With the wheel raised off the ground, apply the brake then free it off, and check that the wheel is about to revolve freely without brake drag.

✔ On disc brakes, examine the disc itself. Check that it is securely mounted and not cracked.

✔ On disc brakes, view the pad material through the caliper mouth and check that the pads are not worn down beyond the limit (see illustration 11).

✔ On drum brakes, check that when the brake is applied the angle between the operating lever and cable or rod is not too great (see illustration 12). Check also that the operating lever doesn't foul any other components.

✔ On disc brakes, examine the flexible hoses from top to bottom. Have an assistant hold the brake on so that the fluid in the hose is under pressure, and check that there is no sign of fluid leakage, bulges or cracking. If there are any metal brake pipes or unions, check that these are free from corrosion and damage. Where a brake-linked anti-dive system is fitted, check the hoses to the anti-dive in a similar manner.

✔ Check that the rear brake torque arm is secure and that its fasteners are secured by self-locking nuts or castellated nuts with split-pins or R-pins (see illustration 13).

✔ On models with ABS, check that the self-check warning light in the instrument panel works.

✔ The MOT tester will perform a test of the motorcycle's braking efficiency based on a calculation of rider and motorcycle weight. Although this cannot be carried out at home, you can at least ensure that the braking systems are properly maintained. For hydraulic disc brakes, check the fluid level, lever/pedal feel (bleed of air if its spongy) and pad material. For drum brakes, check adjustment, cable or rod operation and shoe lining thickness.

Wheels and tyres

✔ Check the wheel condition. Cast wheels should be free from cracks and if of the built-up design, all fasteners should be secure. Spoked wheels should be checked for broken, corroded, loose or bent spokes.

✔ With the wheel raised off the ground, spin the wheel and visually check that the tyre and wheel run true. Check that the tyre does not foul the suspension or mudguards.

✔ With the wheel raised off the ground, grasp the wheel and attempt to move it about the axle (spindle) (see illustration 14). Any play felt here indicates wheel bearing failure.

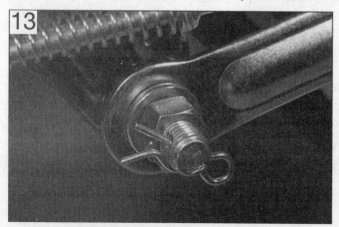

Brake torque arm must be properly secured at both ends

Check for wheel bearing play by trying to move the wheel about the axle (spindle)

Checking the tyre tread depth

Tyre direction of rotation arrow can be found on tyre sidewall

Castellated type wheel axle (spindle) nut must be secured by a split pin or R-pin

Two straightedges are used to check wheel alignment

✔ Check the tyre tread depth, tread condition and sidewall condition (see illustration 15).
✔ Check the tyre type. Front and rear tyre types must be compatible and be suitable for road use. Tyres marked NOT FOR ROAD USE, COMPETITION USE ONLY or similar, will fail the MOT.

✔ If the tyre sidewall carries a direction of rotation arrow, this must be pointing in the direction of normal wheel rotation (see illustration 16).
✔ Check that the wheel axle (spindle) nuts (where applicable) are properly secured. A self-locking nut or castellated nut with a split-pin or R-pin can be used (see illustration 17).
✔ Wheel alignment is checked with the motorcycle off the stand and a rider seated. With the front wheel pointing straight ahead, two perfectly straight lengths of metal or wood and placed against the sidewalls of both tyres (see illustration 18). The gap each side of the front tyre must be equidistant on both sides. Incorrect wheel alignment may be due to a cocked rear wheel (often as the result of poor chain adjustment) or in extreme cases, a bent frame.

General checks and condition

✔ Check the security of all major fasteners, bodypanels, seat, fairings (where fitted) and mudguards.

✔ Check that the rider and pillion footrests, handlebar levers and brake pedal are securely mounted.

✔ Check for corrosion on the frame or any load-bearing components. If severe, this may affect the structure, particularly under stress.

Sidecars

A motorcycle fitted with a sidecar requires additional checks relating to the stability of the machine and security of attachment and swivel joints, plus specific wheel alignment (toe-in) requirements. Additionally, tyre and lighting requirements differ from conventional motorcycle use. Owners are advised to check MOT test requirements with an official test centre.

Preparing for storage

Before you start

If repairs or an overhaul is needed, see that this is carried out now rather than left until you want to ride the bike again.

Give the bike a good wash and scrub all dirt from its underside. Make sure the bike dries completely before preparing for storage.

Engine

● Remove the spark plug(s) and lubricate the cylinder bores with approximately a teaspoon of motor oil using a spout-type oil can (see illustration 1). Reinstall the spark plug(s). Crank the engine over a couple of times to coat the piston rings and bores with oil. If the bike has a kickstart, use this to turn the engine over. If not, flick the kill switch to the OFF position and crank the engine over on the starter (see illustration 2). If the nature on the ignition system prevents the starter operating with the kill switch in the OFF position,

remove the spark plugs and fit them back in their caps; ensure that the plugs are earthed (grounded) against the cylinder head when the starter is operated (see illustration 3).

⚠️ *Warning: It is important that the plugs are earthed (grounded) away from the spark plug holes otherwise there is a risk of atomised fuel from the cylinders igniting.*

HAYNES HiNT *On a single cylinder four-stroke engine, you can seal the combustion chamber completely by positioning the piston at TDC on the compression stroke.*

● Drain the carburettor(s) otherwise there is a risk of jets becoming blocked by gum deposits from the fuel (see illustration 4).

● If the bike is going into long-term storage, consider adding a fuel stabiliser to the fuel in the tank. If the tank is drained completely, corrosion of its internal surfaces may occur if left unprotected for a long period. The tank can be treated with a rust preventative especially for this purpose. Alternatively, remove the tank and pour half a litre of motor oil into it, install the filler cap and shake the tank to coat its internals with oil before draining off the excess. The same effect can also be achieved by spraying WD40 or a similar water-dispersant around the inside of the tank via its flexible nozzle.

● Make sure the cooling system contains the correct mix of antifreeze. Antifreeze also contains important corrosion inhibitors.

● The air intakes and exhaust can be sealed off by covering or plugging the openings. Ensure that you do not seal in any condensation; run the engine until it is hot,

Squirt a drop of motor oil into each cylinder

Flick the kill switch to OFF . . .

. . . and ensure that the metal bodies of the plugs (arrows) are earthed against the cylinder head

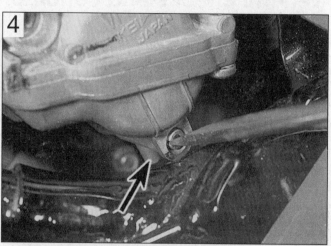
Connect a hose to the carburettor float chamber drain stub (arrow) and unscrew the drain screw

Exhausts can be sealed off with a plastic bag

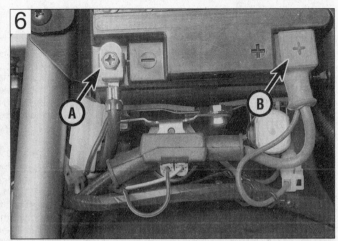

Disconnect the negative lead (A) first, followed by the positive lead (B)

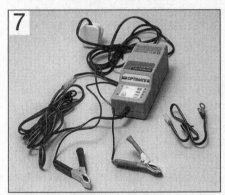

Use a suitable battery charger - this kit also assess battery condition

then switch off and allow to cool. Tape a piece of thick plastic over the silencer end(s) **(see illustration 5)**. Note that some advocate pouring a tablespoon of motor oil into the silencer(s) before sealing them off.

Battery

● Remove it from the bike - in extreme cases of cold the battery may freeze and crack its case **(see illustration 6)**.

● Check the electrolyte level and top up if necessary (conventional refillable batteries). Clean the terminals.
● Store the battery off the motorcycle and away from any sources of fire. Position a wooden block under the battery if it is to sit on the ground.
● Give the battery a trickle charge for a few hours every month **(see illustration 7)**.

Tyres

● Place the bike on its centrestand or an auxiliary stand which will support the motorcycle in an upright position. Position wood blocks under the tyres to keep them off the ground and to provide insulation from damp. If the bike is being put into long-term storage, ideally both tyres should be off the ground; not only will this protect the tyres, but will also ensure that no load is placed on the steering head or wheel bearings.
● Deflate each tyre by 5 to 10 psi, no more or the beads may unseat from the rim, making subsequent inflation difficult on tubeless tyres.

Pivots and controls

● Lubricate all lever, pedal, stand and

footrest pivot points. If grease nipples are fitted to the rear suspension components, apply lubricant to the pivots.
● Lubricate all control cables.

Cycle components

● Apply a wax protectant to all painted and plastic components. Wipe off any excess, but don't polish to a shine. Where fitted, clean the screen with soap and water.
● Coat metal parts with Vaseline (petroleum jelly). When applying this to the fork tubes, do not compress the forks otherwise the seals will rot from contact with the Vaseline.
● Apply a vinyl cleaner to the seat.

Storage conditions

● Aim to store the bike in a shed or garage which does not leak and is free from damp.
● Drape an old blanket or bedspread over the bike to protect it from dust and direct contact with sunlight (which will fade paint). This also hides the bike from prying eyes. Beware of tight-fitting plastic covers which may allow condensation to form and settle on the bike.

Getting back on the road

Engine and transmission

● Change the oil and replace the oil filter. If this was done prior to storage, check that the oil hasn't emulsified - a thick whitish substance which occurs through condensation.
● Remove the spark plugs. Using a spout-type oil can, squirt a few drops of oil into the cylinder(s). This will provide initial lubrication as the piston rings and bores comes back into contact. Service the spark plugs, or fit new ones, and install them in the engine.

● Check that the clutch isn't stuck on. The plates can stick together if left standing for some time, preventing clutch operation. Engage a gear and try rocking the bike back and forth with the clutch lever held against the handlebar. If this doesn't work on cable-operated clutches, hold the clutch lever back against the handlebar with a strong elastic band or cable tie for a couple of hours **(see illustration 8)**.
● If the air intakes or silencer end(s) were blocked off, remove the bung or cover used.
● If the fuel tank was coated with a rust

Hold clutch lever back against the handlebar with elastic bands or a cable tie

preventative, oil or a stabiliser added to the fuel, drain and flush the tank and dispose of the fuel sensibly. If no action was taken with the fuel tank prior to storage, it is advised that the old fuel is disposed of since it will go off over a period of time. Refill the fuel tank with fresh fuel.

Frame and running gear

● Oil all pivot points and cables.
● Check the tyre pressures. They will definitely need inflating if pressures were reduced for storage.
● Lubricate the final drive chain (where applicable).
● Remove any protective coating applied to the fork tubes (stanchions) since this may well destroy the fork seals. If the fork tubes weren't protected and have picked up rust spots, remove them with very fine abrasive paper and refinish with metal polish.
● Check that both brakes operate correctly. Apply each brake hard and check that it's not possible to move the motorcycle forwards, then check that the brake frees off again once released. Brake caliper pistons can stick due to corrosion around the piston head, or on the sliding caliper types, due to corrosion of the slider pins. If the brake doesn't free after repeated operation, take the caliper off for examination. Similarly drum brakes can stick

due to a seized operating cam, cable or rod linkage.
● If the motorcycle has been in long-term storage, renew the brake fluid and clutch fluid (where applicable).
● Depending on where the bike has been stored, the wiring, cables and hoses may have been nibbled by rodents. Make a visual check and investigate disturbed wiring loom tape.

Battery

● If the battery has been previously removal and given top up charges it can simply be reconnected. Remember to connect the positive cable first and the negative cable last.
● On conventional refillable batteries, if the battery has not received any attention, remove it from the motorcycle and check its electrolyte level. Top up if necessary then charge the battery. If the battery fails to hold a charge and a visual checks show heavy white sulphation of the plates, the battery is probably defective and must be renewed. This is particularly likely if the battery is old. Confirm battery condition with a specific gravity check.
● On sealed (MF) batteries, if the battery has not received any attention, remove it from the motorcycle and charge it according to the information on the battery case - if the battery fails to hold a charge it must be renewed.

Starting procedure

● If a kickstart is fitted, turn the engine over a couple of times with the ignition OFF to distribute oil around the engine. If no kickstart is fitted, flick the engine kill switch OFF and the ignition ON and crank the engine over a couple of times to work oil around the upper cylinder components. If the nature of the ignition system is such that the starter won't work with the kill switch OFF, remove the spark plugs, fit them back into their caps and earth (ground) their bodies on the cylinder head. Reinstall the spark plugs afterwards.
● Switch the kill switch to RUN, operate the choke and start the engine. If the engine won't start don't continue cranking the engine - not only will this flatten the battery, but the starter motor will overheat. Switch the ignition off and try again later. If the engine refuses to start, go through the fault finding procedures in this manual. **Note:** *If the bike has been in storage for a long time, old fuel or a carburettor blockage may be the problem. Gum deposits in carburettors can block jets - if a carburettor cleaner doesn't prove successful the carburettors must be dismantled for cleaning.*

● Once the engine has started, check that the lights, turn signals and horn work properly.

● Treat the bike gently for the first ride and check all fluid levels on completion. Settle the bike back into the maintenance schedule.

This Section provides an easy reference-guide to the more common faults that are likely to afflict your machine. Obviously, the opportunities are almost limitless for faults to occur as a result of obscure failures, and to try and cover all eventualities would require a separate book. Indeed, a number have been written on the subject.

Successful fault finding is not a mysterious 'black art' but the application of a bit of knowledge combined with a systematic and logical approach to the problem. Begin by first accurately identifying the symptom and then checking through the list of possible causes, starting with the simplest or most obvious and progressing in stages to the most complex.

Take nothing for granted, but above all apply liberal quantities of common sense.

The main symptom of a fault is given in the text as a major heading below which are listed the various systems or areas which may contain the fault. Details of each possible cause for a fault and the remedial action to be taken are given, in brief, in the paragraphs below each heading. Further information should be sought in the relevant Chapter.

1 Engine doesn't start or is difficult to start
- [ ] Starter motor doesn't rotate
- [ ] Starter motor rotates but engine does not turn over
- [ ] Starter works but engine won't turn over (seized)
- [ ] No fuel flow
- [ ] Engine flooded
- [ ] No spark or weak spark
- [ ] Compression low
- [ ] Stalls after starting
- [ ] Rough idle

2 Poor running at low speed
- [ ] Spark weak
- [ ] Fuel/air mixture incorrect
- [ ] Compression low
- [ ] Poor acceleration

3 Poor running or no power at high speed
- [ ] Firing incorrect
- [ ] Fuel/air mixture incorrect
- [ ] Compression low
- [ ] Knocking or pinking
- [ ] Miscellaneous causes

4 Overheating
- [ ] Engine overheats
- [ ] Firing incorrect
- [ ] Fuel/air mixture incorrect
- [ ] Compression too high
- [ ] Engine load excessive
- [ ] Lubrication inadequate
- [ ] Miscellaneous causes

5 Clutch problems
- [ ] Clutch slipping
- [ ] Clutch not disengaging completely

6 Gearchange problems
- [ ] Doesn't go into gear, or lever doesn't return
- [ ] Jumps out of gear
- [ ] Overselects

7 Abnormal engine noise
- [ ] Knocking or pinking
- [ ] Piston slap or rattling
- [ ] Valve noise
- [ ] Other noise

8 Abnormal driveline noise
- [ ] Clutch noise
- [ ] Transmission noise
- [ ] Final drive noise

9 Abnormal frame and suspension noise
- [ ] Front end noise
- [ ] Shock absorber noise
- [ ] Brake noise

10 Oil pressure warning light comes on
- [ ] Engine lubrication system
- [ ] Electrical system

11 Excessive exhaust smoke
- [ ] White smoke
- [ ] Black smoke
- [ ] Brown smoke

12 Poor handling or stability
- [ ] Handlebar hard to turn
- [ ] Handlebar shakes or vibrates excessively
- [ ] Handlebar pulls to one side
- [ ] Poor shock absorbing qualities

13 Braking problems
- [ ] Brakes are spongy, don't hold
- [ ] Brake lever or pedal pulsates
- [ ] Brakes drag

14 Electrical problems
- [ ] Battery dead or weak
- [ ] Battery overcharged

1 Engine doesn't start or is difficult to start

Starter motor doesn't rotate

- ☐ Engine kill switch OFF.
- ☐ Engine kill switch defective. Check for wet, dirty or corroded contacts. Clean or replace the switch as necessary (Chapter 8).
- ☐ Faulty neutral, sidestand or clutch switch, or starter interlock circuit. Check the wiring to each switch and the switch itself according to the procedures in Chapter 8.
- ☐ Battery voltage low. Check and recharge battery (Chapter 8).
- ☐ Starter motor defective. Make sure the wiring to the starter is secure. Make sure the starter relay clicks when the start button is pushed. If the relay clicks, then the fault is in the wiring or motor.
- ☐ Starter relay faulty. Check it according to the procedure in Chapter 8.
- ☐ Starter switch not contacting. The contacts could be wet, corroded or dirty. Disassemble and clean the switch (Chapter 8).
- ☐ Wiring open or shorted. Check all wiring connections and harnesses to make sure that they are dry, tight and not corroded. Also check for broken or frayed wires that can cause a short to earth (ground) (see Wiring Diagrams, Chapter 8).
- ☐ Ignition switch defective. Check the switch according to the procedure in Chapter 8. Replace the switch with a new one if it is defective.

Starter motor rotates but engine does not turn over

- ☐ Starter clutch defective. Inspect and repair or renew (Chapter 2).
- ☐ Damaged idle/reduction or starter gears. Inspect and renew the damaged parts (Chapter 2).

Starter works but engine won't turn over (seized)

- ☐ Seized engine caused by one or more internally damaged components. Failure due to wear, abuse or lack of lubrication. Damage can include seized valves, followers, camshafts, pistons, crankshaft, connecting rod bearings, or transmission gears or bearings. Refer to Chapter 2 for engine disassembly.

No fuel flow

- ☐ No fuel in tank.
- ☐ Fuel tank breather hose obstructed.
- ☐ Fuel pump failure or filter blocked (Chapter 4).
- ☐ Fuel line blocked. Pull the fuel line loose and carefully blow through it.
- ☐ Injector blocked. Either a very bad batch of fuel with an unusual additive has been used, or some other foreign material has entered the system. Often, after a machine has been stored for many months without running, the fuel turns to a varnish-like liquid and forms deposits on the injector.

Engine flooded

- ☐ Starting technique incorrect. Under normal circumstances the machine should start with no throttle. When the ambient temperature is very low, and the engine is cold, open the throttle slightly and pull the clutch lever in after switching the ignition ON. If the engine floods i.e. fuel is injected but not ignited by the spark plugs, check the ignition system (Chapter 4).

No spark or weak spark

- ☐ Engine kill switch OFF.
- ☐ Battery voltage low. Check and recharge the battery as necessary (Chapter 8).
- ☐ Spark plug(s) dirty, defective or worn out. Locate reason for fouled plugs using spark plug condition chart and follow the plug maintenance procedures (Chapter 1).
- ☐ HT coils or wiring faulty. Check condition. Renew either or both components if cracks or deterioration are evident (Chapter 4).
- ☐ Electronic control unit (ECU) defective. Check the unit, referring to Chapter 4 for details.
- ☐ Ignition timing sensor defective. Check the sensor, referring to Chapter 4 for details.
- ☐ Ignition or kill switch shorted. This is usually caused by water, corrosion, damage or excessive wear. The switches can be disassembled and cleaned with electrical contact cleaner. If cleaning does not help, replace the switches (Chapter 8).
- ☐ Make sure that all wiring connections are clean, dry and tight. Look for chafed and broken wires (Chapters 4 and 8).

Compression low

- ☐ Spark plug(s) loose. Remove the plug(s) and inspect the threads. Reinstall and tighten to the specified torque (Chapter 1).
- ☐ Cylinder head not sufficiently tightened down. If the cylinder head is suspected of being loose, then there's a chance that the gasket or head is damaged if the problem has persisted for any length of time. The head bolts should be tightened to the proper torque in the correct sequence (Chapter 2).
- ☐ Incorrect valve clearance. This means that the valve is not closing completely and compression pressure is leaking past the valve. Check and adjust the valve clearances (Chapter 1).
- ☐ Cylinder and/or piston worn. Excessive wear will cause compression pressure to leak past the rings. This is usually accompanied by worn rings as well. A top-end overhaul is necessary (Chapter 2).
- ☐ Piston rings worn, weak, broken, or sticking. Broken or sticking piston rings usually indicate a lubrication or fuelling problem that causes seizures or excess carbon deposits to form on the pistons and rings. Top-end overhaul is necessary (Chapter 2).
- ☐ Cylinder head gasket damaged. If a head is allowed to become loose, or if excessive carbon build-up on the piston crown and combustion chamber causes extremely high compression, the head gasket may leak. Retorquing the head is not always sufficient to restore the seal, so gasket replacement is necessary (Chapter 2).
- ☐ Cylinder head warped. This is caused by overheating or improperly tightened head bolts. Machine shop resurfacing or head replacement is necessary (Chapter 2).
- ☐ Valve spring broken or weak. Caused by component failure or wear; the springs must be renewed (Chapter 2).
- ☐ Valve not seating properly. This is caused by a bent valve (from over-revving or improper valve adjustment), burned valve or seat (improper fuel/air mix) or an accumulation of carbon deposits on the seat (from fuelling or lubrication problems). The valves must be cleaned and/or renewed and the seats serviced if possible (Chapter 2).

Stalls after starting

- ☐ Ignition malfunction (Chapter 4).
- ☐ Fuel injection malfunction (Chapter 4).
- ☐ Fuel contaminated. The fuel can be contaminated with either dirt or water, or can change chemically if the machine is allowed to sit for several months or more. Drain the fuel system and check that the fuel flows freely and is not being restricted (Chapter 4).
- ☐ Intake air leak. Check for loose throttle body-to-intake manifold connections (Chapter 4).
- ☐ Engine idle speed incorrect. Check engine management system (Chapter 4).

Rough idle

- ☐ Ignition malfunction (Chapter 4).
- ☐ Idle speed incorrect. Check engine management system (Chapter 4).
- ☐ Fuel injection malfunction (Chapter 4).
- ☐ Fuel contaminated. The fuel can be contaminated with either dirt or water, or can change chemically if the machine is allowed to sit for several months or more. Drain the tank and fuel system (Chapter 4).
- ☐ Intake air leak. Check for loose throttle body-to-intake manifold connections (Chapter 4).
- ☐ Air filter clogged. Renew the air filter element (Chapter 1).

2 Poor running at low speeds

Spark weak

- ☐ Battery voltage low. Check and recharge battery (Chapter 8).
- ☐ Spark plug(s) fouled, defective or worn out. Refer to Chapter 1 for spark plug maintenance.
- ☐ HT coils or wiring faulty. Check condition. Renew either or both components if cracks or deterioration are evident (Chapter 4).
- ☐ Incorrect spark plugs. Wrong type, heat range or cap configuration. Check and install correct plugs listed in Chapter 1.
- ☐ Electronic control unit (ECU) defective. See Chapter 4.
- ☐ Ignition timing sensor defective. See Chapter 4.

Fuel/air mixture incorrect

- ☐ Air filter clogged, poorly sealed or missing (Chapter 1).
- ☐ Air intake duct blocked or disconnected (Chapter 1).
- ☐ Intake air leak. Check for loose throttle body-to-intake manifold and air duct connections, loose vacuum hoses, or loose injectors (see Chapter 4).
- ☐ Fuel pump failure or filter blocked (Chapter 4).
- ☐ Fuel tank breather hose obstructed.
- ☐ Injector blocked. Dirt, water or other contaminants can block the injectors. Clean the injectors and renew the fuel strainer (Chapter 4).

Compression low

- ☐ Spark plug(s) loose. Remove the plug(s) and inspect the threads. Reinstall and tighten to the specified torque (Chapter 1).
- ☐ Cylinder head not sufficiently tightened down. If the cylinder head is suspected of being loose, then there's a chance that the gasket or head is damaged if the problem has persisted for any length of time. The head bolts should be tightened to the proper torque in the correct sequence (Chapter 2).
- ☐ Incorrect valve clearance. This means that the valve is not closing completely and compression pressure is leaking past the valve. Check and adjust the valve clearances (Chapter 1).
- ☐ Cylinder and/or piston worn. Excessive wear will cause compression pressure to leak past the rings. This is usually accompanied by worn rings as well. A top-end overhaul is necessary (Chapter 2).
- ☐ Piston rings worn, weak, broken, or sticking. Broken or sticking piston rings usually indicate a lubrication or fuelling problem that causes seizures or excess carbon deposits to form on the pistons and rings. Top-end overhaul is necessary (Chapter 2).
- ☐ Cylinder head gasket damaged. If a head is allowed to become loose, or if excessive carbon build-up on the piston crown and combustion chamber causes extremely high compression, the head gasket may leak. Retorquing the head is not always sufficient to restore the seal, so gasket replacement is necessary (Chapter 2).
- ☐ Cylinder head warped. This is caused by overheating or improperly tightened head bolts. Machine shop resurfacing or head replacement is necessary (Chapter 2).
- ☐ Valve spring broken or weak. Caused by component failure or wear; the springs must be replaced (Chapter 2).
- ☐ Valve not seating properly. This is caused by a bent valve (from over-revving or improper valve adjustment), burned valve or seat (improper fuel/air mix) or an accumulation of carbon deposits on the seat (from fuelling or lubrication problems). The valves must be cleaned and/or replaced and the seats serviced if possible (Chapter 2).

Poor acceleration

- ☐ Timing not advancing. Refer to a BMW dealer equipped with the diagnostic tester.
- ☐ Engine oil viscosity too high. Using a heavier oil than that recommended in *Pre-ride checks* can damage the oil pump or lubrication system and cause drag on the engine.
- ☐ Brakes dragging. Usually caused by debris which has entered the brake piston seals, or from a warped disc or bent axle. Repair as necessary (Chapter 6).

3 Poor running or no power at high speed

Firing incorrect

- [ ] Air filter restricted. Clean or replace filter (Chapter 1).
- [ ] Spark plug(s) fouled, defective or worn out. See Chapter 1 for spark plug maintenance.
- [ ] HT coils or wiring faulty. Check condition. Renew either or both components if cracks or deterioration are evident (Chapter 4).
- [ ] Incorrect spark plugs. Wrong type, heat range or cap configuration. Check and install correct plugs listed in Chapter 1.
- [ ] Electronic control unit (ECU) defective. See Chapter 4.
- [ ] Ignition coils defective. See Chapter 4.

Fuel/air mixture incorrect

- [ ] Air filter clogged, poorly sealed or missing (Chapter 1).
- [ ] Air intake duct blocked or disconnected (Chapter 1).
- [ ] Intake air leak. Check for loose throttle body-to-intake manifold and air duct connections, loose vacuum hoses, or loose injectors (Chapter 4).
- [ ] Fuel pump failure or strainer blocked (Chapter 4).
- [ ] Fuel tank breather hose obstructed.
- [ ] Injector clogged. Dirt, water or other contaminants can clog the injectors. Clean the injectors and renew the fuel strainer (Chapter 4).

Compression low

- [ ] Spark plug(s) loose. Remove the plug(s) and inspect the threads. Reinstall and tighten to the specified torque (Chapter 1).
- [ ] Cylinder head not sufficiently tightened down. If the cylinder head is suspected of being loose, then there's a chance that the gasket or head is damaged if the problem has persisted for any length of time. The head bolts should be tightened to the proper torque in the correct sequence (Chapter 2).
- [ ] Incorrect valve clearance. This means that the valve is not closing completely and compression pressure is leaking past the valve. Check and adjust the valve clearances (Chapter 1).
- [ ] Cylinder and/or piston worn. Excessive wear will cause compression pressure to leak past the rings. This is usually accompanied by worn rings as well. A top-end overhaul is necessary (Chapter 2).
- [ ] Piston rings worn, weak, broken, or sticking. Broken or sticking piston rings usually indicate a lubrication or fuelling problem that causes seizures or excess carbon deposits to form on the pistons and rings. Top-end overhaul is necessary (Chapter 2).
- [ ] Cylinder head gasket damaged. If a head is allowed to become loose, or if excessive carbon build-up on the piston crown and combustion chamber causes extremely high compression, the head gasket may leak. Retorquing the head is not always sufficient to restore the seal, so gasket replacement is necessary (Chapter 2).
- [ ] Cylinder head warped. This is caused by overheating or improperly tightened head bolts. Machine shop resurfacing or head replacement is necessary (Chapter 2).
- [ ] Valve spring broken or weak. Caused by component failure or wear; the springs must be replaced (Chapter 2).
- [ ] Valve not seating properly. This is caused by a bent valve (from over-revving or improper valve adjustment), burned valve or seat (improper fuel/air mix) or an accumulation of carbon deposits on the seat (from fuelling or lubrication problems). The valves must be cleaned and/or replaced and the seats serviced if possible (Chapter 2).

Knocking or pinking

- [ ] Carbon build-up in combustion chamber – remove the cylinder head and decarbonise (Chapter 2).
- [ ] Incorrect or poor quality fuel. Old or improper grades of fuel can cause detonation. This causes the piston to rattle, thus the knocking or pinking sound. Drain old fuel and always use the recommended fuel grade.
- [ ] Spark plug heat range incorrect. Uncontrolled detonation indicates the plug heat range is too hot. The plug in effect becomes a glow plug, raising cylinder temperatures. Install the proper heat range plug (Chapter 1).
- [ ] Improper air/fuel mixture. This will cause the cylinders to run hot, which leads to detonation. Clogged injector or an air leak can cause this imbalance (Chapter 4).

Miscellaneous causes

- [ ] Throttle valve doesn't open fully. Adjust the throttle cable freeplay (Chapter 1). Check operation of throttle valve (see Chapter 4)
- [ ] Clutch slipping. May be caused by loose or worn clutch components. Refer to Chapter 2 for clutch overhaul procedures.
- [ ] Timing not advancing. Refer to a BMW dealer equipped with the diagnostic tester.
- [ ] Engine oil viscosity too high. Using a heavier oil than the one recommended in Pre-ride checks can damage the oil pump or lubrication system and cause drag on the engine.
- [ ] Brakes dragging. Usually caused by debris which has entered the brake piston seals, or from a warped disc or bent axle. Repair as necessary (Chapter 6).

4 Overheating

Engine overheats

☐ Coolant level low. Check and add coolant (see *Pre-ride checks*).
☐ Leak in cooling system. Check cooling system hoses and radiator for leaks and other damage. Repair or replace parts as necessary (Chapter 3).
☐ Thermostat sticking open or closed. Check and renew as described in Chapter 3.
☐ Faulty radiator cap. Remove the cap and have it pressure tested.
☐ Coolant passages clogged. Drain and flush the entire system, then refill with fresh coolant.
☐ Water pump defective. Remove the pump and check the impeller and bearing (Chapter 3).
☐ Clogged radiator fins. Clean them by blowing compressed air through the fins from the rear of the radiator.
☐ Cooling fan fault (Chapter 3).

Firing incorrect

☐ Spark plug(s) fouled, defective or worn out. See Chapter 1 for spark plug maintenance.
☐ Incorrect spark plug(s).
☐ Electronic control unit (ECU) defective (Chapter 4).
☐ Faulty HT coil(s) (Chapter 4).

Fuel/air mixture incorrect

☐ Air filter clogged, poorly sealed or missing (Chapter 1).
☐ Air intake duct blocked or disconnected (Chapter 1).
☐ Intake air leak. Check for loose throttle body-to-intake manifold and air duct connections, loose vacuum hoses, or loose injectors (see Chapter 4).
☐ Fuel pump failure or filter blocked (Chapter 4).
☐ Fuel tank breather hose obstructed.
☐ Injector clogged. Dirt, water or other contaminants can clog the injectors. Clean the injectors and renew the fuel strainer (Chapter 4).

Compression too high

☐ Carbon build-up in combustion chamber. Remove the cylinder head and decarbonised (Chapter 2).
☐ Improperly machined head surface or installation of incorrect gasket during engine assembly.

Engine load excessive

☐ Clutch slipping. Can be caused by damaged, loose or worn clutch components. Refer to Chapter 2 for overhaul procedures.
☐ Engine oil level too high. The addition of too much oil will cause pressurisation of the crankcase and inefficient engine operation. Check Specifications and drain to proper level (Chapter 1 and *Pre-ride checks*).
☐ Engine oil viscosity too high. Using a heavier oil than the one recommended in *Pre-ride checks* can damage the oil pump or lubrication system as well as cause drag on the engine.
☐ Brakes dragging. Usually caused by debris which has entered the brake piston seals, or from a warped disc or bent axle. Repair as necessary (Chapter 6).

Lubrication inadequate

☐ Engine oil level too low. Friction caused by intermittent lack of lubrication or from oil that is overworked can cause overheating. The oil provides a definite cooling function in the engine. Check the oil level (see *Pre-ride checks*).
☐ Poor quality engine oil or incorrect viscosity or type. Oil is rated not only according to viscosity but also according to type. Some oils are not rated high enough for use in this engine.

Miscellaneous causes

☐ Modification to the exhaust system. Most aftermarket exhaust systems cause the engine to run leaner, which make them run hotter. When installing an after market exhaust system, have the bike checked on a dyno, or follow the manufacturer' instructions regarding remapping the ECU.

5 Clutch problems

Clutch slipping

☐ Insufficient clutch cable freeplay. Check and adjust (Chapter 1).
☐ Friction plates worn or warped. Overhaul the clutch assembly (Chapter 2).
☐ Plain plates warped (Chapter 2).
☐ Clutch springs broken or weak. Old or heat-damaged (from slipping clutch) springs should be renewed as a set (Chapter 2).
☐ Clutch release mechanism defective. Replace any defective parts (Chapter 2).
☐ Clutch centre or housing unevenly worn. This causes improper engagement of the plates. Renew the damaged or worn parts (Chapter 2).

Clutch not disengaging completely

☐ Excessive clutch cable freeplay. Check and adjust (Chapter 1).
☐ Clutch plates warped or damaged. This will cause clutch drag, which in turn will cause the machine to creep. Overhaul the clutch assembly (Chapter 2).

☐ Clutch spring tension uneven. Usually caused by a sagged or broken spring. Check and renew the springs as a set (Chapter 2).
☐ Engine oil deteriorated. Old, thin, worn out oil will not provide proper lubrication for the plates, causing the clutch to drag. Renew the oil and filter (Chapter 1 and *Pre-ride checks*).
☐ Engine oil viscosity too high. Using a heavier oil than recommended can cause the plates to stick together, putting a drag on the engine. Change to the correct weight oil (see *Pre-ride checks*).
☐ Clutch housing bearings seized on input shaft. Lack of lubrication, severe wear or damage can cause the bearings to seize on the shaft. Overhaul of the clutch, and perhaps transmission, may be necessary to repair the damage (Chapter 2).
☐ Clutch release mechanism defective. Overhaul the clutch cover components (Chapter 2).
☐ Loose clutch centre nut. Causes housing and centre misalignment putting a drag on the engine. Engagement adjustment continually varies. Overhaul the clutch assembly (Chapter 2).

6 Gear changing problems

Doesn't go into gear or lever doesn't return

- [ ] Clutch not disengaging. See Section 5, *Clutch problems*.
- [ ] Selector fork(s) bent or seized. Overhaul the transmission (Chapter 2).
- [ ] Gear(s) stuck on shaft. Most often caused by a lack of lubrication or excessive wear in transmission bearings and bushes. Overhaul the transmission (Chapter 2).
- [ ] Selector drum binding. Caused by lubrication failure or excessive wear. Replace the drum and bearing (Chapter 2).
- [ ] Gearchange lever return spring weak or broken (Chapter 2).
- [ ] Gearchange lever broken. Splines stripped out of lever or shaft, caused by allowing the lever to get loose or from dropping the machine. Renew necessary parts (Chapter 2).
- [ ] Gearchange mechanism stopper arm broken or worn. Full engagement and rotary movement of selector drum results. Replace the arm (Chapter 2).
- [ ] Stopper arm spring broken. Allows arm to float, causing sporadic gearchange operation. Renew the spring (Chapter 2).

Jumps out of gear

- [ ] Selector fork(s) worn. Overhaul the transmission (Chapter 2).
- [ ] Gear groove(s) worn. Overhaul the transmission (Chapter 2).
- [ ] Gear dogs or dog slots worn or damaged. The gears should be inspected and replaced. No attempt should be made to service the worn parts.

Overselects

- [ ] Stopper arm spring weak or broken (Chapter 2).
- [ ] Gearchange shaft return spring post broken or distorted (Chapter 2).

7 Abnormal engine noise

Knocking or pinking

- [ ] Carbon build-up in combustion chamber. Remove the cylinder head and decarbonised (Chapter 2).
- [ ] Incorrect or poor quality fuel. Old or improper fuel can cause detonation. This causes the pistons to rattle, thus the knocking or pinking sound. Drain the old fuel and always use the recommended grade fuel (Chapter 4).
- [ ] Spark plug heat range incorrect. Uncontrolled detonation indicates that the plug heat range is too hot. The plug in effect becomes a glow plug, raising cylinder temperatures. Install the proper heat range plug(s) (Chapter 1).
- [ ] Improper fuel/air mixture. This will cause the cylinders to run hot and lead to detonation. An air leak can cause this imbalance (Chapter 4).

Piston slap or rattling

- [ ] Cylinder-to-piston clearance excessive. Caused by improper assembly. Inspect and overhaul top-end parts (Chapter 2).
- [ ] Connecting rod bent. Caused by over-revving, trying to start a badly flooded engine or from ingesting a foreign object into the combustion chamber. Replace the damaged parts (Chapter 2).
- [ ] Piston pin or piston pin bore worn or seized from wear or lack of lubrication. Replace damaged parts (Chapter 2).
- [ ] Piston ring(s) worn, broken or sticking. Overhaul the top-end (Chapter 2).
- [ ] Piston seizure damage. Usually from lack of lubrication or overheating. Replace the pistons (Chapter 2).
- [ ] Connecting rod upper or lower end clearance excessive. Caused by excessive wear or lack of lubrication. Replace worn parts.

Valve noise

- [ ] Incorrect valve clearances. Adjust the clearances by referring to Chapter 1.
- [ ] Valve spring broken or weak. Check and replace weak valve springs (Chapter 2).
- [ ] Camshaft or cylinder head worn or damaged. Lack of lubrication at high rpm is usually the cause of damage. Insufficient oil or failure to change the oil at the recommended intervals are the chief causes. Since there are no replaceable bearings in the head, the head itself will have to be replaced if there is excessive wear or damage (Chapter 2).

Other noise

- [ ] Cylinder head gasket leaking.
- [ ] Exhaust pipe leaking at cylinder head connection. Caused by improper fit of pipe(s) or loose exhaust flange. All exhaust fasteners should be tightened evenly and carefully. Failure to do this will lead to a leak.
- [ ] Crankshaft runout excessive. Caused by a bent crankshaft (from over-revving) or damage from an upper cylinder component failure. Can also be attributed to dropping the machine on either of the crankshaft ends.
- [ ] Engine mounting bolts loose. Tighten all engine mounting bolts (Chapter 2).
- [ ] Crankshaft bearings worn (Chapter 2).
- [ ] Camchain defective. Replace according to the procedure in Chapter 2.

8 Abnormal driveline noise

Clutch noise

☐ Clutch housing/friction plate clearance excessive (Chapter 2).
☐ Loose or damaged clutch pressure plate and/or bolts (Chapter 2).

Transmission noise

☐ Bearings worn. Also includes the possibility that the shafts are worn. Overhaul the transmission (Chapter 2).
☐ Gears worn or chipped (Chapter 2).
☐ Metal chips jammed in gear teeth. Probably pieces from a broken clutch, gear or selector mechanism that were picked up by the gears. This will cause early bearing failure (Chapter 2).

☐ Engine oil level too low. Causes a howl from transmission. Also affects engine power and clutch operation (see Pre-ride checks).

Final drive noise

☐ Chain (GS and R) or belt (S and ST) not adjusted properly (Chapter 1).
☐ Front or rear sprocket/pulley loose. Tighten fasteners (Chapter 6).
☐ Sprockets/pulleys worn. Renew (Chapter 6).
☐ Rear sprocket/pulley warped. Renew (Chapter 6).
☐ Rubber dampers in rear wheel hub worn. Check and renew (Chapter 6).

9 Abnormal frame and suspension noise

Front end noise

☐ Low fluid level or improper viscosity oil in forks. This can sound like spurting and is usually accompanied by irregular fork action (Chapter 5).
☐ Spring weak or broken. Makes a clicking or scraping sound. Fork oil, when drained, will have a lot of metal particles in it (Chapter 5).
☐ Steering head bearings loose or damaged. Clicks when braking. Check and adjust or replace as necessary (Chapters 1 and 5).
☐ Fork yokes loose. Make sure all clamp pinch bolts are tightened to the specified torque (Chapter 5).
☐ Fork tube bent. Good possibility if machine has been dropped. Replace tube with a new one (Chapter 5).
☐ Front axle or axle clamp bolts loose. Tighten them to the specified torque (Chapter 6).
☐ Loose or worn wheel bearings. Check and replace as needed (Chapter 6).

Shock absorber noise

☐ Fluid level incorrect. Indicates a leak caused by defective seal. Shock will be covered with oil. Replace shock or seek advice on repair from a suspension specialist (Chapter 5).
☐ Defective shock absorber with internal damage. This is in the body

of the shock and can't be remedied. The shock must be replaced with a new one (Chapter 5).
☐ Bent or damaged shock body. Replace the shock with a new one (Chapter 5).

Brake noise

☐ Squeal caused by dust on brake pads. Usually found in combination with glazed pads. Clean using brake cleaning solvent (Chapter 6).
☐ Contamination of brake pads. Oil, brake fluid or dirt causing brake to chatter or squeal. Clean or renew pads (Chapter 6).
☐ Pads glazed. Caused by excessive heat from prolonged use or from contamination. Do not use sandpaper, emery cloth, carborundum cloth or any other abrasive to roughen the pad surfaces as abrasives will stay in the pad material and damage the disc. A very fine flat file can be used, but pad renewal is recommended (Chapter 6).
☐ Disc warped. Can cause a chattering, clicking or intermittent squeal. Usually accompanied by a pulsating lever and uneven braking. Renew the disc (Chapter 6).
☐ Loose or worn wheel bearings. Check and renew as needed (Chapter 6).
☐ Faulty ABS system, where fitted (Chapter 6).

10 Oil pressure warning light comes on

Engine lubrication system

☐ Engine oil pump(s) defective, blocked oil strainer gauze or failed pressure regulator valve. Carry out an oil pressure check (Chapter 2).
☐ Engine oil level low. Inspect for leak or other problem causing low oil level and add recommended oil (see Pre-ride checks).
☐ Engine oil viscosity too low. Very old, thin oil or an improper weight of oil used in the engine. Change to correct oil (see Pre-ride checks).
☐ Camshaft or journals worn. Excessive wear causing drop in oil pressure. Replace cam and/or cylinder head. Abnormal wear

could be caused by oil starvation at high rpm from low oil level or improper weight or type of oil.
☐ Crankshaft and/or bearings worn. Same problems as above. Check and renew crankshaft and/or bearings (Chapter 2).

Electrical system

☐ Oil pressure switch defective. Check the switch according to the procedure in Chapter 8. Renew it if it is defective.
☐ Oil pressure warning light circuit defective. Check for pinched, shorted, disconnected or damaged wiring (Chapter 8).

11 Excessive exhaust smoke

White smoke

☐ Piston oil ring worn. The ring may be broken or damaged, causing oil from the crankcase to be pulled past the piston into the combustion chamber. Replace the rings with new ones (Chapter 2).

☐ Cylinder worn, cracked, or scored. Caused by overheating or oil starvation (Chapter 2)

☐ Valve oil seal damaged or worn. Replace oil seals with new ones (Chapter 2).

☐ Valve guide worn. Perform a complete valve job (Chapter 2).

☐ Engine oil level too high, which causes the oil to be forced past the rings. Drain oil to the proper level (see Chapter 1 and *Pre-ride checks*).

☐ Head gasket broken between oil return and cylinder. Causes oil to be pulled into the combustion chamber. Replace the head gasket and check the head for warpage (Chapter 2).

☐ Abnormal crankcase pressurisation, which forces oil past the rings. Blocked breather is usually the cause.

Black smoke

☐ Air filter blocked. Renew the element (Chapter 1).

☐ Engine control unit (ECU) defective. Refer to a BMW dealer equipped with the diagnostic tester.

Brown smoke

☐ Fuel strainer clogged - renew the fuel strainer (Chapter 4).

☐ Fuel flow insufficient. Have a BMW dealer perform a fuel pressure check.

☐ Intake manifold clamp loose (Chapter 4).

☐ Air filter poorly sealed or not installed (Chapter 1).

12 Poor handling or stability

Handlebar hard to turn

☐ Steering head bearing adjuster nut too tight. Check adjustment as described in Chapter 1.

☐ Bearings damaged. Roughness can be felt as the bars are turned from side-to-side. Renew bearings and races (Chapter 5).

☐ Races dented or worn. Denting results from wear in only one position (e.g., straight ahead), from a collision or hitting a pothole or from dropping the machine. Renew races and bearings (Chapter 5).

☐ Steering stem lubrication inadequate. Causes are grease getting hard from age or being washed out by high pressure car washes. Disassemble steering head and repack bearings (Chapter 5).

☐ Steering stem bent. Caused by a collision, hitting a pothole or by dropping the machine. Renew damaged part. Don't try to straighten the steering stem (Chapter 5).

☐ Front tyre air pressure too low (see *Pre-ride checks*).

Handlebar shakes or vibrates excessively

☐ Tyres worn or out of balance (Chapter6).

☐ Swingarm bearings worn. Renew worn bearings (Chapter 5).

☐ Wheel rim(s) warped or damaged. Inspect wheels for runout (Chapter 6).

☐ Wheel bearings worn. Worn front or rear wheel bearings can cause poor tracking. Worn front bearings will cause wobble (Chapter 6).

☐ Handlebar clamp bolts loose (Chapter 5).

☐ Fork yoke bolts loose. Tighten them to the specified torque (Chapter 5).

☐ Engine mounting bolts loose. Will cause excessive vibration with increased engine rpm (Chapter 2).

Handlebar pulls to one side

☐ Frame bent. Definitely suspect this if the machine has been dropped. May or may not be accompanied by cracking near the bend. Renew the frame (Chapter 5).

☐ Wheels out of alignment. Caused by improper location of axle spacers or from bent steering stem or frame (Chapter 6).

☐ Swingarm bent or twisted. Caused by age (metal fatigue) or impact damage. Renew the swingarm (Chapter 5).

☐ Steering stem bent. Caused by impact damage or by dropping the motorcycle. Renew the steering stem (Chapter 5).

☐ Fork tube bent. Disassemble the forks and renew the damaged parts (Chapter 5).

☐ Fork oil level uneven. Check and add or drain as necessary (Chapter 5).

Poor shock absorbing qualities

☐ Too hard:
  a) *Fork oil level excessive (Chapter 5).*
  b) *Fork oil viscosity too high. Use a lighter oil (see the Specifications in Chapter 5).*
  c) *Fork tube bent. Causes a harsh, sticking feeling (Chapter 5).*
  d) *Fork internal damage (Chapter 5).*
  e) *Shock shaft or body bent or damaged (Chapter 5).*
  f) *Shock internal damage (Chapter 5).*
  g) *Tyre pressure too high (Pre-ride checks).*

☐ Too soft:
  a) *Fork or shock oil insufficient and/or leaking (Chapter 5).*
  b) *Fork oil level too low (Chapter 5).*
  c) *Fork oil viscosity too light (Chapter 5).*
  d) *Fork springs weak or broken (Chapter 5).*
  e) *Shock internal damage or leakage (Chapter 5).*

13 Braking problems

Brakes are spongy, don't hold

- [ ] Air in brake line. Caused by inattention to master cylinder fluid level or by leakage. Locate problem and bleed brakes (Chapter 6).
- [ ] Pads or disc worn (Chapters 1 and 6).
- [ ] Contaminated pads. Caused by contamination with oil, grease, brake fluid, etc. Renew pads. Clean disc thoroughly with brake cleaner (Chapter 6).
- [ ] Brake fluid deteriorated. Fluid is old or contaminated. Drain system, replenish with new fluid and bleed the system (Chapter 6).
- [ ] Master cylinder internal parts worn or damaged causing fluid to bypass (Chapter 6).
- [ ] Master cylinder bore scratched by foreign material or broken spring. Renew master cylinder (Chapter 6).
- [ ] Disc warped. Renew disc(s) (Chapter 6).
- [ ] Faulty ABS system, where fitted (Chapter 6).

Brake lever or pedal pulsates

- [ ] Disc warped. Renew disc (s) (Chapter 6).
- [ ] Wheel axle bent. Replace axle (Chapter 6).
- [ ] Brake caliper bolts loose (Chapter 6).
- [ ] Brake caliper slider pins damaged or sticking, causing caliper to bind – applies to sliding type caliper only. Lubricate the slider pins or replace them if they are corroded or bent (Chapter 6).
- [ ] Wheel warped or otherwise damaged (Chapter 6).
- [ ] Wheel bearings damaged or worn (Chapter 6).
- [ ] Faulty ABS system, where fitted (Chapter 6).

Brakes drag

- [ ] Master cylinder piston seized. Caused by wear or damage to piston or cylinder bore (Chapter 6).
- [ ] Lever balky or stuck. Check pivot and lubricate (Chapter 5).
- [ ] Brake caliper binds on bracket. Caused by inadequate lubrication or damage to caliper slider pins – applies to sliding type caliper only (Chapter 6).
- [ ] Brake caliper piston seized in bore. Caused by wear or ingestion of dirt past deteriorated seal (Chapter 6).
- [ ] Brake pad damaged. Pad material separated from backing plate. Usually caused by faulty manufacturing process or from contact with chemicals. Renew pads (Chapter 6).
- [ ] Pads improperly installed (Chapter 6).
- [ ] Faulty ABS system, where fitted (Chapter 6).

14 Electrical problems

Battery dead or weak

- [ ] Battery faulty. Caused by sulphated plates which are shorted through sedimentation. Also, broken battery terminal making only occasional contact (Chapter 8).
- [ ] Battery leads making poor contact (Chapter 8).
- [ ] Load excessive. Caused by addition of high wattage lights or other electrical accessories.
- [ ] Ignition switch defective. Switch either grounds (earths) internally or fails to shut off system. Renew the switch (Chapter 8).
- [ ] Regulator/rectifier defective (Chapter 8).

- [ ] Alternator stator coil open or shorted (Chapter 8).
- [ ] Wiring faulty. Wiring grounded (earthed) or connections loose in ignition, charging or lighting circuits (Chapter 8).

Battery overcharged

- [ ] Regulator/rectifier defective. Overcharging is noticed when battery gets excessively warm (Chapter 8).
- [ ] Battery defective. Replace battery with a new one (Chapter 8).
- [ ] Battery amperage too low, wrong type or size. Install manufacturer's specified amp-hour battery to handle charging load (Chapter 8).

A

ABS (Anti-lock braking system) A system, usually electronically controlled, that senses incipient wheel lockup during braking and relieves hydraulic pressure at wheel which is about to skid.

Aftermarket Components suitable for the motorcycle, but not produced by the motorcycle manufacturer.

Allen key A hexagonal wrench which fits into a recessed hexagonal hole.

Alternating current (ac) Current produced by an alternator. Requires converting to direct current by a rectifier for charging purposes.

Alternator Converts mechanical energy from the engine into electrical energy to charge the battery and power the electrical system.

Ampere (amp) A unit of measurement for the flow of electrical current. Current = Volts ÷ Ohms.

Ampere-hour (Ah) Measure of battery capacity.

Angle-tightening A torque expressed in degrees. Often follows a conventional tightening torque for cylinder head or main bearing fasteners (see illustration).

Angle-tightening cylinder head bolts

Antifreeze A substance (usually ethylene glycol) mixed with water, and added to the cooling system, to prevent freezing of the coolant in winter. Antifreeze also contains chemicals to inhibit corrosion and the formation of rust and other deposits that would tend to clog the radiator and coolant passages and reduce cooling efficiency.

Anti-dive System attached to the fork lower leg (slider) to prevent fork dive when braking hard.

Anti-seize compound A coating that reduces the risk of seizing on fasteners that are subjected to high temperatures, such as exhaust clamp bolts and nuts.

API American Petroleum Institute. A quality standard for 4-stroke motor oils.

Asbestos A natural fibrous mineral with great heat resistance, commonly used in the composition of brake friction materials. Asbestos is a health hazard and the dust created by brake systems should never be inhaled or ingested.

ATF Automatic Transmission Fluid. Often used in front forks.

ATU Automatic Timing Unit. Mechanical device for advancing the ignition timing on early engines.

ATV All Terrain Vehicle. Often called a Quad.

Axial play Side-to-side movement.

Axle A shaft on which a wheel revolves. Also known as a spindle.

B

Backlash The amount of movement between meshed components when one component is held still. Usually applies to gear teeth.

Ball bearing A bearing consisting of a hardened inner and outer race with hardened steel balls between the two races.

Bearings Used between two working surfaces to prevent wear of the components and a build-up of heat. Four types of bearing are commonly used on motorcycles: plain shell bearings, ball bearings, tapered roller bearings and needle roller bearings.

Bevel gears Used to turn the drive through 90°. Typical applications are shaft final drive and camshaft drive (see illustration).

Bevel gears are used to turn the drive through 90°

BHP Brake Horsepower. The British measurement for engine power output. Power output is now usually expressed in kilowatts (kW).

Bias-belted tyre Similar construction to radial tyre, but with outer belt running at an angle to the wheel rim.

Big-end bearing The bearing in the end of the connecting rod that's attached to the crankshaft.

Bleeding The process of removing air from an hydraulic system via a bleed nipple or bleed screw.

Bottom-end A description of an engine's crankcase components and all components contained there-in.

BTDC Before Top Dead Centre in terms of piston position. Ignition timing is often expressed in terms of degrees or millimetres BTDC.

Bush A cylindrical metal or rubber component used between two moving parts.

Burr Rough edge left on a component after machining or as a result of excessive wear.

C

Cam chain The chain which takes drive from the crankshaft to the camshaft(s).

Canister The main component in an evaporative emission control system (California market only); contains activated charcoal granules to trap vapours from the fuel system rather than allowing them to vent to the atmosphere.

Castellated Resembling the parapets along the top of a castle wall. For example, a castellated wheel axle or spindle nut.

Catalytic converter A device in the exhaust system of some machines which converts certain pollutants in the exhaust gases into less harmful substances.

Charging system Description of the components which charge the battery, ie the alternator, rectifier and regulator.

Circlip A ring-shaped clip used to prevent endwise movement of cylindrical parts and shafts. An internal circlip is installed in a groove in a housing; an external circlip fits into a groove on the outside of a cylindrical piece such as a shaft. Also known as a snap-ring.

Clearance The amount of space between two parts. For example, between a piston and a cylinder, between a bearing and a journal, etc.

Coil spring A spiral of elastic steel found in various sizes throughout a vehicle, for example as a springing medium in the suspension and in the valve train.

Compression Reduction in volume, and increase in pressure and temperature, of a gas, caused by squeezing it into a smaller space.

Compression damping Controls the speed the suspension compresses when hitting a bump.

Compression ratio The relationship between cylinder volume when the piston is at top dead centre and cylinder volume when the piston is at bottom dead centre.

Continuity The uninterrupted path in the flow of electricity. Little or no measurable resistance.

Continuity tester Self-powered bleeper or test light which indicates continuity.

Cp Candlepower. Bulb rating commonly found on US motorcycles.

Crossply tyre Tyre plies arranged in a criss-cross pattern. Usually four or six plies used, hence 4PR or 6PR in tyre size codes.

Cush drive Rubber damper segments fitted between the rear wheel and final drive sprocket to absorb transmission shocks (see illustration).

Cush drive rubbers dampen out transmission shocks

D

Degree disc Calibrated disc for measuring piston position. Expressed in degrees.

Dial gauge Clock-type gauge with adapters for measuring runout and piston position. Expressed in mm or inches.

Diaphragm The rubber membrane in a master cylinder or carburettor which seals the upper chamber.

Diaphragm spring A single sprung plate often used in clutches.

Direct current (dc) Current produced by a dc generator.

Decarbonisation The process of removing carbon deposits - typically from the combustion chamber, valves and exhaust port/system.

Detonation Destructive and damaging explosion of fuel/air mixture in combustion chamber instead of controlled burning.

Diode An electrical valve which only allows current to flow in one direction. Commonly used in rectifiers and starter interlock systems.

Disc valve (or rotary valve) A induction system used on some two-stroke engines.

Double-overhead camshaft (DOHC) An engine that uses two overhead camshafts, one for the intake valves and one for the exhaust valves.

Drivebelt A toothed belt used to transmit drive to the rear wheel on some motorcycles. A drivebelt has also been used to drive the camshafts. Drivebelts are usually made of Kevlar.

Driveshaft Any shaft used to transmit motion. Commonly used when referring to the final driveshaft on shaft drive motorcycles.

E

Earth return The return path of an electrical circuit, utilising the motorcycle's frame.

ECU (Electronic Control Unit) A computer which controls (for instance) an ignition system, or an anti-lock braking system.

EGO Exhaust Gas Oxygen sensor. Sometimes called a Lambda sensor.

Electrolyte The fluid in a lead-acid battery.

EMS (Engine Management System) A computer controlled system which manages the fuel injection and the ignition systems in an integrated fashion.

Endfloat The amount of lengthways movement between two parts. As applied to a crankshaft, the distance that the crankshaft can move side-to-side in the crankcase.

Endless chain A chain having no joining link. Common use for cam chains and final drive chains.

EP (Extreme Pressure) Oil type used in locations where high loads are applied, such as between gear teeth.

Evaporative emission control system Describes a charcoal filled canister which stores fuel vapours from the tank rather than allowing them to vent to the atmosphere. Usually only fitted to California models and referred to as an EVAP system.

Expansion chamber Section of two-stroke engine exhaust system so designed to improve engine efficiency and boost power.

F

Feeler blade or gauge A thin strip or blade of hardened steel, ground to an exact thickness, used to check or measure clearances between parts.

Final drive Description of the drive from the transmission to the rear wheel. Usually by chain or shaft, but sometimes by belt.

Firing order The order in which the engine cylinders fire, or deliver their power strokes, beginning with the number one cylinder.

Flooding Term used to describe a high fuel level in the carburettor float chambers, leading to fuel overflow. Also refers to excess fuel in the combustion chamber due to incorrect starting technique.

Free length The no-load state of a component when measured. Clutch, valve and fork spring lengths are measured at rest, without any preload.

Freeplay The amount of travel before any action takes place. The looseness in a linkage, or an assembly of parts, between the initial application of force and actual movement. For example, the distance the rear brake pedal moves before the rear brake is actuated.

Fuel injection The fuel/air mixture is metered electronically and directed into the engine intake ports (indirect injection) or into the cylinders (direct injection). Sensors supply information on engine speed and conditions.

Fuel/air mixture The charge of fuel and air going into the engine. See **Stoichiometric ratio**.

Fuse An electrical device which protects a circuit against accidental overload. The typical fuse contains a soft piece of metal which is calibrated to melt at a predetermined current flow (expressed as amps) and break the circuit.

G

Gap The distance the spark must travel in jumping from the centre electrode to the side electrode in a spark plug. Also refers to the distance between the ignition rotor and the pickup coil in an electronic ignition system.

Gasket Any thin, soft material - usually cork, cardboard, asbestos or soft metal - installed between two metal surfaces to ensure a good seal. For instance, the cylinder head gasket seals the joint between the block and the cylinder head.

Gauge An instrument panel display used to monitor engine conditions. A gauge with a movable pointer on a dial or a fixed scale is an analogue gauge. A gauge with a numerical readout is called a digital gauge.

Gear ratios The drive ratio of a pair of gears in a gearbox, calculated on their number of teeth.

Glaze-busting see **Honing**

Grinding Process for renovating the valve face and valve seat contact area in the cylinder head.

Gudgeon pin The shaft which connects the connecting rod small-end with the piston. Often called a piston pin or wrist pin.

H

Helical gears Gear teeth are slightly curved and produce less gear noise that straight-cut gears. Often used for primary drives.

Installing a Helicoil thread insert in a cylinder head

Helicoil A thread insert repair system. Commonly used as a repair for stripped spark plug threads **(see illustration)**.

Honing A process used to break down the glaze on a cylinder bore (also called glaze-busting). Can also be carried out to roughen a rebored cylinder to aid ring bedding-in.

HT (High Tension) Description of the electrical circuit from the secondary winding of the ignition coil to the spark plug.

Hydraulic A liquid filled system used to transmit pressure from one component to another. Common uses on motorcycles are brakes and clutches.

Hydrometer An instrument for measuring the specific gravity of a lead-acid battery.

Hygroscopic Water absorbing. In motorcycle applications, braking efficiency will be reduced if DOT 3 or 4 hydraulic fluid absorbs water from the air - care must be taken to keep new brake fluid in tightly sealed containers.

I

lbf ft Pounds-force feet. An imperial unit of torque. Sometimes written as ft-lbs.

lbf in Pound-force inch. An imperial unit of torque, applied to components where a very low torque is required. Sometimes written as in-lbs.

IC Abbreviation for Integrated Circuit.

Ignition advance Means of increasing the timing of the spark at higher engine speeds. Done by mechanical means (ATU) on early engines or electronically by the ignition control unit on later engines.

Ignition timing The moment at which the spark plug fires, expressed in the number of crankshaft degrees before the piston reaches the top of its stroke, or in the number of millimetres before the piston reaches the top of its stroke.

Infinity (∞) Description of an open-circuit electrical state, where no continuity exists.

Inverted forks (upside down forks) The sliders or lower legs are held in the yokes and the fork tubes or stanchions are connected to the wheel axle (spindle). Less unsprung weight and stiffer construction than conventional forks.

J

JASO Quality standard for 2-stroke oils.

Joule The unit of electrical energy.

Journal The bearing surface of a shaft.

K

Kickstart Mechanical means of turning the engine over for starting purposes. Only usually fitted to mopeds, small capacity motorcycles and off-road motorcycles.

Kill switch Handebar-mounted switch for emergency ignition cut-out. Cuts the ignition circuit on all models, and additionally prevent starter motor operation on others.

km Symbol for kilometre.

kmh Abbreviation for kilometres per hour.

L

Lambda (λ) sensor A sensor fitted in the exhaust system to measure the exhaust gas oxygen content (excess air factor).

Lapping see **Grinding**.

LCD Abbreviation for Liquid Crystal Display.

LED Abbreviation for Light Emitting Diode.

Liner A steel cylinder liner inserted in a aluminium alloy cylinder block.

Locknut A nut used to lock an adjustment nut, or other threaded component, in place.

Lockstops The lugs on the lower triple clamp (yoke) which abut those on the frame, preventing handlebar-to-fuel tank contact.

Lockwasher A form of washer designed to prevent an attaching nut from working loose.

LT Low Tension Description of the electrical circuit from the power supply to the primary winding of the ignition coil.

M

Main bearings The bearings between the crankshaft and crankcase.

Maintenance-free (MF) battery A sealed battery which cannot be topped up.

Manometer Mercury-filled calibrated tubes used to measure intake tract vacuum. Used to synchronise carburettors on multi-cylinder engines.

Micrometer A precision measuring instrument that measures component outside diameters **(see illustration)**.

Tappet shims are measured with a micrometer

MON (Motor Octane Number) A measure of a fuel's resistance to knock.

Monograde oil An oil with a single viscosity, eg SAE80W.

Monoshock A single suspension unit linking the swingarm or suspension linkage to the frame.

mph Abbreviation for miles per hour.

Multigrade oil Having a wide viscosity range (eg 10W40). The W stands for Winter, thus the viscosity ranges from SAE10 when cold to SAE40 when hot.

Multimeter An electrical test instrument with the capability to measure voltage, current and resistance. Some meters also incorporate a continuity tester and buzzer.

N

Needle roller bearing Inner race of caged needle rollers and hardened outer race. Examples of uncaged needle rollers can be found on some engines. Commonly used in rear suspension applications and in two-stroke engines.

Nm Newton metres.

NOx Oxides of Nitrogen. A common toxic pollutant emitted by petrol engines at higher temperatures.

O

Octane The measure of a fuel's resistance to knock.

OE (Original Equipment) Relates to components fitted to a motorcycle as standard or replacement parts supplied by the motorcycle manufacturer.

Ohm The unit of electrical resistance. Ohms = Volts ÷ Current.

Ohmmeter An instrument for measuring electrical resistance.

Oil cooler System for diverting engine oil outside of the engine to a radiator for cooling purposes.

Oil injection A system of two-stroke engine lubrication where oil is pump-fed to the engine in accordance with throttle position.

Open-circuit An electrical condition where there is a break in the flow of electricity - no continuity (high resistance).

O-ring A type of sealing ring made of a special rubber-like material; in use, the O-ring is compressed into a groove to provide the sealing action.

Oversize (OS) Term used for piston and ring size options fitted to a rebored cylinder.

Overhead cam (sohc) engine An engine with single camshaft located on top of the cylinder head.

Overhead valve (ohv) engine An engine with the valves located in the cylinder head, but with the camshaft located in the engine block or crankcase.

Oxygen sensor A device installed in the exhaust system which senses the oxygen content in the exhaust and converts this information into an electric current. Also called a Lambda sensor.

P

Plastigauge A thin strip of plastic thread, available in different sizes, used for measuring clearances. For example, a strip of Plastigauge is laid across a bearing journal. The parts are assembled and dismantled; the width of the crushed strip indicates the clearance between journal and bearing.

Polarity Either negative or positive earth (ground), determined by which battery lead is connected to the frame (earth return). Modern motorcycles are usually negative earth.

Pre-ignition A situation where the fuel/air mixture ignites before the spark plug fires. Often due to a hot spot in the combustion chamber caused by carbon build-up. Engine has a tendency to 'run-on'.

Pre-load (suspension) The amount a spring is compressed when in the unloaded state. Preload can be applied by gas, spacer or mechanical adjuster.

Premix The method of engine lubrication on older two-stroke engines. Engine oil is mixed with the petrol in the fuel tank in a specific ratio. The fuel/oil mix is sometimes referred to as "petroil".

Primary drive Description of the drive from the crankshaft to the clutch. Usually by gear or chain.

PS Pfedestärke - a German interpretation of BHP.

PSI Pounds-force per square inch. Imperial measurement of tyre pressure and cylinder pressure measurement.

PTFE Polytetrafluroethylene. A low friction substance.

Pulse secondary air injection system A process of promoting the burning of excess fuel present in the exhaust gases by routing fresh air into the exhaust ports.

Q

Quartz halogen bulb Tungsten filament surrounded by a halogen gas. Typically used for the headlight **(see illustration)**.

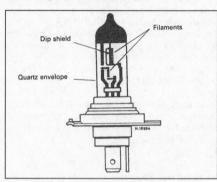

Quartz halogen headlight bulb construction

R

Rack-and-pinion A pinion gear on the end of a shaft that mates with a rack (think of a geared wheel opened up and laid flat). Sometimes used in clutch operating systems.

Radial play Up and down movement about a shaft.

Radial ply tyres Tyre plies run across the tyre (from bead to bead) and around the circumference of the tyre. Less resistant to tread distortion than other tyre types.

Radiator A liquid-to-air heat transfer device designed to reduce the temperature of the coolant in a liquid cooled engine.

Rake A feature of steering geometry - the angle of the steering head in relation to the vertical **(see illustration)**.

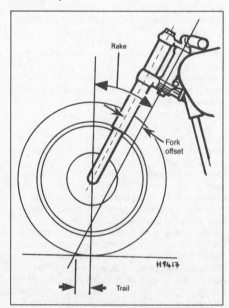

Steering geometry

Rebore Providing a new working surface to the cylinder bore by boring out the old surface. Necessitates the use of oversize piston and rings.

Rebound damping A means of controlling the oscillation of a suspension unit spring after it has been compressed. Resists the spring's natural tendency to bounce back after being compressed.

Rectifier Device for converting the ac output of an alternator into dc for battery charging.

Reed valve An induction system commonly used on two-stroke engines.

Regulator Device for maintaining the charging voltage from the generator or alternator within a specified range.

Relay A electrical device used to switch heavy current on and off by using a low current auxiliary circuit.

Resistance Measured in ohms. An electrical component's ability to pass electrical current.

RON (Research Octane Number) A measure of a fuel's resistance to knock.

rpm revolutions per minute.

Runout The amount of wobble (in-and-out movement) of a wheel or shaft as it's rotated. The amount a shaft rotates 'out-of-true'. The out-of-round condition of a rotating part.

S

SAE (Society of Automotive Engineers) A standard for the viscosity of a fluid.

Sealant A liquid or paste used to prevent leakage at a joint. Sometimes used in conjunction with a gasket.

Service limit Term for the point where a component is no longer useable and must be renewed.

Shaft drive A method of transmitting drive from the transmission to the rear wheel.

Shell bearings Plain bearings consisting of two shell halves. Most often used as big-end and main bearings in a four-stroke engine. Often called bearing inserts.

Shim Thin spacer, commonly used to adjust the clearance or relative positions between two parts. For example, shims inserted into or under tappets or followers to control valve clearances. Clearance is adjusted by changing the thickness of the shim.

Short-circuit An electrical condition where current shorts to earth (ground) bypassing the circuit components.

Skimming Process to correct warpage or repair a damaged surface, eg on brake discs or drums.

Slide-hammer A special puller that screws into or hooks onto a component such as a shaft or bearing; a heavy sliding handle on the shaft bottoms against the end of the shaft to knock the component free.

Small-end bearing The bearing in the upper end of the connecting rod at its joint with the gudgeon pin.

Spalling Damage to camshaft lobes or bearing journals shown as pitting of the working surface.

Specific gravity (SG) The state of charge of the electrolyte in a lead-acid battery. A measure of the electrolyte's density compared with water.

Straight-cut gears Common type gear used on gearbox shafts and for oil pump and water pump drives.

Stanchion The inner sliding part of the front forks, held by the yokes. Often called a fork tube.

Stoichiometric ratio The optimum chemical air/fuel ratio for a petrol engine, said to be 14.7 parts of air to 1 part of fuel.

Sulphuric acid The liquid (electrolyte) used in a lead-acid battery. Poisonous and extremely corrosive.

Surface grinding (lapping) Process to correct a warped gasket face, commonly used on cylinder heads.

T

Tapered-roller bearing Tapered inner race of caged needle rollers and separate tapered outer race. Examples of taper roller bearings can be found on steering heads.

Tappet A cylindrical component which transmits motion from the cam to the valve stem, either directly or via a pushrod and rocker arm. Also called a cam follower.

TCS Traction Control System. An electronically-controlled system which senses wheel spin and reduces engine speed accordingly.

TDC Top Dead Centre denotes that the piston is at its highest point in the cylinder.

Thread-locking compound Solution applied to fastener threads to prevent slackening. Select type to suit application.

Thrust washer A washer positioned between two moving components on a shaft. For example, between gear pinions on gearshaft.

Timing chain See **Cam Chain**.

Timing light Stroboscopic lamp for carrying out ignition timing checks with the engine running.

Top-end A description of an engine's cylinder block, head and valve gear components.

Torque Turning or twisting force about a shaft.

Torque setting A prescribed tightness specified by the motorcycle manufacturer to ensure that the bolt or nut is secured correctly. Undertightening can result in the bolt or nut coming loose or a surface not being sealed. Overtightening can result in stripped threads, distortion or damage to the component being retained.

Torx key A six-point wrench.

Tracer A stripe of a second colour applied to a wire insulator to distinguish that wire from another one with the same colour insulator. For example, Br/W is often used to denote a brown insulator with a white tracer.

Trail A feature of steering geometry. Distance from the steering head axis to the tyre's central contact point.

Triple clamps The cast components which extend from the steering head and support the fork stanchions or tubes. Often called fork yokes.

Turbocharger A centrifugal device, driven by exhaust gases, that pressurises the intake air. Normally used to increase the power output from a given engine displacement.

TWI Abbreviation for Tyre Wear Indicator. Indicates the location of the tread depth indicator bars on tyres.

U

Universal joint or U-joint (UJ) A double-pivoted connection for transmitting power from a driving to a driven shaft through an angle. Typically found in shaft drive assemblies.

Unsprung weight Anything not supported by the bike's suspension (ie the wheel, tyres, brakes, final drive and bottom (moving) part of the suspension).

V

Vacuum gauges Clock-type gauges for measuring intake tract vacuum. Used for carburettor synchronisation on multi-cylinder engines.

Valve A device through which the flow of liquid, gas or vacuum may be stopped, started or regulated by a moveable part that opens, shuts or partially obstructs one or more ports or passageways. The intake and exhaust valves in the cylinder head are of the poppet type.

Valve clearance The clearance between the valve tip (the end of the valve stem) and the rocker arm or tappet/follower. The valve clearance is measured when the valve is closed. The correct clearance is important - if too small the valve won't close fully and will burn out, whereas if too large noisy operation will result.

Valve lift The amount a valve is lifted off its seat by the camshaft lobe.

Valve timing The exact setting for the opening and closing of the valves in relation to piston position.

Vernier caliper A precision measuring instrument that measures inside and outside dimensions. Not quite as accurate as a micrometer, but more convenient.

VIN Vehicle Identification Number. Term for the bike's engine and frame numbers.

Viscosity The thickness of a liquid or its resistance to flow.

Volt A unit for expressing electrical "pressure" in a circuit. Volts = current x ohms.

W

Water pump A mechanically-driven device for moving coolant around the engine.

Watt A unit for expressing electrical power. Watts = volts x current.

Wear limit see **Service limit**

Wet liner A liquid-cooled engine design where the pistons run in liners which are directly surrounded by coolant **(see illustration)**.

Wet liner arrangement

Wheelbase Distance from the centre of the front wheel to the centre of the rear wheel.

Wiring harness or loom Describes the electrical wires running the length of the motorcycle and enclosed in tape or plastic sheathing. Wiring coming off the main harness is usually referred to as a sub harness.

Woodruff key A key of semi-circular or square section used to locate a gear to a shaft. Often used to locate the alternator rotor on the crankshaft.

Wrist pin Another name for gudgeon or piston pin.

Note: *References throughout this index are in the form - "Chapter number" • "Page number"*

A

About this Manual – 0•7
Acknowledgements – 0•7
Air filter – 1•18, 4•3
Air system control valve – 4•5
Air temperature sensor – 4•19, 8•16
Alternator – 8•24
Angle-tightening – REF•13
Antifreeze – 3•1
Anti-lock brake system –
ABS – 6•16
  deactivating the ABS – 6•16
  maintenance – 6•16
  riding conditions – 6•16
Asbestos – 0•8
Axle and eccentric adjuster
  assembly – 6•31

B

Balancer assembly – 2•44
Battery – 0•8, 8•5
  charging – 8•6
  maintenance – 8•6
  removal and refitting – 8•5
Bearings – REF•14
  seal lips lubricant – 1•2
Big-end bearings – 2•45
  oil clearance check – 2•46
Bike spec – 0•16, 0•17
Bleeding and fluid change (brake
  system) – 6•17
Bodywork – 7•1 *et seq*
  centre panel – 7•2, 7•6, 7•12
  front mudguard – 7•5, 7•12, 7•13
  general information – 7•1
  mirrors – 7•5, 7•12, 7•13
  mudguards – 7•4, 7•5, 7•11,
    7•12, 7•13
  passenger handles – 7•3, 7•9,
    7•13
  rear carrier – 7•9
  rear mudguard – 7•4, 7•11, 7•13
  rear panels – 7•4, 7•10, 7•13
  screen – 7•2, 7•9
  seat – 7•1, 7•6, 7•12
  side panels – 7•3, 7•7, 7•12
  sump guard – 7•5
  windshield – 7•13
Bolts – 1•16, REF•5
Brake system – 1•13, REF•30
  bleeding – 6•17
  caliper – 1•14, 6•5, 6•11
  disc – 1•13, 6•7, 6•13
  fittings – 6•17
  fluid – 1•2, 6•17
  fluid change – 1•14, 6•17
  fluid levels – 0•12, 0•13
  hoses – 6•17
  lever – 5•10
  lever pivot lubricant – 1•2
  light bulb – 8•11
  light switches – 8•13
  master cylinder seals – 1•14, 6•8,
    6•14
  pads – 6•2, 6•9
  discs – 1•13

  pedal – 5•3, 5•6
  pedal lubricant – 1•2
  pipes – 6•17
  system check – 1•14
Brakes, wheels and final drive –
6•1 *et seq*
  anti-lock brake system – ABS –
    6•16
  brake system bleeding and fluid
    change – 6•17
  caliper – 6•5, •11
  disc – 6•7, 6•13
  drive belt – 6•27
  drive chain – 6•25
  fittings – 6•17
  general information – 6•2
  hoses – 6•17
  master cylinder – 6•8, 6•14
  pads – 6•2, 6•9
  pipes – 6•17
  pulley coupling bearing(s) – 6•24
  pulley coupling dampers – 6•30
  pulleys – 6•27
  rear axle and eccentric adjuster –
    6•31
  sprocket coupling bearing(s) –
    6•24
  sprocket dampers – 6•30
  sprockets – 6•25
  tyres – 6•32
  wheel bearings – 6•22
  wheels – 6•19, 6•20, 6•21
Bulb replacement – 8•13
Buying spare parts – 0•9

C

Cables
  clutch – 1•12, 2•34
  lubricant – 1•2
  lubrication – 1•13
  throttle – 1•12, 4•9
Caliper – 1•14, 6•5, 6•11
Cam chain – 2•19
  tensioner – 2•19
  guide blades – 2•18
Camshaft position sensor – 4•19
Camshafts and followers – 2•13
CAN-bus technology – 8•2
Carrier – 7•9
Cast wheels – 1•16
Catalytic converter – 4•15
Central vehicle electronics
  control unit – ZFE – 8•2
Centre panel – 7•2, 7•6, 7•12
Centrestand – 5•7
  lubricant – 1•2
Chains – REF•18, REF•28
Charging – 8•6
  system check – 8•23
Circlips – REF•6
Circuit check – 8•13
Clutch – 2•27
  cable – 1•12, 2•34
  lever – 5•11
  lever pivot lubricant – 1•2
  switch – 8•19
Coils – 4•16

Component locations – 1•4 *et seq*
Compression check – 2•5
Compression gauge – REF•12
Connecting rods – 2•45
Continuity checks – 8•4
Conversion factors – REF•26
Coolant – 3•1, 3•2
  draining – 3•2
  flushing – 3•3
  hoses – 3•11
  level – 0•10
  refilling – 3•3
  reservoir – 3•8
  temperature sensor – 3•4
Cooling fan – 3•4
Cooling system – 1•22, 3•1 *et seq*
  antifreeze – 3•1
  coolant – 3•1
  coolant change – 3•2
  draining – 3•2
  fan – 3•4
  flushing – 3•3
  general information – 3•1
  hoses – 3•11
  pressure cap – 3•6
  pressure checks – 3•8
  radiator – 3•6
  refilling – 3•3
  reservoir – 3•8
  temperature sensor – 3•4
  thermostat – 3•5
  water pump – 3•8
Crankcases – 2•40
Crankshaft – 2•48
Crankshaft bearing information
  – 2•45
Cylinder compression
  check – 2•5
Cylinder head
  overhaul – 2•20
  removal and installation – 2•19
Cylinders – 2•50

D

Defective bulb warnings – 8•7
Diagnostic tester – 4•16
Dial gauge – REF•12
Dimensions – 0•16
Discs – 1•13, 6•7, 6•13
Downpipes – 4•14
Drawbolts – REF•15
Drive belt – 0•11, 1•9, 6•27
Drive chain – 0•11, 1•7, 6•25,
  REF•18, REF•28
  lubricant – 1•2
Dust protection – REF•4

E

Earth (ground) checks – 8•5
ECU – 4•16
  removal and installation – 4•17
Electrical system – 8•1 *et seq*,
REF•27
  air temperature sensor – 8•16
  alternator – 8•24
  battery – 8•5, 8•5

  brake light bulb – 8•11
  brake light switches – 8•13
  bulb replacement – 8•13
  CAN-bus technology – 8•2
  central vehicle electronics control
    unit – ZFE – 8•2
  charging – 8•6
  charging system check – 8•23
  circuit check – 8•13
  clutch switch – 8•19
  continuity checks – 8•4
  defective bulb warnings – 8•7
  earth (ground) checks – 8•5
  fault finding – 8•3
  general information – 8•1
  handlebar switches – 8•19
  headlight aim – 8•11
  headlight bulbs – 8•7
  headlight unit – 8•8
  horn – 8•19
  ignition switch – 8•17
  instrument cluster – 8•15
  licence plate light bulb – 8•12
  lighting system check – 8•6
  oil pressure switch – 8•16
  regulator/rectifier – 8•26
  sidelight bulbs – 8•7
  sidestand switch – 8•18
  speed sensor – 8•15
  starter motor – 8•20
  switch continuity checks – 8•4
  tail light bulb – 8•12
  temperature sensor – 8•16
  turn signal units – 8•13
  turn signals – 8•13
  voltage checks – 8•4
  wiring checks – 8•4
  wiring continuity checks – 8•4
  wiring diagrams – 8•27 *et seq*
Electricity – 0•8
Engine management – 4•1 *et seq*
  air filter housing – 4•3
  air temperature sensor – 4•19
  camshaft position sensor – 4•19
  catalytic converter – 4•15
  diagnostic tester – 4•16
  downpipes – 4•14
  ECU – 4•16, 4•17
  engine management system –
    4•16
  engine management system
    sensors – 4•18
  exhaust system – 4•13
  fault identification – 4•16
  fault tracing – 4•17
  fuel level sensor – 4•5
  fuel pressure sensor – 4•8, 4•21
  fuel pump – 4•5
  fuel rail – 4•12
  fuel strainer – 4•5
  fuel system – 4•2
  fuel tank – 4•5
  gear position sensor – 4•20
  general information – 4•2
  HT coils – 4•16
  idle actuator – 4•20
  ignition HT coils – 4•16
  ignition system – 4•2
  ignition system checks – 4•15

Index REF•49

Note: *References throughout this index are in the form - "Chapter number" • "Page number"*

ignition timing sensor – 4•18
injectors – 4•12
intake air temperature sensor – 4•19
oxygen sensor – 4•15, 4•21
precautions – 4•2
roll-over valve – 4•8
secondary air system control valve – 4•5
silencer – 4•13, 4•16
sensors – 4•18
throttle bodies – 4•10
throttle cable – 4•9
throttle position sensor – 4•21
timing sensor – 4•18
Engine numbers – 0•9
Engine oil and filter – 1•10
oil level – 0•11
oil pressure check – 2•6
Engine overhaul information – 2•9
Engine removal and installation – 2•6
Engine wear assessment – 2•5
Engine, clutch and transmission – 2•1 et seq
balancer assembly – 2•44
big-end bearings – 2•45
cam chain – 2•18
cam chain tensioner – 2•12
camshafts and followers – 2•13
clutch – 2•27
clutch cable – 2•34
component access – 2•5
connecting rods – 2•45
crankcases – 2•40
crankshaft – 2•48
crankshaft bearing – 2•45
cylinder compression check – 2•5
cylinder head – 2•19, 2•20
cylinders – 2•50
engine oil pressure check – 2•6
engine overhaul information – 2•9
engine removal and installation – 2•6
engine wear assessment – 2•5
feed pump – 2•35, 2•37
followers – 2•13
gearchange mechanism – 2•37
general information – 2•5
guide blades – 2•18
input shaft – 2•54
main bearings – 2•48
oil cooler – 2•24
oil pressure check – 2•6
oil pressure regulator – 2•39
pumps – 2•35
oil strainer – 2•39
oil sump – 2•39
operations possible with the engine in the frame – 2•5
operations requiring engine removal – 2•5
output shaft – 2•57
output shaft oil seal – 2•54
piston rings – 2•52
pistons – 2•50
running-in procedure – 2•62
scavenge pump – 2•36, 2•37

selector drum and forks – 2•59
starter clutch and gears – 2•25
tensioner – 2•18
transmission shafts – 2•53, 2•54
valve cover – 2•10
valves – 2•20
Exhaust system – 4•13, REF•28
Eye protection – REF•4

F

Fan – 3•4
Fasteners – REF•5
Fault Finding – 8•3, REF•35 et seq
continuity checks – 8•4
earth (ground) checks – 8•5
simple wiring checks – 8•4
switch continuity checks – 8•4
voltage checks – 8•4
wiring continuity checks – 8•4
Fault identification – 4•16
Fault tracing – 4•17
Feed pump – 2•35, 2•37
Feeler gauges – REF•9
Filter
air – 1•18, 4•3
engine oil – 1•10
Final drive – 6•1 et seq, REF•28
Fire – 0•8, REF•4
Fluids – 1•2, REF•4, REF•23 et seq
Followers – 2•13
Footrests – 5•3
brackets – 5•4
pivot lubricant – 1•2
Forks
oil change – 1•21, 5•12
overhaul – 5•14
removal and installation – 5•11
Frame and engine numbers – 0•9
Frame and suspension – 5•1 et seq
brake lever – 5•10
centrestand – 5•7
clutch lever – 5•11
footrests – 5•3
forks – 5•11, 5•12, 5•14
frame – 5•3
gearchange lever – 5•3
general information – 5•3
handlebars – 5•8
heel plates – 5•5
levers – 5•8
pre-load – 5•25
rebound damping – 5•25
shock absorber – 5•23, 5•25
sidestand – 5•7
spring pre-load – 5•25
stands – 5•7
steering head bearings and races – 5•22
steering stem – 5•20
swingarm – 5•25
Frame inspection and repair – 5•3
Front mudguard – 7•5, 7•12, 7•13
Fuel system – 1•22, 4•2
fuel level sensor – 4•5
fuel pressure sensor – 4•8, 4•21
fuel pump – 4•5
fuel rail – 4•12

fuel strainer – 1•22, 4•5
fuel tank – 4•5
Fumes – 0•8, REF•4

G

Gaskets and sealants – REF•17
Gauges – REF•9
Gear position sensor – 4•20
Gearchange lever – 5•3, 5•6
lubricant – 1•2
Gearchange mechanism – 2•37
Guide blades – 2•18

H

Hand protection – REF•4
Handlebars – 5•8
switches – 8•19
Handles – 7•3, 7•9, 7•13
Headlight unit – 8•8
aim – 8•11
beam height – REF•27
bulbs – 8•7
Heel plates – 5•5
Horn – 8•19, REF•27
Hoses – 3•11, REF•19
brake – 6•17
HT coils – 4•16

I

Identification numbers – 0•9
Idle actuator – 4•20
Ignition HT coils – 4•16
Ignition switch – 8•17
Ignition system – 4•2
checks – 4•15
Ignition timing sensor – 4•18
Injectors – 4•12
Input shaft – 2•54
Instrument cluster – 8•15
Intake air temperature sensor – 4•19
Introduction – 0•4

L

Legal and safety – 0•13
Leverage – REF•13
Levers – 5•8
Licence plate light bulb – 8•12
Lighting – 0•13, REF•27
system check – 8•6
Lubricants and fluids – 1•2, REF•23 et seq
Lubrication – 1•15

M

Main bearings – 2•48
oil clearance check – 2•49
Maintenance schedule – 1•3
Master cylinder (brake) – 6•8, 6•14
seals – 1•14
Measuring tools and gauges – REF•9

Micrometers – REF•9
Mirrors – 7•5, 7•12, 7•13
Model development – 0•15
MOT Test Checks – REF•27 et seq
brakes – REF•30
electrical system – REF•27
exhaust system – REF•28
final drive – REF•28
headlight beam height – REF•27
horn – REF•27
lights – REF•27
reflector – REF•27
sidecars – REF•31
steering – REF•28
suspension – REF•28, REF•29
turn signals – REF•27
tyres – REF•30
wheels – REF•30
Mudguards
front – 7•5, 7•12, 7•13
rear – 7•4, 7•11, 7•13

N

Nuts and bolts – 1•16, REF•5

O

Oil
engine – 0•11, 1•10, 2•6
forks – 1•21, 5•12
Oil filter – 1•10
Oil cooler – 2•24
Oil pressure
check – 2•6
gauge – REF•12
regulator – 2•39
switch – 8•16
Oil pumps – 2•35
Oil seals – REF•16
output shaft – 2•54
Oil strainer – 2•39
Oil sump – 2•39
Output shaft – 2•57
oil seal – 2•54
Oxygen sensor – 4•15, 4•21

P

Pads – 1•13, 6•2, 6•9
Parts – 0•9
Passenger handles – 7•3, 7•9, 7•13
Pedals
brake – 5•3
brake lubricant – 1•2
Pipes (brake) – 6•17
Piston rings – 2•52
Pistons – 2•50
Plastigauge – REF•11
Pre-load – 5•25
Pre-ride checks – 0•10 et seq
Pressure cap – 3•6
Pressure checks (cooling system) – 3•8
Pullers – REF•14
Pulley coupling bearing(s) – 6•24
coupling dampers – 6•30
Pulleys – 6•27

Note: *References throughout this index are in the form - "Chapter number" • "Page number"*

R

Radiator – 3•6
Rear axle and eccentric adjuster assembly – 6•31
Rear carrier – 7•9
Rear mudguard – 7•4, 7•11, 7•13
Rear panels – 7•4, 7•10, 7•13
Rear shock absorber – 5•23
  adjustment – 5•25
Rebound damping – 5•25
Reference – REF•1 et seq
Reflector – REF•27
Regulator/rectifier – 8•26
Roll-over valve – 4•8
Routine maintenance and servicing – 1•1 et seq
  air filter – 1•18
  bearing seal lips lubricant – 1•2
  brake caliper seals – 1•14
  brake fluid – 1•2
  brake fluid change – 1•14
  brake lever pivot lubricant – 1•2
  brake master cylinder seals – 1•14
  brake pads – 1•13
  brake pedal lubricant – 1•2
  brake system – 1•13
  cable lubrication – 1•2, 1•13
  cables – 1•12
  cast wheels – 1•16
  centrestand lubricant – 1•2
  clutch cable – 1•12
  clutch lever pivot lubricant – 1•2
  component locations – 1•4 et seq
  cooling system – 1•22
  discs – 1•13
  drive belt and pulleys – 1•9
  drive chain and sprockets – 1•7
  drive chain lubricant – 1•2
  engine oil and filter – 1•10
  fluids – 1•2
  footrest pivot lubricant – 1•2
  fork oil change – 1•21
  servicing front brake lever pivot lubricant – 1•2
  servicing fuel system – 1•22
  gearchange lever lubricant – 1•2
  lubricants and fluids – 1•2
  lubrication – 1•15
  maintenance schedule – 1•3
  nuts and bolts – 1•16
  oil – 1•10
  oil filter – 1•10
  rear brake pedal lubricant – 1•2
  sidestand lubricant – 1•2
  spark plugs – 1•19
  sprockets – 1•7
  stand lubricant – 1•2
  steering head bearings – 1•14
  steering head bearings lubricant – 1•2
  suspension – 1•21

S

Safety First! – 0•8, 0•13
Scavenge pump – 2•36, 2•37
Screen – 7•2, 7•9
Screws – REF•5
Sealants – REF•17
Sealing compound – REF•9
Seals – REF•16
Seat – 7•1, 7•6, 7•12
Secondary air system control valve – 4•5
Security – REF•20 et seq
Seized fasteners – REF•6
Selector drum and forks – 2•59
Sensors
  air temperature – 4•19, 8•16
  camshaft position – 4•19
  coolant temperature sensor – 3•4
  engine management system – 4•18
  fuel pressure – 4•8, 4•21
  gear position – 4•20
  ignition timing – 4•18
  intake air temperature – 4•19
  oxygen – 4•21
  temperature – 3•4, 4•19, 8•16
  throttle position – 4•21
  timing – 4•18
Shock absorber – 5•23
  adjustment – 5•25
Side panels – 7•3, 7•7, 7•12
Sidecars – REF•31
Sidelight bulbs – 8•7
Sidestand – 5•7
  lubricant – 1•2
  switch – 8•18
Signalling – 0•13
Silencer – 4•13
Slide hammers – REF•14
Spare parts – 0•9
Spark plugs – 1•19
Speed sensor – 8•15
Split pins – REF•5
Spring pre-load – 5•25
Sprockets – 1•7, 6•25
  coupling bearing(s) – 6•24
  dampers – 6•30
Stands – 5•7
  lubricant – 1•2
Starter clutch and gears – 2•25
Starter motor – 8•20
swingarm pivot bearings lubricant – 1•2
throttle cable – 1•12
tyres – 1•16
valve clearances – 1•17
wheel bearings – 1•17
wheels and wheel bearings – 1•16
wire spoked wheels – 1•16
Running-in procedure – 2•62

relay – 8•20
Steering – 0•11, REF•28
Steering head bearings – 1•14, 5•22
  lubricant – 1•2
Steering stem – 5•20
Storage – REF•32 et seq
Sump guard – 7•5
Suspension –
Suspension – 0•11, 1•21, 5•1 et seq, REF•28, REF•29
Swingarm – 5•25
  pivot bearings lubricant – 1•2
Switches
  brake light – 8•13
  continuity checks – 8•4
  clutch – 8•19
  handlebar – 8•19
  ignition – 8•17
  oil pressure – 8•16
  sidestand – 8•18

T

Tail light bulb – 8•12
Technical Terms Explained – REF•44 et seq
Temperature sensor – 3•4, 4•19, 8•16
Tensioner – 2•18
Thermostat – 3•5
Thread diameter and pitch – REF•6
Thread locking compound – REF•9
Thread repair – REF•8
Throttle bodies – 4•10
Throttle cable – 1•12, 4•9
Throttle position sensor – 4•21
Timing sensor – 4•18
Tools and workshop tips – REF•2 et seq
  angle-tightening – REF•13
  bearings – REF•14
  bolts – REF•5
  chains – REF•18
  circlips – REF•6
  compression gauge – REF•12
  dial gauge – REF•12
  drawbolts – REF•15
  drive chains – REF•18
  dust protection – REF•4
  eye protection – REF•4
  fasteners – REF•5
  feeler gauges – REF•9
  fire – REF•4
  fluids – REF•4
  fumes – REF•4
  gaskets and sealants – REF•17
  gauges – REF•9
  hand protection – REF•4
  hoses – REF•19
  leverage – REF•13
  measuring tools and gauges – REF•9

micrometers – REF•9
nuts – REF•5
oil pressure gauge – REF•12
oil seals – REF•16
Plastigauge – REF•11
pullers – REF•14
screws – REF•5
sealants – REF•17
sealing compound – REF•9
seals – REF•16
seized fasteners – REF•6
slide hammers – REF•14
split pins – REF•5
thread diameter and pitch – REF•6
thread locking compound – REF•9
thread repair – REF•8
torque and leverage – REF•13
torque wrench – REF•13
vernier caliper – REF•10
washers – REF•5
workbench – REF•4
Torque and leverage – REF•13
Torque wrench – REF•13
Transmission – 2•1 et seq
  shaft – 2•53
  shaft overhaul – 2•54
Turn signals – 8•13, REF•27
Tyres – 0•14, 1•16, 6•32, REF•30
  care – 0•14
  fitting new – 6•32
  pressures – 0•14
  tread depth – 0•14

V

Valves
  clearances – 1•17
  cover – 2•10
  overhaul – 2•20
Vernier caliper – REF•10
Voltage checks – 8•4

W

Washers – REF•5
Water pump – 3•8
Weights – 0•16
Wheels – 1•16, 6•1 et seq, REF•30
  alignment check – 6•19
  bearings – 1•16, 1•17, 6•22
  front – 6•20
  inspection and repair – 6•19
  rear – 6•21
Windshield – 7•13
Wire spoked wheels – 1•16
Wiring checks – 8•4
Wiring diagrams – 8•27 et seq
Workbench – REF•4
Workshop equipment and facilities – REF•4
Workshop Tips – REF•2 et seq

Haynes Motorcycle Manuals – The Complete List

Title	Book No
APRILIA RS50 (99 – 06) & RS125 (93 – 06)	4298
Aprilia RSV1000 Mille (98 – 03) ♦	4255
Aprilia SR50	4755
BMW 2-valve Twins (70 -96) ♦	0249
BMW F650 ♦	4761
BMW K100 & 75 2-valve models (83 - 96) ♦	1373
BMW F800 (F650) Twins (06 – 10) ♦	4872
BMW R850, 1100 & 1150 4-valve Twins (93 – 06) ♦	3466
BMW R1200 (04 – 09) ♦	4598
BMW R1200 dohc Twins (10 – 12) ♦	4925
BSA Bantam (48 – 71)	0117
BSA Unit Singles (58 – 72)	0127
BSA Pre-unit Singles (54 – 61)	0326
BSA A7 & A10 Twins (47 – 62)	0121
BSA A50 & A65 Twins (62 – 73)	0155
CHINESE, Taiwanese & Korean Scooters	4768
Chinese, Taiwanese & Korean 125cc motorcycles	4781
DUCATI 600, 620, 750 & 900 2-valve V-twins (91 – 05) ♦	3290
Ducati Mk III & Desmo singles (69 – 76) ◊	0445
Ducati 748, 916 & 996 4-valve V-twins (94 – 01) ♦	3756
GILERA Runner, DNA, Ice & SKP/Stalker (97 – 11)	4163
HARLEY-DAVIDSON Sportsters (70 – 10) ♦	2534
Harley-Davidson Shovelhead & Evolution Big Twins (70 -99) ♦	2536
Harley-Davidson Twin Cam 88, 96 & 103 models (99 – 10) ♦	2478
HONDA NB, ND, NP & NS50 Melody (81 -85) ◊	0622
Honda NE/NB50 Vision & SA50 Vision Met-in (85-95) ◊	1278
Honda MB, MBX, MT & MTX50 (80 – 93)	0731
Honda C50, C70 & C90 (67 – 03)	0324
Honda XR50/70/80/100R & CRF50/70/80/100F (85 – 07)	2218
Honda XL/XR 80, 100, 125, 185 & 200 2-valve models (78 – 87)	0566
Honda H100 & H100S Singles (80 – 92) ◊	0734
Honda 125 Scooters (00 – 09)	4873
Honda ANF125 Innova Scooters (03 -12) ♦	4926
Honda CB/CD125T & CM125C Twins (77 – 88) ◊	0571
Honda CBF125 (09 – 12) ♦	5540
Honda CG125 (76 – 07) ◊	0433
Honda NS125 (86 – 93)	3056
Honda CBR125R (04 – 10)	4620
Honda MBX/MTX125 & MTX200 (83 – 93) ◊	1132
Honda XL125V & VT125C (99 – 11)	4899
Honda CD/CM185 200T & CM250C 2-valve Twins (77 – 85)	0572
Honda CMX250 Rebel & CB250 Nighthawk Twins (85 – 09)	2756
Honda XL/XR 250 & 500 (78 – 84)	0567
Honda XR250L, XR250R & XR400R (86 – 03)	2219
Honda CB250 & CB400N Super Dreams (78 – 84) ◊	0540
Honda CR Motocross Bikes (86 – 07)	2222
Honda CRF250 & CRF450 (02 – 06)	2630
Honda CBR400RR Fours (88 – 99) ◊♦	3552
Honda VFR400 (NC30) & RVF400 (NC35) V-Fours (89 – 98) ◊♦	3496
Honda CB500 (93 – 02) & CBF500 (03 – 08) ♦	3753
Honda CB400 & CB550 Fours (73 – 77)	0262
Honda CX/GL500 & 650 V-Twins (78 – 86)	0442
Honda CBX550 Four (82 – 86) ◊	0940
Honda XL600R & XR600R (83 – 08) ♦	2183
Honda XL600/650V Transalp & XRV750 Africa Twin (87 – 07)	3919
Honda CB600 Hornet, CBF600 & CBR600F (07 – 12)	5572
Honda CBR600F1 & 1000F Fours (87 – 96) ♦	1730
Honda CBR600F2 & F3 Fours (91 – 98) ♦	2070
Honda CBR600F4 (99 – 06) ♦	3911
Honda CB600F Hornet & CBF600 (98 – 06) ◊♦	3915
Honda CBR600RR (03 – 06) ♦	4590
Honda CBR600RR (07 -12) ♦	4795
Honda CB650 sohc Fours (78 – 84)	0665
Honda NTV600 Revere, NTV650 & NT650V Deauville (88 – 05) ◊♦	3243
Honda Shadow VT600 & 750 (USA) (88 – 09)	2312
Honda NT700V Deauville & XL700V Transalp (06 -13) ♦	5541
Honda CB750 sohc Four (69 – 79)	0131
Honda V45/65 Sabre & Magna (82 – 88)	0820
Honda VFR750 & 700 V-Fours (86 – 97)	2101
Honda VFR800 V-Fours (97 – 01)	3703
Honda VFR800 V-Tec V-Fours (02 – 09) ♦	4196
Honda CB750 & CB900 dohc Fours (78 – 84)	0535
Honda CBF1000 (06 -10) & CB1000R (08 – 11) ♦	4927
Honda VTR1000 Firestorm, Super Hawk & XL1000V Varadero (97 – 08) ♦	3744
Honda CBR900RR Fireblade (92 – 99) ♦	2161
Honda CBR900RR Fireblade (00 – 03) ♦	4060
Honda CBR1000RR Fireblade (04 – 07)	4604
Honda CBR1100XX Super Blackbird (97 – 07)	3901
Honda ST1100 Pan European V-Fours (90 – 02) ♦	3384
Honda ST1300 Pan European (02 -11) ♦	4908

Title	Book No
Honda Shadow VT1100 (USA) (85 – 07)	2313
Honda GL1000 Gold Wing (75 – 79)	0309
Honda GL1100 Gold Wing (79 – 81)	0669
Honda Gold Wing 1200 (USA) (84 - 87)	2199
Honda Gold Wing 1500 (USA) (88 – 00)	2225
Honda Goldwing GL1800 ♦	2787
KAWASAKI AE/AR 50 & 80 (81 – 95)	1007
Kawasaki KC, KE & KH100 (75 – 99)	1371
Kawasaki KMX125 & 200 (86 – 02) ◊	3046
Kawasaki 250, 350 & 400 Triples (72 – 79)	0134
Kawasaki 400 & 440 Twins (74 – 81)	0281
Kawasaki 400, 500 & 550 Fours (79 – 91)	0910
Kawasaki EN450 & 500 Twins (Ltd/Vulcan) (85 – 07)	2053
Kawasaki ER-6F & ER-6N (06 -10) ♦	4874
Kawasaki EX500 (GPZ500S) & ER500 (ER-5) (87 – 08) ♦	2052
Kawasaki ZX600 (ZZ-R600 & Ninja ZX-6) (90 – 06) ♦	2146
Kawasaki ZX-6R Ninja Fours (95 – 02) ♦	3451
Kawasaki ZX-6R (03 – 06) ♦	4742
Kawasaki ZX600 (GPZ600R, GPX600R, Ninja 600R & RX) & ZX750 (GPX750R, Ninja 750R) (85 – 97) ♦	1780
Kawasaki 650 Four (76 – 79)	0373
Kawasaki Vulcan 700/750 & 800 (85 – 04) ♦	2457
Kawasaki Vulcan 1500 & 1600 (87 – 08) ♦	4913
Kawasaki 750 Air-cooled Fours	0574
Kawasaki ZR550 & 750 Zephyr Fours (90 – 97) ♦	3382
Kawasaki Z750 & Z1000 (03 – 08) ♦	4762
Kawasaki ZX750 (Ninja ZX-7 & ZXR750) Fours (89 – 96) ♦	2054
Kawasaki Ninja ZX-7R & ZX-9R (94 – 04) ♦	3721
Kawasaki 900 & 1000 Fours (73 – 77)	0222
Kawasaki ZX900, 1000 & 1100 Liquid-cooled Fours (83 – 97) ♦	1681
KTM EXC Enduro & SX Motocross (00 – 07) ♦	4629
LAMBRETTA Scooters (58 – 00) ♦	5573
MOTO GUZZI 750, 850 & 1000 V-Twins (74 – 78)	0339
MZ ETZ models (81 – 95) ◊	1680
NORTON 500, 600, 650 & 750 Twins (57 – 70)	0187
Norton Commando (68 – 77)	0125
PEUGEOT Speedfight, Trekker & Vivacity Scooters (96 – 08) ◊	3920
PIAGGIO (Vespa) Scooters (91 – 09) ◊	3492
SUZUKI GT, ZR & TS50 (77 – 90) ◊	0799
Suzuki TS50X (84 – 00) ◊	1599
Suzuki 100, 125, 185 & 250 Air-cooled Trail bikes (79 – 89)	0797
Suzuki GP100 & 125 Singles (78 – 93) ◊	0576
Suzuki GS, GN, GZ & DR125 Singles (82 – 05)	0888
Suzuki Burgman 250 & 400 (98 – 11) ♦	4909
Suzuki GSX-R600/750 (06 – 09) ♦	4790
Suzuki 250 & 350 Twins (68 – 78)	0120
Suzuki GT250X7, GT200X5 & SB200 Twins (78 – 83) ◊	0469
Suzuki DR-Z400 (00 – 10) ♦	2933
Suzuki GS/GSX250, 400 & 450 Twins (79 – 85)	0736
Suzuki GS500 Twin (89 – 08) ♦	3238
Suzuki GS550 (77 – 82) & GS750 Fours (76 – 79)	0363
Suzuki GS/GSX550 4-valve Fours (83 – 88)	1133
Suzuki SV650 & SV650S (99 – 08) ♦	3912
Suzuki GSX-R600 & 750 (96 – 00) ♦	3553
Suzuki GSX-R600 (01 – 03), GSX-R750 (00 – 03) & GSX-R1000 (01 – 02) ♦	3986
Suzuki GSX-R600/750 (04 – 05) & GSX-R1000 (03 – 06) ♦	4382
Suzuki GSF600, 650 & 1200 Bandit Fours (95 – 06) ♦	3367
Suzuki Intruder, Marauder, Volusia & Boulevard (85 – 09) ♦	2618
Suzuki GS850 Fours (78 – 88)	0536
Suzuki GS1000 Four (77 – 79)	0484
Suzuki GSX-R750, GSX-R1100 (85 – 92) GSX600F, GSX750F, GSX1100F (Katana) Fours (88 – 96) ♦	2055
Suzuki GSX600/750F & GSX750 (98 – 02)	3987
Suzuki GS/GSX1000, 1100 & 1150 4-valve Fours (79 – 88)	0737
Suzuki TL1000S/R & DL V-Strom (97 – 04) ♦	4083
Suzuki GSF650/1250 (07 – 09) ♦	4798
Suzuki GSX1300R Hayabusa (99 – 04) ♦	4184
Suzuki GSX1400 (02 – 08) ♦	4758
TRIUMPH Tiger Cub & Terrier (52 – 68)	0414
Triumph 350 & 500 Unit Twins (58 – 73)	0137
Triumph Pre-Unit Twins (47 – 62)	0251
Triumph 650 & 750 2-valve Unit Twins (63 – 83)	0122
Triumph 675 (06 – 10) ♦	4876
Triumph 1050 Sprint, Speed Triple & Tiger (05 -13) ♦	4796
Triumph Trident & BSA Rocket 3 (69 – 75)	0136
Triumph Bonneville (01 – 12) ♦	4364
Triumph Daytona, Speed Triple, Sprint & Tiger (97 – 05) ♦	3755
Triumph Triples & Fours (carburetor engines) (91 – 04)	2162
VESPA P/PX125, 150 & 200 Scooters (78 – 12)	0707
Vespa GTS125, 250 & 300 (05 – 10)	4898

Title	Book No
Vespa Scooters (59 – 78)	0126
YAMAHA DT50 & 80 Trail Bikes (78 – 95) ◊	0800
Yamaha T50 & 80 Townmate (83 – 95) ◊	1247
Yamaha YB100 Singles (73 – 91) ◊	0474
Yamaha RS/RXS 100 & 125 Singles (74 – 95)	0331
Yamaha RD & DT125LC (82 – 87) ◊	0887
Yamaha TZR125 (87 – 93) & DT125R (88 – 07)	1655
Yamaha TY50, 80, 125 & 175 (74 – 84) ◊	0464
Yamaha XT & SR125 (82 – 03) ◊	1021
Yamaha YBR125 & XT125R/X (05 – 13)	4797
Yamaha YZF-R125 (08 – 11) ♦	5543
Yamaha Trail Bikes (81 – 00)	2350
Yamaha 2-stroke Motocross Bikes (86 – 06)	2662
Yamaha YZ & WR 4-stroke Motocross Bikes (98 – 08)	2689
Yamaha 250 & 350 Twins (70 – 79)	0040
Yamaha XS250, 360 & 400 sohc Twins (75 – 84)	0378
Yamaha RD250 & 350LC Twins (80 – 82)	0803
Yamaha RD350 YPVS Twins (83 – 95)	1158
Yamaha RD400 Twin (75 – 79)	0333
Yamaha XT, TT & SR500 Singles (75 – 83)	0342
Yamaha XZ550 Vision V-Twins (82 – 85)	0821
Yamaha FJ, FX, XY & YX600 Radian (84 – 92)	2100
Yamaha XT660 & MT-03 (04 – 11) ♦	4910
Yamaha XJ600S (Diversion, Seca II) & XJ600N Fours (92 – 03) ♦	2145
Yamaha YZF600R Thundercat & FZS600 Fazer (96 – 03) ♦	3702
Yamaha FZ-6 Fazer (04 – 08) ♦	4751
Yamaha YZF-R6 (99 – 02) ♦	3900
Yamaha YZF-R6 (03 – 05) ♦	4601
Yamaha YZF-R6 (06 – 13) ♦	5544
Yamaha 650 Twins (70 – 83)	0341
Yamaha XJ650 & 750 Fours (80 – 84)	0738
Yamaha XS750 & 850 Triples (76 – 85)	0340
Yamaha TDM850, TRX850 & XTZ750 (89 – 99) ◊♦	3450
Yamaha YZF750R & YZF1000R Thunderace (93 – 00) ♦	3720
Yamaha FZR600, 750 & 1000 Fours (87 – 96) ♦	2056
Yamaha XV (Virago) V-Twins (81 – 03) ♦	0802
Yamaha XVS650 & 1100 Drag Star/V-Star (97 – 05) ♦	4195
Yamaha XJ900F Fours (83 – 94)	3239
Yamaha XJ900S Diversion (94 – 01)	3739
Yamaha YZF-R1 (98 – 03) ♦	3754
Yamaha YZF-R1 (04 – 06) ♦	4605
Yamaha FZS1000 Fazer (01 – 05) ♦	4287
Yamaha FJ1100 & 1200 Fours (84 – 96) ♦	2057
Yamaha XJR1200 & 1300 (95 – 06) ♦	3981
Yamaha V-Max (85 – 03) ♦	4072

ATV's

Title	Book No
Honda ATC 70, 90, 110, 185 & 200 (71 – on)	0565
Honda Rancher, Recon & TRX250EX ATVs	2553
Honda TRX300 Shaft Drive ATVs (88 – 00)	2125
Honda Foreman (95 – 11)	2465
Honda TRX300EX, TRX400EX & TRX450R/ER ATVs (93 – 06)	2318
Kawasaki Bayou 220/250/300 & Prairie 300 ATVs (86 – 03)	2351
Polaris ATVs (85 – 97)	2302
Polaris ATVs (98 – 07)	2508
Suzuki/Kawasaki/Artic Cat ATVs (03 – 09)	2910
Yamaha YFS200 Blaster ATV (88 – 06)	2317
Yamaha YFM350 & YFM400 (ER & Big Bear) ATVs (87 – 09)	2126
Yamaha YFZ450 & YFZ450R (04 – 10)	2899
Yamaha Banshee and Warrior ATVs (87 – 10)	2314
Yamaha Kodiak and Grizzly ATVs (93 – 05)	2567
ATV Basics	10450

TECHBOOK SERIES

Title	Book No
Twist and Go (automatic transmission) Scooters Service and Repair Manual	4082
Motorcycle Basics Techbook (2nd edition)	3515
Motorcycle Electrical Techbook (3rd edition)	3471
Motorcycle Fuel Systems Techbook	3514
Motorcycle Maintenance Techbook	4071
Motorcycle Modifying	4272
Motorcycle Workshop Practice Techbook (2nd edition)	3470

◊ = not available in the USA ♦ = Superbike

The manuals on this page are available through good motorcycle dealers and accessory shops.
In case of difficulty, contact: **Haynes Publishing**
(UK) **+44 1963 442030**   (USA) **+1 805 498 6703**
(SV) **+46 18 124016**
(Australia/New Zealand) **+61 2 8713 1400**

Preserving Our Motoring Heritage

< The Model J Duesenberg Derham Tourster. Only eight of these magnificent cars were ever built – this is the only example to be found outside the United States of America

Almost every car you've ever loved, loathed or desired is gathered under one roof at the Haynes Motor Museum. Over 300 immaculately presented cars and motorbikes represent every aspect of our motoring heritage, from elegant reminders of bygone days, such as the superb Model J Duesenberg to curiosities like the bug-eyed BMW Isetta. There are also many old friends and flames. Perhaps you remember the 1959 Ford Popular that you did your courting in? The magnificent 'Red Collection' is a spectacle of classic sports cars including AC, Alfa Romeo, Austin Healey, Ferrari, Lamborghini, Maserati, MG, Riley, Porsche and Triumph.

A Perfect Day Out

Each and every vehicle at the Haynes Motor Museum has played its part in the history and culture of Motoring. Today, they make a wonderful spectacle and a great day out for all the family. Bring the kids, bring Mum and Dad, but above all bring your camera to capture those golden memories for ever. You will also find an impressive array of motoring memorabilia, a comfortable 70 seat video cinema and one of the most extensive transport book shops in Britain. The Pit Stop Cafe serves everything from a cup of tea to wholesome, home-made meals or, if you prefer, you can enjoy the large picnic area nestled in the beautiful rural surroundings of Somerset.

John Haynes O.B.E., > Founder and Chairman of the museum at the wheel of a Haynes Light 12.

< The 1936 490cc sohc-engined International Norton – well known for its racing success

The Museum is situated on the A359 Yeovil to Frome road at Sparkford, just off the A303 in Somerset. It is about 40 miles south of Bristol, and 25 minutes drive from the M5 intersection at Taunton.
Open 9.30am - 5.30pm (10.00am - 4.00pm Winter) 7 days a week, *except Christmas Day, Boxing Day and New Years Day*
Special rates available for schools, coach parties and outings Charitable Trust No. 292048